C000184086

EXETER CITY

A COMPLETE
RECORD
1904-1990

EXETER CITY

A COMPLETE RECORD 1904-1990

MAURICE GOLESWORTHY
GARTH DYKES   ALEX WILSON

BREEDON
BOOKS
SPORT

First published in Great Britain by
The Breedon Books Publishing Company Limited
44 Friar Gate, Derby, DE1 1DA, England
1990

ISBN 0 907969 68 2

Printed and bound in Great Britain by
Butler and Tanner Limited, Frome and London.
Jacket printed by Arkle Print Limited, Northampton.

Contents

This book is dedicated to the memory of Alex Wilson.

Photographic Credits

Photographs supplied by Colorsport, Dave Fisher, Chris Howes and the *Exeter Express & Echo*.

Introduction

THIS book is really the brainchild of the late Alex Wilson, an Exeter man who followed the fortunes of the Grecians from his boyhood days in Devon in the 1920s until his death in Leicester in August 1989. Indeed, Alex was working on the manuscript right up to the time he entered hospital and had already delivered several sections of the book to the publishers.

One chapter in particular is uniquely his — the story of his beloved St James' Park. He claimed that there was no better place to be a Saturday afternoon than at the home of Exeter City.

After Alex's death, two of his friends undertook to finish the work in his memory. Maurice Golesworthy, well-known for his work on sports history in general, is based in Exmouth and as a former Exeter City correspondent, his deep local knowledge of the club and its personalities proved invaluable.

Garth Dykes, author of two other books for Breedon, had accompanied Alex on many trips to watch Exeter City when they were in the Midlands and also to Colindale Newspaper Library, where the two studied volumes of crumbling Victorian and Edwardian newspapers, researching details for their respective club history books. It was inevitable that Garth would also want to see Alex's book on Exeter City see the light of day.

Thus, Maurice and Garth took the groundwork laid by Alex and this is the result, the first modern history of one of the oldest football clubs. It is fitting that it should be published in a year when Exeter City Football Club ended one of their most successful seasons as Fourth Division champions.

Richard Young (left) and Shaun Taylor hoist manager Terry Cooper aloft with the Fourth Division Trophy won in 1990.

The
Exeter City
Story

THE Exeter City story is not studded with outstanding success but the club have kept the Football League flag flying at St James' Park for 70 years and there are a lot of people who deserve credit for that (*writes Maurice Golesworthy*).

The early pioneers were scoffed at when they were striving to bring first-class soccer to a rugby stronghold and one wonders what their critics would think today if they could see even the limited achievements of this club.

As with so many other small clubs, the main problem has been lack of money and we shall see in this story how often the directors have had to go cap in hand to the local public, amongst whom it must be said are many Exeter City fanatics, who are more than grateful for the interest and entertainment that has been provided over the years. More than 760 players have worn the team's colours in over 3,400 professional first-team games.

Another problem that existed until comparatively recently was the difficulty in persuading players to move this far west. Before the last war, anywhere west of Bristol was looked upon as the outback and the situation still existed for a few years after the war when it was aggravated by the housing shortage.

One only has to look at the local newspaper files for the latter part of the 19th century to see that the dribbling code was then held in such scant regard in this district that it scarcely got a mention.

It was at Plymouth that soccer first took a hold west of Bristol and when the Devon County FA was formed in 1888, it was in that naval port that its headquarters was based. The earliest members were Argyle Athletic, Exmouth House, Mannamead School, Newtonians, Old Plymothians, Plymouth, Tavistock and Plymouth College. The Devon Challenge Cup was originally put up for competition in the 1889-90 season and for the first 21 years of its existence was won either by clubs in the Plymouth area (including Tavistock) or more often by service teams. Their hold was not broken until 1911, when Torquay Town carried off the trophy.

St Luke's Training College pioneered soccer in Exeter and an Exeter Association club was formed in 1891. This was Exeter United and they first played such teams as Crediton Grammar School, Dunn's Foundation School, Dawlish Town, Dawlish Association, Exeter Grammar School, Collingwood House School, Hele's Past and Present, the Devonshire Regiment and the training college just mentioned. Their home ground was the Horse Show Field, Mount Pleasant.

Exeter United advanced the cause of soccer in the Cathedral City by reaching the Devon Senior Cup Final in 1897-8, when they were beaten 2-1 by the 15th Company Royal Artillery (Western Division) before a crowd of over 6,000 at the Rectory Field, Devonport. Incidentally, the first football excursion train ever to leave Exeter was run to Plymouth for this game, by the London & South Western Railway.

9

Exeter United were not the true antecedents of Exeter City. The latter's story begins with a group of young men who were mostly old boys of St Sidwell's School and members of the local Wesleyan church. When they began playing Association football in an organized fashion at the end of the 19th century, they went under the name of St Sidwell's Wesleyans but in 1901 changed to St Sidwell's United. They originally held their meetings at the Foresters' Arms, then still popularly known as the Drum & Monkey, which was about where the Odeon Cinema now stands, but they soon moved across the road to the Red Lion Inn, a hostelry destroyed by a German bomb in the 1942 blitz. The landlord, Tom Oliver, was to become one of the original directors of Exeter City when a company was formed in 1908.

The first St Sidwell's United team on record in October 1901 reads: Robinson; Flood, Campbell, Avery, Mann, Warner, Morgan, Sellick, Thomas, Eveleigh and Coles.

The most important name as far as this story is concerned is that of the centre-forward, 16-year-old Sid Thomas, who became club secretary in their second season and was subsequently Exeter City's first secretary. He served the City club in that capacity and later as director, chairman and president for nearly 70 years. An outstanding centre-forward, Sid Thomas scored no less than 41 goals in season 1901-02.

St Sidwell's United, rigged out in green and white quartered jerseys with white shorts, played most of their home games on a pitch in Mount Pleasant Road between the L & SW Railway and Monks Road. Other matches in Exeter were played among other locations on the Exeter Training College Ground in Magdalen Road, St James' Park or Field, Blackboy Road, Baring Crescent, Topsham Barracks, Whipton Lane, Marsh Barton, Pinhoe Road and Hoopern Fields. Indeed, some important soccer matches were also played at the County Ground, then as now the home of Exeter RFC.

It was at the County Ground that the citizens of Exeter witnessed their first-ever Association football match played by first-class professionals (albeit an exhibition game). It is obvious that the enterprising enthusiasts who persuaded West Bromwich Albion and Woolwich Arsenal to play this match, on 26 April 1902, included members of St Sidwell's United because as a preliminary to the big game United played a match with the Rest of League in which they were beaten 1-0. West Brom then beat Arsenal by the same score in front of a crowd of about 6,000 and it is worth adding that both sides were at full-strength, which means that the Albion fielded that season's Second Division championship-winning team.

It was in 1904, when the old Exeter United club went out of existence, that the St Sidwell's United enthusiasts decided to change their name to Exeter City, join the East Devon (Senior) League and move to St James' Park. This momentous decision was no doubt taken at a meeting in The Red Lion Inn, although the minutes have long since been lost. Their first match was against the 110th Battery of the Royal Artillery (Topsham Barracks) which City won 2-1. Their team was Peters; Ashford, Aplin, Wallage, Davidson, Morgan, Sellick, Thomas, Revd E.Reid, Eveleigh and Horner. They went on to finish top of the league that season, with a four-point advantage, and moved into the Plymouth & District League.

A star of the team, the Revd Edward Reid, was curate of St James' Church. Newly arrived in Exeter, he had previously played in the Southern League for Swindon Town. A Canadian from St John's, Newfoundland, who had come to England in 1897 to go to Oxford University, his previous first-class experience stood him in good stead, for he emerged as top scorer in that initial season with 16 goals.

The club included other established local footballers who had previously played for Exeter United, St Sidwell's United or both, namely Wallage, Jimmy Sellick,

The Exeter City team which competed in the Plymouth & District League in the final season before the Grecians joined the Southern League. Back row (left to right): Mr C.Fey, Mr W.Bastin, E.Eveleigh, H.Dyer (who went down on the 'Titantic'), W.'Bunker' Wells, S.Bastin, Percy Warner, Sgt Mould, Mr S.H.Thomas (secretary). Sitting: Ben Massey, R.Fenwick, J.Sellick, H.Singlehurst, W.Letheren.

Sid Thomas, 'Ginger' Eveleigh, Keech, Dick Fenwick, 'Bunker' Wells and Horner. Jimmy Sellick, a Devon County player, was Exeter City's first captain.

After three seasons in the Plymouth & District League with no more than moderate success, Exeter City decided to go for broke and become a professional concern as a limited company applying for entry into the Southern League, then the most important competition outside the Football League.

A proposition to go down this road with the public subscribing for £1 shares was made in February 1908 by Norman Kendall, a local sports outfitter. News of this enterprising move met with a good deal of incredulity and pooh-poohing. The majority view seemed to be that a professional soccer club could not be established in Exeter. The rugby enthusiasts were naturally most critical.

However, the Exeter City fanatics persisted in their ambition and at a meeting in March, under the chairmanship of Capt. F.J.Harvey, a former player and secretary of Exeter United, Mr Thomas reported that Mr McGahey (solicitor) had accepted on the proposed company's behalf the terms of a 21-year lease of St James' Park and a promise from Mr J.B.Skeggs, the chairman of Millwall FC, that he would confer with the Exeter committee and advise them on further progress. In passing it is worth noting that an earlier proposal to build a brand new stadium at the Barnfield, in the heart of the city, had been rejected because of the cost.

More enthusiasm was shown at another public meeting with Capt. F.J.Harvey presiding. When the Exeter Football & Athletic Company Limited was formed, he was among the directors, alongside Messrs Michael McGahey (solicitor), Norman Kendall (sports outfitter), Fred Parkhouse (grocer), Charles Collingwood (superintendent of the Blind Institute, St David's Hill), William Fenwick (accountant),

11

Tom Oliver (licensee) and Albert Alford (solicitor). Sidney Thomas (then described as an accountant but subsequently to become a solicitor's clerk) was the company's first secretary.

The man who talked the Southern League into accepting the club as members was Mr Norman Kendall and it is only fitting that St James' Park has a gate which was opened in his honour, for not only was his eloquence so beneficial on this occasion but he also faithfully supported the club for over 50 years.

Nat Whittaker, the Southern League secretary, explained that there were six applicants for five vacancies, including the previous season's bottom two clubs, Leyton and New Brompton. Tottenham Hotspur and Queen's Park Rangers had resigned on making their application to become members of the Football League.

Exeter City were voted in at the top of the poll and it could be said, therefore, that they replaced Tottenham Hotspur. Much to their annoyance, Southern League champions Queen's Park Rangers were left in the wilderness after being surprisingly turned down by the Football League, but were readmitted to the Southern League later that summer with the proviso that they played all fixtures in midweek.

Anticipating the moves that lay ahead, the City had in December 1907 signed Jack Banks as their first professional and player-coach. He made his name with West Bromwich Albion, having appeared in the FA Cup Final team beaten 1-0 by Aston Villa in 1895, and had also served Newton Heath (Manchester United) and Plymouth Argyle, the latter as both player and coach. Now City brought in former England international Arthur Chadwick as player-coach and general adviser, but he was to all intents and purposes the club's first player-manager.

Exeter City registered their colours as green jerseys with white sleeves and white lace-up collars, white knickers and black stockings with two narrow white stripes just below the tops. One wonders if they were influenced by Plymouth Argyle in choosing green, for it is a strange coincidence that this should be the colour of their nearest neighbours in the first-class game, especially considering that only two other clubs in the Football League and Southern League wore green at this time — Burnley and Queen's Park Rangers.

Arthur Chadwick immediately set about getting a team of experienced professionals together and, being a Lancastrian, it was not surprising that all but three of his 15 signings were from northern clubs, and even the three that came from elsewhere — Bill Wakes from Plymouth Argyle, Levi Copestake from Bristol City and Bob Watson from Woolwich Arsenal — were all northerners. There was also one Scot — inside-forward Tommy Drain. Two well known local amateurs, Harry Singlehurst and 'Ginger' Eveleigh, turned professional at this time.

Considering that one of Millwall's original company directors, Jimmy Skeggs, had advised the new club on turning professional, it was a coincidence that City should kick-off in their new environment with a midweek visit to this London club. Accompanied by all but one director, the team acquitted themselves well on a rain-soaked pitch, pulling back a two-goal deficit to force a draw with a couple from 'Daisy' Bell in the last ten minutes. On the train journey home the directors must have been in high spirits as they selected the team for the club's first home game three days later.

There were excursions from all parts of the region for City's Southern League debut at the Park on Saturday, 14 September. Their opponents were Bristol Rovers, who also brought a contingent of supporters to increase the crowd to around 8,000. They saw a good game and went away satisfied with another draw — this time 3-3, with City again coming from behind. Obviously they had a team of fighters.

City had to wait until their fourth game for their first victory and this was obtained at St James' Park, when they beat Norwich City by the odd goal in five. City excited their supporters by running-up a three-goal lead but allowed Norwich to make a comeback. This was the first game in which Arthur Chadwick appeared for the Grecians.

Chadwick's skill and experience had made a difference and this was again in evidence the following week when the first away League victory was gained, 2-1 at Reading.

City went on to finish sixth out of 21 clubs in this initial Southern League campaign, a commendable performance. Add to this their progress through five qualifying rounds to the second round proper of the FA Cup and no-one had any reason to complain.

The highly entertaining and most consistent forward line could certainly be rated among the best the club has ever fielded. Parnell, Watson, McGuigan, Bell and Copestake netted all but three of the 56 goals obtained in Southern League games. All except Fred Parnell had First Division experience.

Whilst skipper Bob Watson was the brains of this attack and centre-forward Andy McGuigan always showed real class, although slowed by leg injuries, everybody's favourite was Jimmy 'Daisy' Bell, a stocky, fast-moving inside-left with an explosive shot which brought him 22 Southern League goals plus nine in the FA Cup. Incidentally, the average attendance for League games from the best estimates available for this season was 5,500, a figure City would have been pleased to attain in the majority of more recent seasons. They were also pleased with the profit of £165 on this first season's working as a professional concern.

However, City had a problem which had to be overcome before they could improve their gate receipts and this was the ground at St James' Park where the pitch was not long enough for FA Cup ties. This meant that receipts suffered in seasons 1909-10 and 1910-11, when three important ties had to be played on the County Ground, with a guarantee of something like £150 having to be paid to Exeter RFC. Another two 'home' ties in that latter season had to be switched to the opposing club's ground. This was not resolved until the summer of 1911 (see *St James' Park, Home of Exeter City*).

After that first flush of reasonable success, the City could best be described as an average side during the remainder of their sojourn in the old Southern League, which continued until 1920 after being interrupted by World War One. At the conclusion of the 1919-20 season all the Southern League clubs, with one exception, formed the new Third Division of the Football League. The exception was Cardiff City, who, although finishing only fourth, were fortunate enough to be elected to the Football League's Second Division. With the initiation of Division Three North in 1921, the original Third Division became the Third Division South.

After Exeter City had dropped to 18th place in their second campaign and began season 1910-11 with only two wins in their first 11 games, the players decided that green was an unlucky colour and so, on 12 November 1910, a change was made to the more familiar red and white striped jerseys but this made little immediate difference to their fortunes.

An exception to the run-of-the-mill fare before the war was provided in season 1912-13, when, although finishing one place lower than in their initial season, City enjoyed their most successful campaign in the old Southern League. By this time the last of the original batch of professionals had left the club. However, new favourites had begun to appear, like goalkeeper Dick Pym from Topsham, full-back Jack Fort from Atherton, wing-half Jimmy Rigby (Accrington) and inside-forward Harry Lockett (Nottingham Forest). All of these joined during the previous season, but injuries had made it impossible to field a settled side. However, with the addition in the summer of 1912 of players like Ellis Crompton (Tottenham Hotspur), a man who could play almost anywhere and took over the captaincy from Bob Watson; and wingers Ben Ives from Barrow and Fred Whittaker from Northampton Town, the side began to look like championship contenders. Indeed, they were leading

Exeter City at the start of the 1910-11 season. Back row (left to right): A.Chadwick (manager), F.Duffy, S.Bassett, W.Wells, W.Whittaker, W.Smith, A.Hughes, A.Coates, C.Pratt, J.Banks (trainer). Middle: E.Whittaker, G.Parnell, Mr N.Kendall, E.Jones, Mr T.Oliver, R.Watson, Mr F.Parkhouse, T.Griffiths, Mr S.Thomas (secretary), F.James, J.Garside. On ground: J.Bell, N.Evans, F.Prideaux, A.Cooke.

the table on Easter Monday, having lost only once at home, but then Millwall, another championship contendor, came to St James' Park and in driving rain City were beaten 4-1. This shook their championship hopes and the season's third home defeat in the next game at St James' Park — 3-1 to a strong Swindon side — knocked City out of the race, Swindon finishing runners-up to Plymouth Argyle.

There were several favourites in the side from now until the war but none more popular than goalkeeper Dick Pym. Taking over from Walter Whittaker in March 1912, this local discovery made 186 consecutive appearances (192 with Cup games). Although the goalkeeper is not the only member of the defence, there is no doubt that many of Pym's brave displays, particularly away from home, were the chief reason for the big drop in the rate of goals conceded once he became established. It was fortunate that the directors had a change of heart in May 1913, when he at first refused to re-sign after being offered summer wages of only ten shillings (50p) per week.

Despite a number of good displays on the field, all was not well in the boardroom at this period of the club's history. Indeed, commencing in season 1910-11 when there was a strong difference of opinion about finding money for summer wages, a subject which nearly brought about the departure of manager Arthur Chadwick, things got worse until there was a complete split in the summer of 1912 when something happened which may have been unique in football at that time but which has, sad to relate, re-occurred at Exeter in not dissimilar circumstances in recent times. Three of their own directors reported the club to the FA alleging payment of illegal bonuses!

The FA appointed a commission of enquiry and after a meeting at The Great Western Hotel in July 1912, it was announced that although no illegal payments had been made there were irregularities regarding the book-keeping and for this the club was fined £20. One of the directors was suspended from acting as a director

Exeter City in 1925-6. Manager Fred Mavin is the man in the suit on the back row. After taking over from Arthur Chadwick at the beginning of 1923, Mavin soon made changes in personnel at a club where morale was at a low ebb. One of his 'star' signings was Billy Compton (third from left of seated players). Players who remained from Chadwick's days included full-back Bob Pollard and inside-forward 'Jazzo' Kirk (third and fifth from left of seated players).

or in any official capacity with Exeter City. Some others were censured but chairman Michael McGahey was completely exonerated.

Just before the outbreak of World War One, Exeter City became one of the first English football clubs to visit the Argentine (more details appear in this volume under a separate section) and they did not return until after war had been declared.

The Great War, as it was known, claimed the lives of five City players — full-backs Kadie White, Fred Hunt and Gus Harding, half-back Arthur Evans and another reserve, Clarke. In addition Fred Goodwin, Billy Smith and Fred Marshall were so badly wounded that they had to give up football.

The club's initial Football League game in 1920 was a 3-0 home win against Brentford, played in front of a crowd of about 6,000 at the Park. Left-half Jimmy Mitton stood out in what was described as 'an ordinary game' and the inimitable John Dockray showed himself as the brains of the attack as well as one of the club's cleverest ball players.

Despite this good start, goals were hard to come by and a new club record of 12 successive games without a win (since beaten) was created while only one victory that season was secured away from home — 1-0 at Reading.

Four pre-war players were still in the side, goalkeeper Dick Pym, wing-half Jimmy Rigby, and forwards John Dockray and Alf Green but, despite the poor playing record, a profit of £4,418 was made on the season's activities, thanks partly to the transfer of Billy Goodwin to Manchester United, Jimmy Mitton to Sunderland

Three Exeter City players of the early 1920s. From left to right: Jimmy Mitton, Billy Goodwin and Harry Fryer. The transfers of Goodwin (to Manchester United) and Mitton (to Sunderland) helped record a profit on season 1920-21.

and Bill Wright to Huddersfield Town. With money in the kitty the board took the opportunity of purchasing the ground at a cost of £5,000.

For the most part City went through a bad spell, including severe financial problems in the 1920s. In 1923-4 they created a Football League record by playing 13 consecutive away games without scoring. This run only ended when they brought in reserve full-back, Andy Flynn, as centre-forward for the game at Swindon and he got the only goal. Flynn, from Mexborough, was a useful man to have around, for in the previous season, when goalkeeper Harry Fryer went down with 'flu, he kept goal in three FA Cup ties.

The 1920s gloom was only relieved by seasons 1924-5 and 1927-8. Manager Arthur Chadwick departed at the end of 1922 and had been immediately replaced by Fred Mavin, a much younger man, who arrived at the Park when morale was at a low ebb. By the start of 1924-5 he had made several changes, his most notable signings being outside-left Billy Compton and half-back Bob Pullan from Bristol City. Stars of the side previously signed by Chadwick and still with the club were full-back Bob Pollard and centre-half Ellis Crompton, who had returned after a spell with Bristol Rovers, outside-right Alf Matthews and inside-forward 'Jazzo' Kirk. Add to these the discovery at Silverton of Harold Blackmore, who was to become one of City's most prolific goalscorers, and the club put together a side that lifted them to fifth place in Division Three South by October 1924. From the beginning of November there was a club record run (since beaten) of 11 games without defeat, during which Bill Compton struck up a fine left-wing partnership with Wilf Lievesley, and City were well up with the leaders. But the loss of Stan Charlton in the last few games, as he journeyed to Australia with the FA touring party, took its toll and City had to settle for seventh position but with a club record bag of points which was not to be exceeded for a further eight years.

Ground improvements had been going on apace during this period, thanks largely to the City Supporters' Club and an appeal to the St Sidwell's Street traders, but the following season was scarcely three months old when a fresh disaster struck — the grandstand burnt down on 17 November and the only item not destroyed was Bob Pollard's boots which were away at the repairers. Manager Fred Mavin was particularly worried about the loss of the players' kit, especially their boots,

16

and this showed four days later when City gave such a mediocre display at Aberdare that they were beaten 5-0, the Welsh club's biggest victory over the City, but one which was to be avenged two seasons later when City thrashed them 9-1 in the first round of the FA Cup.

Eleven days after the fire, City had a home FA Cup tie with Swansea Town and a lot of hard work was put into making the special arrangements necessary for this match. (See *St James' Park, Home of Exeter City*.) Although far from complete inside, the new stand was officially opened on 28 August 1926, when a crowd of 8,000 saw the City make a good start to the season, baffling Merthyr Town with their clever passing and easily beating them 3-0. Harold Blackmore got two of City's goals in that opening game and it was in this season (his third with the club) that he really blossomed into an outstanding centre-forward, especially noted for his powerful and accurate shooting. Indeed, he broke the club scoring record in this campaign with 25 League goals and it was no surprise when, with eight games of the season still to play, he was transferred to Bolton Wanderers after starring in Bob Pollard's benefit match against that First Division club.

The man who inspired so many of City's best displays around this time was the Irishman, Billy McDevitt, and one game in particular deserves more detailed mention. This was the 8-1 home win over Coventry City on 4 December 1926. True, the opposition was weak, but this game was a perfect example of the five-forward attacking formation adopted around this period of soccer's history with the crafty Irishman playing the scheming inside-forward role. We can appreciate this from the fact that each of the forwards except McDevitt scored two goals. The line was Purcell, McDevitt, Blackmore, Dent and Compton. The local reporter tells us that McDevitt received a well deserved ovation 'for his play had borne the hallmark of genius.' Billy McDevitt was soon to play a more important role in the club's history.

In October 1927 manager Fred Mavin left for Crystal Palace and was succeeded

Exeter City, 1928-9. Back row (left to right): Clarke, Davie Wilson (manager), Lowton, Holland, Miller, W.Jones (trainer), Dennington. Front: Purcell, McDevitt, Doncaster, Houghton, Death, Pool.

Charlie Miller clears Exeter City's lines during a Third Division South game against Queen's Park Rangers at Loftus Road in 1929. Alec Sheffield covers him.

by former Scottish international, David Wilson. Mavin had assembled a good side for that 1927-8 campaign in which wily centre-forward Fred Dent was 'stealing' goals whilst stopper centre-half Sam Mason was quite uncompromising in defence. After one run of ten games without defeat, City rose to third place in January-February before dropping back to eighth. This was the side that held the eventual FA Cup winners, Blackburn Rovers, to a 2-2 draw at St James' Park in the fourth round of the competition before going down 3-1 at Ewood Park. Fred Dent broke Blackmore's goalscoring record this season with a total of 26 League goals.

Even the signing by Wilson of another of the outstanding players in the club's history, inside-forward Harold 'Happy' Houghton, did not immediately compensate for the weakening of the defence when Fred Mavin returned to take full-back Stan Charlton away to Crystal Palace, and when City suffered six defeats in a row in 1928-9 Wilson left. Unable to afford another manager, the club persuaded Billy McDevitt to manage as well as continue to play. McDevitt's agreement to take on the dual role marks another turning point in the club's up-and-down career leading to the purple patch of the early 1930s.

Billy McDevitt gathered around him what is arguably the finest team the club has ever fielded and this despite the loss of such outstanding local talent as Wilf Lowton to Wolves and Cliff Bastin to Arsenal, as well as Bob Pollard to Queen's Park Rangers. Indeed, the new player-manager moulded a team on correct lines, bringing in more scientific football and abandoning the old kick-and-rush style of some of the more bustling players.

The nucleus of this fine team already at the Park and playing with Billy McDevitt were Charlie Miller, 'Nobby' Clarke, Les Dennington, 'Happy' Houghton and George Purcell. Billy McDevitt's first notable additions were Dicky Baugh from West Brom and Billy Armfield (Aston Villa) in the close season of 1929, followed during 1929-30 by right-back Jimmy Gray (Liverpool) and Cornish centre-forward, Percy Varco (Norwich City).

Exeter City, 1929-30. Back row (left to right): Sheffield, Gray, Alderson, Shanks, Dennington. Front row: Purcell, Houghton, Guyan, Hemingway, Doncaster, Ditchburn.

The addition of Jack Angus (Scunthorpe United), Stan Barber (Bristol City) and last, but by no means least — in the summer of 1930 — goalkeeper Arthur Davies (Everton), and we have the City team that really put the club on the football map with one of the finest-ever FA Cup runs by a side from the Third Division. It was a team that cost no more than £600 in transfer fees.

The Cup giantkilling story of 1930-31 has been recalled many times but there are still supporters always pleased to relate the details. After disposing of Southern League side Northfleet 3-0 and Third Division South Coventry City 2-1 in a replay at Coventry, after a 1-1 draw at the Park, the Grecians were drawn at home to First Division Derby County in the third round. The feeling of excitement, pride and general amazement was unbounded when City won 3-2 in front of a crowd of 16,500. The standard of the Grecians' display that afternoon can be better appreciated when it is recalled that they were without Dicky Baugh for five minutes in the second half and also lost 'Nobby' Clarke with concussion for the last half-hour. There were no substitutes in those days so one can only wonder at this performance.

At this time, City were a side that believed in attack as the best form of defence and showed this in their 2-1 fourth-round victory against Second Division Bury at gale-swept Gigg Lane. This was the game in which Jack Angus made his Cup debut in place of injured centre-half Les Dennington and proved his worth as a first-time tackler.

Cup fever was now affecting practically everyone in Devon, including even the rugby fans, and when the Grecians were drawn at home to another First Division side, Leeds United, in the fifth round, confidence in a home victory was extraordinary. City obliged in a game in which 'Happy' Houghton showed why there were so many rumours about big clubs seeking his signature, for he set up two of the goals and City won 3-1.

The next round produced an even greater shock as City confounded the prophets once again by holding First Division Sunderland to a 1-1 draw at Roker Park. City's never-say-die spirit came through when they were 1-0 down at the interval and they were even considered the better side in the second half when Houghton got the equalizer.

No wonder the team was greeted on their return to St David's Station by a crowd of several thousands which extended back to The Railway Hotel and on to the higher ground of St David's Hill. With the Exeter City Band in attendance, nothing like it has been seen before or since.

City's football hysteria came to an end in the replay at St James' Park the following Wednesday when they had their backs to the wall, and with Houghton well below form, went down 4-2 to a side whose forwards moved surprisingly fast on the waterlogged pitch. On this occasion City played in red and blue. It was this game that attracted a record crowd of 20,984. The players for this giantkilling Cup run were Davies; Baugh, Miller (captain), Clarke, Dennington or Angus, Barber, Armfield, Purcell, Varco, Houghton and Doncaster. Local amateur outside-right Jimmy Gumm played in place of the injured Armfield in the replay against Coventry City.

City finished no higher than 13th in Division Three South that same season, despite Percy Varco scoring 25 League goals. However, if any further proof is necessary of the class of so many members of this team it should be noted that seven (eight if amateur Jimmy Gumm is included) were also in the side which went so close to gaining promotion to the Second Division two years later, creating several records that are still intact.

Exeter City, under the inspiring captaincy of full-back Charlie Miller, would have won promotion to the Second Division in 1932-3, but for some inexplicable lapses at home in the early part of the season. In addition there was the superb form of Brentford, who were unbeaten in their first 14 matches, building up a substantial lead in those early days when City were throwing points away. While the Grecians' defence was one of the strongest ever fielded by the club, their attack took too many games to settle into any kind of rhythm and despite the fact that Fred Whitlow, who did not come into the team until October, scored a record number of goals this season it was the attack, Fred Whitlow and 'Happy' Houghton excepted, which lacked consistency.

In September the forward line let the side down and they dropped a home point against Crystal Palace. In mid-October the Grecians allowed Bournemouth to turn a 2-0 deficit at the Park into a 3-2 victory. In this game the defence was simply overworked. It was not until the 12th game of the season that the City attack really got into its stride in a 5-2 victory over Watford, when Fred Whitlow scored his first League goal of the season and went on to make it a hat-trick.

After losing 1-0 at Bristol Rovers on 3 December, a run of ten games without defeat took City to the top of the table and they reached their peak on 21 January by beating League leaders Brentford 2-0 at Griffin Park. It was a match which lived long in the memory of those supporters who witnessed it.

When City hit a goalscoring slump in February there was the usual talk about not wanting promotion, but the club gave this the lie when on 13 March they strengthened the team by paying out a club record transfer fee to sign two players from Fulham — wing-half Harry Webb and inside-forward Frank Wrightson.

Promotion was still the talking point when City beat Norwich City 2-1 at the Park in April, for the Canaries had temporarily taken over the lead from Brentford at this time. The Grecians were still in with an outside chance of promotion until their astonishing lapse at League newcomers Aldershot when (with three games still to play) City were thrashed 4-1.

Four days later the lowly placed Aldershot earned a goalless draw at St James' Park and it was this result that clinched promotion for Brentford with City eventually finishing in second position, four points behind the champions. In those days only the top team in each section of the Third Division was promoted. The strength of the club's playing resources this season can be appreciated when we recall that the Reserves finished runners-up in the Southern League and champions of the Western League, thanks largely to the goalscoring prowess of local centre-forward Stan Hurst, who turned professional midway through this campaign in which he scored a total of 34 goals in the two competitions just mentioned.

The goalscorer-in-chief, however, was the highly entertaining centre-forward, Fred Whitlow, whose style was always a delight to watch. He created a new club record, which still stands today, by scoring a total of 33 goals in 32 League appearances. In all games he rattled in 51, including seven League hat-tricks, plus one each in the Southern and Western Leagues. His top score was five in a friendly game against an Army XI which City won 10-5.

The final irony was that in this, their most successful playing season so far, the club lost £1,680, due largely to transfer fees. The comment that this proved the club unable to command sufficient attendances to continue to enter the transfer market, is poignant in view of the fact that the average attendance (estimated only) was just under 6,000, which is more than in the majority of post-World War Two seasons.

With 'Happy' Houghton a marked man and Fred Whitlow losing form after a good start, the Grecians dropped to ninth position the following season, but they became the first cup holders of a new competition, the Third Division South Cup (see Cup Section) after beating Torquay United 1-0 in the Final played at Home

Fred Whitlow's 31st League goal of the season, scored in the win over Bristol City at St James' Park on 15 April 1933.

Park. Fred Whitlow scored six in an early round when City beat Crystal Palace 11-6.

About this time City were again getting into deep financial trouble which necessitated the transfer of players and led, in September 1935, to the departure of manager Billy McDevitt. An emergency committee was set up to consider ways of placing the club on an even keel. Chairman Michael McGahey made some interesting disclosures at a public meeting held in the Civic Hall and in another public meeting, in the Exeter Guildhall in February 1935, it was pointed out that the club needed £5,000 by Easter Monday to save it from extinction. The crisis was partly overcome when Mr F.Blanchard agreed to take over the club's mortgage and guarantee it for a period of ten years. But thousands of copies of a public appeal for money were circulated. This particular crisis seemed to have passed when club president, Lord Mamhead, announced over the public address system at the Park before the kick-off of the game with Watford in April that £5,000 additional share capital had been raised. Then, in an effort to cut expenses, the Reserves were withdrawn from the Western League to play in the East Devon League. They did, however, for the time being continue in the Southern League.

Just how low the morale of the club had sunk was shown immediately after the public meeting in January, when the City suffered their biggest home defeat to date, going down 6-0 to Crystal Palace. Jack Angus and 'Nobby' Clarke were the only City players exempt from criticism of a team whose second half efforts were described as 'bordering on the ludicrous'. Yet City finished 11th in the table and rounded off the season by equalling their League record for a home win with an 8-1 demolition job on Aldershot. The vagaries of football form can be seen in the fact that seven of the players in the Crystal Palace humiliation played in the Aldershot triumph when all of the goals were scored in the second half with the Shots actually opening the scoring! City's outside-left, Jack Dryden, not only had a share in nearly every goal, but also broke the back of net with the powerful shot which got his name on the score-sheet. Incidentally, Harry Poulter scored a hat-trick against Aldershot in that game as well as in the first game of the following season when City beat Aldershot 5-1.

Although he was no more to blame than anyone else, the Crystal Palace defeat just about marked the end of goalkeeper Arthur Davies' career with the Grecians, and, indeed, he had previously lost his place to Arthur Chesters, who proved to be one of the most courageous goalkeepers the Grecians ever had. Of course, when the side were struggling near the foot of the table, he took a hammering and injuries kept his number of appearances down but his spirit was never broken. He went to Crystal Palace in 1937, as, incidentally did his successor, Pat Tierney, a year later.

In the summer of 1935 there was talk of a new era and a new board was formed with no less than 15 directors — yes 15! Two of the newcomers who polled the highest number of votes were Fred Blanchford and former player Jimmy Rigby.

As already mentioned, City lost one of their finest managers, Billy McDevitt, in September 1935. The thought of having to face a board of 15 directors must have had a demoralizing effect, but he had reached a point where a break with the City lifted a load off his mind. The team was at the bottom of the table having gone seven games without a win, a run which eventually extended to 13 before McDevitt's last signing, centre-forward Jimmy McCambridge from Bristol Rovers, clicked in a rearranged forward line and the duck was not only broken but five wins in a row were also registered for the fourth time in the club's professional history. Soon afterwards, however, there followed an even worse run of 15 League games without a win — a dismal record which was not broken until 1983-4.

While City were bottom of the table, and before the break in the run of games without a win, the Grecians appointed a new manager in Jack English, a former Sheffield United full-back who had previously managed Darlington, Nelson and Northampton Town. He was unable to work any miracles and, after City were re-elected at the end of his first season, they had to repeat the application a year later when they finished only one place off the bottom. They came top of the poll on both occasions.

In 1936-7 the Grecians proved once again that League and Cup can bear little resemblance. The FA Cup has often provided something special and so it did for City in this season when they finished next to bottom of Division Three South.

Only 'Nobby' Clarke, who had passed Charlie Miller's club record number of 274 League appearances, and Jack Angus remained of the old Cup giantkilling side when City embarked on their latest Cup run. It was not quite in the same class as that in 1930-31 because the opposition was not so highly rated. However, the excitement was there as City beat Southern League Folkestone, leading amateurs Walthamstow Avenue, Third Division North Oldham Athletic and Second Division Leicester City. The attendance for that fourth-round tie at home to Leicester (13,731) was the biggest since the ground record had been created against Sunderland six years earlier. But whereas in the fifth round of 1930-31, City had drawn First Division Leeds United at home, in this season it was First Division Preston North End away.

There had been much chopping and changing of the side during this campaign, which undoubtedly accounted for the lack of consistency. But when, just two weeks before the Preston game, the Grecians suffered their heaviest defeat to date, being thrashed 8-0 at Crystal Palace, a humiliation followed immediately by a 2-1 home defeat by Aldershot, the weakest side in the Southern Section, it was surprising

Exeter City, 1936-7. Back row (left to right): Clarke, W.Barr (trainer), Hobbs, Chesters, Stimpson, Jack English (manager), Shadwell. Front: Thompson, Scott, Williams, McGill, Urmson, W.Brown.

when the selection committee (the manager was not left to select the team in those days) decided to retain the same side for the visit to Preston.

The game at Deepdale was one of the most thrilling the Grecians have ever engaged in. They twice lost the lead and had a goal ruled offside, but it was still 2-2 after 60 minutes. Ten minutes later the Grecians were ahead again but the O'Donnell brothers, Hugh and Frank, won the match for Preston with two goals in an eight-minute spell before Joe Beresford scored another with the last shot of the match. The score was no reflection of this absorbing Cup tie, for City had really shaken Preston and were drawing 3-3 until 12 minutes from time. This was City's last appearance in the fifth round of the FA Cup for 44 years.

Players had been coming and going at an alarming rate in the second half of the 1930s, especially during 1936-7 when no less than 20 newcomers appeared in the League side, equalling the record of the 1921-2 season which was still in the early post-war rebuilding period.

One of the heroes of that Cup run and the leading League scorer in a poor League season was centre-forward Rod Williams, who, despite having to do a lot of his own foraging, a task he seemed to enjoy, scored a total of 36 League and Cup goals. It was an example of City's continuing difficult financial situation that they had to let him go to Reading, from where he was transferred a few months later to West Ham United for a £4,000 fee.

At the 1938 annual meeting the board was accused of replacing players who had been allowed to leave with inferiors and on the occasion of the City Supporters' Club dinner in March 1939, City's chairman of directors, Capt F.J.C.Hunter, said

24

Centre-forward Harry T. Bowl, was ever-present in 1938-9 when he was City's leading scorer with 24 goals in 42 League games.

that "unless something very drastic happens, I cannot see how this club is going to continue. Unless we get some assistance we shall have to put up the shutters."

How prophetic, for as we all know something drastic did happen — the outbreak of World War Two. Furthermore, City did put up the shutters, although thankfully it was only for a little over five years.

St James' Park was in a poor state when the war in Europe ended in May 1945, with the big bank overgrown and little sign of a recognizable football pitch. During the hostilities the ground had been in possession of the War Department and was mostly used by the US Army.

For a while it was touch and go whether Exeter City would resume first-class football but, after some long and hard discussions, the enthusiasts won through. A lot of hard work was required, much of which was carried out by volunteers, including the spreading of 50 tons of earth to bring the pitch up to standard. A few services games followed late in 1944 before City returned to open their post-war programme with a match against Plymouth Argyle on 20 January 1945. This game, watched by a crowd of around 2,400, resulted in a 2-2 draw. Cpl. Jimmy Wiltshire, one of the finest referees in the land, was the man with the whistle on this historic occasion. The City team was K.Halliday; Corbett (Manchester City), Rich (Stockport County), Ryan (Swindon Town), Helliar (Torquay United), Urquhart, Allen, Walker, Ebdon, Mitcheson (Ipswich Town) and Hodge. Most of these were still in the forces and only Halliday, Walker and Ebdon were on City's books, the last two being pre-war players. Halliday was an amateur goalkeeper from Lyme Regis and not to be confused with pre-war full-back, Tom Halliday.

At the annual meeting in April 1945, Mr Sid Thomas said that an appeal for £5,000 was being launched 'to enable the City to make a successful come-back'. The deficit on the company's profit and loss account stood at over £19,000. It is also important to record that the club's first chairman and a real Exeter City stalwart who had done so much for the club, Mr Michael McGahey, had died during the war, as had his successor in the chair from 1936, Capt F.J.C.Hunter and another director, Mr A.J.Chamberlain.

A notable event in 1945 was the formation of a new supporters' club, The Grecians, due to the initiative of one the City's founders, Mr Norman Kendall. This organization was to be of immense help to the club over the next 25 years, so much so that it is doubtful whether first-class football would have survived in Exeter without their financial assistance which at one period of time was around £1,000 a month. Many fans had been starved of football during the war, especially in the south-west where both Plymouth Argyle and Torquay United, as well as Exeter City, had been out of action.

First-class football was reintroduced gradually with a system of regionalized League and Cup games in 1945-6, but with an official FA Cup competition which was, however, run on a two-leg home and away basis. As during the war, guest players were still permitted during this season and to complete their League and Cup programme, City included nearly 30 of these. Ten pre-war City players returned to resume their careers, although because of continued war service another, Bill Fellowes, did not return until the following season.

One could write a book about the problems in fielding teams during the first post-war season, which was really little better than it had been for the clubs who had continued throughout those dark days. Suffice to say here for the benefit of those statistical fanatics that City's first official post-war League South (South Region) game was played at Swindon on 25 August when City won 4-1 with this team: Joslin (Torquay United); Murray, Rich (Stockport County), Walker, Blood (captain), Jordan, Wardle, Warren, Ebdon, Mitcheson (Ipswich Town) and Casey. The amateur winger Casey scored twice, while Wardle and Ebdon got the others. The attendance was estimated as 11,200.

Apart from mentioning the fact that crowds of 10,000 or even 11,000 were seen at the Park during 1945-6, the season is best glossed over with City finishing near the bottom of the League and League Cup competitions and being knocked out of the FA Cup by Newport County in the second round.

The most important decision taken was to appoint former Huddersfield Town and Manchester United full-back George Roughton as manager. He enjoyed only limited success but no man could have worked harder to drag City back into the game after the wartime break.

City averaged only around 15th in his six post-war seasons with the club, but

Exeter City in 1948-9. Back row (left to right): Jim Clark, Stan Rowe, Ken Powell, Cyril Johnstone, Reg Gibson, Archie Smith, Steve Walker, Bill Dymond. Middle: Ron Johnston, Harry Bartholomew, Arthur Coles, Bert Hoyle, Barney Singleton, Derek Warren, Bob Jeffrey, Fred Davey. Front: Jimmy Gallagher (trainer), Duggie Regan, Peter Fallon, Bill Rowe, Harry Evans, Bill Fellowes (assistant secretary), George Roughton (manager), Angus Mackay, Bernard Grant, Dennis Hutchings, Dick Smart, Stan Cutting (assistant trainer).

this is not to say the St James' Park fans were short of entertainment, for the club had more personalities in the side than in many of the more recent seasons. Who ever provided more thrills than centre-forward 'Digger' Ebdon, who never slackened his efforts for a single moment and had been known to chase forlorn hopes as far as the corner-flag before scoring? What better sliding tackles have ever been seen at the Park than those by full-back George 'Ginger' Thompson? His, indeed, is a lost art made more difficult nowadays by the need for perfect accuracy to avoid the referee's whistle. How many goalscoring wingers can you name who could outstrip Duggie Regan? Or more intelligent inside-forwards than Ray Wright, who, alas, was handicapped by leg injuries. In the same department City have never had a cleverer footballer than Angus Mackay, one of several long-stay players signed by George Roughton. Others who remained more than a half dozen seasons were dedicated players like goalkeeper Barney Singleton and local centre-half Fred Davey. After so many years have passed one is even more puzzled as to why the City did not enjoy more success over this period.

One of the biggest shocks was the club's record League defeat (since equalled) of 9-0 at Notts County in October 1948. But it should be remembered that the County had hit the headlines as a Third Division side by paying out something in the region of £50,000 on transfers and City's £2,000 team really had little chance against one of the game's all-time greats, who led the County attack. This was Tommy Lawton, who had Jackie Sewell on his right and Oscar Hold on his left. Hold opened the scoring then Sewell and Lawton added four each, including half a dozen goals in one 12-minute second-half spell.

Of course the best aspect of these early post-war years was the large crowds which added so much to the atmosphere. The average Third Division attendance at St James' Park for those first six peacetime seasons was 9,140. To put this into perspective the same figure for the six seasons before the latest campaign was 2,580. Of course, this problem is a general one almost throughout the Football League and is certainly not exclusive to Exeter City.

In the 35 years of the clubs existence before the war City had five managers and two chairmen. In the 45 years since hostilities ceased there have been 17 managerial changes and 11 different chairmen. In many cases the chairman has had more affect (good or bad) on the club's fortunes than the manager, so they cannot be ignored. Indeed, as with most football clubs, the stories behind many of the changes of chairmen would make interesting reading. The so called 'power game' is perhaps more prevalent among football clubs than in a good deal of big business.

The highlight of George Roughton's six and a half years at St James' Park was undoubtedly the 1950-51 FA Cup run and in particular the fourth-round tie with First Division Chelsea (see *Matches to Remember*) which City drew 1-1, thanks to a late equalizer by Duggie Regan. This was the first all-ticket match ever played at the Park and 20,000 were sold, with gate receipts of £3,760 easily a record.

The Grecians were without injured full-back Jim Clark, centre-forward Archie Smith and inside-left Angus Mackay for the replay at Stamford Bridge and two goals in the space of six minutes by centre-forward Bobby Smith were enough to put City out of the Cup in front of a crowd of 46,134.

When manager George Roughton left for Southampton he was replaced by Norman Kirkman, who only stayed for a year before being followed by Norman Dodgin. The debacle surrounding the appointment in between of Tim Ward is explained elsewhere under the section on City's managers.

Norman Dodgin arrived at Exeter a month after the opening floodlit match, against Plymouth Argyle on 3 March 1953, and had little time other than to size up the situation with City finishing 17th. Most important of his early moves was to contact Arnold Mitchell and persuade him to continue his career with the City.

This player had been placed on the open to transfer list after only one season and, considering he went on to make a club record number of 495 League appearances, Norman Dodgin deserves thanks for this initiative alone.

This manager, however, was to achieve more, for he pulled the City up by the bootlaces so that they rose from 23rd in 1951-2 to ninth in 1953-4, when the goal-average was the highest since well before the war, and the side also created a new club record (since equalled) of eight consecutive away wins in the League.

Norman Dodgin had signed Andy Donaldson from Middlesbrough in September 1953 and his intelligent leadership was a feature of the attack. Unfortunately, however, this lanky leader was overtaken by illness and faded from the scene in the next season. In 1953-4, though, he scored 16 goals and would have scored more but for some weakness in support. The exception to this criticism was Charlie McClelland, who enjoyed his best scoring season with a bag of 19 League goals. City won eight away games, a club record since only equalled and the defence was the stronger department with goalkeeper Hugh Kelly unlucky not to have gained another Irish cap.

How City dropped from ninth to 22nd in the following season is difficult to explain, although Ray Goddard had gone after a loss of form through injuries and Keith Harvey had not yet reached his peak. Hugh Kelly's form was fading and there was also the loss of Andy Donaldson. Norman Dodgin tried a record number of 28 different players to complete this disastrous League programme and equalled that number in the following campaign, which was only marginally better. This was followed by another two seasons in the bottom four before the Third Division was split in 1958 with City dropping into the new Fourth Division, thus aggravating their financial difficulties with the consequent increase in travelling costs.

There had been a big boardroom shake-up around this time and some of the directors were not smiling. Mr A.S. Line took over the chairmanship from Sid Thomas, who thus ended an active position with the club which stretched back almost to the turn of the century.

Mr Line, who immediately made a public appeal for financial aid, was full of enthusiasm and big ideas but unfortunately he was in poor health, and, indeed, died not long after handing over the chairmanship to George Gillin in October 1959.

Norman Dodgin was one victim of the changes in 1957 when Mr Line decided that his 'new era' necessitated a change of manager and brought in 35-year-old Bill Thompson from Guildford City. Thompson stayed only eight months, leaving in January 1958 when the side was two places off the bottom of the League and the goal-average was at its worst for 35 years. City had paid out a lot of money in transfer fees, all to no avail for they eventually finished bottom with another new manager, Frank Broome, appointed only two days after Thompson's departure, given little time to do more than sign experienced centre-half Ken Oliver to try and bolster the defence. However, even this player could not prevent City from equalling their worst-ever League defeat in April 1958, when they were thrashed 9-0 at Northampton. The ineptness of the side is emphasized by the fact that goalkeeper George Hunter could not be blamed for any of the goals in that débâcle.

Ironically it was around this low point in their playing history that City fans were having the pleasure of watching one of the finest footballers ever to wear the City's colours. Indeed, he may have been too clever, for if centre-forward Ted Calland had converted even half of this talented winger's pin-point centres into goals, then City would certainly have been in a better position. This real entertainer was outside-left Gordon Dale, manager Thompson's best signing and the club's most expensive transfer when they paid Portsmouth a £7,000 fee for his services in October 1957.

Exeter goalkeeper George Hunter makes a despairing grab at the ball during a League game against Gillingham in the late-1950s. The player on the extreme right is City centre-half Ken Oliver, who played alongside Hunter at Derby County before the pair were signed by Frank Broome.

City began their Fourth Division history in 1958-9 with a good season under Frank Broome's management and would have clinched promotion but for the fact that in October, Keith Harvey broke his leg and clever ball-playing inside-forward Brian Birch injured his back. Money was severely restricted with so much having been spent on transfers in the previous campaign. Indeed, only three new first-team players were signed this season. They were Brian Birch, Jim Thompson and Brian Whitnall. City missed promotion by two points, finishing fifth.

There were organized protests by the supporters and disagreement on the board which brought a number of changes from top to bottom before City could produce a promotion-winning side. Not long after George Gillin took over as chairman, Frank Broome decided to try his luck at Southend United and was succeeded by Glen Wilson as player-manager, followed after another two years by the experienced Cyril Spiers, who remained only nine months before handing over to Jack Edwards, the man who had been trainer for a year before being appointed manager in May 1963.

George Gillin resigned in 1961 when Reg Rose became chairman after putting in around £17,000, including buying up the mortgage on the ground. Three directors left the board in the hope of making way for more affluent newcomers and there was an issue of £5 loan receipts to help the finances.

City won promotion for the first time in their history in 1963-4 when a number of club records were equalled and one broken, for this season brought the best goal-average up to then. The crowd's favourite in the scoring department was diminutive newcomer Alan Banks, sometimes referred to as a 'poacher', but in reality

29

Torquay United goalkeeper Terry Adlington falls on the ball during a Fourth Division game at Plainmoor in 1964, with City's Alan Banks still hoping for a scoring opportunity.

a player capable of creating his own openings and scoring from almost any angle. An inspiration to the side, he should not have played in the last game of the season at Workington because of an injured arm, but City needed at least a point to clinch promotion and he turned out to help earn a goalless draw after 90 nail-biting minutes.

One man played in every game in this promotion campaign, local discovery Keith Harvey, a real 90-minute worker, who always played his heart out. Three who missed only one game each were goalkeeper Alan Barnett, left-half John Anderson and outside-right Graham Rees.

Promotion, however, brought the club no long-term benefits. Indeed, it marked the beginning of another period of problems both on and off the field, not the least of which was the loss of £10,986 on the promotion season's working, due mainly to the cost of transfers.

A new supporters' club was formed which marked the beginning of the end for the Grecians' Association, although it continued as part of the new club for a number of years. A shot-shy team made a bad start to their first season in the new Third Division and, after suffering a run of injuries, team morale was really hit by the resignation of manager Jack Edwards, who considered that he had been badly treated. Ellis Stuttard succeeded Edwards in January 1965 but after only two seasons in the Third Division, City were relegated. Stuttard then left, having earlier handed over team control to coach Jock Basford, who was then confirmed as manager.

This time it took 11 seasons, three managerial changes and three more chairmen

30

to regain Third Division status. Jock Basford was fired after a stay of only ten months and Frank Broome was recalled for a second spell of one year and nine months. He was followed in April 1969 by Johnny Newman. In the boardroom Reg Rose (chairman since 1961) handed over to Les Kerslake before the chairmanship passed to Fred Dart in 1970 and Gerald Vallance in 1976. It should also be mentioned that in another effort to sort out the finances, City went without a reserve team for five seasons between 1967 and 1972. At the time the directors had little choice but it was a decision that must have prolonged the club's stay in the Fourth Division.

Before moving on it is worth recalling the case of the unplayed Fourth Division game at Scunthorpe United in April 1974. The Football League fined City £5,000 and ordered them to pay Scunthorpe £1,095 compensation and costs for not fulfilling this fixture. Having only nine fit men — including two goalkeepers — available, the City had made two reasonable requests for a postponement but these were rejected. Considering the number of more recent postponements allowed under similar circumstances it seems that City were, to say the least, unlucky. The game was never played and Scunthorpe were awarded the points.

Johnny Newman's contribution as player, player-manager and manager over a period of nine years was second to none. Indeed, no manager ever left Exeter City in better shape for, when he went to Grimsby Town in December 1976, his side went on to win promotion that season under successor Bobby Saxton who, it must be said, had already helped bring about a great improvement on the field since his arrival from Plymouth Argyle in September 1975.

The 1976-7 promotion side began to build with the transfer of Peter Hatch from Oxford United in 1973 and was completed with the signing in July 1976 of one of City's most powerful goalscorers — Tony Kellow from Falmouth. The team

Exeter City at the start of the 1976-7 promotion season. Back row (left to right): Peter Hatch, Bobby Saxton, Dick Key, Jack Edwards (trainer), Phil Howe, Tony Kellow, John Templeman. Middle row: Alan Hooker, Alan Beer, Keith Clapham, John Newman (manager), Tony Morrin, Nicky Jennings, John Hore. Front row: Harry Holman, Bobby Hodge, Graham Weeks, Mike Green, Mike Jordan.

was a nice blend of youth and experience, the latter provided by John Templeman, Johnny Hore, Nicky Jennings and Bobby Saxton. It is interesting to note that the average age of this promotion side was exactly the same as the previous one in 1963-4, that is 26 years 9 months.

There is little doubt that the introduction of Kellow to help Alan Beer in the goalscoring department was the factor that turned the previous season's side into a promotion-winning combination and he became the first player to top City's League scoring sheet in as many as five seasons.

Clifford Hill took over the chairmanship from Gerald Vallance in 1982. When Clifford Hill became president, Byron Snell had a brief spell as chairman in 1985, before Ivor Doble became the club's 13th different chairman later that same year.

The club and supporters had been sorry to see Bobby Saxton move back to Plymouth Argyle as manager in 1977, after only a year in charge at St James' Park, and Brian Godfrey got the job of keeping City in the Third Division. He enjoyed a couple of above-average campaigns, especially 1980-81 when City almost repeated the FA Cup deeds of 50 years earlier by winning through to the sixth round. This time, however, they were beaten 2-0 at Tottenham Hotspur, instead of forcing a draw on a First Division club's ground. However, in the previous round they had held Second Division Newcastle United to a 1-1 draw at the North Eastern St James' Park before thrashing them 4-0 at home — a victory which ranks among the most remarkable in the club's history with a clever City team making it look so easy.

Brian Godfrey left when the side was on the slide in June 1983 and former England captain, Gerry Francis, was in charge throughout the disastrous campaign of 1983-4. One of the worst in the club's history with a record 11 home defeats, it ended in a return to the Fourth Division after only six wins and going through a record run of 18 games without a victory.

After another bankruptcy scare in November 1982, following a loss of nearly £189,000 on the previous season's working, strict economy measures were taken which reduced losses by 50 per cent the following season. During the two seasons 1983-4 and 1984-5, a record total of 34 players with first team experience were transferred or released by the club, including player-manager Gerry Francis. Around the same time the directors rejected a take-over bid from Dan McCauley, a North Devon millionaire who had been previously voted off the board.

Following relegation in 1984, it took another five years to get the team into shape, due partly to further rapid changes of management. Jim Iley, who had followed Gerry Francis in the summer of 1984, was fired after less than 12 months and his successor, Colin Appleton, remained for about 18 months. But then came the man who put City back on the right track — Terry Cooper.

When this former England international was appointed team manager at St James' Park in May 1988, the club's supporters had endured a run of seven seasons during which City suffered relegation and consistently finished below the half-way mark. Indeed, they were only two places off the bottom when the new manager took charge but, after a little over 12 months, the groans turned to cheers and Football League attendances at St James' Park increased to an average figure which had not been equalled for 17 years.

It has been said in the past that trouble in the boardroom affects the team, but City convincingly disproved this by winning promotion to the Third Division at the end of Cooper's second season. During this memorable 1989-90 campaign, one director resigned under pressure and two were ousted from the board by chairman Ivor Doble. Indeed, there was also a repeat of 1912 with a director reporting the club to the FA for alleged financial irregularities.

Fortunately, Terry Cooper was able to distance himself from these goings on and, not only did his side win promotion, they also achieved it for the first time as champions. Whilst it must be admitted that the standard of much of the opposition was poor, this does not detract from City's outstanding performance, for they won the title by a margin of ten points. Indeed, the fact that City held Sunderland to a draw in the Littlewoods Cup and Norwich City to a draw in the FA Cup confirms that this side, so ably led by Devonian Shaun Taylor, was something special.

City's promotion in this campaign had some quite remarkable aspects, not the least of which was losing 13 away games. No other side has ever lost as many away games and still finished champions of any division of the Football League. It is worth noting, however, that they lost only one away game by a margin of more than one goal.

Teamwork and team spirit were the essential ingredients of this side in which so many individuals improved out of recognition as the season progressed. Important among these was newcomer Danny Bailey, the only ever-present, who had only three Football League appearances to his credit before Terry Cooper spotted his potential. What this player lacks in constructive ability he more than makes up for with sheer hard work and his non-stop running in midfield was a great asset to the side, whilst his never-say-die spirit made him a firm favourite with the fans.

Remember also that City went on to win promotion despite losing leading scorer Darren Rowbotham with a serious knee injury for the last 14 matches after he had netted 20 League goals (plus ten in the Cup). We shall never know whether he would have broken Fred Whitlow's club League scoring record if he had been able to play out the season.

The fact that this 1989-90 side was the youngest of City's three promotion-winning teams sparks the hope that they will be able to build on the rock of this success in a more lasting fashion than their predecessors. One thing is certain — as long as the dedicated Terry Cooper continues as team manager any failure to go further will not be due to lack of effort.

Brian McDermott scores the winner against Southend United on 25 April 1990, in the game that clinched promotion for Exeter City.

This time City ensure the title for themselves. Tony Kelly scores the first of his two penalties against Scarborough on 28 April 1990.

Kelly is on the mark from the spot again as Exeter beat Scarborough 3-2.

City's third goal against Scarborough, scored by Richard Young.

Exeter City receive a cheque for £25,000 after winning the Fourth Division title. From left to right: Bob Gordon (Barclays director of personnel), Norman Thomas (Football League finance officer), City chairman Ivor Doble and manager Terry Cooper.

Exeter City parade the Fourth Division championship trophy. Opposite page shows player-assistant manager Steve Neville with his teammates. This page sees manager Terry Cooper proudly holding aloft the trophy.

St James' Park
Home of Exeter City

by Alex Wilson

AS everybody who knows anything about football is aware, there are two St
James' Parks. One, the big one, is in Newcastle. The other, the small one,
in Exeter. It is the latter with which we are concerned.

From an earlier chapter it will have been seen that the formation of the City
club was not entirely clear-cut. It was a matter of gradual evolution over a period

of time rather than a committee of men standing up on a precise date in history and declaring, "Right — This is Exeter City Football Club."

But, as far as can be ascertained, the first Exeter soccer club was admitted to the Devon County FA in 1891 and became active in the 1891-2 season, when they played a few matches on pitches within the confines of Topsham Barracks. Two years later, the Horse Show Field, or simply the Show Field, in Mount Pleasant was acquired for the purposes of playing football, while the St Luke's College ground in Magdalen Road and an open field in Monks Road also served their purpose around that time.

The earliest mention of St James' Park, or St James' Field, in connection with football is in the early 1890s when rugby games were played there. The first soccer game to take place at this venue was probably that between Exeter and Tavistock Athletic, in good weather and before a fair attendance on 20 October 1894.

And from then onwards, it was generally that piece of land at the north-easterly extent of the town which became, and remains to this day, the home of the Grecians, as we like to call the City club. Its boundaries were enclosed by Well Street and the railway cutting on one side, the school and church on the opposite one, the St James' Road, a street of magnificent Victorian houses behind the goal-posts at the Exeter end and open fields beyond the far end, of which more later.

In those bygone days, the football club had no need of a groundsman, for the grass was maintained at its required length through the agency of the farmer who owned the adjoining field. He would put his livestock out to graze there, an early example of a mutually advantageous ground-sharing scheme, perhaps!

The 'Professional Fever'

IT is not an easy matter for any 'Park-ites' of modern times to conjure up a picture of St James' Park as it would have been at the dawn of the present century. What was the place like in those days? Well, the best that can be said is that it was just a field, reasonably flat but often very wet and muddy, on which football was played by amateur teams. The sun, when it shone at all on a winter's afternoon, beamed its rays from the St James' Road end, so that generations of captains, on winning the toss, have usually directed their men to kick towards the goal at the far end of the ground, one thing at least that does not alter with the passing of the years.

There were neither turnstiles, seated accommodation, banked up terracing or facilities such as toilets and tea bars. There may have, on some occasions, been programmes or match-cards for sale, but most likely not.

However, the relentless march of time, bringing with it the era of progress, modernization and change, was shortly to embrace the little amateur team and a series of quite astonishing developments was just around the corner.

In February 1908 a rumour was circulated by an official of the Plymouth Argyle Club to the effect that a professional club was to be formed in Exeter and an application for enrolment in the Southern League was to be applied for. Unlikely as it appeared to be at the time, there were nevertheless indications that this rumour, as it was called, was founded upon fact.

For 'professional fever' was brewing in Exeter and there were signs that it would become epidemic. At the same time, there were many sentimental objections amongst the natives of the ever-faithful to the idea of paying a troupe of men to play football for the town, as it seemed to lower the noble game to the level of a circus exhibition.

But at the same time it had to be admitted by these critics that, bearing in mind the distance of Exeter from the centre of professional activity and the comparative thinness of the population, it was clear that the object of the promoters of the suggested limited liability football company could not be merely to 'make money', and thus it was assumed that the main purpose of the introduction of the element of professionalism was educational; a laudable endeavour to raise the standard of the play of existing clubs and particularly that of Exeter City. This was the view that met most with the general assent of the townsfolk. Doubts were expressed, however, concerning the suitability of the ground at St James' Park. The most desirable solution would have been to purchase the County Ground at St Thomas's from the Exeter Rugby Club but, to secure this, a bid of £130, or possibly £150, would have had to have been made, and this was out of the question.

The number of people attending matches at St James' Park in those days varied from a few hundred to a little over a thousand, this figure being exceeded on rare occasions only. Exeter City did make an attempt to secure the Barnfield ground with a view to adapting it to the needs of a professional football team but this fell through. In March 1908 it was announced by Mr S.Thomas (secretary) that Mr J.McGahey (solicitor) had accepted, on the proposed Football Company's behalf, the terms offered for a 21 years' lease of the football ground at St James' Park and, at a later date, the architect's plan for the equipment of the St James' Field, exposed to public view, had attracted great attention in Exeter. Many were the exclamations of surprise at the ingenuity which made provision for a crowd of 18,000 souls or thereabouts within so small an enclosure.

This would be made possible, it was explained, by the manufacture of extra space by the aid of stands, flower-pot staging and banking up. And when finished, according to the plans, it was seen that St James' Park would be a cosy and well-furnished ground, one of the best in the west of England.

The first grandstand, a small wooden one, was erected later in the year when it had been confirmed that Exeter City would indeed become a professional outfit in the Southern League's First Division.

On the opposite side of the ground to the grandstand, rows of geraniums were planted just beyond the touch-line and this section was known as the Flower-Pot Stand, becoming known more generally in the fullness of time as the 'Popular Bank', the cheapest part of the ground and the place where the most loyal, noisy and demonstrative of the club's followers assembled. In more recent times this has become the 'Cowshed'.

Trouble Ahead

IT is likely that, when the St James' Park ground was laid out for the purposes of professional football, the directors of the City club were quite unaware of any deficiency in the pitch, regarding its length. But a couple of years later, it became generally known throughout the football world that the distance measured from goal-line to goal-line fell short — by a couple of yards — of the minimum stipulated by the Football Association for matches within the jurisdiction of their Challenge Cup competition.

The consequence was that first Reading, then Nelson and Burnley, refused to send their teams to Exeter for Cup games, which had to be transferred to the grounds of the opposing clubs. Thus, Exeter had to play their home Cup games on opponents' grounds.

Efforts to secure a strip of the adjoining field at the far end of the ground were unsuccessful. The owner, who was the farmer previously referred to, declared that he would sell all or none. Negotiations were then opened for the acquisition of the Rugby Ground at the other end of the city, but these were not followed up for the sportsmanlike reason that it would mean the ousting of the very old-established Exeter RFC from its historic home.

Mr Duke to the Rescue

IN the summer of 1911, Mr H.E.Duke, Exeter's Member of Parliament, came to the rescue by practical assistance of a kind for which the Club had often sought, and sought in vain. Mr Duke footed the bill for the extension of the playing pitch, the enlargement of the grandstand, increased accommodation for spectators and a vast improvement in the ground generally. Mr Duke had, by his timely and generous action, immensely improved the outlook of Exeter City Football Club and relieved the directions of an anxiety which had hung over them like a cloud for a long time. Exeter City now stood on the threshold of what was to prove a new era in its affairs and interest in the club became greater than ever before.

The first match played on the new pitch — City against West Ham United on

14 October 1911 — was to be remembered for more reasons than one. As the spectators entered St James's Park, they saw that across the lower part of the ground where formerly stood the goal-posts had been strung red and white ribbons (Exeter's new colours). The goal-posts, three yards further back, and the new fencing behind were in their permanent positions with cinder banking beyond the fence. The St James' Road end had also been put back a yard or two and the whole ground looked strangely different.

Before the players appeared, Miss Duke, daughter of the MP (who was unable to travel down from Harrogate) cut the ribbons, and while the band played and the crowd cheered, the young lady was presented with suitable mementoes of the occasion by Mr J.Archibald Lewis, the architect, and Mr J.H.Stile, the building contractor. A handsome bouquet of red and white carnations was handed over by little Miss Kendall, daughter of Mr Norman Kendall, a City director. Subsequently the club's new flag was unfurled, amid further loud applause and cheering.

The match resulted in a 3-3 draw. Important men of Exeter were present, numbering about 50 and including some of the 'city fathers', aldermen, members of the city council and the archdeacon of Exeter Cathedral.

For some years after this, the big bank at the lower end, later to be properly laid out in rows of terraces with crush barriers placed at strategic points, was known as the 'Duke Bank.'

On Fire!

THE 1920-21 season, the club's first in the Football League, was remarkable for the continued failure of the team. To the general public the campaign must have been a most disappointing one, of that there could have been no doubt. But in one respect there was much for the management to rejoice about, for one of the principal accomplishments of that year was the securing of the ground as the football club's own property. The purchase was largely made possible with the money received from the transfers of Mitton to Sunderland, Wright to Huddersfield, and Pym to Bolton Wanderers.

The conveyance of the deeds of the ground and offices to Exeter City was made in June at the cost of between £5,000 and £6,000. Four years later, a roof was erected on the Flower-Pot Side but a few months afterwards, on Tuesday 17 November, disaster struck.

For on that day, at about two o'clock in the afternoon, the grandstand was wholly destroyed by a fire which broke out in the boiler-room and developed along the entire range of the building with such amazing rapidity that all the club's football gear, books, accounts, documents and furniture went up in flames.

A few people, including Mr Mavin, the manager, and some of the players, gathered outside the ground in Well Street after smoke had been seen issuing from the top of the grandstand. It was then realized that the whole place was on fire, for with a sudden rush the windows at the back burst outwards and great volumes of dense black smoke belched out and swept across the railway cutting, borne on a brisk autumn breeze. More crowds of people collected in the surrounding streets and then all the players arrived to watch the doomed structure burn out like a gigantic torch.

The pitch was scorched and blackened all along the side nearest the stand — and in four days' time the big FA Cup tie against Swansea Town was due to be played. The players' dressing-rooms, like everything else on that side, were a blazing inferno but, although it sounds impossible, the Cup game did take place — and in a snowstorm what's more. The official attendance was just over 9,500, including a few visitors from Wales.

Tents were provided for the players at half-time and before and after the match, Exeter City were accommodated at the Red Lion Hotel, while Swansea were given the use of Messrs Neal's premises in St James's Road.

'There's a Good Time Coming!'

THE grandstand was replaced by the present one, which is larger, and which was constructed in the summer of 1926, following delays caused by the General Strike. And happier times for the City club were to follow in the early years of the decade which preceded the war.

A popular feature on football days at St James' Park had always been the stirring music of the very fine Exeter City Military Band under the conductorship of Mr George Newman. In their earliest days the City players came out of the tunnel to the strains of the 'Devonshire National Anthem' *Widdecombe Fair.*

In the 1920s, George Newman and his musicians associated themselves with the 'top-of-the-pops' of the day and the Grecians entered the arena while the band belted out the 'number-one' hit *Felix Kept on Walking.*

In 1930, the latest wireless craze was *There's a Good Time Coming, Be it Ever so Far Away* and this is what the band played as the City men ran on to the field. And they were right. There *was* a good time coming indeed, and not so far away either. For in that season, City astonished the football world beyond belief when they knocked out of the Cup two First Division sides at home and one high-riding Second Division team, far away up in Lancashire, and even drew with the mighty Sunderland at Roker Park (which put the Grecians into the hat for the semi-final draw). They lost the replay at the 'Park' on a pouring wet Wednesday afternoon with 21,000 people packed into that little ground.

Record attendances with record gate receipts were the result, and for the first time in the club's entire history, that tight little ground bore an air of prosperity. The following year saw the City players decked out in 'posh' new football shirts, of the 'Corinthians' type, with button-up sleeves, breast pockets, and cricket-style collars, and jet-black silky looking shorts, or knickers as they were called then, in place of the old navy blue ones. And the year after that, Exeter were unlucky not to have gained promotion to the Second Division when they finished runners-up to Brentford at the top.

The Best Place

HOME wins at St James' Park were almost a foregone conclusion in those happy days, the team was strong, powerful, and clever and the general pattern of play was always towards the visiting team's goal.

Further improvements with the money now available were made to the ground, and the roof over the popular side was extended to its present length in the summer of 1933. But those balmy days did not last for much longer and, shortly before the war, various appeals had to be made to the tradesmen and general public of Exeter to 'Save the City' in their fight against extinction.

During the war, St James' Park was given over for part of the time to the American Army, who played their peculiar brand of rugby football there. It can be assumed, therefore, that instead of the usual cries of 'Come on the City' and so on, there would have been heard from the terraces 'Come on you guys, on your marks, get moving, speed it up you knuckle-head sonofabitch' and such-like, from the GIs watching.

Floodlights of rather a poor quality were put up in 1953 and it seems in keeping with the ill-luck that has so often dogged the club that the inauguration match for the new lights had to be scrapped because the ground was enveloped in a thick fog. Typical! Those floodlights have since been replaced by better ones but they do not bear comparison with many others up and down the country.

From my earliest memory of standing behind the goal at that far end to the present-day, St James' Park seems not to have changed a great deal — and a good thing, too, for there is a certain atmosphere there that cannot be put into words. You do not get pushed and shoved about, your ears do not hurt from head-splitting noise, you can stand there or sit in the stand and just enjoy the football and the conversation with people nearby. It is quite ideal and quite unrivalled.

Speaking personally, if I may crave your indulgence for a moment, I do not go there quite so often now because I am unable to, but on Saturday afternoons when the Grecians are playing there, that is where my heart and my mind are, down at St James' Park, standing on the 'Duke Bank' behind the lower goal. Recently, a survey was conducted by a national daily newspaper which, when the results came in, concluded that, out of the whole of England, the best place to live in is Exeter. They were absolutely right, of course. And out of the whole of Exeter, what better place to be than St James's on a Saturday afternoon? There has been a lot of wild talk in recent times about the converting of our soccer grounds for seating only. It is to be earnestly hoped that nothing like this will ever be attempted at 'the Park', for it would quite ruin it.

Exeter City supporters on their way to St James' Park for the vital game against Scarborough in April 1990.

44

EXETER CITY Managers

Arthur Chadwick
April 1908-December 1922

SOON after forming themselves into a limited company in 1908, Exeter City obtained the services of the experienced former England international Arthur Chadwick as player-manager, or as he was officially known at the time, 'adviser'.

The club chose wisely for this Lancastrian performed his difficult task well and Exeter were able to take advantage of his many contacts built up during more than 13 years in the game. Capped twice for England at centre-half, against Wales and Scotland in 1900, he had made well over 200 Football League and Southern League appearances with Burton Swifts, Southampton, Portsmouth and Northampton Town and continued to play during his first two seasons at Exeter. It was when he gave up playing in 1910 that he was officially given the title of 'manager'.

When Chadwick arrived at St James' Park there was only one professional, but he quickly built up a useful team which included several players with First Division experience. As with so many of his successors, Chadwick suffered because of lack of funds which forced him to transfer many of his best players. Indeed, he had to start almost from scratch for a second time after World War One, but it was the 1919-20 team that he always considered to have been his best.

The subsequent transfers of goalkeeper Dick Pym to Bolton Wanderers and leading scorer Billy Goodwin to Manchester United left him with serious gaps to fill and, after the disappointments of the club's first two seasons in the new Third Division, he decided to call it a day shortly before Christmas 1922.

Arthur Chadwick was still the club's longest serving manager, having been in the job for just over 14 years including his time as 'adviser'. He was forever respected at Exeter and though sad, it was perhaps fitting that he should have died in the stand at St James' Park, while watching City and Clapton Orient in March 1936.

Fred Mavin
January 1923-November 1927

CITY were at a low ebb when they secured the services of a Geordie, Fred Mavin, as manager. However, after a difficult spell, he had the satisfaction of leaving them in a far better position than he found them.

A serious injury to his left knee brought Fred Mavin's League career to an end with Reading in 1921. He struggled for a further season in the Southern League, with Boscombe, but was forced to give up. He previously served New Brompton (later Gillingham), Fulham and Bradford, creating a club record run of appearances as an attacking centre-half with the Cottagers.

Football managers are a tough breed and one wonders how Mavin felt when he was appointed manager of Exeter on 23 January 1923. A few weeks earlier they had been knocked out of the qualifying competition of the FA Cup, losing 2-1 at home to Bath City, an event described in the local Press as 'a crowning failure'. True, they had subsequently picked up a couple of victories, but Mavin's task was an uphill struggle.

His most valuable signings included goalkeeper Harry Bailey, full-backs Stan Charlton and Charlie Miller, wingers Billy Compton and George Purcell and half-back Jock Ditchburn. More importantly, Mavin was responsible for signing and nurturing three of the finest stars ever discovered locally — Cliff Bastin, Harold Blackmore and Wilf Lowton. For that alone he must rate highly among City managers.

In 1924-5, City had one of the most successful seasons in their history, finishing seventh, and in 1925 Mavin signed another outstanding player who was to play such an important part in the club's history — Billy McDevitt.

But when, at the end of October 1927, Mavin received the offer of a better salary from ambitious Crystal Palace, he could not afford to refuse. The following season, with the aid of Stan Charlton, he took Palace to within a point of promotion, when they were pipped by Charlton Athletic on goal-average. Had he stayed longer, Mavin might have achieved greater distinction with Exeter City, but he left them well placed and with a ready-made manager in inside-right Billy McDevitt.

David Wilson
March 1928-February 1929

THE directors decided to try another manager before giving Billy McDevitt his chance. McDevitt was going great guns in the team at the time and City were placed fourth in the table when it was announced that a former Scottish international and member of a famous footballing family had been appointed manager.

David Wilson, whose brothers Alex, Andrew and James were also leading professionals (Andrew being another Scottish cap) came to Exeter with excellent credentials. As a left-half, his first-class playing career had begun some 27 years earlier with St Mirren and he had subsequently appeared with Hamilton Academical, Bradford City and Oldham Athletic. He enjoyed one run of 264 consecutive appearances with Oldham, helping the Latics gain promotion to the Second Division before becoming player-manager of Nelson and steering that club up into the Second Division. He did not give up playing until he was 40 years of age.

When he arrived at St James' Park, Exeter were enjoying one of their best-ever runs, being eighth, but the loss of Stan Charlton and Billy Compton hit the side badly and, despite the signing of one of the club's greatest ever stars in Harold 'Happy' Houghton, City suffered a dramatic decline in 1928-9. After a run of six consecutive defeats, club and manager parted company, with some love lost, on St Valentine's Day.

Billy McDevitt
February 1929-September 1935

ARGUABLY the finest manager City ever had, this shrewd Irishman was tailor-made for a club that was living almost from hand to mouth. McDevitt had the happy knack of obtaining good players for practically no financial outlay and then welding them into a successful combination. Indeed, his least successful period was when he started to spend money on players.

Before considering his managerial career at Exeter in any detail, it is worth remembering that within a few months of taking on the job he lost stalwart defender, Wilf Lowton, to Wolves and up-and-coming star, Cliff Bastin, to Arsenal. One wonders what McDevitt might have achieved if the club had been able to keep those players, although, of course, it, must be said that no Third Division club would want to stand in the way of such players furthering their careers in the First Division.

McDevitt played for one more season after his appointment, taking his total of Football League appearances with Swansea Town, Liverpool and City to 134 in nine seasons since crossing the Irish Sea from Belfast Celtic.

Among McDevitt's most notable signings were goalkeeper Arthur Davies, right-back Jimmy Gray, half-backs Jack Angus and Stan Barber and centre-forward Percy Varco. With a side that cost less than £1,000, they enjoyed that great FA Cup giantkilling run of 1930-31, when City went into the hat for the semi-finals and made a profit without the transfer of players for only the second time in their history. Two seasons later they finished runners-up in the Third Division South, at a time when only the top club gained promotion.

In 1933, Billy McDevitt turned down an offer to become manager of Queen's Park Rangers, but the parting of the ways came on 26 September 1935 when most of his stars had moved elsewhere or retired. The season had commenced with only one victory in the first nine games, including three home defeats in a row. A football manager's past efforts count for little in such circumstances. Just before the war, McDevitt returned to Belfast and managed Belfast Celtic and Distillery for brief spells.

Jack English
October 1935-1940

JACK English was appointed manager during one of the club's most critical periods, when at least one director was quoted as saying: 'Thank goodness when this season is over'. An emergency committee had been formed and a new board of no less than 15 directors had been elected. Jack English obviously had nerves of steel with a phlegmatic personality!

At the end of his first season City had to apply for re-election for the third time in their League history and, not surprisingly, Mr English had a clearout of players, reducing his professional staff to only six and signing no less than 14 new players in that summer of 1936.

Unfortunately, there was not a happy atmosphere at St James' Park, despite the excitement of a good FA Cup run, for City had to apply for re-election for the second year in succession. However, the Cup run had at least shown that there was real talent in the side and that English was working along the right lines.

His experience, however, illustrates once again how difficult it is for any club to shake themselves out of the doldrums once they have hit bottom. English must have travelled further than any City manager in his continuous quest for talent. During the four years up to the outbreak of war, he signed nearly 60 new players beginning with former Welsh international Wynne Crompton from Crystal Palace on 28 October 1935 and ending with Ray Freeman on 10 August 1939.

English had a brief playing career with Watford and Sheffield United, helping the latter to win the FA Cup in 1915. After the war he became manager of Darlington, who were then a non-League club. Therefore, as he was still on Sheffield United's books, he was debarred from playing League football for six years. And when he was given permission to play again he found that age and a damaged knee prevented a comeback.

Two of his best discoveries were Mark Hooper, a midget winger who enjoyed much success with Sheffield Wednesday, and Arthur Childs, who became one of the stars of Exeter's promotion-seeking side of 1932-3. Apart from Darlington, English managed Nelson (two years) and Northampton Town (four years) before going to St James' Park. He retired to Darlington during World War Two and died in December 1985.

George Roughton
October 1945-March 1952

TO this affable and much respected manager fell the task of rebuilding Exeter City after World War Two. It was not easy because there was a grave shortage of talent at that time but, in consolation, the people of Exeter and district, like so many other areas of the country, were so starved of football that they crowded into St James' Park eager for the fray.

As a full-back George Roughton had enjoyed eight good seasons with Huddersfield Town in the First Division (164 League appearances) followed by three with Manchester United (86 League appearances) during which United were relegated, but returned to the First Division after only 12 months. He made 14 appearances for City in 1945-6 before finally giving up playing. During his First Division career he had been, for a long time, on the verge of a full international cap. He represented the Football League and also took part in the Football Association's Canadian tour of 1931, along with City inside-forward 'Happy' Houghton.

George Roughton's obvious dedication was not rewarded with outstanding successes, but for the most part he kept the club on an even keel, averaging 13th place over the first five full peacetime seasons. It was not until his final season at St James' Park that things began to go wrong. With 18 months of his contract still to run, the Exeter City directors agreed to let him accept a good offer from Southampton, but only after an agreement was reached for that club to let City have a successor in Norman Kirkman.

George Roughton's expected success with the Saints did not materialize and, partly because of increasingly poor health (he subsequently underwent a heart by-pass operation), he retired in September 1955.

Norman Kirkman
March 1952-March 1953

LIKE all who had preceded him, Norman Kirkman joined the club with bags of enthusiasm especially as this was his first chance to show his paces as a manager, or player-manager as he was then. A full-back, who had begun his professional career with Burnley in 1937, he made his first League appearances after moving to Rochdale in September 1946. In December 1947 he was transferred to Chesterfield for £4,500 and subsequently served Leicester City and Southampton.

During the close season of 1952, he toured the country as well as crossing the sea to Ireland to sign what looked like being a good side, for an outlay of between £4,000 and £5,000. He persuaded his old Southampton teammate, Irish international goalkeeper Hugh Kelly, to return to English football, while other notable signings included centre-forward Jim Dailey and those two outstanding City stalwarts, Keith Harvey and Arnold Mitchell. There was also Eddie Murphy and Jackie Knight.

Unfortunately Norman Kirkman did not remain at St James' Park long enough to build on his promising start. He had lifted the club off the bottom to become a useful middle-of-the-table combination, but before completing his first year at Exeter he announced in the February that he wanted to take over at Bradford and joined the Park Avenue club for a four-figure salary. He stayed on a few more weeks until City thought they had a replacement.

~ ~ ~ ~ ~ ~ ~ ~ ~ ~ ~ ~ ~ ~ ~ ~ ~ ~ ~

IN view of the last sentence under Norman Kirkman, mention should be made here of the débâcle surrounding the appointment of Barnsley half-back and player-coach, Tim Ward, as player-manager of Exeter City in March 1953, lest someone believes that he has been overlooked. The fact is that Tim Ward never legally became player-manager of Exeter City because he was never released by Barnsley. The announcement of his appointment came on 5 March and, although he travelled with the team to Ipswich two days later, he was recalled to Barnsley on 12 March and, after being short-listed, was appointed as their new manager on 30 March.

Norman Dodgin
April 1953-April 1957

AFTER the disappointment over Tim Ward, the City board lost no time in appointing Norman Dodgin as player-manager. City had escaped the possibility of having to apply for re-election again with a midweek victory at Coventry and this appointment was made the following day. Norman Dodgin was then a Northampton Town left-half and the announcement made it clear that he would take over his new job after his contract with that club had expired. At the time, 31-year-old Norman Dodgin became one of the youngest managers in the Football League.

An uncle of Fulham team boss, Bill Dodgin junior, and younger brother of Bill

Dodgin senior, a former Fulham, Brentford and Bristol Rovers manager, Norman Dodgin had a good pedigree. All football managers study tactics, but none was ever more fanatical on this subject than this City manager. He was forthright enough to have told directors and certain journalists that they knew nothing about the game and at board meetings he would often move glasses around the table to show his employers where their ideas may have been wrong. For their part, the directors respected Dodgin and allowed him more control than most of his forerunners had probably enjoyed.

His professional playing career saw him make a total of 116 League appearances with Newcastle United (beginning in 1947-8 when he helped them win promotion to the First Division), Reading and Northampton Town. At Exeter he played for another two seasons, helping the team rise to their highest position (ninth) since 1934, with 30 League appearances in his first season before handing over to Arnold Mitchell, except for four more games, in 1954-5.

His last playing season was disastrous for the City, who just escaped having to apply for re-election. After two more seasons of only limited success, Dodgin was caught up in the great upheaval of March-April 1957 which brought the arrival of a new chairman and the manager's dismissal. Such was Dodgin's popularity that the players were in revolt, demanding to see chairman Mr A.S.Line. An interview was granted but it did not alter the fact that club and manager parted company. Dodgin subsequently managed Yeovil Town, Barrow and Oldham Athletic before retiring to Exeter in 1960 where he opened a newsagents business.

Bill Thompson
May 1957-January 1958

THIS Glaswegian has the doubtful distinction of having served City as manager for a shorter period than anyone either before or since. As a half-back he had played a small part in helping Portsmouth win the League Championship two seasons in succession (1948-50) and subsequently had a couple of seasons with Bournemouth.

His first job as manager was with Guildford City, whom he guided to the Southern League championship in 1955-6. He was brought to Exeter during a period of rapid changes and was unable to make much impression on the club's fortunes in less than eight months before chairman A.S.Line came up with further ambitious plans. The chairman believed that there was no place in the modern game for a manager responsible for both administration and team affairs. He wanted a coach and Bill Thompson either did not, or would not, fit into the new scheme of things. Less than two weeks later he was appointed secretary-manager of Worcester City.

Frank Broome
January 1958-May 1960 and May 1967-February 1969

LESS than 48 hours after parting company with Bill Thompson, the ambitious Mr A.S.Line arranged to meet the cheerful, wise-cracking former England international Frank Broome at The Dell, where Southampton were at home to Exeter City in a Third Division game. A late train meant that Broome missed Southampton's first four goals that afternoon, but he was left in no doubt of the task he could be undertaking when City ended up losing 6-0.

Chairman A.S.Line was a persuasive man, however, and within a few minutes of the referee's final whistle Frank Broome was manager-coach of Exeter City. With the club three places off rock bottom and the Third Divisions North and South due to be split into Third and Fourth Divisions, Broome had no time to achieve anything before the drop. He immediately signed his former Derby County clubmate, centre-half Ken Oliver, in a vain attempt to save the day, but City had to apply for re-election once more.

Broome was one of the most famous footballers ever associated with Exeter City. Just before the war he had played in seven England internationals, appearing in four of the five forward positions together with such all-time greats as Stanley Matthews, Ted Drake, Cliff Bastin and Tommy Lawton. He also played in one wartime international and toured Australia with the FA team in 1952. He made 133 peacetime League appearances for Aston Villa (1934-46), being leading goalscorer in three seasons, and he then brought his final total to 394 appearances and 175 goals after serving Derby County, Notts County, Brentford and Crewe, before joining Shelbourne in 1955.

With the aid of only three new first-team players in 1958-9, Broome turned a bottom of the Third Division South side into one that finished fifth in the Fourth Division, missing promotion by two points. The following season they finished ninth and then Broome dropped a bombshell by taking a better-paid job at Southend United.

It was a move that he subsequently regretted and when, in May 1967, Exeter City cabled him in Australia, where he had been for nearly six years, his happy memories of St James' Park persuaded him to return. Obviously there had been a lot changes since his previous spell of management and he went through a good deal of frustration before being sacked in February 1967 with the side one place off the bottom of the League.

Glen Wilson
June 1960-April 1962

WHEN Frank Broome first quit St James' Park, the club appointed another player-manager in Glen Wilson, a Geordie who had made 410 League appearances in 11 seasons with Brighton. He had been that club's captain for five years, missing only one game when they won promotion to the Second Division in 1957-8.

Wilson was not on City's list of applicants for the vacant position, but the directors had had their eye on him for some time. When he agreed to take the job at Exeter, a transfer fee of about £5,000 was involved. However, although he continued to play in a lot of City's games, the financial restraints placed on managers at this period of the club's history added to the difficulties of being able to create improvements.

Indeed, another application for re-election had to be made at the end of season 1960-61 and, although City climbed to 18th place in the following campaign, Wilson was sacked along with trainer Eddie Nash the day after they beat Chester 5-0 at the Park.

Cyril Spiers
May 1962-February 1963

ONLY a couple of days after Wilson's sacking, the club appointed one of the most experienced of footballing personalities as general manager. Cyril Spiers was a 60-

year-old chief scout with Leicester City and had begun his first-class football career 40 years earlier, in goal for Aston Villa with whom he remained for seven years before transferring to Tottenham Hotspur. A leg injury virtually ended his career after taking his total of League appearances to 262.

He was, however, pressed into service for a further eight games over two seasons with Wolves, after joining their coaching staff. He became assistant manager to Major Frank Buckley whilst at Molineux, as well as having two spells as manager of Cardiff City and one each with Norwich City and Crystal Palace.

Keen to develop youngsters, he brought in Jack Edwards as trainer at Exeter. Edwards had been with him as an amateur at Cardiff City and later as a professional with Crystal Palace. Alas, Spiers did not stay long enough to make any headway, let alone develop a youth policy, for he parted company with the City on amicable terms after only nine months and during a spell when the weather had prevented play for the previous six weeks. He immediately returned to Leicester City as their chief scout for the south of England. Spiers died on 21 May 1967.

Jack Edwards
May 1963-January 1965

WHEN Spiers left Exeter, the directors chose to throw their trainer, Jack Edwards, in at the deep end to run the team on a temporary basis and try and restore the players' shaken confidence in the club's future.

A friendly Welshman, he had spent ten years as a full-back with Crystal Palace (223 League appearances) and two with Rochdale (68 appearances) before turning down a player-manager's job with Ashford to join Exeter as trainer. As temporary manager, Edwards enjoyed immediate success, for City climbed from 22nd to finish 17th at the end of a season that was extended due to appalling weather conditions. On 17 May 1963, his position as manager was confirmed.

Jack Edwards proved to be an excellent choice. In his first full season in charge he steered City through the first promotion-winning campaign in the club's history, when they finished fourth in the Fourth Division. With only three newcomers introduced into the side for Third Division football, continued success eluded City and Edwards handed in his resignation before the 1964-5 season had reached its conclusion. He said that this was because of 'internal squabbling', which was denied by the board, but Edwards insisted that the last straw had been when Ellis Stuttard was appointed chief scout without his (Edwards') prior knowledge.

Subsequently trainer to Torquay United, Jack Edwards was also that club's manager, from October 1971 to January 1973. He then returned to City as trainer under Johnny Newman and included a few weeks as caretaker-manager before going with Bobby Saxton to Plymouth Argyle in 1973.

Ellis Stuttard
February 1965-June 1966

THIS Lancastrian from Burnley was of that generation whose playing careers were shortened by World War Two. He had joined Plymouth Argyle in 1939, but his League appearances for them as a half-back were restricted to the 28 he made in season 1946-7, before having three seasons with Torquay United and becoming assistant manager of Swindon Town.

He had a chequered managerial career for, whereas Plymouth Argyle and Exeter City were only too glad to call on his services in an emergency, he was not allowed time to develop any ideas. Despite this, Stuttard was a 'smiler' who generally did not display any feeling of the anxiety he may have had.

After a spell as assistant manager of Plymouth Argyle, they appointed him manager in November 1961 but dropped him back to assistant under Andy Beattie in September 1963. He came to Exeter City as chief scout in December 1965 and was given the job of caretaker manager just over four weeks later, being confirmed as manager on 11 February 1965.

His sojourn in this capacity, however, was a disaster, for City slid to 22nd in 1965-6, despite the signing of many new players, only one of which — full-back Jimmy Blain — was to make a lasting impression. Indeed, for the last three months of his stay with City, Stuttard was manager in name only, the job of running the team having been given to trainer Jock Basford. It was, therefore, no surprise when Stuttard resigned at the end of that campaign, returning to Plymouth Argyle as chief scout.

There he had another spell as manager (1970-72) before reverting again to chief scout and remaining with Argyle in various capacities until being made redundant two years before his death in 1984, aged 64.

57

Walter 'Jock' Basford
June 1966-April 1967

JOCK Basford was another of that post-war period, when managers stayed at St James' Park scarcely long enough for them to become acquainted with the local Press. Despite being known as 'Jock', he was born in the Midlands and had been on Wolves' books before the war, after which he had spells as trainer and manager of Guildford City and Margate before taking over as Charlton Athletic's trainer-coach for seven years.

He was appointed assistant manager and trainer of Exeter City at a meeting in a London hotel in November 1965. In March 1966, when City were sliding towards the bottom of the table, he was given control of the team in place of Ellis Stuttard, but it was too late for him to save them from relegation. Appointed manager without a contract during the close season, he made more sweeping changes in the team but enjoyed limited success before being sacked after only ten months in the job.

Johnny Newman
April 1969-December 1976

IT was following the dismissal of Frank Broome from his second spell as manager in 1969 that City appointed half-back Johnny Newman as player-manager. The only surprise was the delay of more than two months before the appointment was confirmed, for it had been obvious for some time that Newman was being groomed for the job and he and trainer Bert Edwards had been in charge of the team ever since Broome's departure.

If ever there was an 'Honest John' it was Johnny Newman, who was respected for his conscientious approach to the job and his dealings with the Press, public and players.

Born in Hereford, he had played in the 1956 FA Cup Final, when Birmingham City were beaten by Manchester City. After more than six seasons with Birmingham, he had continued with Leicester City and Plymouth Argyle, making 298 League appearances in nearly eight years at Home Park before being signed by City in an £8,000 deal which included the return of forward Alan Banks to St James' Park. At that time Newman was needed to bolster up a side that was running perilously close to the re-election zone. He helped pull City clear that season and led the club through a much better than average period of their history.

Indeed, there is no doubt that Johnny Newman was one of the club's more successful managers and in October 1971 it was fortunate that, after reconsideration, he tore up a letter of resignation. Although he accepted an offer to manage Grimsby Town in December 1976, it was his Exeter side, that included one of his most important signings in Tony Kellow, that won promotion at the end of that season. Newman did well at Grimsby and subsequently managed Derby County and Hereford United before becoming coach and assistant manager to Notts County. He later joined the backroom staff at neighbouring Mansfield Town.

Bobby Saxton
January 1977-January 1979

IT is something of a coincidence that Newman was succeeded by another former Plymouth Argyle half-back in Bobby Saxton. Newman had secured Bobby Saxton's transfer from his old club in September 1975, for £4,000, and he was the kingpin of the side which won promotion to the Third Division in 1976-7. No doubt it was fortunate that Saxton was already on City's books when Newman left at a critical stage of that campaign, for he was able to keep the momentum going.

A real 90-minute player, Saxton was also an enthusiastic manager and was beginning to make things hum at St James' Park when Plymouth Argyle persuaded him to return to Home Park as their new manager in January 1979. Assistant Bert Edwards, physiotherapist Tony Long and chief scout Jim Furnell also left City and joined Argyle at this time.

Most City supporters believed that Saxton would have achieved a great deal at St James' Park had he remained. As it was, Argyle in turn lost his services a little over a year later when he accepted a better offer from Blackburn Rovers. After five and a half years with that club, he had a short spell as manager of York City before resigning in August 1988.

Brian Godfrey
January 1979-June 1983

WITH the Exeter side well placed in the Third Division, the directors lost no time in replacing Bobby Saxton. Indeed, only nine days had elapsed before they obtained

the services of Brian Godfrey, who came to the club with good credentials having only the previous season steered Bath City to the championship of the Southern League. Even so, his was a surprise appointment.

Born at Flint, North Wales, Godfrey had turned professional with Everton in 1958 and made a total of 557 League appearances with Scunthorpe, Preston, Aston Villa, Bristol Rovers and Newport County over a playing career which spanned 18 years. During this time he had been capped for Wales in one Under-23 international and three full internationals, being well respected as a utility forward. With such a fine playing record and his achievement with Bath City, the Exeter City directors were confident that they had made the right choice.

City finished ninth at the end of his first season and eighth in the next — a position which could be regarded as their highest ever in the Football League and bettered only three times in the old Third Division South before the Third Division was split. Godfrey accomplished a good bit of business in buying Tony Kellow back from Blackpool for £65,000, 16 months after they had paid City £105,000 for his transfer, and this player led City to the sixth round of the FA Cup for only the second time in their history. But the loss of such players as Johnny Hore, Colin Randell and Steve Neville left gaps which proved difficult to fill. True, Steve Neville returned from Sheffield United, but five weeks after the club had narrowly escaped relegation to the Fourth Division in 1982-3, Godfrey decided to quit with a year of his contract still to run. He subsequently returned to manage Bath City and later Weymouth.

Gerry Francis
July 1983-May 1984

CAPPED 12 times for England in the mid-1970s, Gerry Francis had captained the international side in eight of those games. He was, therefore, one of the most highly-rated footballers ever to become associated with Exeter City. Apparently City had been talking to this player before Godfrey quit, but as he still had a year

of his contract to run with Coventry City, a lot of negotiating was needed before Exeter got him on a free transfer.

Francis was then aged 32 and had amassed a total of 419 League appearances with Queen's Park Rangers (two spells), Crystal Palace and Coventry City. In fact, he was still a first-team player at Coventry when City secured his services.

The season under Gerry Francis' charge was one of the worst in the club's history and, even before it had ended with City bottom of the Third Division, rumours abounded that Francis had been sacked. Actually he had been relieved of his duties on 9 May, after only one win in a run of 22 League games, but at his request the official announcement of his departure was not published until five days later.

Francis had made 28 Third Division appearances for City in that dismal campaign and he brought his career total to 492 by adding further games with Cardiff City, Swansea City, Portsmouth and Bristol Rovers — being appointed player-manager of the latter club in July 1987.

Jim Iley
June 1984-April 1985

HERE was another manager to last only a season with the City. When he took the job, he agreed to work within a wages budget of £100,000 a year and was confident enough to announce that this was not the first club he had taken on after being relegated and was experienced enough to bring success to Exeter City.

Including three players on loan, he introduced 16 newcomers to the League side that season, but only Jimmy McNichol and Danny O'Shea really made any impression and with the side standing 16th in the table (they finished 18th) and with four games still to play, he was asked to resign. Iley refused, saying that he had done nothing wrong and could not be judged on ten months with the club. So he was sacked on 22 April.

Despite an uninspiring season, Iley had the sympathy of many supporters, who produced a 1,000-name petition deploring his dismissal, although that was too late to save him. There is no doubt that Iley was extremely bitter about his sacking, for he took the unprecedented step (so far as Exeter City are concerned) of calling a public meeting in a church hall in order to air his grievances. Indeed, so determined was he to get back in charge of Exeter City that he offered to buy the controlling share interest from Clifford Hill.

As a classy and constructive wing-half, Jim Iley had played in 544 League games beginning with Sheffield United in 1953 and playing for Spurs, Nottingham Forest and Newcastle before ending up with Peterborough and going into management with the latter. This was followed by spells in charge at Barnsley, Blackburn Rovers and Bury, who had sacked him four months before he joined Exeter.

Colin Appleton
June 1985-December 1987

COLIN Appleton, who is a native of Scarborough, spent 12 years with Leicester City, playing mostly at left-half and appearing in two FA Cup Finals and two League Cup Finals before moving to Charlton Athletic in 1966. In August 1967 he was appointed player-manager of Barrow, but remained only one and a half years at Holker Street before returning to Scarborough as player-manager and helping them win the FA Challenge Trophy in 1973.

After a short spell on Grimsby's coaching staff, he went back to Scarborough again to steer them to two more FA Challenge Trophy wins, in 1976 and 1977. He spent nearly two years (1982-84) as manager of Hull City, taking them up from the Fourth Division and missing promotion to the Second Division only on goal-difference the following season. Moving to Swansea in May 1984, he was sacked after less than seven months in charge and appointed manager of Exeter City on 4 June 1985.

In his new job, Appleton continued to use seven of the most regular players of season 1984-5 and was able to introduce only a comparatively small number of new regular first-team players in 1985-6. The most notable of his signings were veteran Danny Keough, goalkeeper John Shaw and centre-half Shaun Taylor, but the side had to apply for re-election once more.

Appleton, perhaps surprisingly in view of what happened to some of his predecessors, survived this. His second season at City was nearly four months old, with the side on the slide again after a brief respite, when he was forced to resign for personal reasons on 11 December 1987. John Delve then took over as caretaker manager. Appleton later managed Bridlington Town and had another short spell as Hull City manager for five months in 1989.

Terry Cooper
May 1988 —

WHILST with Bristol City in October 1983, Terry Cooper became the Football League's first player-director this century, but this was not the happiest period of his career, for Cooper is a players' man. That is not to say that he does not criticize players when they deserve it, for he is a blunt Yorkshireman who has proved to be a great motivator.

Born near Castleford on 12 July 1944, Terry Cooper made his name with Leeds United, where he became a star overlapping full-back when that club was one of the most powerful in the land. His England career was shattered when he broke a leg in 1972 and he had to settle for 20 international appearances to add to the 350 senior games played for United, which included three UEFA Cup Finals.

In 1975 he moved to Middlesbrough and three years later to Bristol City. He became player-manager of Bristol Rovers in 1980 and had a brief spell with Doncaster Rovers before returning to Bristol City as player-manager in 1982. He continued to play until he was 40 years of age, taking his aggregate of League appearances to 505. In March 1988, after steering Bristol City up into the Third Division and to two Freight/Rover Trophy Finals (one win) he was surprisingly dismissed. Terry Cooper did not apply for the Exeter City vacancy but fortunately for the club he accepted their invitation to become team-manager and in less than two years turned them into a Fourth Division championship-winning side.

City Stars A-Z

In this section all League appearances up to and including season 1919-20 refer to the old Southern League, while those from 1920-21 are Football League games.

The quiet worker of City's first promotion-winning team in 1963-4, Des Anderson was a laboratory technician in a sandpaper factory and playing part-time for Glenavon when he came to St James' Park for a fortnight's trial at the same time as fellow Irishman, Cec Smyth, in August 1962. His arrival was most opportune, for regular first-team centre-half, Keith Harvey, broke his right ankle in a pre-season trial game and Anderson was immediately signed and pitched into the first team in Harvey's place. The young Irishman was an immediate success, missing only two League games in his initial season. When Harvey returned to the side, Anderson was switched to left-half and kept that position in the following season's promotion team when he missed only one game. Born at Templepatrick on 11 September 1940, Anderson won seven Irish Amateur international caps as a centre-half and was a defender who not only got through a tremendous amount of work but also knew how to cover the gaps. After missing only five League games in his first three seasons at St James' Park he lost his place to Colin Buckingham in 1965-6, requested a transfer and, at the end of that season, was among 14 players allowed to go free in a huge clearout after Exeter had been relegated. He joined Chesterfield that summer.

League debut for City v Torquay United, 18 August 1962.

DES ANDERSON

	LEAGUE		FA CUP		FL CUP		TOTAL	
	App	Gls	App	Gls	App	Gls	App	Gls
1962-63	44	0	1	0	1	0	46	0
1963-64	46	0	2	1	2	0	50	1
1964-65	43	1	1	0	1	0	45	1
1965-66	9/2	0	0	0	1	0	10/2	0
	142/2	1	4	1	5	0	151/2	2

Exeter City were fortunate to have had this young Geordie, signed from Scunthorpe, on their books when centre-half Les Dennington twisted his knee in the middle of that history-making FA Cup giantkilling run of 1930-31. Jack Angus was called in for the fourth-round game at Bury and played in each of the notable Cup ties that followed during this campaign. He was capable of playing anywhere in the half-back line and, while City had other fine centre-halves like Arthur Childs and Harold Webb, he was just as happy at wing-half. But it was in the centre that Angus excelled and he played in this position throughout that other fine Cup run of 1936-7. Indeed, City's 3-1 fourth-round victory over Leicester City in that campaign was one of his finest games, for he certainly held Jack Bowers in a vice-like grip. The tough England centre-forward scored 35 League and Cup goals that season, leading Leicester to promotion, but he got no change out of Angus. At 27 years of age, the City pivot was a master in all phases of centre-half play and became one of the club's most loyal players, enjoying 18 years on the books before retiring from first-class football in 1948.

	LEAGUE		FA CUP		TOTAL	
	App	Gls	App	Gls	App	Gls
1930-31	15	0	4	0	19	0
1931-32	11	0	1	0	12	0
1932-33	11	1	0	0	11	1
1933-34	25	0	1	0	26	0
1934-35	40	0	3	1	43	1
1935-36	39	0	1	0	40	0
1936-37	28	0	5	0	33	0
1937-38	36	0	2	0	38	0
1938-39	38	0	1	0	39	0
1945-46	0	0	1	0	1	0
1946-47	0	0	0	0	0	0
1947-48	3	0	0	0	3	0
	246	1	19	1	265	2

BILLY ARMFIELD

Born Amble, Newcastle-upon-Tyne, on 12 March 1909, he began his career in 1928 with a season on Wolves' books and then played for Wath Athletic and Scunthorpe prior to coming to St James' Park. Even at the age of 39, after leaving the City, he still played a few more games for Sidmouth before calling it a day.

League debut for City v Norwich City, 27 December 1930.

JACK ANGUS

A tall winger, who had only three seasons with City, Billy Armfield nevertheless earns a place in this gallery as another of the Cup giantkilling stars of 1930-31. Born at Handsworth, Birmingham, on 7 July 1903, he joined Exeter in the summer of 1929 after six seasons with Aston Villa, where he had been given very few chances due to the brilliance of another Handsworth boy, Dicky York, an England international. A dislocated shoulder restricted Armfield's appearances in his first season at St James' Park, but he really came into his own in the 1930-31 Cup campaign when he was brought into the side at outside-right with George Purcell moving inside. They struck up a fine partnership and City got a large number of goals from the speedy Armfield's centres. At the end of 1931-2, Billy was sold, along with his partner Purcell, to Gillingham, then managed by former City boss Fred Mavin. He had one moderately successful season with them before returning to the Midlands and joining Brierley Hill Alliance. It was there, in a pre-season practice match in 1933, that he broke a leg. A couple of months later, the leg had to be amputated.

League debut for City v Fulham, 1 February 1930.

	LEAGUE		FA CUP		TOTAL	
	App	Gls	App	Gls	App	Gls
1929-30	7	1	0	0	7	1
1930-31	34	9	7	3	41	12
1931-32	31	4	1	0	32	4
	72	14	8	3	80	17

67

HARRY BAILEY

Before leaving school, Macclesfield-born Harry Bailey kept goal against all-comers at a local fairground. Although injured in World War One, when he was in the Grenadier Guards, he fully recovered and, after making his professional debut with Millwall in 1919-20, became a firm favourite with Luton Town, where he only missed four games in his first two seasons before dropping out of favour and transferring to Exeter City in 1923. Here he went straight into the first team and helped cut the goals conceded from 84 in 1922-3 to 52 in his initial season at St James' Park, when he played in all but one game. The following season he was an ever-present and the number of goals conceded — 48 — was one of City's best-ever figures. Even allowing for the general lack of goals scored at this time (before the change in the offside law) the figures are some indication of his capabilities. At the end of 1926-7, Bailey was transferred to Brentford, where he finished his career after losing his place to former England man, Freddie Fox. That was in season 1929-30, but Harry Bailey was still at Brentford as a gateman for many years after World War Two.

League debut for City v Newport County, 25 August 1923.

	LEAGUE		FA CUP		TOTAL	
	App	Gls	App	Gls	App	Gls
1923-24	41	0	7	0	48	0
1924-25	42	0	5	0	47	0
1925-26	32	0	0	0	32	0
1926-27	28	0	3	0	31	0
	143	0	15	0	158	0

One of the City's most exciting and entertaining post-war players, smiling Alan Banks was born in Liverpool on 5 October 1938 and had one season as an amateur and three as a professional at Anfield before joining Cambridge City. A natural goalscorer, he opened his first-class account with one on his League debut for Liverpool and then scored 120 goals in two and a half seasons with Cambridge City. The Grecians were fortunate to snap him up for only £5,000 in October 1963, for at today's prices Banks blossomed into a forward worth more than 50 times that amount. A human dynamo, the diminutive Banks was always full of fight and could score goals from incredible angles. It was Banks who turned City from a side struggling near the foot of the Fourth Division into a promotion combination in his first season, when he topped the score-sheet with 18 goals. Indeed, he was leading goalscorer in four of his seven most active seasons in City's colours. It was a sad day when he was transferred to Plymouth Argyle in May 1966, but he did not fit so well into their struggling Second Division side and, after a little more than a season, he took up where he had left off with the City. A broken shin-bone kept him out for a spell and then knee trouble slowed him down, but in 1970-71 he enjoyed his best scoring season with 21 League goals. Indeed, Banks was the first Grecian to exceed a century of League goals. Given a free transfer in 1973, he finished his playing career with Poole Town. City's Player of the Year 1968-9, Alan Banks still works in Exeter.

League debut for City v Tranmere Rovers, 28 October 1963.

	LEAGUE		FA CUP		FL CUP		TOTAL	
	App	Gls	App	Gls	App	Gls	App	Gls
1963-64	28	18	0	0	0	0	28	18
1964-65	19	8	0	0	2	1	21	9
1965-66	38	17	1	0	0	0	39	17
1967-68	27	6	4	1	0	0	31	7
1968-69	22	13	3	2	5	2	30	17
1969-70	34/2	10	4	1	2	1	40/2	12
1970-71	40/1	21	0	0	1	0	41/1	21
1971-72	31/5	7	4	0	0	0	35/5	7
1972-73	6/5	1	0/1	0	0	0	6/6	1
	245/13	101	16/1	4	10	4	271/14	109

ALAN BANKS

STAN BARBER

Stan Barber was another Geordie who always displayed enormous enthusiasm for the game. Indeed, it was a great pity that poor health shortened his career with the City, where he was a great favourite. He was born at Wallsend-on-Tyne in 1908 and Newcastle United paid his home-town club £100 for his signature in 1925. He made only one appearance for the First Division club before Bristol City signed him for £500 in the summer of 1928. In those days he was seen at either left-half or centre-half, but it was in the former position that he established himself at St James' Park, arriving there in exchange for Alec Sheffield in the summer of 1930. Scrupulously fair, Barber was a great-hearted wing-half, who always liked to be on the attack and was an ever-present in the 1930-31 FA Cup run, as well as playing in every League game the following season. He missed only a half dozen games when City made their bid for promotion to the Second Division in 1932-3, but then illness overtook him. It was sad to see such a rosy-cheeked, normally big and strong player brought down in this way and although he was allowed to go to Brighton in 1934, his playing career was finished and he returned to Tyneside after only one season.

League debut for City v Bristol Rovers, 17 September 1930.

	LEAGUE		FA CUP		TOTAL	
	App	Gls	App	Gls	App	Gls
1930-31	35	1	8	0	43	1
1931-32	42	4	1	0	43	4
1932-33	36	4	0	0	36	4
1933-34	5	1	0	0	5	1
	118	10	9	0	127	10

Cliff Bastin is undoubtedly the greatest footballer ever born in Exeter and he won every honour open to him before he was 21. Born on 14 March 1912, he became well-known in Exeter as a goalscoring genius with Ladysmith Road School and St Mark's, representing Exeter Schools from the age of 11 and the English Schools in 1926. He scored six goals for his school when they beat Newtown 7-1 in the Exeter Schools' Final at St James' Park in April 1926, and two when making his Southern League debut with Exeter City Reserves as a 15-year-old inside-left, in a 6-1 victory over Bath City on Christmas Eve 1927. With an ice-cool brain, Cliff Bastin developed into one of the finest outside-lefts the game has ever known. Nothing seemed to panic this young man and even when Arsenal came for his signature in 1929, he had to be talked into joining one of the world's most famous clubs before he went out for a game of tennis! 'Boy' Bastin, as he was then known, had already been taking penalties for the City before he was 16, for he could hit a ball with such force that when he grew to full strength, spectators behind the goals would instinctively duck whenever he cracked in a shot. No wonder he scored more League goals for Arsenal than any other player, a total of 150 in the First Division plus 26 in the FA Cup and 12 in 21 England internationals. Arsenal paid City £2,000 for this 16-year-old in 1929, when the British transfer record was still under £11,000. They certainly had their money's worth, for he helped them to five League Championships and two FA Cup Final wins. Bastin returned to his home town after retiring in 1947 and was a pub landlord for many years.

League debut for City v Coventry City, 14 April 1928.

	LEAGUE		FA CUP		TOTAL	
	App	Gls	App	Gls	App	Gls
1927-28	3	3	0	0	3	3
1928-29	14	3	0	0	14	3
	17	6	0	0	17	6

CLIFF BASTIN

Born in Wolverhampton 6 March 1896, Dicky Baugh, a stocky, auburn-haired right-back, joined the Wolves from Stafford Road FC in 1919 and almost immediately became a regular first-team player. One of the regrets of his career was having to miss the 1921 FA Cup Final because of injury. His father, Richard, had appeared in three FA Cup Finals as a full-back with the Wolves and also played for England. Dicky junior moved the short distance to West Bromwich in 1924 and in May 1929 he was persuaded to sign for Exeter City. After a small number of games in his initial season, he was preferred to Jimmy Gray at right-back early in the 1930-31 campaign, teaming up with Charlie Miller. As the finest pair of backs outside the First Division, their fame spread through the great Cup giantkilling feats of that season. In that famous Cup draw at Sunderland, Baugh was described by many critics as the finest full-back on the field. A fearless tackler and noted for his well-timed clearances, this little defender was coming to the end of his playing career in 1931 and eventually lost his place to Jimmy Gray, before joining Kidderminster Harriers in the summer of 1932.
League debut for City v Swindon Town, 2 November 1929.

	LEAGUE		FA CUP		TOTAL	
	App	Gls	App	Gls	App	Gls
1929-30	9	0	1	0	10	0
1930-31	30	4	8	0	38	4
1931-32	14	1	0	0	14	1
	53	5	9	0	62	5

DICKY BAUGH

ALAN BEER

Alan Beer was a Welsh Amateur international who was surely on the way to gaining a full cap when a knee ligament injury ended his brilliant career. Born in Swansea on 11 March 1950, Beer joined Swansea City from local club West End in February 1971 but surprisingly, in view of his later progress, failed to make the grade with them and was allowed to go to Weymouth where he became top scorer before Johnny Newman signed him for the City in November 1974. Beer was a pocket dynamo and City quickly improved with this two-footed sharp-shooter in their attack, linking up with Tony Kellow to panic opposing defenders. Beer rounded off season 1975-6 with a dazzling display and a hat-trick at home to Scunthorpe United and in the next season, when City regained Third Division status, he was again top scorer and the big clubs were taking notice. However, it was in only the third League game of the season 1977-8 (at Shrewsbury) that Alan Beer's playing career came to an end. His playing contract was cancelled a year later, but he remained at St James' Park as assistant to Brian Godfrey until 1983.
League debut for City v Rochdale (scored once), 30 November 1974.

	LEAGUE		FA CUP		FL CUP		TOTAL	
	App	Gls	App	Gls	App	Gls	App	Gls
1974-75	27	9	0	0	0	0	27	9
1975-76	46	20	1	1	4	2	51	23
1976-77	38	21	0	0	3	0	41	21
1977-78	3	2	0	0	4	1	7	3
	114	52	1	1	11	3	126	56

70

When Yorkshireman Jim Bell joined City in 1908, he not only became the team wit, but also their leading goalscorer who did more than most to get the club

JIM 'DAISY' BELL

off to a good start in their first professional campaign. Indeed, 'Daisy' Bell soon showed his talent for getting the ball into the net by scoring four goals in the club's first practice match of the season and got both goals in their initial Southern League game at Millwall, which resulted in a 2-2 draw. He had already scored five goals in his first five appearances at inside-left, when he got six in that farcical Cup tie against Weymouth, which City won 14-0. On being switched to centre-forward against Leyton on 13 February that season, he became the first City player to score a hat-trick in a Southern League game as his side won 3-1 at St James' Park. Born at Eston, Middlesbrough, Bell began his career with Grangetown FC, at the age of 16, before joining Middlesbrough and making ten First Division appearances in 1904-05. He subsequently had three seasons with Barrow in the Lancashire Combination. Bell remained at St James' Park until transferring to Portsmouth in April 1911. He subsequently emigrated to America and resided in Michigan for many years, continuing to play soccer until well into the 1920s.
League debut for City v Millwall (scored twice), 2 September 1908.

	LEAGUE		FA CUP		TOTAL	
	App	*Gls*	*App*	*Gls*	*App*	*Gls*
1908-09	39	22	9	9	48	31
1909-10	38	15	3	3	41	18
1910-11	28	14	2	0	30	14
	105	51	14	12	119	63

There was nothing fancy about Fred Binney's football. Rather he was a throw-back to the days of the tough and energetic centre-forwards, who would go through a brick wall if that was the direction of the goalmouth. Born in Plymouth on 12 August 1946, he was spotted by a Torquay United scout whilst playing with Launceston and, although his first-team chances with Torquay were limited, he scored over 60 goals in three seasons with their reserve side. Exeter City first got him on loan in February 1969 and he returned to Plainmoor at the end of that season. However, in March 1970, when City were struggling to avoid the re-election zone, Johnny Newman signed him for a £5,000 fee. In the best of his three full seasons at the Park he scored 28 League goals, the highest individual total since Rod Williams got one more in 1936-7. Indeed, bustling Fred Binney is the only player to have topped City's Football League scoring record in three consecutive seasons. Binney's goalscoring naturally attracted the attention of other clubs and in May 1974 (just before he was elected City's Player of the Year) Brighton, who had been in danger of relegation to the Fourth Division, paid City £25,000, plus John Templeman and Lammie Robertson, for his transfer. Binney helped revitalize Brighton, although he was

injured the season they gained promotion to the Second Division and in October 1977 he was transferred to Plymouth Argyle, where he was Player of the Year in 1978-9 after netting 26 Third Division goals. Fred Binney finished his League career with Hereford United. After a spell of coaching in Malaysia, he was Exeter City's coach under manager Colin Appleton in 1985-6.
League debut for City v Bradford (scored once), 24 February 1969.

FRED BINNEY

	LEAGUE		FA CUP		FL CUP		TOTAL	
	App	*Gls*	*App*	*Gls*	*App*	*Gls*	*App*	*Gls*
1968-69	17	11	0	0	0	0	17	11
1969-70	7	1	0	0	0	0	7	1
1970-71	30	8	1	0	1	0	32	8
1971-72	39	17	2	1	1	0	42	18
1972-73	46	28	1	0	1	1	48	29
1973-74	38	25	1	0	4	6	43	31
	177	90	5	1	7	7	189	98

No City player, before or since, possessed a harder shot than local discovery Harold Blackmore, who was born at Silverton, near Exeter, in 1904 and used to play with a rag ball during the midday break when he began working at the local paper mills. Indeed, 'Blackie' always believed in practice and it was this that turned him into one of the most accurate shots in the game, for he would play for hours kicking a ball through a rubber tyre. He scored twice on his debut for City Reserves in 1923-4, but was naturally a little slow on the ball when initially brought into

HAROLD BLACKMORE

the first team the following season. However, he soon added pace to his cracking left-foot shot and by his second professional season was attracting the attention of other clubs as a regular scorer. In 1926-7, Blackmore was City's leading scorer, creating a new club record with 25 League goals. When, towards the end of that campaign, he scored twice for City in a benefit match for Bob Pollard against Bolton Wanderers, the visitors were so impressed that soon afterwards they obtained his transfer for a fee of £2,150. Going straight into the Trotters' side, he scored three goals in five appearances before that season had ended. Blackmore remained at Bolton until 1932 and was their leading scorer in three successive seasons, as well as scoring in their FA Cup Final victory over Portsmouth in 1929. He had a season with Middlesbrough prior to becoming top scorer at Bradford and then finished his career with Bury before retiring to Exeter and going into business as a butcher. A goal he scored for Bolton, with a 35-yard shot against Huddersfield in an FA Cup semi-final at Anfield in 1929, was one of the most powerful shots seen in that competition for many years. Harold Blackmore died in Exeter, 28 December 1989. *League debut for City v Swindon Town, 25 October 1924.*

	LEAGUE		FA CUP		TOTAL	
	App	Gls	App	Gls	App	Gls
1924-25	11	6	2	2	13	8
1925-26	27	14	1	0	28	14
1926-27	33	25	3	0	36	25
	71	45	6	2	77	47

This Liverpudlian began his career with Everton in 1959 before becoming an outside-right with Southport in February 1960. From there he moved to Rotherham United for a big fee in December 1962, when the Millers were a middle-of-the-table Second Division side, but he did not stay long before switching to Carlisle United in April 1964. Carlisle also used him as an outside-right and he was transferred to St James' Park in October 1965 as part of a transaction said to be worth £20,000 when City sold Eric Welsh to Carlisle. This proved to be manager Ellis Studdard's best deal, for Blain became one of the club's most popular players. He began as a winger at St James' Park but was a workaholic, allowed to roam all across the attack. A player who always seemed to turn up just where he was needed, he was moved into the midfield in his second season but was always ready to play in any position and even wore the centre-forward shirt. It was not until his fourth season at the Park that manager Frank Broome settled him in at left-back, the position for which he is best remembered by City fans. However, he was always keen to get into the attack and had the powers of recovery to become probably the

Grecians' first modern overlapping full-back or the first to make a success of this tactic. Full of enthusiasm City had no more wholehearted player and one who could produce electrifying bursts of speed. Jimmy Blain was only the fifth player to exceed over 300 League appearances for the City, after 'Nobby' Clarke, Arnold Mitchell, Keith Harvey and Graham Rees. *League debut for City v Swindon Town, 30 October 1965.*

	LEAGUE		FA CUP		FL CUP		TOTAL	
	App	Gls	App	Gls	App	Gls	App	Gls
1965-66	24/1	1	1	0	0	0	25/1	1
1966-67	37/2	3	2	0	3	0	42/2	3
1967-68	44	5	4	1	2	0	50	6
1968-69	42	2	4	0	4	0	50	2
1969-70	41	2	1/1	0	2	0	44/1	2
1970-71	38	0	1	0	2	0	41	0
1971-72	40/2	1	4	0	0	0	44/2	1
1972-73	29/3	0	0	0	1	0	30/3	0
1973-74	15/2	0	1	0	4	0	20/2	0
	310/10	14	18/1	1	18	0	346/11	15

JIMMY BLAIN

A goalkeeper who joined Bristol City as a 14-year-old schoolboy in December 1968, Len Bond remained with the Ashton Gate club until 1977. For the most part he was kept out of the first team by the consistent Ray Cashley and was loaned in turn to Exeter City, Cardiff City, Torquay United, Scunthorpe United and Colchester United before his transfer to Brentford. His spell on loan to Exeter City was in 1974-5, when he took over from Bob Wilson. However, it was at Brentford that he really came to the fore and he enjoyed three good seasons with them. In the summer of 1980 Bond, who had also played for St Louis in the United States, was transferred from Brentford to Exeter City. Brave and daring, Bond soon became a particular favourite with the Exeter fans, with whom he had a good rapport. A great character off the field, he was technically sound on it. He was overworked for most of his stay with the Grecians as they slid towards relegation, but could not be blamed when the drop came in 1983-4. He missed only two League appearances in his last two seasons before leaving in the summer of 1984. Len Bond was born at Ilminster on 12 February 1954.
League debut for City v Crewe Alexandra, 6 November 1974.

	LEAGUE		FA CUP		FL CUP		TOTAL	
	App	Gls	App	Gls	App	Gls	App	Gls
1974-75	30	0	1	0	0	0	31	0
1980-81	17	0	7	0	0	0	24	0
1981-82	31	0	1	0	2	0	34	0
1982-83	45	0	1	0	2	0	48	0
1983-84	45	0	2	0	2	0	49	0
	168	0	12	0	6	0	186	0

LEN BOND

Another player who had two separate spells with the City, Keith Bowker played in several midfield positions before being recognized as a centre-forward. Born at West Bromwich on 18 April 1951, he was apprenticed to Birmingham City in 1966 and after turning professional played in 21 League games before joining

KEITH BOWKER

the Grecians in December 1973. He must have found his League debut with his new club at Workington, before a crowd of only 693 quite a change, but he proved his worth and did not miss a game until midway through the following season. He was top scorer in that campaign with 18 League goals. Bowker's initial spell with the City lasted two and a half seasons and then he went to Cambridge United, where his chances were limited and he was loaned to Northampton Town before Bobby Saxton brought him back to the St James' Park in the summer of 1977. City had just won promotion and the energetic Bowker was an ever-present in the Third Division side, mostly wearing the number-four shirt, before returning to centre-forward the following season. Bowker lost his place when City bought John Sims from Notts County in December 1978 and, although he made a come-back when Sims was sold to Plymouth Argyle for £22,000 in the following season, his City career ended in 1980 when he joined Torquay United.
League debut for City v Workington, 15 December 1973.

	LEAGUE		FA CUP		FL CUP		TOTAL	
	App	Gls	App	Gls	App	Gls	App	Gls
1973-74	25	7	0	0	0	0	25	7
1974-75	43	18	1	0	2	0	46	18
1975-76	42	13	1	1	4	2	47	16
1977-78	46	9	5	1	3	0	54	10
1978-79	26/3	11	2	0	5	1	33/3	12
1979-80	21/6	8	1	0	4/1	5	26/7	13
	203/9	66	10	2	18/1	8	231/10	76

As his balding head indicated, this crafty full-back had plenty of experience when he came to Exeter but, although he may have been past his best, he proved to be a cool and calculating right-back. Over 220 appearances during eight seasons with Watford had taught him how to conserve energy and he was an excellent positional player who used measured clearances. Born at Bishop Auckland in 1907, Bill Brown played for his local amateur club and Crook Town before turning professional with Huddersfield Town in 1927. They, however, were especially well served with full-backs at this time and a year later he moved to Watford. The Grecians were going through a bad spell when Brown moved in, but he was one of the stars of their FA Cup victory over Leicester City in January 1937, being described as 'the best full-back on the field'. During a bad patch in February 1939, Brown suffered the misfortune of scoring in his own goal against Walsall, in what was his last appearance for the City. He lost his place to newly-signed Tom Halliday and was given a free transfer at the end of 1938-9. He then returned north to join Darlington and was scouting for Watford after the war. Bill Brown died on 17 August 1976.

League debut for City v Notts County, 29 August 1936.

	LEAGUE		FA CUP		TOTAL	
	App	*Gls*	*App*	*Gls*	*App*	*Gls*
1936-37	32	0	3	0	35	0
1937-38	26	0	2	0	28	0
1938-39	28	0	1	0	29	0
	86	0	6	0	92	0

BILL BROWN

Born at Eckington, Derbyshire, on 6 December 1904 and turning professional with Midland League Denaby United, Walter Bussey was one of several veteran players City signed in an effort to get themselves out of trouble just before the war. An intelligent inside-

WALTER BUSSEY

forward, he had eight seasons with Stoke, helping them to win promotion to the Second Division in 1926-7. In 1933 he was transferred to Blackpool and played in 25 First Division games for the Seasiders in only one season with them. In 1934 Bussey was one of the first signings new manager Neil Harris made for Swansea Town, where he played under the captaincy of Harry Hanford, a player who came to Exeter as trainer in 1954. Swansea were struggling to avoid relegation to the Third Division at this time but Bussey made his mark as a regular, although not prolific, goalscorer. His finest display for the Swans was scoring four goals in their 8-1 win over Bradford City in February 1936. However, Walter Bussey was more of a schemer than a goalscorer and he proved this after arriving at Exeter in December 1936, helping to settle a much-changed team. He liked to open up the game with his defence-splitting passes and proved a big help to marksman Rod Williams, who had until then been ploughing a lone furrow. Bussey's clever play was one of the features of City's Cup run in his initial season at the Park. He retired in 1939 but remained in Exeter and was assistant-trainer for a brief spell before turning to painting and decorating. He died in January 1982.

League debut for City v Swindon Town, 19 December 1936.

	LEAGUE		FA CUP		TOTAL	
	App	*Gls*	*App*	*Gls*	*App*	*Gls*
1936-37	20	5	3	1	23	6
1937-38	36	6	2	0	38	6
1938-39	19	5	0	0	19	5
	75	16	5	1	80	17

The youngest of three brothers who all played for Torquay United, Ted Calland was born in Durham on 15 June 1932 and turned professional in April 1952, as an outside-left with Fulham. After only one season he moved to Torquay and had just experienced his best season at Plainmoor when City signed him for only £1,500 in July 1957. A strong, 6ft-tall centre-forward with a hard shot, he reached the peak of his career whilst at St James' Park. Showing a fine turn of speed when it mattered, he was one of the Fourth Division's leading scorers in 1958-9 when City just missed promotion, bagging 27 goals, many of them from Gordon Dale's accurate centres. He was at his best when scoring a hat-trick in a 4-3 win over Colchester United during that season and when made captain for the visit to Torquay, he scored one of the fastest goals of his career, inside a minute, helping City to win 4-3. Ted Calland suffered the following season when he moved over to make way for new centre-forward Jack Wilkinson from Port Vale and at the end of that campaign he went to Wilkinson's old club in exchange for Fred Donaldson. Calland finished his League career with Lincoln City in 1961-2, then returned to live in Torquay.
League debut for City v Southend United, 24 August 1957.

	LEAGUE		FA CUP		TOTAL	
	App	Gls	App	Gls	App	Gls
1957-58	34	15	1	1	35	16
1958-59	44	27	1	1	45	28
1959-60	27	7	1	0	28	7
	105	49	3	2	108	51

TED CALLAND

Ray Carter's stay with City was brief, but he was a regular goalscorer in a struggling Fourth Division side and, but for a housing problem, he would have been in City's promotion-winning side, the season after he left. After playing for APV, a Sussex works team, he moved to Brixham to join his brother-in-law's plant-hire business. He did not turn professional with Torquay United until he was 25, but was given very few chances in one of that club's best side's with Tommy Northcott in full flow. City signed him, together with Graham Bond, for a combined fee of £2,000 in October 1960 and the St James' Park fans were treated to some of the best headed goals seen for quite a spell. Carter also possessed a cracking shot and his hat-trick against Oldham Athletic in March 1962 included one delightful overhead kick. Carter was certainly a danger man, especially in the air, and after heading City's score-sheet for two seasons he left in 1963 for a house and a job in a sports shop at Crawley.
League debut for City v Accrington Stanley, 19 November 1960.

	LEAGUE		FA CUP		FL CUP		TOTAL	
	App	Gls	App	Gls	App	Gls	App	Gls
1960-61	25	13	0	0	0	0	25	13
1961-62	40	18	2	1	1	0	43	19
1962-63	40	19	1	2	0	0	41	21
	105	50	3	3	1	0	109	53

RAY CARTER

75

Stan Charlton, a quiet, cheery Lancastrian, who was born at Little Hulton on 16 November 1900, is remembered as one of the most stylish full-backs ever to wear City's colours and was captain of the side for a number of seasons. So highly regarded did he become while at St James' Park that the FA included him in their party which toured Australia in 1925, as well as for the Professionals against Amateurs in the annual FA Charity Shield match that same year. Beginning his professional career with Oldham Athletic in 1920-21, his appearances with them were curtailed by a serious ankle injury. Fortunately he made a full recovery and had a good season with Rochdale before joining City in 1923, to replace Jack Ackroyd who went to Grimsby Town. At the end of his first season with Exeter, the local Press commented that Charlton was 'as fine a full-back as has ever set foot on St James' Park'. Three more good seasons followed until he lost his place to Charlie Miller for long spells in 1927-8, at the end of which campaign he followed former City manager Fred Mavin to Crystal Palace. There he missed only one game in his first season and remained until October 1932, when he finished his League career with Newport County before joining Margate in 1933. His son, Stanley junior, another full-back, became an England Amateur international before playing for Orient (two spells) and Arsenal in the 1950s and 1960s. Stan senior died at South Norwood in 1971.

STAN CHARLTON

| | LEAGUE | | FA CUP | | TOTAL | |
	App	Gls	App	Gls	App	Gls
1923-24	39	1	6	0	45	1
1924-25	30	1	5	0	35	1
1925-26	34	5	1	0	35	5
1926-27	42	3	3	0	45	3
1927-28	18	0	2	0	20	0
	163	10	17	0	180	10

ARTHUR CHILDS

An all-rounder, who played cricket professionally as well as football, Arthur Childs was a 6ft tall centre-half and the king-pin of the City team which finished runners-up to Brentford in the Third Division South in 1932-3. Born at Acomb, Yorkshire, on 25 April 1899, he joined City in 1931 and proved to be a huge success. Childs could control a game and spray accurate passes to his wings, always keeping the side on the move. Before joining the Grecians, he helped Hull City reach the FA Cup semi-final in 1929-30, when they lost in a replay to Arsenal at Villa Park. A relentless tackler, he played for Darlington Railway Athletic and Shildon before turning professional, soon after signing for Darlington in 1923. It was after five seasons at Feethams that he joined Hull City, but he returned to Darlington in the summer of 1934, after losing his place in the Exeter side to Harry Webb. Following his retirement, he was a licensee in Darlington before becoming steward at Whitley Bay Golf Club. He died in 1964.

League debut for City v Thames, 29 August 1931.

| | LEAGUE | | FA CUP | | TOTAL | |
	App	Gls	App	Gls	App	Gls
1931-32	28	1	0	0	28	1
1932-33	30	3	2	0	32	3
1933-34	4	0	0	0	4	0
	62	4	2	0	64	4

Reg Clarke was another of City's best local discoveries and one who stayed with the club to provide them with outstanding service as a right-half. Born at Seaton in 1908, he went to Ladysmith Road school in Exeter, helping them win the Devon County Schools Shield in 1921-2. He later played for Hems Athletic and for Beer and after starting work as an engine cleaner, he also played for the Southern Railway and helped their team win the Railway Cup. Clarke began his long career with City in 1928 and soon got the chance to make his League debut when Harry Gee broke a leg. An immediate success, he missed very few games over the next six seasons, until cartilage trouble intervened midway through the 1934-5 season. He re-established himself at right-half the following season, however. A star of City's 1930-31 Cup run, he played one of his finest-ever games in the shock draw at Sunderland and was also one of City's ever-presents the season they finished runners-up. Clarke was as hard as nails and, without being flashy, one of the club's most consistent performers, noted especially for his first-time passes into the attack. In 1937 he was not retained and joined Aldershot, where he remained until the war. *League debut for City v Newport County, 22 March 1928.*

REG 'NOBBY' CLARKE

	LEAGUE		FA CUP		TOTAL	
	App	Gls	App	Gls	App	Gls
1927-28	9	0	0	0	9	0
1928-29	38	3	2	1	40	4
1929-30	24	0	1	0	25	0
1930-31	31	1	8	0	39	1
1931-32	39	2	1	0	40	2
1932-33	42	2	2	0	44	3
1933-34	41	2	1	0	42	2
1934-35	25	0	2	0	27	0
1935-36	35	6	1	0	36	6
1936-37	31	2	5	0	36	3
	315	18	23	1	338	21

Born Kiveton Park, Sheffield, outside-left Levi Copestake was amongst the first batch of professionals to be signed by City in 1908 and one of the smallest players ever to appear for the club, being just over 5ft 5ins tall. His first professional club was Worksop, but in 1905 he joined Blackpool and made a number of appearances in their Second Division side before his transfer to Bristol City in 1907. There, his First Division appearances were restricted to two before moving to St James' Park. Like most small men, who could get the better of big defenders through tricky ball play and speed off the mark, he became a great favourite. For his part, he took a liking to Exeter and remained in the City for the greater part of his life, resuming his connection for a brief time with the club as late as 1945, when he was put in charge of developing City's Colts. His career as an outside-left with City covered only two seasons, but included the Cup run of 1908-09, when he played in all nine Cup ties. Indeed, this entertaining winger missed few games during his all too brief playing career at the Park before Bristol City regained his services and he had another three seasons at Ashton Gate before retiring to Exeter in 1913. *League debut for City v Norwich City, 19 September 1908.*

	LEAGUE		FA CUP		TOTAL	
	App	Gls	App	Gls	App	Gls
1908-09	32	6	9	4	41	10
1909-10	30	4	1	0	31	4
	62	10	10	4	72	14

LEVI COPESTAKE

A player who 'wore well'· and continued to display his footballing skill until way past his 40th birthday, Ellis Crompton was another of Exeter City's numerous Lancastrians of the pre-World War One era, having been born at Ramsbottom, near Bury in 1886. He

gained First Division experience in over four years with Blackburn Rovers before Tottenham Hotspur paid a substantial fee for his transfer during season 1910-11. Crompton could not settle with Spurs, however, and Arthur Chadwick made one of his finest captures when persuading Crompton to try his luck with Exeter in 1912. His first season with City was one of their most successful to date and, as skipper and inside-forward, he finished leading scorer with ten Southern League goals, forming one of the best left-wing combinations in the Southern League with Ben Ives. However, Ives went to QPR before the season ended and shortly afterwards Ellis Crompton was transferred to Bristol Rovers for a fee of £400. There he had four successful seasons spanning World War One, including many games at centre-half. In 1921 he returned to Exeter as an inside-forward, but soon switched to half-back, captaining the team and being the kingpin of one of City's best sides for many years, in 1924-5, when he missed only five games. One of the most admired aspects of his play was his speed on the ball, but age had caught up with him by this time and after losing his place, he went to Barnstaple Town as player-coach in 1926.
League debut for City v West Ham United, 2 September 1912.

	LEAGUE		FA CUP		TOTAL	
	App	Gls	App	Gls	App	Gls
1912-13	31	10	1	0	32	10
1921-22	39	4	2	0	41	4
1922-23	36	0	3	0	39	0
1923-24	26	0	2	0	28	0
1924-25	37	2	4	0	41	2
1925-26	7	0	0	0	7	0
	176	16	12	0	188	16

ELLIS CROMPTON

Born in Dublin on 26 August 1932, Dermot Curtis was first to gain a full international cap whilst an Exeter City player, a distinction he achieved in September 1963 when he won his 17th cap leading the Republic of Ireland attack in a goalless draw in Austria. This, of course, was near the start of City's first promotion-winning campaign in which he played a vital role, although he missed some games with an ankle injury. Curtis joined Bristol City from Shelbourne in 1956 and scored 13 goals in 15 Second Division appearances in his initial season. Midway through the following season he was transferred to Ipswich Town and, although he helped them win promotion to the First Division, he was generally kept out of the League side by that incredible goalscoring double spearhead, Ted Phillips and Ray Crawford. When he was transfer-listed in 1963, City director Les Kerslake flew to Ireland to persuade him to sign for the Grecians and he liked it at St James' Park so much that he had two spells with the club, spread over six years, with one year

(1966-7) at Torquay United. In July 1969, he joined Bideford. He still lives in Exeter.
League debut for City v Bradford City, 24 August 1963.

DERMOT CURTIS

	LEAGUE		FA CUP		FL CUP		TOTAL	
	App	Gls	App	Gls	App	Gls	App	Gls
1963-64	32	9	2	1	1	0	35	10
1964-65	42	9	2	0	2	2	46	11
1965-66	17	5	1	1	1	1	19	7
1967-68	35	6	4	0	0	0	39	6
1968-69	29/2	4	2	0	1/2	1	32/4	5
	155/2	33	11	2	5/2	4	171/4	39

78

No City player ever displayed more perfect ball control than outside-left Gordon Dale, who was signed from Portsmouth for what was, in October 1957, a club record fee of £7,000. Unfortunately, Exeter's strikers failed to take advantage of many of his pin-point centres and in his first season at the Park the side slid into the Fourth Division. Born at Manton, near

GORDON DALE

Worksop, on 20 May 1928, this cultured footballer began his career with Worksop Town and then played in the Second Division with Chesterfield, where he attracted the attention of First Division Portsmouth, who paid £20,000 for his transfer in 1951. It should be noted that the record transfer fee at this time was no more than £34,000. Gordon Dale made over 100 First Division appearances for Pompey but it is obvious that his unique style was not always appreciated. However, his move to Exeter brought the football connoisseurs at the Park genuine pleasure and many of Ted Calland's 27 League goals in 1958-9 came from this player's centres. Indeed, when making his debut against Bournemouth in 1957, Dale had wandered over to the opposite wing before crossing for Calland to score. Although such a delight to watch, he was sometimes unpredictable and his teammates did not know whether he was about to centre of turn back and beat an opponent a second time. In 1961 he went to Chelmsford.

League debut for City v Bournemouth, 26 October 1957.

	LEAGUE		FA CUP		FL CUP		TOTAL	
	App	Gls	App	Gls	App	Gls	App	Gls
1957-58	31	0	1	0	-	-	32	0
1958-59	41	2	1	0	-	-	42	2
1959-60	26	5	3	1	-	-	29	6
1960-61	26	1	2	0	1	0	29	1
	124	8	7	1	1	0	132	9

It used to be said that City did not make enough use of local talent but after the last war, Fred Davey was amongst the first of several young Devonians to make their mark with the club. Born at Crediton on 13 April 1924, he signed for City as an amateur in 1946-7, when he was already playing some fine games at centre-half for Crediton Town. He turned professional at the end of his first season with the Grecians and few players can ever have made such a notable debut as young Davey when he was brought into the League side on Boxing Day 1947 against Bristol City. Indeed, he succeeded in subduing the visitors' highly-priced centre-forward, Don Clark, in a 3-1 victory. The Notts County manager and a director who had come down to see Davey again before clinching his transfer, after having previously accepted the high price quoted, agreed to sign him. However, after a hastily-called meeting by the City directors it was decided not to part with the player. In 1949, Davey moved to wing-half to make way for Ray Goddard and later in his career at St James' Park, when he was made captain, he played alongside fellow Kyrotonian, Keith Harvey. Davey was often recalled to the centre-half position in subsequent seasons but at the end of his ninth professional

campaign, he was surprisingly placed on the open-to-transfer list and went to Bridgwater Town. Fred Davey, a gentleman both on and off the field, subsequently captained Crediton Town for a number of seasons before hanging up his boots at the age of 41 and moving to Peterborough.

League debut for City v Bristol City, 26 December 1947.

FRED DAVEY

	LEAGUE		FA CUP		TOTAL	
	App	Gls	App	Gls	App	Gls
1947-48	10	0	0	0	10	0
1948-49	7	0	0	0	7	0
1949-50	32	0	3	0	35	0
1950-51	43	1	6	0	49	1
1951-52	45	0	2	0	47	0
1952-53	39	1	1	0	40	1
1953-54	36	0	2	0	38	0
1954-55	33	1	1	0	34	1
1955-56	31	0	4	0	35	0
	276	3	19	0	295	3

A gentleman both on and off the field, Arthur Davies is generally regarded as the most capable goalkeeper ever to play for the City, or at least as good as Dick Pym. Considering that he appeared in no less than 70 First Division games in only his last two seasons with Everton, immediately before his transfer to Exeter in 1930, as well as playing for the Football League, there is no doubt that Billy McDevitt performed something of a miracle in securing his transfer at a fee far less than the £2,000 Everton were originally asking. At the time, City were desperate because first-choice Alderson had still not recovered from an injury sustained in the previous campaign and Davies was signed only five days before the opening of the new season. Born at Wallasey on 3 January 1907, he first signed professional for New Brighton and then joined Flint before moving to Goodison in 1926. When Everton won the League Championship in 1927-8, Davies took part in seven of the last eight critical games. He arrived in Exeter in time for the Cup run of 1930-31, in which his outstanding ability contributed to City's remarkable success. Subsequently, this lanky 'keeper with a long reach and such safe hands enjoyed a run of 124 consecutive League appearances (131 League and Cup), but at the beginning of the 1934-5 season, a wrist injury cost him his place and he found it difficult to oust newcomer Arthur Chesters. At the end of that season, he transferred to Plymouth Argyle and remained with that club, with the exception of 1937-8 when he was with Southport, until his premature death in 1940.

League debut for City v Norwich City, 30 August 1930.

ARTHUR DAVIES

	LEAGUE		FA CUP		TOTAL	
	App	Gls	App	Gls	App	Gls
1930-31	37	0	8	0	45	0
1931-32	42	0	1	0	43	0
1932-33	42	0	2	0	44	0
1933-34	33	0	1	0	34	0
1934-35	11	0	0	0	11	0
	165	0	12	0	177	0

Born in Isleworth, London, on 27 September 1953, this busy midfielder was an apprentice with Queen's Park Rangers and after turning professional played a small part in their promotion to the First Division in 1972-3. In 1974, Plymouth Argyle paid £30,000 for his transfer and he rewarded them in his initial season as a regular in their side which won promotion to the Second Division. In March 1978, when City were fighting to avoid relegation to the Fourth Division, player-manager Bobby Saxton, his former teammate at Home Park, clinched his transfer. He was a great success at St James' Park, helping to keep the side in the top half of the table and captaining them in that grand FA Cup run of 1980-81. Admittedly, City had a bad season in 1982-3 but it was still a big surprise when, at the end of that campaign, Delve was given a free transfer. He was immediately snapped up by Hereford United and enjoyed four seasons with them before returning to St James' Park to help with the lottery. He was re-signed as a player in October 1987 and when Colin Appleton left a couple of months later Delve got the job of caretaker player-manager until the end of the season. However, following Terry Cooper's appointment Delve was again released when it was expected he might continue as Cooper's assistant.
League debut for City v Rotherham United, 8 March 1978.

	LEAGUE		FA CUP		FL CUP		TOTAL	
	App	Gls	App	Gls	App	Gls	App	Gls
1977-78	11	1	0	0	0	0	11	1
1978-79	42	6	2	0	5	3	49	9
1979-80	42	1	1	0	6	0	49	1
1980-81	36	4	8	0	2	0	46	4
1981-82	40	3	1	0	2	0	43	3
1982-83	44	5	1	0	2	0	47	5
1987-88	12/1	1	0	0	0	0	12/1	1
	227/1	21	13	0	17	3	257/1	24

JOHN DELVE

80

Fred Dent had no more than two seasons with the City and held a regular first-team place for only just over half of that time, but he must be included here

FRED DENT

as one of the finest goalscorers the club ever had. Indeed, he might have scored more than he did, for it was not until City were losing 2-0 at Southend in September 1927 and skipper Stan Charlton moved him from inside-right to centre-forward, that Dent really showed his marksmanship. He netted two of City's goals in a 3-2 victory that afternoon and was scoring regularly for the remainder of the season, including all four goals when City beat Bristol Rovers 4-1 at St James' Park in November 1927. At the end of that campaign, Dent had beaten Blackmore's record with 26 League goals. He had a genius for positional play and was a great opportunist. Imagine the shock when, at the end of his record-breaking season, he was one of five City players transferred to a desperate Merthyr Town, who had just been forced to apply for re-election. Born at Sheffield, on 24 January 1896, he began his professional career with the Wednesday in 1920 but, after only one season, moved to Halifax Town. There followed a spell out of the League with Mid-Rhondda, prior to signing for the City. His subsequent stay with Merthyr was only brief, for he was transferred to Norwich in December 1928 and ended his career with one season each at Swindon and Luton before retiring in 1931.
League debut for City v Norwich City (scored twice), 18 September 1926.

	LEAGUE		FA CUP		TOTAL	
	App	Gls	App	Gls	App	Gls
1926-27	14	3	2	0	16	3
1927-28	34	26	6	6	40	32
	48	29	8	6	56	35

Born in Leeds on 13 March 1897, of Scottish parents and brought up in Scotland from the age of three, Jock Ditchburn subsequently played and talked like a Scot. When he returned to England from Blantyre Thistle to sign for Sunderland in 1923, it was as a right-half and that was his recognized position when he joined Exeter City in 1926. However, it is as a centre-half that he is best remembered by older City supporters. Although remaining in the city and working for the Southern Railway, Ditchburn was not on the club's books for the start of season 1928-9, but they re-signed him in November that year after he had played some fine games for the Exeter Loco team. Knee injuries slowed him down after this and he spent most of his last three seasons on City's books as centre-half in the Reserves, who benefited greatly from his experience with one of their most successful periods in the Southern League, before he retired in 1934.
League debut for City v Merthyr Town, 28 August 1926.

	LEAGUE		FA CUP		TOTAL	
	App	Gls	App	Gls	App	Gls
1926-27	30	0	0	0	30	0
1927-28	20	0	4	0	24	0
1928-29	1	0	1	0	2	0
1929-30	18	0	1	0	19	0
1930-31	14	0	0	0	14	0
1931-32	2	0	0	0	2	0
	85	0	6	0	91	0

JOHN 'JOCK' DITCHBURN

81

JOHN DOCKRAY

John Dockray was another of City's skilful outside-lefts, who achieved great popularity at St James' Park. Born at Carlisle and playing for the local team before transferring to Bury in 1912, he was signed by City in 1914, making his Southern League debut at outside-left that year in place of the injured Fred Goodwin, who was subsequently switched to inside-left. Before the war intervened the 'Carlisle Express' was proclaimed as the finest outside-left in the whole of the Southern League, with the possible exception of Northampton's Freeman. Dockray probably enjoyed his best seasons immediately after the war, for he only missed four games in the first three seasons after hostilities ended and it was during this period that he was twice called upon to represent the Southern League in games against the Welsh League. Fast and aggressive, although slightly built, Dockray took some holding. He loved to cut inside to meet crosses from the opposite wing and one of his best games was when he scored twice in a 3-2 win in 1922, at Northampton, during which City had played a long spell with only ten men. In 1924 he refused terms and went to Bideford Town as player-coach.

League debut for City v Reading, 12 December 1914.

	LEAGUE		FA CUP		TOTAL	
	App	Gls	App	Gls	App	Gls
1914-15	23	2	1	0	24	2
1919-20	41	3	1	0	42	3
1920-21	42	2	1	0	43	2
1921-22	39	5	1	0	40	5
1922-23	30	0	0	0	30	0
1923-24	30	5	0	0	30	5
	205	17	4	0	209	17

Exeter City have had some good wingers, but none better than Welshman Arthur Doncaster, who struck up such a remarkable partnership with Harold 'Happy' Houghton in those halcyon years of the early 1930s, before Doncaster was transferred to Crystal Palace, along with inside-forward Les Roberts, in the summer of 1933. Doncaster was tried at inside-forward, as well as on the wing and centre-forward, before the partnership just mentioned was established on a regular basis in 1929-30. In the following season it blossomed throughout City's great Cup run. What a pity that Doncaster left when he did, for such a combination might have been enough to clinch promotion in 1932-3 when Houghton had four different left-wing partners. Born in Barry on 10 May 1909, Doncaster was a Welsh Schoolboy international before playing for his local town club, from where he was transferred to Bolton Wanderers at the age of 18. Fellow countryman, the inimitable Ted Vizard, was outside-left for Bolton in those days and Arthur made no League appearances prior to moving to Exeter in 1928. Here he enjoyed the limelight in the FA Cup, playing three of his best games against First Division Leeds United. He scored in the original draw at St James' Park, in the third round of 1928-9, as well as in the replay when City were well beaten at Leeds. Two season's later, he was in the proud team which took revenge with a 3-1 home victory over the Yorkshire club. A sturdy and tricky winger, Arthur Doncaster had a season each with Palace and Reading before finishing his League career with two years at Gillingham. He joined Yeovil in 1936.

League debut for City v Brentford, 25 August 1928.

ARTHUR DONCASTER

	LEAGUE		FA CUP		TOTAL	
	App	Gls	App	Gls	App	Gls
1928-29	24	7	4	3	28	10
1929-30	29	6	1	0	30	6
1930-31	32	10	8	1	40	11
1931-32	41	8	1	0	42	8
	126	31	14	4	140	35

Born in Salford, Manchester, on 15 July 1930, right-back Brian Doyle was signed by Stoke City in March 1951 from mid-Cheshire League side, Lostock Gralam. After making 17 First Division appearances for the Potters he was spotted by Norman Dodgin whilst playing in their Central League team. The Exeter manager had gone to watch a forward but was more taken with the fast-moving defender and signed him at the first opportunity, which was in April 1954. Brian is not to be confused with another full-back, Leslie 'Paddy' Doyle, who was on City's books at the same time. Brian Doyle originally displaced Norman Douglass at left-back but soon moved to right-back in place of an out-of-form Dick Walton, and that is where he remained for the rest of three seasons with the Grecians before Bristol Rovers completed his transfer in August 1960. At Eastville he made 43 Second Division appearances over three seasons, then lost his place to Doug Hillard after injury. Brian Doyle later managed Workington and Stockport County and assisted Bob Stokoe at Blackpool before going abroad. *League debut for City v Crystal Palace, 21 August 1954.*

	LEAGUE		FA CUP		TOTAL	
	App	Gls	App	Gls	App	Gls
1954-55	39	0	1	0	40	0
1955-56	33	0	2	0	35	0
1956-57	28	0	1	0	29	0
	100	0	4	0	104	0

BRIAN DOYLE

'Digger' Ebdon became one of the Grecians' all-time favourites not only because of his football skills but also because no matter how he played, he always tried his hardest. At his best there was no finer centre-forward in the Third Division, for he had strength,

RICHARD 'DIGGER' EBDON

pace and, above all, persistence. Born at Ottery St Mary on 3 May 1913, Ebdon played several League games for the City before signing professional in December 1935. He was one of those players of the generation who lost their best playing years through World War Two, but he still provided much enjoyment for the three peacetime seasons he was at the Park after the war before going to Torquay United in 1948. In those later seasons he had developed into a complete leader, who knew how to open up the game with well-directed passes to either flank and was still dangerous near goal. Indeed, opposing defences learnt never to leave Ebdon with half a chance, for he would chase every ball in his efforts to score, even when it looked like a lost cause. One of the finest examples of the high standard he could reach was in a 4-1 home win over Bournemouth at the Park in September 1946, when he scored a hat-trick, beating three men by sheer speed before driving home one of these goals. 'Digger' was still playing for Ottery St Mary when he was over 40 years of age. He died on 27 April 1987. *League debut for City v Coventry City, 14 September 1935.*

	LEAGUE		FA CUP		TOTAL	
	App	Gls	App	Gls	App	Gls
1935-36	24	9	0	0	24	9
1936-37	3	0	0	0	3	0
1937-38	22	6	0	0	22	6
1938-39	42	12	1	0	43	12
1945-46	0	0	4	1	4	1
1946-47	29	16	0	0	29	16
1947-48	18	7	0	0	19	7
	138	50	6	1	144	51

Theo Foley arrived at St James' Park from Home Farm (Dublin) as a teenager in February 1955 and his potential was so obvious that he was signed on professional forms within a month. After being allowed to develop at right-back in the Southern League side for a couple of seasons, and vying with Ray John for the right-back position, he came into his own in 1957-8. Once established he never looked back, proving himself to be a most dependable defender. Foley married an Exeter girl but after six seasons at the Park he was surprisingly transferred to Northampton Town for a small fee in 1961, becoming one of the stars of their side that fought its way from Third to First Division in three years. Indeed, the Republic of Ireland recognized his ability by awarding him nine caps during this spell. In 1967 he moved to Charlton Athletic, where he began his coaching career. In 1974 he was with Dulwich Hamlet, but he quit after only two matches and was appointed reserve-team coach to Queen's Park Rangers before becoming assistant manager of Millwall in 1982. In May 1986 he moved to Arsenal as assistant to George Graham and rejoined Northampton as manager in May 1990.
League debut for City v Norwich City, 14 September 1955.

	LEAGUE		FA CUP		TOTAL	
	App	Gls	App	Gls	App	Gls
1955-56	4	0	0	0	4	0
1956-57	0	0	0	0	0	0
1957-58	34	1	0	0	34	1
1958-59	46	0	1	0	47	0
1959-60	45	0	3	0	48	0
1960-61	26	0	0	0	26	0
	155	1	4	0	159	1

THEO FOLEY

JACK FORT

Born at Leigh, Lancashire, on 13 April 1888, Jack Fort played for his local side at inside-forward and centre-half soon after leaving school, but it was after he signed professional for Atherton in the Lancashire Combination that they turned him into a right-back. A fitness fanatic, Fort proved to be one of the most durable defenders of his era. Following three seasons with City, he served Millwall as a player for another 16 years, being nearly 42 when making his final League appearance for them. Arthur Chadwick included him among his many captures from the Lancashire Combination in 1911 and he proved to be one of City's most successful signings to date. Unfortunately, at the end of season 1913-14, City could not resist a good offer for this compactly-built right-back and he began his wonderful service with Millwall, which lasted for over 50 years in various capacities from player to groundsman and chief scout. Indeed, he was still a part-time groundsman until a few days before his death on 23 November 1965. Whilst with City he represented the Southern League against the Football League and, after moving to London, played another game for the Southern League as well as gaining one full England cap.
League debut for City v Swindon Town, 28 October 1911.

	LEAGUE		FA CUP		TOTAL	
	App	Gls	App	Gls	App	Gls
1911-12	18	0	0	0	18	0
1912-13	34	0	1	0	35	0
1913-14	33	0	2	0	35	0
	85	0	3	0	88	0

JIMMY GILES

Jimmy Giles was another player who had two separate spells with the City, where he was one of the club's most popular players. Born at Kidlington, on 21 April 1946, Giles had just over three seasons with Swindon Town before coming to the fore with Aldershot, whom he joined in 1968. He was their Player of the Year in his first season and Johnny Newman did a fine stroke of business in getting him transferred to Exeter in March 1971, for he was a tower of strength in the City defence and helped keep them in the top half of the Fourth Division for four seasons before being transferred to Charlton Athletic in 1975. He therefore, missed City's promotion-winning campaign of 1976-7, but was brought back to St James' Park in December 1977 to play out another three and a half seasons before injury cut short his career and he was released in February 1981. Jimmy Giles was the first player to be voted City's Player of the Year in two seasons — 1971-2 and 1972-3.

League debut for City v Northampton Town (scored once), 16 March 1971.

	LEAGUE		FA CUP		FL CUP		TOTAL	
	App	Gls	App	Gls	App	Gls	App	Gls
1970-71	11	2	0	0	0	0	11	2
1971-72	42	1	4	0	1	0	47	1
1972-73	44	1	1	0	1	0	46	1
1973-74	43	2	1	0	5	0	49	2
1974-75	43	2	1	0	1	0	45	2
1977-78	23	0	2	0	0	0	25	0
1978-79	43	1	1	0	5	0	49	1
1979-80	42	2	1	0	6	0	49	2
1980-81	22	2	0	0	2	0	24	2
	313	13	11	0	21	0	343	13

This experienced centre-half was received like a knight in shining armour when he was signed from Plymouth Argyle for a £5,000 fee in December 1949 to try and stop the rot. Goddard had requested a transfer from Argyle but it took the club's representatives several hours of negotiation to persuade the player to move from one Devon city to another, for Exeter were not the only interested club. His initial appearance for City was a great success, for he certainly tightened up the defence and his generalship was an inspiration. City were bottom of the table when Goddard arrived but he was a wonderful influence in pulling them up to 16th and then 12th the following season. Unfortunately, Ray Goddard had already reached the veteran stage and his hard-tackling style of play made him susceptible to leg injuries which really began to affect his form in 1953-4. Before this season he had lost his place and requested a transfer, going to Bideford Town as player-manager at the end of that campaign. Born in Birmingham on 17 October 1920, Goddard came under Major Buckley's influence when he joined Wolves as a teenager in 1937. He subsequently played for Chelsea before joining Plymouth Argyle in 1948. One of Goddard's finest displays for Exeter, perhaps not surprisingly, was in a 3-2 home win over Argyle in February 1951. He died in 1974.

League debut for City v Watford, 17 December 1949.

	LEAGUE		FA CUP		TOTAL	
	App	Gls	App	Gls	App	Gls
1949-50	22	0	2	0	24	0
1950-51	25	0	2	0	27	0
1951-52	28	0	2	0	30	0
1952-53	37	0	1	0	38	0
1953-54	18	2	0	0	18	2
	130	2	7	0	137	2

RAY GODDARD

Billy Goodwin soon proved himself to be a useful capture after he was signed from Blackburn Rovers in that critical summer of 1914, when World War One broke out and there was doubt as to whether football would continue.

The new centre-forward scored a hat-trick in a practice match and then found the net in each of his first five Southern League games. By the end of that campaign he had claimed the club's League scoring record with 23 goals, which was one better than 'Daisy' Bell in City's initial season as a professional concern. An immaculate footballer, he was an excellent leader of the attack, spraying passes to both wings and showing great skill as a dribbler, as well as a fine shot. Indeed, he became the side's penalty specialist and in his first season would no doubt have been an ever-present, but for the fact that he suffered a bad dislocation of the elbow in his 36th League game. It was perhaps significant that City failed to score in their last three games of that campaign, including the one in which Goodwin was injured. He returned to lead the attack for one more season after the war and was again top scorer, though with six goals less. He wanted a higher grade of football and went to Manchester United for £650. He did not do well there, but found his scoring touch again after joining Southend United in 1922. He finished his playing career with Dartford, in 1928 but retired to Southend and became a wholesale confectioner.

League debut for City v West Ham United (scored once), 5 September 1914.

	LEAGUE		FA CUP		TOTAL	
	App	Gls	App	Gls	App	Gls
1914-15	36	23	1	0	37	23
1919-20	37	17	1	0	38	17
	73	40	2	0	75	40

BILLY GOODWIN

When City lost Dicky Baugh with an ankle injury midway through the 1929-30 season, they were quick to secure a replacement and in January signed Jimmy Gray from Liverpool. Gray, who was born in Glasgow on 16 September 1900, spent five years in South Africa playing for Transvaal prior to joining Liverpool in 1926, but he had little opportunity to show his paces with the Reds. He cost City £75 and proved to be one of the best bargains ever made by the Grecians, for he was one of the stars of that great period when City not only reached the sixth round of the FA Cup but also finished runners-up in the Third Division South. Indeed, it could be argued that Gray and Miller were the finest pair of backs ever to grace City's defence. It will be noted that Gray was already a veteran when City signed him in 1929, but his service extended over seven seasons before he was released at the end of 1935-6. Remembered for his enthusiasm and quick recovery, Jimmy Gray was wonderfully consistent and earned the respect of the City supporters, so much so that 5,000 turned up for his benefit match against Liverpool in May 1935. Jimmy Gray died on 10 May 1978.

League debut for City v Walsall, 19 January 1930.

	LEAGUE		FA CUP		TOTAL	
	App	Gls	App	Gls	App	Gls
1929-30	20	0	0	0	20	0
1930-31	12	0	0	0	12	0
1931-32	30	0	1	0	31	0
1932-33	36	0	2	0	38	0
1933-34	41	0	1	0	42	0
1934-35	41	0	3	0	44	0
1935-36	33	0	1	0	34	0
	213	0	8	0	221	0

JIMMY GRAY

For sheer footballing ability and craftsmanship, very few City players had the better of this Scot in the early post-war years. A polished style with creative skill made Bill Harrower a pleasing footballer to watch and he would have been an even more regular performer in the City colours, but his problem was lack of weight and strength. Nearly 6ft tall but only 10st, he was sometimes too easily brushed off the ball. Torquay United signed him from Third Lanark in 1946 but he was soon called up for National Service in the RAF and Torquay saw very little of him. Whilst in the RAF he played in a number of representative games and in one against an FA XI he was described in a report by Charles Buchan (the former England international) as 'the outstanding player on the field.' Torquay surprisingly lost interest in him but in the summer of 1948, Exeter City manager George Roughton made the long train journey to Scotland to persuade the player to sign for the City at a time when a number of clubs were seeking his transfer. The deal cost City only £1,000, but what pleasure Bill Harrower brought to the footballing connoisseurs among the followers at St James' Park. Originally an inside-forward, he dropped back to wing-half in his final season with the City when leg injuries had slowed him down and when he was transfer-listed in 1952, Harrower joined Bideford. His son, Steve, followed in his footsteps joining City first as an amateur in 1983 and turning professional the following year.

League debut for City v Aldershot, 8 September 1948.

BILL HARROWER

	LEAGUE		FA CUP		TOTAL	
	App	Gls	App	Gls	App	Gls
1948-49	21	5	1	0	22	5
1949-50	20	4	3	0	23	4
1950-51	32	2	5	0	37	2
1951-52	12	0	0	0	12	0
	85	11	9	0	94	11

Keith Harvey was a powerful defender who gave Exeter City 17 seasons of loyal service. His total of League appearances for the club is second only to that of Arnold Mitchell. Born at Crediton on 25 December 1934, he signed professional for City in August 1952 and made his League debut early that season as a right-half. However, it was as a centre-half that he gave such sterling service, being safe in the air and a firm tackler. Never one to hold back, Harvey would have gained the club's appearance record but for a number of serious injuries. He broke his right leg in October 1958, his right ankle in a pre-season practice match in August 1962 and his collarbone on three other occasions. As hard as nails, Harvey was back to the fray as quickly as possible and reached his peak as City's most improved player around 1961-2. In 1963-4 he was an ever-present in the Grecians' first promotion-winning side. He was appointed City's trainer in 1966 but when he continued playing, he gave up this position at the end of one season. He was, however, trainer for two subsequent spells before finally leaving the club in December 1972. Harvey moved to the south coast and now works for the Post Office.

League debut for City v Bristol Rovers, 27 September 1952.

	LEAGUE		FA CUP		FL CUP		TOTAL	
	App	Gls	App	Gls	App	Gls	App	Gls
1952-53	6	0	0	0	0	0	6	0
1953-54	2	0	0	0	0	0	2	0
1954-55	22	0	0	0	0	0	22	0
1955-56	41	0	4	0	0	0	45	0
1956-57	43	6	1	0	0	0	44	6
1957-58	37	2	1	0	0	0	38	2
1958-59	13	3	0	0	0	0	13	3
1959-60	23	0	0	0	0	0	23	0
1960-61	36	0	2	0	2	0	40	0
1961-62	44	2	2	0	1	0	47	2
1962-63	22	2	0	0	0	0	22	2
1963-64	46	5	2	0	2	0	50	5
1964-65	42	5	2	0	2	0	46	5
1965-66	40	3	1	0	1	0	42	3
1966-67	7	0	1	0	0	0	8	0
1967-68	34	0	1	0	0	0	35	0
1968-69	25	0	4	0	5	0	34	0
	483	28	21	0	13	0	517	28

KEITH HARVEY

Whether in the heart of the defence or in midfield, Peter Hatch was always creative. A real football artist, he possessed anticipation and timing to a high degree and was a big help to all around him. Born at Henley-on-Thames on 22 October 1949, he first appeared in the Football League with Oxford United but, considering his ability, was given surprisingly few chances by them in over seven years as a professional after joining as an apprentice. Exeter City certainly made much better use of this player after Johnny Newman signed him in December 1973. The Grecians were then on the upgrade and Peter Hatch helped them to improve still more until they earned promotion in his fourth season at the Park. Although wearing the number-three shirt, he enjoyed overlapping and getting among the attackers, where he helped the side score quite a few goals apart from those he netted himself. One of his finest displays was in the Cup replay against Newcastle United in February 1981, when, playing at outside-left, he scored the first goal and was involved in two of the other three as City caused pandemonium by beating the Magpies 4-0. At the end of the next season he was given a free transfer and joined Bideford. *League debut for City v Workington, 15 December 1973.*

PETER HATCH

	LEAGUE		FA CUP		FL CUP		TOTAL	
	App	Gls	App	Gls	App	Gls	App	Gls
1973-74	24	0	0	0	0	0	24	0
1974-75	41	1	1	0	2	0	44	1
1975-76	43	1	1	0	4	1	48	2
1976-77	43	2	2	1	3	0	48	3
1977-78	38/1	1	5	1	4	0	47/1	2
1978-79	45	2	2	0	4	0	51	2
1979-80	44	6	1	0	6	1	51	7
1980-81	45	2	8	1	2	0	55	3
1981-82	20/2	3	0	0	2	0	22/2	3
	343/3	18	20	3	27	2	390/3	23

Scott Hiley is a product of City's youth policy and was discovered and developed by youth coach Mike Radford. Hiley joined City as a schoolboy in 1983 and signed full professional forms in August 1986. A Devon County youth player, he was brought along as a midfielder and whilst playing at left-half, once headed a hat-trick for City's youth team against Swansea City in an FA Youth Cup tie. Eased into League football gradually as a midfielder when still a teenager, he eventually seemed settled at outside-left. In City's promotion-winning season of 1989-90, however, he was moved to right-back. Although a modern overlapping number-two, these positional moves alone give some indication of his versatility but as season 1989-90 progressed he was often the side's outstanding player, being brimful of sheer talent. Fast, nimble and clever on the ball as well as a keen tackler, he quickly reached the standard displayed by his contemporary, Chris Vinnicombe, when that player was transferred to Glasgow Rangers. Maintaining his present standard, Hiley is surely destined for the highest grade of football. He was born in Plymouth on 27 September 1968. *League debut for City (sub) v Burnley, 17 October 1987.*

	LEAGUE		FA CUP		FL CUP		TOTAL	
	App	Gls	App	Gls	App	Gls	App	Gls
1987-88	12/3	2	0	0	0	0	12/3	1
1988-89	36/1	5	1	0	2	0	39/1	5
1989-90	45/1	0	6	0	7	0	58/1	0
	93/5	6	7	0	9	0	109/5	6

SCOTT HILEY

Born St Austell, 10 February 1947, this curly-haired Cornishman was spotted by Plymouth Argyle playing for East Cornwall Schools and signed professional as soon as he was 17. He is remembered at both Home

JOHNNY HORE

Park and St James' Park as one of the most dependable of defenders, who got through a tremendous amount of work with the minimum of fuss. He made over 400 League appearances for Argyle and helped them regain Second Division status. Johnny Hore first came to Exeter on loan in March 1976, signing a contract in July that year. His consistency was nothing short of amazing, either at left-back or in midfield, for he missed only two League games in four seasons before being released in December 1980. He went into management with Bideford Town and steered them to the Western League championship in two successive seasons before being appointed manager of Plymouth Argyle in October 1984. He had a hard time in this appointment and was dismissed after 12 months, returning to St James' Park in January 1985 to help with the coaching. He became caretaker manager after Jim Iley's dismissal in May that year and fully expected to be confirmed as City's manager but bitterly left, disappointed, when the job went to Colin Appleton.
League debut for City v Rochdale, 9 March 1976.

	LEAGUE		FA CUP		FL CUP		TOTAL	
	App	Gls	App	Gls	App	Gls	App	Gls
1975-76	11	0	0	0	0	0	11	0
1976-77	46	0	2	0	3	0	51	0
1977-78	46	0	2	0	4	0	55	0
1978-79	44	0	2	0	5	0	51	0
1979-80	46	0	1	0	6	0	53	0
	193	0	10	0	18	0	221	0

A quiet man on and off the field, Liverpudlian Harold Houghton was arguably the most skilful inside-forward ever to wear Exeter City's colours. An English Schoolboy international, he joined Everton from Anfield Social Club, signing professional forms in 1921. Considering the amount of praise he attracted when he was at his peak with Exeter, it is perhaps surprising that he made no more than one League appearance for Everton in the seven seasons he was with the club (nine seasons including two as an amateur). But, apart from the fact that he began with them straight from school and needed time to develop, the Toffeemen had numerous international inside-forwards on their books throughout Houghton's stay. Exeter were fortunate enough to obtain his transfer in 1928, for a club record transfer fee of £350. At the time City needed an inside-forward to replace Wilf Lievesley and they could not have made a better signing. For nearly six years Houghton really entertained the City supporters. In 1931 he toured Canada with the FA team. Houghton knew how to hold a ball just long enough to throw the opposing defence off balance and, when City recorded their best-ever goal-average in 1932-3, when they finished runners-up, Houghton appeared in every game and created numerous openings for Fred Whitlow to get his club record total of goals. Houghton was extremely fast with an elusive swerve and if he had a fault, it was an inclination sometimes to overdo the dribbling in the penalty area. After a couple of seasons of rumours about his transfer (Spurs were reported to have offered £3,000), Houghton requested a move and was transferred to Norwich for a small fee, when the Canaries were Third Division South leaders in March 1934. He made his debut for them in a home draw against the Grecians three days after signing. Houghton finished his League career with two seasons

(1935-7) at Bristol Rovers, then joined South Liverpool. He was born on 26 August 1908 and died on 3 February 1986.
League debut for City v Brentford (scored once), 25 August 1928.

HAROLD 'HAPPY' HOUGHTON

	LEAGUE		FA CUP		TOTAL	
	App	Gls	App	Gls	App	Gls
1928-29	27	8	3	0	30	8
1929-30	34	11	1	0	35	11
1930-31	42	23	8	4	50	27
1931-32	33	16	1	0	34	16
1932-33	42	13	2	0	44	13
1933-34	29	8	1	0	30	8
	207	79	16	4	223	83

After a tip-off from former Derby County and England winger Sammy Crooks, who was then chief scout at the Baseball Ground, City manager Norman Dodgin signed George Hunter from the Rams in August 1955 and he proved to be one of the most competent goalkeepers the club had ever had. Unfortunately, a fractured jaw bone and then a fractured arm kept down his number of appearances in five seasons with City, but worst was a fractured leg at home to Port Vale in March 1959, which kept him idle for the whole of the next season. Much to the player's disgust he was given a free transfer when he was returning to fitness in 1960 and he went to Yiewsley that summer. In 1961 he returned to League football with Darlington. A couple of seasons with Burton Albion and a brief spell with Lincoln City ended his playing career, but he was really never the same goalkeeper after leaving Exeter. Born at Troon on 29 August 1930, he won a Scottish FA Cup winners' medal with Glasgow Celtic at the age of 19 before moving to Derby County in June 1954. He returned to Derby after his playing days were over and worked in a factory there. George Hunter died in a Nottingham hospital in May 1990.

League debut for City v Colchester United, 20 August 1955.

GEORGE HUNTER

	LEAGUE		FA CUP		TOTAL	
	App	Gls	App	Gls	App	Gls
1955-56	43	0	4	0	47	0
1956-57	40	0	1	0	41	0
1957-58	28	0	1	0	29	0
1958-59	36	0	1	0	37	0
	147	0	7	0	154	0

Exeter City have had at least three outstanding players from Crediton, just eight miles out of the city, and centre-forward Stan Hurst was one of them. As a

STAN HURST

schoolboy he played rugby at Crediton Grammar School but, after leaving school, he turned to soccer with Jackson's United (a Crediton works team), Newton Poppleford and Tipton St John before joining the City. He led the Devon County XI as an amateur and played for the FA Amateur XI against the Royal Navy at Home Park in 1932. Hurst celebrated turning professional in December that year by scoring five goals in a 10-2 Western League victory over Taunton Town and continued to be a prolific goalscorer as leader of the reserve team. He made his debut as an amateur in 1932-3, when City were bidding for promotion, and made six appearances in all in that illustrious campaign. The following year he succeeded Fred Whitlow as the club's leading scorer, despite playing a lot of games on the wing. Hurst's inclination was to be a centre-forward but his lack of bulk made it difficult for him in the hurly burly of the Third Division and after City's disastrous campaign of 1935-6, he refused terms and went to Brighton, where he remained until the war. At centre-forward he once scored seven goals for the Reserves in a 13-0 Southern League victory over Swindon Town.

League debut for City v Bournemouth, 15 October 1932.

	LEAGUE		FA CUP		TOTAL	
	App	Gls	App	Gls	App	Gls
1932-33	8	0	0	0	8	0
1933-34	34	14	1	0	35	14
1934-35	31	8	3	3	34	11
1935-36	34	3	1	0	35	3
	107	25	5	3	112	28

In the mid 1960s, Plymouth Argyle had one of their finest pair of wingers since the war — Barrie Jones and Nicky Jennings. The latter had joined them from Wellington Town in 1963 and made his Second Division debut soon after his 18th birthday. The fans were delighted with him and more than a little annoyed when he was transferred to Portsmouth in January 1967 for a £25,000 fee. He remained at Fratton Park for nearly seven years, making over 200 Second Division appearances until in May 1974, Johnny Newman added him to his improving promotion-chasing side at St James' Park. He was unfortunate enough to lose the second half of his initial season with a broken arm, but proved to be a classy and determined winger and, but for other injuries which slowed him down, he would have been an even more regular first-team player with the City. He eventually lost his place to Harry Holman midway through his fourth season and was given a free transfer in 1978. *League debut for City v Barnsley, 17 August 1974.*

	LEAGUE		FA CUP		FL CUP		TOTAL	
	App	Gls	App	Gls	App	Gls	App	Gls
1974-75	19	4	1	0	2	3	22	7
1975-76	34	2	0	0	4	0	38	2
1976-77	43	7	2	0	1	0	46	7
1977-78	23/5	2	3	0	4	0	30/5	2
	119/5	15	6	0	11	3	136/5	18

NICKY JENNINGS

Signed in July 1947 from Hamilton Academical, his home-town club, Cyril Johnstone was one of the stalwarts of the Grecians' early post-war period when they generally maintained a better-than-average position. A natural right-back, he got an early chance in City's League side in the second game of 1947-8 when Jack Blood was out with ligament trouble and, although this debut was at left-back, he retained that position for most of the season, missing only two games. It was not until the following season, after 'Ginger' Thompson had departed, that he moved to right-back and struck up a fine partnership with local discovery, Stan Rowe. Johnstone was one of the fastest backs in the Third Division and had terrific powers of recovery. He held a first-team place until suffering a leg injury against Swindon early in 1951-2 and, as so often happens, found it difficult to regain his place permanently after four and a half months on the sidelines. Indeed, a recurrence of this ligament trouble while in training for season 1951-2 ended his playing career and he was released in November of that season. *League debut for City v Reading, 27 August 1947.*

	LEAGUE		FA CUP		TOTAL	
	App	Gls	App	Gls	App	Gls
1947-48	40	0	2	0	42	0
1948-49	37	0	1	0	38	0
1949-50	41	0	4	0	45	0
1950-51	16	0	0	0	16	0
	134	0	7	0	141	0

CYRIL JOHNSTONE

91

Eddie Jones was born in Tyldesley and was a Lancashire lad who might have become a professional Rugby League footballer. As a youngster he played

EDDIE JONES

wing-threequarter and both Wigan and Wakefield Trinity were interested in him. However, when the time came to make up his mind, he chose the dribbling code and turned professional with Bolton Wanderers. He made little progress with them, however, and continued to play for Tyldesley and then Penrith before signing for Chorley in the Lancashire Combination. It was from Chorley that he joined City in 1909 and began an association with the Grecians which, although not continuous, was to be spread over nearly 20 years. He came as a left-back to replace Joe Bulcock, who had been transferred to Crystal Palace. In this position Jones was an outstanding success, missing only a single game in one run of 62 appearances before Bristol City, needing a replacement for Joe Cottle and on the slide out of the First Division, came along with a tempting offer. Eddie Jones went to Ashton Gate in February 1911 and remained with Bristol City for more than 11 years before joining Bristol Rovers as trainer. In 1926 he returned to St James' Park for another three seasons as trainer.
League debut for City v Croydon Common, 4 September 1909.

	LEAGUE		FA CUP		TOTAL	
	App	Gls	App	Gls	App	Gls
1909-10	39	0	4	0	43	0
1910-11	24	2	4	1	28	3
	63	2	8	1	71	3

It is sometimes overlooked that goalscoring is what the game is all about, but here is one player who never fell into that trap. Tony Kellow scored more goals for Exeter City than any other player. In the modern game he did not always wear the centre-forward's shirt, but that is what he was — a bustling, hard-shooting centre-forward, always in the thick of the fray. As hard as nails, he would take all the knocks in his tireless efforts to get the ball into the net and he had one of the hardest right-foot shots ever seen at the Park. City signed him from Falmouth Town, where he had a good grounding in the game's rough-and-tumble which always stood him in good stead. He helped City to regain Third Division status in his first season with the club, but in November 1978 he was transferred to Blackpool for £105,000, when that once-famous club was sliding down the Third Division. Kellow's 23 League goals in around one and a half season for the Seasiders was a valuable contribution. Fortunately for City supporters, he returned to Exeter for a £65,000 fee in March 1980 and stepped up his scoring rate, enjoying his best season in 1980-81 when his total of 33 goals included a hat-trick (with one penalty) in City's

3-1 FA Cup win over Leicester City. This was the first hat-trick by a City player in an FA Cup tie since Dick Smart's against Millwall in 1949. He left City again in November 1983 when transferred to Plymouth Argyle and also played for Swansea City and Newport County before returning to St James' Park in 1985, finishing his playing career in 1988 when he was appointed the club's commercial manager. His total of Football League goals for all clubs was 162.
League debut for City v Hartlepool (scored twice), 21 August 1976.

	LEAGUE		FA CUP		FL CUP		TOTAL	
	App	Gls	App	Gls	App	Gls	App	Gls
1976-77	44	19	2	1	3	2	49	22
1977-78	46	14	5	3	4	0	55	17
1978-79	17	7	0	0	5	2	22	9
1979-80	10	5	0	0	0	0	10	5
1980-81	46	25	8	6	2	2	56	33
1981-82	46	21	1	0	4	1	51	22
1982-83	31/2	10	1	0	2	1	34/2	11
1983-84	7/1	0	0	0	2	1	9/1	1
1985-86	24/9	9	1	1	3	1	28/9	11
1986-87	22/11	15	0	0	0	0	22/11	15
1987-88	5/11	4	0	0	0/2	0	5/13	4
	298/34	129	18	11	25/2	10	341/36	150

TONY KELLOW

92

HUGH KELLY

Born in Lurgan on 17 August 1919, Hugh Kelly was an inside-left with Glenavon before changing to goalkeeper with Belfast Celtic during the war and winning Irish Cup winners' medals in 1943 and 1944. After the Belfast Celtic club went out of existence, Kelly joined Fulham in March 1949. There he made 25 First Division appearances in one season and then signed for Southampton. After 28 Second Division appearances for the Saints in 1950-51, he returned home and played no further League games for them. His former Southampton teammate, Norman Kirkman, flew to Ireland as City's manager in the summer of 1952 and persuaded this classy goalkeeper to return to the Football League. A 'keeper of resource and good judgement, Hugh Kelly was a natural who made the art of goalkeeping look easy. Despite becoming overweight (over 15st), he retained his great positional sense and played many outstanding games for the Grecians until a loss of form during season 1954-5 saw him hand over to Alec Bell. He married an Exeter girl and remained at the club until the end of the 1955-6 season, when he joined Weymouth. Whilst with Fulham and Southampton, he won four full caps for Northern Ireland.

League debut for City v Queen's Park Rangers, 23 August 1952.

	LEAGUE		FA CUP		TOTAL	
	App	Gls	App	Gls	App	Gls
1952-53	37	0	1	0	38	0
1953-54	35	0	2	0	37	0
1954-55	24	0	1	0	25	0
1955-56	3	0	0	0	3	0
	99	0	4	0	103	0

City signed inside-forward Harold Kirk from Plymouth Argyle in a desperate effort to halt the slide towards re-election and he was a big success, putting life into a drab attack. Signed on 1 March, when there were 14 games still to play, he scored in eight of those games but, despite his efforts, City still had to go cap in hand to the League. It was said at the time that it was a pity the club had not moved earlier to strengthen their forward line. Born in Bradford, Kirk joined Bristol City immediately after World War One and moved to Plymouth Argyle in 1921. It appears that City only had him on loan, for at the end of season 1921-2 he was not mentioned among the players retained and during the summer his name was again associated with Argyle. The local Press described the situation as 'peculiar' but the mystery was cleared up when the player re-signed for the Grecians in September 1922. 'Jazzo' Kirk had plenty of dash and often dribbled the ball half the length of the field. A real sharpshooter, he cracked home four goals in a League game against Portsmouth at Fratton Park in March 1923. His best season at St James' Park was 1924-5, when he topped the score-sheet and helped City to seventh place, until then their highest since joining the Football League. An entertainer both on and off the field, 'Jazzo' was a singer and pianist who also kept the players happy on away journeys with his slight-of-hand tricks. The team and fans were sorry when he went to Charlton Athletic in 1926. 'Jazzo' Kirk finished his playing career with Bath City and New Brighton.

League debut for City v Norwich City, 4 March 1922.

HAROLD 'JAZZO' KIRK

	LEAGUE		FA CUP		TOTAL	
	App	Gls	App	Gls	App	Gls
1921-22	14	9	0	0	14	9
1922-23	29	11	3	2	32	13
1923-24	37	8	6	0	43	8
1924-25	33	12	4	3	37	15
1925-26	27	5	1	0	28	5
	140	45	14	5	154	50

93

It was when this local lad was switched from outside-left to left-back at the beginning of 1965-6 that he began to attract attention. In January 1967 he requested a transfer, seeking a higher grade of football, and after watching him a number of times, Portsmouth manager George Smith clinched the 21-year-old defender's transfer for £8,000 in May 1967. City fans, therefore, did not see the best of this player but he made a noteworthy contribution at Fratton Park with 184 Second Division appearances, mostly at left-back. In 1971-2 he was moved into midfield but returned to left-back after his £28,000 transfer to Brighton in September 1972. Ley finished his League career with a couple of seasons at Gillingham, where he was again an accomplished defender, missing only a handful of games. Although born at Exminster, near Exeter, on 7 April 1946, he gained his early experience with Hitchin Town in the Athenian League.
League debut for City v Carlisle United, 11 September 1963.

	LEAGUE		FA CUP		FL CUP		TOTAL	
	App	Gls	App	Gls	App	Gls	App	Gls
1963-64	14	1	0	0	1	0	15	1
1964-65	15	1	2	1	1	0	18	2
1965-66	31	3	1	0	1	0	33	3
1966-67	33	2	2	0	3	0	38	2
	93	7	5	1	6	0	104	8

GEORGE LEY

In each of the two seasons immediately before joining City in 1911, Harry Lockett had gone through the trauma of playing in teams relegated from the First Division. In 1909-10 it had been with Bolton Wanderers and the following season it was with Nottingham Forest, so he was ready for a change of fortune when he arrived at St James' Park. Despite his bad luck, the Grecians were naturally glad to get hold of a player with recent First Division experience, for he had appeared in 16 First Division games for Bolton in their unfortunate season and 23 for Nottingham Forest, most of them at inside-right. Born in Market Drayton, Shropshire, Lockett played for Wilmslow (Cheshire) at 17 and turned professional with Crewe Alexandra, whom he had helped win the Birmingham League and the Cheshire Cup. It was in 1908 that he signed for Bolton Wanderers, where he suffered the misfortune already mentioned. At Exeter he began as an inside-forward but, in the two seasons he was with City, he also appeared at outside-left and left-half. A forager rather than a goalscorer, he had a baffling body swerve which usually threw his opponents off balance and he certainly helped baffle New Brompton (Gillingham) in his first appearance at the Park, when he scored twice in an 8-1 victory. However, he proved more valuable to City as a left-half in his second season, missing only two games in what was one of the Grecians' better pre-World War One campaigns. In 1913 he moved back up country to join Chesterfield.
League debut for City v Watford, 2 September 1911.

HARRY LOCKETT

	LEAGUE		FA CUP		TOTAL	
	App	Gls	App	Gls	App	Gls
1911-12	34	6	3	0	37	6
1912-13	36	0	1	0	37	0
	70	6	4	0	74	6

Wilf Lowton was another local lad from Ladysmith Road School, where their football team swept the board in so many of the inter-war years. Born in Exeter on 3 October 1899, Lowton joined City as an amateur from Heavitree United in 1924 before turning professional in September 1925. Powerfully built, he could kick a dead ball harder than the majority of players and eventually became an expert penalty-taker. Lowton did not establish his first-team place until early in season 1928-9, having to play second fiddle to Bob Pollard in his earliest months at St James' Park. But, once in the side, he quickly impressed as partner to Charlie Miller. Indeed, he was soon being watched by First Division club scouts and at the end of season 1928-9 he transferred to Wolverhampton Wanderers for a fee of £1,400. He went straight into their side and missed only one game when captaining their Second Division championship-winning team in 1931-2. Lowton made 198 League appearances for Wolves in six seasons before being re-signed by City in 1935. Always a most difficult man to beat, Lowton had by now reached the veteran stage and made only a limited number of League appearances in 1935-6 before retiring. He was City's assistant trainer for three months at the start of the following season. He died on 12 January 1963.
League debut for City v QPR, 23 September 1925.

	LEAGUE		FA CUP		TOTAL	
	App	Gls	App	Gls	App	Gls
1925-26	13	1	0	0	13	1
1926-27	19	3	0	0	19	3
1927-28	7	0	0	0	7	0
1928-29	36	5	4	0	40	5
1935-36	18	0	0	0	18	0
	93	9	4	0	97	9

WILF LOWTON

Charlie McClelland had football in his blood, for his Scottish father, Jimmy, had enjoyed a distinguished career between the wars with Raith Rovers, Southend United, Middlesbrough, Bolton Wanderers, Preston, Blackpool and Bradford, winning an FA Cup medal with Bolton. Born in Manchester on 8 January 1924, Charlie McClelland began playing wartime games for Bolton Wanderers in 1943 and signed professional for Blackburn Rovers in December 1946, after opening his peacetime career with Hyde United. Unlike his father, who was primarily a centre-forward, Charlie played in any of the forward positions and it was after three seasons with the Rovers that City manager George Roughton obtained his transfer, for what was then one of the club's highest fees, in close season 1949. There was a good deal of chopping and changing in the City forward line in his earliest seasons with the Grecians and McClelland's form must have suffered as he was constantly switched from one position to another. However, he was a fast-moving and aggressive forward who proved to be a grand opportunist, especially in his best season of 1953-4, when he was allowed to settle into a partnership with Angus Mackay on the left wing and became top scorer with 19 goals. At the end of the next season, when City had a big clear-out after just avoiding having to apply for re-election, McClelland went to Portland United and later appeared for Cheltenham Town.
League debut for the City v Crystal Palace (scored once), 20 August 1949.

CHARLIE McCLELLAND

	LEAGUE		FA CUP		TOTAL	
	App	Gls	App	Gls	App	Gls
1949-50	33	8	2	0	35	8
1950-51	36	8	6	3	42	11
1951-52	35	11	2	2	37	13
1952-53	13	5	1	0	14	5
1953-54	36	19	2	0	38	19
1954-55	30	9	1	0	31	9
	183	60	14	5	197	65

BRIAN McDERMOTT

Brian McDermott is a player whose footballing ability shows that he learnt the finer points of the game in the best company. Born in Slough on 8 April 1961, he signed apprentice forms for Arsenal at the age of 16 and, after six appearances as substitute, got into the side in November 1980. Indeed, this was his best season with the Gunners, for he totalled 16 First Division games plus seven as a substitute. Arsenal finished third in the League in that campaign, when McDermott was competing for his place with such stars as John Hollins and Alan Sunderland. McDermott had a spell on loan to Fulham but totalled 38 League appearances plus 23 as a substitute for Arsenal before his transfer to Oxford United in 1984. After helping United win promotion to the First Division, he had a spell on loan to Huddersfield Town and a season with Cardiff City prior to his transfer to St James' Park in March 1989 after a month on loan. Although he wore the number-six shirt in his first season with the City and then the number-nine shirt he is really used as an outside-right and played a major role in City's promotion-winning race of 1989-90. He is fast and very clever. His body swerve at speed is a delight to watch and usually beats opposing defenders.

League debut for City v Burnley, 18 February 1989.

	LEAGUE		FA CUP		FL CUP		TOTAL	
	App	Gls	App	Gls	App	Gls	App	Gls
1988-89	19	1	0	0	0	0	19	1
1989-90	38/3	3	4	1	4	1	46/3	5
	57/3	4	4	1	4	1	65/3	6

An Irishman from Belfast, who cost City a £300 transfer fee when Fred Mavin signed him as a centre-half in 1925, Billy McDevitt made a major contribution to Exeter City as a player, player-manager and manager. Details of the managerial side of his work can be seen elsewhere in this volume but he must be included here as one of the brainiest inside-forwards to wear the club's colours between the wars. He was switched to inside-forward soon after his arrival and it was his scheming that pulled the side up from the bottom of the table to eighth in 1928-9, which was his best playing season before he agreed to take on the additional managerial work, originally for the same wages, in April 1929. From Belfast Celtic he came into the Football League with Swansea Town in 1921-2 but returned to Belfast before the season had ended. He reappeared in the Football League with Liverpool in 1923-4, but they were so well served by Walter Wadsworth at centre-half at this time that McDevitt made only four League appearances in two seasons before his transfer to St James' Park, where he eventually took over the captaincy. It was his inspiring skill that enabled City to hold mighty Blackburn Rovers to a 2-2 draw at the Park in the FA Cup and his prompting made goalscoring easier for such players as Harold Blackmore and Fred Dent, as well as bringing out the best in outside-right George Purcell. Billy McDevitt was appointed player-manager at a time when he was sidelined with a thigh injury and he made only 16 appearances with this added responsibility, having acquired Harold Houghton as a worthy successor on the field.

League debut for City v Queen's Park Rangers, 23 September 1925.

BILLY McDEVITT

	LEAGUE		FA CUP		TOTAL	
	App	Gls	App	Gls	App	Gls
1925-26	24	2	1	0	25	2
1926-27	28	2	3	1	31	3
1927-28	36	3	6	1	42	4
1928-29	21	2	4	0	25	2
1929-30	16	0	0	0	16	0
	125	9	14	2	139	11

Manager Bill Thompson went back to Portsmouth for his first major signing in the close season of 1957 and brought full-back Les MacDonald to Exeter. Born in Newcastle on 2 April 1934, but brought up in Portsmouth, MacDonald played for Hampshire schoolboy and youth teams before turning professional with the local League club in May 1955. He had, however, been given only one League game by Pompey before his transfer to St James' Park, although he captained their Reserves for a spell. At Exeter he went straight into the League side at left-back but was clearly out of form and it was not until later in the season that he returned, after Arnold Mitchell was switched from left-back to wing-half. These were difficult times for the City defence, constantly under pressure as the side finished bottom of the Third Division, but MacDonald came through it well. He eventually settled down to form an outstanding partnership with Theo Foley and became rated as the club's best left-back since Charlie Miller. He was one of the stars of the 1963-4 promotion side but at the end of the next season, after losing his place to Roy Patrick, he was given a free transfer. However, manager Ellis Stuttard re-signed him for just one more season before he went to Weymouth in 1966. He later played for Waterlooville and has since become a school teacher.
League debut for City v Southend United, 24 August 1957.

LES MacDONALD

	LEAGUE		FA CUP		FL CUP		TOTAL	
	App	Gls	App	Gls	App	Gls	App	Gls
1957-58	31	0	0	0	0	0	31	0
1958-59	39	0	1	0	0	0	40	0
1959-60	40	0	3	0	0	0	43	0
1960-61	46	0	2	0	2	0	50	0
1961-62	43	0	2	0	1	0	46	0
1962-63	28	0	1	0	0	0	29	0
1963-64	42	0	2	0	2	0	46	0
1964-65	15	0	2	0	1	0	18	0
1965-66	10	0	0	0	0	0	10	0
	294	0	13	0	6	0	313	0

Andy McGuigan was born in Wigtown, Dumfries, on 24 February 1878 and was one of the most experienced First Division players signed by City when they first adopted professionalism in 1908. He had begun his professional career in 1898 with Hibernian, where his goalscoring attracted the attention of Liverpool, who obtained his transfer in 1900. In the two seasons he was at Anfield, he not only helped the Reds win the League Championship but also became the first Liverpool player to score five goals in a League game — against Stoke in a 7-0 victory on 4 January 1902. Despite this, he was unable to retain a first-team place and had two seasons with Middlesbrough (1902-04) before serving Burslem Port Vale, Bristol City and Barrow. Exeter City used him mostly at centre-forward and when a knee injury put him out of the side for a spell in his second season at St James' Park, the club tried four other players in this position but none proved to be as fine a leader as McGuigan. The knee trouble which dogged him throughout his second season with City prompted him to retire at the end of that campaign and he returned to Liverpool, where he was on the groundstaff for more than 20 years.
League debut for City v Millwall, 2 September 1908.

	LEAGUE		FA CUP		TOTAL	
	App	Gls	App	Gls	App	Gls
1908-09	28	16	9	9	37	25
1909-10	16	4	1	0	17	4
	44	20	10	9	54	29

ANDY McGUIGAN

A talented footballer in the best traditions of the Scottish style, Angus Mackay was one of City's most entertaining players throughout his eight seasons at St James' Park. Born in Glasgow on 24 April 1925, this diminutive inside-forward began with Hamilton Academical, then joined Ipswich Town in May 1946. After he refused terms to re-sign for that club, negotiations for his transfer, at a substantial fee, were completed when City played at Ipswich in September 1947 and he travelled back to Exeter with his new colleagues to make his debut three days later. Mackay was a clever individualist as well as an inspiring team man, whose subtle touches and dazzling ball play often had the opposition bemused. He played innumerable outstanding games for the Grecians but none better than the FA Cup tie at Grimsby in 1950-51, when he captained the side and scored two of the goals which earned City a 3-3 draw. He missed the winning replay with an ankle injury but at Blundell Park he had given a typical display of his speed and opportunism as well as his ability to get up to head a ball. It was a sad day for City supporters when this dazzling player went to Millwall in 1955. He still lives in Exeter.

League debut for City v Southend United, 20 September 1947.

	LEAGUE		FA CUP		TOTAL	
	App	Gls	App	Gls	App	Gls
1947-48	33	5	1	0	34	5
1948-49	40	8	2	0	42	8
1949-50	26	6	0	0	26	6
1950-51	31	8	4	4	35	12
1951-52	43	20	2	0	45	20
1952-53	23	10	1	0	24	10
1953-54	30	13	2	0	32	13
1954-55	31	8	1	1	32	9
	257	78	13	5	270	83

ANGUS MACKAY

It was a surprise when Exeter City offered this most accomplished defender only a three-month contract at the end of his second season, but the player had just

JIMMY McNICHOL

taken over a pub in Ashburton with his parents-in-law, and manager Colin Appleton was afraid that this could interfere with his commitment to the game. Torquay United had no such doubts and snapped him up in that summer of 1986. McNichol made 124 League appearances for Torquay in three seasons after which City manager Terry Cooper re-signed him. City supporters were glad to see him back at the Park, for his coolness under pressure made him one of the club's reliable defenders who played a major role in helping City to get on the promotion trail in 1989-90. A former Scottish Under-21 international, there is a lot of class about McNichol's play and he also possesses a powerful shot. Born in Glasgow on 9 June 1958, he was an apprentice at Ipswich Town before having a couple of seasons with Luton, who transferred him to Brentford for a fee of £30,000 in 1978. After 155 League appearances for the Bees, he first joined City on a free transfer in 1984, taking over as captain when the club was at a low ebb following their Cup defeat by Enfield.

League debut for City v Northampton Town, 25 August 1984.

	LEAGUE		FA CUP		FL CUP		TOTAL	
	App	Gls	App	Gls	App	Gls	App	Gls
1984-85	42	5	2	0	2	0	46	5
1985-86	45	5	3	0	4	0	52	5
1989-90	33	8	6	0	4	2	43	10
	120	18	11	0	10	2	141	20

98

One of Exeter's numerous local discoveries of recent years, thanks to the existence of a youth policy, this tall, well-built player, who signed apprentice for the club at the age of 16, developed as a centre-half but always retained attacking tendencies. Indeed, he wore at least seven different numbered shirts during his stay at St James' Park, even number-nine. His versatility, therefore, is obvious, but his strength in defence both on the ground and in the air is invaluable. He played a fine attacking game against Plymouth Argyle at the Park when he was among the scorers in a 2-0 League Cup victory in September 1985 and when Argyle came for his transfer a little over two years later, he had been wearing the number-four shirt for some time. But after paying a £95,000 transfer fee for this player and letting City have Darren Rowbotham as part of the deal, Argyle put him back into the number-five shirt. In the more recent Argyle decline, he had to withstand a great deal of pressure. He was born at Budleigh Salterton on 3 May 1965.
League debut for City v Burnley, 7 October 1981.

NICKY MARKER

	LEAGUE		FA CUP		FL CUP		TOTAL	
	App	Gls	App	Gls	App	Gls	App	Gls
1981-82	11/3	1	0	0	1	0	12/3	1
1982-83	18	1	1	0	0	0	19	1
1983-84	28/3	0	0	0	1	0	29/3	0
1984-85	45	0	2	0	2	0	49	0
1985-86	40	0	3	0	4	1	47	1
1986-87	43	1	2	0	1	0	46	1
1987-88	11	0	0	0	2	0	13	0
	196/6	3	8	0	11	1	215/6	4

Born in Bristol on 28 April 1901, Alf Matthews was a speedy little outside-right, who stood only 5ft 5½ins in his stocking feet. He spent 11 seasons in Devon, with City and Argyle. Matthews made his League debut with Bristol City in October 1912, but at the end of that season they let him go to Exeter, where he became a great favourite. Fast, with good ball control, he was always a delight to watch and was one of the more regular first-team men during a little under four seasons that he remained at St James' Park before his transfer to Argyle in March 1926. City got £750 for his transfer and Argyle used his services to the full. While at Exeter he became the penalty specialist and nine of his 17 League and Cup goals for the Grecians were scored from the spot. He was one of the stars of the City side which finished seventh in 1924-5, when he appeared in every game including all six FA Cup ties, one of which was abandoned. After making 142 League appearances for Argyle, he went to Doncaster Rovers in 1933.
League debut for City v Brighton & Hove Albion, 6 September 1922.

	LEAGUE		FA CUP		TOTAL	
	App	Gls	App	Gls	App	Gls
1922-23	39	2	3	1	42	3
1923-24	29	5	6	2	35	7
1924-25	42	4	5	1	47	5
1925-26	28	2	1	0	29	2
	138	13	15	4	153	17

ALF MATTHEWS

99

Although times have changed and comparisons are odious, the reputation of Scotsman Charlie Miller is such that he is still regarded as the finest left-back in the club's history. He is placed at the top of the pile because his strong personality combined with his classy football. Miller learnt his football at Bellshill, Lanarkshire, where he went to the same school as the inimitable international centre-forward Hughie Gallacher. Before joining Plymouth Argyle in 1922, Miller played for Bellshill Athletic and then helped St Roch to win the Scottish Junior Cup. Argyle's well-established Welsh international left-back, Moses

CHARLIE MILLER

Russell, allowed Miller very few League chances in the four seasons he was at Home Park and it was not until his second season with City that he began to make his presence felt. Cartilage trouble led to an operation and kept him out for most of 1929-30, but he came back in time for the Cup run of 1930-31, the season in which he succeeded Les Dennington as captain. He took on this responsibility like a duck to water and was a great inspiration to the team, especially in that exciting promotion bid of 1932-3 when, but for another knee injury, he would certainly have been an ever-present. This classy full-back was placed on the open-to-transfer list at the end of 1932-3, but this caused such an uproar among the supporters that the directors changed their minds and by dint of clever positional play, which conserved energy, he continued to play until the end of season 1935-6, when he retired and later became a licensee. He was appointed assistant trainer in 1947 but resigned after only half a season. His son, Dick, was secretary of Exeter City from 1965 until his untimely death in a road accident in 1968.
League debut for City v Bristol City, 5 March 1927.

	LEAGUE		FA CUP		TOTAL	
	App	Gls	App	Gls	App	Gls
1926-27	10	0	0	0	10	0
1927-28	25	0	4	0	29	0
1928-29	40	0	4	0	44	0
1929-30	6	0	0	0	6	0
1930-31	37	0	8	0	45	0
1931-32	40	0	1	0	41	0
1932-33	35	0	2	0	37	0
1933-34	28	0	0	0	28	0
1934-35	30	0	3	0	33	0
1935-36	23	0	1	0	24	0
	274	0	23	0	297	0

Arnold Mitchell began his career with a number of games in Sheffield Wednesday's 'A' team but was allowed to join Derby County after they had spotted him as an inside-right in the Sheffield & Hallamshire youth team. Three seasons with Derby and one each with Nottingham Forest and Notts County followed before Mitchell joined City in July 1952 to become one of the most accomplished footballers ever to wear the club's colours, being most loyal and always ready to play anywhere in the side. In making a club record 495 League appearances Arnold Mitchell played in every position including 11 minutes in goal when Geoff Morton was injured in a goalless draw at Southend in September 1954. He was signed as an outside-right but eventually settled into his favourite position at right-

half, where his ability to read a game was used to greatest advantage. Mitchell played through thick and thin with the Grecians and recovered from a serious knee injury in his tenth season to captain the 1963-4 promotion-winning side. After ending his City career in 1966, he was persuaded to play a few games for Taunton Town before a broken fibia forced him to call it a day. Born at Rawmarsh on 1 December 1929, he still resides in Exeter.
League debut for City v Northampton Town, 27 August 1952.

ARNOLD MITCHELL

	LEAGUE		FA CUP		FL CUP		TOTAL	
	App	Gls	App	Gls	App	Gls	App	Gls
1952-53	38	10	0	0	0	0	38	10
1953-54	27	3	0	0	0	0	27	3
1954-55	45	1	1	0	0	0	46	1
1955-56	45	4	4	0	0	0	49	4
1956-57	33	3	1	0	0	0	34	3
1957-58	43	4	1	0	0	0	44	4
1958-59	46	7	1	1	0	0	47	8
1959-60	42	0	3	0	0	0	45	0
1960-61	20	0	0	0	0	0	20	0
1961-62	16	0	0	0	0	0	16	0
1962-63	40	5	1	0	1	0	42	5
1963-64	38	3	2	0	2	0	42	3
1964-65	43	3	2	1	0	0	45	4
1965-66	19	1	1	0	1	0	21	1
	495	44	17	2	4	0	516	46

Born at Hamilton on 13 May 1924, this little inside-forward had a season with Hibs before joining the Army in 1943. On his return from the war he played for Morton and was in their Scottish Cup Final team beaten by Rangers in a replay in 1948. He moved into the Football League with Northampton Town and missed only one game when they finished runners-up in the Third Division South in 1949-50. Considering that Barnsley paid £8,000 for his transfer in March 1951, City were fortunate to get him cheaply in the summer of 1952. He proved to be not only another typically skilful Scottish ball player but also one who shone in midfield where as a schemer his quick thinking was sometimes too fast for his teammates. One of his most dazzling displays was on a heavy pitch when his defence-splitting passes bemused a Bournemouth defence at the Park and City won 5-1 in November 1952. However, City's problem was that they had a similar player in Angus Mackay and he was often preferred in the inside-left position after Norman Dodgin took over as player-manager. After four seasons at Exeter, Murphy was given a free transfer and subsequently played for Bridgwater and Trowbridge.

League debut for City v Queen's Park Rangers, 23 August 1952.

	LEAGUE		FA CUP		TOTAL	
	App	Gls	App	Gls	App	Gls
1952-53	38	7	1	1	39	8
1953-54	12	1	0	0	12	1
1954-55	25	2	1	1	26	3
1955-56	19	3	4	1	23	4
	94	13	6	3	100	16

EDDIE MURPHY

It is fortunate for Exeter City that Steve Neville enjoys playing for the club, for apart from his ability as a front runner he has made the Grecians a lot of money in twice agreeing to return to the Park after being transferred. Born at Walthamstow on 18 September 1957, he was apprenticed to Southampton but made only five Second Division appearances before being signed by Bobby Saxton in September 1978 and going straight into the City team at outside-right. On the small side but brave as a lion, it was not long before Sheffield United, on the slide into the Fourth Division, paid £80,000 for his transfer and switched him inside in the hope that he would spark some life into their attack. Neville played a part in their regaining Third Division status the following season but dropped out of the side and in the next campaign was loaned back to the Grecians, who soon clinched his transfer for a £10,000 fee. His talents were wasted on the wing with a Fourth Division side after City were relegated and in November 1984 he was signed by Terry Cooper for Third Division Bristol City, for £12,000 plus Trevor Morgan in part exchange. A couple of months after Terry Cooper became Exeter's manager he brought Neville back to St James' Park, where he has continued as arguably the club's most talented footballer, being an expert at shielding the ball from bigger defenders and then beating them for sheer speed on the turn. He is also the club's assistant manager and was one of the stars of their promotion team.

League debut for City v Swansea City, 14 October 1978.

STEVE NEVILLE

	LEAGUE		FA CUP		FL CUP		TOTAL	
	App	Gls	App	Gls	App	Gls	App	Gls
1978-79	36	9	2	0	1	0	39	9
1979-80	40/3	8	1	1	6	3	47/3	12
1980-81	14	5	0	0	1	0	15	5
1982-83	33	17	1	0	0	0	34	17
1983-84	40/3	9	2	1	2	0	44/3	10
1984-85	16	1	2	1	2	0	20	2
1988-89	38	14	1	0	2	0	41	14
1989-90	42	14	6	1	7	2	55	17
	259/6	77	15	4	21	5	295/6	86

Exeter City did not see the best of this player, which was when he struck up such a great partnership with Ronnie Allen in the West Bromwich Albion team around 1952-4, when he collected an FA Cup winners' medal in 1954 as well as two England caps. Nicholls was born at Wolverhampton on 3 April 1931 and after joining West Brom from Heath Town United in August 1950, following his National Service, he made 145 League and Cup appearances, scoring 64 goals prior to transferring to Cardiff City in June 1957. Nicholls did not fit in at Ninian Park and lost his place after the arrival of Joe Bonson from Wolves. Cardiff allowed Nicholls to go to Exeter City for a fee of only £4,500. At St James' Park he was something of an enigma, brilliant at times but often erratic. A 'poacher', easily his best game for the City was when he got a hat-trick against Plymouth Argyle in a 4-2 win in February 1958, which was shortly before he dropped out of the side with knee trouble which led to an operation. He recovered to play a leading part in pushing the City up to fifth position in the Fourth Division in 1958-9. In that summer he was transferred to Worcester City for a 'satisfactory' fee, rejoining manager Bill Thompson, who had signed him for the Grecians. Johnny Nicholls later played for Wellington, Oswestry and Sankey's.
League debut for City v Reading, 23 November 1957.

	LEAGUE		FA CUP		TOTAL	
	App	Gls	App	Gls	App	Gls
1957-58	17	8	0	0	17	8
1958-59	39	15	1	0	40	15
	56	23	1	0	57	23

JOHNNY NICHOLLS

This experienced centre-half was the first signing made by Frank Broome when he took over as manager at Exeter at a time of crisis in January 1958, when the City were bottom of the table and had conceded 13 goals in their last three matches. Ken Oliver was unable to save City from finishing bottom that season but was outstanding in the following campaign when the Grecians narrowly missed promotion to the Third Division. Born at Loughborough on 10 August 1924, this tall defender was signed by Sunderland from Leicestershire club, Brush Sports, in 1946 but it was with Derby County that he made his reputation. Transferred to Derby in 1949, he played in the same First Division side as Frank Broome in his initial season at the Baseball Ground and made a total of 184 League appearances in eight and a half seasons with them before moving to Exeter. A commanding figure in the middle of the defence, Ken Oliver accomplished what he was signed for at Exeter before a foot injury against Darlington towards the end of 1959-60 finished his career. He returned to Derby and has recently retired as a director of a sports outfitters in that city.
League debut for City v Port Vale, 1 February 1958.

	LEAGUE		FA CUP		TOTAL	
	App	Gls	App	Gls	App	Gls
1957-58	16	0	0	0	16	0
1958-59	46	0	1	0	47	0
1959-60	30	0	3	0	33	0
	92	0	4	0	96	0

KEN OLIVER

Born at Nottingham on 15 January 1945, David Pleat was an England Schoolboy and Youth international outside-right who began his League career with Nottingham Forest. Transferred to Luton Town for £8,000 in August 1964, he was an outstanding prospect until he broke a leg in training at the start of his second season with the Hatters and subsequently suffered a back injury which was to cause him problems for the remainder of his playing career. It was because of these misfortunes that his number of appearances with Luton Town were restricted to 70 in three seasons. He then had a season with Shrewsbury Town before City secured his services in 1968, when they were struggling in the lower half of the table. Despite his back problem, Pleat still showed speed and clever ball control when he was in his best form, but suffered from further injuries and loss of form the following season, at the end of which he joined Peterborough United. After a spell as player-manager of Nuneaton Borough, he returned to Luton as a member of their coaching staff and was appointed manager in 1978, proving to be a great success in steering them back into the First Division in four years. In June 1986 he became one of the game's highest paid managers with Tottenham Hotspur but left under a cloud in October 1987, following newspaper disclosures about his private life. However, after the good work he had done as a manager he was unemployed for only two months before being appointed manager of Leicester City.
League debut for City v Peterborough United, 10 August 1968.

DAVID PLEAT

	LEAGUE		FA CUP		FL CUP		TOTAL	
	App	Gls	App	Gls	App	Gls	App	Gls
1968-69	43	8	3/1	0	5	0	51/1	8
1969-70	23/2	5	3	0	0	0	26/2	5
	66/2	13	6/1	0	5	0	77/3	13

Born in Plattbridge, near Wigan, on 25 August 1899, Bob Pollard was a stockily-built right-back and a consistent first-team performer for almost the entire run of nine seasons he was with the City after joining from Plank Lane (Lancashire Combination) in the summer of 1920. He began his playing career as a teenager during World War One, with Plattbridge United in the Wigan & Distict League, before joining Plank Lane in 1918. City were going through one of their bad spells in Pollard's first two or three seasons and he had to challenge Joe Coleburne for the right-back position in a couple of those campaigns. However, once he was established in 1924, with Stan Charlton as his partner, there was no finer pair of backs in the Third Division. Although on the short side, it was a delight to see the way Pollard could get up to head a ball and when City enjoyed one of their best seasons in 1924-5, he missed only one game. In September 1928, after Stan Charlton had departed, Pollard lost his place to Wilf Lowton. He was tried at right-half for a spell, but at the end of that campaign this aggressive defender joined QPR where he enjoyed another three seasons before having a term with Cardiff City and then going to France to play for Saint-Etienne.
League debut for City v Luton Town, 2 April 1921.

BOB POLLARD

	LEAGUE		FA CUP		TOTAL	
	App	Gls	App	Gls	App	Gls
1920-21	7	0	0	0	7	0
1921-22	24	0	2	0	26	0
1922-23	39	0	3	0	42	0
1923-24	19	0	0	0	19	0
1924-25	41	0	5	0	46	0
1925-26	40	0	1	0	41	0
1926-27	23	0	3	0	26	0
1927-28	36	0	6	0	42	0
1928-29	17	0	3	0	20	0
	246	0	23	0	269	0

Another of the stars of the great Cup run of 1930-31, George Purcell was a Yorkshire miner and keen cricketer from Sheffield, who began his League career with Stockport County and, after a couple of seasons, moved

GEORGE PURCELL

south to join Swindon Town in 1925. At that time, Purcell was an inside-right but, when he joined the City in 1926, he moved to outside-right as partner to Billy McDevitt, a clever tactician who must have helped improve Purcell's game. George Purcell enjoyed a fine run on the wing, missing no more than five games over the same number of seasons. But in 1930-31, when he was an ever-present in both League and Cup, he switched to inside-right, where his brainy play proved even more effective with Billy Armfield as his outside partner. It is inevitable that in writing about City's best players, a lot of superlatives are used but, when one thinks of a trio of forwards like Purcell, Varco and Houghton in the centre of the attack, one can readily appreciate just how entertaining they could be. Indeed, sometimes they were too clever and did not shoot often enough. One of Purcell's finest goals was that scored in the 3-1 Cup victory over Leeds United at St James' Park in February 1931. At the end of the following season he joined Gillingham for a couple of seasons before retiring.
League debut for City v Merthyr Town, 28 August 1926.

	LEAGUE		FA CUP		TOTAL	
	App	Gls	App	Gls	App	Gls
1926-27	41	7	3	1	44	8
1927-28	40	13	6	5	46	18
1928-29	42	8	4	3	46	11
1929-30	40	12	1	0	41	12
1930-31	42	7	8	3	50	10
1931-32	22	4	0	0	22	4
	227	51	22	12	249	63

One of City's finest local discoveries, Dick Pym was a fisherman from Topsham, where he was born on 2 February 1893. He became a centre-forward with the local club before going into goal and developing into one of England's finest 'keepers of the 1920s. Given the nickname 'Pincher', or sometimes 'Scissors', Pym made his debut for City Reserves in December 1911 and, after taking over from the experienced Walter Whittaker for his first-team debut in March 1912, enjoyed a run of 186 consecutive League appearances before injuring his collar-bone two minutes from the end of an FA Cup defeat at Watford in January 1921. City presented him with a gold watch for his long uninterrupted run of games. It was at the end of season 1920-21 that Pym was transferred to Bolton Wanderers. City refused Bolton's original offer but, after a few more days consideration, the Bolton directors increased their bid to nearer £5,000 and the deal was clinched. Dick Pym played in three FA Cup Final victories with Bolton without conceding a single goal. He was also capped three times by England during his stay of ten seasons at Burnden Park, during which he made 301 League appearances — what consistency. A popular man was Dick Pym, both on and off the field, and

someone who made the art of goalkeeping look easy. He played a few games for Yeovil before retiring in 1932, although after he returned home to Topsham it was reported in 1933 that he was still playing for his local team — at centre-forward. He died at the grand old age of 95 in September 1988.
League debut for City v Stoke, 23 March 1912.

	LEAGUE		FA CUP		TOTAL	
	App	Gls	App	Gls	App	Gls
1911-12	8	0	0	0	8	0
1912-13	38	0	1	0	39	0
1913-14	38	0	2	0	40	0
1914-15	38	0	1	0	39	0
1919-20	42	0	1	0	43	0
1920-21	39	0	1	0	40	0
	203	0	6	0	209	0

DICK PYM

This energetic winger, born at Pontypridd on 28 August 1937, joined City from his local youth club team and signed as a part-time professional in September 1954. It is not generally appreciated that Rees was a part-timer for most of his career and this makes his contribution all the more remarkable. He was studying to be an accountant when he came to Exeter and was allowed to develop gradually in the Reserves, playing in nearly every forward position. He was still a part-timer when he became a first-team regular in season 1958-9, bagging 21 League goals, and also when he played a major role in City's promotion success of 1963-4, during which he missed only one game. This rampaging red-head was a real 90-minute player and often City's main danger man, scoring a lot of goals by cutting in front of the opposing full-back to meet crosses from the opposite wing. Although generally remembered as a winger, he played some of his best games at inside-right where he chased everything and spearheaded many attacks.
League debut for City v Norwich City, 15 September 1954.

	LEAGUE		FA CUP		FL CUP		TOTAL	
	App	Gls	App	Gls	App	Gls	App	Gls
1954-55	5	1	0	0	0	0	5	1
1955-56	20	4	4	3	0	0	24	7
1956-57	23	2	1	0	0	0	24	2
1957-58	25	1	0	0	0	0	25	1
1958-59	43	22	1	0	0	0	44	22
1959-60	42	17	3	3	0	0	45	20
1960-61	42	14	1	0	2	1	45	15
1961-62	25	6	2	0	1	0	28	6
1962-63	29	4	1	0	1	0	31	4
1963-64	45	6	2	0	2	0	49	6
1964-65	33	7	1	0	2	0	36	7
1965-66	13	1	1	0	0	0	14	1
	345	85	17	6	8	1	370	92

GRAHAM REES

Born at Stoke-under-Ham, near Yeovil, on 3 June 1922, this goalscoring winger served in the Fleet Air Arm during the war and in 1945 he walked into St James' Park to ask for a trial. His potential was immediately recognized and before the season was out he was already in the first team. The man who helped establish Regan's career was that talented inside-forward, Ray Wright, for Regan delighted in running on to Wright's fine through passes as he cut in to test the goalkeeper with his powerful shooting. Speed, powerful shooting and opportunism were Regan's main attributes and, as a small man, it was especially satisfying for the supporters to see him beat the bigger defenders. He played many exciting games for the City and none better than in the FA Cup tie against Chelsea, when he got City's equalizer four minutes from time at St James' Park. In December 1952 he was signed by Bristol City, less than a week after playing in a 1-1 draw against that club at the Park, and he went straight into the Bristol club's League side the following day. Regan spent just under four seasons at Ashton Gate.
League debut for City v Torquay United, 31 August 1946.

DUGGIE REGAN

	LEAGUE		FA CUP		TOTAL	
	App	Gls	App	Gls	App	Gls
1946-47	37	8	1	1	38	10
1947-48	36	11	2	0	38	11
1948-49	38	15	3	0	41	15
1949-50	27	11	4	4	31	15
1950-51	26	7	6	1	32	8
1951-52	25	5	1	0	26	5
1952-53	17	6	1	0	18	6
	206	63	18	7	224	70

A Bolton lad who was born in 1885, Jimmy Rigby began his playing career with St Mark's Sunday School before joining Atherton in the Lancashire Combination. He first signed professional at 12s 6d (63p) a week, but continued his employment as a cotton spinner until joining Accrington Stanley. It was from that club he signed for Exeter City in 1911 and was introduced to the side as a right-half, where he played fairly consistently in the peacetime campaigns until a muscle strain forced him to take a rest during 1920-21 when he was captain. His experience, coolness and judgement were sorely missed during this season when City were in a bad way, but he did good work in charge of the Western League side for this spell. He returned to the Third Division for another two difficult seasons until an injury to his right knee, sustained in a game at Ashton Gate in February 1923, ended his career. Jimmy Rigby was one of those unobtrusive type of players who just got on with the game, making a consistent contribution, but letting others capture the headlines. He had a tobacconists and newsagents business in Exeter's main thoroughfare for many years and was also a City director.
League debut for City v Bristol Rovers, 21 October 1911.

	LEAGUE		FA CUP		TOTAL	
	App	Gls	App	Gls	App	Gls
1911-12	19	0	1	0	20	0
1912-13	38	1	1	0	39	1
1913-14	37	0	2	0	39	0
1914-15	35	1	1	0	36	1
1919-20	28	0	1	0	29	0
1920-21	7	0	1	0	8	0
1921-22	34	0	2	0	36	0
1922-23	19	0	3	0	22	0
	217	2	12	0	229	2

JIMMY RIGBY

A Scot, who was born at Paisley on 27 September 1947, Lammie Robertson was undoubtedly one of the hardest men to shake off a ball that the Grecians have had in recent years. He joined the City together with John Templeman from Brighton in May 1974, in the deal that took Fred Binney in the opposite direction. Like so many Scots before him at Exeter, he proved to be a brilliant footballer, wearing the number-nine shirt but playing deep. It was this player's craftsmanship that helped turn the City into a promotion-winning side in 1976-7, when he enjoyed a run of 43 consecutive appearances. A cracking shot, he also took over as City's penalty expert and against Southport in the promotion-winning campaign, he scored a hat-trick including two from the spot. At one time he was strongly tipped to take over as City's manager but in September 1977 he was transferred to Leicester City, who were about to drop into the Second Division. Robertson had half a season with Peterborough United before finishing his League career with Bradford City. In July 1981 he was appointed manager of Northwich Victoria.
League debut for City v Barnsley, 17 August 1974.

LAMMIE ROBERTSON

	LEAGUE		FA CUP		FL CUP		TOTAL	
	App	Gls	App	Gls	App	Gls	App	Gls
1974-75	42	10	0	0	2	0	44	10
1975-76	44	4	1	0	3	0	48	4
1976-77	43	9	2	0	0	0	45	9
1977-78	3/1	2	0	0	1/1	3	4/2	5
	132/1	25	3	0	6/1	3	141/2	28

106

Jack Robinson, a former England international goal-keeper, had been out of first-class football for some time and was playing for Green Waves (Plymouth) when signed by City in November 1908. Therefore, despite his past reputation, the signing of this 38-year-old was something of a surprise but he showed his old brilliance in several games after making his debut against one of his former clubs, Plymouth Argyle, in the first-ever League derby between the Devon rivals. Born in Derby on 26 March 1866, Robinson had made his reputation with his local club, for whom he played 163 League games from 1891-97 and won his first England caps before moving on to New Brighton Tower, Southampton, Plymouth Argyle and Millwall. As a matter of fact, he had appeared once for Exeter City before they signed him in 1908 — in 1905-06 in the Plymouth & District League. This spectacular goalkeeper played for Derby Midland and Lincoln City before joining Derby County and, whilst with Southampton, he appeared in two FA Cup Finals and won four Southern League championship medals. Jack Robinson usually hung his watch on the goal net and was so daring that he became deaf through being kicked in the head while flinging himself at the feet of attackers. After he left City he had a season with Stoke before going to America. Towards the end of his life he suffered from fits and died after a long illness on 28 October 1931.

League debut for City v Plymouth Argyle, 11 November 1908.

JACK ROBINSON

	LEAGUE		FA CUP		TOTAL	
	App	Gls	App	Gls	App	Gls
1908-09	29	0	4	0	33	0
	29	0	4	0	33	0

Born at Bristol on 22 April 1953, this skilful forward was signed by the Grecians from Bath City in February 1979 in the hope that his ability would improve a side already on the fringes of the promotion race. He proved to be a strong and determined forward, always keen to take on opponents and also indulged in tricky running through the midfield. Above all, Rogers was industrious and he helped Tony Kellow get a lot of his goals. Another of Rogers' great qualities was his consistency and in each of four of his six seasons at the Park he made at least 40 appearances. Unfortunately for Rogers, he was with the City for that early 1980s spell when they were generally fighting an uphill battle. The exception to this was the 1980-81 FA Cup run, in which he played an outstanding role, especially in the 4-0 beating of Newcastle United, who were unable to find an answer to his speed on the ball.

League debut for City v Rotherham United, 31 March 1979.

	LEAGUE		FA CUP		FL CUP		TOTAL	
	App	Gls	App	Gls	App	Gls	App	Gls
1978-79	11/1	3	0	0	0	0	11/1	3
1979-80	39/4	5	0	0	2	0	41/4	5
1980-81	34/6	6	8	2	1	0	43/6	8
1981-82	42	10	1	0	3	0	46	10
1982-83	43	10	1	0	2	0	46	10
1983-84	25	5	2	0	1	1	28	6
	194/11	39	12	2	9	1	215/11	42

PETER ROGERS

Darren Rowbotham ranks amongst the finest of City forwards and always seems able to snap up goalscoring chances. In a side where some colleagues are often guilty of hesitation near goal, Rowbotham has stood out like a beacon and, of course, his scoring figures prove his ability. Some of his finest goals have been from half-chances, for he likes to shoot at every opportunity and possesses that essential ingredient for a good marksman — timing. As a sharpshooter he has also adopted the role of penalty-taker. Born at Cardiff on 22 October 1966, he was originally with Plymouth Argyle under the YTS scheme in 1983 before signing professional in January 1985. His brother, Jason, also joined him at Home Park. However, it was Darren who progressed the faster and although his first-team appearances were restricted at Plymouth, he created a club record by coming on as substitute in 23 games. He also started 22 League games and in October 1987, City were lucky to get him as part of a deal which took Nicky Marker to Home Park. After a month's trial he was signed by City and has never looked back. Although he is still inclined to be a little static off the ball, it was this player's marksmanship that helped shoot City to the top of the Fourth Division in 1989-90 before a serious knee injury put him out of the game for a long spell.
League debut for City v Hereford United, 31 October 1987.

	LEAGUE		FA CUP		FL CUP		TOTAL	
	App	Gls	App	Gls	App	Gls	App	Gls
1987-88	20/3	2	1	0	0	0	21/3	2
1988-89	45	20	1	1	2	0	48	21
1989-90	31/1	20	6	4	7	6	44/1	30
	96/4	42	8	5	9	6	113/4	53

DARREN ROWBOTHAM

JACK SCOTT

Although on the small side, outside-right Jack Scott was always dangerous and played a major role in City's promotion bid in 1932-3. Born in Sunderland, he began with Seaham Harbour before turning professional with the Roker Park club. Quickly moving on to Kettering, Scott then had a couple of seasons with Nottingham Forest and one with Northampton Town. Billy McDevitt signed him for the City in 1932 and he remained at the Park for four seasons until finishing his League career with Hartlepools. Under 5ft 6ins tall, Scott had a powerful and accurate shot and might have scored a lot more goals as an inside-forward. Despite his lack of stature, he covered a lot of ground and would drop back to help an overworked defence. Coolness under pressure was another of his assets. Two of this player's best performances for the City were in the Cup ties against Charlton Athletic in 1934-5, when City drew 2-2 at The Valley, where Scott had what looked like a winning goal controversially ruled offside. He was amongst the scorers when the Grecians thrashed the Londoners 5-1 in the replay.
League debut for City v Bristol City, 27 August 1932.

	LEAGUE		FA CUP		TOTAL	
	App	Gls	App	Gls	App	Gls
1932-33	37	7	2	0	39	7
1933-34	28	3	0	0	28	3
1934-35	41	7	3	1	44	8
1935-36	27	3	1	0	28	3
	133	20	6	1	139	21

MAURICE SETTERS

	LEAGUE		FA CUP		TOTAL	
	App	Gls	App	Gls	App	Gls
1953-54	1	0	0	0	1	0
1954-55	9	0	1	0	10	0
	10	0	1	0	11	0

One of City's most successful discoveries, Maurice Setters was born at Honiton on 16 December 1936 and turned professional with the Grecians in January 1954. Originally a winger, his potential was soon recognized by player-manager Norman Dodgin, who took a special interest in this stocky, terrier-like player, giving him the benefit of his good advise which the player has since freely acknowledged. Dodgin turned young Setters into a right-half and it was in that position he found fame after being transferred to West Bromwich Albion for at least £3,000 in January 1955. This fearless tackler with the crew-cut hair and bandy legs soon became a well-known figure in the First Division and in January 1960 he was transferred to Manchester United for £30,000, winning an FA Cup medal with them in 1963. Stoke City paid another £30,000 for him in 1964 and he subsequently finished his playing career with Coventry City and Charlton Athletic, bringing his total of League appearances to 434. He has since served Doncaster Rovers as manager, Sheffield Wednesday (coach), Rotherham United (assistant manager), Newcastle United (chief scout) and is currently assistant manager of the Republic of Ireland team under Jackie Charlton. He was an England Schoolboy, Youth and Under-23 international and played for the FA XI twice and for Young England on one other occasion.
League debut for City v Southend United, 6 March 1954.

There was nothing flashy about goalkeeper Barney Singleton but he was a most reliable last line of defence. Born at Conisbrough on 14 April 1924, Singleton was a teenager with Lincoln City just before the war and then became a Wolves player, making his wartime debut for them in 1941-2. The Grecians signed him from Wolves in January 1946 and for four seasons he shared the first-team post with another former Wolves goalkeeper, Bert Hoyle. Eventually, Hoyle was dropped after a bad run in December 1949 and, apart from injuries, Singleton was regular first choice until being succeeded by Irish international, Hugh Kelly. Noted for his unerring judgement, he also goes into the records as one of only two City goalkeepers to score a League goal from the outfield. His was against Aldershot in December 1950 when, after pulling a back muscle in the 25th minute, he went on the right wing with McClelland taking his place between the posts. Although almost unable to walk, he managed to tap in a goal for City in a 4-2 defeat. Given a free transfer in 1954, Singleton remained in Exeter and did some scouting for the club and was coach to Ottery St Mary. He died in Exeter in October 1981.
League debut for City v Northampton Town, 18 September 1946.

	LEAGUE		FA CUP		TOTAL	
	App	Gls	App	Gls	App	Gls
1946-47	23	0	1	0	24	0
1947-48	33	0	2	0	35	0
1948-49	2	0	0	0	2	0
1949-50	28	0	2	0	30	0
1950-51	42	1	6	0	48	1
1951-52	29	0	1	0	30	0
1952-53	9	0	0	0	9	0
1953-54	11	0	0	0	11	0
	177	1	12	0	189	1

BARNEY SINGLETON

109

This diminutive centre-forward was always worth his place if only for his nuisance value, for he was such a relentless pursuer of goalscoring chances that he could be relied upon to take the pressure off his colleagues in the attack. Nimble and big-hearted, he had been a contemporary of Cyril Johnstone with Hamilton Academical and joined City from that club a year after the full-back. Around this period of the club's history there was jocular talk about calling the City 'Exeter Celtic' because Archie Smith was one of nine Scots on the books. Born at Larkhall on 23 October 1924, he played a lot of games at outside-right and even made his debut in that position for the City. But he preferred centre-forward, despite his lack of height, and it is in this position that he is best remembered by City supporters. He could shoot equally well with either foot and mention of this player will bring back memories of that nerve-tingling Cup tie against Chelsea when City held them to a 1-1 draw at St James' Park and Archie Smith played one of his best games in the City's colours, being a constant menace to the visiting defenders. He beat two men to net what looked like a good goal in that tie but was controversially ruled 'offside' after several seconds delay. A foot injury troubled Archie Smith later in his days with the City and when he was transfer-listed at the end of season 1951-2, he went to Carlisle United where he finished his League career with two more seasons. Archie Smith is a nephew of former Scottish international centre-forward, Dave McCulloch.

League debut for City v Norwich City, 28 August 1948.

ARCHIE SMITH

	LEAGUE		FA CUP		TOTAL	
	App	Gls	App	Gls	App	Gls
1948-49	20	7	3	4	23	11
1949-50	31	9	3	1	34	10
1950-51	41	21	5	4	46	25
1951-52	23	6	1	0	24	6
	115	43	12	9	127	52

Born in Belfast on 4 May 1941, Cecil Smyth began his career as a winger with Distillery, being converted into a full-back by new manager George Eastham in 1959. In August 1952 he came to Exeter for a two-week trial and stayed seven seasons, although making three transfer requests before going to Torquay United in August 1969 for a £2,500 fee. Small and slim, his talent was soon appreciated at Exeter, for he went into the first team and stayed there after only five Western League games. A determined two-footed defender who had been a YMCA boxing champion for two years, he was noted for his quick recovery. A clean tackler, this small and slim full-back was one of the stars of City's 1963-4 promotion-winning side, when he missed only two matches. His longest spell out of the first team at Exeter was in 1966-7, when he suffered from ligament trouble. He still lives in Exeter.

League debut for City v Brentford, 8 September 1962.

CECIL SMYTH

	LEAGUE		FA CUP		FL CUP		TOTAL	
	App	Gls	App	Gls	App	Gls	App	Gls
1962-63	39	0	1	0	1	0	41	0
1963-64	44	1	2	0	2	0	48	1
1964-65	40	0	2	0	1	0	43	0
1965-66	44	0	1	0	0	0	45	0
1966-67	25/2	0	2	0	3	1	30/2	1
1967-68	40	0	4	0	2	0	46	0
1968-69	38/1	0	4	0	5	0	47/1	0
	270/3	1	16	0	14	1	300/3	2

Exeter City have been building up a tradition for good local centre-halves and this player is carrying on in the mould of Fred Davey and Keith Harvey. Indeed, he reminds supporters of Harvey, for his is just as brave in the tackle and such a fine all-round performer that Terry Cooper has entrusted him with the captaincy. Shaun Taylor covers a lot of ground in a match for, as can be seen from his record, he has notched up quite a few goals and not all of them have come from moving into the goal area for corner-kicks. Born in Plymouth on 26 March 1963, he attracted attention with Bideford and came to Exeter on a month's trial in December 1986. After making his debut in the number-seven shirt, he was given a contract and has since missed very few games. Taylor shone in City's promotion-winning season of 1989-90, when he proved to be the iron man of the defence, one who never shirked a tackle and shook off a lot of hard knocks. No wonder he was voted 'Player of the Year' in this glorious campaign.

League debut for City v Wolverhampton Wanderers, 27 December 1986.

	LEAGUE		FA CUP		FL CUP		TOTAL	
	App	Gls	App	Gls	App	Gls	App	Gls
1986-87	23	0	0	0	0	0	23	0
1987-88	41	1	1	0	1	0	43	1
1988-89	46	6	1	0	2	0	49	6
1989-90	45	6	6	0	7	0	58	6
	155	13	8	0	10	0	173	13

SHAUN TAYLOR

John Templeman helped Brighton to win promotion to the Second Division in season 1971-2, wearing a number-four shirt. Two years later he joined Exeter City, together with Lammie Robertson, in the deal that took Fred Binney to Brighton. He was moved around a good deal in his first season at the Park before settling down as an overlapping right-back. In this position he was one of the key members of City's 1976-7 promotion-winning team, showing the electrifying speed which enabled him to affect the quick recovery. Born at Yapton, near Bognor Regis, on 21 September 1947, he was spotted by Brighton whilst playing for Arundel Town and signed in July 1966. He made 218/7 League appearances for the Seagulls during his eight seasons at the Goldstone Ground. Another of his best seasons with the City was 1978-9 and it was something of a shock when he was transferred to Swindon in July 1979. He had only one and a half seasons with the Robins before being released from his contract.

League debut for City v Barnsley, 17 August 1974.

	LEAGUE		FA CUP		FL CUP		TOTAL	
	App	Gls	App	Gls	App	Gls	App	Gls
1974-75	39	2	1	0	1	0	41	2
1975-76	42/1	3	0	0	4	0	46/1	3
1976-77	35	1	0	0	3	0	38	1
1977-78	44	0	5	1	4	0	53	1
1978-79	45	1	1	0	5	0	51	1
	205/1	7	7	1	17	0	229/1	8

JOHN TEMPLEMAN

111

Rugby-mad Cornwall has not produced many soccer stars, especially in the period between the two World Wars, but Percy Varco was one of the few. He first attracted attention with Torquay United and was transferred from there to Aston Villa for a fee of £200 in December 1923. Varco managed ten First Division appearances in the star-studded Midland side, then moved to QPR in 1926, but he really made his name after joining Norwich City the following year. He missed only one game in his first season at The Nest, finishing top scorer with 29 goals. It was while with Norwich that the cry 'give it to Varco' was first heard, for he was a difficult man to knock off the ball. Indeed, he always played with such dash and determination that it was no wonder he was eventually injured and lost his place. Exeter City secured his transfer from Norwich in February 1930, and it was against the Canaries that he got his first goal in his new colours. Varco went on to inject his particular brand of dashing football into the famous Cup run, playing between Purcell and Houghton. In this season Varco scored a total of 30 League and Cup goals. One of his outstanding displays was when he scored a hat-trick in the space of 20 minutes of the first-half in a 3-1 home win over Cardiff City in October 1931. He finished his League career with Brighton in 1932-3 before returning home to Fowey, where he later had two spells as Mayor. He died in February 1982.
League debut for City v Clapton Orient, 5 February 1930.

PERCY VARCO

	LEAGUE		FA CUP		TOTAL	
	App	Gls	App	Gls	App	Gls
1929-30	6	0	0	0	6	0
1930-31	39	25	8	5	47	30
1931-32	36	16	1	0	37	16
	81	41	9	5	90	46

There has been no more consistent defender in the City colours in recent years than Keith Viney, who first signed apprentice at the age of 16 for his hometown club Portsmouth, where he was born on 26 October 1957. He joined City on a free transfer in the summer of 1982 but, unfortunately, his efforts during six and a half years at St James' Park may be overlooked in some quarters because his stay coincided with one of the poorest spells in the club's history. The truth is, however, that Viney was one of the players who could not be blamed for the club's poor impression in the League, although even his form began to be affected midway through his third season before he was relieved of the captaincy to lift a load off his mind. Viney was a worrier and giving up this responsibility helped to restore his form at left-back. Voted City's 'Player of the Year' in his first two seasons with the club, he shone in a defence that was almost constantly under pressure. A hard tackler, he was often eager to show his colleagues the way to goal and in a game against Wrexham in February 1983, he scored twice in a 3-3 draw. Before joining the City, Viney had made 160/6 appearances for Portsmouth but he far exceeded this number with Exeter, where he was one of the most regular first-team men the club has ever had over a period of six seasons. Indeed, as can be seen from the figures below, he missed only nine games in those seasons. In 1988-9 he lost his place to Richard Dryden and, after a spell on loan to Bristol Rovers, he was released midway through that campaign.
League debut for City v Huddersfield Town, 28 August 1982.

KEITH VINEY

	LEAGUE		FA CUP		FL CUP		TOTAL	
	App	Gls	App	Gls	App	Gls	App	Gls
1982-83	44	4	1	0	2	0	47	4
1983-84	42	0	2	0	2	0	46	0
1984-85	45	1	2	0	2	1	49	2
1985-86	45	2	3	0	3	0	51	2
1986-87	45	1	2	1	2	0	49	2
1987-88	46	0	1	0	2	0	49	0
1988-89	3	0	1	0	2	0	6	0
	270	8	12	1	15	1	297	10

112

Chris Vinnicombe is yet another of City's local discoveries who has developed into the highest class of football. Born at Exeter on 20 October 1970, he first signed for City as a 14-year-old schoolboy and became a trainee professional in July 1987. He played as a winger but manager Terry Cooper saw him as an overlapping full-back and it was in this position that he attracted so much attention early in season 1989-90. A delightful footballer to watch, the 18-year-old Vinnicombe turned in many immaculate performances at this time, being extremely fast, clever on the ball and with a footballing brain in advance of his years. It was no surprise when, after watching him at least three times, Glasgow Rangers manager Graeme Souness signed this brilliant young prospect for £100,000 down and an agreement to pay up to £500,000 in stages according to the number of first-team appearances he makes for the Ibrox club. After five appearances as a substitute, Chris Vinnicombe made his Premier Division debut from the kick-off against Dundee United on 3 February 1990.
League debut for City (sub) v Doncaster Rovers, 3 September 1988.

	LEAGUE		FA CUP		FL CUP		TOTAL	
	App	Gls	App	Gls	App	Gls	App	Gls
1988-89	21/4	0	0	0	0	0	21/4	0
1989-90	14	1	0	0	5	1	19	2
	35/4	1	0	0	5	1	40/4	2

CHRIS VINNICOMBE

Born in Sheffield on 16 October 1914, this popular footballer had brief spells with Leeds United, Gainsborough Trinity and Sheffield United before joining Exeter on a free transfer in the summer of 1938. He was then a defensive wing-half with a rare turn of speed and got his first chance at left-half when Jack Angus dropped out with injury. Walker proved too good to be relegated to the Reserves when Angus recovered and he held his position with Angus moving almost permanently to centre-half. Steve Walker was capable of playing anywhere and on one occasion he even went in goal during a game when the 'keeper was injured. Apart from that, he played centre-half, inside-right and centre-forward, but was mostly seen at left-half. He returned to the club after wartime military service and continued to hold his place before ending his City career with a couple of games at centre-forward. In 1950, Minehead AFC decided to turn professional and they appointed Steve Walker as their first player-coach.
League debut for City v Newport County, 22 October 1938.

	LEAGUE		FA CUP		TOTAL	
	App	Gls	App	Gls	App	Gls
1938-39	30	0	1	0	31	0
1945-46	0	0	4	5	4	5
1946-47	31	2	1	0	32	2
1947-48	33	0	2	0	35	0
1948-49	39	0	3	0	42	0
1949-50	8	1	1	0	9	1
	141	3	12	5	153	8

STEVE WALKER

113

A skilful footballer, George Wardle was born at Kimbleworth, County Durham, on 24 September 1919 and joined Middlesbrough from Durham BC in 1937, making one First Division appearance as a teenage outside-right before moving to Exeter in 1939. City supporters did not see much of this skilful ball-player, for although he went straight into the first-team in the opening game of season 1939-40 — a Jubilee Fund match against Plymouth Argyle — and played in the season's first three League matches, the outbreak of World War Two then caused the abandonment of the competition. During the war, Wardle played a number of games for Chelsea, appearing at Wembley in the League South Cup Final of 1945 when the Pensioners beat Millwall 2-0 with Wardle scoring one of the goals. He also played in the Cup-winners' match at Stamford Bridge, when the Northern winners, Bolton Wanderers, beat Chelsea 2-1. He returned to Exeter City as an inside-forward in 1945-6 and showed that he was in a class of his own. Often he would beat three or four players with the ball, but sometimes his colleagues did not react quickly enough to his moves. Accommodation was a problem in those days and it was because he could not find a house in Exeter that he went to Cardiff City for a £3,000 fee in May 1947. He subsequently played for Queen's Park Rangers before returning nearer his home and finishing his League career with Darlington.
League debut for City v Torquay United, 31 August 1946 (1939-40 games were expunged from the record).

GEORGE WARDLE

	LEAGUE		FA CUP		TOTAL	
	App	Gls	App	Gls	App	Gls
1945-46	0	0	2	0	2	0
1946-47	38	6	1	0	39	6
	38	6	3	0	41	6

BOB WATSON

Bob Watson was City's first captain when they turned professional in 1908 and one of the most consistent forwards of those early seasons. He was born in Middlesbrough in 1872 and joined the local Second Division club from South Bank in September 1901, scoring on his League debut for them in what was their promotion year. He also appeared with Woolwich Arsenal (1903-05) and Leeds City (1905-08) before Arthur Chadwick persuaded him to try his luck in the West Country. At 36 years of age he was one of the side's most experienced campaigners, who helped place the inside trio of Watson, McGuigan and Bell among the most dangerous in the Southern League. Certainly, clubs not in this class found it quite demoralizing to come up against such seasoned campaigners and they scored a total of 26 goals between them in the 1908-09 FA Cup run, which included the 14-0 victory over Weymouth and the 10-1 win against Longfleet St Mary. Although described as the 'most consistent' member of the attack for the greater part of his stay with City, Watson resigned the captaincy in November 1911 and left the club at the end of that season, returning north to join Stalybridge Celtic.
League debut for City v Millwall, 2 September 1908.

	LEAGUE		FA CUP		TOTAL	
	App	Gls	App	Gls	App	Gls
1908-09	39	6	9	8	48	14
1909-10	40	10	4	2	44	12
1910-11	24	1	4	1	28	2
1911-12	34	8	2	0	36	8
	137	25	19	11	156	36

CLIVE WHITEHEAD

	LEAGUE		FA CUP		FL CUP		TOTAL	
	App	Gls	App	Gls	App	Gls	App	Gls
1989-90	36/2	5	6	0	7	0	49/2	5
	36/2	5	6	0	7	0	49/2	5

Clive Whitehead is a player whose experience proved invaluable to the City in their promotion-winning season of 1989-90, when he was a tower of strength in midfield. Solidly built and as hard as nails, he still showed some fine turns of speed but is obviously a man with a good footballing brain, who has learnt how to pace himself. Born in Birmingham on 24 November 1955, he signed for Bristol City in 1972, after they noted his talent while he was playing against them for Northfield in the FA Youth Cup. He was a winger in those days and it was in that position he helped Bristol City win promotion to the Second Division before being converted into a left-back, although he always retained attacking tendencies. When Bristol City slid back to the Third Division in such a short space of time, he was one of those on their books with an expensive ten-year contract and they transferred him to West Brom, where he had a spell as captain during five and a half seasons with the Throstles. During this time he went on loan to Wolves and when given a free by the Albion in 1987, returned to the First Division with Portsmouth. However, they were relegated that season and in the summer of 1989, manager Terry Cooper got him on a free transfer. This soon proved to be a worthwhile move, for Whitehead's keen tackling and accurate ball distribution made him popular with the City fans. He is also club coach.
League debut for City v Doncaster Rovers, 19 August 1989.

Fred Whitlow, a Bristolian who was born on 3 September 1904, is Exeter City's record goalscorer in a single season and led one of the most exciting and entertaining forward lines the club had ever fielded. An expert positional player, he combined deadly marksmanship with polished artistry. Fred Whitlow was obviously a delight to watch when he was at his best — which was for at least two of the three seasons he was with the club. City got him for £250 from Charlton Athletic in 1931. He had helped the London club win promotion to the Second Division in 1928-9, being their leading scorer with 26 goals. At Exeter, after taking over from Percy Varco at centre-forward with the Cornishman moving to inside-right, Whitlow was soon rattling home more goals. His first hat-trick for City came in his fifth League appearance, but it was in the next season that he really took off. This was when City came closest-ever to winning promotion to the Second Division and no wonder, for Whitlow broke the club record with a total of 33 League goals. Yes, 33 and not 34 which had always been the record attributed to him in the record books. He was originally credited with four goals against Watford in a 5-2 win at St James' Park, but subsequent enquiries by the local reporter found that one of the goals had been scored direct from a corner-kick by Jack Scott, without the ball being touched by Whitlow. However, in this season alone, the man who made scoring look so easy netted seven hat-tricks. For most of the following season Whitlow went through one of those unaccountable lapses of form and made it known that he would like a change. It was no surprise, therefore, when he was transferred to Cardiff City before finishing up where he had begun — with Barry Town.
League debut for City v Fulham, 2 September 1931.

FRED WHITLOW

	LEAGUE		FA CUP		TOTAL	
	App	Gls	App	Gls	App	Gls
1931-32	23	15	0	0	23	15
1932-33	32	33	2	1	34	34
1933-34	28	13	1	0	29	13
	83	61	3	1	86	62

115

After playing for St Catherine's Sunday School, Burnley, Fred Whittaker got his first chance to play for Burnley Reserves when called upon within a couple of hours of the kick-off to fill a vacancy. He scored the winner on that debut and blossomed into an inside-right who became a regular member of the League side in 1906. In November 1908, Bradford City, then a First Division club, secured his transfer but he suffered in a weak team and, in May 1909, joined Southern League Northampton Town, where he was successful as an outside-right. He stayed three seasons before an injury cost him his place and arrived at St James' Park in the close season of 1912. Whittaker was an ever-present in his initial season and, after switching to centre-forward for the majority of games in his second season, he topped the score-sheet with 13 goals. As a former winger he showed plenty of dash at centre-forward and this speed was generally a feature of his goalscoring. In 1914 he was transferred to Millwall, to be joined by Exeter teammate Jack Fort. Whittaker was with Millwall until the outbreak of World War One.

League debut for City v West Ham United, 2 September 1912.

FRED WHITTAKER

	LEAGUE		FA CUP		TOTAL	
	App	Gls	App	Gls	App	Gls
1912-13	38	4	1	0	39	4
1913-14	30	13	2	0	32	13
	68	17	3	0	71	17

One of the most experienced players signed by the City before World War One, goalkeeper Walter Whittaker stood 6ft 2ins and weighed around 14st, so he was a big asset in the days before attacking forwards became 'kinder' to goalkeepers. Born in Manchester on 20 September 1878, 'Big Walt' played for Manchester United, Grimsby Town (two spells), Reading (two spells), Blackburn Rovers, Derby County, Brentford and Clapton Orient before coming to Exeter in the summer of 1910. His League and Southern League appearances up to that time numbered 336. When Derby obtained his transfer from Grimsby in 1903, they paid £400, which was only £50 less than the contemporary British record transfer fee for a 'keeper. Like the majority of big men, Whittaker was of the 'hail fellow, well met' type who seldom resorted to tough tactics. He owned a large sheepdog called 'Laddie', which became the club's first mascot. Whittaker took over the captaincy in November 1911, after Bob Watson resigned the position when the club was going through a bad spell. When he took to his bed with a severe bout of 'flu towards the end of that campaign, City gave amateur Dick Pym his first chance and 'Big Walt' never got another League game. In the summer of 1912 he joined newly-formed Swansea Town as that club's first player-manager, a position he held for two seasons. He was player-manager of Llanelli from the 1914 close season to November that year. He died in 1927.

League debut for City v Brentford, 3 September 1910.

WALTER WHITTAKER

	LEAGUE		FA CUP		TOTAL	
	App	Gls	App	Gls	App	Gls
1910-11	38	0	4	0	42	0
1911-12	21	0	1	0	22	0
	59	0	5	0	64	0

Roderick Williams was a hard-working and tireless centre-forward, who rates a place here, despite the fact that he spent only one season with the City. In that season, however, after signing him from Norwich City, the Exeter supporters were treated to one of the club's finest-ever scorers, for Williams' total of League 29 goals places him second only to the inimitable Fred Whitlow. Rod Williams also scored in one run of six League games as well as finding the net in four out of five FA Cup ties. Born at Newport on 2 December 1909, he was brought up at Wandsworth and played as an amateur for Sutton United, Epsom Town, Uxbridge Town and Crystal Palace, being selected to represent the Athenian League as well as Middlesex County. It was surprising that he did not turn professional with a League club until signing for Norwich City in May 1933, for he helped them win promotion to the Second Division after scoring on his League debut. The Grecians sold him to Reading in 1937, but after three months he was snapped up by West Ham for a fee of £4,000. In September 1938 he moved to Clapton Orient, where he was top scorer before the war ended his career.

League debut for City v Torquay United (scored twice), 2 September 1936.

	LEAGUE		FA CUP		TOTAL	
	App	Gls	App	Gls	App	Gls
1936-37	41	29	5	7	46	36
	41	29	5	7	46	36

RODERICK WILLIAMS

Manager Frank Broome and his players after City defeated Nuneaton Borough at the third attempt in an FA Cup first-round game in December 1967. The Grecians triumphed 1-0 in the second replay held at Ashton Gate.

117

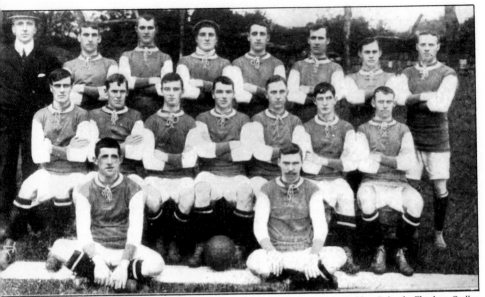

Exeter City, 1908-09. Back row (left to right): A.Chadwick (manager), Ambler, Bulcock, Fletcher, Crelley, Banks, Copestake, Wake. Seated: Drain, Craig, Johnson, Watson, McGuigan, Bell, White. On ground: Tierney, Parnell.

Match to Remember 1   6 February 1909

Plymouth Argyle 2   Exeter City 0

THIS fast, hard-fought but sporting game between the Devonshire rivals at Home Park saw Plymouth Argyle reach the third round of the FA Cup for the first time in their history. Exeter City, meanwhile, were knocked out of the competition after playing right through from the first round of the qualifying series — a total of nine matches including replays.

It was the greatest soccer event ever seen in Devon, the meeting of Exeter City and Plymouth Argyle in the second round of the English Cup. The two earlier contests between the Devon clubs had gone in City's favour, 2-1 in the Southern League match in November and 1-0 in a friendly match at Plymouth on Boxing Day.

For the Cup game, however, each team had been training at home and each was fairly confident of success. Exeter were able to name their strongest side, but Plymouth were handicapped by the absence of centre-half and captain, Charlie Clark, who was under suspension. His deputy was Evenson, a player who had worn the colours of Second Division Leicester Fosse with distinction.

All the week, this match had been almost the sole topic of conversation throughout Devon and there was the promise of a big attendance. That was no false hope and on a brilliant, sunny afternoon the crowd was in the region of 19,000.

Bob Watson won the toss and Argyle faced the sun from the Plymouth End. Hindmarsh kicked off and the home team immediately made ground on the right

118

and forced a corner which was well saved by Jack Robinson. Exeter then had a narrow escape when Hindmarsh hit the crossbar. The Grecians held their own until shortly before half-time, when Hindmarsh put Plymouth ahead following a clever move between Holden and Leavey.

Robinson, the former England international goalkeeper, was in fine form after the interval, despite coming under heavy pressure, and it was almost full-time before he was beaten again. Leavey got past Bulcock and, with Robinson caught in two minds, he shot home. It was an exciting game, but a bitter disappointment for City, who had done so well in the Cup.

Plymouth Argyle: Horne; Butler, Atterbury, McCormick, Evenson, McIntyre, Leavey, Hakin, Hindmarsh, Warburton, Holden.
Exeter City: Robinson; Craig, Bulcock, Ambler, Chadwick, Wake, Parnell, Watson, McGuigan, Bell, Copestake.
Referee: A. McQue (London)   *Attendance: 18,624*

Match to Remember 2   31 January 1914

Exeter City 1   Aston Villa 2

EXETER City earned the right to meet Aston Villa in the second round of the FA Cup with a brilliant victory at Portsmouth in the preceding round. It was arguably Exeter's finest-ever performance and their form that day at Fratton Park gave City supporters hope that their side could even hold the Villains in check.

Villa fielded several internationals — Sam Hardy, Joe Bache, Harry Hampton and Charlie Wallace — and Jimmy Harrop had played for the Football League when with Liverpool. Villa had won the League Championship six times and the FA Cup five times.

Before a crowd of 9,500, who paid ground record receipts of £910, Jimmy Rigby won the toss, Hampton kicked off and Villa were at once away. After only a minute, Harrop flicked the ball to Wallace, from whose centre Hampton was pulled up for offside just as he barged into Jack Fort.

Wallace's next centre went behind the goal and then Exeter showed what they could do, Lyons having to react quickly to clear from Fred Whittaker.

After 15 minutes, Marshall conceded a free-kick after fouling Wallace and from it, Hampton headed Villa into the lead. The kick had been taken so quickly that Exeter were taken completely by surprise.

The Villa team soon settled into their stride on the unfamiliar Exeter pitch, but then Holt was tripped by Weston and Exeter were awarded a penalty. Alas, Fort drove the kick against a post and the ball went behind.

Ten minutes into the second half, Villa scored their second goal — another snap effort by Hampton, who dashed in to meet a centre from the right. McCann reduced Villa's lead, but Exeter had frozen on the day and poor Fort was left to reflect on his chance that would have put the Devon side back in the game.

Exeter City: Pym; Fort, Strettle, Rigby, Lagan, Smith, Holt, Lovett, Whittaker, McCann, Marshall.
Aston Villa: Hardy; Lyons, Weston, Barber, Harrop, Leach, Wallace, Stephenson, Hampton, Bache, Edgley.
Referee: E. W. Child (London)   *Attendance: 9,500*

Jim Carrick (far left) headed the second goal. Joe Colebourne (left) gave a splendid performance at right-back.

Match to Remember 3   11 September 1920

Exeter City 4   Millwall Athletic 0

THIS victory put Exeter at the top of the Third Division and left them the only unbeaten side in the section after a comprehensive victory which certainly did not flatter them. Millwall were fairly beaten by a more skilful, thrustful side and seldom looked capable of hitting back.

Glorious September weather ensured a good attendance at St James' Park, although the players, who were feeling the effects of playing on hard grounds, would have been pleased if the ground had received a good soaking during the week.

Millwall went on the attack from the kick-off and a long shot from Dempsey was gathered by Dick Pym, City's goalkeeper-captain. In the next minute, Pym was faced with a more difficult problem when Broad broke through and bore down on goal. The 'keeper dashed out and bravely took the ball off Broad's toes.

Exeter now took up the running and good work between John Dockray and Makin saw the latter shoot wide when he was well placed. Lansdale then saved from Appleton and a fine shot by Wright scraped the top of the crossbar.

After 20 minutes of almost continuous City pressure, Makin eventually put the Grecians ahead with an angled drive into the top corner from 12 yards. For the next 15 minutes, Millwall were made to look like novices and justice was done when Carrick, jumping high, headed Appleton's cross home for goal number-two.

Six minutes into the second half, Wright made it 3-0 and two minutes later, Vowles netted but was ruled offside. In the 70th minute, however, City's victory was complete when their inside trio tied Millwall's defence into knots. The Lions' goalkeeper came out too far in a vain attempt to collect Appleton's centre and Wright headed the ball into an unguarded net.

It was a glorious victory and not many defences in the Third Division could have held the Grecians on this form. Commented one reporter: 'Now that they are top of the League, the Grecians must see to it that they remain there.'

Exeter City: Pym; Coleburne, Feebury, Crawshaw, Carrick, Mitton, Appleton, Makin, Wright, Vowles, Dockray.
Millwall Athletic: Lansdale; Fort, Hodge, Voisey, Hill, McAlpine, Waterall, Moule, Broad, Sutherland, Dempsey.

Referee: E.Telfree (Southampton)   *Attendance: 7,000*

Portsmouth 3   Exeter City 4

PORTSMOUTH fielded their strongest team for this Third Division South game against Exeter at Fratton Park. Parker, their new centre-half from Luton Town, was making his debut, and Cherrett replaced Alf Strange in attack. Exeter, meanwhile, struggling near the foot of the table, were unchanged.

Ellis Crompton won the toss and City had the wind and sun at their backs in the first half. Pompey kicked-off but were quickly dispossessed and Alf Matthews made progress down the right before being checked by Parker.

After 16 minutes, Portsmouth went ahead through Cherrett, who hammered home a hard, low shot from close range. Five minutes later, however, Exeter drew level when Crockford cut out an opening from which Jazzo Kirk scored a picture-book goal.

Exeter were now playing delightful football and forced several corners in a game which was being played at a fast pace, due partly to the hard ground.

Ten minutes before half-time, Portsmouth regained the lead. The ball was flashed from wing to wing until Cherrett got his chance and beat Pavey with a brilliant hooked shot into the roof of the net.

Not to be outdone, Exeter got back on the attack and Crockford fed John Dockray, who rounded Probert before planting a perfect centre into the goalmouth. Newton got to the ball but Kirk followed up and charged the goalkeeper, the ball dropping over the line to put City back on terms.

There was plenty of excitement in the second half. Pompey should have regained the lead in the first minute, but Cherrett hesitated and was bundled off the ball. Then Kirk broke away and completed his hat-trick.

A curling shot from Shankley was misjudged by Pavey to give Portsmouth their third goal and once more the scores were level. Yet again City pushed forward and this time they found the winning goal.

Again, Kirk was the scorer. Dockray's centre was headed on by Crockford and Kirk found the net with another terrific drive. At the same time he carved a niche for himself in Exeter City folklore by becoming the first of their players to get as many as four goals in a single League match.

Portsmouth: Newton; Probert, Quinn, Abbott, Parker, Martin, Meikle, Shankley, Cherrett, Watson, Beedie.
Exeter City: Pavey; Pollard, Ackroyd, Coopland, Mitton, Crompton, Matthews, Kirk, Crockford, Davis, Dockray.

Referee: H.C.Curtis (Chingford)   *Attendance: 6,000*

Match to Remember 5   25 December 1925
Exeter City 4   Plymouth Argyle 0

THERE were few more dramatic games in the first season of the new offside law than this Christmas Day game at St James' Park when Plymouth Argyle, contenders for promotion to Division Two, suffered a crushing reverse at the hands of Exeter City.

After a run of seven League defeats, the Grecians struck what supporters considered to be their true form and Plymouth Argyle were soundly beaten. Those fans claimed that no club had ever occupied a more false position in the table (19th out of 22) than their side.

Except for rare flashes from Sam Black and Jack Leslie, the Argyle attack was hardly ever in the picture and, almost throughout the game, Exeter dominated play.

A brilliant goal by Harold Blackmore, only three minutes after the start, laid the foundation for Exeter's triumph. Alf Matthews passed to McDevitt, who slipped the ball along the ground to Blackmore. The young Silverton centre-forward let fly and sent a left-foot shot past Craig and into the net.

Although the game was 54 minutes old before Exeter extended that lead, there was never any real danger that Plymouth would regain a toe-hold.

Even when Plymouth resorted to some rough play, City refused to be put off and nine minutes after half-time Lievesley took a pass from Blackmore and crashed home the second goal.

Exeter went 3-0 ahead with a fierce drive from Matthews which thudded into the net off the shoulder of Price, the Plymouth full-back. Then, with the minutes ticking away, City completed the rout when Billy Compton finished off another brilliant attacking move.

Exeter City: Bailey; Pollard, Charlton, Pullan, Potter, Shelton, Matthews, McDevitt, Blackmore, Lievesley, Compton.
Plymouth Argyle: Craig; Price, Russell, Logan, Pullen, Smith, Corcoran, Forbes, Cook, Leslie, Black.

Referee: A.J.Bissex (Midsomer Norton)   *Attendance: 10,000*

Match to Remember 6   28 January 1928

Exeter City 2   Blackburn Rovers 2

AFTER Blackburn Rovers won the FA Cup in 1928, they admitted that their most difficult task on the way to Wembley was the removal of Exeter City in the fourth round, which was achieved only after an extra-time replay.

All the season, bad weather had dogged the Exeter club on big-match days and, although part of the week had been crisp and dry, the wind then veered round to the south-west in the course of Friday night and brought a rainstorm which lasted for several hours on the morning of the match. By the time the teams appeared, the pitch was waterlogged and the attendance was affected adversely.

McDevitt won the toss and Exeter City lined up facing the Duke Bank. Rovers began with a series of long, swinging passes that had the City defence in trouble until Charlie Miller eventually cleared their lines.

When Exeter got within sight of the Rovers goal George Purcell was whistled up for offside. The pace on the slippery turf was fast and the way the City were standing up to their illustrious opponents was heartening. Hutton and Roxburgh did not appear too sure in their tackling and Exeter forced two corners, both of which were cleared with difficulty.

Blackburn nevertheless took the lead after 18 minutes. From a throw-in in front of the grandstand, Puddefoot got the ball across the penalty area and Roscamp, getting the better of Jock Ditchburn, cracked it home.

122

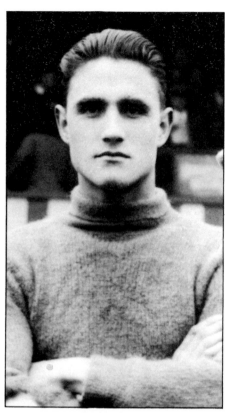

Goalkeeper Tom Holland allowed Rigby to put Blackburn further ahead when the shot went under his body.

After 38 minutes, a miskick by Miller allowed Rigby to put Blackburn further ahead with a low shot which went under Holland's diving body.

Exeter refused to capitulate, however, and Gee got in a free-kick which was punched out by a Blackburn defender. Gee stepped up to convert the penalty and Exeter were back in the hunt.

Some inspired play during the second half saw City gradually gain the upper hand and with a few minutes to play, they drew level. Ditchburn lofted the latest of several free-kicks into the Blackburn goalmouth and Mason crashed the ball home amidst the wildest scenes of bedlam and excitement ever seen on St James' Park.

Exeter pressed forward again during the last seven minutes and on their second half display could be considered unlucky not to have won. It was the greatest day in the history of Exeter City but, alas, the following Thursday it was Blackburn who finally triumphed after extra-time at Ewood Park.

Exeter City: Holland; Pollard, Miller, Ditchburn, Mason, Gee, Purcell, McDevitt, Dent, Vaughan, Compton.

Blackburn Rovers: Crawford; Hutton, Roxburgh, Healless, Rankine, Campbell, Thornewell, Puddefoot, Roscamp, McLean, Rigby.

Referee: H.E. Gray (London)   *Attendance: 17,330*

Cliff Bastin as a young star in Exeter City's colours. He was only 16 at the time of City's fine win over Newport when his fierce shot nearly broke the net.

Exeter City 5   Newport County 0

IN the weeks before this game, all the talk had been about the genius of Cliff Bastin, the 16-year-old locally-born inside-left who, after some brilliant games for City Reserves, had stepped into the first team and proved himself to be a born footballer.

Bastin, playing for the Reserves on Good Friday, in a Southern League match against Taunton, had laid on his team's first goal with a superb pass inside the full-back for Andrews to score. Shortly before the interval, Bastin crowned a dazzling dribble down the left wing with a magnificent goal.

He was then just three weeks past his 16th birthday and the youngest player ever to have appeared in any Exeter City team. The City management felt that, despite his tender years, the talented youngster could no longer be kept out of the first team and he was given his League debut at Highfield Road a week later.

Bastin's clever ball control and thoughtful distribution were early features of the game, but robust defending by Anderson and Hinton, coupled with the liveliness of the new ball, prevented City from threatening the Newport goal.

Two shots from Bastin and one from Fred Dent were diverted for corners by Maidment. Then, in the 27th minute, Newport took the lead, only for Dent to equalize a minute later.

Almost on half-time, Jazzo Kirk slipped the ball through to Bastin just inside the penalty area and the former pupil of Ladysmith Road School beat Maidment with a powerful left-foot shot just inside the far upright.

Bastin soon distinguished himself again, providing Kirk with a pass and then, from the return, hammering in a fierce shot which Maidment did well to save.

But Exeter were on the rampage and further goals were inevitable. George Purcell scored Exeter's third and fourth and then Bastin made it 5-0. His last goal was a thundering left-foot drive of such velocity that it nearly broke the net. For a 16-year-old, Bastin had an amazingly powerful shot and Maidment, acknowledged as one of the Third Division's finest goalkeepers, stood motionless as the ball crashed into the top of the rigging and nearly wrenched the supporting poles from their sockets.

Exeter City: Holland; Pollard, Charlton, Phoenix, Mason, R.Clarke, Purcell, McDevitt, Dent, C.Bastin, Kirk.
Newport County: Maidment; Anderson, Hinton, Richardson, Bowsher, Pugh, Pick, Gittens, Waterston, Thomas, Young.
Referee: H.E.Alray (London)   *Attendance: 6,000*

Match to Remember 8   10 January 1931

Exeter City 3   Derby County 2

THIS was the greatest day in Exeter's history, the day of days when Derby County, one of the best teams in England, were beaten on their first visit to St James' Park.

In mild but overcast weather and on a soft pitch, the third-round FA Cup tie between the City and First Division Derby promised to be a fast and lively game. When the gates opened at 12.30pm there was a big crowd already waiting outside and just before 2.30pm, a rousing cheer greeted England full-back Tom Cooper as he led out the Rams. Seconds later, a massive roar of welcome heralded the appearance of Les Dennington and the Grecians.

'Dido', the famous seagull mascot of Exeter City, flew around the ground and the band thumped out the City signature tune *There's a Good Time Coming*.

It was a really magnificent performance by Exeter, who, despite being without the services of Nobby Clarke throughout the second-half, and Dicky Baugh for part of it, fought their way to victory with gritty determination and a lot of well-planned, clever football.

The genius of Derby and England winger, Sammy Crooks, was there for all to see. His weaving runs along the touch-line in the second-half, ending with immaculately placed centres to the head of Jack Bowers, provided Derby with their two goals, but it was not enough.

Exeter were well served in all departments, particularly at half-back where Barber was as good as any man on the field. And the tough tackling and dogged determination of Dennington was more than a match for Bowers.

Clarke, who was involved in a violent collision with Malloch early in the second-half, was carried off on a stretcher and did not return. Then Baugh and Malloch came to blows, resulting in the Exeter man having to go off for attention to a facial injury.

Percy Varco opened the scoring for Exeter inside 12 minutes. Bowers equalized one minute after the interval and, midway through the second-half, Billy Armfield made the score 2-1 before Harold Houghton grabbed Exeter's third. Derby snatched another copybook goal towards the close and, in mounting excitement, Barber hooked the ball from beneath the Exeter crossbar with the very last kick of the game.

Exeter City: Davies; Baugh, Miller, Clarke, Dennington, Barber, Armfield, Purcell, Varco, Houghton, Doncaster.

Derby County: Kirby; Cooper, Collin, Nicholas, Jessop, Malloch, Crooks, Stephenson, Bowers, Ramage, Mee.

Referee: E.Small (Bristol)   *Attendance: 16,500*

Match to Remember 9   4 March 1931

Exeter City 2   Sunderland 4

THIRTY-SIX hours of continuous rain had rendered the St James's Park pitch almost waterlogged for this sixth-round FA Cup replay between City and Sunderland. The reward for victory was a place in the semi-final against the winners of the Birmingham-Chelsea replay.

Despite the weather, the ground was packed to overflowing and, as the pitch became wetter and wetter, so did most of the spectators, there being very little covered accommodation at St James' Park.

Sunderland, in red and white stripes, were first out, followed immediately by Charlie Miller and the Grecians in blue jerseys with claret shoulders and tops. 'Dido', the seagull mascot, was bathing in the puddles and the Exeter City Military Band had its work cut out to make its customary rendering of *There's a Good Time Coming* heard above the shouting, cheering and the ringing of handbells. McDougall won the toss but it carried no advantage on such a day.

The story of the match is easy to tell. Sunderland showed the class they had failed to display on their own ground four days previously, bringing Exeter's great FA Cup run to an end without too much difficulty.

Their first goal, a simple one, was scored in the 15th minute and they went 2-0 ahead after 22 minutes. Their fast, clever passing game pulled the Exeter defence to pieces, and although the City put up a magnificent and plucky fight right to the end, they could have had no cause for complaint.

Percy Varco scored for Exeter eight minutes before half-time, but Connor got Sunderland's third goal 15 minutes after the interval.

Exeter, though, still fought back. They scored a beautifully headed goal through George Purcell and then were unlucky not to equalize when the ball ran along the goal-line, with no City player near enough to touch it into the net.

When Gurney netted Sunderland's fourth goal ten minutes from time, the game was as good as over and Exeter's dreams of a semi-final appearance faded out of sight.

Yet Exeter City's feats that season had staggered the football world. They kept up their magnificent fighting spirit until the very last kick and McDougall, the Sunderland captain, declared in an interview afterwards that Exeter were 'wonderful Cup fighters' and that both his team's games against them were the hardest ones on their way to the semi-final.

Exeter City, 1930-31. Back row (left to right): Billy McDevitt (manager), Clarke, Baugh, Davies, Miller, Barber. Front: Armfield, Purcell, Varco, Houghton, Doncaster, Angus.

Despite the bitterness of their defeat, the sporting spirit of Exeter players was shown by the fact that they volunteered to accompany the Sunderland players on their walk to St David's Station to catch their north-bound train.

Exeter City: Davies; Baugh, Miller, Clarke, Angus, Barber, Armfield, Purcell, Varco, Houghton, Doncaster.

Sunderland: Middleton; Hall, Shaw, Hastings, McDougall, Andrews, Eden, Devine, Gurney, Leonard, Connor.

Referee: A.E.Fogg (Bolton)   *Attendance: 20,984*

Match to Remember 10   28 January 1933

Exeter City 5   Torquay 0

ON a day when frost-bound pitches might well have produced some freak results, everything went according to plan for Exeter City who, by beating their Devon neighbours, moved to the top of the Third Division South with 36 points from 25 matches. Moreover, Fred Whitlow's three goals gave him the record for most in a single season by an Exeter player.

Exeter fully deserved their sweeping success. They were superior in pace, craft and teamwork. Torquay played scrappy football by comparison and, but for the brilliant and courageous last-ditch efforts of Percy Maggs, they would have been absolutely swamped.

Whitlow opened the scoring in the eighth minute and Higgins made it 2-0 some 15 minutes later. Then Kennedy and Whitlow beat Maggs in rapid succession to give the Grecians a commanding 4-0 half-time lead.

Whitlow received a tremendous ovation when, 13 minutes into the second half, he rounded off excellent work by Harold Houghton by side-stepping a lunging tackle from Maggs and shooting home for a fifth goal for Exeter and his third of the match.

This raised Whitlow's total for the season to 26 and equalled the individual goalscoring record held by Fred Dent. The saves made by Maggs in the second-half were too numerous to detail and, but for him, City's score must have gone well into double figures.

As for Whitlow, although not gaining a place in the team until the eighth match, he had already netted six hat-tricks, including this latest one.

Exeter City: Davies; Gray, Miller, Clarke, Childs, Barber, Scott, Kennedy, Whitlow, Houghton, Higgins.

Torquay: Maggs; Fowler, Tapp, Anderson, Martin, Robinson, Birkett, Tennant, Stabb, Orr, Bird.

Referee: A.Milsom (Bristol)   *Attendance 11,000*

Match to Remember 11   30 January 1937

Exeter City 3   Leicester City 1

GIANTKILLERS once more and shades of 1931 — Exeter City were the shock

team of the FA Cup fourth round in 1937, when they defeated Leicester City after being a goal behind 14 minutes after the start.

There was plenty of drama in this gruelling contest which was fought out on a waterlogged pitch. And how well those mud-spattered, rain-soaked Exeter players stuck to their task. They held Leicester in a vice-like grip for most of the match and Jack Bowers, who must have remembered Exeter City from his Derby County days, had never been more subdued than in this match. The fact that he was marking England's centre-forward did not worry Exeter's Jack Angus one bit. Brown and Boyle were reminiscent of the old Gray-Miller partnership of days gone by.

Leicester deserved some sympathy after losing Sep Smith with the recurrence of a knee injury and this naturally put a tremendous strain on the rest of the City players.

Liddle opened the scoring after 14 minutes, heading home from a corner by O'Callaghan, but Bussey levelled the scores ten minutes later. Ten minutes from half-time, Williams put Exeter in front and, because of the bad light, the interval was curtailed to a couple of minutes. Rain began to fall in torrents and the ground became even more treacherous.

Angus, who had made his name in the 1931 Cup campaign, 'policed' Bowers relentlessly and the former England centre-forward hardly saw the ball. Sep Smith returned, but only to limp along on the left wing, unable to be of much service, and the winning goal was banged home by Williams.

Exeter City: Chesters; Brown, Boyle, Clarke, Angus, Shadwell, F.Smith, Bussey, Williams, Pope, Owen.
Leicester City: McLaren; Frame, Jones, S.Smith, Sharman, Grosvenor, Davis, O'Callaghan, Bowers, Liddle, Stubbs.

Referee: F.J.Lowe (Bristol)   *Attendance: 13,731*

Match to Remember 12   11 September 1946

Exeter City 4   Aldershot 1

THE return of League football to St James' Park, after seven years of wartime fare, brought with it a sizeable increase of public support. Indeed, an attendance of 9,500 spectators on a Wednesday afternoon was unknown before the war, apart from one or two replayed FA Cup-ties.

Exeter City won their third victory of the season to go to the top of the League. Of course, that was all very encouraging and hopes of continued success abounded. But, until the players learned how to stay the full course of 90 minutes, City supporters would be given many frights and anxious moments.

Indeed, inability to stay the course was a noticeably bad feature of their display against Aldershot, despite the fact that the match ended in the Grecians' favour.

For while the City were dominant in the first-half, when all their goals were scored, the initiative passed completely into Aldershot's hands after the change of ends and Exeter's second-half decline was almost unbelievable.

Keeping the ball on the move, the Exeter forwards outplayed the weak Aldershot defence and scored three times — through Richard Ebdon, Duggie Regan and Wright — in a hectic opening spell. There were visions of a big Exeter victory, but things did not work out like that. Anderson crowned a clever attack with a goal from close range and, although George Wardle restored the three-goal margin by shooting into an empty net a minute later, that was just about the end of Exeter City's dominance.

Distress signals were flying in the second-half. There was panic in the ranks and an alarming lack of speed and staying power. Against a team stronger than Aldershot, City would have been in real trouble.

Exeter City: Hoyle; Thompson, Long, Cutting, Hanford, Walker, Wardle, Hydes, Ebdon, Wright, Regan.
Aldershot: Gage; Rodgers, Sheppard, Brinton, White, Brown, Hobbs, Griffiths, Anderson, Fitzgerald, Hassell.

Referee: W.E. Plyer (Weymouth)   *Attendance: 9,538*

Match to Remember 13   26 November 1949

Millwall 3   Exeter City 5

ALL the West Country's soccer clubs made progress in the first round of the 1949-50 FA Cup. As expected, Torquay United won at Gravesend, whilst Yeovil Town beat Romford. But Exeter City's 5-3 victory at The Den was one of the most surprising results of the day.

The East London club were unlucky, though, as Ted Hinton, their goalkeeper, was taken to hospital with concussion before the interval and Jim Constantine, their centre-forward, fractured his shoulder later in the game.

The referee pleased impartial observers by his handling of the match, but not a section of the Millwall supporters, who were resentful at the award of a free-kick which led to the scoring of City's fourth goal. Spectators attempted to invade the pitch when the teams and officials were leaving the field. Missiles were thrown and Mr Meads left the ground heavily protected by police.

Exeter City broke one record and preserved another in this game. They won at Millwall for the first time and maintained their record of never having lost an FA Cup match in London.

The order of scoring (Exeter first) was 0-1, 1-1, 2-1, 3-1, 4-1 in the first-half. Second-half: 4-2, 4-3, 5-3.

Three of City's goals were netted by Dick Smart and the others by Duggie Regan and Archie Smith. After Hinton's injury, Chris Simmonds went into goal and was later replaced by Ernie Forrest. Exeter City's best players were Smart, Bert Hoyle, Cyril Johnstone, John Greenwood and Billy Harrower.

Millwall: Hinton; Evans, Fisher, Brolly, Reeves, Forrest, Johnson, Simmonds, Constantine, Morgan, Hodgetts.
Exeter City: Hoyle; Johnstone, Rowe, Doyle, Davey, Greenwood, Harrower, Smart, Smith, McClelland, Regan.
Referee: R.H.Meads (Wiltshire)   *Attendance: 19,487*

Match to Remember 14   27 January 1951

Exeter City 1   Chelsea 1

SIX hours before the kick-off of Exeter City's fourth-round FA Cup tie against Chelsea, a small queue of enthusiasts were waiting patiently outside the entrances to St James' Park. They were the first arrivals of the advance guard of a crowd which packed into the stand and terraces.

It was a quiet and orderly crowd, but excitement quickened when the main body of the Chelsea contingent, which numbered about 2,000, arrived in Exeter and marched to the ground headed by a chromium banner on which the printed word 'Chelsea' was surmounted by a modelled Chelsea Pensioner. By kick-off time, the crowd numbered 20,000, the biggest crowd at St James' Park since the replayed Sunderland tie of 1930-31.

Both teams received an enthusiastic welcome and there was another roar from the Chelsea section when John Harris won the toss. The first threat, however, came from Exeter, who advanced from the kick-off and had the Chelsea defence on the retreat.

Collecting Angus Mackay's pass, Doug Regan beat Bathgate and centred, but Harris headed the ball away. Forceful work by Mackay kept play at the Chelsea end and anything might have happened when a shot from Joe Lynn hit a defender and then bounced off Archie Smith's shins before going behind the goal.

When Chelsea got forward, Ray Goddard three times broke up attacks with perfectly-timed tackles. Pickering then had to save from Regan and Smith inside a minute.

Following a good move involving four men, Williams put Chelsea ahead in the 32nd minute and it was not until four minutes from the end that Regan got Exeter's equalizer.

Considering that Exeter had a goal disallowed and a penalty claim refused earlier in the game, and the fact that Mackay's effectiveness was reduced after he suffered a foot injury, City came out of the match with great credit and fully earned their right to a replay which they lost 2-0 at Stamford Bridge. The gate receipts of £3,760 for the first game were, incidentally, easily a record for St James' Park.

Exeter City: Singleton; Warren, Clark, Harrower, Goddard, Davey, McClelland, Lynn, A.Smith, Mackay, Regan
Chelsea: Pickering; Bathgate, Hughes, Armstrong, Harris, Mitchell, Gray, Campbell, R.Smith, Bentley, Williams.
Referee: R.C.Carter (Swindon)   *Attendance: 20,000*

131

Exeter City 3   Plymouth Argyle 2

AFTER a lapse of 21 years, Exeter City and Plymouth Argyle met in a Football League match. The Plymouth invasion began before midday, when several hundred supporters wearing the Argyle colours crowded into the city centre. Those early arrivals were the vanguard of the main army which arrived at lunch-time.

Three special trains were run and nearly every motor-coach in Plymouth was commissioned. Further large contingents came from other parts of Devon, whilst Cornwall and Somerset were also represented. A moderate estimate was that nearly 10,000 football supporters from outside Exeter converged upon St James' Park for the second all-ticket game there within the space of seven days.

All the ingredients possible were blended into this excellent and exciting feast of football, Exeter's doggedness and Plymouth's poise providing several thrilling goalmouth incidents and many pleasing constructive moves. It was, indeed, one of the best derby games in the long series of meetings between the Devon rivals.

The Argyle began like masters and Exeter reeled from two damaging blows, a goal by George Dews in the 27th minute and another by him 15 minutes later. But then Major allowed a centre from Charles McClelland to spin out of his hands and Angus Mackay was on hand to apply the finishing touch.

Exeter equalized early in the second-half and it was easily the best goal of match. A long ball to Doug Regan was followed by a perfect centre and Archie Smith's header flashed into the Plymouth net.

McClelland scored the winning goal from close range as Argyle's players protested that the player was offside. With half an hour remaining, Argyle staked everything on attack but the erstwhile craft was missing from these late onslaughts against a very dependable Exeter defence.

Exeter City: Singleton; Warren, Rowe, Harrower, Goddard, Lynn, McClelland, Smyth, Smith, Mackay, Regan.
Plymouth Argyle: Major; Ratcliffe, Jones, McShane, Chisholm, Porteous, Astall, Dougall, Tadman, Dews, Govan.

Referee: G.Clark (London)   *Attendance: 20,000*

Exeter City 6   Leyton Orient 1

IN gaining their biggest win for more than three seasons, Exeter City — with Brian Doyle for Ray Goddard the only change from the team which went down so heavily at Torquay on Boxing Day — were a transformed side in the second half of this encounter with Orient at St James' Park.

A goal down at the interval, the Grecians had frittered away several good chances and the initiative looked to have passed to the Londoners before City took command in no uncertain manner.

Lacking pace and strength in the muddy conditions, Exeter City were rarely dangerous before the interval and most of the play was in their half of the field. Leyton Orient took the lead through Bryant, ten minutes before half-time, but the entire picture changed in the second period when Exeter scored six times without reply.

The first two goals were from penalty-kicks, converted by Charles McClelland. Walton headed the third, then McClelland completed his hat-trick with a shot into the roof of the net from one of Dennis Hutchings's well-placed corner kicks. Ivan Armes, playing only for the third time in Exeter's team since his transfer from Norwich just before Christmas, beat Groombridge with the rebound off a free-kick taken by himself. Richard Walton rounded off a splendid afternoon's work when he banged in goal number-six.

Exeter City: Singleton; Warren, Rowe, Armes, Doyle, Davey, Hutchings, Smart, Walton, Mackay, McClelland.
Leyton Orient: Groombridge; Evans, Banner, Blizzard, Aldous, Brown, Woan, Pacey, Bryant, Rees, Blatchford.

Referee: G.W.Pullin (Bristol)   *Attendance: 7,363*

Match to Remember 17   9 January 1954

Exeter City 7   Crystal Palace 0

EXETER City, without Norman Dodgin, made two changes from the team which drew at Shrewsbury and against Palace at St James' Park the injured player-manager was replaced by Ray Goddard, who captained the side. Andy Donaldson returned to lead the attack after a five-week lay-off.

Freezing weather was followed by the milder and damp variety during the morning but conditions continued to be uninviting, and there was only a small attendance by kick-off time.

Goddard won the toss and saw his colleagues get off to a flying start. From John Knight's pass, Gerald Priestley had a clear run, but his low centre went behind Donaldson and a good chance was lost. Then neat play by the Palace was effectively countered by a sound defence in which Norman Douglass and Richard Walton were prominent.

Hugh Kelly had to move quickly to save a header from Andrews and Bailey had to do likewise when Angus Mackay connected with Knight's centre at the other end. Then Thomas, for the Londoners, and Charles McClelland, for Exeter, each came within an ace of scoring.

A corner, given away by Choules, eventually brought City a goal. McClelland's kick was headed out by a defender, Knight's overhead volley returned the ball into the goalmouth and Donaldson's head did the rest.

Another header by Donaldson put Exeter 2-0 ahead after 28 minutes and clever triangular play on the left flank might have resulted in goal number-three, but McClelland's shot went just wide.

Palace began brightly after the interval but, after McLean had broken up two attacks, Exeter took up the running again and in the 55th minute, Priestley scored City's third.

The unhappy Palace defence was bewildered by the speed and precision of the moves which kept the ball in their half. Donaldson completed his hat-trick and then Mackay got his name on the score-sheet with two cleverly-taken goals. The tally was completed by McClelland, five minutes from time.

No Third Division team would have held the City on that form and Palace must have wondered what they had come up against. It was Exeter's biggest win of the season and their first seven-goal haul for many years.

Exeter City: Kelly; Walton, Douglass, McLean, Davey, Goddard, Priestley, Knight, Donaldson, Mackay, McClelland.
Crystal Palace: Bailey; Choules, Edwards, Willard, Briggs, Simpson, Fell, Bennett, Andrews, Thomas, Hanlon.

Referee: A.Hill (Newport)   *Attendance: 7,382*

Match to Remember 18   12 April 1958

Northampton Town 9   Exeter City 0

ON 16 October 1948, Notts County beat Exeter City 9-0 with goals by Jack Sewell (4), Tommy Lawton (4) and Oscar Hold. But since then, another score of the same magnitude has gone into the City's 'black file' — this humiliation at the hands of Northampton.

Apart from listing the scorers — Tabbutt (3), Hawkins, Woan (3) and Mills (2) there was so little to be said about that latest reverse, apart from the obvious. Exeter City were overwhelmed, bemused, baffled, completely outplayed — all that and a lot more. It was a defeat for which there were no excuses and no extenuating circumstances.

The Cobblers, a strong and confident team, running into form over Easter and playing with all the self-assurance in the world, started as if they knew they were going to win. Every man in the team wanted to get on with the game, wanted to help his teammates out of any difficulties, wanted the ball. And having got it, knew there would be someone else moving into position, also wanting and calling for the ball.

So, City were only white-shirted shadows. No Exeter player, barring one, did well. Some fought ferociously, like Arnold Mitchell for instance. Some did not. The one exception was goalkeeper George Hunter, who was not in any way to be faulted for any of the goals. Not one goal was scored from a range greater than 15 yards and most of them were hammered in from far closer than that.

With Yeoman and Smith coming through untroubled to spray out their endless supply of passes, Northampton's attack consisted for nearly all the game of seven men, not five. And with hardly a second's breather, no defence could have held out for very long. City's just cracked more quickly and more often than others might have done.

The Exeter defence was so demoralized that Hunter was often faced with three Northampton forwards, all just waiting for the ball before slamming in another goal. And it was only by bare inches that the home side failed to get into double figures.

City's attacking shots? Two from Dilwyn Hill — one blocked on the line and one saved by Elvy — and one from Keith Harvey that went over the bar. That was the lot.

Northampton Town: Elvy; Claypole, Patterson, Yeoman, Gale, Smith, Mills, Tebbutt, Hawkings, Woan, Fowler.

Exeter City: Hunter; Foley, MacDonald, Mitchell, Oliver, Harvey, Stiffle, Hill, Calland, Rees, Dale.

Referee: J. Cook (Pontefract)   *Attendance: 9,465*

Match to Remember 19   21 April 1964

Exeter City 6   Chesterfield 1

'IT'S a long time', reported the *Express and Echo*, 'since a 9,000-strong crowd stood to cheer an Exeter City side off the field at St James' Park.' But that is exactly what happened on this Tuesday evening in April 1964. After 90 minutes of furious football, City swept their way to victory over Chesterfield and regained their position in the Third Division promotion race.

As the teams left the pitch, hundreds of schoolboys ran on, milling around Alan Banks. Once again the little Liverpudlian was City's hero and their inspiration. Banks was the heart and life of the City attack, pulling them from the stumbling shambles they had been against Bradford in the previous match into a hard-hitting, quick-striking goal machine.

Still nursing an injured arm, he made two goals and scored twice himself. There was no stopping him or any of the Exeter forwards as they ran up their highest score of the season. It was a game in which Exeter silenced all their critics.

135

Alan Banks (out of picture) scores one of his two goals against Chesterfield.

It was not then known exactly what City would have to do at Workington in the last match of the season to ensure promotion. Depending on the results of the other midweek games, they might need one or even no points at all. Of course, if they turned on the form they showed against Chesterfield, then they would have no worries at all.

As events turned out, City drew with Workington the following Saturday and won their promotion after years of slogging it out in the Fourth Division.

Exeter City: Barnett; Smyth, MacDonald, Mitchell, Harvey, Anderson, Rees, Banks, Curtis, Hancock, Thorne.

Chesterfield: Powell; Holmes, Poole, Clarke, Blakey, Lovie, Duncan, Frear, Hughes, Rackstraw, Armstrong.

Referee: J.Finney (Hereford)   *Attendance: 9.449*

Match to Remember 20   4 January 1969

Exeter City 1   Manchester United 3

THIS visit of Manchester United in the third round of the FA Cup was, without doubt, the most notable event ever to have taken place at St James' Park. In the

City goalkeeper Peter Shearing punches clear from Manchester United's Denis Law.

past, ten First Division sides had visited Exeter for Cup games, but never before had Exeter City and their supporters had the privilege of welcoming such an illustrious team as Manchester United, holders of the European Cup.

City, like many other clubs, had suffered in the bad winter and had not played for three weeks, apart from their defeat at Aldershot on Boxing Day. Two places off the bottom rung of the Fourth Division, they could have entertained only scant hopes of any success against United's star-studded team.

Despite the frosty ground and some variable gusts of wind, the game went according to the form-book. There was no surprise result and no 'giantkilling' this time. The biggest crowd at St James' Park since the Cup tie against Chelsea and the League game against Plymouth Argyle in 1951 saw a top-class display of scientific, thrustful football in the second-half, when United scored their last two goals.

City, to their credit, had played a whole lot better than their League placing suggested and were level at the interval, thanks to a goal from Alan Banks.

A few comparisons showed the gulf that divided Exeter City and Manchester United. The previous season 1.5 million people paid to watch United at Old Trafford. That was as many as had watched City at St James' Park in the previous ten seasons. Manchester United's profit for the same season would not only cancel out Exeter's deficit, but also leave them with something like £200,000 in the bank.

Exeter City: Shearing; Smyth, Blain, Harvey, Sharples, Newman, Corr, Banks, Pinkney, Mitten, Balson.

Manchester United: Stepney; Dunne, Burns, Fitzpatrick, James, Stiles, Best, Kidd, Charlton, Law, Sartori.

Referee: E.D.Wallace (Swindon)   *Attendance: 18,500*

137

Exeter City 6   Swansea Town 0

IT may have been that the criticisms levelled at the City players after their flop at Port Vale the previous Saturday went home with penetrating effect. Certainly their display against Swansea a few days later was nothing short of unbelievable.

The Exeter men simply went on the rampage from the word go and produced by far their best display of the season, if not for a few seasons, to eclipse Swansea Town.

Exeter outplayed the Swans and produced everything — effort, pace, running and chasing, good teamwork, bags of ability and clever football. The Grecians had the lot.

City played fast, direct football that cut the Swansea defence to pieces as five of the goals came in the first half. 'Mr Utility' himself, Jimmy Blain, was a huge success as a striker. He was moved from full-back to inside-right for this game and how well he played. He was not alone, it should be added, and on this display, no one man could be particularly singled out. It was a huge all-round team success.

Swansea, on the other hand, must have felt that the Severn Bridge had hit them. They came to St James' Park full of confidence, being unbeaten in their previous five matches. The Welshmen did occasionally show, however, that they were no mean performers themselves and they moved the ball around smartly, although City were in no mood to let them do this too often.

Blain (2), John Corr (2), John Wingate and John Mitten were Exeter City's marksmen on this night to remember.

Exeter City: Shearing; Crawford, Morris, Parker, Sharples, Balson, Corr, Blain, Wingate, Mitten, Walker.
Swansea Town: Millington; Lawrence, Gomersall, A.Williams, Rosser, Thomas, Allchurch, Slattery, H.Williams, Gwyther, Evans.

Referee: E.T.Jennings (Stourbridge)   *Attendance: 5,183*

Doncaster Rovers 0   Exeter City 3

EXETER City hauled themselves back to the Third Division for the first time in 13 years after this sparkling victory at Belle Vue and defeats for the other promotion hunters, Swansea Town and Colchester United. City clinched their place with a determined display of fast, skilful football and first-half goals by Alan Beer (2) and Tony Kellow.

Hundreds of Exeter supporters flooded into the huge Belle Vue ground, having travelled up from Devon by coach or rail. Some even hitch-hiked all the way to Yorkshire. But with Rovers having won their last ten home matches on the trot, it was realized that City had a stiff task in front of them.

Doncaster enjoyed the balance of play in the early stages and when City were penalized for a foul just outside their penalty-area, things looked far from rosy.

Exeter City, 1976-7. Back row (left to right): Peter Hatch, Bobby Saxton, Dick Key, Jack Edwards (trainer), Phil Howe, Tony Kellow, John Templeman. Middle row: Alan Hooker, Alan Beer, Keith Clapham, John Newman (manager), Tony Morrin, Nicky Jennings, John Hore. Front row: Harry Holman, Bobby Hodge, Graham Weeks, Mike Green, Mike Jordan.

However, McConville, taking the ball from Olney's free-kick, headed straight at John Baugh, who cleared.

Exeter made the perfect start when Beer scored after only 14 minutes and from that moment they were on top. Combining together expertly, with the players moving into the right position to receive the ball, they exuded confidence and when Beer netted again after 21 minutes, everyone thought it was a good goal except the referee, who disallowed it — and then gave Exeter a free-kick.

Peacock saved from Graham Weeks and Beer in succession, but there was no let-up and as Exeter maintained the pressure they went further ahead inside 34 minutes. A shrewd pass split the defence and Kellow made no mistake with a firm shot into the bottom corner. It was all Exeter now and a minute later, Beer scored their third goal.

Doncaster Rovers: Peacock; Olney, Brooks, Robinson, Reed, Taylor, Miller, McConville, O'Callaghan, Laidlaw, Murray.
Exeter City: Baugh; Templeman, Hore, Weeks, Roberts, Hatch, Hodge, Kellow, Robertson, Beer, Jennings.

Referee: J.Hunting (Leicester)

Attendance: 3,447

139

Aston Villa goalkeeper Jimmy Rimmer dives at the feet of Exeter's Nicky Jennings.

Match to Remember 23   31 August 1977

Exeter City 1   Aston Villa 3

EXETER City were put out of the Football League Cup by Aston Villa, but they could certainly hold their heads up high and feel proud. City put up a wonderfully plucky fight in front of their biggest crowd for nearly ten years.

It was not until the very last minute of the match, when Andy Gray scored his third goal, that Villa made absolutely sure of going through to the next round.

There was only one goal in it at half-time, Gray having put Villa ahead in the 22nd minute. When Gray scored again in the 58th minute, all seemed lost for Exeter, but the goal and the replacement of Graham Weeks by substitute Lammie Robertson sparked off a rousing climax by the Grecians.

Within five minutes, Robertson scored and Exeter rolled up their sleeves with renewed vigour and launched a series of attacks that had the visitors' defence reeling. From then on, the Midlanders had to soak up a huge amount of pressure, albeit without losing any material advantage, before they finally clinched the result with that late goal.

It was not the first time that Villa had played at St James' Park in a Cup tie, although the earlier occasion was too long ago for anyone to remember it. It was in the 1913-14 season, in the FA Cup, when Villa were the holders. This time they were the holders of the League Cup, having beaten Everton in the 1977 Final.

Exeter City: Baugh; Templeton, Hore, Weeks(Robertson), Saxton, Hatch, Hodge, Kellow, Bowker, Beer, Jennings.

Aston Villa: Rimmer; Gregory, Smith, Phillips, McNaught, Mortimer, Deehan, Little, Gray, Cropley, Carrodus.

Referee: D.Nippard (Bournemouth)   *Attendance: 13,768*

Match to Remember 24   18 February 1981

Exeter City 4 Newcastle United 0

IT WAS just as well that the television cameras were at St James' Park for this fifth-round FA Cup replay. Otherwise those people who were not among the crowd that packed the tiny ground would not have fully comprehended how Exeter City mauled the Magpies of Newcastle, to record a famous victory in this historic match.

United, held to a draw on their own St James' Park, made the 365-mile return journey to Devon, full of confidence. But as the drama unfolded, Peter Hatch emerged as the seasoned artist intent on stealing the scene.

After 13 minutes, a right-wing corner was volleyed goalwards by Peter Hatch, chest-high from outside the penalty area. Carr fumbled the ball and it bounced from his shoulder on to the inside of the upright before coming to rest in the net. The cheering must have been heard all over the city.

Six minutes later, Hatch took a throw-in and got the ball to Lee Roberts, who passed to Pearson. With his back to goal, Pearson hooked the ball acrobatically over his shoulder, past the bewildered Carr and into the net for Exeter's second goal. This was more than anyone expected and pandemonium reigned around the terraces.

Five minutes before half-time, Newcastle rushed out in a futile effort to throw Exeter offside, forgetting that Wharton, knocked out in a collision with Lee Roberts and lying inert on the six-yard line, was keeping the Grecians on-side. Phil Roberts nodded the ball back to Hatch, who drove it into the penalty area for Peter Rogers to find the net with the simplest of goals.

Newcastle were shattered, Exeter's supporters were triumphant and the night sky echoed with the volume of noise coming out of that little football ground. The cauldron was bubbling and about to burst — the 'joint was jumping' as they say in the jazz clubs.

In addition to the three goals, Lee Roberts, Tony Kellow and Pearson each had shots either saved or kicked off the goal-line and nothing had been seen of the Geordies as an attacking force. The game was 56 minutes old before Bond was called upon to make his first and only real save of the match.

Martyn Rogers volleyed the fourth goal after nice work between Kellow and John Sparrow, with the Newcastle defence again spreadeagled. Peter Rogers ran through unchecked to miss the near post by the narrowest of margins. There were now seven First Division clubs, plus Exeter City, left in the Cup.

Exeter City: Bond; M.Rogers, L.Roberts, P.Roberts, Delve, Sparrow, Forbes, P.Rogers, Kellow, Pearson, Hatch.

Newcastle United: Carr; Carney, Boam, Halliday, Johnson, Wharton, Trewick, Walker, Shoulder, Clark, Waddle.

Referee: R.Bridges (Deeside)   *Attendance: 17,668*

Above: *John Delve (left), Tony Kellow (on ground) and scorer Peter Rogers (9) in a goalmouth mêlée.*
Below: *Tony Kellow (right) again threatens the visitors' goal with goalkeeper Kevin Carr sprawling.*

Match to Remember 25   5 January 1986

Everton 1   Exeter City 0

THIS third-round FA Cup tie was played on a Sunday so as to avoid an unmanageable crush of people on Merseyside because Liverpool were also drawn at home. But the crowd at Goodison Park was disappointing, with only 22,000 turning up. Perhaps the local people felt that their Sunday dinners were more important than watching Exeter City.

With 82 minutes of the match played, Stevens, one of Everton's internationals, finally broke through the plucky and well-organized City defence, lashing a low, 20-yard shot beyond John Shaw's reach.

Everton, FA Cup winners in 1984 and runners-up in each of the last two Finals, were on the attack for most of the 90 minutes of the game, but their tactics lacked any hint of invention or flair. The continuous succession of lofted centres into the City penalty area played right into the hands of the tall Exeter defenders, Nick Marker, Aiden McCaffery and Keith Viney. And if any of this trio missed the ball, then Jim McNichol was always there. Strange though it may seem, Shaw had very little to do.

Apart from that goal, nothing much went right for Everton. After 23 minutes, Shaw did well to tip a shot from Sharp over the crossbar and Lineker found Exeter's goalkeeper in a similarly unbeatable mood eight minutes later.

Heath, Lineker and Richardson all wasted good chances by shooting wide, yet the best chance of the match fell to Alan Crawford, when Ratcliffe misjudged the flight of a long kick from Viney. But, with only Southall to beat, the little Exeter forward sent a weak shot straight at the goalkeeper.

The spirit of resistance and determination, the quality of their play and the stubborn refusal to accept defeat by Crawford and his men, took the First Division side by surprise. City supporters were left to wonder what the outcome might have been had the tie been played on St James' Park.

Everton: Southall; Stevens, Pointon, Ratcliffe, Van den Hauwe, Heath, Harper, Lineker, Sharp, Richardson, Wilkinson.

Exeter City: Shaw; Harrower, Viney, NcNichol, Marker, McCaffery, Ling, Jackson, Gale, Keough, Crawford.

Referee: R. Milford (Bristol)   *Attendance: 22,276*

Martin Ling (centre) gets after Everton's Pat Van den Hauwe during Exeter's narrow defeat at Goodison Park.

143

City Against Other League Clubs

Exeter City have played 83 clubs in the Football League since 1920-21. Below is City's record against each club. Some clubs changed their names (eg Clapton Orient became Leyton Orient then Orient and then Leyton Orient again) and some clubs modified their titles (eg Swansea Town became Swansea City). In all cases the current name used by each club covers all games under previous names.

		HOME					AWAY			
	P	W	D	L	F	A	W	D	L	F	A
Aberdare Athletic	12	4	1	1	11	4	1	1	4	5	14
Accrington Stanley	2	0	0	1	2	4	1	0	0	1	0
AFC Bournemouth	70	17	7	11	68	44	3	8	24	34	71
Aldershot	74	23	9	5	79	31	8	13	16	34	54
Barnsley	20	8	0	2	22	9	1	4	5	9	15
Barrow	18	4	3	2	23	11	1	5	3	8	15
Blackburn Rovers	2	1	0	0	2	0	0	1	0	1	1
Blackpool	8	2	2	0	5	1	0	2	2	1	5
Bolton Wanderers	4	0	2	0	3	3	0	0	2	0	2
Bradford	16	6	1	1	24	9	2	1	5	12	15
Bradford City	28	6	4	4	22	15	5	4	5	18	23
Brentford	72	16	10	10	65	48	8	4	24	29	73
Brighton & Hove Albion	66	16	6	11	56	52	5	5	23	39	79
Bristol City	44	8	8	6	27	17	2	6	14	20	44
Bristol Rovers	62	15	9	7	48	32	5	12	14	41	64
Burnley	16	4	2	2	12	7	0	2	6	4	18
Bury	14	3	2	2	9	11	0	2	5	8	20
Cambridge United	24	4	3	5	19	22	3	4	5	14	17
Cardiff City	24	7	2	3	18	11	2	2	8	14	33
Carlisle United	28	7	4	3	20	11	2	4	8	15	23
Charlton Athletic	22	8	2	1	22	14	0	2	9	2	14
Chester City	44	13	7	2	39	16	8	3	11	28	35
Chesterfield	30	5	6	4	28	20	3	3	9	11	23
Colchester United	54	14	8	5	47	32	8	6	13	26	47
Coventry City	34	10	2	5	39	18	1	7	9	13	35
Crewe Alexandra	40	11	3	6	38	23	3	8	9	17	27
Crystal Palace	60	15	6	9	65	44	4	11	15	26	54
Darlington	38	8	7	4	30	19	4	5	10	15	29
Doncaster Rovers	34	10	1	6	24	17	2	3	12	17	37
Fulham	12	4	0	2	8	10	1	2	3	7	13
Gateshead	4	1	1	0	3	2	1	0	1	2	2
Gillingham	90	24	14	7	88	52	10	13	22	61	80
Grimsby Town	20	5	2	3	21	13	2	1	7	8	19
Halifax Town	22	7	3	1	17	8	4	2	5	12	14
Hartlepool United	44	17	4	1	47	14	4	9	9	27	32
Hereford United	16	6	2	0	13	5	1	2	5	6	15
Huddersfield Town	10	3	0	2	11	9	2	2	1	4	7
Hull City	12	2	1	3	9	13	0	2	4	7	16
Ipswich Town	22	4	4	3	15	12	2	4	5	13	18

		HOME					AWAY			
	P	W	D	L	F	A	W	D	L	F	A
Leyton Orient	52	12	7	7	52	38	6	6	14	37	66
Lincoln City	40	8	4	8	25	18	3	6	11	23	44
Luton Town	40	7	5	8	32	33	2	5	13	20	54
Maidstone United	2	1	0	0	2	0	0	0	1	0	1
Mansfield Town	32	7	4	5	23	17	3	4	9	21	32
Merthyr Town	20	8	2	0	26	8	3	2	5	13	21
Millwall	64	18	6	8	61	46	2	6	24	27	81
Newport County	94	26	12	9	96	52	10	13	24	46	76
Northampton Town	88	22	12	10	83	55	4	14	26	50	110
Norwich City	52	14	5	7	44	26	6	7	13	24	53
Nottingham Forest	4	0	1	1	0	5	0	1	1	2	7
Notts County	30	3	8	4	20	23	2	5	8	12	35
Oldham Athletic	18	6	1	2	21	14	2	2	5	11	18
Oxford United	20	5	3	2	17	11	4	4	2	12	8
Peterborough United	34	8	3	6	27	24	2	10	5	20	29
Plymouth Argyle	42	9	8	4	29	22	3	7	11	18	40
Portsmouth	16	1	4	3	9	12	1	1	6	8	22
Port Vale	36	10	3	5	30	22	2	4	12	15	37
Preston North End	12	5	0	1	17	7	0	3	3	6	9
Queen's Park Rangers	58	10	10	9	40	30	4	7	18	23	56
Reading	74	17	6	14	69	57	3	6	28	32	84
Rochdale	34	9	5	3	31	16	3	6	8	13	25
Rotherham United	16	3	3	2	6	7	1	1	6	4	14
Scarborough	6	3	0	0	5	2	1	0	2	4	6
Scunthorpe United	*33	10	6	1	34	15	1	3	12	13	38
Sheffield United	8	1	1	2	5	7	0	1	3	4	11
Sheffield Wednesday	6	2	1	0	5	3	1	0	2	3	4
Shrewsbury Town	26	7	3	3	20	10	3	3	7	13	23
Southend United	98	21	17	11	78	59	11	14	24	37	85
Southampton	14	3	2	2	10	9	0	1	6	2	23
Southport	26	7	4	2	19	13	3	4	6	12	19
Stockport County	38	14	2	3	37	19	3	5	11	17	23
Swansea City	36	10	4	4	33	16	3	3	12	12	28
Swindon Town	78	16	12	11	65	50	5	9	25	45	91
Thames	4	2	0	0	8	4	0	1	1	0	1
Torquay United	78	17	15	7	74	39	15	8	16	56	57
Tranmere Rovers	24	7	0	5	18	12	2	3	7	15	21
Walsall	58	15	5	9	49	42	6	5	18	40	71
Watford	76	19	8	11	71	48	7	8	23	34	71
Wigan Athletic	4	1	1	0	3	2	0	1	1	1	2
Wimbledon	6	1	0	2	2	6	0	2	1	4	5
Wolverh'ton Wanderers	4	0	0	2	3	7	0	1	1	2	5
Workington	36	12	4	2	24	10	4	3	11	16	33
Wrexham	28	6	5	3	25	18	2	6	6	10	22
York City	26	10	0	3	25	13	4	2	7	18	29
TOTALS	2803	711	350	341	2472	1630	246	368	787	1404	2693

* Scunthorpe match in April 1974 not played because Exeter could not raise a team.

Exeter City in the Football League 1920-21 to 1989-90

	Pos	P	W	D	L	F	A	Pts	Top Goalscorer
				EAST DEVON LEAGUE					
1904-05	1st	14	11	2	1	40	17	24	...................E.Reid 16
				PLYMOUTH & DISTRICT LEAGUE					
1905-06	6th	12	3	1	8	16	27	7	....................E.Reid 7
1906-07	9th	24	10	2	12	42	53	22	...................Tipping 6
1907-08	5th	26	15	2	9	50	50	*34	...............E.Eveleigh 15

Exeter City v Millbrook Rangers played for 4 points, Exeter won 3-0.

	Pos	P	W	D	L	F	A	Pts	Top Goalscorer
				SOUTHERN LEAGUE FIRST DIVISION					
1908-09	6th	40	18	6	16	56	65	42	.....................J.Bell 23
1909-10	18th	42	14	6	22	60	69	34	.....................J.Bell 15
1910-11	13th	38	14	9	15	51	53	37	.....................J.Bell 14
1911-12	15th	38	11	11	16	48	62	33	...................A.Rutter 10
1912-13	7th	38	18	8	12	48	44	44	...............E.Crompton 10
1913-14	12th	38	10	16	12	39	38	36	...............F.Whittaker 13
1914-15	11th	38	15	8	15	50	41	38	.............W.Goodwin 23
1919-20	10th	42	17	9	16	57	52	43	.............W.Goodwin 17
				DIVISION THREE SOUTH					
1920-21	19th	42	10	15	17	39	54	35	......C.Vowles 9, W.Wright 9
1921-22	21st	42	11	12	19	38	59	34	...............C.Vowles 11
1922-23	20th	42	13	7	22	47	84	33	............H.Crockford 17
1923-24	16th	42	15	7	20	37	52	37	....................H.Kirk 8
1924-25	7th	42	19	9	14	59	48	47	...................H.Kirk 12
1925-26	20th	42	15	5	22	72	70	35	.............W.Lievesley 18
1926-27	12th	42	15	10	17	76	73	40	............H.Blackmore 25
1927-28	8th	42	17	12	13	70	60	46	...................F.Dent 26
1928-29	21st	42	9	11	22	67	88	29	...............E.Cameron 9
1929-30	16th	42	12	11	19	67	73	35	...........C.Hemingway 19
1930-31	13th	42	17	8	17	84	90	42	...................P.Varco 25
1931-32	7th	42	20	7	15	77	62	47	H.Houghton 16, P.Varco 16
1932-33	2nd	42	24	10	8	88	48	58	.............F.Whitlow 33
1933-34	9th	42	16	11	15	68	57	43	....................S.Hurst 14
1934-35	11th	42	16	9	17	70	75	41	H.Poulter 16, F.Wrightson 16
1935-36	22nd	42	8	11	23	59	93	27	..........J.McCambridge 14
1936-37	21st	42	10	12	20	59	88	32	.............R.Williams 29
1937-38	17th	42	13	12	17	57	70	38	..................H.Bowl 18
1938-39	14th	42	13	14	15	65	82	40	..................H.Bowl 24
1946-47	15th	42	15	9	18	60	69	39	..................R.Ebdon 16
1947-48	11th	42	15	11	16	55	63	41	................D.Regan 11
1948-49	12th	42	15	10	17	63	76	40	................D.Regan 14
1949-50	16th	42	14	11	17	63	75	39	.................R.Smart 13
1950-51	14th	46	18	6	22	62	85	42	..................A.Smith 22
1951-52	23rd	46	13	9	24	65	86	35	................A.Mackay 20
1952-53	17th	46	13	14	19	61	71	40	..................J.Dailey 13
1953-54	9th	46	20	8	18	68	58	48	............C.McClelland 19
1954-55	22nd	46	11	15	20	47	73	37	.............C.McClelland 9
1955-56	16th	46	15	10	21	58	77	40	..................R.Burke 10
1956-57	21st	46	12	13	21	61	79	37	..................J.Currie 14
1957-58	24th	46	11	9	26	57	99	31	...............E.Calland 15

146

	Pos	P	W	D	L	F	A	Pts	Top Goalscorer
				DIVISION FOUR					
1958-59	5th	46	23	11	12	87	61	57	...............E.Calland 27
1959-60	9th	46	19	11	16	80	70	49	..................G.Rees 17
1960-61	21st	46	14	10	22	66	94	38	..................G.Rees 14
1961-62	18th	44	13	11	20	62	77	37	..................R.Carter 19
1962-63	17th	46	16	10	20	57	77	42	................R.Carter 19
1963-64	4th	46	20	18	8	62	37	58	................A.Banks 18
				DIVISION THREE					
1964-65	17th	46	12	17	17	51	52	41	.................D.Curtis 9
1965-66	22nd	46	12	11	23	53	79	35	................A.Banks 17
				DIVISION FOUR					
1966-67	14th	46	14	15	17	50	60	43	...............R.McNeil 11
1967-68	20th	46	11	16	19	45	65	38	....................J.Corr 7
1968-69	17th	46	16	11	19	66	65	43	................A.Banks 13
1969-70	18th	46	14	11	21	57	59	39	................J.Gadston 10
1970-71	9th	46	17	14	15	67	68	48	................A.Banks 21
1972-73	15th	46	16	11	19	61	68	43	................F.Binney 17
1972-73	8th	46	18	14	14	57	51	50	................F.Binney 28
1973-74	10th	*45	18	8	19	58	55	44	................F.Binney 25
			*Scunthorpe United v Exeter City not played						
1974-75	9th	46	19	11	16	60	63	49	...............K.Bowker 18
1975-76	7th	46	18	14	14	56	47	50	..................A.Beer 20
1976-77	2nd	46	25	12	9	70	46	62	..................A.Beer 21
				DIVISION THREE					
1977-78	17th	46	15	14	17	49	59	44	................A.Kellow 14
1978-79	9th	46	17	15	14	61	56	49	...............K.Bowker 11
1979-80	8th	46	19	10	17	60	68	48	................D.Pullar 10
1980-81	11th	46	16	13	17	62	66	45	................A.Kellow 25
1981-82	18th	46	*16	9	21	71	84	57	................A.Kellow 21
			*Three points for a win from now on						
1982-83	19th	46	14	12	20	81	104	54	................S.Neville 17
1983-84	24th	46	6	15	25	50	84	33	.................R.Pratt 16
				DIVISION FOUR					
1984-85	18th	46	13	14	19	57	79	53	.................R.Pratt 20
1985-86	21st	46	13	15	18	47	59	54	.................A.Kellow 9
1986-87	14th	46	11	23	12	53	49	56	................A.Kellow 15
1987-88	22nd	46	11	13	22	53	68	46	..............D.Edwards 12
1988-89	13th	46	18	6	22	65	68	60	...........D.Rowbotham 20
1989-90	1st	46	28	5	13	83	48	89	...........D.Rowbotham 20

1904-05 East Devon Senior League

Secretary: S.H.Thomas

1	Sep	10	(h)	110 Battery RA	W	2-1	Eveleigh, Thomas	600
2		17	(a)	Belmont *	W	3-1	Davidson, Sellick, Eveleigh	
3	Oct	8	(h)	St Luke's College	W	3-1	Reid 3 (1 pen)	400
4		15	(a)	111 Battery RA	W	5-1	Reid 5	
5		29	(a)	110 Battery RA	D	3-3	Sellick, Thomas, Reid (pen)	
6	Nov	5	(a)	Dawlish	W	3-2	Coles, Sellick, Thomas	
7	Dec	17	(a)	Friernhay	W	4-2	Reid, Thomas 2, Sellick	
8		24	(h)	Newton Town	W	3-1	Sellick, Thomas, Reid	500
9		31	(a)	Newton Town	W	1-0	Ashford (pen)	800
10	Feb	4	(h)	112 Battery RA	W	2-0	Sellick, Thomas	1,500
11		18	(a)	St Luke's College	W	3-0	Reid 2 (1 pen), Thomas	500
12	Mar	18	(a)	112 Battery RA	D	2-2	Reid (pen), Thomas	1,500
13	Apr	1	(h)	Dawlish	L	2-4	Russell (pen), Thomas	
14		8	(h)	Friernhay	W	6-0	Davidson, Reid 2, Thomas 2, Andrews (pen)	1,300
15		22	(h)	111 Battery RA	W	1-0	Andrews	

FINAL LEAGUE POSITION: 1st in East Devon Senior League

Appearances

*Belmont withdrew, match excluded from results.

Goals

East Devon Challenge Cup

1	Jan	28	(h)	Belmont	W	4-0
2	Feb	25	(h)	Exmouth U	W	4-1
SF	Mar	25	(n†)	Newtown T	L	1-2

†Played at Dawlish

Friendly matches

Sep	24	(h)	Torquay U	W	5-0
Oct	1	(a)	112 Battery RA	L	0-3
	22	(h)	N Devon School	W	8-0
Nov	12	(h)	Devon Cnty School	W	5-1
	19	(a)	Crediton G School	W	4-0
	26	(h)	111 Battery RA	W	1-0
Dec	3	(a)	Dawlish	W	3-1
	7	(h)	Exmouth U	W	3-2
	26	(h)	Plym Garr Choir	W	6-3
	29	(a)	Holsworthy	L	0-3
Jan	7	(h)	Belmont	W	4-0
	21	(a)	111 Battery RA	D	1-1
Feb	11	(a)	Torquay U	W	6-3
Mar	4	(h)	111 Battery RA	W	8-0
	11	(h)	Friernhay	W	6-2
Apr	15	(a)	Exmouth U	W	4-1
	24	(n‡)	Triumph (Plym)	W	2-0

‡Played at the County Ground, Exeter.

Match	Peters	Ashford	Aplin	Wallage	Davidson	Morgan	Sellick	Thomas	Reid	Eveleigh	Horner	Russell	Keech	Campbell	Smeath	Coles	Fenwick	Andrews	Bailey	Wells	Henderson	Sturge
1	1	2	3	4	5	6	7	8	9	10	11											
2																						
3	1	2		4	5	6	7	8	9	10	3	11										
4	1	2		4	5	6	7	8	9	11	3		10									
5	1	2		4	5	6	7	8	9	11			10	3								
6	1	2			5	6	7	8		10	3				9	11	4					
7	1	2		4	5	6	7	8	9	10	3	11										
8	1	2			5	6	7	8	9	10	3	11		4								
9	1	2		4	5	6	7	8		10	3	9				11						
10	1	2		4	5	6	7	8	9	11	3	10										
11	1	2		4	5	6	7	8	9		3	10				11						
12	1			4	5	6	7	8	9		2	11					3	10				
13	1			4		6	10	8			2	9		3					5	7		11
14	1			4	5	6	7	8	9		2	11					3	10				
15				4	5	6	7	8	9		2	11					3	10			1	
Totals	13	10	1	12	13	14	13	14	11	9	12	10	2	4	1	3	4	3	1	2	1	1
Goals		1			1				5	12	16	1		1			1	2				

Goals scored by Davidson, Sellick and Eveleigh in the excluded Match 2 not included in totals.

149

1905-06   Plymouth & District League

Secretary: S.H.Thomas

#				Opponent	Result	Scorers	
1	Sep	16	(a)	Torpoint	L 2-3	Andrews, Reid	
2		30	(a)	Plymouth A Res	L 0-6		
3	Oct	14	(a)	Essa	W 2-0	Fenwick, Sellick	
4	Dec	2	(h)	Plymouth A Res	L 1-4	Sellick	2,000
5		16	(a)	Green Waves	L 0-1		
6	Jan	20	(a)	Millbrook Ran	L 1-4	Reid	1,000
7	Feb	3	(h)	Tavistock	D 1-1	Thomas	800
8	Mar	3	(h)	Millbrook Ran	W 2-0	Reid, Andrews	1,500
9		31	(h)	Torpoint	L 1-3	Andrews	
10	Apr	7	(h)	Tavistock	W 4-1	Reid 3, Andrews	
11		14	(h)	Essa	L 1-2	Thomas	
12		28	(h)	Green Waves	L 1-2	Reid	

FINAL LEAGUE POSITION: 6th in Plymouth & District League

Appearances
Goals

East Devon Challenge Cup

2	Feb	24	(h)	Bovey Tr St John's	W 10-0
SF	Mar	24	(n*)	United Batteries RA	L 1-3

*Played at Magdalen Road

Friendly matches

	Sep	23	(h)	112 Battery RA	W 3-1
	Oct	7	(h)	United Batteries	D 2-2
		21	(h)	Royal Marines	W 6-2
	Nov	4	(a)	United Batteries	W 2-0
		11	(a)	112 Battery RA	L 2-3
		25	(h)	Royal Marines	D 2-2
	Dec	9	(h)	East Devon League	L 1-6
		23	(h)	R.F.A.	L 2-4
		24	(h†)	Plymouth A	W 3-2
		26	(a)	Pympton	L 1-2
		30	(a)	Holsworthy	W 7-2
	Jan	6	(a)	Taunton Casuals	L 0-1
		13	(h)	Exmouth U	W 4-1
		27	(h)	Millbrook Ran	L 0-2
	Feb	10	(h)	Holsworthy	W 3-1
		17	(a)	St Luke's	L 1-4
	Mar	17	(h)	United Batteries	D 2-2
	Apr	16	(h)	Plympton	D 2-2
		18	(h)	111 Battery RA	L 2-3

†Played at the County Ground, Exeter.

Sturge	Reid	Wells	Morgan	Bastin	Fitzgerald	Sellick	Thomas	Davidson	Andrews	Russell	Clarke	Fenwick	Keech	Kendrick	Robinson	Brooks	Reed	Selley	West	Horner	Hill	Richardson	
1	2	3	4	5	6	7	8	9	10	11													1
1	9	2	4			7		5	10	11	3	6	8										2
1	9	2	4			7		5	10	11	3	6		8									3
	9	3	4			7	8	5	10	11		2			1	6							4
1	9	2	4		3		8	5	10	11						6	9						5
	9	3	2		4		8	5	10	11						6	7	1					6
1	9	2	4			7	8	5	10	11	3					6							7
1	9	2	4			7	8	5	10	11	3					6							8
1	11	2	4			7	8	6	9	10	3					5							9
1	9	2			6		8	5	10	11	3					4			7				10
1	9	6				7	8	5	10	11	2					4				3			11
1	10		4	6		7	8	5		11	2										3	9	12
10	12	11	10	3	3	9	10	12	11	12	2	8	2	1	1	8	2	1	1	1	1	1	
	7					2	2			4		1											

1906-07 Plymouth & District League

Secretary: S.H.Thomas

1	Oct	6	(a)	D.C.L.I.	W	4-3	Tipping, Massey, Turner 2	
2		13	(h)	Plymouth A Res	L	3-5	Tipping 3	3,000
3		20	(a)	2nd Devons	L	2-4	Reid, Turner	
4	Nov	3	(a)	Rifle Brigade	L	1-4	Tipping	2,000
5		10	(h)	Millbrook Ran	W	2-1	Youlden 2	300
6		17	(h)	Royal Marines	L	1-4	Tipping	
7	Dec	8	(h)	St Michael's	W	1-0	Reid	200
8		22	(h)	Essa	D	1-1	Fenwick (pen)	700
9		26	(h)	Gunnislake	L	1-2	Massey	
10	Jan	5	(h)	Torpoint	W	3-2	Massey 2, Wilson	3,000
11		12	(a)	Millbrook Ran	W	3-0	Ebery, Thomas, Youlden	
12		19	(h)	D.C.L.I.	W	2-0	Youlden, Massey	1,000
13		26	(a)	St Michael's	W	3-1	Thomas, Aspey, Sellick	
14	Feb	2	(a)	Torpoint	L	1-8	Eveleigh	
15		9	(a)	Royal Marines	L	1-3	Reid	
16		16	(a)	Plymouth A Res	L	1-3	Wilson	2,000
17		23	(h)	Green Waves	L	0-2		
18	Mar	9	(a)	Gunnislake	D	2-2	Singlehurst, Reid	
19		16	(h)	Tavistock	W	2-1	Fenwick, Pryce	
20		23	(h)	Rifle Brigade	W	3-0	Reid, Pryce 2	
21		30	(a)	Green Waves	L	0-3		
22	Apr	1	(h)	2nd Devons	L	0-1		
23		6	(a)	Essa	L	0-1		
24		20	(a)	Tavistock	W	5-2	Sellick 3, Russell 2	

FINAL LEAGUE POSITION: 9th in Plymouth & District League

Appearances
Goals

Friendly matches

Sep	8	(h)	RAUnited	L	1-4
	15	(a)	112 Battery RA	L	1-3
	22	(a)	Barnstaple	W	7-0
	29	(h)	Taunton Casuals	W	5-2
Dec	1	(h)	St Luke's College	L	0-1
	15	(a)	Holsworthy	L	2-3
	25	(h*)	Green Waves	W	3-2
	27	(a)	North Devon	L	1-3
Mar	2	(h)	Holsworthy	D	2-2
Apr	3	(h*)	15 Brigade RA	L	3-6
	13	(h)	Friernhay	W	2-0

*Played at the County Ground, Exeter.

Season appearance and goalscoring grid (players across the top, matches down the side; player numbers indicate the shirt worn in each match).

Antliff	Wells W	Fenwick	Muncey	Davidson	Bastin	Sellick	Massey	Tipping	Turner	Andrews	Reid	Smith	Thomas	Russell	Sturge	Vibart	Youlden	Hyde	Robins	Lintott	Henry	Oliver	Warner	Hill	Morgan	Wilson	Ebery	Wells E	Aspey	Eveleigh	Kelly	Campbell	Brown	Haswell	Hawke	Singlehurst	Chapman	Tomlinson	Pryce	Coates	Vansinter	
1	2	3	4	5	6	7	8	9	10	11																																1
1	2	3	4	5		7	8	9	10	11	6																															2
	2	3	4	5	6	7			10		8	1	9	11																												3
	3	2	4	10	5	7	9	8	6		11		1																													4
	3	2	6		5	7	9	8			4		11			1	10																									5
	2	3	5	4	8	9	7	10			6		11		1																											6
	9	3	4	8	6	7			10				1								2	5	11																			7
	3	2	6	5	4	7	9		10		11		8			1																										8
	3	2	10		6	7	8				11		9	1		4	5																									9
	5	2	6			7	9				11		8			1									3	4	10															10
	2	3	4			7	9				10		1			8								5	6			11														11
	5	3	4		6	7	9				11		8			1	10						2																			12
	5	3	4			7	8				6		9			1													2	10	11											13
	5	3	6			7	9						8			1							2							10		4	11									14
		3	6			7	8				11					1							2	9						4		10		5								15
	5	3	4			7	9				6		8			1							2	10					11													16
	2	3			6	7	9									1							11	10					4	5							8					17
1	3	2	4			7					6		9	11															5	10							8					18
	2	3	4		11	6	8																						5	10								7	1	9		19
	3	2	4			5	7																						6	10						11	8	9	1			20
	3	2	6			9	4																						5							11	8	7	1	10		21
	3		6			7	9				10		8	11															4	5									1		2	22
	3		4			9					11																		5	6							8	7	1	10	2	23
	2	4	6			7	9				11																		5								8	3	1	10		24
3	23	21	18	8	16	23	13	5	8	2	18	1	12	9	1	12	3	1	1	1	1	1	5	5	2	3	1	1	9	7	1	2	1	1	1	3	6	4	5	4	2	
	2				4	5	6	3			5		2	2			4						5		2	1			1	1						1			3			

153

1907-08 Plymouth & District League

Secretary: S.H.Thomas

1	Sep	21	(a)	Torpoint	L 0-6	
2	Oct	5	(h)	Gunnislake	W 7-2 Eveleigh 2, Fenwick, Mudd 4	
3		12	(a)	Gunnislake	L 1-3 Mudd	
4		19	(h)	Plymouth A Res	L 0-5	2,000
5		26	(a)	Oreston R	L 1-3 Letheren	
6	Nov	2	(h)	Looe	L 1-3 Eveleigh	
7		9	(a)	Essa	W 1-0 Singlehurst	
8		16	(h)	Plympton	W 2-1 Drew, Eveleigh	
9		23	(a)	St Michael's	D 1-1 Eveleigh	
10		30	(a)	Tavistock	W 1-0 Mudd	
11	Jan	4	(h)	Torpoint	L 1-3 Eveleigh	
12		11	(a)	Plympton	D 0-0	
13		18	(a)	Woodland Villa	W 2-1 Eveleigh, Singlehurst	
14		25	(h)	Green Waves	L 0-2	700
15	Feb	1	(h)	Royal Marines	W 2-1 Banks, Singlehurst	
16		22	(h)	St Michael's	W 1-0 Eveleigh	300
17		29	(a)	Plymouth A Res	L 1-8 Massey	500
18	Mar	7	(h)	Tavistock	W 3-1 Eveleigh 2, Massey	
19		14	(h)	Millbrook Ran	W 3-0 Massey 3	
20		21	(a)	Royal Marines	W 3-1 Massey 2, Singlehurst	
21		28	(h)	2nd Devons	W 2-1 Badcock, Singlehurst	
22	Apr	4	(h)	Woodland Villa	W 3-0 Eveleigh, Massey 2	
23		11	(h)	Essa	W 6-1 Eveleigh 2, Sellick 2, Singlehurst 2	500
24		18	(a)	Looe	L 1-4 Singlehurst	
25		20	(h)	2nd Devons	W 4-1 Singlehurst, Banks, Sellick, Eveleigh	
26		25	(h)	Oreston R	W 3-2 Massey, Eveleigh, Singlehurst	

FINAL LEAGUE POSITION: 5th in Plymouth and District League

Appearances
Goals

Results of Other Matches

Sep	7	(h)	Friernhay	D 2-2	
	14	(h)	Exmouth U	W 2-1	
	28	(h)	1st Rifle Brigade	L 1-3	
Dec	7	(h)	St Luke's College	W 1-0	
	21	(h)	Yeovil Casuals	W 1-0	
	25	(h*)	East Devon	D 3-3	
	26	(h)	Friernhay	W 2-1	
Feb	8	(h)	Exmouth U	W 4-1	
	15	(h)	15 Brigade RA	L 1-3	

*Played at the County Ground, Exeter.

Exeter City v Millbrook Rangers on 14 December was abandoned at three-quarter time. The return match was not played and the second match (at Exeter) was played for four points. The twice-postponed match with Green Waves was also played for four points on 25 January and the return match not played. Both matches with 2nd Devons played on Exeter City's ground.

Antliff	Wells E	Fenwick	Oliver	Wells W	Letheren	Singlehurst	Sellick	Aspey	Mudd	Eveleigh	Warner	Chenneour	Clark	Hyde	Dyer	Blunden	Jones	Thomas	Bastin	Drew	Goodchild	Sercombe	Massey	Ashford	Banks	Murch	Smith	Johnson	Parsons	Stoneman	Badcock	#
1	2	3	4	5	6	7	8	9	10	11																						1
1		3	6	2	4	7			9	8	5	10	11																			2
		3		4	7	5	9	8	6	10	11	1	2																			3
1		2		3		7		5	4	8	6	10			9	11																4
1		3		4	5	7	10	9	8	6			11		2																	5
1		2		5	4	7		9	8	6			11		3					10												6
		2		1	4	8	7		10	9	6		11		3					5												7
		2		1	4	8	7			9	6		11		3			5	10													8
		2		1	4	8	7			9	6		11		3			10	5													9
	2			1	4	8	7		10	9	5				3					6	11											10
		5		1	6	8	7			9					2					11			10	3	4							11
		5		1	6	8	7			9					2					11			10	3	4							12
				1	4	8	7		5	9					2					11			10	3	6							13
	2			1	4	8	7		5	9										11			10	3	6							14
	6	2		1	10	7			5	8										11			9	3	4							15
	3	2	6	1	4	10	7		5	8										11			9									16
				1	4	11	7		5														10	2	6	3	8	9				17
	2			1	4	10	6			8							11						9		5				3	7		18
	3	2		1	4	10	7		5	8													9		6						11	19
	3	2		1	4	10	7		5	8													9		6						11	20
	3	2		1	4	10	7		5	8													9		6						11	21
	3	2		1	4	10	7		5	8													9		6						11	22
	3	2		1	4	10	7		5	8													9		6						11	23
	2	6		1	10	7			5	8													9	3	4						11	24
	2	5		1	10	7				8					4							6	9	3							11	25
	2	6	1	3	10	7			5	8													9		4						11	26
5	12	18	8	25	22	26	21	4	20	25	9	3	7	1	11	1	1	2	2	9	1	1	17	7	15	1	1	1	1	1	8	
	1				1	10	3		6	15										1			10	2							1	

1908-09 Southern League

Manager: A.Chadwick

1	Sep	2	(a)	Millwall	D 2-2 Bell 2	2,500
2		5	(h)	Bristol R	D 3-3 Watson, Parnell 2	8,000
3		12	(a)	Watford	L 1-3 Bell	4,000
4		19	(h)	Norwich C	W 3-2 McGuigan, Chadwick (pen), Bell	5,000
5		26	(a)	Reading	W 2-1 Bell, Watson	7,000
6	Oct	7	(a)	Swindon T	L 1-2 Copestake	3,000
7		10	(a)	Leyton O	L 2-4 McGuigan 2	5,000
8		14	(h)	Southampton	L 1-2 McGuigan	6,000
9		24	(a)	Brighton & HA	W 2-1 McGuigan 2	6,500
10		31	(h)	Crystal P	D 1-1 Bell	10,000
11	Nov	11	(h)	Plymouth A	W 2-1 Bell 2	7,000
12		14	(h)	Luton T	W 2-1 Bell, McGuigan	4,000
13		16	(a)	Brentford	W 2-0 McGuigan, Copestake	7,000
14		28	(h)	Portsmouth	W 4-1 Chadwick (pen), Copestake, McGuigan, Bell	5,000
15	Dec	12	(a)	Northampton T	L 0-1	6,000
16		19	(h)	New Brompton	L 1-3 Bell	5,000
17		25	(h)	Millwall	W 2-1 Bell, McGuigan	11,500
18	Jan	2	(a)	Bristol R	L 1-5 McGuigan	6,000
19		9	(h)	Watford	W 1-0 Watson	6,000
20		23	(a)	Norwich C	L 0-2	7,000
21		30	(h)	Reading	W 5-1 Bell 2, Copestake, Watson, McGuigan	5,000
22	Feb	8	(h)	Coventry C	L 0-3	2,500
23		13	(h)	Leyton	W 3-1 Bell 3	4,500
24		20	(a)	Queen's Park R	D 1-1 Bell	8,000
25		24	(h)	Queen's Park R	W 1-0 Parnell	5,000
26		27	(h)	Brighton & HA	W 1-0 Bell	4,500
27	Mar	6	(a)	Crystal P	D 0-0	1,000
28		8	(h)	Southend U	W 2-1 McGuigan, Bell	1,500
29		10	(a)	Plymouth A	L 0-4	8,000
30		13	(h)	Brentford	L 1-2 Bell	4,000
31		17	(h)	Swindon T	L 1-4 McGuigan (pen)	2,000
32		20	(a)	Luton T	W 2-0 Copestake, Watson	4,500
33		22	(a)	Coventry C	W 1-0 McGuigan	1,000
34		24	(a)	Southend U	D 0-0	5,000
35	Apr	1	(a)	West Ham U	L 1-4 McGuigan	9,000
36		3	(a)	Portsmouth	L 0-2	10,000
37		13	(a)	Southampton	L 0-2	5,000
38		17	(h)	Northampton T	W 2-1 Drain, Watson	8,500
39		21	(h)	West Ham U	W 1-0 Copestake	5,000
40		24	(a)	New Brompton	L 1-3 Bell	4,000

FINAL LEAGUE POSITION: 6th in Southern League, Division One.

Appearances
Goals

FA Cup

Q1	Oct	3	(h)	Weymouth	W 14-0
Q2		17	(a)	Longfleet St Mary	D 1-1
R		21	(h)	Longfleet St Mary	W 10-1
Q3	Nov	7	(h)	Whiteheads	W 4-0
Q4		21	(a)	Kingswood R	W 2-0
Q5	Dec	5	(a)	Barnet Alston	W 3-0
1	Jan	16	(a)	Wrexham	D 1-1
R		20	(h)	Wrexham	W 2-1
2	Feb	6	(a)	Plymouth A	L 0-2

Fletcher	Craig	Bulcock	Ambler	Johnson	Wake	Parnell	Watson	McGuigan	Bell	White	Tierney	Drain	Chadwick	Copestake	Robinson	Crelley	Plant	Banks	#
1	2	3	4	5	6	7	8	9	10	11									1
1	2	3	4	5		7	8		10	11	6	9							2
1	2	3	4	5	6	7	8	9	10	11									3
1	2	3	4		6	7	8	9	10				5	11					4
1	2	3	4		6	7	8	9	10				5	11					5
1	2	3	4		6	7	8	9	10				5	11					6
1	2	3			6		8	9		11		10	5	7					7
1	2	3		4	6	7	8	9	10				5	11					8
1	2	3	4	6			8	9	10	7			5	11					9
1	2	3	4	5	6		8	9	10	7				11					10
	2	3	4	6			8	9	10	7			5	11	1				11
	2	3	4	6			8	9	10	7			5	11	1				12
	2	3	4		6		8	9	10	7			5	11	1				13
	2	3	4	6			8	9	10	7			5	11	1				14
	2		4	6		7	8	9	10				5	11	1	3			15
	2	3	4	5	6	7	8	9	10					11	1				16
	2		4	6		7	8	9	10				5	11	1	3			17
	2	3	4		6		8	9	10	7			5	11	1				18
	2	3	4	5	6	7	8	9	10					11	1				19
	2		4	5	6	7	8	9	10					11	1	3			20
	2	3	4	5	6	7	8	9	10					11	1				21
	2	3	4	5	6	7	8	9	10					11	1				22
	2		4		6	7	8	9		11		10	5		1	3			23
	2		4		6	7	8	9		11		10	5		1	3			24
	2		4		6	7	8	9		11		10	5		1	3			25
	2		4		6	7	8	9		11		10	5		1	3			26
	2	3	4		6		8	9		7		10	5	11	1				27
	2	3	4		6	7	8		10		9		5	11	1				28
1	3	2		4	6	7	8		10		5	9	1						29
	2			4	6	7	8		10		5	9		11	1	3			30
	2			4	6		8	9	10	7	5			1	3	11			31
	2			4	6	7	8	9	10		5			11	1	3			32
	2			4	6	7	8	9	10		5			11	1	3			33
	2			4			8	9	10	7	5			11	1	3	6		34
	2			4	6	7	8	9	10		5			11	1	3			35
	2				6	7	8	9	10	11	5			4	1	3			36
	2		4	5	6	7	8		10			9		11	1	3			37
	2		4	5	6	7	8		10			9		11	1	3			38
	2		4	5	6	7	8		10			9		11	1	3			39
			2		6	7	8		10		5	9		11	1	3	4		40
11	38	23	35	23	30	29	39	28	39	19	11	14	19	32	29	18	1	2	
						3	6	16	22		1	2	6						

1909-10 Southern League

Manager: A.Chadwick

1	Sep	2	(a)	West Ham U	L	1-2	McGuigan	5,000
2		4	(a)	Croydon Com	L	1-2	Chadwick (pen)	5,000
3		11	(h)	Bristol R	D	1-1	Watson	8,000
4		13	(a)	Southampton	L	2-3	Bell, Watson	2,000
5		18	(a)	Millwall	D	0-0		10,000
6		25	(h)	Norwich C	D	2-2	Bell, Watson	8,000
7	Oct	2	(a)	Gillingham	L	2-3	McGuigan, Bell	8,000
8		9	(h)	Brentford	W	4-1	Chadwick (pen), Bell 3	7,000
9		16	(a)	Northampton T	D	0-0		6,000
10		20	(a)	Portsmouth	L	1-4	Harrison	5,000
11		23	(h)	Coventry C	W	3-0	Hartley (pen), Harrison, Tierney	5,000
12		30	(a)	Queen's Park R	L	0-2		11,000
13	Nov	6	(h)	Watford	D	1-1	Green	5,000
14		10	(h)	Portsmouth	W	5-0	Harrison 3, Watson, Bell	2,000
15		13	(a)	Luton T	L	1-3	Green	5,000
16		27	(a)	Swindon T	L	1-3	Tierney	5,000
17	Dec	11	(a)	Crystal P	L	0-3		5,000
18		18	(h)	Leyton	W	2-1	Chadwick (pen), Evans	8,000
19		25	(a)	Plymouth A	L	0-1		14,000
20		27	(h)	Plymouth A	L	2-4	Evans, Bell	13,000
21		28	(h)	Reading	W	3-1	Watson, Bell, Chadwick (pen)	5,000
22	Jan	1	(h)	Southampton	W	2-0	Green, Hartley	6,000
23		8	(h)	Croydon Com	W	3-1	Bell, Hartley, Watson	4,000
24		22	(a)	Bristol R	L	0-1		8,000
25		26	(h)	Southend U	W	3-1	Bell 2, Hartley	3,000
26		29	(h)	Millwall	W	5-0	Green 2, Watson, Copestake, Bell	5,000
27	Feb	5	(a)	Norwich C	L	0-1		3,000
28		12	(h)	Gillingham	W	3-2	Green, Copestake, Garside	6,000
29		19	(a)	Brentford	L	0-3		4,000
30		26	(h)	Northampton T	L	2-3	Garside, Green	5,000
31	Mar	5	(h)	West Ham U	W	1-0	Copestake	6,500
32		12	(h)	Queen's Park R	D	0-0		5,000
33		19	(a)	Watford	W	3-1	Watson, McGuigan 2	1,500
34		25	(a)	Brighton & HA	L	1-2	Bell	11,000
35		26	(h)	Luton T	L	1-2	Green	7,000
36		28	(h)	Brighton & HA	L	0-1		7,000
37	Apr	2	(a)	Reading	W	1-0	Garside	6,000
38		9	(h)	Swindon T	L	0-1		6,000
39		16	(a)	Southend U	L	0-2		5,000
40		23	(h)	Crystal P	W	2-0	Garside, Copestake	4,000
41		25	(a)	Coventry C	L	0-6		3,000
42		30	(a)	Leyton	L	1-5	Bell	4,000

FINAL LEAGUE POSITION: 18th in Southern League, Division One.

Appearances
Goals

FA Cup

Q4	Nov	20	(h)	Nunhead	W	7-1
Q5	Dec	4	(a)	Stoke	D	0-0
R		8	(h*)	Stoke	D	1-1
2R		13	(n†)	Stoke	L	1-2

*Played at the County Ground, Exeter. †Played at Craven Cottage, Fulham.

Southern Charity Cup

1	Sep	29	(a)	Plymouth A	W	1-0
2	Oct	27	(a)	Swindon T	L	0-4

158

Crossthwaite	Craig	Crelley	Ambler	Chadwick	Atkinson	Green	Watson	McGuigan	Bell	Copestake	Jones	Garside	Tierney	Hartley	Harrison	Sturge	Evans	No.
1	2	3	4	5	6	7	8	9	10	11								1
1		3	4	5	6	7	8	9	10	11	2							2
1	2	3	4	5	6		8	9	10	7		11						3
1	2	3	4		6		8	9	10	7		11	5					4
1		3	6	5	4		8	9	10	7	3	11						5
1		3		5	4		8	9	10	7	2	11		6				6
1	2		4	5	6		8	9	10	7	3	11						7
1	2			5	4	7	8		10		3	11		6	9			8
1	2			5	4	7	8		10		3	11		6	9			9
1	2			5	4	7	8		10		3	11		6	9			10
1	2				4		8		10	7	3	11	5	6	9			11
1	2			5	4	7	8		10		3	11	5	6				12
1	2			4		7	8	9	10		3	11	5	6				13
1	2			4		7	8		10		3	11	5	6	9			14
1	2			4		7	8		10		3	11	5	6	9			15
1	2		4		6	7	8		10		3	11	5		9			16
	2			4	9	8	10		7		3	11	5	6		1		17
1		2		5	6	7	8			11	3		4	10	9			18
1		2		5	6		8			7	3	11	4	10	9			19
1		2			4		8		10	7	3	11	5	6	9			20
1	2		4	5	6	9	8		10	7	3	11						21
1		2		5	6	9	8			7	3	11	4	10				22
1		2		5	4	7	8	9		11	3		6	10				23
1		2		5	6	7	8	9		11	3		4	10				24
1		2		5	6	7	8	9		11	3		4	10				25
1		2			4	9	8		10	7	3	11	5	6				26
1		2			4	9	8		10	7	3	11	5	6				27
1	2			5	4	9	8		10	7	3	11		6				28
1	2		4	6		9	8		10	7	3	11		6				29
1		2		5	4	9	8		10	7	3	11		6				30
1		2	5		4	9	8		10	7	3	11		6				31
1		2	5		4	9	8		10	7	3	11		6				32
1		2	5			7	8	9	10	11	3		4	6				33
1		2	5		4	7	8	9	10		3			6				34
1	2		5		4	9	8		10	7	3	11		6				35
1		2	5		6	7	8	9			3	11	4	10				36
1	2	4	5	8	7		9	10			3	11		6				37
1		2	5		4	7		9	8		3	11	6	10				38
1		2	5		4	9	8		10	7	3	11		10				39
1		5	2			8	9		10	7	3	11	4	6				40
1		5	2			8	9		10	7	3	11	4	6				41
1	2	5		4		8	9		10	7	3	11		6				42
41	13	30	21	21	40	31	40	16	38	30	39	35	21	34	8	1	3	
			4		8	8	4	15	4			4	2	4	5		2	

1910-11 Southern League

Manager: A.Chadwick

1	Sep	3	(h)	Brentford	D 0-0	7,000
2		10	(a)	Leyton	L 0-1	5,000
3		14	(h)	Crystal P	L 3-4 Collyer 2 (2 og's), Bell	4,000
4		17	(h)	Watford	W 2-0 Bell, James	6,000
5		24	(a)	Plymouth A	D 0-0	7,000
6	Oct	1	(h)	Southampton	D 0-0	5,000
7		8	(a)	Southend U	W 2-1 Hughes, Garside	3,000
8		15	(h)	Coventry C	L 2-3 Hughes, Garside	3,000
9		22	(a)	New Brompton	L 0-1	3,000
10		29	(h)	Millwall	L 1-2 Garside	4,500
11	Nov	5	(a)	Queen's Park R	L 0-1	8,000
12		12	(h)	West Ham U	D 0-0	6,000
13		26	(h)	Portsmouth	L 0-2	4,000
14	Dec	10	(a)	Brighton & HA	W 2-1 Parnell, Watson	5,000
15		17	(h)	Norwich C	W 3-1 Garside, McKenzie (og), Jones (pen)	5,000
16		24	(a)	Swindon T	W 1-0 Bell	7,000
17		26	(h)	Bristol R	W 2-1 Hughes, Jones (pen)	6,000
18		27	(a)	Bristol R	W 3-1 Bell, Hughes, Garside	5,000
19		28	(a)	Northampton T	L 0-2	6,000
20		31	(a)	Brentford	L 1-3 Bell	5,000
21	Jan	7	(h)	Leyton	W 3-0 Garside 2, Hughes	5,000
22		21	(a)	Watford	D 2-2 E.Whittaker, Hughes	5,000
23		28	(h)	Plymouth A	L 1-3 Hughes	7,500
24	Feb	4	(a)	Southampton	W 3-1 Bell 2, Smith	8,000
25		11	(h)	Southend U	W 1-0 Smith	4,500
26		18	(a)	Coventry C	W 3-1 Bell 2, Smith	5,000
27		25	(h)	New Brompton	D 2-2 James, Bell	4,000
28	Mar	4	(a)	Millwall	L 1-3 Smith	6,000
29		11	(h)	Queen's Park R	D 2-2 Bell 2	4,000
30		18	(a)	West Ham U	L 1-4 Bell	7,000
31		25	(h)	Luton T	W 4-2 Evans, Pratt, Garside, Bell	3,500
32	Apr	1	(a)	Portsmouth	D 0-0	3,000
33		8	(h)	Northampton T	L 1-4 James	4,500
34		15	(a)	Brighton & HA	W 2-0 Parnell, Kent	6,000
35		17	(a)	Crystal P	L 0-1	20,000
36		18	(a)	Luton T	L 1-3 James	5,000
37		22	(a)	Norwich C	D 0-0	4,500
38		29	(h)	Swindon T	W 2-1 James 2	4,000

FINAL LEAGUE POSITION: 13th in Southern League, Division One.

Appearances
Goals

FA Cup

Q4	Nov	19	(a)	Reading	D 1-1
R		23	(h*)	Reading †	D 1-1
2R		28	(h*)	Reading	W 1-0
5	Dec	3	(h‡)	Nelson	W 4-3
1			(h§)	Burnley	L 0-2

*Played at the County Ground, Exeter. Abandoned ten minutes from time.
‡Played at Nelson. §Played at Burnley

Southern Charity Cup

1		(a)	Bristol R	L 0-1

160

Whittaker W	Evans	Jones	Bassett	Pratt	Prideaux	Parnell	Hughes	James	Bell	Garside	Coates	Griffiths	Watson	Smith	Duffy	Maxsted	Cooke	Whittaker E	Kent	No.
1	2	3	4	5	6	7	8	9	10	11										1
1		3	4	5		7			10	11	2	6	8	9						2
1		3	4	5	6	7			10	11	2		8	9						3
1		3	4	5	6	7		9	10	11	2		8							4
1		3	4	5	6	7		9	10	11	2		8							5
1		3	4	5	6	7	9		10	11	2		8							6
1		3	4	5	6	7	9		10	11	2		8							7
																				8
1	2	3	4		6	7	10		8	11		5		9						9
1	2	3			6	7	10		8	11		5		9	4					10
1	2	3	4	5	6	7	9		10	11			8							11
1	2	3	4	5	6	7	9		10	11			8							12
1		3	4		6	7	10		8		2	5				9	11			13
1	2	3	4	5	6	7	9		10	11			8							14
1	2	3	4	5	6	7	9		10	11			8							15
1	2	3	4	5	6	7	9	8	10	11										16
1	2	3	4	5	6		8	9	10	11								7		17
1	2		4	5	6		9	8	10	11	3							7		18
1		3	4	5	6		9	8	10	11	2							7		19
1	2	3	4	5	6		9		10				8				11	7		20
1	2	3	4	5	6		9	8	10	11								7		21
1	2	3	4	5	6		9		10	11			8					7		22
1	2	3	4	5	6	7	9		10	11			8							23
1	2	3	4	5	6	7			10	11			8	9						24
1	2	3	4	5	6	7			10	11			8	9						25
1	2		4	5	6	7	8		10	11	3			9						26
1	2		4	5	6	7	8		10		3			9			11			27
1	2		4	5	6		8		10		3			9			11	7		28
1	2		4	5	6	7	8		10	11	3			9						29
1	2		4	5	6	7	8		10	11	3			9						30
1	2			5	6	7	9		10	11	3		8		4					31
1	2	6	5			7	9		10	11	3		8		4					32
1	2		4	5	6	7	9		10	11	3		8							33
1	2			5	6	7	9			11	3		8		4				10	34
1	2			5	6		11				3		8	9	4			7	10	35
1	2			5	6		11	9			3		8		4			7	10	36
1	2			5	6	7	9			11	3		8		4				10	37
1	2		4	5		7	9			11	3	6	8						10	38
38	29	24	32	35	35	33	18	24	28	32	23	5	24	12	7	1	4	9	5	
	1	2		1		3	7	6	14	8				1	4				1	

3 own-goals

1911-12 Southern League

Manager: A.Chadwick

1	Sep	2	(a)	Watford	D	0-0	6,000
2		9	(h)	New Brompton	W	8-1 Watson 3, Rutter 2, Garside, Lockett 2	6,000
3		16	(h)	Luton T	W	2-0 Evans (pen), Watson	6,500
4		23	(a)	Brentford	L	1-3 Lockett	8,000
5		30	(h)	Queen's Park R	D	1-1 Rutter	6,000
6	Oct	7	(a)	Millwall	L	0-5	11,000
7		14	(h)	West Ham U	D	3-3 Watson, Parnell (pen), Griffiths	7,000
8		21	(a)	Bristol R	L	1-2 Cornan	6,000
9		28	(h)	Swindon T	L	1-4 Rutter	5,000
10	Nov	4	(a)	Northampton T	L	1-2 Watson	5,000
11		6	(a)	Stoke	W	3-1 Garside 3	6,000
12		11	(h)	Brighton & HA	L	1-3 Kent	2,500
13		25	(h)	Coventry C	D	0-0	3,000
14	Dec	2	(a)	Leyton	D	0-0	2,000
15		9	(h)	Norwich C	W	1-0 Lockett	2,000
16		16	(a)	Crystal P	L	0-5	10,000
17		23	(h)	Southampton	D	2-2 Cornan, E.Whittaker	4,000
18		25	(a)	Plymouth A	L	1-3 Kent	10,000
19		26	(h)	Plymouth A	L	0-1	8,000
20		30	(h)	Watford	L	0-1	5,000
21	Jan	6	(a)	New Brompton	L	1-4 Tompkinson	2,000
22		20	(a)	Luton T	L	2-4 Lockett, Garside	4,000
23		27	(h)	Brentford	W	1-0 Garside	5,000
24	Feb	3	(a)	Queen's Park R	D	0-0	4,000
25		10	(h)	Millwall	W	3-1 E.Whittaker, Lockett, Bassett	5,000
26		17	(a)	West Ham U	L	2-3 Cornan, Rutter	8,000
27		24	(h)	Bristol R	W	2-1 Cornan, Rutter	5,000
28	Mar	2	(a)	Swindon T	W	1-0 Rutter	6,000
29		9	(h)	Northampton T	L	0-2	5,000
30		16	(a)	Brighton & HA	L	1-2 Watson	4,000
31		23	(h)	Stoke	D	1-1 Parnell (pen)	4,000
32		30	(a)	Coventry C	D	1-1 Rutter	6,000
33	Apr	5	(a)	Reading	W	2-1 Griffiths, Rutter	7,000
34		6	(h)	Leyton	W	1-0 Cornan	5,000
35		8	(h)	Reading	W	2-0 Rutter, Garside	7,000
36		13	(a)	Norwich C	D	1-1 Cornan	3,000
37		20	(h)	Crystal P	D	1-1 Watson	5,000
38		27	(a)	Southampton	L	0-3	5,000

FINAL LEAGUE POSITION: 15th in Southern League, Division One.

Appearances
Goals

FA Cup

Q4	Nov	18	(h)	Merthyr T	D	1-1
R		23	(a)	Merthyr T	D	0-0
2R		27	(n*)	Merthyr T	L	0-2

*Played at Bristol

Southern Charity Cup

1	Sep	20	(h)	Swindon T	W	2-0
2	Oct	18	(h)	Plymouth A	D	0-0
R	Dec	13	(a)	Plymouth A	L	1-2

	Whittaker W	Evans	Coates	Bassett	Pratt	Prideaux	Whittaker E	Watson	Rutter	Lockett	Garside	Griffiths	Parnell	Kent	Chapman	Rigby	Cornan	Fort	Chenneour	Crute	Caddy	Chadwick	Tompkinson	Pym
1	1	2	3	4	5	6	7	8	9	10	11													
2	1	2	3	4	5	6	7	8	9	10	11													
3	1	2	3	4	5	6	7	8	9	10	11													
4	1	2	3	4	5			8	9	10			6	7	11									
5	1	2	3	4	5		11	8	9	10			6	7										
6	1	2	3	4	5			8		9	11		6	7	10									
7		2	3	4	5			9	8	11			6	7	1	4	10							
8			3	4	5			9	8	11			6	7	1		10	2						
9		2	3	4	5			8	9		11		6	7	1		10							
10		2	3	4	5			10		9	11		6	7	1		8							
11		2	3	4			7	8	9		11	5		10	1	6								
12	1	2	3	4		6	7		9	8	11	5			10									
13	1	2	3		5		6	7	8			11				4	10		9					
14	1	2	3		5		6	7	8		11					4	10		9					
15	1		3	4		6		8	9	10		5	7		11		2							
16			3	5		6	7	9		11			8		1	4	10	2						
17		4	3	5		6	7	9		11			8			10	2			1				
18	1	2		6			7	9		11			8			4	10			5	3			
19		2		5			7	9	11	8		6				4	10			3				
20		3		5	6	7			11	8			4	10		1					9			
21	1	2		5	6		9		8	11		7			4	10	3							
22	1	3		5		7	9		8	11	6				4	10	2							
23	1	3		5		7	8	9	6	11					4	10	2							
24	1	3		5		7	8	9	6	11					4	10	2							
25	1			5		7	8	9	6	11					4	10	2					3		
26	1	3		4	5	7	8	9	6	11							10	2						
27	1	3		4	5	7	8	9	6	11							10	2						
28	1	3		4	5	6	7	8	9		11						10	2						
29	1	3		6	5		7	9		8	11				4	10	2							
30		3		4	5		7	8	9	6	11					1	10	2						
31		3		4	5			8	9	6	11	7					10	2						1
32		3		4	5			8	9	6	11	7					10	2						1
33		3		2	5			8	9	6	11		7		4		10							1
34		3		2				8	9	6	11	5	7		4		10							1
35		3		2	5		7	8	9	6	11				4		10							1
36		3		2	5		7	8	9	6	11				4		10							1
37		3		2	5			8	9	6	11		7		4		10							1
38		3		2	5			8	9	6	11		7		4		10							1
	21	34	18	38	21	12	24	34	28	34	24	17	17	8	6	19	28	18	2	3	2	1	1	8
	1		1				2	8	10	6	7		2	2	2		6					1		

163

1912-13 Southern League

Manager: A.Chadwick

1	Sep	2	(a)	West Ham U	L	0-4	9,000
2		7	(h)	Watford	W	1-0 Rutter	4,000
3		14	(a)	Merthyr T	L	0-2	10,000
4		21	(h)	Crystal P	D	1-1 Brooksbank	4,000
5		28	(a)	Plymouth A	L	0-3	8,000
6	Oct	5	(h)	Southampton	W	1-0 Ives	2,500
7		12	(a)	Reading	D	2-2 Rutter, Whittaker	6,000
8		19	(h)	Norwich C	W	1-0 Crompton	4,000
9		23	(h)	Bristol R	W	4-0 Crompton 2, Rutter 2	3,000
10		26	(a)	Gillingham	W	4-0 Cooper 2, Crompton, Garside	3,000
11		30	(h)	West Ham U	D	0-0	3,000
12	Nov	2	(h)	Northampton T	D	1-1 Cooper	5,000
13		9	(a)	Queen's Park R	L	1-2 Ives	7,000
14		16	(h)	Brentford	W	1-0 Crompton	5,000
15		23	(a)	Millwall	L	0-1	15,000
16	Dec	7	(a)	Swindon T	D	2-2 Kay (og), Brooksbank	6,000
17		14	(h)	Portsmouth	W	2-1 Ives 2	5,000
18		21	(a)	Stoke	W	2-0 Rigby, Crompton	4,000
19		25	(a)	Brighton & HA	L	0-1	3,000
20		26	(h)	Brighton & HA	W	2-1 Rutter, Cooper	5,000
21		28	(a)	Watford	L	0-1	5,000
22	Jan	4	(h)	Merthyr T	L	2-4 Ives, Brooksbank	4,000
23		18	(a)	Crystal P	W	1-0 Ives	8,000
24		25	(h)	Plymouth A	W	1-0 Cooper	12,000
25	Feb	8	(a)	Southampton	D	2-2 Rutter, Ives	2,000
26		15	(h)	Reading	W	1-0 Crompton	4,000
27		22	(a)	Norwich C	D	1-1 Cooper	4,000
28	Mar	1	(h)	Gillingham	W	2-0 Cooper, Crompton	3,500
29		8	(a)	Northampton T	L	0-4	6,000
30		15	(h)	Queen's Park R	W	3-1 Ives, Whittaker (pen), Crompton	4,000
31		21	(a)	Coventry C	W	1-0 Rutter	3,000
32		22	(a)	Brentford	W	1-0 Whittaker	6,000
33		24	(h)	Coventry C	W	3-0 Cooper, Bassett, Ives	5,000
34		29	(h)	Millwall	L	1-4 Bassett	3,000
35	Apr	5	(a)	Bristol R	D	1-1 Whittaker	5,000
36		12	(h)	Swindon T	L	1-3 Rutter	4,000
37		19	(a)	Portsmouth	L	1-2 Rutter	9,000
38		26	(h)	Stoke C	W	1-0 Crompton	1,000

FINAL LEAGUE POSITION: 7th in Southern League, Division One.

Appearances
Goals

FA Cup

Q4	Nov	30	(a)	Cardiiff C	L	1-5

Season appearances and goals grid (shirt number played by each man in each match).

Pym	Fort	Hurst	Rigby	Bassett	Lockett	Whittaker	Rutter	Crompton	Golightly	Ives	Nevin	Pratt	Brooksbank	Garside	Cooper	Lagan	Match
1	2	3	4	5	6	7	8	9	10	11							1
1	2	3	4	5	6	7	9	8	10	11							2
1	2		4	5	6	7	9	8	10	11	3						3
1	2	3	4		6	7	10	8				5	9	11			4
1	2	3	4		6	7	10	8				5	9	11			5
1	2	3	4		6	7		9	10	11		5		8			6
1	2	3	4		6	10	7	9		11		5		8			7
1	2	3	4		6	10	7	9	8	11		5					8
1		3	4		6	7		9	10		2	5	11		8		9
1		3	4		6	7		9	10		2	5	11		8		10
1	2	3	4		6	7		9	10			5	11		8		11
1	2	3	4		6	7		9	10	11		5		8			12
1	2	3	4		6	7		9	10	11		5		8			13
1	2	3	4		6	7		9	10	11		5		8			14
1	2	3	4		6	7		9	10	11		5		8			15
1	2	3	4		6	7			10	11		5	9	8			16
1	2	3	4		6	7			10	11		5	9	8			17
1	2	3	4		6	7		9	10	11					8	5	18
1	2	3	4		6	7		9		11		10			8	5	19
1	2	3	4		6	7		9		11		10			8	5	20
1		3	4		6	7		9		11	2	10			8	5	21
1	2	3	4		6	7		9		11		10			8	5	22
1	2	3	4		6	7		9		11		10			8	5	23
1	2	3	4		6	7		9	10	11					8	5	24
1	2	3	4		6	7		9	10	11					8	5	25
1	2	3	4		6	7		9	10	11					8	5	26
1	2		4		6	7		9	10	11	3				8	5	27
1	2	3	4		6	7		9	10	11					8	5	28
1	2	3	4		6	7		9	10	11					8	5	29
1	2	3	4	5		7		9	10	11			6		8		30
1	2	3	4	5	6	7		9	10	11					8		31
1	2	3	4	5	6	7		9	10	11					8		32
1	2	3	4	5	6	7		9	10	11					8		33
1	2	3	4	5	6	7		9	10	11					8		34
1		3	4		6	7	9	8	10		2		11			5	35
1	2		4		6	7	9	8	10		3		11			5	36
1	2	3	4		6	7	9	8	10				11			5	37
1	2	3	4		6	7	9	8	10				11			5	38
38	34	35	38	11	36	38	36	31	7	29	7	14	10	10	28	16	
		1	2		4	9	10		8		3	1			9		

1 own-goal

Manager: A.Chadwick

1	Sep	6	(a)	Southampton	L	0-2	7,000
2		13	(h)	Reading	L	0-1	6,000
3		20	(a)	Crystal P	D	0-0	5,000
4		27	(h)	Coventry C	D	0-0	4,000
5	Oct	1	(h)	Merthyr T	W	3-0 McCann, Brooksbank, Whittaker	2,000
6		4	(a)	Watford	W	1-0 Lee	6,000
7		11	(h)	Norwich C	L	0-1	4,000
8		18	(a)	Gillingham	L	0-2	4,000
9		25	(h)	Northampton T	W	2-0 Whittaker 2	4,000
10	Nov	1	(a)	Southend U	L	0-1	3,000
11		8	(h)	Brighton & HA	W	4-1 Marshall, McCann, Whittaker, Holt	4,000
12		15	(a)	Portsmouth	D	2-2 Whittaker 2	8,000
13		22	(h)	Millwall	W	3-1 Whittaker 2, Marshall	5,000
14		29	(h)	Queen's Park R	D	0-0	5,000
15	Dec	6	(a)	Cardiff C	D	1-1 Whittaker	3,000
16		13	(h)	Swindon T	L	0-2	4,000
17		20	(a)	Bristol R	D	1-1 McCann	5,000
18		25	(a)	West Ham U	D	1-1 Marshall	11,000
19		26	(h)	West Ham U	D	1-1 Holt	7,000
20		27	(h)	Southampton	W	2-0 Lovett, McCann	8,000
21	Jan	3	(a)	Reading	D	2-2 Lovett, McCann	6,000
22		17	(h)	Crystal P	D	1-1 Marshall	5,000
23		24	(a)	Coventry C	W	2-1 Goodwin, Holt	10,000
24	Feb	7	(a)	Watford	D	1-1 McCann	3,000
25		14	(h)	Norwich C	L	1-3 McCann	6,000
26		21	(h)	Gillingham	W	2-0 McCann, Goodwin	2,500
27		28	(a)	Northampton T	L	1-2 Whittaker	5,000
28	Mar	7	(h)	Southend U	D	0-0	4,000
29		14	(a)	Brighton & HA	L	1-2 Whittaker	5,000
30		21	(h)	Portsmouth	W	1-0 Brooksbank	4,000
31		28	(a)	Millwall	L	1-3 McCann	8,000
32	Apr	4	(a)	Queen's Park R	W	3-2 Whittaker 2, Lovett	7,000
33		10	(a)	Plymouth A	D	0-0	15,000
34		11	(h)	Cardiff C	L	0-1	7,000
35		13	(h)	Plymouth A	D	0-0	11,000
36		15	(a)	Merthyr T	L	0-1	3,000
37		18	(a)	Swindon T	D	1-1 McCann	8,000
38		25	(h)	Bristol R	D	1-1 McCann	3,500

FINAL LEAGUE POSITION: 12th in Southern League, Division One.

Appearances
Goals

FA Cup

1	Jan	10	(a)	Portsmouth	W	4-0
2		31	(h)	Aston Villa	L	1-2

Southern Charity Cup

1	Sep	15	(a)	Merthyr T	L	1-2

Pym	Fort	Strettle	Rigby	Pratt	Evans	Whittaker	Kirby	Lovett	McCann	Lee	Brooksbank	Orr	Marshall	Harding	Lewis	Smith	Holt	Lagan	Pridham	Goodwin F	
1	2		4	5	6	7	8	9	10	11											1
1	2	3	4	5	6	7	8		10			9	11								2
1	2	3	4	5		7	10	8			11	9		6							3
1	2	3	4	5		7	10	8			11	9		6							4
1		3	4	5		7		10		11	9		6	2	8						5
1		3	4	5		7	8	10		11	9		6	2							6
1	2	3	4	5		7	8		10		9					6	11				7
1	2	3	4			9		10				11	8	6	7	5					8
1		3	4		6	9		10				11	8	6	7	5					9
1	2	3	4			9		10	8		11			6	7	5					10
1	2	3	4			9		10	8		11			6	7	5					11
1	2	3	4			9		10	8		11			6	7	5					12
1	2	3	4			9		10	8		11			6	7	5					13
1	2	3	8		11	9		10			4			6	7	5					14
1	2	3	4		11	9		10						6	7	5	8				15
1	2	3	4	5			8	10	9		11			6	7						16
1	2	3	4	5			8	10	9		11			6	7						17
1	2	3	4	5			8	10	9		11			6	7						18
1	2	3	4				8	10	9					6	7	5			11		19
1	2	3	4				8	10	9		11			6	7	5					20
1	2	3	4		9		8	10			11			6	7	5					21
1		3	4	5			8	10	9			2		6	7				11		22
1	2	3	4		9		8	10						6	7	5			11		23
1	2	3	4			8	10	9					6	7	5	11					24
1	2	3	4		8		10	9					6	7	5	11					25
1	2	3	4		8		10	9					6	7	5	11					26
1	2	3	4		8			9	10				6	7	5	11					27
1	2	3	4		7		10	9					6		5	8	11				28
1	2	3	4		8		10	9					6	7	5	11					29
1	2	3	4		8		10	9	11			6	7	5							30
1	2	3	4		9		8	10					6	7	5	11					31
1	2	3	4		9		8	10					6	7	5	11					32
1	2	3	4	6	9		8	10						7	5	11					33
1	2	3	4	5	9		8	10					6	7		11					34
1		3	4	5			8	10	9		11	2	6	7							35
1	2	3	4	5	9		8	10					6	7		11					36
1	2	3		5	6	9		8	10		11		4	7							37
38	33	38	37	17	6	30	5	21	35	6	25	2	19	6	3	29	30	22	2	14	38
			13		3	11	1	2		4			3				2				

1914-15 Southern League

Manager: A.Chadwick

							Attendance
1	Sep	5	(h)	West Ham U	W 3-1	Lovett 2, W.Goodwin	4,000
2		12	(a)	Norwich C	L 1-3	W.Goodwin (pen)	3,500
3		19	(h)	Gillingham	W 2-0	W.Goodwin, Lovett	4,000
4		23	(h)	Northampton T	W 2-1	Green, W.Goodwin	2,000
5		26	(a)	Brighton & HA	L 1-2	W.Goodwin	4,000
6	Oct	3	(h)	Cardiff C	W 2-0	W.Goodwin (pen), Green	5,000
7		10	(a)	Crystal P	D 0-0		3,500
8		17	(a)	Luton T	W 2-0	W.Goodwin 2	5,000
9		24	(h)	Portsmouth	D 1-1	W.Goodwin	5,000
10		31	(a)	Swindon T	L 0-4		6,000
11	Nov	7	(h)	Southend U	W 7-1	Green 3, W.Goodwin 2, Lovett, F.Goodwin	5,000
12		14	(a)	Queen's Park R	W 2-0	Green 2	4,000
13		21	(h)	Millwall	L 0-1		5,000
14		28	(a)	Bristol R	L 1-2	W.Goodwin	5,000
15	Dec	5	(h)	Croydon Com	W 3-1	W.Goodwin 3 (1 pen)	2,000
16		12	(a)	Reading	L 0-1		3,000
17		19	(h)	Southampton	L 1-2	Hunter	4,000
18		25	(a)	Watford	D 1-1	W.Goodwin	2,000
19		26	(h)	Watford	W 4-1	Dockray, Lovett, W.Goodwin 2	6,000
20		28	(a)	Northampton T	D 1-1	W.Goodwin	6,000
21	Jan	2	(a)	West Ham U	L 1-4	W.Goodwin	8,000
22		16	(h)	Norwich C	W 2-0	Dockray, Holt	2,500
23		23	(a)	Gillingham	D 0-0		2,000
24	Feb	6	(a)	Cardiff C	L 0-1		6,000
25		13	(h)	Crystal P	D 1-1	Evans	2,000
26		20	(h)	Luton T	L 1-2	Holt	3,000
27		24	(h)	Brighton & HA	W 1-0	Lovett	1,500
28		27	(a)	Portsmouth	W 2-0	F.Goodwin, Rigby (pen)	6,000
29	Mar	6	(h)	Swindon T	L 0-1		6,000
30		13	(a)	Southend U	W 2-0	W.Goodwin, F.Goodwin	5,000
31		20	(h)	Queen's Park R	L 0-1		4,000
32		27	(a)	Millwall	L 1-2	W.Goodwin	8,000
33	Apr	2	(a)	Plymouth A	W 3-1	Holt, Butler (og), W.Goodwin (pen)	7,000
34		3	(h)	Bristol R	W 1-0	Holt	5,000
35		5	(h)	Plymouth A	D 1-1	Lovett	5,000
36		10	(a)	Croydon Com	D 0-0		5,000
37		17	(h)	Reading	L 0-1		3,000
38		24	(a)	Southampton	L 0-3		5,500

FINAL LEAGUE POSITION: 11th in Southern League, Division One.

Appearances
Goals

FA Cup

| 1 | Jan | 9 | (a) | Aston Villa | L 0-2 | |

Southern Charity Cup

| 1 | Oct | 14 | (h) | Merthyr T | W 2-1 | |
| 2 | Feb | 10 | (a) | Plymouth A | L 0-1 | |

Pym	Harding	Strettle	Rigby	Lagan	Smith	Holt	Green	Goodwin W	Lovett	Goodwin F	Marshall	Pratt	Evans	Cowie	Hunter	Dockray	Cox	
1	2	3	4	5	6	7	8	9	10	11								1
1		3	4	5	6	7	8	9	10	11	2							2
1		3	4	5	6	7	8	9	10	11	2							3
1		3	4		6	7	8	9	10	11	2	5						4
1		3	4		6	7	8	9	10	11	2	5						5
1		3	4		5	7	8	9	10	11	2		6					6
1		3	4	5	6	7	8	9	10	11	2							7
1		3	4	5	6	7	8	9	10	11	2							8
1		3	4	5	6	7		9	8	11	2		10					9
1		3	4	5	6	7	8	9	10	11	2							10
1		3	4	5	6	7	8	9	10	11	2							11
1		3	4	5	6	7	8	9	10	11	2							12
1		3		5	4	7	8	9	10	11	2		6					13
1		3	4	5	6	7	8	9	10	11	2							14
1		3		5	4	7		9	10		2		6		8	11		15
1		3		5	4	7		9	10		2		6		8	11		16
1		3	4	5	6	7		9	10		2				8	11		17
1		3	4	5	6	7		9	10		2				8	11		18
1		3	4	5	6	7		9	10		2				8	11		19
1		3	4	5	6	7	8	9	10		2					11		20
1		3	4	5	6	7		9	10		2		8			11		21
1		3	4	5	6	7		9	10		2		8			11		22
1		3	4	5	6	7		9	10		2		8			11		23
1		3	4	5	6	7		9	10		2		8			11		24
1		3	4	5	6	7		9	10		2		8			11		25
1		3	4	5	6	7		9	10		2		8			11		26
1		3	4	5	6	7		9		10	2		8			11		27
1		3	4	5		7	8	9	10		2		6			11		28
1		3	4		6	7		9	10		2	5	8			11		29
1		3	4		6	7		9	10		2	5		8		11		30
1		3	4		6	7		9	10		2	5	8			11		31
1		3	4		6	7		9	10		2	5	8			11		32
1		3	4		6	7		9	10		2	5	8			11		33
1		3	4		6	7	8	9	10		2	5				11		34
1		3	4		6	7		9	10		2	5	8			11		35
1		3	4		6	7	8	9	10		2	5				11	2	36
1		3	4		6	7		9	10		2	5	8			11	2	37
1		3	4		6	7		9	10		2	5	8			11		38
38	1	38	35	25	37	38	14	36	32	26	36	11	20	1	5	23	2	
			1		4	7	23	7	3			1			1	2		

1 own-goal

1919-20 Southern League

Manager: A.Chadwick

				Result	Scorers	Attendance
1	Aug	30	(a) Southampton	D 1-1	Connor	7,000
2	Sep	3	(h) Reading	D 2-2	Makin, Goodwin	3,000
3		6	(h) Luton T	W 3-2	Dockray, Lovett, Makin	5,000
4		10	(a) Reading	W 1-0	Goodwin	3,500
5		13	(a) Gillingham	D 0-0		6,000
6		20	(h) Swansea T	W 2-1	Lovett, Oldacre	6,000
7		24	(h) Brentford	D 0-0		3,000
8	Oct	4	(a) Cardiff C	L 0-1		13,000
9		8	(h) Southend U	W 3-0	Dockray, Goodwin, Oldacre	2,000
10		11	(h) Queen's Park R	L 0-1		5,000
11		18	(a) Swindon T	D 1-1	Goodwin	10,000
12		25	(h) Millwall	W 3-1	Makin 2, Popplewell	6,500
13	Nov	1	(a) Brighton & HA	D 0-0		8,000
14		8	(h) Newport C	L 1-2	Goodwin	5,000
15		15	(a) Portsmouth	L 0-2		8,000
16		22	(h) Northampton T	L 2-4	Makin, Oldacre	6,000
17		26	(a) Watford	W 1-0	Makin	6,000
18	Dec	13	(a) Norwich C	D 0-0		8,000
19		25	(a) Plymouth A	L 1-3	Oldacre	15,000
20		26	(h) Plymouth A	L 0-1		9,500
21		27	(a) Merthyr T	L 1-2	Goodwin	4,000
22	Jan	3	(h) Southampton	W 4-1	Henderson, Lovett, Popplewell (pen), Reader	5,000
23		17	(a) Luton T	L 1-3	Henderson	5,000
24		24	(h) Gillingham	W 2-1	Oldacre, Goodwin	5,000
25		31	(a) Swansea T	W 1-0	Henderson	10,000
26	Feb	7	(h) Watford	W 3-0	Goodwin 2, Oldacre	6,000
27		14	(h) Cardiff C	D 1-1	Goodwin	8,000
28		21	(a) Queen's Park R	D 0-0		7,000
29		28	(h) Swindon T	W 3-1	Makin 2, Goodwin	7,000
30	Mar	6	(a) Millwall	L 0-1		12,000
31		13	(h) Brighton & HA	W 4-1	Makin 2, Lovett, Goodwin	5,000
32		17	(a) Crystal P	L 0-1		5,000
33		20	(a) Newport C	L 1-4	Dockray	5,000
34		27	(h) Portsmouth	W 2-0	Popplewell (pen), Green	7,500
35	Apr	2	(a) Bristol R	L 2-4	Popplewell (pen), Makin	14,000
36		3	(a) Northampton T	L 1-3	Oldacre	6,000
37		5	(h) Bristol R	W 2-1	Goodwin, Makin	11,000
38		10	(h) Crystal P	W 2-1	Makin, Goodwin	6,000
39		17	(a) Southend U	L 0-2		5,000
40		24	(h) Norwich C	W 2-1	Goodwin, Lovett	5,000
41		26	(a) Brentford	L 1-2	Goodwin	3,000
42	May	1	(h) Merthyr T	W 3-0	Makin, Goodwin, Oldacre	6,000

FINAL LEAGUE POSITION: 10th in Southern League, Division One.

Appearances
Goals

FA Cup

6	Dec	20	(a) Newport C	L 0-1	

170

Appearances and goals grid (cell value = shirt number worn; final right-hand column = match number). Totals rows at foot give appearances and goals.

Pym	Coleburne	Strettle	Rigby	Popplewell	Mitton	Connor	Makin	Goodwin	Lovett	Dockray	Shreeve	Lincoln	Oldacre	Nutland	Pratt	Potter	Medcalf	Southcombe	Henderson	Reader	Crawshaw	Gill	Green	Hetherington	
1	2	3	4	5	6	7	8	9	10	11															1
1	2	3	4	5	6	7	8	9	10	11															2
1	2		4	5	6	7	8	9	10	11	3														3
1	2	3	4	5	6	7	8	9	10	11															4
1	2	3	4	5	6	7	8	9	10			11													5
1	2	3	4	5	6	7		9	10	11			8												6
1	2	3	4	5	6	7		9		11		10	8												7
1	2	3	4	5	6	7		9	10	11			8												8
1	2	3	4	5	6	7		9	10	11			8												9
1	2	3	4	5	6				10	11		7	9	8											10
1	2	3	4	5	6			9	10	11			7		8										11
1	2	3	4	5	6	7	8	9	10	11															12
1	2	3	4	5	6	7	8	9	10	11															13
1	2	3	4	5	6	7	8	9	10	11															14
1	2		4	5	6	7	8	9	10	11							3								15
1	2		4	5	6	7	8		10	11			9				3								16
1	2		4	5	6		8		10	11			9			7	3								17
1	2		4	5	6		8	9	10	11			7				3								18
1	2	3	4	5	6		8	9		11			7						10						19
1	2		4	5	6		8	9		11			7				3		10						20
1	2	3	4	5	6		8	9	10	11			7												21
1	2		4	5	6		8			11			7				3		10	9					22
1	2		4	5	6		8	9		11			7				3		10						23
1	2	3	4	5	6		8	9		11			7						10						24
1	2	3		5	6		8	9		11			7						10		4				25
1	2	3	4	5	6		8	9	10	11			7												26
1	2	3		5	6		8	9	10	11			7								4				27
1	2	3	4	5	6		8	9	10	11			7												28
1	2	3		5	6		8	9	10	11			7								4				29
1	2	3	4	5	6		8	9	10	11			7												30
1	2	3	4	5	6		8	9	10	11			7												31
1	2	3	4	5	6		8	9	10	11			7												32
1	2	3	4	5	6		8		10	11			7									9			33
1	2	3		5	6		8		10	11			7								4	9			34
1	2	3		5	6		8	9		11			7								4		10		35
1	2	3		5	6		8	9		11			10								4		7		36
1	2	3		5	6		8	9		11			10								4	7			37
1	2	3		5	6		8	9	10	11			7								4				38
1	2	3		5	6		8	9		11			7								4		10		39
1	2	3		5	6		8	9	10	11			7								4				40
1	2	3		5	6		8	9	10	11			7								4				41
1	2	3		5	6		8	9	10	11			7								4				42
42	42	34	28	41	42	14	31	37	34	41	2	2	33	1	1	2	5	1	6	1	15	3	3	1	
			4		1	14	17	5	3				8				3	1			1				

171

1920-21

Manager: A.Chadwick

#		Date		Opponent	Result	Scorers	Attendance
1	Aug	28	(h)	Brentford	W 3-0	Wright, Vowles, Feebury (pen)	6,000
2	Sep	1	(h)	Norwich C	D 1-1	Makin	4,000
3		4	(a)	Brentford	D 0-0		10,000
4		8	(a)	Norwich C	D 0-0		6,000
5		11	(h)	Millwall	W 4-0	Wright 2, Makin, Carrick	7,000
6		18	(a)	Millwall	L 0-2		10,000
7		25	(h)	Newport C	L 0-1		7,000
8	Oct	2	(a)	Newport C	L 0-2		8,000
9		9	(h)	Gillingham	W 2-1	Appleton, Vowles	7,000
10		16	(a)	Gillingham	L 1-2	Wright	5,000
11		20	(h)	Southend U	D 0-0		2,000
12		23	(h)	Swindon T	W 1-0	Makin	9,000
13		30	(a)	Swindon T	D 1-1	Carrick	10,000
14	Nov	6	(h)	Watford	L 1-2	Wright	7,000
15		13	(a)	Watford	D 0-0		10,000
16		20	(h)	Crystal P	D 1-1	Vowles	5,000
17		27	(*)	Crystal P	L 1-2	Vowles	13,000
18	Dec	4	(h)	Northampton T	W 4-0	Wright 2, Vowles, Dockray	5,000
19		11	(a)	Northampton T	D 3-3	Wright 2, Dockray	6,000
20		25	(a)	Plymouth A	D 0-0		17,500
21		27	(h)	Plymouth A	D 1-1	Shields	14,664
22	Jan	1	(a)	Southend U	D 0-0		3,000
23		15	(h)	Brighton & HA	W 1-0	Shields	5,000
24		22	(a)	Brighton & HA	D 1-1	Makin	6,000
25		29	(a)	Merthyr T	L 1-7	Shields	12,000
26	Feb	5	(h)	Merthyr T	D 3-3	Vowles, Shields, Appleton	5,000
27		12	(h)	Grimsby T	D 1-1	Feebury (pen)	6,000
28		19	(a)	Grimsby T	L 0-2		10,000
29		26	(h)	Queen's Park R	L 0-1		6,000
30	Mar	5	(a)	Queen's Park R	L 1-2	Carrick	12,000
31		12	(h)	Swansea T	L 1-2	Hinton	5,000
32		19	(a)	Swansea T	L 1-2	Makin	9,000
33		25	(a)	Portsmouth	L 1-2	Hetherington	24,000
34		26	(a)	Luton T	L 0-3		8,000
35		28	(h)	Portsmouth	D 0-0		8,000
36	Apr	2	(h)	Luton T	W 1-0	Vowles	5,000
37		9	(a)	Southampton	L 0-3		12,000
38		16	(h)	Southampton	W 1-0	Vowles	5,500
39		23	(a)	Reading	W 1-0	Vowles	7,500
40		30	(h)	Reading	L 0-1		6,000
41	May	2	(a)	Bristol R	L 0-5		7,000
42		7	(h)	Bristol R	W 1-0	Makin	4,000

FINAL LEAGUE POSITION: 19th in Division Three

*Played at The Dell, Southampton. Crystal Palace's ground, The Nest, closed.

Appearances
Goals

FA Cup

1	Jan	8	(a)	Watford	L 0-3

172

Pym	Coleburne	Feebury	Crawshaw	Carrick	Mitton	Appleton	Makin	Wright	Vowles	Dockray	MacIntyre	Brayshaw	Hetherington	Betteridge	Lakin	Green	Hesmondhalgh	Shields	Waller	Rigby	Taylor	Hinton	Pollard	Hilton	
1	2	3	4	5	6	7	8	9	10	11															1
1	2	3	4	5	6		8	9	10	11	7														2
1	2	3	4	5	6	7	8	9		11		10													3
1	2	3	4	5	6	7	8	9	10	11															4
1	2	3	4	5	6	7	8	9	10	11															5
1	2	3	4	5	6	7	8	9		11		10													6
1	2	3	4	5	6	7	8	9		11			10												7
1		3		5	6	7	8		10	11				2	4	9									8
1		3		5	6	7	8		10	11				2	4										9
1	2	3		5	6	7	8	9	10	11					4										10
1	2	3	4	5	6	7	8	9	10	11															11
1	2	3	4	5		7	8	9	10	11						6									12
1	2	3	4	5		7	8	9	10	11						6									13
1	2	3	4	5		7	8		10	11						6	9								14
1	2	3	4	5		7	8	9	10	11						6									15
1	2	3	4	5		7	8	9	10	11						6									16
1	2	3	4	5		7	8	9	10	11						6									17
1	2	3	4	5		7	8	9	10	11						6									18
1	2	3	4	5		7	8		10	11						6		9							19
1	2	3	4	5		7	8		10	11						6		9							20
1	2	3	4	5		7	8		10	11						6		9							21
		3		5		10	8			11	7			2		6		9	1	4					22
		3	4	5		7	8			11			10	2		6		9	1						23
		3	4	5		7	8			11			10	2		6		9	1						24
1	2	3	4	5		7	8		10	11						6		9							25
1	2	3	4	5		7	8		10	11						6		9							26
1	2	3	4				8			11	7		10			5		9			6				27
1	2	3	4	5		7				11			10			8		9			6				28
1	2	3		4		7	8		10	11						6		5							29
1	2	3		4		7	8			11						5		9			6	10			30
1	2	3	4	5		7	8			11							9				6				31
1	2	3	4	5		7	8			11			10			6		9							32
1	2	3	4	5			8			11	7		10			6		9							33
1	2	3		5		7	8		10	11						6		9	4						34
1		3	4	5		7	8		10	11						6		9			2				35
1		3		5					10	11	7		8					4		9	2	6			36
1		3		5		7	8		9	11						6		4			10	2			37
1		3		5		7	8		9	11						6		4			10	2			38
1		3		5			8		9	11	7					6		4				2			39
1		3		5			8		9	11	7					6		4				2			40
1		3		5			8		9	11						6		4				2			41
1		3		5		7	8		9	11	10					6		4				2			42
39	30	42	28	41	11	37	39	17	31	42	5	5	8	2	6	31	1	19	3	7	6	4	7	1	
2		3		2	6	9	9	2						1		4					1				

1921-22

Manager: A.Chadwick

1	Aug	27	(a)	Charlton A	L 0-1	9,000
2		31	(h)	Brighton & HA	L 0-3	6,000
3	Sep	3	(h)	Charlton A	W 1-0 Vowles	7,000
4		7	(a)	Brighton & HA	L 1-3 Crompton	13,000
5		10	(h)	Portsmouth	L 1-4 Crompton	6,000
6		14	(a)	Luton T	L 0-4	7,000
7		17	(a)	Portsmouth	L 0-2	12,000
8		24	(h)	Southend U	W 4-1 Williams, Vowles 2, Crompton (pen)	2,300
9	Oct	1	(a)	Southend U	W 1-0 Vowles	4,000
10		8	(a)	Swansea T	L 1-2 Vowles	12,000
11		15	(h)	Swansea T	D 1-1 Crompton	5,000
12		22	(a)	Swindon T	D 1-1 Mitton	7,000
13		29	(h)	Swindon T	L 1-4 Dockray	6,550
14	Nov	5	(a)	Millwall	L 0-1	14,000
15		12	(h)	Millwall	W 1-0 Hill	6,000
16		19	(h)	Gillingham	D 1-1 Vowles	3,000
17	Dec	10	(h)	Luton T	L 0-1	4,000
18		17	(a)	Watford	D 0-0	7,000
19		24	(h)	Watford	L 1-3 Dockray	5,000
20		26	(h)	Plymouth A	L 0-2	16,000
21		27	(a)	Plymouth A	D 0-0	22,000
22		31	(h)	Newport C	D 2-2 Hill, Bullock	4,000
23	Jan	14	(a)	Newport C	D 1-1 Dockray	5,000
24		21	(a)	Northampton T	W 3-2 Dockray 2, Bullock	4,000
25	Feb	4	(a)	Southampton	L 0-2	10,000
26		11	(h)	Southampton	D 0-0	5,000
27		18	(a)	Queen's Park R	L 1-2 Bullock	10,000
28		25	(h)	Queen's Park R	L 0-1	4,000
29	Mar	4	(a)	Norwich C	D 0-0	6,000
30		*6	(a)	Gillingham	L 0-3	4,000
31		11	(h)	Norwich C	W 2-0 Kirk, Newman	3,000
32		18	(h)	Reading	L 1-3 Kirk	4,000
33		25	(a)	Reading	D 0-0	4,000
34	Apr	1	(h)	Bristol R	D 2-2 Kirk, Vowles	5,000
35		3	(h)	Northampton T	W 2-0 Kirk, Vowles	4,000
36		8	(a)	Bristol R	W 3-1 Kirk 2 (1 pen), Vowles	10,000
37		14	(a)	Merthyr T	D 0-0	5,000
38		15	(h)	Brentford	W 1-0 Kirk	5,000
39		17	(h)	Merthyr T	W 1-0 Kirk	5,000
40		22	(a)	Brentford	L 2-5 Kirk, Vowles	5,000
41		29	(h)	Aberdare A	L 0-1	5,000
42	May	6	(a)	Aberdare A	W 2-0 Bullock, Vowles	5,000

FINAL LEAGUE POSITION: 21st in Division Three South   Appearances
*Original game on 26 November postponed through fog.   Goals

FA Cup

Q5	Dec	3	(a)	Bristol R	D 0-0
R		7	(h)	Bristol R	L 0-2

Football appearances / shirt-number grid (matches 1–42).

Match	Fryer	MacKechnie	Stewart	Mitton	Brown	Green A	Edge	Crompton	Bullock	Green J	Dockray	Vowles	Gaskell	Rigby	Newman	Williams	Pollard	Watson	Graham	Congdon	Hill	McCulloch	Wilson	Townsend	Kirk	Squires
1	1	2	3	4	5	6	7	8	9	10	11															
2	1	2	3	4	5	6	7	8	9		11	10														
3	1		3	5		6		8	9		11	10	2	4	7											
4	1		3	5		6		8		9	11	10	2	4	7											
5	1		3	5		6		8			11	10	2	4	7	9										
6	1			5		6		8			11	10	2	4	7	9	3									
7				5				8			11	9	2	4	7	10	3	1	6							
8		2		5				10			11	9		4	7	8	3	1	6							
9		2		5				8			11	9		4	7		3	1	6	10						
10		2		5				10	9		11	8		4	7		3	1	6							
11		2		5				10	9		11	8		4	7		3	1	6							
12		2		5				10	9		11			4	7		3	1	6	8						
13		2		5				10	9		11			4	7	8	3	1	6							
14				5		6		8			11	9		4	7	2		1	3	10						
15				5		6	7	8			11			4			3	1	2	10	9					
16				5		6		8			11	9		4	7		3	1	2	10						
17	1	2		5		6		10	8	9				4	7		3			11						
18	1	2		5				8	9		11			4	7		3		6	10						
19	1		3	5				4	9		11	10		2	7					8	6					
20	1		3	5				4	9		11			2	7		10			8	6					
21	1		3	5		6			9		11			2	7		10			8		4				
22	1		3	5		6			9		11			2	7		10			8						4
23	1		3	5		6			9		11		2	4	7		10			8						
24	1		3	5		6			9		11		2	4	7		10			8						
25	1		3	5		6			9		11		2	4	7		10			8						
26	1		3	5					9		11	8	2	4	7						6		10			
27	1		3	5		6			9		11		2	4	7						8		10			
28	1	2	3	5		6			9		11			4	7								10	8		
29	1	2	3	5		6			9		11			4	7								10	8		
30	1	2	3	5		6									7					11	8		10	9		4
31	1	2	3	5				8							7					11	6		10	9		4
32	1		3	5		6			9		11			4	7		2						10		8	
33	1		3	5		6			9		11	10		4	7		2								8	
34	1		3	5		6			9		11	10		4	7		2								8	
35	1		3	5		6			9		11	10		4	7		2								8	
36	1		3	5		6			9		11	10		4	7		2								8	
37	1		3	5		6			9		11	10		4	7		2								8	
38	1		3	5		6			9		11	10		4	7		2								8	
39	1		3	5		6			9		11	10		4	7		2								8	
40	1		3	5		6			9		11	10		4	7		2								8	
41	1		3	5		6			9		11	10		4	7		2								8	
42	1		3	5		6			9		11	10		4	7		2								8	
Totals	32	18	25	40	6	12	3	39	27	6	39	23	14	34	39	11	24	10	12	6	14	1	4	7	14	2
(goals)				1				4	4		5	11					1	1			2				9	

1922-23

Manager: A.Chadwick/F.Mavin

1	Aug	26	(a)	Aberdare A	L 1-3	Devlin	8,000
2		30	(h)	Brighton & HA	W 1-0	Mathieson	5,000
3	Sep	2	(h)	Aberdare A	W 1-0	Devlin	7,000
4		6	(a)	Brighton & HA	L 0-3		11,000
5		9	(h)	Charlton A	D 0-0		6,500
6		16	(a)	Charlton A	D 0-0		5,000
7		23	(h)	Watford	L 1-2	Crockford	5,000
8		30	(a)	Watford	L 0-4		5,000
9	Oct	7	(h)	Brentford	L 0-2		6,000
10		14	(a)	Brentford	W 1-0	Matthews	7,000
11		21	(a)	Swansea T	L 1-5	Devlin	10,000
12		28	(h)	Swansea T	W 1-0	Mitton	5,000
13	Nov	4	(h)	Norwich C	W 2-0	Crockford, Matthews	4,000
14		11	(a)	Norwich C	L 0-6		6,000
15		25	(a)	Northampton T	L 0-3		7,000
16	Dec	9	(h)	Southend U	W 2-1	Devlin, Kirk	4,000
17		16	(a)	Southend U	L 0-5		3,000
18		23	(h)	Merthyr T	W 2-1	Mathieson, Devlin	1,000
19		25	(a)	Bristol R	D 3-3	Kirk 2 (1 pen), Mathieson	10,000
20		26	(h)	Bristol R	D 0-0		10,000
21		30	(a)	Reading	W 3-1	Crockford 3	8,000
22	Jan	6	(h)	Reading	W 4-0	Kirk 2, Crockford 2 (1 pen)	5,000
23		13	(h)	Northampton T	L 1-2	Crockford (pen)	4,500
24		20	(h)	Swindon T	W 2-1	Crockford, Kirk	5,000
25		27	(a)	Swindon T	L 1-2	Weston (og)	5,000
26	Feb	3	(a)	Newport C	L 2-6	Crockford, Davis	6,000
27		10	(h)	Newport C	W 4-0	Crockford 3, Carr (og)	4,000
28		17	(a)	Bristol C	D 1-1	Davis	12,000
29		24	(h)	Bristol C	D 0-0		7,000
30	Mar	3	(a)	Portsmouth	W 4-3	Kirk 4	6,000
31		10	(h)	Portsmouth	L 2-3	Newton (og), Kirk	6,000
32		17	(h)	Millwall	W 2-1	Davis, Mathieson	5,000
33		24	(a)	Millwall	L 0-3		10,000
34		30	(a)	Plymouth A	L 1-5	Crockford (pen)	16,000
35		31	(h)	Luton T	L 1-2	Crockford (pen)	5,000
36	Apr	2	(h)	Plymouth A	D 0-0		14,000
37		7	(a)	Luton T	L 0-6		8,000
38		12	(a)	Merthyr T	L 1-3	Crockford	3,000
39		14	(h)	Queen's Park R	L 1-2	Davis	4,000
40		21	(a)	Queen's Park R	L 0-2		6,000
41		28	(h)	Gillingham	L 0-1		4,000
42	May	5	(a)	Gillingham	L 1-2	Crockford (pen)	4,000

FINAL LEAGUE POSITION: 20th in Division Three South

Appearances
Goals

FA Cup

Q4	Nov	18	(h)	Bournemouth	D 0-0	
R		22	(a)	Bournemouth	W 3-1	
Q5	Dec	2	(h)	Bath C	L 1-2	

Fryer	Pollard	Ackroyd	Rigby	Mitton	Crompton	Newman	Vowles	Devlin	Crockford	Dockray	Southway	Clarke	Mathieson	Matthews	Shelton	Kirk	Bell	Flynn	Davis	Pavey	Coopland	Duke	
1	2	3	4	5	6	7	8	9	10	11													1
1	2	3			4	7	8	9		11	5	6	10										2
1	2	3			4	7	8	9		11	5	6	10										3
1	2	3			4		8	9		11	5	6	10	7									4
1	2	3			4		8	9		11	5	6	10	7									5
1	2	3			4		8		9		5	6	10	7	11								6
1	2	3		5				9			4	6	10	7	11	8							7
1		2			4			9			5	6	10	7	11	8	3						8
1	2	3	4	5	6			9					10	7	11	8							9
1	2	3	4	5	6			9					10	7	11	8							10
1	2	3	4	5	6				10				9	7	11	8							11
1	2	3	4	5	6				10				9	7	11	8							12
1	2	3	4	5	6				10				9	7	11	8							13
1	2	3	4		6			9				5	10	7	11	8							14
1	2			5	6			9		11		4	10	7		8		3					15
1	2		4	5	6			9		11			10	7		8		3					16
1	2	3	4	5				9		11		6	10	7		8							17
1	2	3	4	5					9	11		6	10	7		8							18
1	2	3	4	5	6				9	11			10	7		8							19
1	2	3	4	5					9	11		6	10	7		8							20
1	2	3	4		5				9	11		6	10	7		8							21
1	2	3	4	5					9	11		6	10	7		8							22
1		3	4	5				9	10	11		6		7		8		2					23
1	2	3	4	5	6			9	10	11				7		8							24
1	2	3	4	5	6			9		11				7		8			10				25
	2	3	4	5	6			9		11				7		8			10	1			26
	2	3	4	5	6			9		11				7		8			10	1			27
	2	3		5	6			9		11				7		8			10	1	4		28
	2	3		5	6			9		11				7		8			10	1	4		29
	2	3		5	6			9		11				7		8			10	1	4		30
	2			5	6			9		11	4		10	7				3	8	1			31
	2			5	6			9		11	4		10	7				3	8	1			32
	2	3		5	6			9		11	4		10	7					8	1			33
	2			5	6			9		11	4			7				3	8	1	10		34
	2			5	6			9					10	7	11			3	8	1	4		35
	2			5	6			9						7	10			3	8	1	4		36
				5	6			9	2					7	11	8		3	10	1	4		37
				5	6			9						7	11	8		3	10	1	4		38
	4			5	6				10	11	2			7		8		3	9	1			39
	2			5	6			9		11				7		8		3	10	1	4		40
	2				6			9		11	5			7		8		3	10	1	4		41
26	39	30	19	32	36	3	10	12	30	30	15	16	26	39	13	29	1	13	17	16	9	1	42
	1						5	17		4	2		11			4							

3 own-goals

1923-24

Manager: F.Mavin

#	Month	Date		Opponent	Result	Scorers	Attendance
1	Aug	25	(a)	Newport C	L 0-2		10,000
2		29	(h)	Merthyr T	W 1-0	Kirk	6,000
3	Sep	1	(h)	Newport C	W 5-0	Kirk 2, Matthews, Batten, Davis	8,000
4		6	(a)	Merthyr T	L 0-3		8,000
5		8	(h)	Bournemouth	L 0-2		7,000
6		12	(h)	Portsmouth	D 0-0		5,000
7		15	(a)	Bournemouth	L 0-1		6,000
8		22	(h)	Reading	W 3-2	Kirk, Edmondson, Matthews (pen)	6,000
9		29	(a)	Reading	L 0-1		8,000
10	Oct	6	(h)	Luton T	W 2-1	Dockray, Matthews (pen)	6,000
11		13	(a)	Luton T	L 0-1		6,000
12		20	(a)	Brighton & HA	L 0-1		7,000
13		27	(h)	Brighton & HA	L 0-1		5,000
14	Nov	3	(a)	Bristol R	D 0-0		9,000
15		10	(h)	Bristol R	W 3-1	Matthews (pen), Davis 2	5,000
16		24	(a)	Brentford	L 0-1		4,000
17	Dec	8	(a)	Portsmouth	L 0-4		8,000
18		22	(a)	Southend U	D 0-0		3,000
19		25	(a)	Plymouth A	L 0-4		14,500
20		26	(h)	Plymouth A	L 0-4		13,000
21		29	(a)	Aberdare A	D 0-0		3,000
22	Jan	5	(h)	Aberdare A	D 1-1	Davis	4,000
23		26	(h)	Charlton A	D 0-0		4,000
24	Feb	9	(h)	Norwich C	L 1-2	Kirk	3,000
25		14	(a)	Norwich C	L 0-4		4,000
26		16	(a)	Swindon T	W 1-0	Flynn	6,000
27		23	(h)	Southend U	W 2-0	Lievesley, Charlton (pen)	4,000
28	Mar	1	(a)	Watford	L 1-4	Davis	7,000
29		8	(h)	Watford	W 1-0	Gallogley	5,000
30		15	(h)	Swansea T	W 1-0	Kirk	6,000
31		19	(h)	Swindon T	W 3-1	Shelton, Kirk, Dockray	4,000
32		22	(a)	Swansea T	L 0-1		10,000
33		29	(h)	Northampton T	W 2-1	Gilchrist, Dockray	4,000
34	Apr	2	(h)	Brentford	W 1-0	Coleburne	3,500
35		5	(a)	Northampton T	L 0-1		7,000
36		7	(a)	Charlton A	L 0-1		950
37		12	(h)	Gillingham	W 2-1	Coleburne, Matthews (pen)	4,000
38		18	(a)	Millwall	L 1-3	Lievesley	11,000
39		19	(a)	Gillingham	D 1-1	Lievesley	5,000
40		21	(h)	Millwall	W 2-0	Kirk, Coleburne	11,000
41		26	(h)	Queen's Park R	W 3-0	Dockray 2, Murray	5,000
42	May	3	(a)	Queen's Park R	L 0-2		7,000

FINAL LEAGUE POSITION: 16th in Division Three South

Appearances
Goals

FA Cup

Q4	Nov	17	(a)	Newport C	W 2-0
Q5	Dec	1	(h)	Bristol R	D 2-2
R		5	(a)	Bristol R	W 1-0
Q6		15	(a)	Sittingbourne	W 2-0
1	Jan	12	(h)	Grimsby T	W 1-0
2	Feb	2	(h)	Watford	D 0-0
R		6	(a)	Watford	L 0-1

178

Bailey	Coleburne	Flynn	Hunter	Whelan	Crawshaw	Lievesley	Batten	Kirk	Davis	Dockray	Charlton	Crompton	Gilchrist	Matthews	Lowson	Murray	Edmondson	Pollard	McIntosh	Gallogley	Shelton	Potter	Pavey	
1	2	3	4	5	6	7	8	9	10	11														1
1	2		4			7	9	8	10	11	3	5	6											2
1	2		4				9	8	10	11	3	5	6	7										3
1	2		4				9	8	10	11	3	5	6	7										4
1	2		4	6			9	8	10	11	3	5		7										5
1	2		4				9	8		11	3	5	6	7	10									6
1	2	5					8	9		11	3		6	7	10	4								7
1	2		4				8			11	3	5	6	7		10	9							8
1	2		4				8			11	3	5	6	7		10	9							9
1			4				8			11	3			7		6	9	2	5	10				10
1	3		4				8			11	3		6	7		9			5	10				11
1	2		4								3		6	7	10	9			5	8	11			12
1	2		4								3		6	7	10	9			5	8	11			13
1	2		4				8	9			3		6	7					5	10	11			14
1	2		4				8	9			3		6	7					5	10	11			15
1	2	3	4				8	9					6	7					5	10	11			16
1	2	3	4				8	9			6			7					5	10	11			17
1	2						8	9			3		6	7	4				5	10	11			18
1	2						8	9			3		6	7	4				5	10	11			19
1		6	4			9				11	3		5		10	8		2				7		20
1		4				7	8	9			3				10			2	5		11	6		21
1	2				4	7	8	9			3	5	6							10	11			22
1	2				6	7	9	8	10		3	5						4			11			23
1	2				6	7		8	9	11	3	5			10			4						24
1	4	9				7	8	10	11		3		6					2	5					25
1	4	9				7	8	10	11		3	5	6					2						26
1	4	6				7		10	11		3							2	5	8	9			27
1	4						8			11	3	5	6	7				2		10	9			28
1	4						8			11	3	5	6	7				2		10	9			29
1	4						8		10	11	3	5	6	7				2			9			30
1	4						8		10	11	3	5	6	7				2			9			31
1	4						8	9		11	3	5	6	7				2			10			32
1	4						8	9		11	3	5	6	7				2		10				33
1	4						8			11	3	5	6	7				2		10	9			34
1	4					9			10	11	3	5	6	7				2		8				35
1	4					9		8		11	3	5		7				2		10		6		36
1	4					9		8		11	3	5		7				2		10		6		37
1	2					9		8		11	3	4		7	10			5				6		38
	4					9		8		11	3	5			10			2			7	6	1	39
1	4					9		8		11	3	5			10			2			7	6		40
1	4					9		8		11	3	5			10			2			7	6		41
1	4					9		8		11	3	5			10			2			7	6		42
41	39	7	18	2	5	16	9	37	24	30	39	26	29	29	4	14	6	19	16	21	23	7	1	
3	1				3	1	8	5	5	1		1	5		1	1			1	1				

1924-25

Manager: F.Mavin

1	Aug	30	(h)	Reading	W 1-0 Matthews (pen)	6,500
2	Sep	1	(a)	Bristol C	W 1-0 Appleyard	15,000
3		6	(a)	Merthyr T	W 1-0 Compton	5,000
4		8	(a)	Luton T	D 1-1 Compton	6,000
5		10	(h)	Bristol C	L 0-2	8,000
6		13	(h)	Queen's Park R	L 1-3 Kirk	7,000
7		20	(a)	Charlton A	L 0-1	6,000
8		24	(h)	Swansea T	W 2-0 Davis 2	4,500
9		27	(h)	Northampton T	D 0-0	7,000
10	Oct	4	(a)	Watford	L 0-3	7,000
11		11	(h)	Southend U	L 0-1	6,000
12		18	(a)	Newport C	L 1-2 Davis	7,000
13		25	(h)	Swindon T	W 1-0 Kirk	8,000
14	Nov	1	(a)	Aberdare A	L 1-3 Blackmore	2,500
15		8	(h)	Norwich C	W 1-0 Matthews (pen)	6,000
16		15	(a)	Brentford	W 5-2 Matthews, Pullan, Blackmore 2, Compton	2,500
17		22	(h)	Millwall	D 0-0	6,000
18	Dec	6	(h)	Gillingham	D 3-3 Lievesley, Compton, Blackmore	6,000
19		20	(h)	Brighton & HA	W 2-0 Davis, Pullan	5,000
20		25	(a)	Plymouth A	D 1-1 Compton	15,000
21		26	(h)	Plymouth A	W 3-0 Kirk, Compton, Potter	14,000
22		27	(a)	Reading	D 1-1 Lievesley	10,000
23	Jan	3	(h)	Merthyr T	W 2-1 Davis 2	6,000
24		17	(a)	Queen's Park R	W 4-1 Kirk, Compton, Matthews (pen), Davis	6,000
25		24	(a)	Charlton A	W 2-1 Davis, Compton	6,500
26		31	(a)	Northampton T	L 1-2 Crompton	5,000
27	Feb	7	(h)	Watford	W 4-0 Davis, Charlton, Crompton, Kirk	5,000
28		14	(a)	Southend U	L 0-3	5,000
29		21	(h)	Newport C	W 4-3 Kirk 3, Lievesley	7,000
30		28	(a)	Swindon T	L 0-1	8,0000
31	Mar	7	(h)	Aberdare A	W 3-1 Blackmore, Smelt, Compton	4,000
32		14	(a)	Norwich C	W 1-0 Compton	6,000
33		21	(h)	Brentford	W 5-1 Compton, Lievesley 2, Shelton 2	3,000
34		25	(a)	Bournemouth	D 1-1 Kirk	5,000
35		28	(a)	Millwall	L 0-2	6,000
36	Apr	4	(h)	Luton T	L 0-1	5,000
37		10	(a)	Bristol R	W 1-0 Kirk	3,000
38		11	(a)	Gillingham	D 1-1 Kirk	5,000
39		13	(h)	Bristol R	D 1-1 Sambridge (og)	10,000
40		18	(h)	Bournemouth	W 2-1 Kirk, Shelton	5,000
41		25	(a)	Brighton & HA	L 0-2	6,500
42	May	2	(a)	Swansea T	L 1-2 Blackmore	25,000

FINAL LEAGUE POSITION: 7th in Division Three South

Appearances
Goals

FA Cup

Q5	Nov	29	(h)	Newport C	D 1-1
R	Dec	4	(a)	Newport C	D 3-3
2R	Dec	8	(n*)	Newport C	W 1-0
Q6	Dec	13	(h)	Barnet	W 3-0
1	Jan	10	(a)	Southampton †	L 0-5
	Jan	14	(a)	Southampton	L 1-3

*Played at Bristol. †Match abandoned after 77 minutes, fog.

Football appearances and goals grid (numbers indicate shirt positions worn in each match).

Match	Bailey	Pollard	Charlton	Coleburne	Crompton	Potter	Matthews	Pullan	Lievesley	Davis	Compton	Appleyard	Flynn	Jones	Kirk	Crawshaw	Murray	Shelton	Smelt	Blackmore
1	1	2	3	4	5	6	7	8	9	10	11									
2	1	2	3	4	5	6	7	8		10	11	9								
3	1	2		4	5	6	7	8		10	11	9	3							
4	1	2		4		6	7	8		10	11	9	3	5						
5	1	2		4		6	7			10	11	9	3	5	8					
6	1	2	3		5	6	7		9		11				8	4	10			
7	1	2	3		5		7	4	9		11				8	6	10			
8	1	2	3		5		7	4	9		11				8	6	10			
9	1		3		5	6	7	8	9		11		2			4	10			
10	1	2	3		5	6	7	4			11				8		10	9		
11	1	2	3		5		7	4		10	11	9		6	8					
12	1	2	3		5		7	4		10	11			6	8			9		
13	1	2	3		5		7			10	11			6	8	4		9		
14	1	2	3		5		7	4		10	11			6	8			9		
15	1	2	3		5		7	4		10	11			6	8			9		
16	1	2	3		5		7	4			11	9		6	8			10		
17	1	2			5		7		9		11		3		8	4	6	10		
18	1	2	3		5		7	4	9	10	11			6	8					
19	1	2	3		5	6	7	4	9	10	11				8					
20	1	2	3		5	6	7	4	9	10	11				8					
21	1	2	3		5	6	7	4	9	10	11				8					
22	1	2	3		5	6	7	4	9	10	11				8					
23	1	2	3		5	6	7	4	9	10	11				8					
24	1	2			5	6	7	4	9	10	11		3		8					
25	1	2	3		5	6	7	4	9	10	11				8					
26	1	2	3		5	6	7	4	9	10	11				8					
27	1	2	3		5	6	7	4	9	10					8		11			
28	1	2	3		5	6	7	4		10					8		11	9		
29	1	2	3		5	6	7	4	9	10					8		11			
30	1	2	3		5	6	7	4			11						10		8	9
31	1	2	3		5		7	4	9	10	11				8	6				
32	1	2	3		5	6	7	4	9		11				8		10			
33	1	2	3		5	6	7	4	9		11				8		10			
34	1	2	3		5	6	7	4	9		11				8		10			
35	1	2			5	6	7	4	9	10	11		3		8					
36	1	2			5	6	7	4	9		11		3		8		10			
37	1	2			5		7	4		10	11		3		8	6				9
38	1	2			5	6	7	4	9		11		3		8		10			
39	1	2			5	6	7	4			11		3		8		10			9
40	1	2			5	6	7	4		10	11		3		8					9
41	1	2			5	6	7	4		10	11		3		8				9	
42	1	2			5	6	7	4		10	11		3						8	9
Apps	42	41	30	6	37	32	42	37	24	27	39	8	13	10	33	6	6	13	5	11
Goals		1			2	1	4		2	5	9	11	1		12			3	1	6

1 own-goal

1925-26

Manager: F.Mavin

#	Month	Date		Opponent	Result	Scorers	Att.
1	Aug	29	(a)	Reading	L 2-3	Compton 2	12,834
2		31	(a)	Bristol R	W 1-0	Matthews (pen)	10,000
3	Sep	5	(h)	Bournemouth	L 0-1		5,000
4		9	(h)	Bristol R	W 3-0	Myers, Casson, Compton	5,500
5		12	(a)	Charlton A	L 0-1		5,000
6		19	(h)	Gillingham	W 2-1	Compton, Casson	5,500
7		23	(h)	Queen's Park R	W 3-0	Myers, Kirk, Lowton (pen)	5,000
8		26	(a)	Merthyr T	L 1-3	Myers	8,000
9	Oct	3	(h)	Newport C	W 2-1	Compton, Casson	7,000
10		8	(a)	Queen's Park R	D 0-0		3,000
11		10	(a)	Luton T	D 1-1	Blackmore	5,000
12		17	(h)	Bristol C	D 1-1	Charlton (pen)	8,000
13		24	(a)	Crystal P	L 2-3	Shelton, Kirk	5,000
14		31	(h)	Norwich C	L 0-1		6,000
15	Nov	7	(a)	Southend U	L 1-3	Blackmore	5,000
16		14	(h)	Brighton & HA	L 2-4	Charlton (pen), Kirk	5,000
17		21	(a)	Aberdare A	L 0-5		5,000
18	Dec	5	(a)	Millwall	L 0-3		8,000
19		19	(a)	Watford	L 1-3	Blackmore	7,500
20		25	(h)	Plymouth A	W 4-0	Blackmore, Lievesley, Price (og), Compton	10,000
21		26	(a)	Plymouth A	D 2-2	Compton, Blackmore	20,000
22		28	(h)	Brentford	W 6-1	Shelton, Blackmore 3, Matthews, Potter	7,000
23	Jan	2	(h)	Reading	W 3-2	McDevitt, Lievesley 2	5,000
24		16	(a)	Bournemouth	L 1-2	Charlton (pen)	2,000
25		23	(h)	Charlton A	W 5-3	Blackmore 2, Lievesley 2, McDevitt	5,000
26		30	(a)	Gillingham	L 0-2		4,000
27	Feb	6	(h)	Merthyr T	W 6-2	Lievesley 3, Blackmore, Shelton, Charlton (pen)	7,000
28		13	(a)	Newport C	L 0-3		6,000
29		20	(h)	Luton T	D 2-2	Lievesley, Compton	7,000
30		27	(a)	Bristol C	L 0-1		15,000
31	Mar	6	(h)	Crystal P	L 0-1		6,000
32		13	(a)	Norwich C	L 1-3	Newman	7,000
33		20	(h)	Southend U	L 0-1		5,000
34		27	(a)	Brighton & HA	W 3-1	Kirk, Compton, Lievesley	6,000
35	Apr	2	(a)	Swindon T	L 1-2	Compton	9,000
36		3	(h)	Aberdare A	W 4-0	Lievesley 3, Shelton	7,000
37		5	(h)	Swindon T	L 1-2	Lievesley	11,000
38		10	(a)	Northampton T	L 1-2	Charlton (pen)	4,000
39		14	(h)	Northampton T	W 1-0	Lievesley	3,500
40		17	(h)	Millwall	W 3-1	Compton, Lievesley, Kirk	6,000
41		24	(a)	Brentford	L 0-2		5,000
42	May	1	(h)	Watford	W 6-1	Lievesley 2, Blackmore 3, Compton	6,000

FINAL LEAGUE POSITION: 20th in Division Three South

Appearances
Goals

FA Cup

1	Nov	28	(h)	Swansea T	L 1-3		

Player appearance and goalscoring grid (matches 1–42):

Bailey	Pollard	Hawkins	Pullan	Crompton	Potter	Matthews	Kirk	Blackmore	Myers	Compton	Lievesley	Charlton	Casson	Bolam	Flynn	Shelton	Lowton	McDevitt	Pavey	Anderson	Newman	Garratt	
1	2	3	4	5	6	7	8	9	10	11													1
1	2	3	4	5	6	7	8		10	11	9												2
1	2		4	5	6	7	8		10	11	9	3											3
1	2	3	4	5	6	7	8		10	11			9										4
1	2	3	4	5	6	7				11	10		9	8									5
1	2		4	5	6	7	8		10				9		3	11							6
1	2		4		6	7	8		10	11			9				3	5					7
1	2		4			7	8		10	11			9			6	3	5					8
	2		4			7	8		10	11		3	9			6		5	1				9
	2		4			7	8		10	11		3	9			6		5	1				10
	2		4			7	8	9	10	11		3				6		5	1				11
	2		4			7	8		10	11		3	9			6		5	1				12
	2		4			7	8	9	10	11		3				6		5	1				13
	2		4			7	8	9	10	11		3				6		5	1				14
	2		4					9		11	10	3				6		5	1	8	7		15
	2		4	5			8	9		11		3				6		10	1		7		16
	2				6		8	9		11	10	3				4		5	1		7		17
	2		4	5		7	8	9	10	11		3				6			1				18
1	2		4		5	7		9		11	10					6	3	8					19
1	2		4		5	7		9		11	10	3				6		8					20
1	2		4		5	7		9		11	10	3				6		8					21
1	2		4		5	7		9		11	10	3				6		8					22
1	2		4		5	7		9		11	10	3				6		8					23
1	2		4		5	7		9		11	10	3				6		8					24
1	2		4		5	7		9		11	10	3				6		8					25
1	2		4		5	7		9		11	10	3				6		8					26
1	2		4		5	7		9		11	10	3				6		8					27
1	2		4		5	7		9		11	10	3				6		8					28
1			4		5	7		9		11	10	3				6	2	8					29
1	2		4		5	7		9		11	10	3				6		8					30
1	2		4		5	7		9		11	10	3				6		8					31
1	2		4				8	9	6	11	10	3									7	5	32
1	2		4		6		8	9		11	10	3									7	5	33
1	5		4		6		8		10	11	9	3					2				7		34
1	5		4		6		8		10	11	9	3					2				7		35
1	5		4		6		8			11	9	3				10	2				7		36
1	5		4		6		8			11	9	3				10	2				7		37
1	5		4		6		8		10	11	9	3					2				7		38
1	5		4		6		8	9		11	10	3					2				7		39
1	5		4		6		8	9		11	10	3					2				7		40
1			4		6		8	9	5	11	10	3					2				7		41
1	5		4		6		8	9		11	10	3					2				7		42
32	40	4	40	7	33	28	27	27	19	42	29	34	8	1	1	26	13	24	10	1	14	2	
					1	2	5	14	3	12	18	5	3			4	1	2			1		

1 own-goal

1926-27

Manager: F.Mavin

1	Aug	28	(h)	Merthyr T	W	3-0	Walker, Blackmore 2	8,000
2		30	(a)	Swindon T	L	2-4	Purcell, Pool	4,500
3	Sep	4	(a)	Southend U	W	2-1	Blackmore, Walker	6,000
4		11	(h)	Luton T	L	1-2	Charlton (pen)	8,000
5		15	(h)	Bristol R	D	1-1	Blackmore	6,000
6		18	(a)	Norwich C	D	4-4	Hannah (og), Blackmore 2, Phoenix	8,500
7		25	(h)	Brighton & HA	D	0-0		7,000
8	Oct	2	(a)	Northampton T	D	2-2	Phoenix 2	5,000
9		9	(h)	Brentford	W	3-1	Blackmore 2, Phoenix	7,000
10		16	(a)	Bristol C	L	2-3	Lievesley, Compton	14,000
11		23	(h)	Bournemouth	W	4-0	Blackmore 3, Lievesley	6,000
12		30	(a)	Newport C	L	0-2		7,000
13	Nov	6	(h)	Aberdare A	W	2-1	Blackmore, Charlton	6,000
14		13	(a)	Gillingham	L	2-3	Blackmore, Compton	4,000
15		20	(h)	Watford	W	2-0	Compton, Blackmore	5,000
16	Dec	4	(h)	Coventry C	W	8-1	Dent 2, Compton 2, Purcell 2, Blackmore 2	6,000
17		18	(a)	Charlton A	W	1-0	Blackmore	6,000
18		25	(a)	Plymouth A	L	0-2		15,000
19		27	(h)	Plymouth A	L	0-2		19,221
20		28	(a)	Bristol R	L	1-3	Parkin	17,000
21	Jan	1	(h)	Swindon T	W	3-1	Charlton (pen), Phoenix 2	8,000
22		15	(a)	Merthyr T	D	3-3	Lievesley, Blackmore, McDevitt	2,000
23		22	(h)	Southend U	W	2-0	Lievesley, Blackmore	5,000
24		29	(a)	Luton T	D	2-2	Phoenix, Potter	6,000
25	Feb	5	(h)	Norwich C	W	1-0	Campbell (og)	5,000
26		9	(a)	Crystal P	L	0-1		8,000
27		12	(a)	Brighton & HA	L	2-5	Purcell, Blackmore	10,000
28		19	(h)	Northampton T	W	3-2	Blackmore 2, Lowton (pen)	6,000
29		24	(a)	Queen's Park R	D	1-1	McDevitt	3,000
30		26	(a)	Brentford	L	1-6	Compton	7,000
31	Mar	5	(h)	Bristol C	D	1-1	Blackmore	8,000
32		12	(a)	Bournemouth	L	3-4	Blackmore 2, Lievesley	7,000
33		19	(h)	Newport C	W	2-1	Compton, Purcell	5,000
34		26	(a)	Aberdare A	L	1-3	Lowton (pen)	6,000
35	Apr	2	(h)	Gillingham	W	5-1	Lowton (pen), Lievesley 4	3,000
36		9	(a)	Watford	L	0-1		3,000
37		15	(a)	Millwall	L	2-4	Lievesley 2	15,000
38		16	(h)	Crystal P	W	3-1	Dent, Lievesley, Purcell	6,000
39		18	(h)	Millwall	D	1-1	Purcell	10,500
40		23	(a)	Coventry C	D	0-0		8,000
41		30	(h)	Queen's Park R	L	0-2		6,000
42	May	7	(a)	Charlton A	L	0-1		8,000

FINAL LEAGUE POSITION: 12th in Division Three South

Appearances
Goals

FA Cup

1	Nov	27	(h)	Aberdare A	W	3-0
2	Dec	11	(h)	Northampton T	W	1-0
3	Jan	8	(h)	Accrington S	L	0-2

Bailey	Pollard	Charlton	Ditchburn	Pool	Garratt	Purcell	McDevitt	Blackmore	Walker	Compton	Randall	Pullan	Good	Phoenix	Dent	Potter	Lievesley	Parkin	Lowton	Newman	Miller	
1	2	3	4	5	6	7	8	9	10	11												
1	2	3	4	5	6	7	8	9	10	11												1
	2	3		5	6	7	8	9	10	11	1	4										2
	2	3		5	6	7	8	9	10	11	1	4										3
1	2	3		5	6	7	8	9	10	11		4										4
1	2	3	4		6	7		9		11			5	8	10							5
1	2	3		5		7		9		11		4		8	10	6						6
1	2	3		5		7		9		11		4		8		6	10					7
1	2	3		5		7		9		11		4		8		6	10					8
1	2	3		5		7		9		11		4		8		6	10					9
1	2	3		5		7		9		11		4		8		6	10					10
1	2	3		5		7		9		11		4		8		6	10					11
1	2	3		5		7		9	10	11		4		8		6						12
1	2	3		5		7	8	9		11		4				6	10					13
1	2	3		5		7	8	9		11		4			10	6						14
1	2	3		5	6	7	8	9		11		4			10							15
1	2	3		5	6	7	8	9		11		4			10							16
1	2	3		5		7		9				4		8	10	6	11					17
1	2	3		5		7	8	9				4			10	6	11					18
1	2	3		5		7	8	9				4			6	10	11					19
1	2	3		5		7	8		10			4			6	9	11					20
1	2	3		5		7	8	9		11		4				6	10					21
1	2	3		5		7	8	9		11		4				6	10					22
1		3	4			7		9		11			5	8	6	10			2			23
		3				7		9		11		4	5	8	10	6			2			24
		3	4	5		7		9	6	11	1			8	10				2			25
		3	6	5			8	9	10		1	4				11		7	2			26
		3		5		7	8	9		11	1	4			10	6			2			27
		3		5		7	8	9		11	1	4			10	6			2			28
		3		5		7	8	9		11	1	4			10	6			2			29
1		3	4	5		7	8	9		11					10				2		6	30
		3	4	5		7	8	9		11	1					6	10		2			31
		3	4	5		7	8	9		11	1						10		2		6	32
		3	4	5		7		9		11	1			8			10		2		6	33
		3	4	5		7	8			11	1					10	9		2		6	34
		3	4	5			8			11	1					10	9	7	2		6	35
		3	4	5			8			11	1					10	9	7	2		6	36
		3		5		7	8			11	1					10	9		2		6	37
1		3	4	5		7	8			11						10	9		2		6	38
1		3	4	5		7	8			11						10	9		2		6	39
1		3	4	5		7	8			11						10	9		2		6	40
1		3	4	5		7	8			11					9	10			2		6	41
1		3	4	5		7	8			11					9	10			2		6	42
28	23	42	30	27	8	41	28	33	12	37	14	26	4	16	14	17	26	5	19	2	10	
		3		1		7	2	25	2	7				7	3	1	12	1	3			

2 own-goals

1927-28

Manager: F.Mavin/D.Wilson

#	Month	Date		Opponent	Result	Scorers	Attendance
1	Aug	27	(a)	Torquay U	D 1-1	Vaughan	11,625
2		29	(a)	Crystal P	L 0-2		12,000
3	Sep	3	(h)	Norwich C	D 2-2	Phoenix, McDevitt	8,000
4		7	(h)	Crystal P	D 2-2	Pool, Phoenix	7,000
5		10	(a)	Northampton T	L 0-5		7,000
6		17	(h)	Southend U	W 3-2	Dent 2, Purcell	6,000
7		24	(a)	Brighton & HA	W 2-0	Compton, Dent	10,000
8	Oct	1	(h)	Bournemouth	W 4-1	Compton 2, Dent, Purcell	6,000
9		8	(a)	Brentford	D 1-1	Dent	9,000
10		15	(h)	Luton T	W 3-2	Purcell 2, Dent	8,000
11		22	(h)	Watford	D 3-3	Purcell 2, Compton	6,000
12		29	(a)	Charlton A	D 0-0		10,000
13	Nov	5	(h)	Bristol R	W 4-1	Dent 4	5,500
14		12	(a)	Queen's Park R	W 1-0	Dent	5,750
15		19	(h)	Swindon T	D 0-0		5,500
16	Dec	3	(h)	Coventry C	L 0-1		5,000
17		17	(h)	Walsall	W 3-0	Vaughan 2, Purcell	6,000
18		24	(a)	Merthyr T	W 3-0	Compton, Dent 2	4,000
19		26	(h)	Plymouth A	W 2-0	Dent, Purcell	10,000
20		27	(a)	Plymouth A	W 2-1	Compton, Russell (og)	13,000
21		31	(h)	Torquay U	W 5-0	Compton, Dent 2, McDevitt, Vaughan	7,000
22	Jan	7	(a)	Norwich C	D 2-2	Dent 2	7,000
23		21	(h)	Northampton T	D 1-1	Vaughan	5,000
24	Feb	4	(h)	Brighton & HA	L 0-3		5,000
25		11	(a)	Bournemouth	L 0-2		6,000
26		15	(a)	Southend U	W 2-1	Mason, Gee (pen)	3,500
27		18	(h)	Brentford	L 0-1		7,000
28		25	(a)	Luton T	L 1-2	Compton	8,000
29	Mar	3	(a)	Watford	L 2-3	Dent, Gee (pen)	8,000
30		10	(h)	Charlton A	W 2-1	Vaughan, Purcell	5,000
31		17	(a)	Bristol R	W 2-1	McDevitt, Dent	9,000
32		22	(a)	Newport C	L 0-1		6,000
33		24	(a)	Queen's Park R	W 4-0	Dent 2, Purcell, Vaughan	6,000
34		28	(a)	Gillingham	D 1-1	Vaughan	5,000
35		31	(a)	Swindon T	L 0-3		3,000
36	Apr	6	(a)	Millwall	L 0-2		4,000
37		7	(h)	Gillingham	D 2-2	Dent, Vaughan	6,000
38		9	(h)	Millwall	L 2-4	Purcell (pen), Dent	12,500
39		14	(a)	Coventry C	D 0-0		7,000
40		21	(h)	Newport C	W 5-1	Dent, Purcell 2, Bastin 2	6,000
41		28	(a)	Walsall	L 1-5	Bastin	5,000
42	May	5	(h)	Merthyr T	W 2-0	Compton, Dent	5,000

FINAL LEAGUE POSITION: 8th in Division Three South

Appearances
Goals

FA Cup

1	Nov	26	(h)	Aberdare A	W 9-1	
2	Dec	10	(h)	Ilford	W 5-3	
3	Jan	14	(a)	Rotherham U	D 3-3	
R		18	(h)	Rotherham U	W 3-1	
4		28	(h)	Blackburn R	D 2-2	
R	Feb	2	(a)	Blackburn R	L 1-3	

Player appearances and goals grid (27 players, 42 matches):

Wainwright	Lowton	Charlton	Ditchburn	Pool	Warren	Purcell	McDevitt	Lievesley	Vaughan	Kirk	Gee	Jenkins	Phoenix	Dent	Compton	Mason	Andrews	Holland	Miller	Pollard	McDade	Edwards	Parkin	Clarke	Bastin	Chambers	#
1	2	3	4	5	6	7	8	9	10	11																	1
1	2	3	4	5			8		10	11	6	7	9														2
1	2	3	4	5			8			7	6		9	10	11												3
1	2	3	4	5		7	10	9		11	6		8														4
1	2	3	4			7				11	6		8	10		5	9										5
	2	3	4	5		7			10				9	8	11			1	6								6
				5		7	8		10		6		4	9	11			1	3	2							7
				5		7	8		10		6		4	9	11			1	3	2							8
				5		7	8		10		6		4	9	11			1	3	2							9
				5		7	8		10		6		4	9	11			1	3	2							10
				5		7	8		10		6		4	9	11			1	3	2							11
				5		7	8		10		6		4	9	11			1	3	2							12
				5		7	8		10		6		4	9	11			1	3	2							13
		3		5		7	8		10		6		4	9	11			1		2							14
		3		5		7	8		10		6		4	9	11			1		2							15
			4			7	8		10		6			9	11	5		1	3	2							16
			4			7	8		10		6			9	11	5		1	3	2							17
			4			7	8		10		6			9	11	5		1	3	2							18
			4			7	8		10		6			9	11	5		1	3	2							19
			4			7	8		10		6			9	11	5		1	3	2							20
			4			7	8		10		6			9	11	5		1	3	2							21
			4			7	8		10		6			9	11	5		1	3	2							22
			4			7	8		10		6		9		11	5		1	3	2							23
			4			7	8		10		6			9	11	5		1	3	2							24
			4			7	8		10		6		9		11	5		1	3	2							25
			4			7	8		10		6				11	5		1	3	2	9						26
			4			7			10		6				11	5		1	3	2	8	9					27
			4			7	8				6				11	5		1	3	2		9	10				28
			4			7	8		10		6				11	5		1	3	2		9					29
1				5		7	8		10		6		4	9	11				3	2							30
1				5		7	8		10				4	9	11				3	2				6			31
1		3		5			8		10			7	4	9						2			11	6			32
1		3		5			8		10			7	4	9						2			11	6			33
1		3		5		7	8		10				4	9	11					2				6			34
1		3		5		7	8		10				4	9	11	5				2							35
1		3		5		7	8		10				4	9	11					2				6			36
1		3		5			8		10			7	4	9	11					2				6			37
		3		5		7	8			11			4	9				1		2				6	10		38
		3				7	8			11			4	9		5		1		2				6	10		39
		3				7	8			11			4	9				1		2				6	10	5	40
		3				7	8						4	10	11	5	9	1		2				6			41
		3				7	8		10				4	9	11	5		1		2				6			42
13	7	18	20	23	1	40	36	2	33	8	29	4	28	34	33	20	2	29	25	36	2	3	3	9	3	1	
			1			13	3		9		2		2	26	9	1								3			

1 own-goal

1928-29

Manager: D.Wilson/W.McDevitt

							Att
1	Aug	25	(a)	Brentford	L 2-4	Houghton, Doncaster	11,000
2		27	(a)	Southend U	L 0-1		7,000
3	Sep	1	(h)	Luton T	D 1-1	Cameron	7,000
4		5	(h)	Southend U	L 1-2	Cameron	7,000
5		8	(a)	Coventry C	D 1-1	Cameron	13,000
6		15	(h)	Northampton T	W 2-0	Cameron, Purcell	6,000
7		22	(a)	Charlton A	L 1-3	Pool	11,000
8		29	(h)	Norwich C	W 3-1	Wade 2, Houghton	6,000
9	Oct	6	(a)	Brighton & HA	L 2-3	Wade 2	8,000
10		13	(h)	Torquay U	L 1-3	Houghton	12,000
11		20	(a)	Gillingham	W 3-1	Death 3	5,000
12		27	(h)	Plymouth A	L 1-2	Death	14,000
13	Nov	3	(a)	Fulham	D 0-0		18,000
14		10	(h)	Queen's Park R	D 1-1	McDevitt	4,000
15		17	(a)	Bristol R	D 1-1	Cameron	8,000
16	Dec	1	(a)	Walsall	L 2-7	Doncaster, Houghton	8,000
17		15	(a)	Crystal P	L 0-1		5,000
18		22	(h)	Swindon T	D 1-1	Purcell	5,000
19		25	(a)	Bournemouth	L 1-3	Houghton	10,000
20		26	(h)	Bournemouth	W 6-3	Houghton, Doncaster 2, Purcell 3	8,000
21		29	(h)	Brentford	L 2-3	Lowton, Streets	5,000
22	Jan	5	(a)	Luton T	L 0-4		5,000
23		19	(h)	Coventry C	L 2-3	Cameron, McDevitt	6,000
24		26	(a)	Northampton T	L 0-4		7,000
25	Feb	2	(h)	Charlton A	L 2-5	Streets, Smith (og)	5,000
26		9	(a)	Norwich C	L 0-5		4,000
27		23	(a)	Torquay U	W 3-1	Doncaster, Purcell, Lowton (pen)	7,000
28	Mar	2	(h)	Gillingham	W 4-2	Doncaster, Purcell, Cameron, Hick	4,000
29		9	(a)	Plymouth A	D 0-0		10,000
30		16	(h)	Fulham	L 1-4	Hick	6,000
31		20	(h)	Newport C	W 6-1	Hick 2, Purcell, Death, Clarke, Bastin	1,500
32		23	(a)	Queen's Park R	L 0-1		12,000
33		30	(h)	Bristol R	D 2-2	Houghton, Bastin	7,000
34	Apr	1	(h)	Merthyr T	W 5-0	Lowton (pen), Hick, Cameron, Bastin (pen), Houghton	10,000
35		2	(a)	Merthyr T	L 1-2	Hick	4,000
36		6	(a)	Watford	L 0-3		9,350
37		10	(h)	Watford	D 2-2	Wade, Clarke	2,000
38		13	(h)	Walsall	D 1-1	Doncaster	4,000
39		17	(h)	Brighton & HA	W 4-1	Hick 2, Clarke, Lowton	2,000
40		20	(a)	Newport C	D 1-1	Cameron	4,000
41		27	(h)	Crystal P	L 1-2	Lowton (pen)	7,000
42	May	4	(a)	Swindon T	L 0-2		3,000

FINAL LEAGUE POSITION: 21st in Division Three South

Appearances
Goals

FA Cup

1	Nov	24	(h)	Barking T	W 6-0
2	Dec	8	(a)	Torquay U	W 1-0
3	Jan	12	(h)	Leeds U	D 2-2
R		16	(a)	Leeds U	L 1-5

188

Player appearance and goalscoring grid (shirt numbers shown per match; matches numbered 1–42 down the right-hand side).

	Campbell	Pollard	Miller	Phoenix	Mason	Christie	Purcell	McDevitt	Cameron	Houghton	Doncaster	Clarke	Wade	Kirk	Taylor	Streets	Bastin	Lowton	Pool	Death	Ditchburn	Dennington	Hick	Holland	Sheffield	
1	1	2	3	4	5	6	7	8	9	10	11															1
2	1	2	3		5	6	7	8		10	11	4	9													2
3	1	2	3		5	6	7	8	9	10		4		11												3
4	1		3				7		9			6	11	4	8	10										4
5	1		3				7	8	9	10	11	6			4		2	5								5
6	1		3	4			7	8	9	10		6					2	5	11							6
7	1		3	4			7	8		10		6	9				2	5	11							7
8	1		3				7	8		10		6	9		4		2	5	11							8
9	1		3				7	8		10		6	9		4		2	5	11							9
10		4	3				7			10		6	9		8		2	5	11					1		10
11		4	3				7			10		6	9		8		2	5	11					1		11
12		4	3				7	8	9	10		6					2	5	11					1		12
13		4	3				7	8	9	11	10	6					2	5						1		13
14			3				7	8	9	11	10	6					2	5			4			1		14
15			3				7	8		10	9	4					2	5					6	1		15
16		4	3				7	8		10	9	6					2	5	11					1		16
17	1	4	3				7	8		10	9	6					2	5	11							17
18	1	4	3				7	8	11	10	9	6					2	5								18
19	1	4	3				7	8	11	10	9	6					2	5								19
20		4	3				7		11	10	9	6			8		2	5						1		20
21			3				7	8	11	10	9	6					2	5			4			1		21
22	1		3				7	8	11		10	4					2	5	9	6						22
23	1		3				7	8	11		10	4					2	5		6	9					23
24	1		3		6		7		11			4					8	10	2	6	9					24
25	1	2		4			7		10							8		3	5	11	6	9				25
26			3	4			7	8	11		10	6					2	5				9	1			26
27			3	4			7		11	10	8	6					2	5				9	1			27
28			3	4			7		11	10	8	6					2	5				9	1			28
29			3	4			7		11	10	8	6					2					5	9	1		29
30			3				7			8		6					10	2		11		5	9	1	4	30
31			3				7			8		6					10	2		11		5	9	1	4	31
32			3	5			7			8							10	2		11	1	6	9	1	4	32
33			3				7		11	8		6					10	2				5	9	1	4	33
34		2	3	5			7		11	8							10					6	9	1	4	34
35		2	3				7		11	8	6	9					10					5		1	4	35
36			3				7			8	6	9					10	2		11		5		1	4	36
37			3				7			8	6	9					10	2		11		5		1	4	37
38			3	5			7		11			8					10	2				6	9	1	4	38
39			3	5			7	11				8					10	2				6	9	1	4	39
40			3	5			7					8					10	2		11		6	9	1	4	40
41			3	5			7										2			11		6	9	1	4	41
42			3	5			7			10	8						2			11		6	9	1	4	42
	17	17	40	8	10	4	42	21	24	27	24	38	9	2	2	9	14	36	24	21	1	19	16	25	12	
			8	2	9	8	7	3	5			2	3	5	1	5						8				

1 own-goal

189

1929-30

Manager: W.McDevitt

#	Month	Date		Opponent	Result	Scorers	Attendance
1	Aug	31	(h)	Luton T	D 2-2	Hemingway, Guyan	9,000
2	Sep	4	(h)	Gillingham	W 3-0	Purcell, Death, Guyan	7,000
3		7	(a)	Bournemouth	L 0-3		5,000
4		11	(a)	Gillingham	L 0-2		6,000
5		14	(h)	Walsall	L 0-2		7,000
6		18	(h)	Torquay U	D 0-0		7,000
7		21	(a)	Queen's Park R	L 0-2		10,000
8		28	(h)	Fulham	W 2-1	Purcell, Guyan	7,000
9	Oct	5	(a)	Norwich C	L 1-3	Hannah (og)	6,000
10		12	(h)	Crystal P	W 6-1	Houghton, Guyan 2, Hemingway, Purcell 2	6,000
11		19	(h)	Merthyr T	D 1-1	Houghton	6,000
12		26	(a)	Plymouth A	L 1-4	Hemingway	17,000
13	Nov	2	(h)	Swindon T	W 5-1	Hemingway 3, Doncaster, Guyan	6,000
14		9	(a)	Brighton & HA	D 1-1	Doncaster	7,000
15		16	(h)	Bristol R	W 5-2	Guyan 2, Hemingway 2, Houghton	5,000
16		23	(a)	Brentford	L 0-2		5,000
17	Dec	7	(a)	Coventry C	D 3-3	Purcell, Houghton (pen), Doncaster	6,000
18		21	(a)	Newport C	L 1-4	Houghton (pen)	5,000
19		25	(a)	Southend U	L 0-1		7,000
20		26	(h)	Southend U	W 3-1	Guyan, Doncaster, Purcell	11,000
21		28	(a)	Luton T	W 4-0	Houghton 2, Purcell, Guyan	5,000
22	Jan	4	(h)	Bournemouth	L 1-2	Houghton (pen)	4,000
23		18	(a)	Walsall	L 2-5	Purcell, Guyan	7,000
24		25	(h)	Queen's Park R	L 0-2		5,000
25	Feb	1	(a)	Fulham	D 2-2	Houghton, Guyan	18,000
26		5	(h)	Clapton O	W 4-0	Purcell, Doncaster, Hemingway 2	4,000
27		8	(h)	Norwich C	W 3-0	Purcell, Houghton, Guyan	7,000
28		15	(a)	Crystal P	D 1-1	Purcell	12,000
29		19	(h)	Watford	W 1-0	Doncaster	4,000
30		22	(a)	Merthyr T	W 2-0	Guyan, Hemingway	3,000
31	Mar	1	(h)	Plymouth A	D 1-1	Shanks	16,000
32		8	(a)	Swindon T	L 0-1		5,000
33		15	(h)	Brighton & HA	L 1-4	Purcell (pen)	5,000
34		22	(a)	Bristol R	L 0-1		8,000
35		29	(h)	Brentford	D 0-0		7,000
36	Apr	5	(a)	Clapton O	L 0-3		8,000
37		12	(h)	Coventry C	D 1-1	Hemingway	6,000
38		19	(a)	Watford	L 1-2	Hemingway	8,000
39		21	(h)	Northampton T	W 6-4	Hemingway 4, Armfield, Mason	8,000
40		22	(a)	Northampton T	D 2-2	Hemingway 2	6,000
41		26	(h)	Newport C	L 0-4		6,000
42	May	3	(a)	Torquay U	L 1-2	Houghton	5,000

FINAL LEAGUE POSITION: 16th in Division Three South

Appearances
Goals

FA Cup

1	Nov	30	(a)	Walsall	L 0-1

190

Football season line-up grid (shirt numbers by player and match). Player columns run left to right; match numbers are in the right-hand column.

Alderson	Howson	Miller	Ditchburn	Mason	McMullan	Purcell	McDevitt	Guyan	Hemingway	Death	Shanks	Sheffield	Henderson	Houghton	Doncaster	Gurkin	Thomas	Clarke	Baugh	Dennington	Armfield	Gray	Varco	Holland	
1	2	3	4	5	6	7	8	9	10	11															1
1	2	3	4	5	6	7	8	9	10	11															2
1	2		4	5	6	7	8	9	10	11	3														3
1	2			5	6	7	8		11		3	4	9	10											4
1	2			5	6	7	8		10	11	3	4	9												5
1	2			5	6	7			10		3	4	9	8	11										6
1	2	3			6	7	5	9	10			4		8	11										7
1	2	3			6	7	5	9	10			4			11			8							8
1	2	3		5	6	7		9	10		3			8	11			4							9
1	2			5	6	7		9	10		3			8	11			4							10
1	2	3		5	6	7		9	10					8	11			4							11
1				5		7		9	10		3			8	11			4	2	6					12
1				5		7		9	10		3			8	11			4	2	6					13
1				5		7		9	10		3			8	11			4	2	6					14
1				5				9	10		3			8	11			4	2	6	7				15
1				5		7		9	10		3			8	11			4	2	6					16
1				5		7		9	10		3			8	11			4	2	6					17
1				5		7		9	10		3	4		8	11				2	6					18
1				5		7		9	10		3	4		8	11				2	6					19
1				5		7		9	10		3	4		8	11				2	6					20
1	2			5		7		9	10		3	4		8	11					6					21
1				5		7		9	10		3	4		8	11					6		2			22
1				5		7		9	10		3	4		8	11					6		2			23
1				5				9	10		3			8	11			4		6	7	2			24
1				5		7			10		3			8	11			4		6		2	9		25
1				5		7	8	9	11		3			10				4		6		2			26
1				5		7	8	9	11		3			10				4		6		2			27
1				5		7		9	10		3			8	11			4		6		2			28
1				5		7	8	9	11		3			10				4		6		2			29
1				5		7	8	9	11		3			10				4		6		2			30
1				5		7	8	9	11		3			10				4		6		2			31
1				5		7		9	10		3			8	11			4		6		2			32
1	2			5		7	8	9	10		3							4		6		2			33
1	2			5		7	8				3			10	11			4		6		2	9		34
1				5	11	7	8				3			10				4		6		2	9		35
				5	11	7					3			10				4		6		2	9		36
				5	11	7		10			3			8				4		6		2	9	1	37
				5	6	8		10			3				11			4		7		2	9	1	38
				5	6	8		9			3			10	11			4		7		2		1	39
				5	6	8		9			3			10	11			4		7		2		1	40
				5	1	8		9			3			10	11			4		6	7	2			41
						8		9			3			10	11	5		4		6	7	2		1	42
36	13	6	18	23	19	40	16	28	39	4	36	12	5	34	29	2	1	24	9	30	7	20	6	5	
		1		12		14	19	1	1					11	6					1					

1 own-goal

1930-31

Manager: W.McDevitt

							Att.
1	Aug	30	(h)	Norwich C	W	1-0 Varco	6,000
2	Sep	3	(h)	Luton T	D	1-1 Houghton	5,000
3		6	(a)	Brighton & HA	L	2-3 Varco 2	5,000
4		8	(a)	Bristol R	D	1-1 Houghton	6,000
5		13	(h)	Torquay U	D	2-2 Halliday, Houghton	8,000
6		17	(h)	Bristol R	L	0-3	3,000
7		20	(a)	Northampton T	L	0-1	7,000
8		27	(h)	Brentford	W	4-0 Armfield, Baugh (pen), Doncaster, Houghton	5,000
9		29	(a)	Luton T	L	1-3 Varco	2,000
10	Oct	4	(a)	Crystal P	L	2-7 Varco, Greener (og)	12,000
11		11	(h)	Southend U	D	1-1 Doncaster	6,000
12		18	(h)	Thames	W	4-3 Varco, Purcell, Armfield, Houghton	6,000
13		25	(a)	Clapton O	W	3-2 Doncaster, Armfield, Varco	4,000
14	Nov	1	(h)	Notts C	D	3-3 Varco, Purcell, Baugh (pen)	5,000
15		8	(a)	Watford	W	1-0 Varco	6,000
16		15	(h)	Bournemouth	W	4-1 Armfield, Houghton 2, Varco	6,000
17		22	(a)	Swindon T	L	1-2 Armfield	5,000
18	Dec	6	(a)	Coventry C	L	1-3 Purcell	9,000
19		20	(a)	Queen's Park R	L	2-7 Varco, Houghton	5,000
20		25	(a)	Newport C	L	0-4	6,000
21		26	(h)	Newport C	W	3-0 Houghton, Varco, Doncaster	7,000
22		27	(a)	Norwich C	W	2-1 Houghton 2	5,000
23	Jan	3	(h)	Brighton & HA	D	2-2 Varco, Wilkinson (og)	5,000
24		14	(h)	Fulham	W	3-2 Varco 2, Lister	3,000
25		17	(a)	Torquay U	D	0-0	6,000
26		28	(h)	Northampton T	D	3-3 Doncaster 2, Armfield	3,000
27		31	(a)	Brentford	L	1-2 Houghton	10,000
28	Feb	7	(h)	Crystal P	W	4-3 Varco 2, Houghton, Doncaster	5,000
29		18	(h)	Walsall	L	2-5 Varco 2	3,000
30		21	(a)	Thames	L	0-1	4,000
31	Mar	7	(a)	Notts C	W	2-1 Varco, Houghton	12,000
32		14	(h)	Watford	W	2-1 Houghton, Armfield	6,000
33		18	(a)	Southend U	L	1-5 Varco	4,000
34		21	(a)	Bournemouth	L	1-3 Houghton	6,000
35		28	(h)	Swindon T	W	3-1 Armfield, Baugh (pen), Houghton	5,000
36	Apr	3	(a)	Gillingham	W	5-3 Varco, Doncaster, Houghton 2, Purcell	6,000
37		4	(a)	Fulham	L	2-4 Purcell, Barber	14,000
38		6	(h)	Gillingham	W	3-0 Baugh (pen), Varco, Houghton	7,000
39		11	(h)	Coventry C	L	2-3 Houghton, Varco	5,000
40		15	(h)	Clapton O	W	6-1 Houghton (pen), Purcell, Armfield, Doncaster 2, Clarke	2,500
41		18	(a)	Walsall	L	1-2 Houghton	4,000
42		25	(h)	Queen's Park R	W	2-0 Purcell, Varco	5,000

FINAL LEAGUE POSITION: 13th in Division Three South

Appearances
Goals

FA Cup

1	Nov	29	(a)	Northfleet U	W	3-0
2	Dec	13	(h)	Coventry C	D	1-1
R		18	(a)	Coventry C	W	2-1
3	Jan	10	(h)	Derby C	W	3-2
4		24	(a)	Bury	W	2-1
5	Feb	14	(h)	Leeds U	W	3-1
6		28	(a)	Sunderland	D	1-1
R	Mar	4	(h)	Sunderland	L	2-4

Davies	Gray	Miller	Clarke	Inglis	Dennington	Purcell	Houghton	Varco	Halliday	Lister	Shanks	Parsons	Doncaster	Barber	Baugh	Ditchburn	Armfield	Jones	McCosh	Angus	Courtney	Gumm	
1	2	3	4	5	6	7	8	9	10	11													1
1	2	3	4	5	6	7	8	9	10	11													2
1	2		4	5	6	7	8	9	10	11	3												3
1	2		4	5	6	7	8		10	11	3	9											4
1	2	3	4	5		7	8		10			9	11	6									5
1		3	4			8	10	9					11	6	2	5	7						6
1		3	4			8	10	9					11	6	2	5	7						7
1		3	4			8	10	9					11	6	2	5	7						8
1		3	4			8	10	9					11	6	2	5	7						9
		3	4			8	10	9					11	6	2	5	7	1					10
		3	4			8	10	9					11	6	2	5	7	1					11
		3	4	5		8	10	9					11	6	2		7	1					12
1		3	4	5		8	10	9					11	6	2		7						13
1		3	4	5		8	10	9					11	6	2		7						14
1		3	4	5		8	10	9	11					6	2		7						15
1		3	4	5		8	10	9	11					6	2		7						16
1		3	4	5		8	10	9					11	6	2		7						17
1			4	5		7	10	9			3		11	6	2				8				18
1		3	4	5		8	10	9					11	6	2		7						19
1	2	3	4	5		8	10	9					11	6			7						20
1	2		4			8	10	9			3		11	6			7			5			21
1		3	4	5		8	10	9					11	6	2		7						22
	2	3	4			8	10	9		11				6			7	1		5			23
1	2	3	4	5		8	10	9		11				6			7						24
1		3	4			8	10	9					11	6	2		7			5			25
		3	4		6	8	10	9					11		2		7	1		5			26
1		3	4			8	10	9					11	6	2		7			5			27
1	2	3	4	4		8	10	9					11				7			5			28
1		3	4			8	10	9					11	6	2		7			5			29
1		3				8	10	9					11	6	2	4	7			5			30
1		3				8	10	9					11	6	2	4	7			5			31
1		3				8	10	9					11	6	2	4	7			5			32
1		3				8	10	9						6	2	4	7			5	11		33
1		3	4			8	10					9		6	2	5	7			5	11		34
1		3				8	10	9					11	6	2	5	7						35
1			4			8	10	9			3		11	6	2	5	7						36
1		3	4			8	10	9					11	6	2	5	7						37
1		3	4			8	10	9					11	6	2					5	7		38
1	2	3	4			8	10	9					11	6			7			5			39
1		3	4			8	10	9					11	6	2		7			5			40
1		3	4			8	10	9					11	6	2		7			5			41
37	**12**	**37**	**31**	**15**	**16**	**42**	**42**	**39**	**6**	**8**	**5**	**3**	**32**	**35**	**30**	**14**	**34**	**5**	**1**	**15**	**2**	**1**	42
		1				7	23	25	1	1			10	1	4		9						

2 own-goals

1931-32

Manager: W.McDevitt

1	Aug	29	(a)	Thames	D 0-0	10,000
2	Sep	2	(h)	Fulham	L 0-3	7,000
3		5	(h)	Brentford	W 4-1 Whitlow, Houghton, Baugh (pen), Doncaster	6,000
4		7	(a)	Northampton T	L 1-2 Whitlow	7,000
5		12	(a)	Bournemouth	L 2-5 Varco 2	6,000
6		16	(h)	Northampton T	D 0-0	7,000
7		19	(a)	Coventry C	L 0-4	12,000
8		26	(h)	Gillingham	W 4-0 Childs, Houghton, Purcell, Barber	6,000
9		30	(h)	Brighton & HA	W 3-1 Varco 2, Clarke	4,000
10	Oct	3	(a)	Luton T	L 3-6 Houghton 2, Varco	5,500
11		10	(h)	Cardiff C	W 3-1 Varco 3	8,000
12		17	(h)	Queen's Park R	W 6-2 Whitlow 3, Armfield, Houghton 2	7,000
13		24	(a)	Bristol R	W 4-2 Whitlow, Houghton 2 (1 pen), Armfield	7,000
14		31	(h)	Torquay U	W 3-1 Clarke, Armfield, Varco	10,000
15	Nov	7	(a)	Clapton O	D 2-2 Whitlow, Houghton	5,000
16		14	(h)	Swindon T	D 1-1 Whitlow	2,500
17		21	(a)	Norwich C	W 1-0 Doncaster	12,000
18	Dec	5	(a)	Mansfield T	L 1-3 Houghton	6,000
19		16	(h)	Watford	W 2-0 Armfield, Whitlow	2,000
20		19	(a)	Crystal P	L 0-3	8,000
21		25	(a)	Southend U	W 1-0 Whitlow	10,000
22		26	(h)	Southend U	W 3-0 Houghton, Woodward, Whitlow	14,000
23	Jan	2	(h)	Thames	W 4-1 Houghton (pen), Doncaster 2, Whitlow	6,000
24		16	(a)	Brentford	D 2-2 Houghton 2 (1 pen)	15,000
25		27	(h)	Bournemouth	W 1-0 Houghton	3,000
26		30	(h)	Coventry C	W 3-0 Doncaster, Varco, Purcell	6,000
27	Feb	6	(a)	Gillingham	W 1-0 Varco	7,000
28		13	(h)	Luton T	D 1-1 Doncaster	6,000
29		20	(a)	Cardiff C	L 2-5 Barber, Purcell	8,000
30		27	(a*)	Queen's Park R	L 0-1	14,000
31	Mar	5	(h)	Bristol R	W 1-0 Woodward	7,500
32		12	(a)	Torquay U	L 1-2 Whitlow	5,500
33		19	(h)	Clapton O	W 4-3 Whitlow, Roberts, Houghton (pen), Doncaster	6,000
34		25	(a)	Reading	L 0-2	20,000
35		26	(a)	Swindon T	L 1-2 Varco	4,000
36		28	(h)	Reading	W 4-0 Whitlow, Barber, Varco, Doncaster	11,000
37	Apr	2	(h)	Norwich C	W 3-0 Varco 2, Purcell	8,000
38		9	(a)	Brighton & HA	D 1-1 Roberts	4,000
39		16	(h)	Mansfield T	W 3-0 Roberts 2, Barber	5,000
40		23	(a)	Watford	L 0-1	7,000
41		30	(h)	Crystal P	L 0-1	4,000
42	May	7	(a)	Fulham	L 1-3 Varco	15,000

FINAL LEAGUE POSITION: 7th in Division Three South

*Played at the White City, London.

Appearances
Goals

FA Cup

3	Jan	9	(a)	Grimsby T	L 1-4

194

Davies	Baugh	Miller	Clarke	Childs	Barber	Armfield	Purcell	Varco	Houghton	Doncaster	Woodward	Whitlow	Gray	Robinson	Bright	Ditchburn	Angus	Gumm	Halliday	Roberts	Courtney	
1	2	3	4	5	6	7	8	9	10	11												
1	2	3	4	5	6	7	8			11	9	10										1
1	2	3	4	5	6	7	8		10	11			9									2
1		3		5	6	7	8		10	11			9	2	4							3
1	2				6	7	4	9	10	11			8		5	3						4
1	2	3	4		6	7	8	9	10	11						5						5
1	2	3			6	7	8	9		11	10		4			5						6
1	2	3	4	5	6	7	8	9	10	11												7
1	2	3	4	5	6	7	8	9	10	11												8
1	2	3	4	5	6	7	8	9	10	11												9
1		3	4	5	6	7	8	9	10	11			2									10
1		3	4	5	6	7		8	10	11		9	2									11
1		3	4		6	7		8	10	11		9	2				5					12
1		3	4		6	7		8	10	11		9	2				5					13
1		3	4		6	7		8	10	11		9	2				5					14
1		3	4		6	7		8	10	11		9	2				5					15
1	2	3	4		6	7		8	10	11		9					5					16
1	2	3	4		6	7		8	10	11		9					5					17
1	2	3	4		6	7		8	10	11		9					5					18
1	2	3	4		6			8	10	11		9					5	7				19
1		3	4		6			8	10	11	7	9	2				5					20
1		3	4		6			8	10	11	7	9	2				5					21
1		3	4		6			8	10	11	7	9	2				5					22
1		3	4	5	6		9	8	10	11	7		2									23
1		3	4	5	6	7	8	9					2									24
1		3	4	5	6	7	8	9	10	11			2									25
1		3	4	5	6	7	8	9	10	11			2									26
1		3	4	5	6	7	8	9		11			2						10			27
1		3	4	5	6	7	8	9		11			2						10			28
1		3	4	5	6	7		8		11		9	2					10				29
1		3	4	5	6			8		11	7	9	2					10				30
1		3	4	5	6	7			10	11		9	2				8					31
1		3	4	5	6	7			10	11		9	2				8					32
1		3	4	5	6	7			10	11		9	2				8					33
1		3	4	5	6	7		9	10	11			2				8					34
1		3	4	5	6			8	9			7	2						10			35
1		3	4	5	6			8	9	11		7	2						10			36
1		3	4	5	6			7	9	11			2					8	10			37
1		3	4	5	6			7	9	10	11		2				8					38
1		3	4	5	6	7			9	10	11		2				8					39
1		3	4	5	6			7	9	10	11		2				8					40
1		3	4	5	6	7			9	10			2				8					41
1		3	4	5	6	7			9	10			2				8			11		42
42	14	40	39	28	42	31	22	36	33	41	7	23	30	2	1	2	11	1	5	11	1	
1		2	1	4	4	16	16	8	2	15			4									

1932-33

Manager: W.McDevitt

#				Opponent	Result	Scorers	Attendance
1	Aug	27	(h)	Bristol C	W 2-0	Welsby, Poulter	9,500
2		29	(a)	Northampton T	L 3-5	Connaboy, Childs, Poulter	5,000
3	Sep	3	(a)	Coventry C	L 0-4		14,000
4		7	(h)	Northampton T	W 3-1	Barber, Scott, Poulter	6,300
5		10	(h)	Brentford	L 1-2	Houghton	8,000
6		17	(a)	Torquay U	W 3-1	Poulter, Scott, Higgins	6,000
7		24	(h)	Crystal P	D 1-1	Barber	7,150
8	Oct	1	(h)	Luton T	W 2-0	Higgins 2	6,000
9		8	(a)	Newport C	D 1-1	Welsby	6,000
10		15	(h)	Bournemouth	L 2-3	Higgins 2	6,000
11		22	(a)	Gillingham	W 2-1	Higgins, Houghton	5,500
12		29	(h)	Watford	W 5-2	Welsby, Whitlow 3, Scott	5,000
13	Nov	5	(a)	Cardiff C	W 3-1	Whitlow, Houghton, Higgins	3,000
14		12	(h)	Reading	W 4-1	Whitlow 3, Childs	6,000
15		19	(a)	Norwich C	D 0-0		8,000
16	Dec	3	(a)	Bristol R	L 0-1		9,000
17		17	(a)	Queen's Park R	W 3-1	Clarke, Whitlow 2	2,500
18		24	(h)	Southend U	W 3-0	Whitlow 3	10,000
19		26	(a)	Swindon T	D 2-2	Whitlow 2	10,000
20		27	(h)	Swindon T	W 5-0	Whitlow 3, Houghton, Welsby	12,000
21		31	(a)	Bristol C	W 1-0	Houghton	5,000
22	Jan	7	(h)	Coventry C	W 5-0	Houghton 2, Whitlow 2, Kennedy	7,000
23		18	(h)	Brighton & HA	W 4-1	Scott, Whitlow 3	2,000
24		21	(a)	Brentford	W 2-0	Houghton, Whitlow	16,000
25		28	(h)	Torquay U	W 5-0	Whitlow 3, Higgins, Kennedy	11,000
26	Feb	4	(a)	Crystal P	D 2-2	Scott, Higgins	10,000
27		11	(a)	Luton T	L 0-4		8,000
28		18	(h)	Newport C	W 4-0	Whitlow 3, Scott	6,000
29		25	(a)	Bournemouth	D 1-1	Houghton	5,000
30	Mar	4	(h)	Gillingham	W 2-1	Whitlow, Welsby	7,000
31		11	(a)	Watford	D 0-0		5,000
32		18	(h)	Cardiff C	W 1-0	Kennedy	7,000
33		25	(a)	Reading	D 2-2	Houghton, Angus	10,000
34	Apr	1	(h)	Norwich C	W 2-1	Houghton, Scott	15,000
35		8	(a)	Brighton & HA	L 1-2	Houghton	6,000
36		14	(a)	Clapton O	D 2-2	Webb, Barber	4,000
37		15	(h)	Bristol R	W 1-0	Whitlow	7,000
38		17	(h)	Clapton O	W 3-0	Barber, Whitlow 2	11,000
39		22	(a)	Aldershot	L 1-4	Childs (pen)	5,000
40		26	(h)	Aldershot	D 0-0		5,000
41		29	(h)	Queen's Park R	W 2-0	Clarke (pen), Wrightson	6,000
42	May	6	(a)	Southend U	W 2-1	Poulter, Houghton	8,000

FINAL LEAGUE POSITION: 2nd in Division Three South

Appearances
Goals

FA Cup

1	Nov	26	(a)	Southend U	D 1-1
R		30	(h)	Southend U	L 0-1

Davies	Gray	Miller	Clarke	Childs	Barber	Scott	Connaboy	Poulter	Houghton	Welsby	Kennedy	Higgins	Robinson	Whitlow	Hurst	Hughes	Angus	Webb	Wrightson	Gumm	No.
1	2	3	4	5	6	7	8	9	10	11											1
1	2	3	4	5	6	7	8	9	10	11											2
1	2	3	4	5	6	7	8	9	10	11											3
1	2	3	4	5	6	7	8	9	10	11											4
1	2	3	4	5	6	7		9	10	11	8										5
1	2	3	4	5	6	7		9	10	11	8										6
1	2	3	4		6	7		9	10	11	8	5									7
1	2	3	4	5	6	7			10	11	8			9							8
1	2	3	4	5	6	7			10	11	8			9							9
1	2	3	4	5	6	7			10		8			9	11						10
1	2	3	6	5		7			10	11	8	4		9							11
1	2	3	6	5		7			10	11	8	4		9							12
1	2	3	6	5		7			10	11	8	4		9							13
1	2	3	6	5		7			10	11	8	4		9							14
1	2	3	6	5		7			10	11	8	4		9							15
1	2		4	5	6	7			10	11	8			9	3						16
1	2	3	4	5	6	7			10	11	8			9							17
1	2	3	4	5	6	7			10	11	8			9							18
1	2	3	4	5	6	7			10	11	8			9							19
1	2		4	5	6	7		8	10	11				9	3						20
1	2		4	5	6	7		8	10	11				9	3						21
1	2		4	5	6	7			10	11	8			9	3						22
1	2	3	4	5	6	7			10		8	11		9							23
1	2	3	4	5	6	7			10		8	11		9							24
1	2	3	4	5	6	7			10		8	11		9							25
1	2	3	4	5	6	7			10		8	11		9							26
1	2		4		6	7			10		8	11		9	3	5					27
1	2		4	5	6	7			10		8	11		9	3						28
1	2	3	4	5	6	7			10	11	8			9							29
1	2	3	4		6	7			10	11	8			9			5				30
1		3	4		6	7			10	11	8			9		2	5				31
1		3	4			7			10	11				9		2	5	6	8		32
1		3	4		6	7			10	11				9		2	5		8		33
1		3	4		6	7			10	11				9		2	5		8		34
1		3	4		6	7			10	11				9		2	5		8		35
1		3	4		6	7			10		8			9		2	5		11		36
1	2		4	5	6	7			10		8			9	3				11		37
1	2	3	4	5	6				10	11	8			9		7					38
1	2	3	4	5	6				10	11	8			9		7					39
1	2	3	4		6	7		9	10	11	8						5				40
1	2	3	4		6				10	11				9			5		8	7	41
1	2	3	4		6			9	10	11							5		8	7	42
42	36	35	42	30	36	37	4	11	42	27	15	22	6	32	8	13	11	5	6	2	
	2	3	4	7	1	5	13	5	3	9	33						1	1	1		

1933-34

Manager: W.McDevitt

1	Aug	26	(a)	Reading	L 1-3	Whitlow		8,000
2		30	(h)	Coventry C	W 1-0	Whitlow		8,0000
3	Sep	2	(h)	Watford	W 3-1	Whitlow 2, Houghton		8,000
4		4	(a)	Coventry C	W 3-1	Welsby, Houghton, Walters		15,000
5		9	(a)	Charlton A	L 1-4	Barnes		10,000
6		13	(h)	Brighton & HA	W 3-0	Whitlow 3		6,000
7		16	(h)	Bournemouth	W 4-0	Walters 2, Welsby, Whitlow		7,000
8		23	(a)	Cardiff C	L 1-2	Welsby		10,000
9		30	(h)	Queen's Park R	D 1-1	Walters		7,000
10	Oct	7	(h)	Gillingham	W 2-0	Houghton 2		7,000
11		14	(a)	Crystal P	D 0-0			10,000
12		21	(a)	Newport C	L 0-1			6,000
13		28	(h)	Norwich C	L 3-4	Houghton, Poulter, Hurst		7,000
14	Nov	4	(a)	Bristol C	D 1-1	Hurst		7,000
15		11	(h)	Clapton O	L 0-3			6,000
16		18	(a)	Swindon T	D 1-1	Houghton		8,000
17	Dec	2	(a)	Aldershot	W 2-0	Poulter, Clarke (pen)		3,000
18		9	(h)	Luton T	W 4-2	Poulter 2, Hurst 2		4,000
19		16	(a)	Northampton T	L 3-5	Poulter, Clarke, Wrightson		5,000
20		23	(h)	Torquay U	W 4-0	Wrightson, Poulter 2, Hurst		6,000
21		25	(h)	Southend U	W 2-0	Poulter, Wrightson		9,000
22		26	(a)	Southend U	L 1-3	Poulter		10,000
23		30	(h)	Reading	W 4-1	Whitlow 2, Hurst, Houghton		5,000
24	Jan	6	(a)	Watford	L 0-2			4,000
25		20	(h)	Charlton A	W 2-0	Wrightson, Hurst		5,000
26		27	(a)	Bournemouth	W 3-1	Wrightson 2, Scott		5,000
27	Feb	3	(h)	Cardiff C	W 4-0	Houghton, Hurst, Whitlow 2		6,000
28		10	(a)	Queen's Park R	L 0-2			15,000
29		17	(a)	Gillingham	D 1-1	Wrightson		6,000
30		24	(h)	Crystal P	L 1-2	Barber		5,000
31	Mar	3	(h)	Newport C	D 1-1	Hardie		5,000
32		10	(a)	Norwich C	D 1-1	Wrightson		15,000
33		17	(h)	Bristol C	W 2-0	Whitlow, Scott		5,000
34		24	(a)	Clapton O	L 0-4			8,000
35		30	(a)	Bristol R	D 1-1	Scott		10,000
36		21	(h)	Swindon T	D 2-2	Hurst, Risdon		8,000
37	Apr	2	(h)	Bristol R	D 0-0			10,000
38		7	(a)	Brighton & HA	L 1-2	Hurst		9,000
39		14	(h)	Aldershot	D 0-0			4,000
40		21	(a)	Luton T	L 2-3	Hurst 2		5,000
41		28	(h)	Northampton T	L 0-2			2,500
42	May	5	(a)	Torquay U	W 2-0	Hurst 2		4,000

FINAL LEAGUE POSITION: 9th in Division Three South

Appearances

Goals

FA Cup

1	Nov	25	(a)	Northampton T	L 0-2	

Third Division South Cup

1	Jan	24	(h)	Crystal P	W 11-6
2	Feb	21	(h)	Watford	W 4-2
3	Mar	14	(h)	Coventry C	D 1-1
R		22	(a)	Coventry C	W 1-0
SF	Apr	12	(n*)	Brighton & HA	D 1-1
R		23	(h)	Brighton & HA	D 1-1
2R		26	(a)	Brighton & HA	W 4-3
F	May	2	(n†)	Torquay U	W 1-0

*Played at Craven Cottage, Fulham. †Played at Home Park, Plymouth.

Davies	Gray	Hughes	Clarke	Angus	Webb	Welsby	Wrightson	Whitlow	Kennedy	Barnes	Houghton	Walters	Hurst	Miller	Hardie	Risdon	Childs	Scott	Poulter	Gumm	Chesters	Barber	Smith	Boundy	Jasper	No.
1	2	3	4	5	6	7	8	9	10	11																
1	2	3	4	5	6	7	8	9		11	10															1
1	2	3	4	5	6	7	8	9		11	10															2
1	2	3	4	5	6	7		9		11	10	8														3
1	2	3	4	5	6	7		9		11	10	8														4
1	2	3	4	5	6	7		9		11	10	8														5
1	2	3	4	5	6	7		9		11	10	8														6
1	2	3	4	5	6	7		9			10	8	11													7
1	2		4	5	6	7		9			10	8	11	3												8
1	2		4	5		7		9			10		11	3	6	8										9
1	2		4				8	9			10		11	3	6		5	7								10
1	2	6	4				8	9			10		11	3			5	7								11
1	2		4	5			8				10		11	3	6			7	9							12
1	2		4	5							10		11	3	6	8		7	9							13
1	2		4			7		9			10		11	3	6		5		8							14
1	2	3	4	5				9			10		11		6			7		8						15
1	2	3	4	5			8				10		11		6			7	9							16
1	2	3	4	5			8	7			10		11		6				9							17
1	2	3	4	5			8				10		11		6			7	9							18
1	2		4	5			8				10		11	3	6			7	9							19
1	2		4	5			8				10		11	3	6			7	9							20
1	2		4	5			8				10		11	3	6			7	9							21
1	2		4	5			8	9			10		11	3	6			7								22
1	2		4	5			8	9			10		11	3	6			7								23
1	2		4	5			8	9			10		11	3	6			7								24
	2		4	5			8	9			10		11	3				7	1		6					25
	2		4	5			8	9					10	11	3			7	1		6					26
	2		4	5			8	9					10	11	3			7	1		6					27
	2		4	5			8				10	11	9	3	6			7	1							28
	2	8	4	5				9			10	11		3				7	1		6					29
1	2		4	5			8	9			10		11	3	6			7								30
1	2		4	6	5		8	9			10		11	3				7								31
1	2		4	6	5		8	9			10		11	3				7								32
1	2		4	6	5			10					11	9	3	8		7								33
1	2		4	6	5		8	10					11	9	3			7								34
1	2		4	6	5			10					11	9	3	8		7								35
1	2		4	6	5		8						11	9				7				3	10			36
1	2		4	6	5			10					11	9		8		7				3				37
	2	8	4										3	6	10	5			1	11	9	7				38
	2		4	6	5			10					11	9	3	8		7	1							39
	2		4	5	11			10						9	3	8		7	1		6					40
	2		4	4	5			10					11	9	3	8		7	1							41
33	41	13	41	25	35	12	28	28	1	18	29	6	34	28	18	8	4	28	11	1	9	5	3	2	1	42
	2		3	8	13	1	8	4		14			1	1	3	9		1								

1934-35

Manager: W.McDevitt

#		Date		Opponent	Result	Scorers	Att
1	Aug	25	(h)	Newport C	L 0-1		7,500
2		27	(a)	Northampton T	L 1-2	Dudley	4,000
3	Sep	1	(a)	Southend U	W 2-1	Hurst 2	10,000
4		5	(h)	Northampton T	W 3-0	Wrightson 3	6,000
5		8	(a)	Bristol C	L 0-2		7,000
6		15	(h)	Millwall	L 0-1		7,000
7		22	(a)	Coventry C	D 1-1	J.Scott	10,000
8		29	(h)	Clapton O	D 1-1	Hurst	6,000
9	Oct	6	(a)	Gillingham	L 1-2	McArthur	7,000
10		13	(h)	Reading	L 2-3	Lewis, Wrightson	6,000
11		20	(h)	Luton T	L 1-2	Lewis	4,000
12		27	(a)	Brighton & HA	L 0-6		8,000
13	Nov	3	(h)	Charlton A	W 3-1	T.Scott, Webb (pen), Poulter	4,000
14		10	(a)	Bristol R	D 5-5	Webb (pen), Poulter 2, Wrightson 2	9,500
15		17	(h)	Swindon T	D 3-3	Wrightson, J.Scott, T.Scott	5,000
16	Dec	1	(h)	Queen's Park R	W 3-0	Wrightson, Poulter, T.Scott	6,000
17		15	(h)	Cardiff C	W 2-1	Dryden, J.Scott	3,000
18		22	(a)	Aldershot	D 0-0		3,000
19		25	(a)	Bournemouth	L 2-3	Hurst, Poulter	8,000
20		26	(h)	Bournemouth	W 4-1	Wrightson 2, Webb (pen), Dryden	7,000
21		29	(a)	Newport C	W 3-1	Hurst, Dryden, Wrightson	3,000
22	Jan	5	(h)	Southend U	W 4-3	Wrightson, Hurst 2, McArthur	4,000
23		12	(a)	Torquay U	L 0-3		6,000
24		19	(h)	Bristol C	W 3-0	Webb (pen), J.Scott, Hurst	4,000
25		26	(h)	Crystal P	L 0-6		5,000
26		31	(a)	Millwall	L 0-1		8,000
27	Feb	2	(h)	Coventry C	W 2-0	Poulter 2	5,000
28		9	(a)	Clapton O	W 3-0	Poulter 3	8,000
29		16	(h)	Gillingham	W 2-0	Wrightson 2	5,000
30		23	(a)	Reading	L 0-2		10,000
31	Mar	2	(a)	Luton T	L 0-4		6,000
32		9	(h)	Brighton & HA	W 3-1	Tierney, Dryden, Wrightson	3,000
33		16	(a)	Charlton A	L 0-1		10,000
34		23	(h)	Bristol R	D 2-2	Poulter, J.Scott	4,000
35		30	(a)	Swindon T	L 1-6	J.Scott	6,000
36	Apr	6	(h)	Torquay U	D 1-1	McArthur	4,000
37		13	(a)	Queen's Park R	D 1-1	Poulter	4,000
38		19	(a)	Watford	W 1-0	Poulter	6,000
39		20	(a)	Crystal P	W 1-0	Owens (og)	15,000
40		22	(h)	Watford	D 1-1	McArthur	9,000
41		27	(a)	Cardiff C	L 0-5		4,000
42	May	4	(h)	Aldershot	W 8-1	J.Scott, Poulter 3, Dryden, Summerbee (og), McArthur, Wrightson	2,000

FINAL LEAGUE POSITION: 11th in Division Three South

Appearances
Goals

FA Cup

1	Nov	24	(a)	Charlton A	D 2-2
R		28	(h)	Charlton A	W 5-2
2	Dec	8	(a)	Yeovil & Petters	L 1-4

Third Division South Cup

1	Oct	24	(h)	Aldershot	W 4-0
2	Feb	20	(h)	Millwall	W 5-0
SF	Mar	27	(a)	Bristol R	L 1-2

Davies	Gray	Miller	Clarke	Webb	McClure	Scott J	Dudley	Poulter	McArthur	Dryden	Chesters	Angus	Lewis	Hurst	Wrightson	Smith	Tierney	Scott T	Risdon	Keefe	Bamsey	
1	2	3	4	5	6	7	8	9	10	11												
1	2	3	4	5	6	7	8	9	10	11												1
	2	3	4			7			10	11		1	5	6	9	8						2
	2	3	4			7			10	11		1	5	6	9	8						3
	2	3			4	7		9	10	11		1	5	6		8						4
	2	3	4			7			10	11		1	5	6	9	8						5
	2	3	4			7			10	11		1	5	6	9	8						6
	2		4			7			10			1	5	6	9	8	3	11				7
	2		4			7			10			1	5	6	9	8	3	11				8
	2		4			7						1	5	6	9	10	3	11	8			9
	2				4	7						1	5	6	9	10	3	11	8			10
	2	6	5	4		7		9				1		3	6				8			11
1	2		4	5		7		9				3	6	11	8		10					12
1	2			5		7		9				4	6	11	8	3	10					13
1	2		4	5		7		9				3	6	11	8		10					14
	2	3	4	5		7						1	6	11	8		10					15
	2	3	4	5		7			11	1		6		9	8		10					16
	2		4	5		7		9				1	6	11	8	3	10					17
	2	3	4	5		7		9				1	6	11	8		10					18
1	2	3	4	5		7			11			6		9	8		10					19
1	2	3	4	5		7		10	11			6		9	8							20
1	2	3	4	5		7		10	11			6		9	8							21
1	2		4	5		7		10	11			6		9	8	3						22
1	2		4	5		7		10	11			6		9	8	3						23
1	2		4	5		7		10	11			6		9	8	3						24
	2	3		5		7		9				1	6	11	8		10	4				25
	2	3		5		7		9				1	6	11	8		10	4				26
	2	3		5		7		9				1	6	11	8		10	4				27
	2	3				7		9		11		1	6		8		10	4	5			28
	2	3				7		9				1	6	11	8		10	4	5			29
		3	5			7		9				1	6	11	8	2	10	4				30
	2	3		5		7		9		11		1	6		8		10	4				31
	2	3		5		7		9		11		1	6		8		10	4				32
	2	3		5		7		9				1	6	11	8		10	4				33
	2	3		5		7		9		11		1	6		10	8		4				34
	2	3		5		7	9	11				1	6		10	8		4				35
	2	3				7		9	10			1	6		8		11	4	5			36
	2	3	6			7		9	10			1	5		8		11	4				37
	2	3	7	5		8		9	10			1	4	6			11					38
	2	3		5		8		9	10			1	4	6	7		11					39
	2	3	7	5					10			1	4	6	9	8	11					40
	2	3		5		7		9	10	11		1	6		8				4			41
																						42
11	41	30	25	29	5	41	8	26	15	20	31	40	16	31	37	10	18	11	14	2	1	
			4			7	1	16	5	5		2	8	16			1	3				

2 own-goals

1935-36

Manager: W.McDevitt/J.English

1	Aug	31	(h)	Aldershot	W 5-1 Poulter 3, Fantham, Clarke	10,000
2	Sep	4	(h)	Watford	L 1-3 Clarke (pen)	8,000
3		7	(a)	Swindon T	D 1-1 McArdle	12,000
4		11	(a)	Watford	L 0-1	8,000
5		14	(h)	Coventry C	L 1-3 McArthur	8,000
6		18	(h)	Bristol C	L 0-1	6,000
7		21	(a)	Newport C	L 1-2 Dunn	6,500
8		25	(a)	Torquay U	L 1-2 McArthur	5,000
9		28	(h)	Gillingham	L 2-5 Dunn, Robinson	5,000
10	Oct	5	(h)	Brighton & HA	D 3-3 Ebdon 2, McCambridge	5,000
11		12	(a)	Queen's Park R	L 1-3 McCambridge	10,000
12		19	(a)	Bournemouth	D 1-1 T.Scott	6,000
13		26	(h)	Luton T	L 1-2 Ebdon	4,000
14	Nov	2	(a)	Notts C	L 1-3 McCambridge	5,000
15		9	(h)	Cardiff C	W 2-0 Hoyle, Hurst	4,000
16		16	(a)	Clapton O	W 2-1 McCambridge, McLean	6,000
17		23	(h)	Southend U	W 1-0 McCambridge	5,000
18	Dec	7	(h)	Crystal P	W 1-0 Ebdon	3,000
19		21	(h)	Bristol R	W 3-1 Ebdon, Clarke, T.Scott	4,000
20		25	(a)	Millwall	D 2-2 Clarke, McCambridge	8,000
21		26	(h)	Millwall	W 4-3 Clarke, T.Scott 2, Hurst	9,383
22		28	(a)	Aldershot	L 0-3	2,950
23	Jan	4	(h)	Swindon T	L 0-3	4,000
24		11	(a)	Northampton T	D 1-1 Dunn	6,000
25		18	(a)	Coventry C	L 0-3	10,000
26		25	(h)	Newport C	D 3-3 Dunn, Ebdon, T.Scott	3,000
27	Feb	1	(a)	Gillingham	D 2-2 Merrie 2	6,000
28		8	(a)	Brighton & HA	L 1-3 Hurst	6,000
29		15	(h)	Queen's Park R	D 0-0	4,000
30		22	(h)	Bournemouth	L 1-3 J.Scott	4,000
31		29	(a)	Cardiff C	L 2-5 T.Scott, McCambridge	5,000
32	Mar	7	(h)	Reading	L 4-5 McCambridge 2, T.Scott, Clarke (pen)	4,000
33		14	(a)	Luton T	L 1-3 J.Scott	12,000
34		18	(a)	Reading	L 0-2	3,000
35		21	(h)	Clapton O	L 2-3 McCambridge 2	4,000
36		28	(a)	Southend U	L 0-4	7,000
37	Apr	4	(h)	Northampton T	W 3-1 McCambridge 2, T.Scott	2,000
38		11	(a)	Crystal P	D 2-2 J.Scott, Ebdon	12,000
39		13	(h)	Torquay U	D 1-1 Ebdon	8,657
40		18	(h)	Notts C	D 0-0	4,000
41		25	(a)	Bristol R	L 1-6 McCambridge	3,000
42	May	2	(a)	Bristol C	L 1-2 Ebdon	5,000

FINAL LEAGUE POSITION: 22nd in Division Three South

Appearances
Goals

FA Cup

1	Nov	30	(h)	Gillingham	L 0-4

Third Division South Cup

1	Oct	2	(a)	Gillingham	D 0-0
R		16	(h)	Gillingham	W 4-2
2		28	(a)	Crystal P	L 2-4

Chesters	Gray	Miller	Clarke	Angus	Fantham	Hurst	Dunn	Poulter	McLean	McArdle	Scott J	Lowton	Robinson	McArthur	Risdon	Ebdon	Scott T	McCambridge	Bamsey	Hoyle	Kirk	Crompton	Merrie	Beby	#
1	2	3	4	5	6	7	8	9	10	11															1
1	2	3	4	5	6	9	8		10	11	7														2
1	2		4		6		8		10	11	7	3	5	9											3
1	2		4		6		8		10	11	7	3	5	9	4										4
1	2			5	6		8			11	7	3		10	4	9									5
1	2		4	6					10			3	5	11	8	9									6
1	2			5	6				10	11	7	3		9	4	8									7
1		3		6		7	8		10			3	5	11	4	9									8
1	3	10	6							11	7		4	8		9	5								9
1	2		4		6	11	8			3	5		9			10		7							10
1	2		4	6		7		10		3	5		9	8				11							11
1	2		4	6		7		10		3	5		9	8				11							12
1	2		4	6		7		10		3	5	11	8	9											13
1	2	3		6		7	8	10		5		4		9				11							14
1	2	3		6		11	8	10		7	5	4		9											15
1	2	3		6		11	8	10		7	5	4		9											16
1	2	3	4	6		11		10		7	5		9	8											17
1	2	3	4	6		11		10		7	5		9	8											18
1	2	3	4	6		11		10		5		9	8	7											19
1	2	3	4	6		11		10		7	5		9	8											20
1		3	4	6		11		10		7	5		9	8					2						21
1		3	4	6		11		10		7	5		9	8					2						22
		3	4	6		11	10			5		7	8	9				1	2						23
		3	4	6		11	10			5		7	8	9				1	2						24
1	2	3	4	6		11	10	9		5		7	8												25
1	2		4	6		11	10			5		7	8						3	9					26
1	2		4	6		7	10		11	5			8						3	9					27
1	2	3	4	6		7	10		11	5			8							9					28
1	2	3	4	6		7		10	11	5		8								9					29
	2	3	4	6		7		10	11	5			8	9			1								30
			4	6		7	10			2			8	9	5	11		3		1					31
	2	3	4	6		7	10		11		5		8	9						1					32
	2	3	4	6		7	10		11		5		8	9						1					33
	2	3	4	6				11	7		5		8	8	9					1					34
	2	3	4	6		11		10	7		5		8	9						1					35
	2		4	6		7				3		8	10	9	5	11				1					36
	2		4	6		7		11	3		8	10	9	5						1					37
	2		4	6		7		11	3		8	10	9	5						1					38
			4	6		7		11	3		2	8	10	9	5					1					39
			4	6		7			7	3	2	8	10	9	5					1					40
1			4	6		11		10		7	3	2	8		9	5									41
29	33	23	35	39	6	34	22	2	21	9	27	18	30	8	13	24	28	23	8	6	3	7	4	10	42
		6		1	3	4	3	1		1	3		1	2		9	9	14			1	2			

203

1936-37

Manager: J.English

#					Result	Scorers	Attendance
1	Aug	29	(a)	Notts C	L 1-3	Scott	10,000
2	Sep	2	(h)	Torquay U	W 2-1	Williams 2	8,766
3		5	(h)	Clapton O	L 0-2		7,000
4		9	(a)	Torquay U	W 1-0	Williams	4,000
5		12	(a)	Walsall	L 2-4	Shadwell, Scott	4,422
6		16	(a)	Reading	L 0-1		7,231
7		19	(h)	Luton T	L 2-4	Williams, Scott	8,000
8		26	(a)	Cardiff C	L 1-3	Clarke	20,000
9	Oct	3	(h)	Crystal P	W 3-2	Williams 2, Scott	6,000
10		10	(a)	Aldershot	D 1-1	Williams	4,000
11		17	(h)	Gillingham	D 1-1	Scott	5,000
12		24	(a)	Newport C	L 0-2		11,650
13		31	(h)	Southend U	D 2-2	Williams, Clarke	5,000
14	Nov	7	(a)	Watford	D 1-1	Keane	6,000
15		14	(h)	Brighton & HA	L 0-4		6,000
16		21	(a)	Bournemouth	D 0-0		6,000
17	Dec	5	(a)	Bristol R	L 2-4	Williams 2	8,000
18		19	(a)	Swindon T	L 1-3	Williams	6,000
19		25	(a)	Queen's Park R	L 0-4		14,000
20		26	(h)	Notts C	L 1-3	Williams	11,000
21		28	(h)	Queen's Park R	L 0-3		5,000
22	Jan	2	(a)	Clapton O	L 0-1		9,000
23		9	(h)	Walsall	W 3-0	Williams, Pope, Owen	4,000
24		20	(a)	Northampton T	L 2-5	Williams 2	2,000
25		23	(a)	Luton T	D 2-2	Williams, Owen	10,000
26	Feb	3	(h)	Cardiff C	W 3-1	F.Smith, Pope, Bussey	3,000
27		6	(a)	Crystal P	L 0-8		12,000
28		13	(h)	Aldershot	L 1-2	F.Smith	4,000
29		24	(a)	Gillingham	D 2-2	Johnson, Williams	5,000
30		27	(h)	Newport C	W 3-1	Owen, Williams 2	4,000
31	Mar	6	(a)	Southend U	D 4-4	Pope 2, Owen (pen), Williams	7,000
32		13	(h)	Watford	W 2-1	F.Smith 2	6,000
33		17	(h)	Millwall	D 1-1	Williams	3,000
34		20	(a)	Brighton & HA	L 0-1		11,000
35		26	(a)	Bristol C	L 1-2	Owen (pen)	10,000
36		27	(h)	Bournemouth	D 1-1	Williams	6,000
37		29	(h)	Bristol C	W 3-0	Williams 2, Bussey	9,000
38	Apr	3	(a)	Northampton T	L 1-2	Williams	6,343
39		10	(h)	Bristol R	W 3-2	Williams 2, Owen	2,500
40		17	(a)	Millwall	D 3-3	Bussey, Williams, McGill	16,000
41		24	(h)	Swindon T	D 1-1	Williams	3,500
42	May	1	(h)	Reading	W 2-0	Bussey 2	3,000

FINAL LEAGUE POSITION: 21st in Division Three South

Appearances
Goals

FA Cup

1	Nov	28	(h)	Folkestone	W 3-0	
2	Dec	12	(a)	Walthamstow A	D 1-1	(abandoned due to fog)
		17	(a)	Walthamstow A	W 3-2	
3	Jan	16	(h)	Oldham A	W 3-0	
4		30	(h)	Leicester C	W 3-1	
5	Feb	20	(a)	Preston NE	L 3-5	

Third Division South Cup

| 1 | Oct | 28 | (h) | Cardiff C | W 1-0 | |
| 2 | Nov | 11 | (a) | Torquay U | L 1-2 | |

Chesters	Brown	Stimpson	Shadwell	Hobbs	Young	Smith F	Scott	Johnson	McGill	Urmson	Angus	Williams	Pollard	Ebdon	Clarke	Thompson	Boyle	Smith C	Bamsey	Keane	Tierney	Pope	Bussey	Owen	#
1	2	3		5	6	7	8	9	10	11															1
1	2	3		5	4	7	8			11	6	9	10												2
1	2	3		5	4	7				11	6	9	8	10											3
1	2	3	6	5			8		10	11		9			4	7									4
1	2	3	6	5			8		10	11		9			4	7									5
1		3	6	5			8		10	11		9			4	7	2								6
1		3	6	5			8		10	11		9			4		2	7							7
1		3	6	5			8		10	11		9			4		2	7							8
1	2	3	6	5			8		10	11		9			4			7							9
1	2		6				8		10			9			4		3	7	5	11					10
1	2		6				8		10			9			4		3	7	5	11					11
1	2		6		4	7	8		10			9			5		3			11					12
1	2		6				10		8	11	5	9			4		3			7					13
	2		6				8			11	5	9			4		3			7	1	10			14
	2		6				10			11	5	9		8	4		3			7	1				15
	2	6					10		8	11	5	9			4		3			7	1				16
	2	6					8			11	5	9			4		3			7	1	10			17
	2	6									5	9			4		3			7	1	10	8	11	18
	2		6				10				5	9			4		3			7	1		8	11	19
	2			5	6			9			10				4		3			7	1		8	11	20
1	2			5	6		8		10			9			4		3			7				11	21
1	2	3			6	7					5	9			4							10	8	11	22
1	2	3			6	7					5	9			4							10	8	11	23
1	2	3			4	7	8		6		5	9										10		11	24
1	2		6			7	8		10			9			4		3		5					11	25
1	2		6			7					5	9			4		3					10	8	11	26
1	2		6			7					5	9			4		3					10	8	11	27
1	2		6			7					5	9			4		3					10	8	11	28
1	2	3	6		4		8		10			9					5			7				11	29
1		3			6	7					5	9			4		2					10	8	11	30
1		2			6	7					5	9			4		3					10	8	11	31
1		2			6	7	10				5	9			4		3						8	11	32
1	2	3			6	7					5	9			4							10	8	11	33
	2	3	4	6	7		8		10		5	9									1			11	34
	2	3	6	4	7				10		5	9									1		8	11	35
	2	3	4	6	7				10		5	9									1		8	11	36
	2	3	4	6	7						5	9									1	10	8	11	37
	2	3		6	7		11		10		5	9			4						1		8		38
	2	3	6		7				10		5	9			4						1		8	11	39
	2	3	6		7				10		5	9			4						1		8	11	40
	2	3	6		7				10		5	9			4						1		8	11	41
	2		4		7						6	9		10			3		5		1		8	11	42
26	32	29	30	11	19	24	17	11	25	10	28	41	3	3	31	3	23	5	5	13	16	13	20	24	
		1		4	5	1	1					29			2					1		4	5	6	

1937-38

Manager: J.English

					Result	Scorers	Attendance
1	Aug	28	(a)	Newport C	D 2-2	Farrell 2	15,000
2	Sep	1	(h)	Notts C	L 0-3		8,614
3		4	(h)	Bristol C	W 3-2	Bowl 2, Storey	7,000
4		8	(a)	Notts C	D 0-0		15,000
5		11	(a)	Watford	D 0-0		9,000
6		13	(a)	Millwall	L 1-2	B.Clarke	5,000
7		18	(h)	Gillingham	L 3-5	Storey, Liddle 2 (1 pen)	5,856
8		25	(a)	Torquay U	L 1-2	Liddle	7,000
9	Oct	2	(a)	Swindon T	L 0-3		9,000
10		9	(h)	Aldershot	L 0-1		6,000
11		16	(h)	Mansfield T	W 4-0	Bowl 2, Pope 2	5,000
12		23	(a)	Bristol R	D 1-1	Pope	7,000
13		30	(h)	Northampton T	W 4-1	Bowl 2, Pope 2	6,000
14	Nov	6	(a)	Walsall	W 2-0	Bowl, W.Clarke	4,000
15		13	(h)	Cardiff C	W 2-1	Bowl, Bussey	10,000
16		20	(a)	Bournemouth	D 2-2	Bowl, Bussey	6,000
17	Dec	4	(a)	Queen's Park R	L 0-4		10,000
18		18	(a)	Clapton O	L 1-2	Farrell	4,309
19		27	(h)	Crystal P	D 2-2	Liddle, Farrell	12,893
20		28	(a)	Crystal P	D 2-2	Bowl 2	20,000
21	Jan	1	(h)	Newport C	W 2-0	Pope, Bowl	5,272
22		12	(h)	Brighton & HA	W 4-0	Liddle, Stephens (og), Bowl 2	2,700
23		15	(a)	Bristol C	L 1-4	Bowl	7,425
24		22	(h)	Watford	L 1-2	Bowl (pen)	7,000
25		29	(a)	Gillingham	L 1-2	Coulston	5,000
26	Feb	5	(h)	Torquay U	W 2-0	Stokes (og), Liddle	7,000
27		12	(h)	Swindon T	D 0-0		6,000
28		19	(a)	Aldershot	W 1-0	Liddle	5,000
29		26	(a)	Mansfield T	W 3-2	Ebdon, Bowl, Coulston	7,000
30	Mar	5	(h)	Bristol R	D 0-0		6,000
31		12	(a)	Northampton T	L 0-1		7,000
32		19	(h)	Walsall	W 3-2	Bussey 3 (2 pens)	4,321
33		26	(a)	Cardiff C	D 1-1	Liddle	8,000
34		30	(h)	Southend U	D 1-1	Ebdon	3,000
35	Apr	2	(h)	Bournemouth	W 3-1	Bowl, Bussey, Shadwell	5,000
36		9	(a)	Brighton & HA	L 0-6		6,000
37		15	(a)	Reading	L 0-1		11,000
38		16	(h)	Queen's Park R	L 0-4		7,000
39		18	(h)	Reading	L 0-2		7,990
40		23	(a)	Southend U	D 1-1	Ebdon	4,375
41		30	(h)	Clapton O	W 2-0	Ebdon 2	5,000
42	May	7	(h)	Millwall	L 1-5	Ebdon	9,436

FINAL LEAGUE POSITION: 17th in Division Three South

Appearances

Goals

FA Cup

1	Nov	27	(h)	Folkestone	W 1-0
2	Dec	11	(h)	Hull C	L 1-2

Third Division South Cup

1	Sep	22	(a)	Southend U	W 2-1
2	Nov	17	(a)	Swindon T	L 0-2

Player appearance and scorers grid (shirt numbers by match, 1–42).

Tierney	Brown	Wallace	Shadwell	Angus	Davies	Miles	Storey	Ebdon	Farrell	Liddle	Bamsey	Bowl	Kavanagh	Coulston	Bussey	Clarke B	McGill	Clarke W	Miller	Pope	Church	Pollard	Coles	Topping	
1	2	3	4	5	6	7	8	9	10	11															1
1	2	3	4	5	6	7	8	9	10	11															2
1	2	3	4		6	7	10	8		11	5	9													3
1	2	3	6		5	11	10	8				9	4	7											4
1	2	3	4		5	11		9	10				6	7	8										5
1	2	3	4	6	5	7									8	9	10	11							6
1	2		4		5	7	8	10		11		9	6			3									7
1	2	3	6		5	7		10		11		9	4		8										8
1	2	3	6		5	7				11		10	4		8	9			1						9
1	2	3	6	5		7		10		11		9	4		8										10
1	2	3	4	6							5	9		7	8			11		10					11
1	2	3	4	6							5	9		7	8			11		10					12
1	2	3	4	6							5	9		7	8			11		10					13
1	2	3	4	6							5	9		7	8			11		10					14
	2	3	4	6							5	9		7	8			11		10	1				15
	2	3	4	6							5	9		7	8			11		10	1				16
	2	3	4	6							5	9		7	8			11		10	1				17
		3	4	6					10	11	5	9			8	2		7			1				18
		3	4		5				10	11	5	9		7	8	2					1				19
		3	4	2	5				10	11	5	9		7	8						1				20
		3	4	2	5					11	5	9		7	8					10	1				21
		3	4	6						11	5	9		7	8	2				10	1				22
		3	4	6						11	5	9		7	8	2				10	1				23
	2	3	4	6						11	5	9		7	8					10	1				24
	2	3	4	6						11		9		7	8		10				1	5			25
	2	3	4	6						11	5	9		7	8		10				1				26
	2	3	4	6						11	5	9		7	8		10				1				27
		3	4	6						11	5	9		7	8	2	10				1				28
		3	4	6				10		11	5	9		7	8	2					1				29
		3	4	6				9		11	5			7	8	2				10	1				30
	2		4	6				9		11	5			7	8	3				10	1				31
	2		4	6				10		11	5	9		7	8	3					1				32
		3	4	6				10		11		9		7	8	2					1		5		33
		3	4	6				10		11		9			8	2	7				1		5		34
		3	4	6	5			10		11		9		7	8	2					1				35
		3	4	6	5			10		11		9		7	8	2					1				36
		3	4	6				10			5	9		7	8	2		11			1				37
		3		6				4			5	9		7	8	2	10	11			1				38
		3	4	6				10		11	5	9		7	8	2					1				39
	2		4	6				8		11	5			7	9			10			1			3	40
	2	3	4	6				10			5			7	8	9		11			1				41
	2		4	6				10			5	9		7	8	3		11			1				42
13	26	37	40	36	14	10	5	22	6	28	28	34	6	32	36	22	9	12	1	13	28	1	2	1	
		1					2	6	4	8		18			2	6	1	1		6					

2 own-goals

1938-39

Manager: J.English

#	Month	Date		Opponent	Result	Scorers	Attendance
1	Aug	27	(a)	Cardiff C	W 2-1	Rich, Bowl	25,000
2	Sep	1	(a)	Queen's Park R	L 0-5		12,000
3		3	(h)	Ipswich T	W 3-0	McLuckie (og), Ebdon, Millar	10,000
4		7	(h)	Mansfield T	W 2-0	Turnbull, Ebdon	6,427
5		10	(a)	Reading	D 1-1	Bowl	10,066
6		17	(h)	Bristol R	W 2-1	Ebdon 2	8,500
7		24	(a)	Brighton & HA	L 1-6	Millar	9,372
8	Oct	1	(h)	Bournemouth	D 0-0		7,000
9		8	(a)	Walsall	W 2-1	Bussey, Rich	6,786
10		15	(h)	Torquay U	L 1-2	Millar	9,014
11		22	(a)	Newport C	D 0-0		11,261
12		29	(h)	Port Vale	L 1-3	Bowl	6,874
13	Nov	5	(a)	Watford	L 2-4	Ebdon, Rich	7,256
14		12	(h)	Crystal P	D 4-4	Collins (og), Liddle, Bowl, Riley	5,510
15		19	(a)	Bristol C	L 1-4	Bowl	8,302
16	Dec	3	(a)	Notts C	L 1-3	Rich	11,000
17		10	(h)	Northampton T	W 3-2	Ebdon, Riley, Bowl	3,560
18		17	(a)	Swindon T	L 1-2	Fellowes	6,819
19		24	(h)	Cardiff C	D 1-1	Riley	4,000
20		27	(h)	Southend U	D 3-3	Bussey, Mackenzie (og), Ebdon	9,6533
21		31	(a)	Ipswich T	D 2-2	Bussey (pen), Ebdon	13,000
22	Jan	7	(h)	Aldershot	D 3-3	Bowl 2, Ebdon	5,876
23		14	(h)	Reading	W 3-2	Bowl, Bussey, Riley	4,662
24		21	(a)	Bristol R	D 1-4	Riley	5,000
25		28	(h)	Brighton & HA	D 2-2	Bowl 2	5,152
26	Feb	4	(a)	Bournemouth	L 0-2		5,692
27		15	(h)	Walsall	W 3-2	Bussey, Ebdon, Bowl	2,228
28		18	(a)	Torquay U	W 1-0	Riley	7,050
29		25	(h)	Newport C	W 3-1	Bowl 2 (1 pen), Riley	9,370
30	Mar	4	(a)	Port Vale	L 2-3	Bowl, Riley	6,240
31		11	(h)	Watford	L 1-3	Riley	5,150
32		18	(a)	Crystal P	L 2-3	Bowl 2	9,521
33		25	(h)	Bristol C	D 1-1	Bowl	4,847
34	Apr	1	(a)	Aldershot	L 0-2		3,642
35		7	(a)	Clapton O	D 3-3	Bowl 2, Hearty (og)	8,700
36		8	(h)	Notts C	W 1-0	Ebdon	5,931
37		10	(h)	Clapton O	W 2-1	Bowl, Ebdon	7,329
38		12	(a)	Southend U	W 1-0	Bowl	2,657
39		15	(a)	Northampton T	D 0-0		4,207
40		22	(h)	Swindon T	D 0-0		4,622
41		29	(h)	Queen's Park R	D 1-1	Sutherley	3,348
42	May	6	(a)	Mansfield	L 2-4	Bowl 2	2,500

FINAL LEAGUE POSITION: 14th in Division Three South

Appearances
Goals

FA Cup

1	Nov	26	(a)	Torquay U	L 1-3

Third Division South Cup

1	Oct	19	(a)	Swindon T	W 3-2
2	Feb	1	(h)	Bournemouth	L 1-2

208

	Church	Brown	Wallace	Shadwell	Fellowes	Angus	Rich	Bussey	Bowl	Ebdon	Liddle	Little	Millar	Clarke	Turnbull	Walker	Riley	Blore	Halliday	Sutherley	Southcombe
1	1	2	3	4	5	6	7	8	9	10	11										
2	1	2		4	5	6	7	8	9	10		3	11								
3	1	2		4	5	6	7	8	9	10		3	11								
4	1	2		4	5	6	7		9	10			11	3	8						
5	1	2		4	5	6	7		9	10			11	3	8						
6	1	2		4	5	6	7		9	10			11	3	8						
7	1	2		4	5	6	7		9	10			11	3	8						
8	1	2		4	5	6	7	8	9	10		3	11								
9	1	2		4	5	6	7	8	9	10		3	11								
10	1	2		4	5	6	7	8	9	10		3	11								
11	1	2		4	5		7		8	10	11	3		9		6					
12	1	2		4	5		7		8	10	11	3		9		6					
13	1	2		4	5		7		9	8	11	3				6	10				
14		2		4	5		7		9	8	11	3				6	10	1			
15		2			5	4	7		9	8	11	3				6	10	1			
16	1	2			6	5	7		9	10	11			3		4	8				
17	1	2			6	5	7		9	10	11			3		4	8				
18	1	2			6	5	7		9	10	11			3		4	8				
19	1	2			6	5	7		9	10	11			3		4	8				
20	1	2		4	6	5	7	8	9	10	11			3							
21	1	2			6	5	11	8	9	10				3	7	4					
22	1	2			6	5		8	9	10	11			3		4	7				
23		2			6	5	7	8	9	10				3		4	11	1			
24		2			6	5	7	8	9	10				3		4	11	1			
25	1	2			6	5		8	9	10		3			7	4	11				
26	1	2			6	5	4		9	10	11	3			7		8				
27	1	2			6	5	8	11	9	10		3			7	4					
28	1				6	5	11		9	10		3			7	4	8		2		
29	1				6	5	11		9	10				3	7	4	8		2		
30	1				6	5	11		9	10				3	7	4	8		2		
31	1				6	5	11		9	10				3	7	4	8		2		
32	1				6	5	7		9	10	11	3				4	8		2		
33	1				6	5	7		9	10	11	3				4	8		2		
34	1				6	5		8	9	7		3				4	10		2	11	
35	1				6	5		8	9	10		3				4	7		2	11	
36	1				6	5		7	9	10		3				4	8		2	11	
37	1				6	5		7	9	10		3				4	8		2	11	
38	1	2			6	5			9	10		3				4	8			11	7
39	1				6	5		7	9	10		3				4	8		2	11	
40	1				6	5		8	9	10		3				4			2	11	7
41	1				6	5			9	10		3			7	4	8		2	11	
42	1				6	5			9	10		3			7	4	8		2	11	
	38	28	1	15	42	38	32	19	42	42	15	25	9	18	13	30	26	4	14	9	2
					1		4	5	24	12	1		3		1		9			1	

4 own-goals

1945-46

Manager: George Roughton (from 17 Oct 1945)

#		Date		Opponent	Result	Scorers	Att.
1	Aug	25	(a)	Swindon T	W 4-1	Casey 2, Warren, Ebdon	11,200
2	Sep	1	(h)	Swindon T	D 1-1	Mitcheson	6,301
3		5	(a)	Aldershot	W 5-3	Ebdon 2, Wardle, Challis, Kernick	1,500
4		8	(h)	Reading	W 5-1	Ebdon 2, Kernick 2, Challis	9,000
5		15	(a)	Reading	D 1-1	Challis	6,905
6		19	(h)	Aldershot	L 1-4	Challis	7,000
7		22	(a)	Bristol R	L 1-2	Kernick	9,200
8		29	(h)	Bristol R	D 2-2	Challis, Haddington	9,000
9	Oct	6	(h)	Crystal P	L 0-1		10,259
10		13	(a)	Crystal P	L 1-2	Walker	15,000
11		20	(a)	Bournemouth	L 1-3	Ebdon	6,151
12		27	(h)	Bournemouth	L 0-3		6,500
13	Nov	3	(h)	Cardiff C	W 3-2	Kernick, Walker 2	9,484
14		10	(a)	Cardiff C	D 0-0		18,000
15	Dec	1	(h)	Bristol C	W 1-0	Challis	9,000
16		19	(a)	Brighton & HA	L 2-3	Jones, Blood	
17		22	(h)	Brighton & HA	W 3-2	Challis 2, Ebdon	4,578
18		25	(a)	Torquay U	L 1-3	Mitcheson	4,000
19		26	(h)	Torquay U	L 0-2		9,387
20		27	(a)	Bristol C	L 1-5	Wardle	7,465

FINAL LEAGUE POSITION: 9th in Division Three South (South of Thames)

Appearances
Goals

#		Date		Opponent	Result	Scorers	Att.
21	Jan	12	(a)	Bristol R	L 1-2	Walker	7,000
22		19	(h)	Bristol R	L 0-1		5,166
23		26	(h)	Cardiff C	W 2-1	Walker, Bowden	8,000
24	Feb	2	(a)	Cardiff C	L 1-5	Regan	8,000
25		9	(h)	Bristol C	W 3-0	Walker, Ebdon 2	8,000
26		16	(a)	Bristol C	L 0-3		12,891
27		23	(h)	Brighton & HA	D 0-0		6,783
28	Mar	2	(a)	Brighton & HA	D 2-2	Ebdon, Walker	3,000
29		9	(h)	Torquay U	D 1-1	Tickell	6,000
30		16	(a)	Torquay U	W 2-0	Wright, Regan	6,400
31		23	(a)	Crystal P	L 0-3		12,000
32		30	(h)	Crystal P	L 2-3	Walker, Wardle	8,824
33	Apr	6	(a)	Bournemouth	D 1-1	Ebdon	10,000
34		13	(h)	Bournemouth	W 3-1	Ebdon 3	7,805
35		20	(a)	Aldershot	L 3-5	Wardle 2, Wright	4,901
36		22	(h)	Aldershot	W 1-0	Ebdon	8,000

FINAL LEAGUE POSITION: 8th in Division Three South Cup (Southern Section)

Appearances
Goals

FA Cup

1	Nov	17	(a)	Trowbridge T	W 3-1
		24	(h)	Trowbridge T	W 7-2
2	Dec	8	(a)	Newport C	L 1-5
		15	(h)	Newport C	L 1-3

Joslin	Murray	Rich	Walker	Blood	Jordan	Wardle	Warren	Ebdon	Mitcheson	Casey	Goodfellow	Brown	Challis	Kernick	Lewis	Latham	Franklin	Staveley	Roughton	Haddington	Sutherley	Boye-Karlsen H	Elliott	Angus	Baxter	Bowden	Dalgleish	Gallagher	Tickell	Thomson	Haddock	Purvis	Harris	Gadsby	Regan	Topham	Hydes	Singleton	Coles	Match
1	2	3	4	5	6	7	8	9	10	11																														1
	2	3	4	5	6	8	7	9	10	11	1																													2
	2		4	5	6	8		9					1	3	7	10	11																							3
	2		4	5	6			9	10				1	3	7	8	11																							4
	2		4	5									1	3		11	6																							5
3			4		6	8		9					1	2	7	10	11	5																						6
	2		4	5	6			9					1	3	7	10	11	8																						7
			4	5	6			9	10					3	7				1	2	8	11																		8
3			4	5	6				10				1	2	7	8							9	11																9
	2	9	5	4	8				10				1		11			3							6	7														10
	2		4	5	6			9					1		7			3	10	11						8														11
	2		4	5					10				1		11			3							6		8	7	9											12
	2	9	6	5	8								1		11	10		3									4	7												13
	2	9	5	4	8		6						1		11	10		3										7												14
	2	10	5	4	8			9							11			3										7		1	6									15
	2	9	5	4	8										11	10														1			3							16
	2		5	4	8			9							11			3								10				7	1	6								17
	2														11	7	4													1	6				3					18
		10	5	4	8													3								9				1	6				2					19
	2		6	5	4	8									7															1										20
1	**18**	**2**	**19**	**17**	**18**	**14**	**2**	**16**	**9**	**2**	**12**	**7**	**16**	**8**	**6**	**2**	**1**	**1**	**10**	**2**	**2**	**1**	**1**	**2**	**1**	**4**	**1**	**2**	**4**	**6**	**6**	**4**	**1**					**2**		
	3	**1**			**2**	**1**	**7**	**2**	**2**				**8**	**5**						**1**																					
	2	9	3	4	8			11																6		10		7							2		1	5		21
	2	9	3	4	8			11																6		10		7									1	5		22
	2	8	3	4		7		9																6		10									11		1	5		23
		8	3	4		7		9																6		10									11		1	5		24
	2	10	3	4		7		9																6								11		8		1	5		25
	2	6	3	4		7		9																5		10						11		8			1			26
	2	10		4	8			9																6				7				11	3				1	5		27
		10	3	4	8			9																6				7				11	2				1	5		28
		10	3	4		7																		6			11						2				1	5		29
			3		7			9																6								2	11		8		1	5		30
	2		3		7			9																6								11		8		1	5		31
		8			7			9																								2	11			8		5		32
	7		2					9				11												4									3				1	5		33
		4	2		7			9				11																					3	11			1	5		34
		8	2		7			9																									3	11				5		35
	7		2		7			9								15																	2							36
7	**12**	**14**	**9**	**14**	**15**							**2**											**12**		**5**		**5**					**2**	**8**	**9**	**1**	**5**	**13**	**15**	
	5			**3**	**8**																		**1**		**1**										**2**					

Attwood played number 9 in Match 29; Cutting played number 6 in Match 16, number 4 in Matches 30, 31, 32 & 36 and number 8 in Matches 34 & 35; Crawshw played number 9 in Match 20; Davison played number 2 in Match 24; Eastham played number 6 in Matches 32, 34 & 36; Jones played number 7 in Match 16, scoring once, and number 8 in Match 29; Lambton played number 1 in Matches 33, 35 & 36; Langford played number 11 in Match 20; Long played number 3 in Matches 32 & 33; Perkins played number 7 in Match 19; Petherbridge played number 7 in Match 33; Wright played number 10 in Matches 30, scoring once, 31, 32, 33, 34, 35, scoring once, & 36.

1946-47

Manager: George Roughton

1	Aug	31	(h)	Torquay U	D 1-1	Wright	11,468
2	Sep	2	(a)	Northampton T	W 2-1	Regan, Wright	11,000
3		7	(a)	Port Vale	W 2-1	Regan, Ebdon	10,000
4		11	(h)	Aldershot	W 4-1	Ebdon, Regan, Wright, Wardle	9,538
5		14	(h)	Bristol C	L 1-3	Wardle	13,100
6		18	(h)	Northampton T	W 1-0	Ebdon	8,000
7		21	(a)	Swindon T	L 0-2		20,831
8		28	(h)	Bournemouth	W 4-1	Ebdon 3, Wardle	12,000
9	Oct	5	(a)	Cardiff C	L 0-5		32,000
10		12	(h)	Norwich C	W 3-0	Ebdon, Wright, Regan	9,160
11		19	(h)	Crystal P	W 2-1	Regan, Ebdon	12,000
12		26	(a)	Reading	L 0-4		11,042
13	Nov	2	(h)	Walsall	D 2-2	Ebdon 2	9,102
14		9	(a)	Watford	L 1-3	Wright	6,900
15		16	(h)	Ipswich T	D 0-0		8,849
16	Dec	7	(a)	Southend U	D 2-2	Walton (og), Owen	10,000
17		14	(h)	Bristol R	W 3-2	Holman 2, Wright	7,000
18		21	(a)	Mansfield T	L 0-1		4,236
19		25	(a)	Brighton & HA	W 6-1	Owen 3, Wright 2, Wardle	7,777
20		26	(h)	Brighton & HA	W 2-1	Cutting, Blood	12,000
21		28	(a)	Torquay U	L 1-2	Head (og)	11,000
22	Jan	4	(h)	Port Vale	D 1-1	Jones	8,165
23		11	(a)	Leyton O	L 1-3	Regan	8,577
24		18	(a)	Bristol C	D 2-2	Ebdon, Regan	20,153
25		25	(h)	Swindon T	D 1-1	Owen	8,000
26	Feb	15	(a)	Norwich C	W 3-1	Ebdon 2, Regan	12,696
27		22	(a)	Crystal P	L 0-1		7,100
28	Mar	1	(h)	Reading	L 1-3	Ebdon	10,000
29		5	(h)	Queen's Park R	W 3-0	Cutting, Wright, Walker	5,000
30		15	(h)	Watford	W 1-0	Wright	5,500
31		22	(a)	Ipswich T	L 1-2	Wright	12,000
32		29	(h)	Leyton O	W 3-1	Wardle 2, Ebdon	7,387
33	Apr	4	(a)	Notts C	D 0-0		10,000
34		5	(a)	Queen's Park R	L 0-2		18,000
35		7	(h)	Notts C	D 2-2	Owen 2	12,000
36		12	(h)	Southend U	L 1-5	Ebdon	10,000
37		19	(a)	Bristol R	L 0-1		13,775
38		26	(h)	Mansfield T	W 1-0	Walker	6,000
39	May	3	(a)	Aldershot	L 0-2		4,500
40		10	(a)	Bournemouth	L 1-4	Owen	8,000
41		17	(h)	Cardiff C	L 0-2		12,431
42		24	(a)	Walsall	L 1-2	Challis (pen)	10,000

FINAL LEAGUE POSITION: 15th in Division Three South

Appearances

Goals

FA Cup

| 1 | Nov | 30 | (a) | Bournemouth | L 2-4 | | |

Football appearance grid (shirt numbers worn by each player in each match). Players are columns; matches are rows (numbered 1–42 at right). The two bottom rows are totals.

Hoyle	Thompson	Blood	Cutting	Hanford	Walker	Wardle	Hydes	Ebdon	Wright	Regan	Fellowes	Hammond	Long	Murray	Singleton	Coles	Mustard	Vaughan	Owen	Granville	Haddock	Challis	Holman	Hutchings	Sutherland	Smart	#
1	2	3	4	5	6	7	8	9	10	11																	1
1	2	3	4	5	6	7	8	9	10	11																	2
1	2	3		5	6	7	8	9		11	4	10															3
1	2		4	5	6	7	8	9	10	11			3														4
	2		4	5	6	8		9	10	11					1	3	7										5
	2		4	5	6	8		9		11					1	3	7	10									6
	2		4	5		8		9	10	11	6				1	3	7										7
	2	3	4			8		9	10	11	6				1	5	7										8
	2		4	5		8		9	10	11	6				1	3	7										9
	2	3	4			8		9	10	11	6				1	5	7										10
	2	3				7		9	10	11	6				1	5		4	8								11
1		2				8		9	10	11	6					5	7	4		3							12
	2	3		5		8		9	10	11	6				1		7	4									13
	2	3		5	9	8			10	11	6				1		7	4									14
	2	3		5	6	8			10	11	4				1		7					9					15
	2	3	4	5	6	8			10	11					1		7					9					16
	2	3	4	5	6	8			10	11					1				7			9					17
	2	3	4	5	6	8			10	11					1				7			9					18
	2	3	4	5	6	8			10	11					1					7		9					19
	2	3	4	5	6	8			10	11					1			9	7								20
	2	3	4	5	6	8			10	11					1			9	7								21
	2	3	4	5	6	8				11					1		10	9	7								22
	2	3	4	5	6			9	10	11					1			8	7								23
1	2	3	4	5	6	11		9	10									8	7								24
1	2	3	4	5	6	8		9	10	11									7								25
1		3		5	6	8		9	10	11	4				2				7								26
1	2	3	4	5	6	8		9	10	11									7								27
1	2	3	4	5	6	8		9	10	11						7											28
1	2	3	4	5	6	8		9	10	11						7											29
1	2	3	4	5	6	8		9	10	11						7											30
1	2	3	4	5	6	8		9	10	11									7								31
1	2	3	4	5	6	8		9		11								10	7								32
1	2	3	4	5		7		9		11						6		10	8								33
1	2	3	4	5	6	8			10	11						7				9							34
1	2	3	4	5	6	8			10	11								9						7			35
	2	3		5	6	8		9	10						1			4				11		7			36
	2	3	4	5	6	7		9	10	11					1									8			37
	2	3	4	5		8			10	11					1	6		9						7			38
		3	4	5		8			10	11	6				1	2			9	7							39
	2	3	4			8	7	9	10						5								11				40
1	2	3	4						10										5	9			11	7	8	9	41
19	38	36	35	36	31	38	4	29	38	37	14	2	1	1	23	13	14	4	20	13	1	4	4	5	1	1	42
	1	2			2	6		16	11	8									9			1	2				

2 own-goals

1947-48

Manager: George Roughton

#		Date		Opponent	Result	Scorers	Attendance
1	Aug	23	(a)	Walsall	L 0-4		15,096
2		27	(h)	Reading	W 1-0	Evans	10,000
3		30	(h)	Leyton O	D 1-1	Granville	10,000
4	Sep	3	(a)	Reading	L 1-2	Ebdon	10,713
5		6	(a)	Torquay U	W 2-1	W.Fallon, Ebdon	11,100
6		10	(h)	Ipswich T	W 1-0	Bell (og)	7,000
7		13	(a)	Newport C	L 0-3		13,161
8		17	(a)	Ipswich T	L 0-2		12,500
9		20	(h)	Southend U	D 0-0		10,000
10		25	(a)	Queen's Park R	L 1-3	Ebdon	12,000
11		27	(a)	Notts C	D 1-1	Ebdon	20,756
12	Oct	4	(h)	Swansea T	W 3-1	Hutchings, Thompson, Regan	12,000
13		11	(h)	Crystal P	W 2-0	Ebdon, Hutchings	11,000
14		18	(a)	Aldershot	D 0-0		8,000
15		25	(h)	Northampton T	D 1-1	W.Fallon	11,000
16	Nov	1	(a)	Bristol R	D 2-2	Thompson (pen), Regan	14,389
17		8	(h)	Norwich C	W 2-0	Guy (og), Hutchings	9,000
18		15	(a)	Brighton & HA	W 1-0	Smart	8,600
19		22	(h)	Watford	W 3-1	Regan, Ebdon, Thompson (pen)	9,623
20	Dec	26	(h)	Bristol C	W 3-1	Thompson (pen), Sutherland, Mackay	12,627
21		27	(a)	Bristol C	D 1-1	Dymond	11,148
22	Jan	3	(a)	Leyton O	W 4-2	Sutherland 2, Mackay, Regan	12,000
23		17	(h)	Torquay U	L 0-2		12,751
24		31	(h)	Newport C	D 4-4	Mackay, Hutchings, Evans, Regan	10,154
25	Feb	7	(a)	Southend U	L 0-2		9,500
26		14	(h)	Notts C	L 0-1		16,942
27		21	(a)	Swansea T	L 0-2		14,000
28		28	(a)	Crystal P	W 2-1	Evans, Mackay	17,500
29	Mar	6	(h)	Aldershot	W 4-0	Dymond 2, Regan, Evans	7,718
30		13	(a)	Northampton T	L 1-3	Regan	7,000
31		20	(h)	Bristol R	W 4-0	Hutchings, Bamford (og), Evans, Bartholomew (pen)	8,000
32		26	(h)	Bournemouth	D 1-1	Wilson (og)	15,833
33		27	(a)	Norwich C	L 0-3		24,755
34		29	(a)	Bournemouth	L 1-2	Regan	24,000
35	Apr	3	(h)	Brighton & HA	W 1-0	Evans	7,853
36		7	(h)	Port Vale	D 0-0		7,643
37		10	(a)	Watford	L 1-3	Regan	10,000
38		14	(a)	Swindon T	L 2-3	Mackay, Regan	8,000
39		17	(h)	Queen's Park R	L 1-2	Bartholomew (pen)	12,000
40		21	(h)	Walsall	L 0-6		6,501
41		24	(a)	Port Vale	D 1-1	Regan	5,561
42	May	1	(h)	Swindon T	W 2-1	Ebdon, Smart	6,924

FINAL LEAGUE POSITION: 11th in Division Three South

Appearances
Goals

FA Cup

1	Nov	29	(h)	Northampton T	D 1-1
R	Dec	6	(a)	Northampton T	L 0-2

Hoyle	Thompson	Blood	Cutting	Bartholomew	Walker	Hutchings	Evans	Ebdon	Wright	Regan	Johnstone	Granville	Sutherland	Fallon W	Gibson	Angus	Singleton	Rowe S	Mackay	Vaughan	Smart	Dymond	Davey	Jeffrey	Fallon P	No.
1	2	3	4	5	6	7	8	9	10	11																1
1	2		4	5	6		8		10		3	7	9	11												2
1	2		4		6		8	9	10		3	7		11	5											3
1	2				6		8	9		11	3		10	7	5	4										4
1	2				6		8	9		7	3		10	11	5	4										5
1	2				6		8	9		7	3		10	11	5	4										6
	2			4	6		8	9	10	11	3	7			5		1									7
	2			4	6			9	10		3	7			5		1		8	11						8
	2			4	6			9	10		3				5		1		8	11	7					9
	2			4	6			9	10	11	3				5		1		8		7					10
	2			4	6	7		9	10	11	3				5		1		8							11
	2			4	6	7		9	10	11	3				5		1		8							12
	2			4	6	7		9	10		3		11		5		1		8							13
	2			4	6	7		9	10		3		11		5		1		8							14
	2			4	6	7			10	11	3				5		1		8		9					15
	2			4	6	7			10	11	3				5		1		8		9					16
	2			4	6	7			10	11	3				5		1		8		9					17
	2			4	6	7		9	10	11	3				5		1		8							18
	2			4	6				10	11	3		9		5		1		8		7					19
				4	6				10	11	3		9		5		1	2	8		7					20
	2			4	6				10	11	3		9		5		1		8		7					21
	2			4	6				10	11	3		9		5		1		8		7					22
	2			4	6	7			10	11	3		9		5		1		8							23
	2			4	6	7			10	11	3		9		5		1		8							24
	2			4	6	7			10	11	3		9		5		1		8							25
	2			4	6	7	8			11					5		1	3	10			9				26
				4	6	7	8			11	2				5		1	3	10			9				27
				4	6	7	8			11	2				5		1	3	10			9				28
				4	6	7	8			11	2				5		1	3	10			9				29
				4	6	7	8			11	2				5		1	3	10			9				30
				4	6	7	8			11	2						1	3	10			9	5			31
				4	6	7	8			11	2				5		1	3	10			9				32
				4		7	8			11	2						1	3	10			9	5	6		33
				4		7	8			11	2						1	3	10			9	5	6		34
		3		4		7	8			11	2						1		10			9	5	6		35
		3		4		7	8			11	2						1		10			9	5	6		36
				4		7	8			11	2						1	3	10			9	5	6		37
				4		7	8	9		11	2						1	3	10				5	6		38
				4		7	8	9		11	2						1	3	10				5	6		39
1				4	5			9		11	2							3	10			8	7		6	40
1				4	5			9		11	2							3	10			8	7		6	41
9	25	3	3	32	33	26	30	18	18	36	40	7	13	8	30	3	33	16	33	2	8	17	10	7	2	42
	4			2		5	6	7		11		1	3	2					5		2	3				

4 own-goals

1948-49

Manager: George Roughton

#		Date		Opponent	Result	Scorers	Att.
1	Aug	21	(h)	Northampton T	W 5-1	Johnston, Regan 3, Smart	9,586
2		25	(h)	Southend U	D 0-0		11,229
3		28	(h)	Norwich C	W 4-1	Smart 2, Regan, Mackay	10,000
4		31	(a)	Southend U	D 0-0		14,000
5	Sep	4	(a)	Torquay U	L 1-2	Dymond	14,000
6		8	(h)	Aldershot	D 3-3	Dymond, Mackay, Bartholomew (pen)	11,500
7		11	(a)	Bristol C	L 0-1		16,519
8		15	(a)	Aldershot	W 2-1	Regan, Harrower	6,500
9		18	(h)	Swindon T	W 3-1	Regan, Smith 2	11,578
10		22	(a)	Bournemouth	L 0-1		15,119
11		25	(a)	Leyton O	L 2-5	Bartholomew, Mackay	20,000
12	Oct	2	(h)	Port Vale	W 2-1	Bartholomew 2 (1 pen)	10,672
13		9	(h)	Walsall	W 2-1	Smith, Dymond	10,844
14		16	(a)	Notts C	L 0-9		37,647
15		23	(h)	Reading	L 1-2	Regan	10,534
16		30	(a)	Swansea T	L 0-6		29,000
17	Nov	6	(h)	Watford	W 2-1	Mackay, Dymond	7,739
18		13	(a)	Crystal P	D 1-1	Regan	14,000
19		20	(h)	Ipswich T	L 1-3	Smith	9,167
20	Dec	18	(a)	Northampton T	L 0-4		7,850
21		25	(h)	Brighton & HA	D 1-1	Mackay	7,000
22		27	(a)	Brighton & HA	L 0-2		17,000
23	Jan	1	(a)	Norwich C	L 0-3		18,915
24		15	(h)	Torquay U	W 2-0	Harrower, Smith	12,988
25		22	(h)	Bristol C	D 1-1	Regan	9,762
26	Feb	5	(a)	Swindon T	D 1-1	Regan	13,444
27		12	(a)	Bristol R	L 1-3	Regan	16,802
28		19	(h)	Leyton O	W 3-1	Durrant, Mackay, Harrower	9,375
29		26	(a)	Port Vale	D 1-1	Durrant	8,300
30	Mar	5	(a)	Walsall	L 3-4	Harrower 2, Hutchings	6,000
31		12	(h)	Notts C	W 3-1	Regan 2, Fallon	14,000
32		19	(a)	Reading	L 0-2		13,877
33		26	(h)	Swansea T	D 1-1	Regan	13,000
34	Apr	2	(a)	Watford	W 1-0	Johnston	7,337
35		9	(h)	Crystal P	W 3-1	Mackay, Durrant, Hutchings	7,656
36		15	(a)	Millwall	L 1-2	Hutchings	27,000
37		16	(a)	Ipswich T	D 2-2	Smith, Powell	15,000
38		18	(h)	Millwall	W 3-0	Clark (pen), Smart, Rew	10,920
39		23	(h)	Bournemouth	L 2-3	Smith, Clark (pen)	9,088
40		30	(a)	Newport C	W 2-0	Smart, Regan	8,000
41	May	4	(h)	Newport C	L 1-2	Smart	6,593
42		7	(h)	Bristol R	W 2-1	Durrant, Mackay	7,000

FINAL LEAGUE POSITION: 12th in Division Three South

Appearances
Goals

FA Cup

#		Date		Opponent	Result
1	Dec	4	(a)	Barnet	W 6-2
2		11	(h)	Hereford U	W 2-1
3	Jan	8	(a)	Grimsby T	L 1-2

Batting order / appearance grid. Columns are players (left→right): Hoyle, Johnstone, Rowe, Bartholomew, Gibson, Walker, Hutchings, Smart, Johnston, Mackay, Regan, Smith, Dymond, Davey, Harrower, Evans, Clark, Grant, Coles, Fallon, Warren, Singleton, Gallagher, Durrant, Powell, Rew. The right-hand numbers (1–42) label each row.

Hoyle	Johnstone	Rowe	Bartholomew	Gibson	Walker	Hutchings	Smart	Johnston	Mackay	Regan	Smith	Dymond	Davey	Harrower	Evans	Clark	Grant	Coles	Fallon	Warren	Singleton	Gallagher	Durrant	Powell	Rew	#
1	2	3	4	5	6	7	8	9	10	11																
1	2	3	4	5	6	7	8	9	10	11																1
1	2	3	4	5	6		8	9	10	11	7															2
1	2	3	4	5	6		8	9	10	11		7														3
1	2	3	4		6		8	9	10	11		7	5													4
1	2	3	4		6		8		10	11		7	5	9												5
1	2	3	4		5		8		10	11	9	7			6											6
1		3	4		5				8	11	9	7		10	6	2										7
1	2	3	4		5				8	11	9	7		10	6											8
1	2	3	4		5				8	11	9	7			6		10									9
1	2	3	4						10	11	9	7		8	6			5								10
1	2	3	4		5				10	11	9	7		8	6											11
1	2	3	4		5	11			10		9	7		8	6											12
1	2	3	4		5	11			10		9	7		8	6											13
1	2	3	4		5			9	10	11	8	7			6											14
1	2	3			6			9	10	11		7	5	8		4										15
1					6			9	10	11		7	5	8	3	4	2									16
1			4		6		8	9	10	11		7	5		3		2									17
			4		6		8		10	11	9	7	5		3		2	1								18
1		3	4		5				10	11	9	7		8	6		2									19
1	2		4		5				10	11	9	7		8	3				6							20
1	2		4		5	9			10	11		7		8	3				6							21
1	2		4				8			11	9	7		10		3			6		5					22
1	2		4	5			8			11	9	7		10		3			6							23
1	2		4	6			8			11	9	7	5	10		3										24
1	2		4		5		8			11		7		10		3			6				9			25
1	2		4		5		8			11		7		10		3			6				9			26
1	2		4		5	7	8			11				10		3			6				9			27
1	2		4		5	7	8			11				10		3			6				9			28
1	2		4		5	7	8			11				10		3			6				9			29
1	2		4		5	7	8			11				10		3			6				9			30
1	2		4		5	7	8			11				10		3							9	6		31
1	2		4		5	7	8			11				10		3							9	6		32
1	2				5	7	8		10	11						3	4						9	6		33
1	2		4		5	7	8		10	11						3							9	6		34
1	2		4		5	7	8		10	11						3							9	6		35
1	2		4		5	7	8		10	11	9					3			6							36
1	2		4		5	7	8		10	11						3			6				9			37
1	2		4		5	7	8		10		9					3						11		6		38
1	2		4		5	7	8		10	11	9					3			6							39
	2		4		5	7	8		10	11						3			6		1		9			40
1	2		4		5	7	8		10	11						3							9	6		41
							8		10	11						3							9	6		42
40	37	17	34	10	39	19	20	10	40	38	20	24	7	21	11	26	2	1	16	4	2	1	13	9	1	
			4			3	6	2	8	15	7	4		5		2			1				4	1	1	

1949-50

Manager: George Roughton

1	Aug	20	(h)	Crystal P	W 2-1	Durrant, McClelland	12,180
2		24	(a)	Bournemouth	L 0-2		19,041
3		27	(a)	Watford	W 2-1	Mackay, Regan	11,000
4		31	(h)	Bournemouth	L 1-2	Regan	12,055
5	Sep	3	(h)	Reading	L 3-4	Hutchings 2, Regan	10,853
6		8	(a)	Notts C	D 3-3	Regan 2, McClelland	32,167
7		10	(a)	Leyton O	L 1-4	McClelland	16,000
8		17	(h)	Aldershot	W 1-0	Hutchings	10,108
9		24	(h)	Ipswich T	D 1-1	Mackay	9,107
10	Oct	1	(a)	Port Vale	L 0-1		12,000
11		8	(a)	Nottingham F	L 0-5		25,908
12		15	(h)	Northampton T	L 1-3	Regan	8,323
13		22	(a)	Norwich C	W 2-1	Smith, Smith	22,697
14		29	(h)	Newport C	D 3-3	McClelland, Smart, Regan	8,000
15	Nov	5	(a)	Bristol C	L 0-1		18,880
16		12	(h)	Brighton & HA	L 2-3	Clark, Harrower	7,615
17		19	(a)	Walsall	L 0-3		8,700
18	Dec	3	(a)	Swindon T	L 1-7	Smart	10,785
19		17	(a)	Crystal P	L 3-5	Smith, Greenwood, Regan	15,000
20		24	(h)	Watford	W 3-1	Greenwood, Smart, Fallon	7,565
21		26	(h)	Southend U	D 1-1	Smart	14,105
22		27	(a)	Southend U	L 0-1		20,000
23		31	(a)	Reading	L 2-3	Smart, Regan	12,999
24	Jan	14	(h)	Leyton O	D 1-1	Smart	8,917
25		21	(a)	Aldershot	W 2-1	Walker, Smart	4,677
26	Feb	4	(a)	Ipswich T	L 0-1		11,431
27		11	(h)	Torquay U	D 1-1	Smart	14,833
28		18	(h)	Port Vale	W 3-1	Smart 2, Smith	9,472
29		25	(h)	Nottingham F	D 0-0		11,680
30	Mar	4	(a)	Northampton T	D 3-3	Smith, Regan, Mackay	11,571
31		11	(h)	Norwich C	W 3-1	Smart, Regan, Mackay	9,875
32		18	(a)	Newport C	W 2-1	Clark (pen), Smith	6,414
33		25	(h)	Bristol C	D 0-0		10,937
34	Apr	1	(a)	Brighton & HA	D 0-0		9,610
35		7	(h)	Bristol R	W 2-0	Mackay, Smart	12,121
36		8	(h)	Walsall	W 2-1	Harrower 2	9,291
37		10	(a)	Bristol R	L 0-1		9,698
38		15	(a)	Millwall	L 1-3	McClelland	15,924
39		22	(h)	Swindon T	W 3-0	Smith, Harrower, Mackay	8,664
40		26	(h)	Millwall	W 2-1	Smith, Clark (pen)	6,128
41		29	(a)	Torquay U	W 4-1	Smith, McClelland 3	9,500
42	May	6	(h)	Notts C	D 2-2	Hutchings, Smith	10,241

FINAL LEAGUE POSITION: 16th in Division Three South

Appearances
Goals

FA Cup

1	Nov	26	(a)	Millwall	W 5-3	
2	Dec	10	(h)	Chester	W 2-0	
3	Jan	7	(h)	Nuneaton Boro	W 3-0	
4		28	(a)	Liverpool	L 1-3	

218

Hoyle	Johnstone	Rowe	Greenwood	Walker	Powell	Hutchings	Smart	Durrant	McClelland	Regan	Davey	Mackay	Rew	Doyle	Singleton	Roy	Squires	Harrower	Smith	Fallon	Mitchell	Murphy	Clark	Goddard	№
1	2	3	4	5	6	7	8	9	10	11															1
1	2	3	4	5	6	7	8	9	10	11															2
1	2	3	6		4	7			10	11	5	8	9												3
1	2	3	6	4		7			10	11	5	8	9												4
1	2	3	6	4		7			10	11	5	8		9											5
	2	3	6		4	7			9	11	5	10			1	8									6
	2	3	6			7			9	11	5	10			1	8	4								7
	2	3	6	5	4	7				11	10	9			1			8							8
	2	3	6	5	4	7			9		10				1			8	11						9
	2	3	6		4	11			9		5	10			1			8	7						10
	2	3	6			7			10	11	5			4	1			8	9						11
	2	3	6				8		10	11	5			4	1				9		7				12
	2	3	6				8		10	11	5			4	1				9		7				13
1	2	3	6			7	8		10		5			4					9			11			14
1	2	3	6				8		10		5			4				7	9			11			15
1	2	3	6				8		10	11	5			4				7	9			11			16
1	2	3	6				8		10	11	5			4				7	9						17
1	2		10		6		8			11	5							7	9	4			3		18
1	2		10		6		8			11								7	9	4			3	5	19
1	2		10		6		8			11								7	9	4			3	5	20
1		3	10				8			11				6				7	9	4	2			5	21
1	2		10		6		8			11								7	9	4			3	5	22
	2		10		6		8			11					1			7	9	4			3	5	23
	2		6	9	7	8			10						1				4		11		3	5	24
	2		10	9	7	8			11	6					1				4				3	5	25
	2		10			8				11	6	7			1				9	4			3	5	26
	2		10			8				11	6	7			1				9	4			3	5	27
	2		10			8				11	6	7			1				9	4			3	5	28
	2		10			8				11	6	7			1				9	4			3	5	29
	2					8			10	11	6	7			1				9	4			3	5	30
	2					8			10	11	6	7			1				9	4			3	5	31
	2					8			10	11	6	7			1				9	4			3	5	32
	2					8			10	11	6	7			1				9	4			3	5	33
	2					8			10	11	6	7			1				9	4			3	5	34
	2					8				11	6	10			1			7	9	4			3	5	35
	2				8					11	6	10			1			7	9	4			3	5	36
	2	10								11	6	8			1			7	9	4			3	5	37
	2								10	11	6	8			1			7	9	4			3	5	38
	2						8		10		6	11			1			7	9	4			3	5	39
	2		10							11	6	8			1			7	9	4			3	5	40
	2		10							11	6	8			1			7	9	4			3		41
	2									11	6	8			1	5		7	9	4			3		42
14	41	19	31	8	13	18	25	4	33	27	32	26	3	10	28	2	1	20	31	25	2	2	25	22	
		2	1		4	13	1	8	11		6							4	9	1			3		

1950-51

Manager: George Roughton

								Attendance
1	Aug	19	(h)	Millwall	L	0-1		12,844
2		23	(a)	Bristol C	L	1-3	Smith	21,700
3		26	(a)	Watford	W	2-1	Smith 2	11,800
4		30	(h)	Bristol C	W	1-0	Smith	9,546
5	Sep	2	(h)	Walsall	W	1-0	Lynn	10,711
6		6	(a)	Swindon T	L	0-1		9,467
7		9	(a)	Leyton O	W	3-1	Smart 2, Smith	20,000
8		13	(h)	Swindon T	W	1-0	McClelland	12,000
9		16	(h)	Ipswich T	W	2-0	McClelland, Davey	9,789
10		23	(a)	Plymouth A	W	1-0	Smith	25,424
11		30	(h)	Reading	L	1-3	Smith (pen)	11,116
12	Oct	7	(a)	Colchester U	W	1-0	Smith	12,000
13		14	(h)	Bristol R	L	0-2		13,325
14		21	(a)	Crystal P	W	1-0	Regan	16,081
15		28	(h)	Brighton & HA	W	4-2	Mackay 3, McClelland	10,803
16	Nov	4	(a)	Newport C	W	3-0	McClelland 2, Smith	10,653
17		11	(h)	Norwich C	L	1-2	Lynn	12,385
18		18	(a)	Northampton T	L	1-4	Regan	11,458
19	Dec	2	(a)	Nottingham F	D	2-2	Regan, Mackay	24,240
20		23	(h)	Watford	D	3-3	Eggleston (og), Fallon 2	7,252
21		25	(a)	Aldershot	L	2-4	Smith, Singleton	
22		26	(h)	Aldershot	W	3-0	McClelland 2, Smith	11,899
23		30	(a)	Walsall	W	2-0	Mackay, Smith	4,275
24	Jan	13	(h)	Leyton O	D	0-0		9,327
25		17	(a)	Gillingham	L	4-9	Kingsnorth (og), Smith 2, Regan	4,061
26		20	(a)	Ipswich T	L	0-1		10,466
27	Feb	3	(h)	Plymouth A	W	3-2	Mackay, Smith, McClelland	20,000
28		7	(h)	Gillingham	L	1-2	Mackay	5,140
29		10	(h)	Port Vale	L	0-3		7,832
30		17	(a)	Reading	L	2-4	Short, Regan	15,695
31		24	(h)	Colchester U	W	5-0	Rochford (og), Smith 3, Regan	7,334
32	Mar	3	(a)	Bristol R	L	1-3	Mackay	25,294
33		10	(h)	Crystal P	L	1-2	Smart	6,474
34		17	(a)	Brighton & HA	L	1-4	Smith (pen)	8,013
35		23	(a)	Bournemouth	D	1-1	Harrower	12,000
36		24	(h)	Newport C	D	2-2	Regan, Harrower	7,505
37		26	(h)	Bournemouth	W	2-1	Smith, Hutchings	9,853
38		31	(a)	Norwich C	L	0-3		21,732
39	Apr	4	(h)	Torquay U	D	0-0		6,924
40		7	(h)	Northampton T	W	1-0	Smart	6,476
41		18	(h)	Southend U	W	1-0	Smith (pen)	6,033
42		21	(h)	Nottingham F	L	0-5		10,928
43		25	(a)	Millwall	L	0-5		13,361
44		28	(a)	Torquay U	L	0-2		9,503
45		30	(a)	Port Vale	L	0-2		2,600
46	May	5	(a)	Southend U	L	1-5	Fallon	10,850

FINAL LEAGUE POSITION: 14th in Division Three South

Appearances
Goals

FA Cup

1	Nov	25	(a)	Glastonbury	W	2-1
2	Dec	9	(h)	Swindon T	W	3-0
3	Jan	6	(a)	Grimsby T	D	3-3
R		10	(h)	Grimsby T	W	4-2
4	Jan	27	(h)	Chelsea	D	1-1
R		31	(a)	Chelsea	L	0-2

Singleton	Johnstone	Clark	Fallon	Doyle	Davey	Mackay	Smart	Smith	Lynn	McClelland	Rowe	Dunlop	Goddard	Harrower	Warren	Regan	Dare	Lear G	Smyth	Short	Hutchings	Salter	Wilkinson	Greenaway	Carter	
1	2	3	4	5	6	7	8	9	10	11																1
1	2		4	5	6	7		9	10	11	3	8														2
1	2		4		6	7		9	10	11	3	8	5													3
1	2		4		6			9	10	11	3	8	5	7												4
1	2		4	5	6			9	10	11	3			7												5
1	2		4	5	6		8	9	10	11	3			7												6
1	2		4	5	6		8	9	10	11	3			7												7
1			4	5	6		8	9	10	11	3			7	2											8
1			4	2	6		8	9	10	11	3		5	7												9
1			4	2	6		8	9	10	11	3		5	7												10
1		2	4		6		8	9	10	11	3		5	7												11
1		2	4		6		8	9	10	11	3		5	7												12
1		2	4		6	8		9	10	11	3		5	7												13
1		2	4		6	8		7	10	11	3		5		9											14
1		2	4		6		8		10	11	3		5	7	9											15
1		2	4		6	8			10	11	3		5	7	9											16
1		2			6	10		8		7	3		5	4	11	9										17
1		2	8	5	6	10		9		7	3		4		11											18
1		2	8	5	6	10		9		7	3		4		11											19
1		2	4	5	6	10	8	9		7	3				11											20
	3	4	5	6	10		8	9							2	11	1									21
	3	4	5	6	8	9	10	7							2	11	1									22
1	3		8	5	6			9	10	7			4		2	11										23
1	3		8	5	6			9	10	7			4		2	11										24
1	3		8	5	6			9	10	7					2	11										25
1					10			9	6	7	3		5	4	2	11		8								26
1	2		6		10			9	8	7	3		5	4		11										27
1	2		6	10			8			3			5	4		11	9									28
1		3			6	10		9					5	4	2	11				8	7					29
1		3			6	10		9					5	4	2	11				8	7					30
1		3			6	10		9					5	4	2	11				8	7					31
1		3			6	10	8	9					5	4	2	11					7					32
1		3		5	6	10	8	9						4	2	11					7					33
1		3	4		6	10		9		7			5	8	2	11										34
	2		4		6	10		9		7	3		5	8		11					1					35
1	2		4		6	10		9			3		5	8		11				7						36
1	2		4		6	10		9		11	3		5	8						7						37
	2		4	5	6	10	8	9		11	3						1			7						38
1	2		4	5	6	10	8			11	3				9					7						39
1	2			5	6	10		9	8		3		4		11					7						40
1	2		4	5	6	10		9		11	3				7		8			7						41
1		2	4			9				11	3		5	8						7			6	10		42
1		2	4		6	10	9	11	8		3		5	7												43
1		2	4		6	10	9	11	8		3			7											5	44
1			8		6	10	9			11	3		5	4	2					7						45
42	16	26	37	22	43	31	17	41	29	36	34	4	25	32	14	26	6	3	5	5	8	1	1	1	1	46
1		3		1	8	4	21	2	8				2		7					1	1					

3 own-goals

1951-52

Manager: George Roughton/Norman Kirkman (from 8 March 1952)

							Attendance
							15,404
1	Aug	18	(a)	Crystal P	L 1-2	Mackay	
							7,758
2		22	(h)	Gillingham	W 4-2	McClelland (pen), Smith, Smart 2	
							9,005
3		25	(h)	Swindon T	L 1-2	Smart	
							12,378
4		29	(a)	Gillingham	L 1-2	Fallon	
							18,000
5	Sep	1	(a)	Leyton O	L 0-3		
							8,304
6		5	(h)	Norwich C	L 2-4	Mackay, McClelland	
							8,000
7		8	(h)	Walsall	W 1-0	Smith	
							15,000
8		12	(a)	Norwich C	D 1-1	Mackay	
							10,402
9		15	(a)	Shrewsbury T	L 1-2	Mackay	
							7,756
10		22	(h)	Aldershot	L 0-4		
							10,029
11		29	(a)	Watford	D 1-1	Smith	
							7,749
12	Oct	6	(h)	Ipswich T	W 2-1	Regan, Smart	
							17,349
13		13	(a)	Bristol C	D 1-1	Mackay	
							7,500
14		20	(h)	Port Vale	W 2-0	Smart, Mackay	
							12,576
15		27	(a)	Northampton T	L 1-3	Smart	
							8,795
16	Nov	3	(h)	Reading	L 1-4	Regan	
							10,920
17		10	(a)	Newport C	L 0-4		
							7,102
18		17	(h)	Southend U	D 2-2	Mackay, Smith	
							8,906
19	Dec	1	(h)	Millwall	L 0-3		
							10,831
20		8	(a)	Brighton & HA	L 1-2	Fallon	
							8,614
21		22	(a)	Swindon T	L 1-3	Digby	
							8,429
22		25	(h)	Torquay U	W 4-0	Smart, Walton, Armes, Mackay	
							13,000
23		26	(a)	Torquay U	L 1-5	McClelland (pen)	
							7,363
24		29	(h)	Leyton O	W 6-1	McClelland 3 (2 pens), Walton 2, Armes	
							5,717
25	Jan	5	(a)	Walsall	W 2-1	Mackay, Walton	
							25,494
26		12	(a)	Plymouth A	L 1-2	Mackay	
							7,088
27		16	(h)	Bristol R	L 0-1		
							7,890
28		19	(h)	Shrewsbury T	W 4-2	McClelland 2, Smart, Mackay	
							5,560
29		26	(a)	Aldershot	L 1-4	McClelland	
							7,692
30	Feb	2	(a)	Colchester U	L 0-1		
							9,597
31		9	(h)	Watford	W 3-0	Mackay, McClelland, Nolan (og)	
							9,839
32		16	(a)	Ipswich T	W 4-2	Mackay 2, McClelland, Smith	
							7,860
33		23	(h)	Colchester U	D 0-0		
							8,204
34	Mar	1	(h)	Bristol C	D 0-0		
							12,300
35		8	(a)	Port Vale	L 0-3		
							7,848
36		15	(h)	Northampton T	L 0-3		
							15,839
37		22	(a)	Reading	L 1-2	Regan	
							5,600
38		26	(h)	Crystal P	L 0-1		
							4,076
39		29	(h)	Newport C	L 3-4	Digby, Regan, Smith	
							8,000
40	Apr	5	(a)	Southend U	D 0-0		
							7,836
41		12	(h)	Bournemouth	D 2-2	Howells, Mackay	
							19,000
42		14	(h)	Plymouth A	W 1-0	Regan	
							14,572
43		19	(a)	Millwall	L 0-4		
							7,000
44		23	(a)	Bournemouth	W 4-0	Fallon, Howells, Mackay 2	
							8,836
45		26	(h)	Brighton & HA	W 2-0	Mackay 2	
							9,124
46	May	1	(a)	Bristol R	D 2-2	Mackay, Howells	

Appearances
Goals

FINAL LEAGUE POSITION: 23rd in Division Three South

FA Cup

1	Nov	24	(a)	King's Lynn	W 3-1
2	Dec	15	(a)	Ipswich T	L 0-4

Singleton	Warren	Clark	Davey	Goddard	Coley	McClelland	Smart	Smith	Mackay	Regan	Lear	Fallon	Harrower	Digby	Brown	Howells	Rowe	Mitchell	Wilkins	Doyle	Carter	Hutchings	Booth	Walton	Armes	Kirkman	
1	2	3	4	5	6	7	8	9	10	11																	1
1	2	3	4	5	6	7	8	9	10	11																	2
1	2	3	4	5	6	7	8	9	10	11																	3
	2	3	6	5		7	9		10	11	1	4	8														4
	2	3	4	5		11	9		10		1	8	6	7													5
	2	3	4	5		11	9	7	10		1	8	6														6
	2	3	4	5	6	11	8	9	10		1				7												7
	2	3	4	5	6	11	8	9	10		1				7												8
	2	3	4	5	6	11	8	9	10		1				7												9
	2	3	4	5	6	7	8	9	10		1					11											10
	2	3	6	5			8	9	10	7	1	4				11											11
	2	3	6	5		11	8	9	10	7	1	4															12
	2	3	6	5		11	8	9	10	7	1	4															13
	2		6	5		11	8	9	10	7	1	4					3										14
	2		6	5		11	8		10	7	1	4					3	9									15
	2	3	6	5	4	11			10	7	1							9	8								16
	2	3		5		7	8		10	11	1	4							9	6							17
	2	3	6	5			8	9	10	11	1	4	7														18
	2	3	6			10	8	9		11	1	4									5	7					19
	2		6			11	8		10		1	4		7			3	9		5							20
1	2		6	5		11	8		10					7			3						4	9			21
1	2		6	5		11	8		10					7			3							9	4		22
1	2		6	5		11	8		10								3					7		9	4		23
1	2		6			11	8		10								3			5		7		9	4		24
1	2		6			11	8		10					7			3			5				9	4		25
1	2		6				8		10					7			3			5		11		9	4		26
1	2		6				8		10					7		11	3			5				9	4		27
1	2		6			11	8		10					7			3			5				9	4		28
1	2		6			11	8							7			3		10	5				9	4		29
1	2		4			11		8	10					7			3			5				9	6		30
1	2		4			11		8	10					7			3			5				9	6		31
1	2		5			11	8	9	10				4	7			3								6		32
1	2		4			11	8	9	10	7			6				3			5							33
1	2		4			9	8		10	11			6				3			5		7					34
1	2		4			11		8	10				6				3			5		7		9			35
1	2		6			11		8	10				4	7		9				5						3	36
1	2		4				10	8		11			6	7		9	3			5							37
1			4					9	8	11			10	7			3			5				2	6		38
1			4					9	8	11			10	7			3			5				2	6		39
1			6	5		7			8	11					10	9							4	2		3	40
1			6	5					8	11				7	10	9							4	2		3	41
1			6	5					8	11		4		7	10	9								2		3	42
1			6	5					8	11		4		7	10	9								2		3	43
1			6	5					8	11		10		7		9							4	2		3	44
1			6	5		7			8	11		10				9							4	2		3	45
1			6	5		7			8	11		10				9							4	2		3	46
29	37	17	45	28	8	35	32	23	43	25	17	17	12	20	7	12	21	3	3	17	1	6	6	21	13	8	
						11	8	6	20	5		3		2		3								4	2		

1 own-goal

1952-53

Manager: Norman Kirkman

1	Aug	23	(h)	Queen's Park R	D	2-2	Murphy, Regan
2		27	(h)	Northampton T	W	2-0	Knight, Dailey
3		30	(a)	Shrewsbury T	W	3-1	Regan, Dailey, Murphy
4	Sep	4	(a)	Northampton T	L	1-3	Regan
5		6	(h)	Walsall	W	6-1	Murphy 2, Regan, Dailey 3
6		10	(h)	Norwich C	W	1-0	Dailey
7		13	(a)	Gillingham	L	0-1	
8		17	(a)	Norwich C	L	0-2	
9		20	(h)	Millwall	W	1-0	Rose
10		24	(a)	Brighton & HA	L	2-4	Mitchell, Mackay
11		27	(a)	Bristol R	D	0-0	
12		29	(a)	Coventry C	L	0-1	
13	Oct	4	(h)	Torquay U	W	4-1	Mitchell 2 (1 pen), Kirkman, Murphy
14		11	(a)	Leyton O	L	0-2	
15		18	(h)	Ipswich T	D	1-1	Murphy
16		25	(a)	Reading	L	1-3	Regan
17	Nov	1	(h)	Bournemouth	W	5-1	Dailey, Mackay, Regan, McClelland, Murphy
18		8	(a)	Southend U	D	1-1	Dailey
19		15	(h)	Watford	D	1-1	McClelland
20		29	(h)	Newport C	W	3-2	Mackay 2, McClelland
21	Dec	6	(a)	Bristol C	L	1-4	Mackay
22		13	(h)	Bristol C	D	1-1	Mackay
23		20	(a)	Queen's Park R	D	1-1	Mackay
24		26	(h)	Swindon T	L	1-2	Mitchell
25		27	(a)	Swindon T	L	2-5	Mitchell, Dailey
26	Jan	3	(h)	Shrewsbury T	D	2-2	Mackay, Mitchell
27		17	(a)	Walsall	D	2-2	Dailey, Mitchell
28		21	(h)	Colchester U	W	2-0	Mitchell, Dailey
29		24	(h)	Gillingham	D	0-0	
30		31	(a)	Colchester U	L	1-3	Walton
31	Feb	7	(a)	Millwall	D	0-0	
32		14	(h)	Bristol R	D	0-0	
33		21	(a)	Torquay U	L	2-5	Mitchell, G.Webster (og)
34		28	(h)	Leyton O	L	0-1	
35	Mar	7	(a)	Ipswich T	W	1-0	Knight
36		14	(h)	Reading	W	2-0	Mackay 2
37		21	(a)	Bournemouth	L	1-2	Dailey
38		28	(h)	Southend U	L	0-2	
39	Apr	3	(a)	Aldershot	D	1-1	Davey
40		4	(a)	Watford	L	1-3	Knight
41		6	(h)	Aldershot	D	2-2	Rose 2
42		11	(h)	Brighton & HA	L	1-5	Mitchell
43		15	(a)	Crystal P	L	0-2	
44		18	(a)	Newport C	L	0-1	
45		22	(h)	Coventry C	W	1-0	McClelland
46		25	(h)	Crystal P	W	2-0	Knight, McClelland

	15,078
	12,745
	10,797
	11,986
	11,955
	15,720
	13,763
	18,681
	14,620
	14,695
	23,773
	8,588
	13,773
	12,800
	11,503
	12,202
	10,069
	9,500
	10,097
	6,848
	17,589
	10,597
	8,000
	13,620
	10,580
	9,318
	6,775
	3,951
	9,305
	5,643
	18,825
	13,116
	10,147
	9,509
	8,867
	9,074
	10,336
	7,300
	7,419
	12,500
	8,000
	8,000
	4,808
	8,220
	5,785
	7,357

FINAL LEAGUE POSITION: 17th in Division Three South

Appearances
Goals

FA Cup

1	Nov	22	(a)	Port Vale	L	1-2

Kelly	Walton	Kirkman	Booth	Goddard	Fallon	Digby	Mackay	Dailey	Murphy	Regan	Rowe	Mitchell	Knight	Anderson	Davey	Rose	Harvey	McClelland	Armes	Singleton	Doyle	Black	Howells	Wood	Clark	
1	2	3	4	5	6	7	8	9	10	11																1
1	2		4	5	6			9	10	11		3	7	8												2
1	2		4	5	6			9	10	11		3	7	8												3
1			4	5				9	10	11		3	7	8	2	6										4
1			4	5				9	10	11		3	7	8	2	6										5
1			4	5				9	10	11		3	7	8	2	6										6
1			4	5				9	10	11		3	7	8	2	6										7
1			4	5					10	11		3	7	8	2	6	9									8
1			4	5					10	11		3	7	8	2	6	9									9
1	2			5			11		10			3	7	8	6		9	4								10
1	2			5			11		10			3	7	8	6		9	4								11
1	2	9	4	5			8		10	11		3	7		6											12
1	2		4	5			11	9	10			3	7	8	6											13
1	2	3		5			7	9	10	11			8		6			4								14
1	2			5			7	9	10	11		3		8	6			4								15
1	2		4	5			8	9	10	11		3			6		7									16
1	2		4	5			8	9	10	11		3			6		7									17
1	2		4				8	9	10	11		3			6	5	7									18
1	2		4	5			10	9			11	3		8	6		7									19
1	2		4	5			10	9			11	3	7	8	6											20
1	2		4	5			10	9			11	3	7	8	6											21
1	2		4	5			10	9			11	3	7	8	6											22
1	2		4	5			10	9			11	3	7	8	6											23
1	2		4	5			10	9			11	3	7	8	6											24
	2		4	5			10	9			11	3	7	8	6					1						25
1	2			5			8	9	10			7			6			4	11		3					26
1	2		4	5			8	9	10			7			6			11			3					27
1	2		4	5	6			9	10			7	8					11			3					28
1	2		4	5				9				7	8		6			11			3	10				29
1	2		4	5			8					7			6		9				3	10	11			30
	2		4	5			8					7			6		9			1	3	10	11			31
1	2		4	5			8				11	7			6		9				3	10				32
	2		4	5							11	7	8		6		9			1	3	10				33
	2		4	5							11	7	8		6		9			1	3	10				34
	2		4				7	9	10				8		6					1	3		11	5		35
	2		4				11	9	10			7	8		6					1	3			5		36
	2		4				11	9	10			7	8		6					1	3			5		37
1	2		5	4		11		9	10			7	8		6						3					38
1	2		5	4		11		9	10			7	8		6						3					39
1	2		5	4		11			10			7	8		6		9				3					40
1	2		5	4		11			10			7	8		6		9								3	41
1	2		4					9	10			7	8		6			11			3			5		42
1	2		4					9	10			7	8		6			11			3			5		43
	2		4					9	10			7	8		6			11		1	3			5		44
	2		4						10			7	8		6		9	11		1	3			5		45
	2		4						10			7	8		6		9	11			3			5		46
37	40	3	33	37	13	11	23	36	38	17	25	38	36	6	39	11	6	13	1	9	18	4	3	8	1	
1	1						10	12	7	6		10	4		1	3		5								

1 own-goal

1953-54

Manager: Norman Dodgin

#		Date		Venue	Opponent	Result	Scorers	Att.
1	Aug	19	(h)	Leyton O		W 2-1	Knight, Parker	10,412
2		22	(a)	Walsall		D 1-1	Goddard	10,428
3		26	(h)	Colchester U		L 1-2	Priestley	10,589
4		29	(h)	Shrewsbury T		L 0-1		11,000
5	Sep	3	(a)	Colchester U		W 1-0	Murphy	7,500
6		5	(a)	Torquay U		L 2-3	Mitchell, McClelland (pen)	10,583
7		9	(h)	Bristol C		L 0-1		10,310
8		12	(a)	Newport C		W 3-0	Mitchell, Donaldson 2	6,949
9		15	(a)	Bristol C		L 1-5	Goddard	15,302
10		19	(h)	Norwich C		L 0-2		11,412
11		23	(h)	Swindon T		W 3-1	Mackay 2, Priestley	8,162
12		26	(a)	Queen's Park R		D 0-0		12,943
13		30	(a)	Swindon T		W 4-2	Mackay 2, McClelland 2	7,727
14	Oct	3	(h)	Southampton		W 4-0	Dailey, Mackay 2, McClelland	13,691
15		7	(h)	Brighton & HA		L 0-1		12,044
16		17	(a)	Southend U		W 1-0	Donaldson	8,000
17		24	(h)	Reading		W 2-0	McClelland 2	10,284
18		31	(a)	Leyton O		L 1-3	Mackay	11,342
19	Nov	7	(h)	Millwall		W 4-1	McClelland, Samuels, Donaldson, Mackay	10,000
20		14	(a)	Ipswich T		D 1-1	Donaldson	15,125
21		28	(a)	Coventry C		L 0-2		10,224
22	Dec	5	(h)	Gillingham		L 1-2	McClelland	7,948
23		19	(h)	Walsall		W 2-1	McClelland 2	6,500
24		25	(a)	Aldershot		W 2-1	Mitchell, McClelland	4,425
25		26	(h)	Aldershot		L 1-3	McClelland	8,892
26	Jan	2	(a)	Shrewsbury T		D 1-1	Mackay	6,000
27		9	(h)	Crystal P		W 7-0	Donaldson 3, Priestley, Mackay 2, McClelland	7,382
28		16	(h)	Torquay U		L 1-2	Knight	15,518
29		23	(h)	Newport C		W 1-0	Mackay	8,038
30		30	(a)	Crystal P		D 0-0		5,535
31	Feb	6	(a)	Norwich C		W 2-1	Priestley, Donaldson	24,728
32		13	(h)	Queen's Park R		D 0-0		8,133
33		20	(a)	Southampton		L 0-2		16,327
34		27	(a)	Brighton & HA		L 1-2	Ellaway	20,217
35	Mar	6	(h)	Southend U		D 1-1	McClelland (pen)	8,392
36		13	(a)	Bournemouth		L 1-4	Donaldson	8,263
37		20	(h)	Coventry C		W 4-0	Donaldson 2, Parker, Dodgin	8,000
38		27	(a)	Millwall		L 1-2	Mackay	8,620
39	Apr	3	(h)	Ipswich T		L 1-2	Donaldson	8,578
40		8	(a)	Northampton T		D 2-2	Donaldson, Ellaway	5,597
41		10	(a)	Gillingham		W 1-0	Donaldson	9,500
42		16	(a)	Watford		W 2-0	McClelland 2	14,161
43		17	(h)	Northampton T		W 1-0	McClelland	8,844
44		19	(h)	Watford		W 2-1	Priestley, McClelland	9,000
45		24	(a)	Reading		L 1-4	McClelland	7,900
46		28	(h)	Bournemouth		W 1-0	Donaldson	5,357

FINAL LEAGUE POSITION: 9th in Division Three South

Appearances
Goals

FA Cup

1	Nov	21	(h)	Hereford U		D 1-1	
R		25	(a)	Hereford U		L 0-2	

226

Kelly	Walton	Douglass	McLean	Goddard	Dodgin	Priestley	Samuels	Mitchell	Knight	Parker	Doyle	McClelland	Dailey	Murphy	Booth	Mackay	Donaldson	Davey	Singleton	Storey	Rowe	Owens	Ellaway	Setters	Harvey	#
1	2	3	4	5	6	7	8	9	10	11																1
1	2	3	4	5	6	7	8	9	10	11																2
1	2	3	4	5	6	7	8	9	10	11																3
1	2		4	5	6		8			11	3	7	9	10												4
1	2			5	6		8	9		11	3	7			10	4										5
1	2			5	6		8	9		11	3	7			10	4										6
1	2			5	6				7		3	11			10	4	8	9								7
1	2			5	6				7		3	11			10	4	8	9								8
1	2				6				7		3	11			10	4	8	9	5							9
1	2				6	7					3	11			8	4	10	9	5							10
1	2				6	7					3	11			8	4	10	9	5							11
	2				6	7					3	11			8	4	10	9	5	1						12
	2				6	7		9			3	11			8	4	10		5	1						13
	2				6	7		9			3	11			8	4	10		5	1						14
	2				6	7	8					11				4	10	9	5	1	3					15
	2				6	7	8					11				4	10	9	5	1	3					16
	2				6		8		7			11				4	10	9	5	1	3					17
1	2				6		8					11		7		4	10	9	5		3					18
1					6		8					11		7		4	10	9	5		3	2				19
1	2	11			6		8		7							4	10	9	5		3					20
1	2	3			6		8					11		7	10	4		9	5							21
	2		4		6	7	8	9				11					10		5	1	3					22
	2		4		6	7	8	9				11					10		5	1	3					23
	2		4		6	7	8	9				11					10		5	1	3					24
1	2	3	4		6	7	8	9				11					10		5							25
1	2	3	4		6	7	8					11					10	9	5							26
1	2	3	4		6	7	8					11					10	9	5							27
1	2	3	4		6	7	8					11					10	9	5							28
1	2	3	4		6	7	8					11					10	9	5							29
1	2		4		6	7	8					11					10	9	5		3					30
1	2	3	4		6	7	8					11					10	9	5							31
1	2	3	4		6	7	8					11					10	9	5							32
1		3			6				10			9				8	7	5		2		4	11			33
1		3			6							11					10	9	5	2		4	8	7		34
1		3			6	7						11					10	9		2		4	8	5		35
1	2				6	7						11			8	4	10	9	5		3					36
1	2				6	7						11			8	4	10	9	5		3					37
1	2	3			6	7						11			8	4	10	9	5							38
1	2	3			6	7						11			8	4	10	9	5							39
1	2	3			6	7						11			8	4	10	9	5							40
1	2	3				7	6	8	10			11				4		9	5							41
1	2	3				7	6	8	10			11				4		9	5							42
1	2	3				7	6	8	10			11				4		9	5							43
	2	3				7	6	8	10			11				4		9	5	1						44
	2	3				7	6	8				11				4	10	9	5	1						45
	2	3				7	6	8				11					10	9	5	1			4			46
35	42	22	15	18	30	33	12	27	20	18	12	36	9	12	23	30	33	36	11	9	7	5	8	1	2	
		2	1	5	1	3	2	2				19	1	1			13	16	2							

227

1954-55

Manager: Norman Dodgin

#		Date		Opponent	Result	Scorers	Attendance
1	Aug	21	(h)	Crystal P	W 2-0	McClelland, Houghton	12,467
2		25	(h)	Colchester U	D 2-2	Houghton, Ellaway	9,100
3		28	(a)	Northampton T	L 0-2		9,248
4	Sep	2	(a)	Colchester U	W 2-1	Ellaway, McClelland	7,063
5		4	(h)	Watford	D 0-0		9,304
6		8	(h)	Norwich C	L 0-1		9,770
7		11	(a)	Bournemouth	L 0-2		11,310
8		15	(a)	Norwich C	L 0-3		15,929
9		18	(h)	Queen's Park R	W 2-1	Ellaway, Mackay (pen)	8,901
10		21	(a)	Southend U	D 0-0		10,000
11		25	(a)	Newport C	L 1-2	Rees	10,000
12		29	(h)	Southend U	W 2-1	Ellaway, Mackay (pen)	7,142
13	Oct	2	(a)	Torquay U	L 0-1		11,027
14		9	(h)	Brentford	W 3-2	Mackay 2 (1 pen), Callan	9,700
15		16	(a)	Coventry C	D 1-1	Ellaway	13,619
16		23	(a)	Southampton	L 0-1		10,125
17		30	(a)	Bristol C	L 0-2		26,230
18	Nov	6	(h)	Leyton O	L 1-7	McClelland (pen)	8,874
19		13	(a)	Gillingham	D 1-1	Kaile	9,100
20		27	(a)	Shrewsbury T	D 1-1	Priestley	5,733
21	Dec	4	(h)	Walsall	D 1-1	Ellaway	8,000
22		18	(a)	Crystal P	D 1-1	Thomas	6,906
23		25	(h)	Swindon T	W 2-1	John, Murphy	6,527
24		27	(a)	Swindon T	L 0-2		9,550
25	Jan	1	(h)	Northampton T	W 3-1	Mackay, McClelland, John	7,040
26		22	(h)	Bournemouth	D 1-1	McClelland	7,476
27		29	(h)	Brighton & HA	W 3-1	Houghton, Dunne, McClelland	7,042
28	Feb	5	(a)	Queen's Park R	W 2-1	Houghton, Murphy	9,576
29		12	(h)	Newport C	D 1-1	John	6,545
30		19	(h)	Torquay U	L 1-2	Mackay	11,160
31		26	(a)	Brentford	L 0-1		7,450
32	Mar	5	(h)	Coventry C	D 0-0		7,581
33		12	(a)	Southampton	L 0-3		12,419
34		19	(h)	Bristol C	L 0-1		12,111
35		23	(a)	Brighton & HA	L 3-5	Houghton, Mitchell, John	3,624
36		26	(a)	Leyton O	L 0-5		11,500
37	Apr	2	(h)	Gillingham	D 1-1	Thomas	5,179
38		8	(a)	Aldershot	L 2-4	Houghton, Thomas	6,183
39		9	(a)	Reading	D 0-0		8,271
40		11	(h)	Aldershot	L 0-1		6,959
41		16	(h)	Shrewsbury T	W 1-0	McClelland	4,944
42		23	(a)	Walsall	L 0-1		10,953
43		27	(h)	Reading	W 3-1	Davey, Mackay, McClelland	4,968
44		30	(h)	Millwall	L 1-4	Mackay (pen)	6,426
45	May	2	(a)	Millwall	D 2-2	Walton, McClelland	4,930
46		6	(a)	Watford	D 1-1	Thomas	4,125

FINAL LEAGUE POSITION: 22nd in Division Three South

Appearances
Goals

FA Cup

1	Nov	20	(a)	Millwall	L 2-3	

228

Football appearance/selection grid (players as columns, matches 1–46 as rows; cell values are shirt numbers worn).

	Kelly	Walton	Doyle B	Dunne	Davey	Mitchell	Priestley	Ellaway	Houghton	Mackay	McClelland	Anderson	Bell	Douglass	Doyle L	Callan	Murphy	Owens	Morton	John	Rees	Kaile	Dodgin	Donaldson	Setters	Thomas	Williams	Harvey	
	1	2	3	4	5	6	7	8	9	10	11																		
1	1	2	3	4	5	6	7	8	9	10	11																		1
2	1	2	3	4	5	6	7	9		10	11		8																2
3		2		4	5	6	7		9	10	11	1	8	3															3
4		2		4	5	6	7			10	11	1	8	3			9												4
5		2		4	5	6			9	10		1	8	3		7	11												5
6		2			5	6				10	11	1	8	3		7	9	4											6
7		2			5			8	9	10				3		6		4	1	7	11								7
8		2			5		7	8	10					3		6		4	1	9	11								8
9		2			5		7	8	10					3		6		4	1	9	11								9
10		2			5		7	8	10					3		6		4	1	9	11								10
11		2		4	5	6	7	8	10					3					1	9	11								11
12	9	2			5	6		8			11 10			3		7		4	1										12
13	1	9	2		5	6		8		10				3		7		4			11								13
14	1		2		5	6		8		10				3		7		4	9		11								14
15		2			5	4		10						1 3	7			8		11	6	9							15
16	1		2		5	4		10						3	7			8		11	6	9							16
17	1		2	8	5				7					3			10			11	6	9		4					17
18	1		2		5	6		8	7					3			10			11		9	4						18
19	1		2		5	6	7	9	8	11				3			10							4					19
20	1		2		5	6	7	9	8	11				3			10							4					20
21	1		2		5	6		9	8					3			10			11				4		7	3		21
22	1		2		5	6		8	11					3			10			9				4		7			22
23	1		2		5	6		8	11					3			10			9				4		7			23
24	1	2				6		10						3					8	11				9		4 7		3 5	24
25	1	2				6			8					3			10			9				4 7				5	25
26	1	2		4		6			8	11				3			10			9						7		5	26
27	1	2		4		6			8	11				3			10			9						7		5	27
28	1	2		4		6		11		8				3			10			9						7		5	28
29	1	2		4		6		10	8	11				3						9						7		5	29
30	1		2	4		6		10	8					3			11			9						7		5	30
31	1		2			6		8	11					3			10	4		9						7		5	31
32	1	2		4		6	9							3						8						7		5	32
33	1		2	4		6	9		8					3			10			11						7		5	33
34	1		2	4		6	9		10 8					3			11									7		5	34
35		2		4		6	9		10 8					1 3												7		5	35
36		2		4		6	9			8	11			1 3			10			9						7		5	36
37		2		4		6		8						1 3			10									7		5	37
38		2		4		6		8						1 3			10						9			7		5	38
39		2		4		6		8						1 3			10						9			7		5	39
40		2		4		6	7							1 3			10			9				9				5	40
41		2		4		6		8						1 3			10									7		5	41
42		2		4	9	6		8	11					1 3			10									7		5	42
43		2		4	9	6		8	11					1 3			10									7		5	43
44	9	2		4		6		8	11					1 3			10									7		5	44
45	9	2		4		6		8	11					1 3			10									7		5	45
46																													46
Totals	24	14	39	25	33	45	9	19	18	31	30	7	16	41	3	10	25	9	6	26	5	6	3	6	9	24	1	22	
	1		1	1	1	1	6	6	8	9			1	2			4	1	1						4				

229

1955-56

Manager: Norman Dodgin

1	Aug	20	(h)	Colchester U	D	0-0		11,871
2		22	(a)	Millwall	L	0-2		8,140
3		27	(a)	Leyton O	D	1-1	Worthington	15,000
4		31	(h)	Millwall	W	3-1	John 2, Mitchell	10,561
5	Sep	3	(h)	Torquay U	D	0-0		13,991
6		7	(a)	Norwich C	L	1-2	John	14,014
7		10	(h)	Southend U	L	0-1		9,231
8		14	(h)	Norwich C	D	1-1	Burke	8,443
9		17	(a)	Coventry C	D	2-2	John, Buckle	20,790
10		21	(a)	Gillingham	L	1-2	Burke	8,400
11		24	(h)	Brentford	L	2-3	Burke 2	8,454
12		28	(h)	Reading	L	0-2		6,536
13	Oct	1	(a)	Watford	W	3-2	John 2, Simpson	9,785
14		8	(a)	Swindon T	W	1-0	Buckle	6,783
15		15	(h)	Queen's Park R	W	2-0	Burke 2	8,741
16		22	(a)	Northampton T	L	0-3		10,805
17		29	(h)	Aldershot	W	2-1	Iggleden, Jefferson (og)	7,851
18	Nov	5	(a)	Crystal P	W	1-0	Rees	12,440
19		12	(h)	Brighton & HA	L	0-5		9,019
20		26	(h)	Shrewsbury T	W	3-0	Rees, Simpson, Burke	6,000
21	Dec	3	(a)	Ipswich T	D	2-2	Rees, Simpson	14,703
22		17	(a)	Colchester U	L	1-5	Murphy	6,179
23		24	(h)	Leyton O	D	1-1	Murphy	8,931
24		26	(a)	Bournemouth	D	0-0		8,342
25		27	(h)	Bournemouth	W	2-0	Iggleden 2	10,540
26		31	(a)	Torquay U	L	1-3	Iggleden	12,128
27	Jan	14	(a)	Southend U	L	0-6		7,500
28		21	(h)	Coventry C	L	2-3	Rees, Murphy	7,472
29		28	(h)	Walsall	D	1-1	Whiteside	7,147
30	Feb	4	(a)	Brentford	L	0-2		6,300
31		11	(h)	Watford	L	1-2	John	4,207
32		18	(h)	Swindon T	L	1-2	Houghton	4,937
33		25	(a)	Queen's Park R	L	0-1		6,859
34	Mar	3	(h)	Northampton T	W	3-1	Mitchell (pen), Sword, Willis	6,996
35		10	(a)	Aldershot	L	0-1		5,367
36		17	(h)	Crystal P	W	6-1	Sword 3, Iggleden 2, Thomas	6,826
37		24	(a)	Brighton & HA	L	0-1		13,274
38		30	(h)	Newport C	W	2-1	Buckle, John	5,960
39		31	(a)	Southampton	L	0-5		9,924
40	Apr	2	(h)	Newport C	W	2-0	Burke, Buckle	7,363
41		7	(a)	Shrewsbury T	L	0-2		6,676
42		11	(h)	Southampton	W	3-2	Iggleden, Burke 2	6,933
43		14	(h)	Ipswich T	D	2-2	Mitchell (pen), Buckle	6,606
44		21	(a)	Walsall	L	1-3	Simpson	13,656
45		25	(a)	Reading	W	2-1	Iggleden, Ellaway	5,234
46		28	(h)	Gillingham	W	2-1	Willis, Mitchell (pen)	6,887

FINAL LEAGUE POSITION: 16th in Division Three South

Appearances

Goals

FA Cup

1	Nov	15	(a)	Coventry C	W	1-0
2	Dec	10	(h)	Hendon	W	6-2
3	Jan	7	(h)	Stoke C	D	0-0
R		9	(a)	Stoke C	L	0-3

Football appearances and goals grid (shirt numbers by match). Columns = players; rows = matches 1–46.

Hunter	Walton	Parr	Dunne	Harvey	Mitchell	Simpson	Worthington	Burke	Iggleden	Buckle	Doyle	Packer	Davey	John	Foley	Thomas PJ	Ellaway	Murphy	Rees	Whiteside	Grinney	Kelly	Houghton	Sword	Porteous	Willis	Thomas WK	#
1	2	3	4	5	6	7	8	9	10	11																		1
1	2			5	6	7	8	9	10	11	3	4																2
1	2			5	6	7	8	9		11	3			4	10													3
1	2			5	6	7	8	9		11	3			4	10													4
1	2			5	6	7	8	9		11	3			4	10													5
1	2			5	6	7	8	9		11	3			4	10													6
1	2			5	6	7	8	9	10	11	3			4														7
1				5	6	7	8	9	10	11	3			4		2												8
1				5	6	7	8	9		11	2			4		3		10										9
1				5	6	7	8	9		11	2			4		3		10										10
1				5	6	7	8	9		11	2			4		3		10										11
1	2			5	3		8	9		11				4		7	10	6										12
1	2			5	3	7	8	9						4			10	6	11									13
1	2			5	3	7	8	9		11				4			10	6										14
1	2			5	3	7	8	9		11				4			10	6										15
1	2			5	3	7	8	9		11				4			10	6										16
1	2			5	3	7	8	9	10					4				6	11									17
1	2			5	3	7	8	9	10					4				6	11									18
1	2			5	3		8	9	10					4		7		6	11									19
1	2		6	5	3	7		9					8	4				10	11									20
1	2		6	5	3	7		9					8	4				10	11									21
1	2		6	5	3	7		9					8	4				10	11									22
1			6	5	3	7		9			2		8	4				10	11									23
1			6	5	3	7		9			2		8	4				10	11									24
1			6	5	3			9			2		8	4		7		10	11									25
1			6	5	3			9			2		8	4				10	11				7					26
1			7	5	3		8	9			2			4	6			10	11									27
1	4	2		5	3		8	9							6			10	11			7						28
				5	3		8	9			2			4	6			10	11	7			1					29
	3			5	6			9			2			4			10	8	11	7	1							30
			4	5	3			9			2					7		6	11				1					31
1			4	5	3	7	8	9			2								11				10	9				32
1	3		4	5		7	8				2				6				11				10	9				33
1				5	3	7					2			4					11				8	9	6	10		34
1				5	3						2			4					11				8	9	6	10	7	35
1				5	3		8			11	2			4										9	6	10	7	36
1					3		8			11	2		5	4										9	6	10	7	37
1					3		8			11	2		5	4										9	6	10	7	38
1					3		8			11	2		5	4										9	6	10	7	39
1					3		8			11	2		5	4										9	6	10	7	40
1					3		8				2		5	4				11						9	6	10	7	41
1				5	3		8	9		11	2			4											6	10	7	42
1				5	3		8	9		11	2			4											6	10	7	43
1				5	3	7	8			11	2			4											6	10	8	44
1				5	3	7	8			11	2			4											6	10		45
1				5	3	7		9		11	2			4											6	10		46
43	18	5	12	41	45	27	16	30	27	28	33	1	31	40	4	5	4	19	20	3	2	3	4	9	13	13	10	
					4	4	1	10	8	5				8				1	3	4	1			1	4	2	1	

1 own-goal

1956-57

Manager: Norman Dodgin (until 8 April 1957)

						Attendance
1	Aug	18	(a)	Coventry C	L 0-1	20,100
2		22	(h)	Norwich C	D 0-0	9,530
3		25	(h)	Southampton	L 0-4	9,127
4		29	(a)	Norwich C	L 0-1	12,073
5	Sep	1	(h)	Torquay U	D 1-1 Burke	10,936
6		5	(h)	Newport C	W 2-0 Burke, Currie	5,074
7		8	(a)	Crystal P	D 0-0	11,801
8		13	(a)	Newport C	D 1-1 Burke	5,000
9		15	(h)	Southend U	W 6-1 Beer 2, Buckle 2, Currie, Burke	7,809
10		19	(h)	Colchester U	L 0-2	8,360
11		22	(a)	Northampton T	D 1-1 John	9,431
12		24	(a)	Colchester U	L 0-4	6,754
13		29	(h)	Queen's Park R	D 0-0	7,312
14	Oct	6	(a)	Brighton & HA	L 0-3	13,139
15		13	(h)	Gillingham	W 4-0 Currie 2, Thomas, Mitchell	6,524
16		20	(a)	Swindon T	W 5-3 Currie 2, Buckle 2, Thomas	8,441
17		27	(h)	Brentford	D 1-1 Currie	8,482
18	Nov	3	(a)	Aldershot	W 4-1 Currie 2, Willis, Rees	4,701
19		10	(h)	Watford	L 1-2 Currie	7,391
20		24	(h)	Walsall	L 0-1	4,617
21	Dec	1	(a)	Ipswich T	L 0-3	11,731
22		15	(h)	Coventry C	W 4-2 Thomas, Harvey 2 (2 pens), Houghton	4,119
23		22	(a)	Southampton	D 2-2 John 2	12,239
24		26	(h)	Plymouth A	W 2-1 Houghton 2	10,301
25		29	(a)	Torquay U	L 0-1	8,065
26	Jan	5	(a)	Plymouth A	L 0-5	9,857
27		12	(h)	Crystal P	W 2-1 Lackenby, Buckle	5,015
28		19	(a)	Southend	L 0-2	8,321
29		26	(h)	Reading	D 1-1 Rees	5,492
30	Feb	2	(h)	Northampton T	D 0-0	5,931
31		9	(a)	Queen's Park R	L 3-5 Currie 2, Harvey (pen)	8,593
32		16	(h)	Brighton & HA	L 1-3 Tennant (og)	6,545
33		23	(a)	Gillingham	L 1-2 Buckle	3,398
34	Mar	2	(h)	Swindon T	W 3-2 John 2, Harvey (pen)	5,244
35		9	(a)	Bournemouth	L 1-3 Currie	11,257
36		13	(a)	Reading	L 0-4	6,714
37		16	(h)	Aldershot	D 1-1 Thomas	4,798
38		23	(a)	Watford	D 1-1 Divers	7,395
39		30	(h)	Shrewsbury T	W 5-1 Thomas, Currie 2, Mitchell 2	4,739
40	Apr	6	(a)	Walsall	L 0-2	10,500
41		13	(h)	Ipswich T	L 1-2 Harvey (pen)	5,953
42		19	(a)	Millwall	W 3-1 Lackenby, Buckle, Currie	11,414
43		20	(a)	Brentford	L 0-3	9,200
44		22	(h)	Millwall	D 1-1 Currie	6,485
45		27	(a)	Shrewsbury T	W 2-1 Harvey (pen), Lackenby	5,729
46	May	1	(h)	Bournemouth	L 1-2 Lackenby	5,708

FINAL LEAGUE POSITION: 21st in Division Three South

Appearances

Goals

FA Cup

1	Nov	17	(h)	Plymouth A	L 0-2

232

Appearance and goalscoring grid (shirt numbers per match):

Hunter	Doyle	Mitchell	John	Parr	Porteous	Simpson	Divers	Burke	Currie	Buckle	Ferrier	Harvey	Thomas WK	Phoenix	Willis	Beer	Rees	Lackenby	Houghton	Packer	Simpson N	Churms	Bell	#
1	2	3	4	5	6	7	8	9	10	11														1
1	2	3	4	5	6	7	10	8	9	11														2
1	2	3	4	5	6	7	10	8	9	11														3
1	2		4		6			8	9	11	3	5	7	10										4
1	2		4		6			8	9	11	3	5	7	10										5
1	2		4		6			8	9	11	3	5	7	10										6
1	2		4		6			8	9	11	3	5	7	10										7
1	2		4		6			8	9	11	3	5	7		10									8
1	2		4		6			8	9	11	3	5			10	7								9
1	2		4		6			8	9	11	3	5			10	7								10
1	2	4	8		6				9		3	5			10	7	11							11
1	2	4	8		6				9		3	5			10	7	11							12
1	2	4	10		6				9	7	3	5	8				11							13
1	2	9	4		6				10	7	3	5	8				11							14
1	2	9	4		6				10	7	3	5	8				11							15
1	2	9	4		6				10	7	3	5	8				11							16
1	2	9	4		6				10	7	3	5	8				11							17
1	2		4		6				10	7	3	5	8		9		11							18
1	2		4		6				10	7	3	5	8		10		11							19
1	2	6	4					10	9	7	3	5	8				11							20
1	2	9	4				10			7	3	5	8				11							21
1	2		9		6				10	11	3	5	7					4	8					22
1	2		9		6				10	11	3	5	7					4	8					23
1	2		9		6				10	11	3	5	7					4	8					24
1	2		9		6				10	11	3	5	7					4	8					25
1	2		9						10	11	3	5	7	6				4	8					26
1	2		10		6			9		11	3	5	7					8	4					27
1	2		10		6			9		11	3	5	7					8	4					28
1	2		10				8	9			3	5	7				11	4		6				29
1	2		10				8	9			3	5	7				11	4		6				30
1	2		10				8	9			3	5	7				11	4		6				31
1	2		10				8	9			3	5	7				11	4		6				32
1	3	4	10							7		5	8	9			11	2		6				33
1	10	4	8							7	3	5		9			11	2		6				34
1	2	4	8							7	3	5		10			11	9		6				35
1	2	3	9							8		7		5	10		11	4		6				36
1	2	3	4						9			7	5	8			11			6	10			37
1	3	2	11						8			5	7	9			4			6	10			38
1	2	3	3						11		9	5	7				4			6	10			39
1	3	2	11						9	7		5	8				4			6	10			40
	3	2	11						9	7		5			10		4			6	8	1		41
	3	2	11						9	7		5			10		4			6	8	1		42
	3	2	11						9	7		5			10		4			6	8	1		43
	3	2							10	11		5	7				9	4	6		8	1		44
	3	2							9	11		5	7				8	4	6		10	1		45
	3	2							9	11		5	7				8	4	6		10	1		46
40	28	33	46	3	27	3	12	12	45	37	31	43	33	5	13	4	23	24	5	7	16	16	10	6
		3	5				1	4	17	7		6	5				1	2	2		4	3		

1 own-goal

1957-58

Manager: Bill Thompson/Frank Broome from January 1958

1	Aug	24	(h)	Southend U	L	0-5	10,234
2		27	(a)	Brentford	L	0-1	12,300
3		31	(a)	Brighton & HA	D	2-2 Churms, Currie	16,036
4	Sep	4	(h)	Brentford	L	3-5 Wilson, Harvey (pen), Churms	8,948
5		7	(h)	Southampton	D	2-2 Hill, Calland	9,457
6		11	(h)	Millwall	W	2-0 Churms, Robinson	8,434
7		14	(a)	Newport C	D	0-0	9,213
8		16	(a)	Millwall	L	0-3	13,840
9		21	(h)	Port Vale	W	1-0 Robinson	9,397
10		25	(h)	Gillingham	L	1-3 Calland	5,965
11		28	(a)	Plymouth A	L	0-1	23,418
12	Oct	2	(a)	Gillingham	D	1-1 Robinson	5,297
13		5	(h)	Aldershot	W	3-0 Harvey (pen), Currie, Atkinson	7,398
14		12	(a)	Colchester U	L	0-3	7,930
15		19	(h)	Norwich C	D	2-2 Foley, Robinson	7,414
16		26	(a)	Bournemouth	L	1-2 Calland	11,893
17	Nov	2	(h)	Walsall	W	2-1 Churms 2	8,272
18		9	(a)	Coventry C	L	1-6 Atkinson	12,707
19		23	(a)	Reading	L	0-2	10,916
20		30	(h)	Northampton T	L	0-1	7,933
21	Dec	7	(a)	Watford	L	4-5 Rapley 2, Rees, Atkins	4,361
22		14	(h)	Crystal P	L	0-1	5,570
23		21	(a)	Southend U	L	0-2	4,000
24		25	(a)	Torquay U	W	3-1 Rapley, Mitchell, Nicholls	6,774
25		26	(h)	Torquay U	W	5-1 Churms 2, Nicholls 2, John	11,581
26		28	(h)	Brighton & HA	W	2-0 Rapley, Nicholls	10,701
27	Jan	4	(a)	Swindon T	L	1-5 Churms	11,292
28		11	(a)	Southampton	L	0-6	12,668
29		18	(h)	Newport C	L	0-2	7,471
30	Feb	1	(a)	Port Vale	L	2-3 Calland 2	9,300
31		8	(h)	Plymouth A	W	4-2 Nicholls 3, Mitchell (pen)	13,598
32		15	(a)	Aldershot	D	2-2 Nicholls, Calland	5,62
33		22	(h)	Colchester U	W	4-3 Calland 3, Mitchell	7,636
34	Mar	1	(a)	Norwich C	L	2-3 Calland 2 (1 pen)	16,761
35		8	(h)	Bournemouth	L	1-2 Calland	8,075
36		15	(a)	Walsall	L	0-3	8,903
37		22	(h)	Reading	D	1-1 Calland	5,725
38		29	(a)	Crystal P	L	0-2	10,506
39	Apr	4	(a)	Queen's Park R	D	1-1 Mitchell	10,098
40		5	(h)	Coventry C	W	1-0 Calland	5,304
41		7	(h)	Queen's Park R	D	0-0	7,104
42		12	(a)	Northampton T	L	0-9	9,465
43		16	(h)	Shrewsbury T	W	2-1 Calland, Hill	3,500
44		19	(h)	Watford	L	1-2 Wilson	5,230
45		23	(h)	Swindon T	L	0-1	5,255
46		26	(a)	Shrewsbury T	L	0-1	3,358

FINAL LEAGUE POSITION: 24th in Division Three South

Appearances

Goals

FA Cup

1	Nov	16	(a)	Bath C	L	1-2

234

Appearance and scoring grid (player line-ups by match):

Hunter	John	MacDonald	Lightly	Packer	Simpson	Wilson	Currie	Calland	Atkinson	Churms	Mitchell	Harvey	Robinson	Bell	Foley	Butterworth	Hill	Rees	Waterman	Dale	Nicholls	Atkins	Rapley	Beer	Oliver	Stiffle	No.
1	2	3	4	5	6	7	8	9	10	11																	1
1		3	4		6	7	8	9	10	11	2	5															2
1		3	4		6	7	8	9	10	11	2	5															3
1		3	4		6	7	8	9		10	2	5	11														4
					6	7		9		10	3	5	11	1	2	4	8										5
					6	7		9	8	10	3	5	11	1	2	4											6
					6	7		9		10	3	5	11	1	2	4			8								7
					6	7	8	9		10	3	5	11	1	2	4											8
						7		9		10	3	5	11	1	2	4	8	6									9
	2	3			6					11		5	7	1		4		9	8	10							10
	2				6		8			10	3	5	11	1	2	4		7									11
1					6		8	9		10	3	5	11		2	4		7									12
1					6		8	9		10	3	5	11		2	4		7									13
1	4				6	7	8	9		10	3	5	11		2												14
1					6			9		10	3	5	7		2	4	8	11									15
1					6	7		9		10	3	5			2	4	8	11									16
1					6	7		9	8	10	3	5			2	4		11									17
	2							9			3	5	7	1		4		10	6	11	8						18
	2							9			3	5	7	1		4		10	6	11	8						19
	2	3									6	5		1		4		10		11	9	7	8				20
	4	3								8	6	5		1	2			10		11	9		7				21
	4	3								8	6	5		1	2			10		11	9		7				22
	4	3								8	6	5		1	2			10		11	9		7				23
	4	3								8	6	5		1	2			10		11	9		7				24
	4	3								8	6	5		1	2			10		11	9		7				25
	4	3								10	6	5		1	2				8	11	9		7				26
		3								10		5		1	2	6			8	11	9		7		4		27
1	4	3	5		7			9			6				2		8			11	10						28
1	4	3						9	8		6				2					11	10		7		5		29
1	4	3	2					9	8		6				2					11	10				5		30
1	4	3	2					9	8		6				2					11	10				5		31
1	4	3	2					9	8	10		5						7		11			6				32
1	4	3				7		9	8		6				2			10		11					5		33
1	4	3						9	8		6				2			10	7	11					5		34
1	7	3						9			6	4			2			10		11					5	8	35
1	4	3					8	9		10	6				2					11					5	7	36
1	4	3					8	9		10	6				2					11					5	7	37
1	4	3					8	9		10	6				2					11					5	7	38
1	4	3					8	9		10	6				2					11					5	7	39
1	4	3						9		10	6				2			8		11					5	7	40
1		3						9		4	6				2		8	10		11					5	7	41
1		3	4					9		10	6				2		8			11					5	7	42
1		3	4			7		9		10	6				2		8			11					5		43
1	10	3				7		9		4	6				2		8			11					5		44
1		3			10			9		4	6				2		8			11					5	7	45
		3			10			9		4	6			1	2		8			11				1	5	7	46
28	26	31	4	7	17	22	9	34	8	34	43	37	15	18	34	17	10	25	4	31	16	1	9	1	16	9	
	1				2	2	15	2	8	4	2	4		1		2	1			8	1		4				

235

1958-59

Manager: Frank Broome

#	Month	Date		Opponent	Result	Scorers	Attendance
1	Aug	23	(h)	Walsall	W 3-0	Rees, Calland, Harvey (pen)	8,750
2		28	(h)	Barrow	W 4-0	Rees, Calland, Dale, Harvey	8,836
3		30	(a)	Darlington	D 1-1	Harvey (pen)	7,716
4	Sep	1	(a)	Barrow	L 0-1		5,707
5		6	(h)	Shrewsbury T	W 1-0	Dale	8,442
6		10	(h)	Oldham A	W 3-2	Calland, Mitchell, Rees	9,562
7		13	(a)	Coventry C	L 0-2		14,537
8		15	(a)	Oldham A	L 1-2	Rees	5,139
9		20	(h)	Torquay U	D 2-2	Calland, Rees	13,102
10		27	(h)	Gillingham	W 3-0	Rees, Stiffle, Birch	8,524
11	Oct	4	(a)	Carlisle U	W 2-1	Rees, Calland	10,260
12		8	(h)	Aldershot	W 2-0	Calland, Rees	8,528
13		11	(a)	Northampton T	D 1-1	Nicholls	10,077
14		18	(h)	Workington	W 1-0	Nicholls	9,257
15		25	(a)	York C	W 2-0	Calland 2	9,748
16		27	(a)	Gateshead	W 2-1	Nicholls, Stiffle	3,347
17	Nov	1	(h)	Bradford	W 4-0	Rees 2, Nicholls 2	10,808
18		8	(a)	Port Vale	L 3-5	Rees 3	14,314
19		22	(a)	Chester	L 2-4	Nicholls, Calland	8,040
20		29	(h)	Watford	W 3-0	Nicholls 2, Calland	8,866
21	Dec	13	(h)	Southport	W 3-2	Mitchell (pen), Nicholls 2	8,321
22		27	(h)	Crewe A	W 3-0	Rees 2, Calland	11,478
23	Jan	3	(h)	Darlington	D 2-2	Calland, Rees	9,336
24		24	(a)	Hartlepools U	D 3-3	Rees, Thompson, Calland	4,157
25		31	(h)	Coventry C	W 2-1	Calland 2	12,578
26	Feb	7	(a)	Torquay U	W 4-3	Calland, Mitchell, Stiffle, Nicholls	11,511
27		14	(a)	Gillingham	W 2-0	Nicholls, Mitchell	6,545
28		21	(h)	Carlisle U	W 2-1	Calland 2	10,097
29		28	(h)	Northampton T	L 3-4	Calland 2, Mitchell (pen)	9,870
30	Mar	5	(a)	Crewe A	D 0-0		7,092
31		7	(a)	Workington	D 2-2	Calland 2	4,200
32		14	(h)	York C	L 0-2		9,000
33		17	(a)	Walsall	L 0-3		4,656
34		21	(a)	Bradford	W 3-0	Calland 2, Rees	7,203
35		27	(a)	Millwall	D 1-1	Calland	16,868
36		28	(h)	Port Vale	L 3-4	Rees, Stiffle, Calland	12,088
37		30	(h)	Millwall	W 3-1	Rees, Calland, Stiffle	8,950
38	Apr	4	(a)	Crystal P	D 1-1	Rees	20,979
39		6	(h)	Gateshead	D 1-1	Mitchell	7,670
40		11	(h)	Chester	D 1-1	Hill	6,400
41		15	(h)	Crystal P	W 3-1	Rees, Nicholls, Stiffle	8,352
42		18	(a)	Watford	L 1-2	Stiffle	6,150
43		22	(a)	Aldershot	L 0-1		3,143
44		25	(h)	Hartlepools U	W 3-0	Stiffle, Mitchell, Nicholls	6,561
45		28	(a)	Southport	W 1-0	Nicholls	2,646
46		30	(a)	Shrewsbury T	L 0-3		15,318

FINAL LEAGUE POSITION: 5th in Division Four

Appearances
Goals

FA Cup

| 1 | Nov | 15 | (a) | Brentford | L 2-3 | | |

236

#	Hunter	Foley	MacDonald	Mitchell	Oliver	Harvey	Stiffle	John	Calland	Rees	Dale	Nicholls	Birch	Packer	Robinson	Thompson	Butterworth	Lobbett	Whitnall	Hill
1	1	2	3	4	5	6	7	8	9	10	11									
2	1	2	3	4	5	6	7		9	10	11	8								
3	1	2	3	4	5	6	7		9	10	11	8								
4	1	2	3	4	5	6	7		9	8	11	10								
5	1	2	3	4	5	6	7		9	8	11	10								
6	1	2	3	4	5	6	7		9	8	11	10								
7	1	2	3	4	5	6	7		9	8	11	10								
8	1	2	3	4	5	6	7		9	8	11		10							
9	1	2	3	4	5	6	7		9	8	11		10							
10	1	2	3	4	5	6	7		9	8	11		10							
11	1	2	3	4	5	6	7		9	8	11		10							
12	1	2	3	4	5	6	7		9	8	11	10								
13	1	2	3	4	5		7		9	8	11	10		6						
14	1	2	3	4	5		7		9	8	11	10		6						
15	1	2	3	4	5		7	6	9	8	11	10								
16	1	2	3	4	5		7	6	9	8	11	10								
17	1	2	3	4	5		7	6	9	8	11	10								
18	1	2	3	4	5		7	6	9	8	11	10								
19	1	2	3	4	5			6	9	8	11	10			7					
20	1	2	3	4	5		7		9	8	11	10				6				
21	1	2	3	4	5		7		9	8	11	10				6				
22	1	2	3	4	5		7		9	8	11	10				6				
23	1	2	3	4	5		7		9	8	11	10				6				
24	1	2	3	4	5		7		9	8	11	10				6				
25	1	2	3	4	5		7		9	8	11	10				6				
26	1	2	3	4	5		7		9	8	11	10				6				
27	1	2	3	4	5		7		9	8	11	10				6				
28	1	2	3	4	5		7		9	8	11	10				6				
29	1	2	3	4	5		7		9		11	10	8			6				
30	1	2	3	4	5		7		9		11	10	8			6				
31	1	2	3	4	5		7		9	8	11	10				6				
32	1	2	3	4	5		7		9		11	8	10			6				
33	1	2	3	6	5		7		9	8	11				10	4				
34	1	2	3	6	5		7		9	8	11				10	4				
35	1	2	3	8	5		7		9		11	10				6	4			
36		2	3	8	5		7		9		11	10				6	4	1		
37		2	3	8	5		7		9		11	10				6	4	1		
38		2		8	5				9	7	11	10				6	4	1	3	
39		2		4	5		7		9		11	10				6		1	3	8
40		2		4	5		7		9	8	11	10				6		1	3	
41		2		4	5		7		9	8	11	10				6		1	3	
42		2		4	5		7		9	8	11	10				6		1	3	
43		2		4	5		7		9	8	11	10				6		1	3	
44		2		4	5		7		9	8	11	10				6		1	3	
45		2		9	5		7				11	10				6	4	1	3	
46		2	3	9	5		7				11	10				6	4	1		8
	36	46	39	46	46	13	44	6	44	43	41	39	7	2	1	26	8	10	7	2
		7		3	8				27	22	2	15	1			1			1	

1959-60

Manager: Frank Broome

					Result	Scorers	Attendance
1	Aug	22	(h)	Northampton T	D 1-1	Micklewright	9,678
2		24	(a)	Stockport C	L 0-1		5,000
3		29	(h)	Watford	W 2-0	Micklewright 2	8,323
4	Sep	2	(h)	Stockport C	W 2-1	Calland, Micklewright	8,732
5		5	(a)	Oldham A	W 2-1	Calland, Rees	9,720
6		7	(a)	Chester	L 0-1		6,482
7		12	(h)	Carlisle U	L 1-3	Thompson (pen)	7,480
8		17	(h)	Chester	W 2-0	Micklewright 2	7,555
9		19	(a)	Notts C	L 0-3		11,982
10		21	(a)	Bradford	L 0-1		4,615
11		26	(h)	Walsall	L 1-2	Dale	8,142
12		30	(h)	Bradford	W 3-1	Thompson, Rees 2	6,414
13	Oct	3	(a)	Hartlepools U	L 3-4	Rees 2, Micklewright	3,604
14		7	(h)	Crewe A	L 2-4	Dale 2	6,340
15		10	(h)	Millwall	D 2-2	Brady (og), Micklewright	7,000
16		14	(a)	Crewe A	D 1-1	Bennett	11,993
17		17	(a)	Southport	L 2-3	Stiffle, Rutherford (og)	4,569
18		24	(h)	Gillingham	W 2-0	Wilkinson, Stiffle	7,119
19		31	(a)	Barrow	D 3-3	Wilkinson, Stiffle, Rees	5,193
20	Nov	7	(h)	Aldershot	W 3-1	Rees, Calland, Dale	7,621
21		21	(h)	Gateshead	W 2-1	Atkins 2	6,992
22		28	(a)	Rochdale	L 0-3		4,856
23	Dec	12	(a)	Doncaster R	W 1-0	Rees	3,754
24		19	(a)	Northampton T	D 1-1	Wilkinson	4,709
25		26	(a)	Torquay U	W 3-2	Wilkinson, Rees, Stiffle	10,231
26		28	(h)	Torquay U	W 1-0	Thompson (pen)	12,947
27	Jan	2	(a)	Watford	L 2-5	Wilkinson, Stiffle	8,893
28		16	(h)	Oldham A	W 4-3	Thompson, Wilkinson 2, Rees	5,515
29		23	(a)	Carlisle U	W 4-0	Stiffle, Wilkinson, Calland, Rees	4,304
30		30	(h)	Workington	W 1-0	Rees	7,690
31	Feb	6	(h)	Notts C	D 3-3	Rees, Wilkinson 2	8,000
32		20	(h)	Hartlepools U	W 5-0	Stiffle 2, Wilkinson 2, Thompson	7,066
33		27	(a)	Millwall	W 3-2	Rees, Stiffle, Calland	12,826
34	Mar	5	(h)	Southport	D 1-1	Rees	7,920
35		12	(a)	Gillingham	L 1-2	Dale	7,431
36		19	(h)	Barrow	D 2-2	Wilkinson, Micklewright	6,000
37		22	(h)	Walsall	D 2-2	Calland 2	10,568
38		26	(a)	Aldershot	L 0-1		8,014
39	Apr	2	(h)	Darlington	D 0-0		6,000
40		9	(a)	Gateshead	L 0-1		2,056
41		15	(a)	Crystal P	L 0-1		15,731
42		16	(h)	Rochdale	W 4-1	Wilkinson, Micklewright, Rees 2	6,669
43		18	(h)	Crystal P	D 2-2	Wilkinson, Micklewright	6,661
44		23	(a)	Workington	L 1-2	Bennett	2,600
45		25	(a)	Darlington	W 1-0	Wilkinson	3,446
46		30	(h)	Doncaster R	W 4-2	Bennett 3, Thompson	5,000

FINAL LEAGUE POSITION: 9th in Division Four

Appearances

Goals

FA Cup

1	Nov	14	(h)	Barnstaple T	W 4-0
2	Dec	5	(h)	Brentford	W 3-1
3	Jan	9	(h)	Luton T	L 1-2

	Lobbett	Foley	Whitnall	Mitchell	Oliver	Thompson	Stiffle	Rees	Calland	Micklewright	Dale	Harvey	Birch	MacDonald	Rapley	Jones	Bennett	Wilkinson	Atkins	Butterworth	Hill	Welsh	#
	1	2	3	4	5	6	7	8	9	10	11												1
	1	2	3	4	5	6	7	8	9	10	11												2
	1	2	3	4		6	7		9	8	11	5	10										3
	1	2		4		6	7		9	8	11	5	10	3									4
	1	2		4		6	7	11	9	8		5	10	3									5
	1	2		4		6	7	11	9	8		5	10	3									6
	1	2				6	7		9	8	11	5	10	3	4								7
		2		4	5	10	7	11		9		6	8	3		1							8
		2		4	5	6	7	8	11	9			10	3		1							9
		2	8	5	4		7	11	9	10		6		3		1							10
		2		4	5		7	10	9	8	11	6		3		1							11
		2	3	4	5	6	7	8		9	11		10			1							12
		2	3	4	5	6	7	8		9	11		10			1							13
	1	2			5	6		8	9	7	11	4	10	3									14
	1	2			5	6		8		7	11	4	10	3				9					15
	1	2			5	6	7	8			11	4	10	3				9					16
		2		4	5		7	8	11	10		6		3		1		9					17
		2		4	5	6	7	8	10	11				3		1		9					18
		2		4	5	6	7	8	10		11			3		1		9					19
		2		4	5	6		8		10	11			3		1		9	7				20
		2		4	5	6		8	10		11			3		1		9	7				21
				4	5	6	7	8	10		11			3		1		9		2			22
		2		4	5	6	7	8	10		11			3		1		9					23
		2		4	5	6	7	8	10		11			3		1		9					24
		2		4	5	6	7	8	10		11			3		1		9					25
		2		4	5	6	7	8	10		11			3		1		9					26
	1	2		4	5	6	7	8	9	11				3				10					27
		2		4	5	6	7	8	9	11				3		1		10					28
		2		4	5	6	7	8	9	11				3		1		10					29
		2		4	5	6	7	8	11	10				3		1		9					30
		2		4		6	7	8	11	10	5			3		1		9					31
		2		4		6	7	8	10	11	5			3		1		9					32
		2		4		6	7	8	10	11	5			3		1		9					33
		2		4		6	7	8		10	11	5		3		1		9					34
		2		4	5	6	7		10	8	11			3		1		9					35
		2		4	5	6	7	8		10	11			3		1		9					36
	1	2		4	5	6	7	8		10	11			3				9					37
	1	2		4	5	6	7	8		10	11			3				9					38
	1	2		4		6	7		10		11	5		3				9			8		39
		2		4		6			10	11	7	5		3		1		9			8		40
		2		4		6	7	8		10	11	5		3		1		9					41
		2		4		6	7	8	10	11	5			3		1		9					42
		2		4		6	11	8	10		5			3		1		9				7	43
		2		4		6	11	8	10		5			3		1		9				7	44
		2		4		6	11	8	10		5			3		1		9				7	45
		2		4		6	11	8	10		5			3		1		9				7	46
	14	45	6	42	30	44	41	42	27	38	26	23	12	40	1	32	5	29	2	1	2	4	
						6	9	17	7	11	5			5				16	2				

2 own-goals

1960-61

Manager: Glen Wilson

#	Month	Date	Venue	Opponent	Result	Scorers	Attendance
1	Aug	20	(h)	Carlisle U	D 0-0		9,933
2		25	(a)	Wrexham	L 1-3	Wilkinson	8,000
3		27	(a)	Rochdale	L 1-3	Wilkinson	2,514
4		31	(h)	Wrexham	W 1-0	Rees	6,138
5	Sep	3	(h)	Mansfield T	L 0-2		5,576
6		6	(a)	Doncaster R	L 1-2	Harrison	5,121
7		10	(a)	Stockport C	D 0-0		8,035
8		14	(h)	Doncaster R	W 2-0	Harrison, Gordon	5,015
9		17	(a)	Bradford	L 2-5	Donaldson 2	6,124
10		19	(a)	Hartlepools U	D 0-0		2,926
11		24	(h)	Peterborough U	L 3-4	Wilson, Wilkinson 2	9,146
12		26	(h)	Hartlepools U	W 2-1	Gordon, Wilkinson	5,000
13	Oct	1	(a)	Southport	L 0-2		4,413
14		5	(h)	Darlington	L 1-3	Rees	5,400
15		8	(h)	Aldershot	W 1-0	Rees	3,107
16		15	(a)	Oldham A	L 2-5	Donaldson, Harrison	17,116
17		22	(h)	Workington	D 0-0		4,000
18		29	(a)	Chester	D 4-4	Bond 2, Harrison, Donaldson	5,173
19	Nov	12	(a)	York C	L 1-6	Wilkinson	5,281
20		19	(h)	Accrington S	L 2-4	Bond, Dale	6,000
21	Dec	3	(h)	Barrow	D 2-2	Wilkinson 2	3,042
22		10	(a)	Gillingham	L 2-4	Carter, Rees	4,925
23		17	(a)	Carlisle U	D 2-2	Rees, Wilkinson	2,484
24		26	(h)	Crystal P	L 2-3	Jenkins, Thompson	7,551
25		27	(a)	Crystal P	D 0-0		28,551
26		31	(h)	Rochdale	W 1-0	Wilkinson	4,365
27	Jan	7	(a)	Millwall	D 2-2	Carter 2	7,974
28		14	(a)	Mansfield T	W 3-2	Carter 2, Donaldson	4,485
29		21	(h)	Stockport C	W 2-1	Carter, Rees	4,582
30	Feb	4	(h)	Bradford	W 4-2	Carter 2, Jenkins, Thompson	4,916
31		11	(a)	Peterborough U	L 1-7	Rees	11,518
32		18	(h)	Southport	W 2-1	Thompson (pen), Jenkins	4,774
33		25	(a)	Aldershot	L 1-3	Carter	5,042
34	Mar	4	(h)	Oldham A	W 3-0	Carter, Rees 2	4,483
35		11	(a)	Workington	L 1-3	Rees	2,011
36		16	(h)	Crewe A	L 0-1		3,632
37		18	(h)	Chester	W 4-1	Bond, Jenkins 2, Carter	3,642
38		25	(a)	Crewe A	L 0-2		3,000
39	Apr	1	(h)	York C	W 2-1	Gordon, Rees	5,090
40		3	(h)	Northampton T	L 1-3	Williams (pen)	5,903
41		4	(a)	Northampton T	L 1-3	Rees	12,402
42		8	(a)	Accrington S	W 1-0	Donaldson	2,700
43		15	(h)	Millwall	L 2-3	Rees, Carter	4,641
44		22	(a)	Barrow	D 1-1	Jenkins	2,754
45		24	(a)	Darlington	L 0-3		2,267
46		29	(h)	Gillingham	W 2-0	Carter, Rees	3,602

FINAL LEAGUE POSITION: 21st in Division Four

Appearances
Goals

FA Cup

1	Nov	5	(h)	Bournemouth	D 1-1
R		9	(a)	Bournemouth	L 1-3

League Cup

1	Oct	19	(h)	Manchester U	D 1-1
R		26	(a)	Manchester U	L 1-4

240

Jones	Foley	MacDonald	Mitchell	Harvey	Thompson	Harrison	Gordon	Wilkinson	Donaldson	Dale	Rees	Lobbett	Whitnall	Bennett	Wilson	Packer	Welsh	Grant	Williams A	Bond	Carter	Jenkins	Williams P	No.
1	2	3	4	5	6	7	8	9	10	11														1
1	2	3	4	5	6	7	8	9	10	11														2
1	2	3	4	5	6	7	8	9		11	10													3
	2	3	4	5	6	7	8	9		11	10	1												4
	2	3	4	5	6	7	8	9		11	10	1												5
		3	4	5	6	7		10		11	8	1	2	9										6
		3	4	5	6	7	8	9	10	11		1	2											7
		3	4	5	6	7	10	9	8	11		1	2											8
		3	4	5	6	7	10	9	8	11		1	2											9
		3		5	6	7	10	9	8	11		1	2		4									10
		3		5	6	11	10	9	8	7		1	2		4									11
		3		5	6	11	10	9	8	7		1			4	2								12
		3		5	6	11	10	9	8	7		1	2		4									13
		3		5	6	11	9	8	10			1	2		4		7							14
1		3		5	6	11	8	9	10				2		4		7							15
		3		5	6	11	8	9	10				2		4		7							16
		3			6	11	7	9	10			1	2		4			5	8					17
		3	4		6	7		9	11	10		1	2					5	8					18
	2	3		5	6			9		11	10	1			4		7		8					19
	2	3		5	6			9		11		1			4		7		8		10			20
	2	3		5	6			9		11	8	1			4		7				10			21
	2	3		5	6			10		11	8	1			4		7					9		22
	2	3		5	6			9		11	10	1			4		7		8					23
	2	3		5	6	7				11	10	1			4				8			9		24
1	2	3		5	6	7				11	10				4				8			9		25
1		3		5	6	7	8			11			2		4						10	9		26
1		3			6	7				11	8		2		4				5		10	9		27
1	2	3			6	7				11	8				4				5		10	9		28
1	2	3			6	7				11	8				4				5		10	9		29
1	2	3			6	7				11	8				4				5		10	9		30
1	2	3			6	7				11	8				4				5		10	9		31
1	2	3			6	7				11					4				5	8	10	9		32
1	2	3	4		6	7				11	8								5		10	9		33
1	2	3	4		6	7				11	8								5		10	9		34
1	2	3	4		6	7				11	8								5		10	9		35
1	2	3	4	5						11	8						6		7		10	9		36
1	2	3	4	5		7				11	8						6				10	9		37
1		3	4	5		7				11	8		2				6				10	9		38
1		3	4		6	7				11	8		2					5	9		10			39
1		3	4		6	7				11	8		2					5	9		10			40
1	2	3	4		6	7				11	8								5		10	9		41
1	2	3	4		6	7				11	8								5		10	9		42
1	2	3	4		6	7				11	8								5		10	9		43
1		3			6	7				11	8		2		4				5		10	9		44
1		3			6	7				11	8		2		4				5		10	9		45
1	2	3			6	7				11	8				4				5		10	9		46
26	26	46	20	36	35	18	24	19	36	26	42	20	19	1	25	1	7	4	19	10	25	20	1	
		3	4	3	10	6	1	14					1				1	4	13	6				

1961-62

Manager: Glen Wilson

								Appearances
1	Aug	19	(a)	Mansfield T	L 1-3	Welsh	7,611	
2		23	(h)	Chesterfield	W 4-1	Carter 2, Rees, Gordon	5,944	
3		26	(h)	Barrow	W 3-0	Blue, Gordon, Jenkins	6,153	
4		28	(a)	Chesterfield	L 0-2		4,300	
5	Sep	2	(a)	Rochdale	L 0-3		5,062	
6		4	(a)	York C	L 1-2	Jenkins (pen)	9,241	
7		9	(h)	Crewe A	W 2-1	Gordon, Wilson	5,494	
8		16	(a)	Tranmere R	W 4-3	McGugan (og), Rees, Carter, Blue	7,889	
9		19	(h)	Southport	D 1-1	Carter	5,739	
10		23	(a)	Wrexham	W 2-1	Carter, Jenkins	13,138	
11		25	(a)	Southport	D 1-1	Blue	4,969	
12		30	(h)	Doncaster R	L 1-5	Gordon	6,424	
13	Oct	4	(a)	Workington	L 1-3	Jenkins	3,472	
14		7	(h)	Hartlepools U	D 1-1	Welsh	4,173	
15		11	(h)	Workington	W 3-1	Gordon, Carter 2	4,301	
16		14	(a)	Darlington	L 0-1		5,462	
17		28	(a)	Oldham A	D 1-1	McMillan	12,491	
18	Nov	11	(a)	Aldershot	D 1-1	Jenkins	5,336	
19		18	(h)	Bradford C	L 1-2	Carter	4,405	
20	Dec	2	(h)	Colchester U	L 0-2		4,530	
21		9	(a)	Chester	D 1-1	Harvey (pen)	3,192	
22		16	(h)	Mansfield T	W 2-1	Blue, Carter	3,592	
23		23	(a)	Barrow	L 0-3		4,094	
24		26	(h)	Gillingham	L 1-3	Rees	4,326	
25		30	(a)	Gillingham	D 2-2	Carter 2	6,786	
26	Jan	6	(h)	Stockport C	W 4-3	Brown, Gordon, Welsh, Rees	4,135	
27		13	(h)	Rochdale	L 1-3	Carter	4,000	
28		20	(a)	Crewe A	L 1-3	Brown	4,078	
29		27	(a)	Carlisle U	L 1-2	Carter	4,993	
30	Feb	3	(h)	Tranmere R	W 1-0	Jenkins	3,628	
31		10	(h)	Wrexham	D 1-1	Gordon	4,257	
32		16	(a)	Doncaster R	L 1-3	Malloy (og)	2,089	
33		24	(a)	Hartlepools U	D 0-0		2,933	
34	Mar	3	(h)	Darlington	L 0-1		3,341	
35		17	(h)	Oldham A	D 3-3	Carter 3	3,187	
36		23	(a)	Stockport C	L 0-1		4,148	
37		31	(h)	Aldershot	W 2-1	Welsh, Gordon	2,740	
38	Apr	7	(a)	Bradford C	L 1-5	Brown	5,697	
39		11	(h)	York C	W 2-1	Welsh, Carter	2,919	
40		14	(h)	Carlisle U	W 4-0	Welsh, Harvey (pen), Jenkins 2	3,278	
41		20	(a)	Milwall	L 0-2		19,666	
42		21	(a)	Colchester U	L 0-2		5,530	
43		23	(h)	Millwall	D 1-1	Carter	5,031	
44		28	(h)	Chester	W 5-0	Blue 2, Jenkins, Rees 2	3,310	

FINAL LEAGUE POSITION: 18th in Division Four   Appearances

Accrington Stanley resigned from the League and their record expunged   Goals

FA Cup

1	Nov	4	(h)	Dartford	D 3-3	
R		8	(a)	Dartford	L 1-2	

League Cup

1	Sep	11	(a)	Mansfield T	L 2-5	

Jones	Hudson	MacDonald	Mitchell	Harvey	Sullivan	Welsh	Rees	Blue	Gordon	Jenkins	Wilson	Carter	Whitnall	Hughes	McMillan	Tinsley	Brown	No.
1	2	3	4	5	6	7	8	9	10	11								1
1	2	3		5	6		7	9	8	11	4	10						2
1	2	3		5	6		7	9	8	11	4	10						3
1	2	3		5	6		7	9	8	11	4	10						4
1	2	3		5	6		7	9	8	11	4	10						5
1		3		5	6		7	9	8	11	4	10	2					6
1		3		5	6		7	9	8	11	4	10	2					7
1		3		5	6		8	9	7	11		10	2	4				8
1	2	3		5	6		8	9	7	11		10		4				9
1	2	3		5	6		8	9	7	11	4	10						10
1	2	3		5	6		8	9	7	11	4	10						11
1	2	3		5	6		8	9	7	11	4	10						12
1	2	3		5	6		8	9	7	11	4	10						13
1	2	3		5	6	7		9	8	11	4	10						14
1	2	3		5	6	7		9	8	11		10		4				15
1	2	3		5	6	7		9	8	11		10		4				16
1	2	3		5	6			9	8	11		10		4	7			17
1	2	3		5	6			9	8	11		10		4	7			18
1	2	3		5	6		8	9		11		10		4	7			19
	2	3		5	6			9	8	11		10		4	7	1		20
	2	3		5	6	7		9	8	11		10		4		1		21
	2	3		5	6	7		9	8	11		10		4		1		22
	2	3		5	6	7	10	9	8	11				4		1		23
	2	3		5	6	7	10	9	8	11				4		1		24
	2	3	4	5	6	7	8			11		10				1	9	25
	2	3	4	5	6	7	8			11		10				1	9	26
	2	3	4	5	6	7	8			11		10				1	9	27
1		3		5	6				8	11		10	2	4	7		9	28
1	2	3		5	6		8		7	11		10		4			9	29
1	2	3		5	6	7			8	11		10		4			9	30
1	2	3		5	6	7			8	11		10		4			9	31
1	2	3		5	6				8	11		10		4	7		9	32
1	2	3	4	5	6				8	11		10			7		9	33
1	2	3	4	5	6				8	11		10			7		9	34
1	2	3	4	5	6		8	9	7	11		10						35
1	2	3	4	5	6		8	9	7	11		10						36
1	2	3	4	5	6		8	9	7	11		10						37
	2	3	4	5	6	7	8		10	11						1	9	38
	2	3	4	5	6		8	9	7	11		10				1		39
	2	3	4	5	6		8	9	7	11		10				1		40
1	2	3	4	5	6		8	9	7	11		10						41
1	2	3	4	5	6		8	9	7	11		10						42
	2	3	4	5	6		8	9	7	11		10				1		43
1	2	3	4	5	6		8	9	7	11		10						44
32	41	43	16	44	44	20	25	34	43	39	11	40	4	17	8	12	11	
		2			6	6	6	9	8	1		18		1			3	

2 own-goals

1962-63

Manager: Cyril Spiers until February 1963, then Jack Edwards.

1	Aug	18	(h)	Torquay U	L	0-3		9,676
2		22	(h)	Mansfield T	L	0-3		5,862
3		25	(a)	Chesterfield	D	1-1	Green	6,000
4		27	(a)	Mansfield T	L	0-1		11,173
5	Sep	1	(h)	Rochdale	L	0-2		4,524
6		8	(a)	Brentford	L	1-3	Carter	11,150
7		12	(h)	Doncaster R	L	0-1		4,136
8		15	(h)	York C	W	2-1	Carter 2	3,922
9		20	(h)	Workington	W	1-0	Tinsley	
10		22	(a)	Chester	L	1-3	Welsh	
11		24	(a)	Workington	L	1-3	Carter	3,870
12		29	(h)	Crewe A	D	1-1	Carter	3,928
13	Oct	3	(h)	Lincoln C	D	1-1	Sanders	4,490
14		6	(a)	Oldham A	W	2-1	Jenkins (pen), Carter	15,790
15		10	(a)	Lincoln C	L	1-4	Carter	
16		13	(h)	Barrow	L	0-2		4,258
17		20	(a)	Hartlepools U	W	2-0	Carter, Rees	4,969
18		27	(h)	Darlington	L	1-3	Carter	3,857
19	Nov	10	(h)	Aldershot	W	4-2	Pierce, Carter 2, Mitchell	3,007
20		17	(a)	Newport C	L	0-4		
21	Dec	1	(a)	Bradford C	W	3-2	Carter, Pierce 2	
22		8	(h)	Tranmere R	W	2-1	Rees, Carter	2,737
23		15	(a)	Torquay U	L	0-3		5,703
24		22	(h)	Chesterfield	D	2-2	Carter, Henderson	
25		26	(h)	Stockport C	L	0-1		
26		29	(a)	Stockport C	L	3-4	Mitchell, Rees, Welsh	
27	Feb	23	(h)	Oldham A	W	2-1	Mitchell, Henderson	3,488
28	Mar	2	(a)	Barrow	W	2-0	Pierce, Carter	
29		9	(h)	Hartlepools U	W	3-1	Henderson, Mitchell, Jenkins	2,815
30		16	(a)	Darlington	W	1-0	Henderson	
31		18	(a)	York C	D	3-3	Carter 2, Jenkins	4,381
32		23	(h)	Southport	W	2-1	Harvey (pen), Carter	4,465
33		30	(a)	Oxford U	W	3-0	Mitchell, Harvey (pen), Henderson	4,192
34	Apr	2	(a)	Doncaster R	D	1-1	Henderson	5,206
35		6	(h)	Newport C	W	1-0	Rathbone (og)	5,258
36		12	(a)	Gillingham	L	0-4		9,272
37		13	(a)	Aldershot	D	1-1	Rees	4,886
38		15	(h)	Gillingham	D	0-0		7,001
39		20	(h)	Bradford C	L	0-2		3,938
40		27	(a)	Tranmere R	L	1-2	Carter	
41		29	(a)	Southport	W	3-1	Sells, Welsh 2	3,160
42	May	4	(h)	Chester	W	2-1	Fleming (og), Sells	3,917
43		8	(h)	Oxford U	D	1-1	Henderson	3,374
44		11	(a)	Rochdale	L	0-3		1,403
45		17	(h)	Brentford	D	2-2	Henderson, Sells	4,940
46		22	(a)	Crewe A	L	0-1		8,000

FINAL LEAGUE POSITION: 17th in Division Four

Appearances
Goals

FA Cup

1	Nov	3	(a)	Gravesend U	L	2-3

League Cup

1	Sep	5	(a)	Aldershot	L	0-2

Appearances and goals grid (figures are shirt numbers; the right-hand column is the match number).

Tinsley	Johnston	MacDonald	Mitchell	Anderson	Hughes	Carter	Sells	Pierce	Welsh	Jenkins	Sanders	McMillan	Rees	Grace	Green	Smyth	Rutley	Boag	Henderson	Harvey	Patrick	#
1	2	3	4	5	6	7	8	9	10	11												1
1	2	3		4	6		10	9		11	5	7	8									2
1	2	3	4	5	6	7	10			11			8	9								3
1	2	3	4	5	6	7	9			11			8		10							4
1	2	3	4	5	6	7	9			11			8		10							5
1		3	8	5	4	10		7	11	6					9	2						6
1		3	8	5	4	10		7	11	6					9	2						7
1		3		5		10	8	7	11	6					9	2	4					8
1		3		5		10	11	9	7	8	6					2	4					9
1	9	3		5	8	10			7	11	6					2	4					10
1		3	9	5	4	10				11	6	7				2	8					11
1		3	9	5	4	10				11	6	7				2	8					12
1		3	9	5	4	10		8		11	6	7				2						13
		3	9	5	4	10		11			6	7				2	8	1				14
		3	8	5	4			10		11	6	7	9			2		1				15
1	5	3			10			9		11	6	7	8			2	4					16
1	5	3			10					11	6	7	8		9	2	4					17
1		3	8	5	4	10		9	7		6		11			2						18
1		3	8	5	4	10		9	7		6		11			2						19
1		3	4	5		10		9	7		6		11			2			8			20
1		3	8	5	4	10		9	7		6		11			2						21
1		3	8	5	4	10		9	7		6		11			2						22
1		3	4	5		10		9	7		6		11			2			8			23
1	2	3	8	5	4	10				11			7						9	6		24
1	2	3	4	6		9	10		7	11									8	5		25
1	2	3	4	6		9	10		7				11						8	5		26
1		3	4	6		8		10		11	7					2			8	5		27
1			4	6		8		10		11	7					2			9	5	3	28
1			4	6		8		10		11	7					2			9	5	3	29
1			4	6		8		10		11	7					2			9	5	3	30
1			4	6		8		10		11	7					2			9	5	3	31
1			4	6		8		10		11	7					2			9	5	3	32
1			4	6		8		10		11	7					2			9	5	3	33
1			4	6		8		10		11	7					2			9	5	3	34
1			4	6		8		10		11	7					2			9	5	3	35
1			4	6		10		7		11			8			2				5	3	36
1			4	6		10		7		11			8			2				5	3	37
1			4	6		8		10		11			7			2				5	3	38
1			4	6		10	8		7				11			2				5	3	39
1			4	6		10	8		7	11						2				5	3	40
1			4	6		10	8		7	11						9				5	3	41
1			4	6		10	8		7				11			2				5	3	42
1			4	6		10	8			11			7			2				5	3	43
1		10	6			10	8			11		7	4			2				5	3	44
1			6	4		10	8		7				11			2				5	3	45
1			4	6		10	8		7				11			9				5	3	46
44	10	28	40	44	19	40	14	28	21	34	20	12	29	1	9	39	8	2	24	22	18	
1		5		19	3	4	4	3	1		4		1						8	2		

2 own-goals

1963-64

Manager: Jack Edwards

1	Aug	24	(a)	Bradford C	W	2-1	Henderson 2	4,668
2		26	(a)	Carlisle U	L	0-3		6,454
3		31	(h)	Lincoln C	D	0-0		5,449
4	Sep	7	(a)	Gillingham	D	0-0		8,381
5		11	(h)	Carlisle U	W	1-0	Curtis	5,671
6		14	(h)	Southport	D	1-1	Curtis	5,335
7		18	(a)	Aldershot	W	1-0	Henderson	7,603
8		21	(h)	Doncaster R	W	3-1	Henderson 2, Curtis	5,775
9		28	(a)	Hartlepools U	D	1-1	Harvey	2,000
10	Oct	2	(h)	Aldershot	D	0-0		7,000
11		5	(h)	Darlington	D	1-1	Curtis	5,965
12		9	(h)	Halifax T	D	0-0		7,317
13		12	(a)	Chester	L	0-2		6,966
14		14	(a)	Halifax T	L	0-2		3,760
15		19	(h)	York C	W	1-0	Smyth	5,549
16		23	(h)	Tranmere R	W	5-0	Phoenix, Mitchell, Curtis, Henderson, Rees	5,701
17		26	(a)	Barrow	D	1-1	Harvey (pen)	3,214
18		28	(a)	Tranmere R	L	1-2	Harvey (pen)	5,471
19	Nov	2	(h)	Rochdale	L	0-1		6,249
20		9	(a)	Oxford U	W	2-0	Curtis, Banks	7,185
21		23	(a)	Newport C	W	1-0	Banks	3,339
22		29	(h)	Stockport C	W	2-0	Rees, Banks	7,058
23	Dec	14	(h)	Bradford C	W	4-1	Banks, Mitchell, Ellam (og), Grace	5,566
24		21	(a)	Lincoln C	D	1-1	Grace	3,673
25		26	(a)	Brighton & HA	W	2-1	Thorne, Banks	10,250
26		28	(h)	Brighton & HA	D	0-0		9,873
27	Jan	4	(h)	Workington	W	2-1	Banks, Grace	7,286
28		11	(h)	Gillingham	D	0-0		10,905
29		18	(a)	Southport	D	1-1	Banks	1,618
30		25	(a)	Bradford	L	2-3	Banks, Grace	6,273
31	Feb	1	(a)	Doncaster R	L	0-1		8,083
32		8	(h)	Hartlepools	W	2-1	Banks, Rees	6,177
33		15	(a)	Darlington	D	1-1	Rees	
34		22	(h)	Chester	W	3-0	Banks, Mitchell, Ley	6,589
35		28	(a)	York C	W	2-1	Banks 2	3,817
36	Mar	7	(h)	Barrow	D	0-0		
37		14	(a)	Rochdale	W	3-1	Banks, Thorne 2	2,113
38		21	(h)	Oxford U	W	3-2	Thorne, Kyle (og), Curtis	6,602
39		27	(h)	Torquay U	D	0-0		16,141
40		30	(a)	Torquay U	D	1-1	Curtis	13,655
41	Apr	4	(h)	Newport C	W	3-1	Banks 2, Harvey	6,077
42		11	(a)	Stockport C	D	0-0		2,773
43		13	(a)	Chesterfield	W	1-0	Banks	4,442
44		18	(h)	Bradford	L	2-3	Harvey (pen), Rees	9,722
45		21	(h)	Chesterfield	W	6-1	Curtis, Banks 2, Thorne 2, Rees	9,449
46		25	(a)	Workington	D	0-0		8,600

FINAL LEAGUE POSITION: 4th in Division Four (Promoted)

Appearances
Goals

FA Cup

1	Nov	16	(h)	Shrewsbury T	W	2-1
2	Dec	7	(h)	Bristol C	L	0-2

League Cup

1	Sep	25	(a)	Hull C	L	0-1

Barnett	Smyth	Patrick	Mitchell	Harvey	Anderson	Rees	Henderson	Curtis	Edgar	Spiers	Cochrane	MacDonald	Grace	Ley	Phoenix	Rutley	Northcott	Banks	Thorne	Hancock	Parkhill	
1	2	3	4	5	6	7	8	9	10	11												1
1	2	3	4	5	6	7	8	9	10	11												2
1	2	3	4	5	6	10	8	9		11	7											3
1	2		4	5	6	11	8	9			7	3	10									4
1	2		4	5	6	7	8	9				3	10	11								5
1	2		4	5	6	7	8	9				3	10	11								6
1	2		4	5	6	7	8	9				3	10	11								7
1	7	2	4	5	6	11	8	9				3	10									8
1	2		4	5	6	7	8	9				3	10	11								9
1	2		4	5	6	7	8	9				3	10	11								10
1	2		4	5	6	7		9	10			3		11	8							11
1	2		4	5	6	7		9	10			3		11	8							12
1	2		4	5	6	7		9				3		11	10	8						13
1	2			5	6	7		8	10			3		11	4	9						14
1	2		4	5	6	7	10	9	8			3		11								15
1	2		4	5	6	7	10	9	8			3		11								16
1	2		4	5	6	7		9	10			3		11								17
1	2	3	4	5	6	7	10	9						11				8				18
1	2		4	5	6	7		9				3	10	11				8				19
1	2		4	5	6	7		9				3	10		11			8				20
1	2		4	5	6	7		9				3	10		11			8				21
1	2		4	5	6	7						3	10		11			8	9			22
1	2		4	5	6	7						3	10		11			8	9			23
1	2		4	5	6	7						3	10		11			8	9			24
1	2		4	5	6	7						3	10		11			8	9			25
1	2		4	5	6	7						3	10		11			8	9			26
1	2		4	5	6	7		9				3	10					8	11			27
1	2		4	5	6	7		9				3	10					8	11			28
1	2		4	5	6	7		9				3	10					8	11			29
1		2	4	5	6	11		7				3	10					8	9			30
1		2	4	5	6	7		9				3	10					8	11			31
1	2		4	5	6	7						3	10		11			8	9			32
1	2		4	5	6			9				3	10		11			8	7			33
1	2		4	5	6	7						3	10		11			8	9			34
1	2		4	5	6	7						3	10		11			8	9			35
1	2			5	6	7	10	9				3	4					8	11			36
1	2			5	6	7		9				3	4					8	11	10		37
1	2		10	5	6	7		9				3						8	11	4		38
1	2			5	6	7		9				3	10					8	11	4		39
	2			5	6	7		9				3	10					8	11	4	1	40
1	2			5	6	7		9				3	10					8	11	4		41
1	2			5	6	7		9				3	10					8	11	4		42
1	2			5	6	7	8	9				3	10						11	4		43
1	2		4	5	6	7		9				3						8	11	10		44
1	2		4	5	6	7		9				3						8	11	10		45
1	2		4	5	6	7		9				3						8	11	10		46
45	44	7	38	46	46	45	22	32	6	5	2	42	32	14	15	2	1	28	24	9	1	
	1		3	5			6	6	9				4	1	1				18	6		

2 own-goals

1964-65

Manager: Jack Edwards/Ellis Stuttard (from Jan 1965)

1	Aug	22	(h)	Peterborough U	W 4-2	Harvey (pen), Rees, Mitchell, Curtis	10,218
2		26	(a)	Bournemouth	D 2-2	Hancock, Curtis	12,342
3		29	(a)	Grimsby T	L 1-2	Carter	7,737
4	Sep	5	(h)	Mansfield T	L 2-3	Carter, Harvey (pen)	8,357
5		8	(a)	Shrewsbury T	L 0-1		6,557
6		12	(a)	Luton T	W 2-1	Carter, Curtis	10,461
7		16	(h)	Shrewsbury T	L 0-1		7,671
8		19	(h)	Carlisle U	D 0-0		7,502
9		26	(a)	Port Vale	W 1-0	Banks	7,006
10		28	(a)	Oldham A	L 0-2		9,879
11	Oct	3	(h)	Colchester U	W 2-0	Welsh, Rees	5,859
12		8	(h)	Oldham A	W 2-1	Welsh, Hancock	5,939
13		10	(a)	Southend U	D 0-0		6,552
14		14	(h)	Brentford	D 0-0		7,500
15		17	(h)	Barnsley	W 3-0	Rees, Harvey (pen), Curtis	6,306
16		20	(a)	Brentford	L 1-2	Mitchell	12,100
17		24	(a)	Scunthorpe U	D 0-0		4,086
18		31	(h)	Walsall	L 0-1		6,667
19	Nov	7	(a)	Watford	L 0-1		7,818
20		21	(a)	Hull C	L 1-3	Carter	11,786
21		28	(h)	Gillingham	D 1-1	Rees	5,088
22	Dec	12	(a)	Peterborough U	D 0-0		7,817
23		19	(h)	Grimsby T	W 4-1	Anderson, Thorne, Banks, Curtis	5,291
24		26	(h)	Reading	D 2-2	Banks, Thorne	8,712
25	Jan	2	(a)	Mansfield T	L 1-2	Rees	6,768
26		8	(h)	Scunthorpe U	L 1-3	Banks	6,092
27		16	(h)	Luton T	W 5-1	Curtis, Banks, Harvey (pen), Welsh, Mitchell	4,686
28		30	(a)	Bristol C	D 1-1	Banks	8,450
29	Feb	6	(h)	Port Vale	W 2-1	Banks 2	5,456
30		13	(a)	Colchester U	D 1-1	Curtis	3,073
31		20	(h)	Southend U	D 1-1	Welsh	4,946
32		27	(a)	Barnsley	D 0-0		2,822
33	Mar	6	(h)	Bristol C	L 0-1		7,319
34		9	(a)	Carlisle U	L 1-2	Curtis	11,544
35		13	(a)	Walsall	L 1-2	Hancock	6,463
36		20	(h)	Watford	W 1-0	Welsh	5,161
37		22	(h)	Workington	D 0-0		4,952
38		26	(a)	Workington	W 1-0	Curtis	3,495
39		31	(h)	Queen's Park R	D 2-2	Rees, Welsh	5,615
40	Apr	3	(h)	Hull C	L 0-2		6,571
41		7	(a)	Reading	D 2-2	Rees, Harvey	4,923
42		10	(a)	Gillingham	W 1-0	Burgess (og)	10,567
43		16	(a)	Bristol R	D 1-1	Welsh	12,194
44		19	(h)	Bristol R	L 0-1		8,165
45		23	(a)	Queen's Park R	D 0-0		4,060
46		28	(h)	Bournemouth	L 1-3	Ley	4,956

FINAL LEAGUE POSITION: 17th in Division Three

Appearances
Goals

FA Cup

1	Nov	14	(h)	Hayes	W 1-0
2	Dec	5	(h)	Shrewsbury T	L 1-2

League Cup

1	Sep	2	(h)	Gillingham	W 2-0
2		23	(h)	Bradford C	L 3-5

248

Barnett	Smyth	MacDonald	Mitchell	Harvey	Anderson	Welsh	Curtis	Carter	Hancock	Rees	Fulton	Banks	Shearing	Patrick	Grace	Ley	Rutley	Redwood	Thorne	
1	2	3	4	5	6	7	8	9	10	11										1
1		3	4	5	6	7	8	9	10	11	2									2
1		3	4	5	6		7	9	10	11	2	8								3
1		3		5	4	7	10	9	6	11	2	8								4
1		3	4	5	6	7	8	9	10	11	2									5
		3	4	5	6	7	8	9	10	11	2		1							6
		3	4		5	7	9	10	6	11	2	8	1							7
	2		4	5	6	7		9	10	11		8	1	3						8
	2		4	5	6	7	9	3				8	1		10	11				9
	2		4	5	6	7	9	3				8	1		10	11				10
	2			5	6	7	9	4		11		8	1	3	10					11
	2			5	6	7	9	4		11		8	1	3	10					12
	2	3		5	6	7	9	4		11		8	1		10					13
	2		4	5	6	7	9	3	10	11		8	1							14
	2		4	5	6		9		10	7		8	1	3		11				15
	2		4	5	6				10	11		8	1	3			7	9		16
	2		4	5	6		9		10	7			1	3		11	8			17
	2		4	5	6	7	8	9	10	11			1	3						18
	2		4	5	6	7	9		10	8			1	3		11				19
	2	3	4	5	6	7	8	9	10	11			1							20
	2	3		5	6	7	8	9		11			1			10	4			21
	2	3	4	5	6	7	8	10					1				9		11	22
	2	3	4	5	6	7	9					8	1			10			11	23
	2	3	4	5	6	7	9					8	1			10			11	24
	2	3	4	5	6		9	10		7		8	1						11	25
	2	3	4	5	6		10	9		7		8	1						11	26
	2	3	4	5	6	7	9	10				8	1						11	27
	2		4	5	6	7	9	10				8	1	3					11	28
	2		4	5	6	7	9	10				8	1	3					11	29
	2		4	5	6	7	9	8	10				1	3					11	30
	2		4	5	6	7	9	8	10				1	3					11	31
	2		4	5	6	7	9	8	10				1	3					11	32
	2		4	5	6	7	9	8	10				1	3					11	33
	2		4	5	6	7	9	8	10				1	3					11	34
	2		4	5	6	7	9	10	8				1	3		11				35
	2		4	5	6	7	9	8					1	3	10				11	36
	2		4	5	6	7	9	8					1	3	10				11	37
	2			5	4	7	9	8		6			1	3		11	10			38
	2			5	4	7	9	8		6			1	3		11	10			39
	2		4	5		7	9	10	8	6			1	3		11				40
	2		4	5	10	7	9	8		6			1	3		11				41
	2		4	5	10	8	9	7	11	6			1	3						42
	2		4	5	10	7	9	8	11	6			1	3						43
	2		4	5	10	7	9	8	11	6			1	3						44
	2		4	5		7	9			6		8	1	3		11			10	45
	2		4	5		7	9			6		8	1	3		11			10	46
5	40	15	43	42	43	40	42	26	31	33	15	19	41	25	7	15	6	1	17	
		3	5	1	7	9	4	3	7	8						1			2	

1 own-goal

1965-66

Manager: Ellis Stuttard/Jock Basford (from April 1966)

1	Aug	21	(h)	Oldham A	W	4-0	Banks 2, McLean, Welsh	7,271
2		25	(a)	Gillingham	D	1-1	Banks	10,540
3		28	(a)	Watford	L	0-3		10,580
4	Sep	4	(h)	Scunthorpe U	W	4-0	McLean 2, Welsh, Curtis	5,818
5		11	(a)	Brighton & HA	L	1-2	Carter	13,252
6		13	(a)	Millwall	L	0-3		12,288
7		18	(h)	Queen's Park R	D	0-0		6,223
8		25	(a)	Mansfield	D	0-0		7,511
9	Oct	2	(h)	Hull C	L	1-4	Banks	7,125
10		6	(h)	Millwall	L	1-2	Banks	6,770
11		9	(a)	Workington	L	1-6	Ley	3,903
12		16	(h)	Bournemouth	W	1-0	Harvey (pen)	5,383
13		23	(a)	Southend U	L	2-4	Curtis 2	7,212
14		30	(h)	Swindon T	D	1-1	Curtis	6,722
15	Nov	6	(a)	Shrewsbury T	L	0-4		4,559
16		20	(a)	Brentford	W	2-1	Peapell, Banks	5,943
17		27	(h)	Bristol R	W	1-0	Ley	5,964
18	Dec	4	(h)	Gillingham	W	3-1	McLean 2, Kennedy	5,000
19		11	(h)	Oxford U	L	1-2	Ley	7,000
20		17	(a)	Bournemouth	W	1-0	Banks	4,655
21		27	(h)	Swansea T	D	1-1	Banks	9,132
22	Jan	1	(h)	Workington	W	2-1	Blain, Stuckey	6,000
23		8	(a)	Grimsby T	D	1-1	Harvey (pen)	7,514
24		15	(h)	Southend U	D	1-1	Banks	4,845
25		22	(a)	Swansea T	L	0-1		7,212
26		29	(a)	Oldham A	L	1-3	McLean	13,449
27	Feb	5	(h)	Watford	L	1-2	Banks	4,775
28		19	(a)	Scunthorpe U	L	1-2	Rees	4,396
29	Mar	5	(h)	Peterborough U	L	2-5	Kennedy, Harvey (pen)	5,362
30		12	(a)	Queen's Park R	L	0-1		7,542
31		19	(h)	Mansfield T	D	2-2	Keeley, Carter	5,055
32	Apr	2	(h)	Shrewsbury T	D	0-0		4,515
33		9	(a)	York C	L	0-2		2,726
34		11	(a)	Walsall	D	1-1	Banks	9,478
35		13	(h)	Walsall	L	0-2		4,700
36		16	(h)	Brentford	W	5-0	Banks 2, McLean 2, Kennedy	4,975
37		20	(a)	Hull C	L	1-6	Banks	28,055
38		23	(a)	Bristol R	L	0-2		6,803
39		27	(h)	Reading	L	1-2	Kennedy	4,500
40		30	(h)	York C	L	0-2		3,985
41	May	3	(h)	Brighton & HA	W	2-0	Curtis, Banks	3,344
42		7	(a)	Oxford U	W	1-0	Mitchell	6,703
43		9	(a)	Peterborough U	L	0-2		4,467
44		18	(a)	Reading	L	1-4	Banks	4,160
45		21	(h)	Grimsby T	W	2-0	McLean, Banks	3,770
46		28	(a)	Swindon T	D	2-2	McLean 2	6,593

FINAL LEAGUE POSITION: 22nd in Division Three (Relegated)

Appearances
Sub Appearances
Goals

FA Cup
1 Nov 13 (h) Bedford T L 1-2

League Cup
1 Sep 1 (a) Colchester U L 1-2

250

Shearing	Smyth	Peapell	Mitchell	Harvey	Fulton	Welsh	Banks	McLean	Carter	Ley	Curtis	MacDonald	Anderson	Rees	Barnett	Buckingham	Blain	Stuckey	Kennedy	Tolchard	Riding	Harford	Evans	Keeley	Elliott	
1	2	3	4	5	6	7	8	9	10	11																1
1	2	3	4	5	6	7	8	9	10	11																2
1	2	3	4	5	6	7		9	10	11	8															3
1		2	4	5	6*	7		9	8	11	10	3	12													4
		2	4	5		7		9	10	11	8	3	6													5
1	2		4	5	6	7		9	10		8	3		11												6
	2		4	5	6	7		9		11		3	8	1	10											7
1	2		4	5	6	7	8	9				3		11		10										8
1	2	3		5	4	7	8	9			10			11		6										9
1	2	3*		5	6	7	8		4	11	9		12			10										10
1	2	11		5	4	7	8	9			3	10				6										11
1	2	11		5	4	7	8	9			3	10				6										12
1	2	11	4	5	6		8	9			3	10					7									13
1	2	12	4	5	6		8				3	9*		11		10	7									14
1	2		4	5			8	9			3			10		6	11	7								15
1	2	4		5			8	9				3				6	11	7	10							16
1	2	4		5			8	9				3				6	11	7	10							17
1	2	4		5			8	9				3				6	11	7	10							18
1	2	4		5			8	9				3				6	11	7	10							19
1	2	4		5			8	9				3				6	11	7	10							20
1	2	4		5			8	9				3				6	11	7	10							21
1	2	4		5			8	9				3				6	11	7	10							22
1	2	4		5			8	9				3				6	11	7	10							23
1	2	4		5			8	9				3				6	11	7	10							24
1	2	4		5			8	9				3				6	11	7	10							25
1	2		4	5			8					3	9			6		7	10	11						26
1	2	4		5			8					3			11	6	7		10		9					27
1	3							10	9			2			7	6	11		8			4				28
	2		6	5			8		9	3				1			11	7	10			4				29
	2		6	5		7		9				3			11	1						4	8	10		30
	2			5	3			9				6		1			11	7				4	8	10		31
	2			5	3			9				6		1			12	7				4	8*	10	11	32
	2			5	3		8*	10				6		1			11	12				4		7	9	33
	2			5	3		8	10				6		1			11					4		7	9	34
1	2			5	3		9	10	7			6	11						8			4				35
1	2			5	3		8	9	7			6	11						10			4				36
1	2			5	3		8	9	7			6	11						10			4*	12			37
1	2			5	3		8	9				6	11						7			4	10			38
1	2		4	5			8	9					11	6	7									10		39
1	2		4				8	9	7			10	3	6	11							5				40
1	2		4				8	10	7				9	3		6	11					5				41
1	2		4				8	10	7				9	3		6	11					5				42
1	2		4				10			11	9	3				6	7					5	8			43
1	2						10	9	7	3	11					6						5	8			44
1	2						9		3							6		11	4			5	8	10	7	45
39	44	23	19	40	22	13	38	34	22	31	17	10	9	13	7	28	24	14	22	1	1	17	7	7	4	46
	1	1	3		2	17	11	2	3	5		1				1	1	4				1				

1966-67

Manager: Jock Basford

1	Aug	20	(a)	Wrexham	D 0-0	7,133
2		27	(h)	Southend U	L 0-1	4,346
3	Sep	3	(a)	Tranmere R	D 1-1 Thompson	3,495
4		5	(a)	Crewe A	D 2-2 Elliott, Blain	4,152
5		10	(h)	Bradford C	D 2-2 Evans 2	4,600
6		17	(h)	Port Vale	L 0-1	5,000
7		24	(a)	Hartlepools U	L 1-3 Smith	4,227
8		27	(h)	Crewe A	W 2-0 Godfrey, McNeil	3,831
9	Oct	1	(h)	Halifax T	W 3-2 Smith 2, McNeil	4,559
10		8	(a)	Barrow	L 0-5	4,163
11		15	(h)	York C	W 3-1 Ley, McNeil, Keeley	4,174
12		22	(a)	Lincoln C	D 1-1 Godfrey	2,894
13		24	(h)	Barnsley	L 1-2 McNeil	3,573
14		29	(h)	Chesterfield	D 1-1 McNeil	4,102
15	Nov	4	(a)	Stockport C	L 0-1	8,960
16		12	(h)	Rochdale	D 0-0	3,625
17		16	(h)	Barnsley	L 0-3	2,753
18		19	(a)	Southport	D 1-1 McLean	3,085
19	Dec	3	(a)	Chester	W 2-0 Keeley, Blain (pen)	3,347
20		10	(h)	Bradford	W 4-1 Kennedy, McNeil 2, Keeley	4,285
21		17	(h)	Wrexham	W 4-1 Keeley 3 (1 pen), Stuckey	7,044
22		26	(h)	Newport C	D 0-0	4,082
23		27	(a)	Newport C	L 2-3 Kennedy, McNeil	6,581
24		31	(a)	Southend U	D 0-0	6,090
25	Jan	14	(a)	Bradford C	D 1-1 Keeley	3,450
26		21	(a)	Port Vale	L 0-2	4,300
27		28	(h)	Tranmere R	L 1-4 Ryan	3,702
28	Feb	4	(h)	Hartlepools U	W 1-0 Ryan	6,775
29		11	(a)	Halifax T	D 0-0	3,764
30		18	(h)	Luton T	W 2-1 Elliott, Keeley	3,550
31		25	(h)	Barrow	L 1-2 Ryan	3,141
32	Mar	3	(a)	York C	W 4-2 Ryan, Godfrey, Elliott, Keeley	6,045
33		11	(a)	Luton T	L 0-4	3,142
34		18	(h)	Lincoln C	W 1-0 Blain	4,642
35		24	(a)	Aldershot	L 0-1	4,258
36		25	(a)	Notts C	W 1-0 Godfrey	4,248
37		27	(h)	Aldershot	D 1-1 McNeil	4,059
38	Apr	1	(h)	Stockport C	L 0-3	1,294
39		8	(a)	Rochdale	L 0-1	7,800
40		11	(a)	Brentford	L 1-3 Ley	3,044
41		15	(h)	Southport	D 0-0	3,665
42		22	(a)	Chesterfield	L 0-1	2,934
43		25	(h)	Brentford	W 1-0 Ryan	3,077
44		29	(h)	Chester	W 2-0 Singleton (og), McNeil	3,172
45	May	6	(a)	Bradford	D 2-2 McNeil, Harford	3,417
46		13	(h)	Notts C	W 1-0 Stuckey	

FINAL LEAGUE POSITION: 14th in Division Four

Appearances
Sub Appearances
Goals

FA Cup

1	Nov	26	(h)	Luton T	D 1-1
R	Dec	1	(a)	Luton T	L 0-2

League Cup

1	Aug	24	(h)	Torquay U	D 2-2
R		31	(a)	Torquay U	W 2-1
2	Sep	14	(a)	Cardiff C	W 1-0
3	Oct	5	(h)	Walsall	L 1-2

Jones	Smyth	Ley	Wilkinson	Harford	Thompson	Godfrey	Keeley	McLean	Kennedy	McNeil	Elliott	Evans	Blain	Nash	Embury	Smith	Smout	Buckingham	Harvey	Stuckey	Ryan	Balsom	Match
1	2	3	4	5	6	7	8	9	10	11													1
1	2	3	4	5	6	7	8	9	10				11										2
1	2	3	4	5	6	7	8			9	10	11											3
1	2	3	4	5	6	7	8			9	10	11											4
1	2		4	5	6	7	8	9			10	11		3									5
1		3	4	5	6	7	8			9		11			2	10							6
1		3	4	5	6	7	8		10	9					2	11							7
1		3	4	5	6	7	8		10	9					2	11							8
1		3	4	5	6	7	8		10	9					2	11							9
1		3	4	5	6	7	8		10	9					2								10
1		3*	4	5	6	7	8		10	11	9		12		2								11
1		3	4	5	6*	7	8		11	10	9		12		2								12
1		3	4	5		7	8		11	10	9		6		2								13
1		3	4	5		7	8		11	10	9		6		2								14
		3	4	5		7	8	9	11	10			6		2		1						15
	3	9	4*	5			8	10	11	7			6		2		1			12			16
	2	3	4	5	10	7	8	9					6				1	11					17
	2		4	5	6	7	8	9	11	10			3				1						18
	2		4		6	7	11	9	10	8			3				1			5			19
	2		4*		6	11	9	8	10				3				1		12	5			20
	2		4		6	11	7	9	8	10			3				1			5			21
1	2		4	5	6	11	7	9	8	10			3										22
	2		4		6	11	7	9	8	10			3				1			5			23
			4		6	11	7		8	10			3		2		1			5	9		24
		3	4		6	11	7		8	10			2				1			5	9		25
		3	4		12	11	8		10				6		2		1			5*	7	9	26
		3	4	5	6	11	7			8			10		2		1				9		27
	12	3	4	5	6						10		8*		2	11	1			7	9		28
		3	4	5	6		12		10*				8		2	11	1			7	9		29
		3	4	5	6	11	7			8			10		2		1				9		30
	12	3	4*	5	6	11	7			8			10		2		1				9		31
		3	4	5	6	11	7			8			10		2		1				9		32
		3	4	5	6	11	7			8			10		2		1				9		33
			4	5	6	11	7			10		8	3		2		1				9		34
	2		4	5	6	11	7			10		8	3				1				9		35
	2		4	5	6	11	7			10		8	3				1				9		36
	2	3	4	5	6	11	7			10			8				1				9		37
1	2	3	4	5		7	11						6						10		9		38
	2	3	4	5*	6					10			8		12		1			7	9		39
	2	3	4	5	6					10			8				1			7	9		40
	2	3	4	5	6					10			8				1			7	9		41
	2	3	4	5*	6					10			8		12		1			7	9		42
	2	3	4		6					10			8		5		1			11	9		43
	2	3	4		6	7				10			8		12		1			11	9		44
	2	3	4	5						10			7		6		1			11		9	45
	2		4	5		7				11	10	3			6		1			8		9	46
17	25	33	46	38	38	42	38	13	18	31	24	4	37	1	25	6	29	1	7	11	20	2	
	2				1		1						2	2					2				
	2		1	1	4	9	1	2	11	3	2	3		3			3				2	5	

1 own-goal

1967-68

Manager: Frank Broome

					Result	Scorers	Attendance
1	Aug	19	(a)	Bradford C	L 1-2	Fudge	5,000
2		26	(h)	Crewe A	L 1-4	Whatling	4,647
3	Sep	2	(a)	Notts C	L 0-1		3,741
4		4	(a)	Halifax T	D 1-1	Huxford	4,752
5		9	(h)	Port Vale	W 3-1	Stuckey, Whatling, Fudge	3,722
6		16	(a)	Chester	L 1-3	Stuckey	4,000
7		23	(h)	Chesterfield	D 1-1	Fudge	3,845
8		27	(h)	Halifax T	D 0-0		3,948
9		30	(a)	Swansea T	D 1-1	Curtis	6,712
10	Oct	4	(a)	Workington	L 0-1		2,770
11		7	(h)	Wrexham	D 2-2	Stuckey, Blain	3,500
12		14	(a)	Southend U	L 0-1		9,000
13		21	(h)	Luton T	L 0-5		3,500
14		25	(h)	Workington	W 1-0	Tugman (og)	3,090
15		28	(a)	Doncaster R	L 1-3	Hamilton	6,000
16	Nov	11	(a)	Brentford	L 1-5	Fudge	7,215
17		15	(h)	Notts C	D 3-3	Crawford, Hart, Blain	4,002
18		18	(h)	Rochdale	W 3-1	Curtis, Banks 2	4,072
19		25	(a)	York C	L 0-4		2,795
20	Dec	2	(h)	Newport C	W 2-1	Fudge, Collins (og)	4,208
21		16	(h)	Bradford C	W 4-1	Curtis 2, Corr 2	3,861
22		23	(a)	Crewe A	L 0-2		4,595
23		26	(a)	Aldershot	D 0-0		6,532
24		30	(h)	Aldershot	W 3-0	Corr 2, Curtis	5,046
25	Jan	20	(h)	Chester	W 1-0	Corr	4,336
26		27	(a)	Barnsley	L 1-2	Newman	11,612
27	Feb	3	(a)	Chesterfield	D 1-1	Blain	11,631
28		10	(h)	Swansea T	L 1-3	Fudge	3,961
29		17	(a)	Darlington	W 1-0	Curtis	2,888
30		24	(a)	Rochdale	D 2-2	Blain, Corr	2,159
31	Mar	2	(h)	Southend U	L 0-2		3,705
32		9	(h)	Barnsley	W 2-0	Banks 2	3,840
33		16	(a)	Luton T	D 0-0		12,409
34		23	(h)	Doncaster R	L 0-1		3,323
35		25	(a)	Port Vale	L 0-1		3,395
36		30	(a)	Bradford	W 1-0	Banks	1,956
37	Apr	1	(a)	Hartlepools U	L 1-3	Coughlin	4,502
38		6	(h)	Brentford	L 0-3		3,900
39		12	(h)	Lincoln C	L 0-1		3,853
40		13	(a)	Wrexham	D 0-0		5,000
41		15	(a)	Lincoln C	D 1-1	Pinkney	8,129
42		20	(h)	York C	W 3-1	Blain (pen), Corr, Coughlin	3,526
43		27	(a)	Newport C	D 1-1	Banks	1,605
44	May	1	(h)	Bradford	D 0-0		3,535
45		4	(h)	Hartlepools U	D 0-0		3,693
46		11	(h)	Darlington	D 0-0		3,515

FINAL LEAGUE POSITION: 20th in Division Four

Appearances
Sub Appearances
Goals

FA Cup

1	Dec	9	(a)	Nuneaton B	D 0-0	
R		13	(h)	Nuneaton B	D 0-0	
2R		18	(n*)	Nuneaton B	W 1-0	*Played at Ashton Gate, Bristol.
2	Jan	6	(h)	Walsall	L 1-3	

League Cup

1	Aug	22	(a)	Torquay U	D 0-0
R		28	(h)	Torquay U	L 0-3

254

Smout	Smyth	Crawford	Curtis	Wilkinson	Huxford	Blain	Stuckey	Balson	Fudge	Whatling	Embury	Hart	Harvey	Hamilton	Newman	Banks	Corr	Pinkney	Coughlin	
1	2	3	4*	5	6	7	8	9	10	11	12									1
1	2	3		5	12	6	8	9*	10	11	4	7								2
1	2	3	9*	4	6	8	11	12	10			7	5							3
1	2	3			6	4	8	9	10	11		7	5							4
1	2	3	9		6	4	8		10	11		7	5							5
1	2	3	9		6	4	10	7	8	11			5							6
1	2	3	9	12	6	4	10	7*	8	11			5							7
1	2	3	9		6	4	11	8	10			7	5							8
1	2	3	9		6	4	11	8	10			7	5							9
1	2	3	9	8	6	4	11		10			7	5							10
1	2	3		4	6	8	11		10			7	5	9						11
1	2	3		4	6	9		8	11			7	5	10						12
1		8	6*	5	4	3		9	12	11	2	7		10						13
1		8	4	5	6	3		9	11		2	7		10						14
1			10	4	6	3		9	7	11	2		5		8					15
1		10	9	5	3	6			11		2	7	4		8					16
1		10	9	5		6		3	11		2	7	4		8					17
1		10	9	5		6		3	11		2	7	4		8					18
1	3	10	9			4				11	2	7	5	6	8					19
1	3	10	9		6	4		7			2		5		8	11				20
1	3	10	9		6	4		7			2		5		8	11				21
1	2	11	9		6	10		3				7	5	4	8					22
1	2	12	9		6	10		3				7*	5	4	8	11				23
1	2	10	9		6	7		3					5	4	8	11				24
1	2	10			6	7		9	8		3		5	4		11				25
1	2	10	9		6	7		3					5	4	8	11				26
1	2	10	9		6	7		3	11				5	4	8					27
1	2	10	9		6	7		3	11				5	4			8			28
1	2	10	9	6		7		3	8				5	4		11				29
1	2	10	9		6	4		3	7				5		8	11				30
1	2	7*			6	10		3	11			5	4		8	12			9	31
1	2		10		6	11		3	7			5	4		8				9	32
1	2	7	10		6	11		3				5	4		8				9	33
1	2	8*	10		6	7		3	11		12	5	4						9	34
1	2		10		6	7		3				5	4		8	11			9	35
1	2		10		6	9		3	11		7	5			8				4	36
1	2				4			3	11		7	5	6		8			10	9	37
1	2			6	11*			3	12			5	4		8	7		10	9	38
1	2	7		6				3				5	4		8	11		10	9	39
1	2	7		6				3				5	4		8	11		10	9	40
1	2		10		6	11		3				5	4		8		7		9	41
1	2		10		6	8		3				5	4			11	7		9	42
1	2		10		6	4		3	7			5			8	11			9	43
1	2	10	9		6	8		3				5	4			11	7			44
1	2	10*	9		6	8		3			12	5	4			11	7			45
46	40	36	35	13	40	44	12	37	32	10	11	20	34	4	30	27	17	5	13	46
	1		1	1			1	2		1	2						1			
	1	6		1	5	3		6	2		1		1	1	6	7	1	2		

2 own-goals

1968-69

Manager: Frank Broome until February 1968, then John Newman.

No	Month	Date		Opponent	Result	Scorers	Att
1	Aug	10	(a)	Peterborough U	D 1-1	Corr	8,532
2		17	(h)	Chesterfield	W 3-0	Bullock, Pleat, Blain	7,241
3		24	(a)	Rochdale	D 1-1	Mitten (pen)	3,225
4		31	(h)	Brentford	D 2-2	Banks 2	8,835
5	Sep	7	(a)	Doncaster R	L 1-3	Blain	8,590
6		9	(a)	Bradford	L 1-2	Bullock	2,591
7		14	(h)	Chester	D 2-2	Kirkham, Corr	5,121
8		18	(h)	Bradford C	L 2-3	Banks 2	6,182
9		21	(a)	Scunthorpe U	L 1-2	Mitten (pen)	3,620
10		28	(h)	Colchester U	D 1-1	Banks	5,146
11		30	(a)	Port Vale	L 0-1		5,235
12	Oct	5	(h)	Aldershot	D 0-0		4,595
13		8	(h)	Port Vale	W 3-1	Kirkham, Banks 2	3,981
14		11	(a)	Southend U	L 1-6	Banks	9,935
15		19	(h)	Notts C	D 0-0		4,123
16		26	(a)	Darlington	W 2-1	Corr, Balson	6,868
17		28	(a)	York C	W 2-0	Banks 2	2,594
18	Nov	2	(h)	Grimsby T	D 2-2	Banks, Pleat	5,178
19		6	(h)	Lincoln C	W 3-0	Corr, Balson, Banks	4,332
20		9	(a)	Workington	L 0-3		2,165
21		23	(a)	Halifax T	L 1-2	Whatling	3,186
22		30	(h)	Swansea T	L 0-1		3,851
23	Dec	14	(h)	Southend U	L 1-2	Pleat	12,714
24		21	(a)	Notts C	L 1-3	Corr	4,605
25		26	(a)	Aldershot	L 0-2		8,642
26	Jan	11	(a)	Grimsby T	W 2-1	Kirkham, Pleat	2,981
27		25	(a)	Lincoln C	L 2-3	Kirkham, Pleat	9,105
28	Feb	1	(a)	Newport C	L 1-2	Kirkham	1,427
29		24	(h)	Bradford	W 4-2	Crawford, Kirkham, Binney, Mitten (pen)	3,745
30	Mar	1	(h)	Peterborough U	L 0-1		4,604
31		8	(a)	Chesterfield	L 0-2		5,124
32		12	(h)	Newport C	W 2-0	Binney 2	3,264
33		15	(h)	Rochdale	D 2-2	Mitten, Binney	4,067
34		18	(h)	Wrexham	W 5-3	Curtis, Binney 2, Pleat, Sharples	3,999
35		22	(a)	Brentford	W 1-0	Binney	5,240
36		24	(h)	Darlington	W 2-0	Pleat, Curtis	4,989
37		29	(h)	Doncaster R	D 0-0		6,744
38		31	(h)	Workington	W 1-0	Curtis	4,829
39	Apr	5	(a)	Colchester U	L 0-1		5,650
40		7	(a)	Bradford C	L 0-1		9,382
41		9	(h)	York C	W 5-0	Mitten 2 (1 pen), Wingate 2, Binney	5,083
42		12	(h)	Scunthorpe U	W 3-1	Pleat, Mitten (pen), Wingate	4,566
43		19	(a)	Chester	W 1-0	Curtis	2,821
44		21	(a)	Wrexham	D 2-2	Binney 2	3,228
45		24	(h)	Halifax T	W 2-1	Banks, Binney	
46	May	5	(a)	Swansea T	L 0-2		

FINAL LEAGUE POSITION: 17th in Division Four

Appearances
Sub Appearances
Goals

FA Cup

1	Nov	16	(h)	Newport C	D 0-0
R		18	(a)	Newport C	W 3-1
2	Dec	7	(a)	Colchester U	W 1-0
3	Jan	4	(h)	Manchester U	L 1-3

League Cup

1	Aug	14	(a)	Plymouth A	D 0-0
R		21	(h)	Plymouth A	D 0-0
2R		26	(n†)	Plymouth A	W 1-0*
2	Sep	4	(h)	Sheffield W	W 3-1
3		25	(a)	Tottenham H	L 3-6

†Played at Plainmoor, Torquay. *After extra-time

256

Shearing	Smyth	Balson	Kirkham	Harvey	Newman	Corr	Banks	Bullock	Mitten	Pleat	Blain	Crawford	Curtis	Whatling	Sharples	Pinkney	Rowlands	Binney	Parker	Wingate	
1	2	3	4	5	6	7	8	9	10	11											1
1	2	3	4	5	6		8	9	10	11	7										2
1	2	3	4	5	6		8	9	10	11*	7	12									3
1	2	3	4	5	6		8	9*	10	11	7		12								4
1	2	3		5	6	7		9	10	11	8		4								5
1	2	3	4	5	6	7		9	10	11	8										6
1		3	4	5*	12	7		9	10	11	8	2	6								7
1		3	4		6	7	8	9	10	11		2	5								8
1		3	4	5	6	7	8	9	10	11		2									9
1	2		4*	5	6	7	8	9	10	11	3		12								10
1	2	4		5	6		8	9	10	11	3	7									11
1	2	3		5	6*	7	8		10	11	4		9	12							12
1	2	6	4	5		7	8	9	10	11	3										13
1	2	6	4	5		7	8	9	10	11	3										14
1	2	6	4	5		7	8	9	10	11*	3			12							15
1	2	9	4	5		7	8		10	11	3		6								16
1	2	9	4	5		7	8		10	11	3		6								17
1	2	9	4	5		7	8		10*	11	3	12	6								18
1	2	9	10	5	4	7	8			11	3		6								19
1	2	9	10	5	4	7	8			11	3		6								20
1	2		9	5	6	7				8	3	4	10	11							21
1	2	9	4	5	6	7			10	11	3		8								22
1	2	8	10	5	6	7				11*	3	4	9	12							23
1	2	4	10		6	7				11	3		9		5	8					24
1	2	9		6	4	7			10	11	3				5	8					25
1		8	12	4	6	7			10	11	3	2	9		5*						26
1	2	4	8		6				10	7	3*	12	9	11	5						27
1	2	3	4		6				10	7			8	11	5		9				28
1	2	10	4		6				11	7	3	8			5			9			29
1	2	10	4	5	6	12			11	7	3	8*						9			30
1	2		10		6				11	7	3	12			5*			8	4	9	31
1	2		10		6				11	7	3				5			8	4	9	32
1	2		10		6				11	7	3				5			8	4	9	33
1	2				6					7	3		10	11	5			8	4	9	34
1	2				6					7	3		10	11	5			8	4	9	35
1	2	6			5				12	7	3		10	11				8	4*	9	36
1	2	4			6				10	7	3		5	11				8		9	37
1	2	6	4		5					7	3		10	11				8		9	38
1	2	6			5				12	7*	3		10	11				8	4	9	39
1	2	6			5				11	7	3		8					10	4	9	40
1	2				5	7			10	11	3		6					8	4	9	41
1	2				5	7	8		10	11	3		6						4	9	42
1		6	4		5		7		11		3	2	10					8		9	43
1		6	4		5		7		11		3	2	10					8		9	44
1		6			5	7	8			11	3	2	4					10		9	45
1	12	6			5		7		11		3	2	10					8*	4	9	46
46	38	37	31	25	39	25	22	14	35	43	42	13	29	9	11	2	1	17	11	16	
	1		1		1	1			2			4	2	3							
		2	6			5	13	2	7	8	2	1	4	1	1			11		3	

1969-70

Manager: John Newman

1	Aug	9	(a)	Wrexham	L 0-3		6,300
2		16	(h)	Darlington	L 1-2	Morris	5,125
3		23	(a)	Newport C	L 0-2		2,525
4		25	(a)	York C	L 0-1		6,200
5		30	(h)	Bradford	W 3-0	Giles, Wingate 2	4,457
6	Sep	6	(a)	Scunthorpe U	D 0-0		4,073
7		13	(h)	Workington	W 5-1	Wingate, Mitten 2 (1 pen), Pleat, Banks	4,536
8		17	(h)	Aldershot	W 2-1	Pleat, Banks	6,119
9		20	(a)	Notts C	L 0-4		6,358
10		27	(h)	Port Vale	L 1-2	Sharples	5,348
11	Oct	1	(h)	Swansea T	W 6-0	Blain 2, Corr 2, Wingate, Mitten	5,183
12		4	(a)	Lincoln C	L 0-1		5,791
13		6	(a)	Darlington	L 0-4		2,888
14		11	(h)	Crewe A	W 3-0	Walker, Crawford, Corr	5,101
15		18	(a)	Southend U	D 1-1	Mitten (pen)	
16		25	(h)	Grimsby T	L 0-1		5,459
17	Nov	1	(a)	Chester	L 0-2		4,387
18		8	(h)	Brentford	D 2-2	Pleat, Mitten	4,897
19		22	(a)	Oldham A	D 1-1	Corr	4,351
20		24	(a)	Chesterfield	L 1-2	Gadston	7,977
21		29	(h)	Peterborough U	D 1-1	Wingate	5,027
22	Dec	13	(a)	Workington	W 2-1	Gadston 2	1,342
23		20	(h)	Scunthorpe U	W 4-1	Balson, Gadston, Wingate, Walker	3,534
24		26	(h)	Newport C	D 1-1	Banks	6,700
25		27	(a)	Bradford	L 1-2	Pleat	
26	Jan	10	(h)	Notts C	D 1-1	Gadston	3,872
27		17	(a)	Port Vale	L 0-2		4,633
28		24	(h)	Hartlepool	W 6-0	Banks 3, Mitten (pen), Gadston, Gill (og)	4,341
29		31	(h)	Lincoln C	L 1-2	Banks	
30	Feb	7	(a)	Crewe A	D 1-1	Gadston	3,000
31		14	(h)	Wrexham	W 1-0	Banks	4,210
32		21	(a)	Grimsby T	L 0-2		2,767
33		24	(a)	Swansea C	D 0-0		
34		28	(h)	Southend U	W 3-0	Gadston, Pleat, Sharples	4,343
35	Mar	2	(a)	Northampton T	L 0-2		4,974
36		7	(h)	Oldham A	L 0-2		4,440
37		11	(h)	Colchester U	W 2-1	Mitten, Banks	4,017
38		14	(a)	Peterborough U	D 1-1	Wingate	5,283
39		16	(a)	Hartlepool	L 0-2		1,980
40		21	(h)	Northampton T	W 1-0	Gadston	4,981
41		27	(a)	Brentford	L 0-2		10,110
42		28	(a)	Colchester U	L 1-2	Wingate	3,842
43		30	(h)	Chester	W 1-0	Mitten	5,722
44	Apr	4	(a)	York C	W 2-1	Binney, Mitten (pen)	4,111
45		7	(h)	Chesterfield	D 1-1	Banks	5,443
46		15	(a)	Aldershot	L 0-1		5,000

FINAL LEAGUE POSITION: 18th in Division Four

Appearances
Sub Appearances
Goals

FA Cup

1	Nov	15	(h)	Fulham	W 2-0
2	Dec	6	(a)	Northampton T	D 1-1
R		10	(h)	Northampton T	D 0-0* *After extra-time
2R		15	(n†)	Northampton T	L 1-2 †Played at the County Ground, Swindon.

League Cup

1	Aug	13	(h)	Bristol C	D 1-1
R		19	(a)	Bristol C	L 2-3

	Shearing	Crawford	Blain	Parker	Newman	Balson	Pleat	Banks	Wingate	Giles	Walker	Morris	Corr	Mitten	Sharples	Gadston	Wilson	Binney
1	1	2	3	4	5	6	7	8	9	10	11							
2	1	2	3	6	5			9	12	8	11	4	7*	10				
3	1	2	3	4		6	12	8	9	7	11*			10	5			
4	1	2		4	6	3	11	8	9	7				10	5			
5	1	2		4		6	11	8	9	7		3		10	5			
6	1	2		4		6	11	8	9	7		3		10	5			
7	1	2		4		6	11	8	9	7		3		10	5			
8	1	2		4		6	11	8	9	7		3		10	5			
9	1	12	2	4		6	11*		9	7	8	3		10	5			
10	1	2		4		6	11		9	8*	12	3	7	10	5			
11	1	2	8	4		6			9	12	11	3	7	10	5*			
12	1	2	8	4	5	6			9		11	3	7	10				
13	1	2		4	6		5	12	8	10*	11	3	7	9				
14	1	2	8		5	6			9	4	11	3	7	10				
15	1	2	8		6		4		7	9	11	3		10	5			
16	1	2	8	4		6	7	12	9*		11	3		10	5			
17	1	2	8			6		7	9	4	11	3		10	5			
18	1	2	3			6	11	8		4*	12	7	10	5	9			
19	1	2	3			6	11	8			4	7	10	5	9			
20	1	2	3			6	11	8			4	7	10	5	9			
21	1	2		4		6		8	12		11	3	7*	10	5	9		
22	1	2		6		3		8			11	4	7	10	5	9		
23	1	2	3			6		9			11	4	7	10	5	8		
24	1	2	3	4		6	8*	12			11		7	10	5	9		
25	1	2	3	4		6	7		9		11			10	5	8		
26	1	2	3	4		6	7	8	10		12		11	5*	9			
27	1	2	3	4		6	7	10	8			11	5	9				
28		2	3	4		6	7	8			11		10	5	9	1		
29		2	3	4		6	7	8	12		11		10	5	9*	1		
30		2				6	3	8	9	7	4		10	5	11	1		
31			3	4		2	8	9	7	6			11	5	10	1		
32		2	6			3	8	9	7	4*	12	11	5	10		1		
33		2	3	4*		6	11	8	12		7		10	5	9	1		
34		2	3	4		6	7	8			11		10	5	9	1		
35		2	3	4		6	7		8		11		10	5	9	1		
36		2	3	4		6*	7	8	12		11		10	5	9	1		
37		2	3	6			8	10	7		4		11	5	9	1		
38		2	3	6			8	10	7		4		11	5	9	1		
39		2	3	6			8	10	7	12	4*		11	5	9	1		
40		2	3	4*		6		10	7		12		11	5	9	1	8	
41	2*		3	4		6		10	7		12		11	5	9	1	8	
42		2		6		3	8	10	7		4		11	5		1	9	
43		2	3	4*			8	10	6		12		11	5	9	1	7	
44		2	3			6	12	10	7		4		11*	5	9	1	8	
45		2	3			6	11	8	10		4	7		5		1	9	
46		2		4		3	11	8	6	10		7		5		1	9	
	27	37	41	39	4	41	23	34	31	28	21	28	16	43	41	26	19	7
	1							2	2	6	1	2		5	1			
	1	2				1	5	10	8	1	2	1	4	9	2	9		1

1 own-goal

1970-71

Manager: Johnny Newman

#	Month	Date		Opponent	Result	Scorers	Attendance
1	Aug	15	(h)	Scunthorpe U	D 1-1	Binney	5,456
2		22	(a)	Oldham A	L 1-2	Gadston	6,352
3		29	(h)	Peterborough U	W 3-2	Gadston 2, Rowan	4,537
4	Sept	2	(h)	Southend U	W 2-0	Corr, Gadston	5,190
5		5	(a)	Darlington	L 2-3	Horner (og), Sharples	3,472
6		12	(h)	Crewe A	W 6-2	John Giles, Gadston 2, Banks 2, Corr	4,769
7		19	(a)	Chester	L 1-3	Banks	4,337
8		21	(a)	Southport	W 2-0	Rowan 2	3,842
9		26	(h)	Notts C	L 0-1		6,093
10		29	(a)	Newport C	W 1-0	Gadston	2,169
11	Oct	3	(a)	Lincoln C	L 1-4	Gadston	6,548
12		10	(h)	Hartlepool	D 1-1	Mitten (pen)	4,590
13		17	(a)	Scunthorpe U	L 0-3		3,684
14		21	(h)	Grimsby T	W 4-0	Banks 3, Binney	4,087
15		24	(h)	Cambridge U	W 1-0	Rowan	5,631
16		31	(a)	Brentford	L 0-5		5,270
17	Nov	7	(h)	Colchester U	D 2-2	Gadston, Banks	4,420
18		11	(h)	Aldershot	W 4-1	Gadston 2, Banks, Corr	4,434
19		14	(a)	Barrow	D 1-1	Gadston	2,244
20		28	(a)	Workington	L 0-1		2,013
21	Dec	5	(h)	York C	L 0-2		4,403
22		12	(h)	Southport	W 2-1	Wingate, Binney	3,437
23		19	(h)	Oldham A	L 0-2		4,185
24	Jan	9	(h)	Newport C	D 1-1	Binney	4,142
25		16	(a)	Grimsby T	W 2-1	Gadston, Parker	2,926
26		22	(a)	Stockport C	W 3-0	Banks, Parker, Binney	1,992
27		27	(a)	Bournemouth	L 1-4	Gadston	9,184
28	Feb	6	(a)	York C	D 2-2	Rowan, Banks	3,234
29		9	(h)	Northampton T	D 1-1	Banks	5,016
30		13	(h)	Stockport C	W 2-1	Banks 2	4,223
31		16	(h)	Workington	L 0-1		4,609
32		20	(a)	Aldershot	D 2-2	Gadston, Banks	5,505
33		27	(h)	Brentford	W 1-0	Binney	3,892
34	Mar	6	(a)	Cambridge U	L 0-2		3,803
35		13	(h)	Barrow	W 4-2	Rowan, Gadston, Binney, Banks	3,999
36		16	(a)	Northampton T	D 2-2	Banks, Jimmy Giles	5,724
37		20	(a)	Colchester U	D 1-1	Banks	5,630
38		27	(h)	Darlington	W 2-1	Wingate, Banks	4,136
39	Apr	3	(a)	Peterborough U	W 3-1	Jimmy Giles, Gadston, Banks	3,880
40		9	(a)	Crewe A	L 1-4	Wingate	3,748
41		10	(h)	Bournemouth	D 0-0		7,918
42		12	(h)	Lincoln C	D 0-0		4,614
43		17	(a)	Hartlepool	L 0-3		1,515
44		24	(h)	Chester	W 3-1	Banks 2, Binney	4,024
45		28	(a)	Southend U	D 0-0		4,471
46	May	1	(a)	Notts C	D 1-1	Gadston	18,002

FINAL LEAGUE POSITION: 9th in Division Four

Appearances
Sub Appearances
Goals

FA Cup

1	Nov	21	(a)	Swansea C	L 1-4

League Cup

1	Aug	18	(h)	Swansea C	D 0-0
R		25	(a)	Swansea C	L 2-4* *After extra-time

260

Wilson	Crawford	Balson	Morris	Newman	Parker	Rowan	Banks	Gadston	Giles, John	Corr	Sharples	Shearing	Blain	Wingate	Binney	Mitten	Molyneux	Giles, Jimmy	
1	2	6			4		8		10	7	5		3		9	11			1
1	2	6	12		4		8	9	7		5		3	10		11*			2
1	2	6	4			7		9		11	5		3	10		8			3
1	2	6	4			7		9		11	5		3	10		8			4
1	2	6	4			7		9	8	11	5		3	10					5
1	2	3	4	5	6	7	8	9	10	11									6
	2	3	4	6	10	7	8	9	11		5								7
	2	6			4	7	12		10	11	5*	1	3	8	9				8
	2	6		5	4	7	8	9	10	11		1	3						9
	2	5			4	7		9		11		1	3	6	8	10			10
	2	5			4	7		9		11		1	3	6	8	10			11
	2	5	3		4	7	8	9		11		1		6		10			12
	2	6	3		4	7	8	9	10		5*	1		12	11				13
1	2	6			5	4*	7	8		10			3	12	9	11			14
1	2	6	3	5			7	8	10				4	9	11				15
1	2	6	3	5	4	7	8	9					10	11					16
1	2	6		5	4	7	8	9		11		3		10					17
1	2	4		5		7	8	9		11		3	6	10					18
1	2	6		5		7	8	9		11		3	4	10					19
1	2		4			7	8	9	10		5		3	6	11				20
1	2	12	4			7	8	9	10		5		3	6	11*				21
1	2	6			4	7	10			11	5	3	9	8					22
1	2	6			10	7	8			11	5	3	4	9					23
1	2	6			4	12	8	9	11*		5	3	7	10					24
1	2	6			4	12	8	9	11*		5	3	7	10					25
1	2	6			4	7	8	9			5	3	11	10					26
1	2	6			4	7	8	9			5	3	11	10					27
1	2	6			4	7	8	9				3	11	10		5			28
1	2	6			4	7	8	9				3	11*	10	12	5			29
1	2	6		5	4	7	8	9				3		10	11				30
1	2	6		5	4	7	8	9				3		10	11				31
1	2	6	11	5	4	7	8	9				3		10					32
1	2	6	11	5	4	7	8	9				3		10					33
1	2	6	11	5	4	7	8	9				3		10					34
1	2	6	11			7	8	9				3	4	10		5			35
1	2	6	11			7	8	9*		12		3	4	10		5			36
1	2	5	11		4	7	8	9*		12		3	6	10		5			37
1	2	6			4	7	8	9				3	11	10		5			38
1	2	6			4	7	8	9				3	11	10		5			39
1	2	6			4	7	8	9		12		3	11	10*		5			40
1	2	6	11				8	9		7		3	10			5			41
1	2	6	11		4		8	9*	12	7		3	10			5			42
1	2	6	4			7	8		9			3	10		11	5			43
1	2	6	3		4	7	8		11				10	9		5			44
1	2	8		4		6	7	9				3	11	10		5			45
1	2	6	3	4*			8	9	11				7	10	12	5			46
40	46	44	22	14	35	38	40	39	17	15	16	6	38	33	30	18	2	11	
	1	1			2	1		1	3				2	2					
			2	6	21	18	1	3	1		3	8	1		2				

1 own-goal

1971-72

Manager: Johnny Newman

#		Date		Opponent	Result	Scorers	Att.
1	Aug	14	(a)	Southport	L 0-4		2,467
2		21	(h)	Grimsby T	L 3-4	Wingate 2, Morrin	4,052
3		28	(a)	Northampton T	D 1-1	Blain	5,886
4	Sep	1	(a)	Workington	D 0-0		2,595
5		4	(h)	Peterborough U	W 3-2	Parker, Wingate 2	4,125
6		11	(a)	Doncaster R	L 1-2	Brookes (og)	3,616
7		18	(h)	Chester	D 1-1	Wingate	4,040
8		25	(a)	Bury	L 3-4	Wingate, Gadston, Binney	2,627
9		29	(a)	Cambridge U	W 1-0	Wingate	4,924
10	Oct	2	(h)	Crewe A	W 3-1	Rowan, Gadston, Banks	3,962
11		9	(a)	Lincoln C	L 1-4	Rowan	5,985
12		16	(h)	Southport	L 1-3	Binney	3,408
13		20	(h)	Gillingham	D 1-1	Wingate	3,656
14		23	(h)	Stockport C	W 2-0	Rowan, Morrin	3,545
15		30	(a)	Reading	L 1-3	Binney	4,877
16	Nov	6	(h)	Scunthorpe U	W 1-0	Parker	3,556
17		12	(a)	Southend U	L 0-3		10,107
18		26	(a)	Colchester U	L 0-3		5,116
19	Dec	4	(h)	Brentford	L 0-1		3,809
20		18	(a)	Peterborough U	D 3-3	Rowan, Banks 2	5,341
21		27	(h)	Aldershot	W 1-0	Morris	5,144
22	Jan	1	(a)	Chester	W 2-1	Binney 2	3,610
23		8	(h)	Northampton T	L 1-3	Binney	4,485
24		15	(a)	Darlington	L 1-2	Morrin	2,127
25		22	(h)	Cambridge U	L 3-4	Morrin, Binney, Jimmy, Giles	3,649
26		29	(a)	Gillingham	W 2-0	Rowan 2 (1 pen)	3,755
27	Feb	5	(h)	Newport C	W 1-0	Binney	3,732
28		12	(a)	Stockport C	W 4-0	Gibson, Parker, Binney, Banks	2,166
29		19	(h)	Reading	D 0-0		4,971
30		26	(a)	Scunthorpe U	L 0-3		6,250
31	Mar	4	(h)	Southend U	D 0-0		3,336
32		11	(h)	Lincoln C	L 1-2	Rowan (pen)	2,970
33		15	(h)	Darlington	W 3-0	Binney 2, Gadston	3,497
34		20	(a)	Barrow	D 0-0		2,153
35		25	(h)	Doncaster R	W 1-0	Balson	3,370
36		27	(a)	Hartlepool	L 0-1		3,501
37		31	(a)	Crewe A	W 1-0	Wingate	2,355
32	Apr	1	(a)	Aldershot	D 0-0		2,918
33		3	(h)	Bury	W 3-2	Binney 3	4,942
34		8	(a)	Newport C	D 0-0		2,362
35		15	(h)	Colchester U	D 3-3	Binney, Rowan, Banks	4,052
36		19	(h)	Hartlepool	W 1-0	Banks	3,791
37		22	(a)	Brentford	L 0-1		14,520
38		26	(h)	Workington	L 0-2		3,564
39		29	(h)	Barrow	W 7-1	Knox (og), Binney 2, Parker, Morrin, Neale, Banks	3,050
40	May	2	(a)	Grimsby T	L 0-3		22,484

FINAL LEAGUE POSITION: 15th in Division Four

Appearances
Sub Appearances
Goals

FA Cup

1	Nov	20	(a)	Crawley T	D 0-0
R		24	(h)	Crawley T	W 2-0
2	Dec	11	(a)	Swansea C	D 0-0
R		15	(h)	Swansea C	L 0-1

League Cup

1	Aug	18	(h)	Bristol R	L 0-3

Football club season appearance & goalscorer grid. Players (columns left→right): Wilson, Crawford, Stacey, Parker, Giles Jimmy, Balson, Morrin, Banks, Gadston, Blain, Binney, Wingate, Giles John, Newman, Morris, Rowan, Gibson, Neale. Match number in right margin.

Wilson	Crawford	Stacey	Parker	Giles, Jimmy	Balson	Morrin	Banks	Gadston	Blain	Binney	Wingate	Giles, John	Newman	Morris	Rowan	Gibson	Neale	#
1	2	3	4	5	6	7	8	9*	12	10	11							1
1	2	3	4	5	6	7	8		12	9*	10	11						2
1	2	3	4		6	7	8	10*		9	11	5	12					3
1	2	3	4		6	7	8	10*		9	11	5	12					4
1	2	3	4		6	11	8			9	10	5		7				5
1	2	3	4		6	7*	8		10		9	5	11	12	7			6
1	2	3	4*	5	6	7		9		10	11		12	8				7
1	2	3		5	6				9	4	8	10		11	7			8
1	2	3		5	6		12	9		4	8	10		11*	7			9
1	2	3		5	6				9	4	8	10		11	7			10
1	2	3*	4	5	6		12	9	10	8	11			7				11
1	2		4	5	6	8			3	9	10	11		7				12
1	2		4	5	6	8			3	9	10	11		7				13
1	2*		4	5	6	10			3	8	11	9	12	7				14
1		2	4	5	6	7	8		3	9	10	11						15
1		2*	4	5	6	7	8		3	9	10	11	12					16
1	2			5	6	10	12	9	3	8*	11		4	7				17
1		2		5	6		8		3	9	10	11	4	7				18
1	2			5	6		8	9	3		10	11	4	7				19
1		2		5	6	4	8	9	3		10		11	7				20
1	2	4	5	6		8			3	9	10		11	7				21
1		6	3	5	8	12		2	9	10		4	7	11*				22
1	6	4	3	5	8	10		2	9				7	11				23
1	2	4	5	6	8	10		3	9				7	11				24
1	2	4	5	6	8	10		3	9				7	11				25
1	2	4	5	6	8	10		3	9				7	11				26
1	2	4	5	6	8	10		3	9				7	11				27
1	2	4	5	6	8	10		3	9				7	11				28
1	2	4	5	6	8	10		3	9				7	11				29
1	2	3	4	5	6	8			9	10*	12		7	11				30
1	12	2	4	5	6	8	10*		3	9			7	11				31
1	12	2	4	5	6	7*		9	3	8				10	11			32
1	2	4		5	6		12	9	3	8	10	7*		11				33
1	2			5	6		8	9	3	10	4		7	11				34
1	2			5	6		8*	9	3	10	4		7	11	12			35
1	2	12	5	6			8	9	3	10	4	7*		11				36
1	2			5	6		8	9	3	10	4		7	11				37
1	2			5	6		8	9	3	10	4		7	11				38
1	2	4	5	6		8	9	3	10	11			7					39
1	2	3	4	5	6	8			10	9			7	11				40
1	2	4	5	6	7	8	9	3		12			11*	10				41
1	2	4	5	6		8	9	3	10				7	11				42
1	2	4	5*	6	7		9	3	8	10	12			11				43
1	2	4	5	6	7	8		3	10*	9				11	12			44
1	2	4	5	6	7	8		3	10	9				11				45
46	30	30	33	42	46	31	31	20	40	39	35	10	4	11	33	23	2	
	2	1							5	2	1	3		5	1		2	
	4	1	1	5	7	3	1	17	9			1	8		1	1		

2 own-goals

1972-73

Manager: Johnny Newman

#		Date		Opponent	Result	Scorers	Att.
1	Aug	12	(a)	Southport	L 0-1		2,600
2		19	(h)	Bradford C	W 5-1	Binney 2, Howell (og), Parker, Wingate	3,849
3		26	(a)	Mansfield T	L 0-3		4,177
4		28	(h)	Hartlepool	D 1-1	Gibson	4,304
5	Sep	2	(h)	Cambridge U	W 3-1	Wingate, Binney, Morrin	3,249
6		9	(a)	Workington	L 1-3	Plumb	1,345
7		16	(h)	Stockport C	W 3-0	Parker, Binney, Plumb	3,384
8		20	(h)	Aldershot	W 1-0	Binney	4,013
9		23	(a)	Torquay U	W 2-0	Wingate, Binney	8,026
10		25	(a)	Darlington	D 0-0		1,374
11		30	(h)	Colchester U	W 1-0	Plumb	5,005
12	Oct	7	(a)	Crewe A	L 0-1		1,911
13		11	(a)	Reading	L 0-2		4,138
14		14	(h)	Hereford U	W 1-0	Banks	4,516
15		21	(a)	Bury	L 1-2	Binney	2,870
16		28	(h)	Newport C	D 0-0		4,588
17	Nov	4	(h)	Darlington	D 1-1	Binney	3,991
18		6	(h)	Lincoln C	W 2-0	Wingate, Binney	4,319
19		11	(a)	Aldershot	D 0-0		3,737
20		25	(a)	Northampton T	W 2-1	Balson, Binney	2,263
21	Dec	2	(h)	Barnsley	W 2-1	Balson 2	3,882
22		16	(h)	Gillingham	W 3-2	Parker, Binney 2	3,866
23		23	(a)	Chester	W 1-0	Binney	2,560
24		26	(h)	Torquay U	W 3-2	Binney 2 (1 pen), Plumb	11,296
25		30	(a)	Bradford C	L 0-4		5,498
26	Jan	6	(h)	Mansfield T	W 4-2	Plumb 3 (1 pen), Morrin	6,744
27		13	(a)	Lincoln C	D 2-2	Plumb, Binney	3,729
28		20	(a)	Cambridge U	W 3-1	Balson, Gibson, Binney	3,979
29		27	(h)	Workington	W 4-2	Plumb 2, Binney 2 (1 pen)	6,892
30	Feb	9	(a)	Stockport C	L 0-1		3,164
31		12	(h)	Peterborough U	D 1-1	Binney	5,403
32		17	(h)	Southport	L 0-1		10,122
33		24	(a)	Gillingham	L 0-1		4,695
34	Mar	3	(h)	Crewe A	D 0-0		5,731
35		10	(a)	Hereford U	L 0-1		11,302
36		17	(h)	Bury	D 1-1	Binney	4,560
37		19	(a)	Doncaster R	L 1-5	Binney	1,823
38		24	(a)	Newport C	L 0-2		4,817
39		31	(h)	Northampton T	W 4-1	Binney 3 (1 pen), Plumb	3,137
40	Apr	3	(h)	Reading	D 0-0		3,898
41		6	(a)	Barnsley	D 1-1	Binney	1,428
42		14	(h)	Doncaster R	L 0-1		3,609
43		16	(a)	Colchester U	W 2-1	Binney 2	3,489
44		21	(a)	Peterborough U	D 1-1	Giles	4,593
45		23	(h)	Chester	D 0-0		3,863
46		28	(a)	Hartlepool	D 0-0		1,868

FINAL LEAGUE POSITION: 8th in Division Four

Appearances
Sub Appearances
Goals

FA Cup
1 Nov 18 (a) Walton & H L 1-2

League Cup
1 Aug 16 (a) Brighton & HA L 1-2

Player appearance and goal grid (shirt numbers by match; `*` denotes substituted):

Wilson	Stacey	Blain	Parker	Giles	Balson	Wingate	Banks	Binney	Gibson	Scott	Morrin	Plumb	Rowan	Crawford	Clapham	Neale	Clarke	Benson	#
1	2	3	4	5	6	7	8	9	10	11*	12								1
1	2	3	4	5	6	7		8	11*		10	9	12						2
1	2	3	4	5	6			8	10	11	7	9							3
1		3	4	5	6			8	10	11	7	9	2						4
1		3	4*	5	6	12		8	10	11	7	9	2						5
1		3	4	5	6	8		10	11		7	9	2						6
1		3	4	5	6	10		8		11	7	9	2						7
1		3		5	6	10	12	8		11*	4	9	7	2					8
1		3		5	6	10		8		11	7	9		2	4				9
1	12	3		5	6	10*		8		11	7	9		2	4				10
1	12	3		5	6	10*		8		11	7	9		2	4				11
1	10	3		5	4		12	8		11	7	9		2	6*				12
1	11*	3	4	5	6		12	8			7	9		2	10				13
1		3	4	5	6		8	9		11		7		2	10				14
1	10	3	4	5	6		8	9		11	7			2*	12				15
1	10	3	4	5			8*	9		11	7		12	2	6				16
1		3*	4	5	6		12	9	10	11	8			2		7			17
1	2	3		5	6	8		9	10	11*	4		12	7					18
1	2	3		5	6	7		8	11		10	9		4					19
1	2	3*		5		7	8	10	11	6	9		12	4					20
1		3			6		12	8	10	11*	4	9	7	2	5				21
1		3	4	5	6	12		8	11*	7	10	9		2					22
1		3	4	5	6	12		8	11	7*	10	9		2					23
1		3	4	5	6	12		8	11		10	9	7*	2					24
1		3	4	5	6			8	11		10	9	7	2					25
1		3	4	5	6	12		8*	11	7	10	9		2					26
1	3*	12	4	5		10		8	11	7		9		2	6				27
1		3	4	5	6	10		8	11*	7		9		2	12				28
1	3	10	4*	5	6	11		8		7		9		2	12				29
1		3	4	5	6	11		8	12	7	10*	9		2					30
1		3	4	5	6			8	11	7	10	9		2					31
1	2	3	4	5	6	12		8	11	7*	10	9							32
	2	3	4*	5		12	8	11			10	9			6	7	1		33
1	3	2		5		4		8	11		10	9			6	7			34
1	2		4	5	6	7		8	11		10	9				3			35
	2		4	5	6	11		8			10	9*			12	7	1	3	36
	2		6	3	4	11		9		7	10				8		1	5	37
	2	12		5	6	7		8			11	10	9		4*		1	3	38
	3		5	2	10			8	11	7*	4	9			6		1		39
	3		5	2	4			8	10	7*	9			12	6	11	1		40
	3		5	4	11			8	10		9			2	6	7	1		41
1	3		5	2	4			8	9	10	11				6	7			42
	2		5	3	10			8	11	4	9				6	7	1		43
1	12		5	3	10	9		8*	11	4				2	6	7			44
1	3		5	6	10			8	11	7	4	9		2					45
1	11		5	3	10			8		4	9			2	6	7			46
38	27	29	30	44	42	28	6	46	30	30	39	38	5	29	21	12	8	4	
2	3					7	5		1	1					2	2	5		
		3	1	4	4	1		28	2		2	11							

1 own-goal

1973-74

Manager: Johnny Newman

#		Date		Opponent	Result	Scorers	Attendance
1	Aug	25	(h)	Bradford C	D 0-0		4,176
2	Sep	1	(a)	Brentford	W 1-0	Giles	4,820
3		8	(h)	Workington	D 1-1	Plumb	3,815
4		12	(h)	Darlington	W 3-0	Binney (pen), Balson, Scott	4,403
5		15	(a)	Chester	W 1-0	Binney (pen)	2,884
6		17	(a)	Hartlepool	W 3-1	Plumb, Wingate, Binney	2,606
7		22	(h)	Reading	L 0-1		6,822
8		28	(a)	Colchester U	L 0-1		5,466
9	Oct	3	(h)	Hartlepool	W 2-0	Giles, Binney	4,461
10		6	(h)	Gillingham	W 2-1	Plumb, Binney	4,744
11		13	(a)	Rotherham U	L 0-4		2,958
12		20	(a)	Northampton T	W 2-1	Binney, Plumb	4,923
13		22	(a)	Darlington	L 0-1		1,804
14		27	(h)	Crewe A	W 2-0	Binney 2	4,804
15	Nov	3	(a)	Peterborough U	L 0-2		9,641
16		10	(h)	Barnsley	W 6-1	Plumb 2, Binney 2, Scott, Wingate	4,697
17		14	(h)	Doncaster R	L 1-2	Wallace	5,259
18		17	(a)	Lincoln C	L 1-2	Neale	4,100
19	Dec	1	(a)	Swansea C	L 0-2		2,046
20		8	(h)	Newport C	L 0-1		3,476
21		15	(a)	Workington	L 1-3	Parker	693
22		22	(h)	Colchester U	W 1-0	Binney	3,638
23		26	(a)	Torquay U	D 0-0		9,107
24	Jan	1	(h)	Brentford	W 2-1	Binney (pen), Morrin	5,754
25		5	(a)	Stockport C	W 1-0	Binney	1,803
26		12	(h)	Chester	W 2-1	Bowker, Wingate	5,047
27		20	(a)	Bradford C	L 0-1		9,041
28		27	(a)	Newport C	L 1-2	Bowker	3,812
29	Feb	10	(a)	Reading	L 1-4	Parker	5,232
30		23	(a)	Gillingham	L 1-2	Bowker	7,994
31	Mar	2	(h)	Torquay U	W 4-2	Binney 2, Harrison (og), Morrin	5,928
32		9	(h)	Mansfield T	D 1-1	Binney	3,669
33		10	(a)	Crewe A	W 5-2	Binney 3, Morrin, Bowker	1,801
34		16	(h)	Northampton T	D 1-1	Binney	4,052
35		18	(a)	Mansfield T	D 3-3	Bowker, Parker, Wingate	2,406
36		23	(a)	Barnsley	L 0-3		3,067
37		27	(h)	Stockport C	W 2-1	Binney, Charter (og)	3,337
38		30	(h)	Peterborough U	L 1-2	Wingate	3,592
39	Apr	6	(a)	Doncaster R	L 0-1		1,373
40		12	(a)	Bury	D 0-0		5,043
41		13	(h)	Lincoln C	L 0-1		3,687
42		15	(h)	Bury	L 0-3		2,992
43		22	(h)	Scunthorpe U	W 4-0	Binney 3, Bowker	2,226
44		27	(h)	Swansea C	W 2-0	Binney, Bowker	2,915
45		30	(h)	Rotherham U	D 0-0		2,945

FINAL LEAGUE POSITION: 10th in Division Four

Exeter City could not fulfil the fixture against Scunthorpe United (a) who were awarded the points

Appearances
Sub Appearances
Goals

FA Cup

1	Nov	24	(h)	Alvechurch	L 0-1

League Cup

1	Aug	28	(a)	Swansea C	D 1-1	
R	Sep	5	(h)	Swansea C	W 2-1*	*After extra-time
2	Oct	10	(a)	Rotherham U	W 4-1	
3		31	(a)	West Brom A	W 3-1	
4	Nov	20	(a)	Wolves	L 1-5	

266

Wilson	Crawford	Balson	Parker	Giles	Clapham	Scott	Binney	Plumb	Blain	Wingate	Neale	Joy	Gibson	Clarke	Morrin	Wallace	Hatch	Bowker	Devlin	#
1	2	3	4	5	6	7	8	9	10*	11	12									1
1	2	10	4	5	6*	7	8	9	3	11		12								2
1	2	10		5	6	7	8	9	3	11		4								3
1	2	10		5	6	7	8*	9	3	11	12	4								4
1	2		4	5	6	7	8	9	3	11		10								5
1	2		4	5	6	7	8	9	3	11		10								6
1	2	12	4	5	6		8	9	3	11	7*		10							7
1	2	3	4	5	6	7	8	9		11		10								8
	2	3	4	5	6	7	8	9		11		10		1						9
	2	2	4	5	6	7	8	9		11		10		1						10
1	2	3	4	5	6		8	9		10		7	11							11
1	2	3	4	5	6	7	8	9		11	10*		12							12
1	2	3	4	5	6	7	8	9				11	10							13
1	2			5	6	7	8	9		11		3	10	4						14
1	2			5			8	9		6	11	3	10	4	7					15
	2			5	6	7	8	9		11		3	10	1	4					16
	2			5	6		8*	9		11	12	3	10	1	4	7				17
	2			5	6			9		11	8	3	10	1	4	7				18
	2			5	6	11		9	3	10			8	1	4	7				19
1	2			10	5		7	8	9		6		3	11*		4	12			20
1	2			11	5			9			6		8		4	7	3	10		21
1				11	5	6		8	9		7		2		4		3	10		22
1				10	5	6	7*	8		12	11		2		4		3	9		23
1				10	5	6	11*	8			7	12	2		4		3	9		24
1	2	5	10			6	11	8			7				4		3	9		25
1	2	6	10	5			11	8			7				4		3	9		26
1	2	6	10	5			11	8*			7	12			4		3	9		27
1	2	6	10	5			11				7	9			4		3	9		28
1	2	6	10	5							7	9	11		4		3	9		29
1		6	8	5	11					10	7	2			4		3	9		30
1		6	10	5	12		8			11	7	2			4		3	9*		31
1		6	10	5			8			11	7	2			4		3	9		32
1		6	10*	5	12		8			11	7	2			4		3	9		33
1		6	10	5			8			11	7	2			4		3	9		34
1		6	10	5	9			12		11	7	2*			4		3	8		35
1	2	3	10	5	6		8			11	7				4			9		36
	2	5			6		8		4	10	7		11	1			3	9		37
	2	6		5					4	10	7		11	1		12	3	8	9*	38
1	2		10	5	6		8			11	7				4		3	9		39
1			10	5	6		8			11	7	2			4		3	9		40
1			10	5	6		8		7	11		2	12		4		3	9*		41
1			10	5	6		8		7	11		2			4		3	9		42
1	2			5	6		8		4	11			10			7	3	9		43
1	2			5	4		8		6	10			11			7	3	9		44
1	2			5			8		4	11	12	3	10			7*	6	9		45
37	33	24	32	43	32	21	38	21	15	44	16	29	16	8	28	8	24	25	1	
	1		2			2		6	1	1		1	2							
	1	3	2		2	25	6		5	1		3	1			7				

2 own-goals

267

1974-75

Manager: Johnny Newman

#	Month	Date		Opponent	Result	Scorers	Attendance
1	Aug	17	(a)	Barnsley	L 0-1		4,704
2		24	(h)	Doncaster R	W 2-1	Bowker 2	3,704
3		31	(a)	Lincoln C	L 0-5		2,751
4	Sep	4	(a)	Bradford C	W 1-0	Neale	3,146
5		7	(h)	Mansfield T	L 0-1		3,276
6		14	(a)	Torquay U	D 2-2	Rutter, Jennings	5,306
7		21	(h)	Reading	L 0-2		3,493
8		25	(h)	Darlington	W 4-1	Bowker 2, Jennings, Steele	2,271
9		28	(a)	Workington	W 1-0	Jennings	1,213
10	Oct	2	(h)	Bradford C	W 1-0	Robertson (pen)	2,874
11		5	(a)	Newport C	W 2-1	Joy, Robertson	3,130
12		12	(h)	Swansea C	L 1-2	Jennings	3,867
13		18	(a)	Cambridge U	D 1-1	Templeman	1,840
14		23	(a)	Crewe A	L 1-2	Hatch	2,059
15		26	(h)	Chester	W 1-0	Bowker	3,664
16	Nov	2	(a)	Southport	L 0-3		1,505
17		6	(h)	Crewe A	W 2-0	Robertson (pen), Bowker	2,565
18		9	(h)	Scunthorpe U	D 0-0		3,058
19		16	(a)	Rotherham U	D 1-1	Hodge	4,623
20		30	(a)	Rochdale	D 1-1	Beer	1,033
21	Dec	7	(h)	Northampton T	D 2-2	Robertson 2 (1 pen)	3,597
22		14	(h)	Barnsley	W 4-2	Hodge, Giles, Bowker 2	2,916
23		21	(a)	Shrewsbury T	D 2-2	Bowker 2	3,097
24		26	(h)	Torquay U	D 0-0		7,271
25		28	(a)	Brentford	L 0-2		5,610
26	Jan	4	(h)	Hartlepool	W 1-0	Templeman	3,424
27		11	(a)	Northampton T	D 1-1	Robertson (pen)	4,104
28		18	(h)	Rochdale	W 2-1	Bowker, Robertson (pen)	3,560
29		24	(h)	Stockport C	W 4-1	Bowker 2, Neale 2	4,438
30	Feb	1	(a)	Scunthorpe U	L 1-2	Beer	1,846
31		8	(h)	Southport	W 1-0	Giles	3,594
32		15	(a)	Stockport C	L 2-3	Morrin 2	1,551
33		22	(h)	Rotherham U	L 0-4		3,548
34	Mar	1	(h)	Lincoln C	L 1-2	Robertson	2,978
35		8	(a)	Darlington	L 0-2		1,692
36		10	(a)	Hartlepool	W 3-0	Beer, Bowker, Hodge	2,178
37		15	(h)	Workington	W 1-0	Bowker	2,581
38		21	(a)	Mansfield T	L 2-3	Beer 2	8,412
39		29	(h)	Shrewsbury T	W 1-0	Morrin	3,240
40		31	(h)	Brentford	W 1-0	Beer	3,301
41	Apr	2	(a)	Reading	L 0-3		4,474
42		5	(a)	Chester	D 1-1	Beer	3,318
43		12	(h)	Newport C	W 3-1	Bowker, Joy, Beer	2,755
44		19	(a)	Swansea C	W 2-0	Bowker, Robertson	2,000
45		22	(a)	Doncaster R	D 3-3	Hodge, Beer, Robertson	4,251
46		26	(h)	Cambridge U	L 1-4	Bowker	2,924

FINAL LEAGUE POSITION: 9th in Division Four

Appearances
Sub Appearances
Goals

FA Cup

1	Nov	23	(h)	Newport C	L 1-2

League Cup

1	Aug	21	(h)	Swansea C	W 3-1
2	Sep	11	(h)	Hereford U	L 0-1

268

Wilson	Rutter	Hatch	Morrin	Giles	Steele	Neale	Bowker	Robertson	Templeman	Jennings	Joy	Clapham	Hodge	Bond	Beer	Hooker	Munks	#
1	2	3	4	5	6	7	8	9	10	11								
1	2	3	4	5	6	12	8	9	7	11	10*							1
1	2	3	4	5	6	12	8*	9	7	11	10							2
1	2		4	5		7	8	9	10	11	3	6						3
1	2		4	5	6	7	8	9	10	11	3							4
1	2	3	4	5		7	8	9		11	10	6						5
1	2	3	4		5	7*	8	9		11	10	6	12					6
1	2	3	4		5		8	9		11	10	6	7					7
1	2	3	4			7*	8	9	10	11	5	6	12					8
1	2	3	4	5		8	9	7	11	10	6							9
1	2	3	4	5		8	9	7	11	10	6							10
1	2	3	4*	5	12	8	9	7	11	10	6							11
1	2	3	4	5	12	8	9	7	11	10*	6							12
1	2	3	4	5	12	8*	9	7	11	10	6							13
1	2	3	4	5		8	9	7	11	10	6							14
1	2*	3	4	5		7	9		10	11	8	6	12					15
1	2	3	4	5		8	9	7	11	10	6			1				16
	3	4	5			7*	8	9	2	11	10	6	12	1				17
	2	3	4	5	12	7*	9		8	10	6	11		1				18
	2	3	4	5		8	9	7	11*	6	12			1	10			19
	2	6	4	5		8	10	7	3	11				1	9			20
	2	6	4	5		8	9	7	3	11				1	10			21
	2	3	4	5		8	9	7	6	11				1	10			22
	2	6	4	5		8	9	7	3	11				1	10			23
	2	3	4	5		9	7	6	11					1	10	8		24
	3	4	5			8	9	7	2	11				1	10	6		25
	3	4	5			8	9	7	2	11				1	10	6		26
	7	3	4	5		8	9		2	11				1	10	6		27
	2	6	4	5		7	8	9	3	11				1	10			28
	2	6	4	5		7	8	10	3	11				1	9			29
	2	6	4	5		7	8*	9	3	11				1	10	12		30
	2*	6	4	5		7	9	8	3	11				1	10	12		31
	3	4	5			7	9	8	2	6	11			1	10			32
	6	4	5			7	8	9	2	3	11			1	10			33
	11	4	5			7	8	9	2	3				1	10	6		34
		4	5			8	9	2	3	7				1	10	11	6	35
		4	5			8	9	2	3	11				1	10	7	6	36
		4	5			8	9	2	3	7				1	10	11	6	37
	6	4*	5			8	9	2	3	12	7			1	10	11		38
	6		5	12		8	9	2	3	4*	7			1	10	11		39
	6		5			8	9	2	3	4	7			1	10	11		40
2	3			5		7	8	9	6	4	11			1	10			41
2	3			5		7	8	9	6	11				1	10	4		42
	3			5		7	8	9	2	6	11			1	10	4		43
	3			5		7	8	9	2	4	12	11*		1	10	6		44
	3			5		7	8	9	2	4	11			1	10	6		45
16	31	41	39	43	6	21	43	42	39	19	45	19	27	30	27	7	11	46
											1	6		2	5		2	
1	1	3	2	1	3	18	10	2	4	2	4	9						

269

1975-76

Manager: Johnny Newman

#	Month	Date		Opponent	Result	Scorers	Attendance
1	Aug	16	(h)	Southport	W 2-0	Beer, Hodge	2,844
2		23	(a)	Scunthorpe U	W 1-0	Bowker	1,660
3		29	(h)	Tranmere R	L 0-2		3,861
4	Sep	6	(a)	Workington	L 0-1		1,004
5		13	(h)	Cambridge U	L 1-2	Beer	2,471
6		20	(a)	Lincoln C	L 1-4	Robertson	5,088
7		24	(a)	Torquay U	L 0-1		3,705
8		27	(h)	Crewe A	D 2-2	Saxton, Bowker	2,116
9	Oct	4	(a)	Rochdale	W 1-0	Bowker	1,234
10		11	(a)	Darlington	D 0-0		2,314
11		13	(a)	Hartlepool	L 1-2	Bowker	1,323
12		18	(h)	Hartlepool	W 3-1	Beer, Jennings, Potter (og)	2,406
13		21	(a)	Barnsley	D 0-0		3,619
14		25	(a)	Newport C	D 3-3	Beer 2, Bowker	2,871
15		31	(h)	Stockport C	W 2-0	Beer, Hodge	2,856
16	Nov	4	(h)	Bradford C	D 0-0		2,723
17		8	(a)	Reading	L 3-4	Beer 2, Hodge	6,341
18		14	(h)	Swansea C	W 3-0	Wingate, Harris (og), Bowker	2,967
19		28	(h)	Doncaster R	W 1-0	Bowker	2,848
20	Dec	6	(a)	Huddersfield T	W 1-0	Morrin	4,981
21		13	(h)	Northampton T	D 0-0		3,394
22		20	(a)	Northampton T	L 1-3	Beer	5,212
23		26	(h)	Brentford	D 0-0		4,912
24		27	(a)	Watford	L 0-2		5,055
25	Jan	2	(h)	Bournemouth	W 1-0	Templeman	3,031
26		9	(a)	Tranmere R	D 1-1	Beer	4,661
27		17	(h)	Lincoln C	D 0-0		3,858
28		24	(a)	Cambridge U	W 1-0	Jordan	2,188
29		31	(h)	Barnsley	W 2-0	Hatch, Bowker	2,449
30	Feb	7	(a)	Bradford C	D 0-0		3,049
31		13	(h)	Reading	W 4-1	Robertson, Jordan, Beer, Templeman	3,641
32		20	(a)	Swansea C	W 3-0	Beer 2, Bowker	4,252
33		25	(h)	Torquay U	D 0-0		8,112
34		28	(h)	Newport C	W 3-0	Templeman, Bowker, Jennings	3,447
35	Mar	5	(a)	Stockport C	L 1-2	Bowker	2,440
36		9	(h)	Rochdale	W 1-0	Morrin	3,102
37		13	(h)	Darlington	D 1-1	Beer	3,196
38		20	(a)	Doncaster R	D 0-0		4,149
39		27	(h)	Huddersfield T	W 4-1	Beer 2, Robertson, Bowker	3,925
40	Apr	2	(a)	Southport	L 0-1		1,514
41		7	(a)	Crewe A	D 0-0		2,034
42		10	(h)	Workington	W 1-0	Beer	2,603
43		16	(a)	Bournemouth	L 0-1		4,651
44		17	(a)	Brentford	L 1-5	Jordan	3,980
45		19	(h)	Watford	L 1-3	Bowker	2,480
46		23	(h)	Scunthorpe U	W 5-4	Beer 3, Robertson, Wingate	1,863

FINAL LEAGUE POSITION: 7th in Division Four

Appearances
Sub Appearances
Goals

FA Cup
1	Nov	22	(a)	Cardiff C	L 2-6

League Cup
1	Aug	19	(a)	Newport C	D 1-1
R		26	(h)	Newport C	W 2-0
2	Sep	10	(a)	Torquay U	D 1-1
R		17	(h)	Torquay U	L 1-2

Wilson	Templeman	Hooker	Joy	Wingate	Hatch	Hodge	Beer	Robertson	Bowker	Jennings	Morrin	Jordan	Moxham	Key	Saxton	Munks	Hore	Clapham	Rutter	
1	2	3	4	5	6	7	8	9	10	11										1
1	2	3	4	5	6	8	11	9	10	7										2
1	2	3	4	5	6		11	9	8	7	10									3
1	2	3	4	5	6		11	10	9	7*	8	12								4
1	2		3	5	6	7*	10	9	8	11	4	12								5
1	2		3	5	6	7	10	9	8	11	4									6
	2		3	5	6	7	10	9	8		4			11	1					7
	2		3		6	7	10	9	8		4			11	1	5				8
	2		3	7	6		10	9	8	11	4				1	5				9
	2	7	3		6		10	9	8	11	4				1	5				10
	2	3	4	7	6		10	9	8	11					1	5				11
	2	3		4	6	7	10	9	8	11					1	5				12
	2	3		7	6	4	10	9	8	11					1	5				13
	2	3		4	6	7	10	9	8	11					1	5				14
1	2	3		7	6	4	10	9	8	11						5				15
1	2	3		7	6	4	10	9	8	11						5				16
1	2	3		4	6	7	10	9	8	11						5				17
	2*	3		7	6	4	10	9	8			12		11	1	5				18
	3	2		7	6		10*	9	11	8	4	12			1	5				19
	2			7	6		10	9	8	11	4				1	5		3		20
	2			7	6		10	9	8	11	4				1	5		3		21
12	2*			4	6	7	10	9	8	11					1	5		3		22
	2			7	6	4	10	9	8	11					1	5	6			23
	2			4	3	7	10	9	8	11					1	5	6			24
	2			7	3		10	9	8	11	4				1	5	6			25
	2			7	3	9	10		8	11	4				1	5	6			26
	2	3		7	12		10	9	8*	11	4				1	5	6			27
	2	3		8	7		10	9			4	11			1	5	6			28
	2	3		7	6		10	9	8		4	11			1	5				29
	2	3		7	6		10	9	8		4	11			1	5				30
	2	3		7	6	4	10	9	8			11			1	5				31
	2	3		7	6		10	9	8		4	11			1	5				32
	2	3		7	6		10	9	8		4	11			1	5				33
	2	3		7	6		10	9	8	11	4				1	5				34
	2	3		7	6		10	9	8	11	4				1	5				35
	2			7	6		10	9	8	11	4				1	5		3		36
	2			7	6		10	9	8	11	4				1	5		3		37
	2			7	6		10	9	8	11	4				1	5		3		38
	2	12		7	6		10	9	8	11	4				1	5		3*		39
	2			7	6		10	9	8	11	4				1	5		3		40
	2			7	6		10	9	8	11	4				1	5		3		41
	2	12		7	6		10	9	8	11	4*				1	5		3		42
	2	3		7	6	11	10	9		8					1	5	4			43
	2	3		7*	6	8	10	9		11					1	5	4	12		44
	2	3		12	6	7	10	8*	11	9					1	5	4			45
	2			7	6	12	10	9		11	4*		8		1	5		3		46
9	42	26	15	44	43	23	46	44	42	34	28	10	4	37	39	9	11			
1	2		2							1	2			1	1					
3			2	1	3	20	4	13	2	2	3			1						

2 own-goals

271

1976-77

Manager: Johnny Newman until December 1976, then Bobby Saxton.

1	Aug	21	(a)	Hartlepool	D	2-2	Kellow 2	1,602
2		28	(h)	Cambridge U	D	1-1	Kellow	3,606
3	Sep	4	(a)	Colchester U	L	1-3	Smith (og)	2,516
4		11	(h)	Rochdale	W	2-1	Beer, Kellow	2,829
5		18	(a)	Halifax T	W	2-1	Kellow, Beer	1,424
6		25	(a)	Watford	L	1-4	Beer	5,079
7		29	(h)	Scunthorpe U	W	2-0	Beer 2	2,934
8	Oct	2	(h)	Crewe A	W	3-0	Beer 2, Hatch	3,337
9		9	(a)	Bournemouth	L	0-2		4,621
10		16	(h)	Workington	D	0-0		2,958
11		23	(a)	Southend U	L	0-2		4,605
12		25	(a)	Stockport C	D	0-0		5,490
13		30	(h)	Southport	W	3-1	Robertson 3 (2 pens)	2,835
14	Nov	3	(h)	Brentford	W	3-2	Kellow 2, Robertson	2,779
15		6	(a)	Swansea C	D	0-0		3,856
16		12	(h)	Huddersfield T	W	2-0	Kellow, Robertson	3,657
17		27	(a)	Darlington	L	1-2	Kellow	2,997
18	Dec	4	(h)	Doncaster R	L	0-2		2,891
19		27	(h)	Torquay U	W	3-0	Saxton, Kellow, Jennings	6,446
20	Jan	1	(h)	Swansea C	W	2-0	Kellow 2	3,596
21		3	(a)	Southport	D	1-1	Jennings	1,840
22		8	(h)	Barnsley	W	1-0	Kellow	3,784
23		22	(h)	Hartlepool	W	3-1	Hodge, Kellow, Robertson (pen)	3,285
24		29	(a)	Bradford C	D	1-1	Hodge	4,979
25	Feb	5	(a)	Cambridge U	D	1-1	Beer	4,428
26		12	(h)	Colchester U	W	1-0	Hodge	6,132
27		19	(a)	Rochdale	W	2-1	Weeks, Beer	1,523
28		26	(h)	Halifax T	W	1-0	Beer	5,995
29	Mar	2	(a)	Aldershot	D	2-2	Kellow, Templeman	3,789
30		5	(h)	Watford	D	2-2	Beer, Kellow	5,867
31		11	(a)	Crewe A	L	0-2		2,500
32		15	(a)	Scunthorpe U	L	1-4	Jennings	2,147
33		19	(h)	Bournemouth	D	1-1	Robertson	4,065
34		26	(a)	Workington	W	3-1	Beer, Jennings 2	1,365
35	Apr	2	(h)	Southend U	W	3-1	Kellow, Beer, Saxton	4,156
36		8	(a)	Torquay U	W	1-0	Beer	7,900
37		9	(h)	Newport C	W	1-0	Hodge	5,243
38		12	(a)	Brentford	L	0-1		7,640
39		16	(h)	Stockport C	W	2-1	Robertson (pen), Hodge	4,474
40		20	(h)	Bradford C	D	0-0		7,827
41		23	(a)	Huddersfield T	W	1-0	Hatch	4,717
42		26	(a)	Newport C	W	3-0	Jennings, Beer, Hodge	3,550
43		30	(h)	Darlington	W	1-0	Beer	6,722
44	May	3	(a)	Barnsley	W	4-3	Beer 2, Kellow, Robertson (pen)	5,141
45		7	(a)	Doncaster R	W	3-0	Beer 2, Kellow	3,447
46		14	(h)	Aldershot	W	3-0	Hodge, Beer, Jennings	10,751

FINAL LEAGUE POSITION: 2nd in Division Four

Appearances
Sub Appearances
Goals

FA Cup

1	Nov	20	(h)	Southend U	D	1-1	
R		22	(a)	Southend U	L	1-2*	*After extra-time

League Cup

1	Aug	14	(a)	Plymouth A	W	1-0	
		18	(h)	Plymouth A	W	1-0	
2		31	(h)	Norwich C	L	1-3	

272

Key	Templeman	Hooker	Hore	Saxton	Hatch	Hodge	Kellow	Clapham	Beer	Jordan	Morrin	Jennings	Weeks	Robertson	Phillipson-Masters	Holman	Green	Darke	Gay	Roberts	Baugh	
1	2	3	4	5	6	7	8	9	10	11												1
1	2	3	4	5	6	7	8		10	11	9											2
1	2	3	4		6		8	5	10	7*	9	11	12									3
1	2	3	4	5*	6		8	12	10		9	11		7								4
1	2		3		6		8	5	10		4	11	7	9								5
1	2		3	5*	6		8		11	12	4	7	10	9								6
1	2		3		6	7	8		10		4	11		9	5							7
1	2		3		6	7	8		10		4	11		9	5							8
1	2		3		6	7	8		10*		4	11	12	9	5							9
1	2*	8	3		6	7					4	11	12	9	5	10						10
1		3	2		6	7*					4	11	8	9	5	10			12			11
1		3	2		6		8				4	11	7	9	5	10						12
1		3	2		6		8				4	11	7	9	10	5						13
1		3	2		6		8				4	11	7	9	10	5						14
1		3	2		6		8				4	11	7	9	10	5						15
1		3	2		6		8				4	11	7	9	10	5						16
1		3	4	5	6		8		10			11	7	9	2							17
1	2	3	4				8	5	10	12		11	7*	9								18
1	2		3	5		7	8	6	10			11	4	9								19
1	2		3	5	6		8	4	10			11	7	9								20
1	2		3	5		7	8	6	10			11	4	9								21
1	2		3	5*	6	7	8	12	10			11	4	9								22
1	2		3	5	6	7	8		10			11	4	9								23
1	2		3	5	6	7	8		10			11	4	9								24
1	2		3	5	6	7	8		10			11	4	9								25
1	2		3	5	6	7	8		10			11	4	9								26
1	2		3	5	6	7	8		10			11	4	9								27
1	2		3	5	6	7	8		10			11	4	9								28
1	2		3	5	6	7	8		10			11	4	9								29
1	2		3	5	6	7	8		10			11	4	9								30
1*			3	5	6	7	8		10			11	4	9				2	12			31
			3	5	6	7	8		10			11	4	9				2			1	32
			3	5	6	7	8		10			11	4	9				2			1	33
			3	5	6	7	8		10			11	4	9				2			1	34
	2		3	5	6	7	8		10			11	4*	9					12		1	35
	2		3	5	6	7	8		10			11	4	9							1	36
	2		3	5	6	7	8		10			11	4	9							1	37
	2		3	5	6	7	8		10			11*		9				4	12		1	38
	2		3	5	6	7	8		10			11	4	9							1	39
	2		3	5	6	7	8		10			11	4	9							1	40
	2		3		6	7	8		10			11	4	9						5	1	41
	2		3		6	7	8		10			11	4	9						5	1	42
	2		3		6	7	8		10			11	4	9						5	1	43
	2		3		6	7	8		10			11	4	9						5	1	44
	2		3		6	7	8		10			11	4	9						5	1	45
			3	5	6	7	8		10			11	4	9							1	46
31	35	13	46	28	43	35	44	7	38	5	15	43	37	43	6	7		5	5	5	15	
									2		2				3		1		1		2	
	1			2	2	7	19		21			7	1	9								

1 own-goal

1977-78

Manager: Bobby Saxton

1	Aug	20	(a)	Walsall	W 3-1 Beer 2, Kellow	5,174
2		27	(h)	Bury	D 2-2 Hodge, Kellow	5,236
3	Sep	3	(a)	Shrewsbury T	W 2-0 Atkins (og), Kellow	3,302
4		10	(h)	Port Vale	W 4-1 Robertson 2 (2 pens), Hodge, Holman	5,026
5		13	(a)	Rotherham U	L 0-1	4,889
6		17	(a)	Peterborough U	D 1-1 Kellow	5,016
7		24	(h)	Portsmouth	L 0-1	5,875
8		26	(h)	Carlisle U	L 0-1	5,106
9	Oct	1	(a)	Chesterfield	D 0-0	3,771
10		3	(a)	Tranmere R	L 1-2 Roberts	3,807
11		8	(h)	Wrexham	L 0-1	4,722
12		12	(h)	Sheffield W	W 2-1 Jennings, Holman	4,564
13		15	(a)	Lincoln C	W 2-1 Randell, Kellow	4,704
14		22	(h)	Preston NE	W 2-0 Jennings, Kellow	5,444
15		29	(a)	Swindon T	L 0-4	7,021
16	Nov	5	(h)	Oxford U	W 2-1 Hodge (pen), Bowker	4,830
17		12	(a)	Gillingham	L 0-1	5,714
18		19	(h)	Bradford C	W 1-0 Hodge (pen)	4,747
19	Dec	3	(h)	Cambridge U	L 2-4 Kellow 2 (2 pens)	4,932
20		9	(a)	Colchester U	L 1-3 Holman	3,267
21		26	(a)	Plymouth A	D 2-2 Roberts, Kellow	12,349
22		27	(h)	Hereford U	W 1-0 Bowker	6,722
23		31	(a)	Oxford U	D 0-0	4,688
24	Jan	2	(h)	Chester	D 1-1 Ingham	6,193
25		14	(h)	Walsall	D 1-1 Kellow	5,149
26		17	(a)	Sheffield W	L 1-2 Bowker	9,596
27		21	(a)	Bury	L 0-5	3,730
28		28	(h)	Shrewsbury T	D 1-1 Kellow	3,906
29	Feb	8	(a)	Port Vale	L 0-4	3,333
30		11	(h)	Peterborough U	W 1-0 Holman	4,017
31		28	(a)	Portsmouth	D 1-1 Cahill (og)	10,260
32	Mar	4	(a)	Wrexham	L 1-2 Bowker	15,317
33		8	(h)	Rotherham U	W 1-0 Kellow	4,016
34		11	(h)	Lincoln C	W 3-0 Bowker, Holman 2	4,280
35		18	(a)	Preston NE	D 0-0	9,189
36		22	(h)	Swindon T	D 0-0	4,449
37		25	(a)	Hereford U	L 0-4	4,436
38		28	(h)	Plymouth A	D 0-0	8,334
39	Apr	1	(a)	Chester	L 1-2 Holman	1,996
40		3	(a)	Carlisle U	L 0-2	3,693
41		8	(h)	Gillingham	W 2-1 Bowker, Kellow	3,982
42		15	(a)	Bradford C	W 2-1 Holman, Kellow	4,924
43		18	(h)	Chesterfield	D 0-0	3,200
44		22	(h)	Colchester U	D 0-0	3,853
45		26	(h)	Tranmere R	W 4-2 Bowker 2, Delve, Hatch	3,156
46		29	(a)	Cambridge U	L 1-2 Bowker	8,741

FINAL LEAGUE POSITION: 17th in Division Three

Appearances
Sub Appearances
Goals

FA Cup

1	Nov	26	(a)	Newport C	D 1-1
R		30	(h)	Newport C	W 4-2
2	Dec	17	(a)	Minehead	W 3-0
3	Jan	7	(h)	Wolves	D 2-2
R		10	(a)	Wolves	L 1-3

League Cup

1	Aug	13	(h)	Plymouth A	D 2-2
		16	(a)	Plymouth A	D 0-0
R		23	(a)	Plymouth A	W 1-0
2		31	(h)	Aston Villa	L 1-3

274

Baugh	Templeman	Hore	Weeks	Saxton	Hatch	Hodge	Kellow	Bowker	Beer	Jennings	Robertson	Holman	Key	Randell	Roberts	Heale	Giles	Ingham	Delve	Forbes	
1	2	3	4	5	6	7	8	9	10	11											1
1	2	3	4	5	6	7*	8	9	10	11	12										2
1	2	3		5	6	4	8	7	10*	11	9	12									3
1	2	3		5	6	4	8	7		11	9	10									4
	2	3		5	6	7	8	4		11	9	10	1								5
	2	3		5	6	7	8	4		11		9	1	10							6
	2	3		5	6	7	8	4		11		10*	1	9	12						7
	2	3		5	6	7	8	4		11		10*	1	9	12						8
	2	3		5	6	7	8	4		11			1	9	10						9
	2	3		5	6	7	8	4		11			1	9	10						10
	2	3		5	6	7	8	4		11			1	9	10						11
		3		5	6	7	8	4		11		10	1	9	2						12
	2			5	6	7	8	4		11		10	1	9	3						13
	2	3		5	6	7	8	4		11		10	1	9							14
	2	3		5	6	7	8	4		11		10	1	9							15
	2	3		5	6	7	8	4		11		10	1	9							16
	2	3		5	6	7	8	4		11		10	1	9							17
	2	3		5	6	7	8	4		11		10	1	9							18
	2	3	4		6		8	9		7			1	10	5	11					19
	2	3	7		6*		8	4		12		11	1	9	5	10					20
	2	3		5	6		8	4	7*			11	1	9	10	12					21
	2	3		5	6		8	4				11	1	9	10	7					22
	2	3	4*		6		8	9		12		11	1	7	10		5				23
	2	3			6		8	4	7			11	1		10		5	9			24
	2		4		6	3	8	9				11	1	7	10		5				25
	2	3	7		6		8	4				11	1	9	10		5				26
	2		4		6	3	8	9				11	1	7	10		5				27
	2		4		6*	3	8	9				11	1	7	10		5	12			28
	2	3	7		6		8	4		11			1	9	10*		5	12			29
1	2	3	4			7	8	10				9	11	6			5				30
	2	3	4			7	8	10				11	1	9	6		5				31
	2	3	4			7	8	10				11	1	9	6		5				32
	2	3				7	8	10				11	1	9	6		5	4			33
	2	3				7	8	10				11	1	9	6		5	4			34
	2	6		11			8	4				10	1	9	3		5	7			35
	2	3		12		7	8	10				11	1	9	6		5*		4		36
	2	3	12	5		7	8	10				11	1	9	6*				4		37
	2	3		11	6		7	9				10	1	8			5		4		38
	2	3		11	6*		7	9		12		10	1	8			5		4		39
	2	3	7*		6		8	10		12		11	1	9			5		4		40
	2	3	4		6		8	9		11		10	1	7			5		4		41
	2	3	4		6	7	8	9				10	1	11			5		4		42
	2	3	4		6*	7	8	10		12		11	1	9			5		4		43
	2	3				7	8	6				11	1	9			5	10	4		44
	2	3		11			8	6					1	9			5	10	4	7	45
	2	3			6	12	8	10					1	9			5	11*	4	7	46
5	44	46	12	25	38	31	46	46	3	23	3	36	41	40	24	3	23	4	11	2	
	1		1	1					5	1	1			2	1		2				
			1	4	14	9	2	2	2			8	1	2				1	1		

2 own-goals

1978-79

Manager: Bobby Saxton until January 1979, then Brian Godfrey.

1	Aug	19	(h)	Mansfield T	D	0-0		3,704
2		26	(a)	Chester	L	0-3		3,431
3	Sep	2	(h)	Brentford	D	2-2	Bowker 2	3,604
4		9	(a)	Chesterfield	W	1-0	Kellow	3,936
5		13	(h)	Shrewsbury T	L	0-1		3,732
6		16	(a)	Oxford U	L	2-3	Bowker, Templeman	5,441
7		23	(h)	Hull C	W	3-1	Kellow, Delve, Bowker	3,733
8		27	(h)	Colchester U	W	2-1	Kellow, Bowker	3,421
9		30	(a)	Peterborough U	D	1-1	Holman	6,714
10	Oct	7	(h)	Gillingham	D	0-0		4,241
11		14	(a)	Swansea C	L	0-1		10,957
12		18	(h)	Blackpool	W	3-0	Kellow 2, Bowker	3,993
13		21	(h)	Bury	W	2-1	Kellow, Bowker	3,840
14		24	(a)	Sheffield W	L	1-2	Kellow	11,139
15		28	(a)	Watford	L	0-1		14,797
16	Nov	4	(h)	Tranmere R	W	3-0	Bowker 2, Hatch	3,526
17		11	(a)	Brentford	D	0-0		6,390
18		18	(h)	Chester	L	0-1		3,985
19	Dec	2	(h)	Southend U	D	0-0		3,195
20		9	(a)	Carlisle U	D	1-1	Roberts	4,568
21		26	(h)	Walsall	W	3-1	Sims, Randell, Pearson	4,159
22		30	(h)	Lincoln C	W	3-2	Sims 2, Pearson	3,810
23	Jan	13	(h)	Chesterfield	W	3-1	Neville (pen), Delve, Roberts	3,671
24		20	(h)	Oxford U	W	2-0	Neville, Randell	4,532
25	Feb	2	(a)	Colchester U	D	2-2	Neville 2	2,767
26		10	(h)	Peterborough U	W	1-0	Pearson	3,844
27		24	(h)	Swansea C	W	2-1	Delve, Sims	7,697
28		27	(a)	Plymouth A	L	2-4	Delve, Sims	12,637
29	Mar	3	(a)	Bury	L	2-4	Hatch, Giles	3,425
30		10	(h)	Watford	D	0-0		7,082
31		16	(a)	Tranmere R	D	2-2	Sims, Roberts	984
32		24	(h)	Sheffield W	D	2-2	Neville, Sims	4,521
33		26	(a)	Mansfield T	D	1-1	Bowker	4,562
34		31	(h)	Rotherham U	W	2-0	Randell, Sims	3,349
35	Apr	3	(a)	Swindon T	D	1-1	Sims	7,923
36		6	(a)	Southend U	W	1-0	Neville (pen)	6,733
37		11	(h)	Swindon T	L	1-2	Sims	5,548
38		14	(a)	Walsall	D	2-2	Rogers, Delve	3,118
39		17	(h)	Plymouth A	W	1-0	Rogers	8,022
40		21	(a)	Lincoln C	W	1-0	Neville (pen)	2,675
41		24	(a)	Blackpool	D	1-1	Sims	3,136
42		28	(h)	Carlisle U	W	3-2	Neville 2 (1 pen), Rogers	4,229
43	May	5	(a)	Rotherham U	L	1-2	Bowker	2,217
44		7	(a)	Hull C	L	0-1		4,079
45		14	(a)	Gillingham	L	0-2		8,788
46		17	(a)	Shrewsbury T	L	1-4	Delve	14,441

FINAL LEAGUE POSITION: 9th in Division Three

Appearances
Sub Appearances
Goals

FA Cup

1	Nov	25	(h)	Brentford	W	1-0
2	Dec	16	(a)	Maidstone	L	0-1

League Cup

1	Aug	12	(a)	Bournemouth	W	1-0
		15	(h)	Bournemouth	D	1-1
2		29	(h)	Blackburn R	W	2-1
3	Oct	4	(h)	Bolton W	W	2-1
4	Nov	8	(h)	Watford	L	0-2

276

No.	O'Keefe	Templeman	Hore	Randell	Giles	Roberts L	Hodge	Kellow	Bowker	Delve	Hatch	Ingham	Williams	Holman	Mitchell	Neville	Forbes	Pearson	Sims	Main	Rogers	Ireland	Roberts P
1	1	2	3	4	5	6	7	8	9	10	11												
2	1	2	3	4	5	6	7*	8	9	10	11	12											
3	1	2	3	4	5	6	7*	8	9	10	11		12										
4	1	2	3	4	5	6	7	8	9	10	11												
5	1	2	3	4	5	6		8	9	10	11		7										
6	1	2	3	4	5	6		8	9	10	11	7*	12										
7	1	2	3	4	5	6		8	9	7	11			10									
8	1	2	3	4	5	6		8	9	10	11		7										
9	1	2	3	4	5	6		8	9	10			7										
10	1	2	3*	4	5	6		8	9	10	11		12			7							
11	1	2	3	4	5	6		8	9	10	11					7							
12	1	2	3	4	5	6		8	9	10	11					7							
13	1	2	3	4	5	6		8	9		11		12	10*		7							
14	1	2	3	4	5	6		8	9	10*	11		12			7							
15	1	2		4	5	6		8	9	10	11		3			7							
16	1	2	3			6		8	9	10	11		5			7							
17	1	2	3			6			9	10	11		5			7	4						
18	1	2			5	6			9	10	11		5			7	4	8					
19	1		3		5	6			9	10	11		3			7	4	8					
20	1		3		5	6			9	10	11		2			7	4	8					
21	1	2	3	10	5	6			4		11					7	8	9					
22	1	2	6	4	5	3				10	11					7	8	9					
23	1	2	3	4	5	6				10	11					7	8	9					
24	1	4	3	6	5	2*				10	11					7	12	9	8				
25	1	2	3	4	5	6				10	11					7	8	9					
26	1	2	3	4	5	6				10	11					7	8	9					
27	1	2	3	4		5				11	6					7	8	9	10				
28	1	2	3	4	5	6				10	11					7	8	9					
29	1	2	3	4	5	6				10	11					7	9	8					
30	1	2	3	4	5	6				10*	11	12				7	8	9					
31	1	2	3		5	6				9	11					7	4	8	10				
32	1	2	3	4	5	6				10	11					7	8	9					
33		2	3	4	5	6				10	11					7	8*	9	1	12			
34		2	3	4	5	6				10	11					7	9		1	8			
35		2	3	4	5	6				10	11					7	9		1	8			
36		2	3		5	6			4	10	11					7	9		1	8			
37		2	3		5	6			4	10	11					7	9		1	8			
38		2	3	4	5	6				10	11					7	9		1	8			
39		3	2		5	6				10	11					7	4	9	1	8			
40		2	3	4	5	6				10	11					7	9		1	8			
41		2	3	4	5				12	10	11					7	8		1	9*			
42		2	3	4	5				12	10	11*				6	7		8	1	9*			
43		3	2	4	5				12	10	11*				6	7		9	1	8			
44		2	3	4	5				12	10	11*				6	7		9	1	8			
45		2	3	4	5				8	10	11					7	9*		1		12		6
46		2	3	4	5					10	11					7	9		1	8	6		
	33	45	44	38	43	41	4	17	26	42	45		2	4	10	36	7	18	25	13	11		2
												3		2	1	4			1			1	1
	1		3	1	3		7	11	6	2			1		9		3	11			3		

277

1979-80

Manager: Brian Godfrey

#	Month	Date		Opponent	Result	Scorers	Att
1	Aug	18	(a)	Grimsby T	L 1-4	Neville	5,937
2		22	(h)	Wimbledon	L 0-2		4,051
3		25	(h)	Mansfield T	W 2-1	P.Rogers, Pullar	3,475
4	Sep	1	(a)	Sheffield U	L 1-3	L.Roberts	12,617
5		8	(h)	Bury	W 1-0	Bowker	2,995
6		15	(a)	Millwall	L 1-5	Pullar	5,567
7		17	(a)	Brentford	W 2-0	Bowker, Neville	7,810
8		22	(h)	Carlisle U	L 1-2	Neville (pen)	3,409
9		29	(a)	Gillingham	L 0-1		7,538
10	Oct	3	(h)	Brentford	D 0-0		3,297
11		6	(h)	Blackpool	W 1-0	Hatch	3,769
12		9	(a)	Wimbledon	D 2-2	Bowker, Neville (pen)	2,999
13		13	(h)	Chester	W 1-0	Bowker	3,454
14		20	(a)	Reading	L 1-2	Pearson	6,083
15		24	(h)	Southend U	W 4-2	Forbes, Neville (pen), Bowker, Pearson	3,246
16		27	(a)	Hull C	D 2-2	Bowker, Pullar	5,196
17	Nov	3	(h)	Grimsby T	L 1-2	Forbes	4,356
18		5	(a)	Southend U	L 0-4		2,787
19		10	(a)	Barnsley	D 2-2	Hunter (og), Pearson	11,739
20		17	(h)	Oxford U	D 0-0		3,550
21	Dec	1	(h)	Rotherham U	D 1-1	Hatch	3,354
22		8	(a)	Sheffield W	W 1-0	P.Rogers	11,530
23		21	(h)	Colchester U	W 3-1	L.Roberts, Dowman (og), Pullar	2,648
24		26	(a)	Swindon T	W 3-2	Bowker 2, Pullar	11,606
25		29	(a)	Mansfield T	W 1-0	Neville	3,711
26	Jan	1	(h)	Plymouth A	D 2-2	Hatch, P.Rogers	10,489
27		12	(h)	Sheffield U	W 3-1	Moore (og), Hatch, Pullar	6,632
28		19	(a)	Bury	L 0-3		3,5790
29		26	(h)	Chesterfield	L 1-2	Hatch	4,325
30	Feb	2	(h)	Millwall	W 2-1	L.Roberts, P.Rogers	4,538
31		9	(a)	Carlisle U	L 1-4	Pullar	4,085
32		16	(h)	Gillingham	W 3-1	Delve, Hatch, P.Rogers	3,466
33		27	(a)	Blackburn R	D 1-1	Pullar	10,601
34	Mar	1	(h)	Reading	W 1-0	Giles	4,390
35		8	(h)	Hull C	D 2-2	Giles, Pullar	3,771
36		15	(a)	Blackpool	L 0-1		4,155
37		22	(h)	Barnsley	W 2-1	Kellow (pen), Pullar	4,700
38		26	(a)	Chester	W 3-1	Kellow (pen), Pratt 2	2,867
39		29	(a)	Oxford U	L 0-2		2,910
40	Apr	2	(a)	Colchester U	D 0-0		2,780
41		5	(h)	Swindon T	W 4-1	Kellow 2 (1 pen), Neville, Stroud (og)	5,442
42		7	(a)	Plymouth A	L 0-2		10,214
43		12	(h)	Blackburn R	W 2-0	Forbes, Neville	5,407
44		19	(a)	Rotherham U	L 0-2		3,241
45		26	(h)	Sheffield W	W 1-0	Kellow	10,461
46	May	3	(a)	Chesterfield	L 0-3		5,770

FINAL LEAGUE POSITION: 8th in Division Three

Appearances
Sub Appearances
Goals

FA Cup

1	Nov	24	(a)	Aldershot	L 1-4

League Cup

1	Aug	11	(a)	Hereford U	W 3-1	
		15	(h)	Hereford U	W 2-1	
2		28	(a)	Doncaster R	L 1-3	
	Sep	5	(h)	Doncaster R	W 5-1*	*After extra-time
3		26	(a)	Birmingham C	W 2-1	
4	Oct	30	(a)	Liverpool	L 0-2	

278

O'Keefe	Roberts F	Rogers M	Hore	Giles	Hatch	Neville	Pearson	Rogers P	Delve	Pullar	Sims	Roberts I	Bowker	Mitchell	Forbes	Ireland	Bell	Main	Kellow	Pratt	#
1	2	3	4	5	6	7	8	9	10	11											1
1	2	3	4	5	6	7	8	9*	10	11	12										2
1	2	3*	4	5	6	7		9	10	11	8	12									3
1	2		4	5	6	7		8	10	11	9	3									4
1	2	3	4	5	6	7		8*	10	11	9		12								5
1	2	3	4	5	6	7			10	11	8		9								6
1			4	5	3	7*	12	10	11	9		8	2	6							7
1		2	5	6	7			10	11	8		9	3	4							8
1			4	5	3	7		12	10	11*	9		8	2	6						9
1			4	5	3	7		12	10	11	9		8*	2	6						10
1			4	5	3	7		9	10	11			8	2	6						11
1			4	5	3	7		8	10	11			9	2	6						12
1			4	5	3	7		8	10	11			9	2	6						13
1			4	5	2	7	12	8	10	11			9	3	6*						14
1			4	5	3	7	8		10	11			9	2	6						15
1			4	5	3	7	8	12	10*	11			9	2	6						16
1			4	5	3	7		8	10*	11			9	2	6	12					17
1			4	5	3	7		8		11*		10	9	2	6		12				18
1	12		4	5			7	10	8			2*	9	3	6	11					19
1			4	5	3	7	8	11	10				9	2	6						20
			4	5	3	7	8	9	10	11		6		2				1			21
	5		4		3	7	8	9	10	11		6		2				1			22
	5		4		3	7	8*	9	10	11		6	12	2				1			23
	5		4		3	7		8	10	11		6	9	2				1			24
	3		4	5	6	7		8	10	11			9	2				1			25
	6		4	5	3	7		8	10	11		12	9	2*				1			26
	6		4	5	3	7		9	10	11			8	2				1			27
	6		2	5	4	7*		9	10	11			8	3	12			1			28
	6	2	4	5	3	7		8	10	11			9					1			29
	6		4	5	3			8	10	11		7		2		9		1			30
	6		4	5	3	12		8	10	11		7*		2		9		1			31
	6		4	5	3	7		8	10	11		9*	12	2				1			32
	6		4	5	3	7		8	10	11		9*	12	2				1			33
	6		4	5	3	7*		8	10	11		9	12	2				1			34
	6		4	5	3	7		8	10	11		9*	12	2				1			35
	6		2	5	4			8	10	7			3					1	9	11	36
	6		4	5	3	12		8	10	11			2					1	9	7*	37
	6		4	5	3			8	10	11			2					1	9	7	38
	6		4	5	3	12		8	10	11*			2					1	9	7	39
	6	2	4	5	3	11		8	10					9				1	7		40
	6	2	4	5	3	7		8	10	11								1	9*	12	41
	6	2	4	5	3	7*		8	10	11		12						1	9		42
	6	2	4	5	3	7		8		11				10				1	9		43
	3	2	4			7		8		11		5		6*	10			1	9	12	44
	6		4	5	3	7		8	10	11			2					1	9		45
	6		3	5	4	7		8	10	11			2					1	9		46
20	31	11	46	42	44	40	9	39	42	43	8	14	21	34	16	3	2	26	10	5	
	1				3	1	4			1		3	6		1	1	1			2	
		2	6	8	3	5	1	10				3	8	3				5	2		

4 own-goals

1980-81

Manager: Brian Godfrey

1	Aug	16	(h)	Gillingham	W 2-1	Kellow, Neville	3,630
2		20	(a)	Oxford U	W 2-1	Neville, Kellow	3,751
3		23	(a)	Hull C	D 3-3	Neville 2, Hatch	3,559
4		30	(h)	Colchester U	W 4-0	Neville, Giles, Delve, Kellow (pen)	3,918
5	Sep	6	(a)	Chester	L 0-1		1,974
6		13	(h)	Burnley	D 0-0		4,534
7		17	(h)	Fulham	W 1-0	Kellow	5,300
8		20	(a)	Millwall	L 0-1		3,638
9		27	(h)	Charlton A	W 4-3	Kellow 3, Prince	4,916
10	Oct	1	(a)	Fulham	W 1-0	P.Rogers	4,509
11		4	(a)	Rotherham U	L 1-3	Giles	6,889
12		8	(h)	Brentford	D 0-0		4,665
13		11	(h)	Huddersfield T	L 1-4	P.Rogers	4,769
14		18	(a)	Sheffield U	L 1-3	Kellow	10,608
15		21	(a)	Walsall	W 3-1	P.Rogers, Kellow, Pratt	3,703
16		25	(h)	Swindon T	L 3-4	Kellow 2 (1 pen), Pratt	4,688
17	Nov	1	(a)	Reading	L 1-2	Kellow	4,622
18		3	(a)	Brentford	W 1-0	Kellow	6,590
19		8	(h)	Barnsley	L 0-1		4,019
20		12	(h)	Oxford U	D 1-1	Delve	3,241
21		15	(a)	Gillingham	W 5-1	Delve, Kellow 3, Pullar	3,725
22		29	(h)	Carlisle U	W 2-0	P.Rogers, Forbes	3,940
23	Dec	6	(a)	Blackpool	D 0-0		3,597
24		20	(h)	Chesterfield	D 2-2	P.Rogers, Pratt	4,075
25		26	(a)	Plymouth A	W 2-0	Kellow (pen), Pullar	14,792
26		27	(h)	Newport C	D 2-2	Pullar, Kellow (pen)	6,295
27	Jan	10	(h)	Walsall	L 0-3		4,590
28		14	(h)	Portsmouth	W 2-0	Pearson, Pullar	3,722
29		31	(h)	Hull C	L 1-3	Hoolickin (og)	5,022
30	Feb	3	(a)	Colchester U	W 2-1	Forbes, Pullar	2,357
31		7	(a)	Burnley	L 0-1		5,585
32		10	(a)	Portsmouth	L 0-5		12,743
33		21	(a)	Charlton A	L 0-1		7,245
34		28	(h)	Millwall	W 2-0	Kellow, Hatch	5,408
35	Mar	18	(h)	Rotherham U	W 2-1	Sparrow, Delve	4,494
36		21	(h)	Sheffield U	D 1-1	Kellow	4,224
37		28	(a)	Swindon T	D 2-2	Pearson, Kellow	6,509
38		31	(a)	Carlisle U	D 1-1	P.Rogers	4,385
39	Apr	4	(h)	Reading	W 3-1	Pearson 2, Kellow	3,890
40		7	(a)	Huddersfield T	L 0-5		12,009
41		10	(a)	Barnsley	L 0-1		13,445
42		18	(a)	Newport C	L 1-2	Kellow (pen)	5,231
43		21	(h)	Plymouth A	D 1-1	Kellow	8,491
44		29	(h)	Chester	D 2-2	Kellow, Pratt	3,056
45	May	2	(h)	Blackpool	D 0-0		3,864
46		8	(a)	Chesterfield	L 0-1		3,448

FINAL LEAGUE POSITION: 11th in Division Three

Appearances
Sub Appearances
Goals

FA Cup

1	Nov	22	(h)	Leatherhead	W 5-0	
2	Dec	13	(a)	Millwall	W 1-0	
3	Jan	3	(a)	Maidstone U	W 4-2	
4		24	(a)	Leicester C	D 1-1	
R		28	(h)	Leicester C	W 3-1	
5	Feb	14	(a)	Newcastle U	D 1-1	
R		18	(h)	Newcastle U	W 4-0	
6	Mar	7	(a)	Tottenham H	L 0-2	

League Cup

1	Aug	9	(h)	Bristol R	D 1-1	
		12	(a)	Bristol R	D 1-1*	*After extra-time. Bristol Rovers won 7-6 on penalties.

Main	Ireland	Hatch	Prince	Giles	Roberts P	Pearson	Neville	Kellow	Delve	Pullar	Rogers P	Rogers M	Forbes	Bond	Pratt	Roberts L	Sparrow	Mitchell	Nute	Fisher	
1	2	3	4	5	6	7*	8	9	10	11	12										1
1	2	3	4	5	6	7	8	9*	10	11	12										2
1	2	3	4	5	6	7	8	9	10	11											3
1	2	3	4	5	6	7	8	9*	10	11	12										4
1	2*	3	4	5	6	7	8	9	10	11	12										5
1	2	3	4	5	6	7	8	9	10	11											6
1	2	3	4	5	6	7	8	9	10	11											7
1	2*	3	4	5	6	7	8	9	10	11	12										8
1		3	4	5	6	7	8	9	10	11		2									9
1		3	4	5	6	7	8	9	10	11		2									10
1		3	4	5	6	7	8	9	10	11		2									11
1		3	4	5	6	7	8	9	10	11		2									12
1		3	4	5	6	7*	8	9	10	11		2	12								13
1		3	4	5	6		8	9	10	11		2	7								14
		3	4	5	6			9	10	11	8*	2	7	1	12						15
		3	4*	5	6	12		9	10	11		2	7	1	8						16
		3		5	6	7		9	10	11	8	2	4	1							17
		3		5	6	7		9	10	11	8	2	4	1							18
		3		5	6	7		9	10	11*	8	2	4	1	12						19
		3			6	7		9	10	11		2	4	1	8	5					20
		3			6	7		9	10	11	8	2	4	1		5					21
	10	3			6	7		9		11	8	2	4	1		5					22
	10	3			6	7		9		11	8	2	4	1		5					23
		3			6	7*		9	10	11	8	2	4	1	12	5					24
		3			6	7		9	10	11	8	2	4	1		5					25
		3			6	7		9	10	11	8	2	4	1		5					26
		3			6	7*		9	10	11	8	2	4	1	12	5					27
		3			6	7		9	10	11	8	2	4	1		5					28
1		3			6	7		9	10	11	8	2	4		12	5*					29
1		3		5	6	7		9	10	11	8	2	4								30
1		3		5	6	7		9	10	11*	8	2	4		12						31
1	11	10	5	6	7		9*				8	2	4		12	3					32
	11			7		9	10				2	4	1	8	5	3	6				33
	11		6*	7		9	10				8	2	4	1		5	3				34
	11		6	7		9	10				8	2	4	1		5	3				35
1	11		6	7		9	10				8	2	4*			5	3				36
1	11		6	7		9	10				8	2	4*	12		5	3				37
1	10	11	6	7		9					8	2	4			5	3				38
	10	11	6	7		9					8	2	4			5	3		1		39
	10*	11	6	7		9					8	2	4	12		5	3		1		40
	12	11	6	7		9	10				2	4*	8			5	3		1		41
	12	11	6	7		9					8	2	4*	10		5	3		1		42
1	11	7	6		9	10*					8	2	4	12		5	3				43
1	11	4	6		9						8	2	12	10		5	3			7*	44
1	11	4	6	8	9						12		10	5	3	2				7*	45
	11	4		9	12	8*	2					10	5	3	6	1	7				46
24	14	45	21	22	44	40	14	46	36	24	34	37	30	17	8	24	15	3	5	3	
2				1				1	6		2		9	2							
	2	1	2		4	5		25	4	5	6		2		4		1				

1 own-goal

1981-82

Manager: Brian Godfrey

1	Aug	29	(a)	Huddersfield T	D	1-1	Pratt	8,647
2	Sep	5	(h)	Carlisle U	W	2-1	Hatch, Kellow	3,533
3		11	(a)	Doncaster R	L	0-3		4,369
4		19	(h)	Swindon T	L	1-2	Kellow (pen)	4,372
5		23	(h)	Bristol R	L	1-3	Kellow	5,510
6		26	(a)	Gillingham	W	3-2	Lester, L.Roberts, P.Rogers	4,158
7		29	(a)	Portsmouth	L	0-2		10,989
8	Oct	3	(h)	Millwall	W	5-4	Kellow, Lester 3, P.Rogers	7,169
9		10	(h)	Brentford	W	3-1	Kellow, Cooke, Prince	3,689
10		17	(a)	Burnley	D	3-3	Kellow, Lester, Cooke	3,975
11		20	(a)	Fulham	L	1-4	Cooke	4,500
12		24	(h)	Preston NE	W	4-3	P.Rogers, Kellow 2 (1 pen), L.Roberts	3,642
13		31	(a)	Wimbledon	D	1-1	Lester	2,152
14	Nov	4	(h)	Oxford U	L	1-2	L.Roberts	3,349
15		7	(h)	Reading	W	4-3	Kellow 2 (1 pen), P.Rogers, Pullar	3,765
16		14	(a)	Chester	W	2-0	Sparrow, Pratt	2,125
17		28	(a)	Newport C	D	1-1	Hatch	4,149
18	Dec	5	(h)	Chesterfield	L	0-3		3,947
19		28	(h)	Plymouth A	D	1-1	Kellow	9,144
20	Jan	1	(a)	Southend U	L	1-2	Fisher	5,985
21		16	(h)	Walsall	W	2-0	Kellow 2	3,118
22		31	(a)	Swindon T	L	2-3	M.Rogers, Pullar	5,656
23	Feb	6	(h)	Doncaster R	W	2-1	M.Rogers, Delve	3,193
24		9	(a)	Bristol R	L	2-3	M.Rogers, Kellow (pen)	4,987
25		14	(a)	Millwall	L	1-5	P.Rogers	3,628
26		20	(h)	Gillingham	D	1-1	Kellow (pen)	2,888
27		23	(a)	Bristol C	L	2-3	L.Roberts, P.Rogers	6,612
28		27	(a)	Brentford	L	0-2		4,931
29	Mar	6	(h)	Burnley	W	2-1	P.Rogers 2	3,136
30		10	(h)	Fulham	W	1-0	P.Rogers	3,367
31		13	(a)	Preston NE	L	0-1		4,770
32		17	(a)	Oxford U	D	0-0		5,098
33		20	(h)	Wimbledon	W	2-1	Pratt, Kellow	3,002
34		24	(h)	Lincoln C	L	1-2	M.Rogers	3,081
35		27	(a)	Reading	L	0-4		3,365
36	Apr	3	(h)	Chester	W	3-0	Raynor (og), Kellow (pen), Giles	2,498
37		9	(a)	Plymouth A	L	1-2	Kellow (pen)	9,458
38		10	(h)	Bristol C	W	4-0	Kellow 2 (1 pen), Pratt, P.Rogers	4,580
39		17	(a)	Chesterfield	L	1-2	Pratt	2,867
40		20	(a)	Carlisle U	L	2-3	Pratt, Delve	5,220
41		24	(h)	Newport C	W	1-0	Delve	3,168
42	May	1	(a)	Walsall	L	1-2	Pratt	2,487
43		5	(h)	Portsmouth	D	3-3	Kellow, Pratt 2	2,596
44		8	(h)	Southend U	D	1-1	Marker	3,174
45		12	(h)	Huddersfield T	W	1-0	Hatch	2,888
46		15	(a)	Lincoln C	L	0-2		5,447

FINAL LEAGUE POSITION: 18th in Division Three

Appearances
Sub Appearances
Goals

FA Cup

1	Nov	21	(a)	Brentford	L	0-2

League Cup

1	Sep	2	(a)	Cardiff C	L	1-2
		16	(h)	Cardiff C	W	3-1
2	Oct	7	(a)	Liverpool	L	0-5
		28	(h)	Liverpool	L	0-6

Main	Rogers M	Hatch	Davey	Cooke	Roberts L	Rogers P	Pratt	Kellow	Lester	Pullar	Bond	Roberts P	Prince	Mitchell	Sparrow	Fisher	Delve	Marker	Shaw	Foster	Howarth	Kirkup	Giles	Robertson	
1	2	3	4	5	6	7	8	9	10	11															1
2	11	4	5	3	7*	8	9	10		1	6	12													2
2	11*	4	5	3	7	8	9	10		1	6	12													3
	11	4	5	3		8	9	10		1	6	12	2*			7									4
	11*	2	5	6			8	9	4	1				12	3	7	10								5
2		5*	6	7			9	4	11	1	12	8			3		10								6
2		5	6	7			9	4	11	1		8			3		10								7
2			5	6	8		9	4	11	1		7			3		10								8
12		2	5	6	8		9	4	11*	1		7			3		10								9
2			4	7	6	8		9	11	1					3		10			5					10
2			4*	7	6	8		9	11	1	12				3		10			5					11
2			4		6	8		9	11	1	7				3		10			5					12
2		6	7*		8	12	9	4	11	1	5				3		10								13
1	2*		4		6	7	12	9	11	8					3		10			5					14
1	2			6	8	11	9	4	7						3		10			5					15
1	2	7*		6	8	12	9	4	11						3		10			5					16
1	2	11		7	6*	8		9	4	12		5			3		10								17
1	2	11		5		8		9	4	7		6*			3		10	12							18
1	3		7	6	8		9		11			4	2				10			5					19
1	3		7*	6		12	9		11			4	2	8			10			5					20
1	4			8		9		11		6		2	3			7	10			5					21
1	4			8		9	12	11		6		2	3			7*	10			5					22
4	7			6	8	9		11	1			2	3				10			5					23
4	11			6	8	9		7	1			2	3				10			5					24
4	11*			6	8	9		7	1			2	3	12			10			5					25
4	11*			6	8	9		7	1			2	3	12			10			5					26
4				6	8	12	9	11	1			2*	3	7			10			5					27
2				8	12	9		7	1	6		3					10	4		5	11*				28
				8	7	9*		11	1	6		3					10	4		5		12	2		29
11				8	7	9		1	6			3					10	4		5			2		30
11				8	7	9		12	1	6		3					10	4*		5			2		31
				8	7	9		11	1		6	3					10	4		5			2		32
1	4			8	7	9*		10		6		3					11	12		5			2		33
4				8	7	9		11	1	6		3					10			5			2		34
				8	12	9		11	1	6	4*	3								5		2	7	10	35
2	12			8	7	9		11*	1	6		3								5			4	10	36
2	12			8	7*	9		1	6	3		3					10			5			4	11	37
2	11			8	7	9		1	6			3					10			5			4		38
2	11			8	7	9		1	6			3					10			5			4		39
1	2	11		8	7	9		6				3*					10			5			4	12	40
1	2	3		8	7	9		6									10			5			4	11	41
1	2	4		8	7	9		6				3					10	12		5				11*	42
1		11	12	8*	7	9		6				3					10	4		5			2		43
	2	11		8		9		1	6			3					10	4		5			7		44
	2	11		8	7	9		1	6			3					10	4		5			4		45
	2	11	12	8*	7	9		1	6			3					10			5			4		46
15	35	20	15	17	23	42	23	46	18	27	31	26	6	13	38	6	40	11	3	28	1	8	9	5	
1	2		2		7		1	3		1	4		2		3				1				1		
4	3		3	4	10	9	21	6	2			1		1	1	1	3	1					1		

1 own-goal

1982-83

Manager: Brian Godfrey

1	Aug	28	(a)	Huddersfield T	D	1-1	Pullar	5,168
2	Sep	4	(h)	Gillingham	D	2-2	Kellow, Pullar	2,409
3		8	(h)	Portsmouth	D	1-1	Howe (og)	3,146
4		10	(a)	Doncaster R	L	1-6	P.Rogers	3,205
5		18	(h)	Preston NE	W	5-1	Pratt 2, Kellow, Harle, P.Rogers	2,310
6		25	(a)	Bournemouth	L	0-2		7,547
7		28	(a)	Cardiff C	L	0-2		4,867
8	Oct	2	(h)	Chesterfield	L	2-3	Rogers, Pullar	2,389
9		9	(a)	Wrexham	W	2-1	Hatter, McEwan	2,110
10		16	(h)	Millwall	W	2-1	Rogers, Pratt	2,640
11		20	(a)	Lincoln C	L	1-4	Kellow (pen)	3,699
12		23	(h)	Sheffield U	L	0-3		3,858
13		30	(a)	Oxford U	D	1-1	Viney	4,689
14	Nov	3	(h)	Wigan A	W	2-1	Rogers, Kellow	2,399
15		6	(h)	Walsall	W	4-3	Kellow, Delve 2, Neville	2,614
16		13	(a)	Bradford C	D	3-3	Harle, Pullar, Delve	4,576
17		27	(h)	Orient	W	2-0	Kellow, Harle	2,611
18	Dec	4	(a)	Reading	L	1-3	Pullar	1,971
19		11	(h)	Reading	D	2-2	Kellow, Delve	2,272
20		18	(a)	Brentford	L	0-4		5,296
21		27	(h)	Plymouth A	W	1-0	Neville	9,168
22		29	(a)	Bristol R	D	4-4	P.Rogers 2, Delve, McEwan	8,160
23	Jan	1	(h)	Newport C	L	0-1		3,505
24		3	(a)	Southend U	D	1-1	Marker	3,570
25		8	(a)	Gillingham	D	4-4	McEwan, Neville 3	2,970
26		15	(h)	Huddersfield T	L	3-4	McEwan (pen), Neville, M.Rogers	2,882
27		22	(a)	Preston NE	D	2-2	Pratt, Neville	3,767
28		29	(h)	Cardiff C	L	0-2		4,019
29	Feb	5	(h)	Bournemouth	W	4-2	Viney, McEwan, Neville, Pratt	3,008
30		12	(a)	Portsmouth	L	2-3	Neville 2	10,622
31		15	(a)	Wigan A	L	0-1		2,764
32		19	(h)	Wrexham	D	3-3	Viney 2, Neville	2,507
33		26	(a)	Millwall	L	2-5	Neville, Harle	2,806
34	Mar	2	(h)	Lincoln C	W	3-1	McEwan, Pratt, Neville	2,505
35		5	(a)	Sheffield U	L	0-3		9,703
36		12	(h)	Oxford U	W	3-1	Harle 2, Kellow	2,957
37		19	(a)	Walsall	L	2-3	P.Rogers 2	2,669
38		26	(h)	Bradford C	W	2-1	Crown, Pratt	2,639
39	Apr	1	(a)	Plymouth A	L	0-1		8,856
40		2	(h)	Bristol R	L	0-1		5,741
41		16	(a)	Chesterfield	W	3-1	Sparrow, Pratt, Crown	1,788
42		23	(h)	Brentford	L	1-7	Gibson	2,759
43		30	(a)	Orient	L	1-5	Neville	2,407
44	May	2	(h)	Southend U	W	4-3	Neville 3, Crown	2,956
45		7	(h)	Doncaster R	W	3-0	Kellow 2, Pratt	3,110
46		14	(a)	Newport C	D	1-1	P.Rogers	3,520

FINAL LEAGUE POSITION: 19th in Division Three

Appearances
Sub Appearances
Goals

FA Cup

| 1 | Nov | 20 | (a) | Plymouth A | L | 0-2 | |

League Cup

| 1 | Sep | 1 | (h) | Newport C | L | 1-2 | |
| | | 14 | (a) | Newport C | L | 0-6 | |

Football League Trophy

G1	Aug	14	(h)	Bristol C	W	2-1	
G2		18	(a)	Newport C	L	1-5	
G3		21	(a)	Torquay U	L	2-3	

Bond	Kirkup	Viney	McEwan	Roberts	Rogers M	Harle	Rogers P	Kellow	Delve	Pullar	Pratt	Gibson	Hatter SJ	Neville	Howarth	Marker	Sparrow	Davies G	Thomas	Ling	Phillips	Burke	Shepherd	Crown D	No.
1	2	3	4	5	6	7	8	9	10	11															1
1	2	3	4	5	6		8	9	10	11	7														2
1	2	3	4	5	6	7	8	9	10	11															3
1	2	3	4	5	6	7	8	9	10	11*	12														4
1		3	4	5	2	6		8	9	10		7	11												5
1	2	3		5		6	8	9	10	12	7*	11	4												6
1	2	3		5		6	8	9	10	12	7	11*	4												7
1		3	4	6	2	7	8	9	10	11				5											8
1	2		6	5	3	7	8	9	10	11			4												9
1	2	3	4		6	7	8	9	10	11*	12			5											10
1	2	3	6		4	7*	8	9	10		12			5	11										11
1	2*	3	6		4	7	8	9	10	11				5	12										12
1		3	6		4		8	9	10			7		5	11	2									13
1		3	6		4		8	9	10	11				5		7	2								14
1		3	6		4		8	9	10	11	12			5		7	2*								15
1		3	6	2	4		8	9	10	11				5		7									16
1		3	4	2	6		8	9	10	11						7	5								17
1		3	6	2	4		8	9	10	11						7	5								18
1		3	4	2	6		8	9*	10	11	12					7	5								19
1		3	6	2	4		8		10	11	12					7	5	9*							20
1		3	6	2	4		8	9	10	11						7	5								21
1		3	6	2	4		8	9*	10	11						7	5	12							22
1	12	3	6		2		8		10	11	9*					7	5	4							23
1		3	6		2		8	10*	11		9					7	12	5	4						24
1		3	6		10	4*	8		11	12	9					7	5	2							25
1		3	6		4		8	10	11	12	9					7	5	2*							26
1		3	6		11	4	8	10		12	9					7	5	2*							27
1	2	3			4	12	8	10	6	11	9					7	5*								28
1		3	4		2	6	8	10	11	9						7	5								29
1	12	3	6		4		8	10	9	11						7	2*	5							30
1	2	3*	6		4		8	10	11	9						7	5	12							31
1		3	6		2		8	9	10	4	12	11*				7	5								32
1		3	6		2	6	10*	8	7	12	11	9				4									33
1		3	6		2	4	9	10	11	8						7	5								34
1		3		2	4	8	9*	10	6	7	11			5	12										35
1		3		6	4	8	9	10	2	11				7	5										36
1		3		6		8	9	10	2	12	7*			5							4	11				37
		3		2	4	8	9*	10	12					5						6	7	1	11		38
1		3		2	4	8	10*	9	12					7	5					6		11			39
1		3	6		2	4	12		8					7	5				10	9	11*				40
1	2		6			8		10	9	5	7		3		4					11					41
1		2	6			8	12	10	9	5	7		3*		4					11					42
1		3	6		2	8	10	12	9*	7	5				4					12					43
1		3	5		2	4	7	9*	10	11	8			6	12										44
1	6	3		2	4	8	9	10	11					7	5										45
1	11	3	6	2	4	8	9*	10	12					7	5										46
45	15	44	37	9	37	36	43	31	44	30	17	17	11	33	3	18	9	7		10	3	1	6		
	2		1	1		2		2	14	1		2		1	1		1			1					
		4	6		1	6	10	10	5	5	9	1	1	17		1	1						3		

1 own-goal

285

1983-84

Manager: Gerry Francis

1	Aug	27	(h)	Walsall	L	0-1	4,742
2	Sep	3	(a)	Scunthorpe U	L	1-3	McEwan (pen)	2,768
3		6	(a)	Wigan A	D	1-1	McEwan	2,569
4		10	(h)	Rotherham U	L	0-1		3,193
5		17	(a)	Bristol R	L	0-2		4,813
6		24	(h)	Wimbledon	L	0-3		3,046
7		28	(h)	Lincoln C	L	0-3		2,775
8	Oct	1	(a)	Bradford C	W	3-1	McEwan, Rogers 2	2,505
9		8	(h)	Bolton W	D	2-2	McEwan 2 (1 pen)	3,478
10		15	(a)	Southend U	W	3-0	Rogers, Francis, Pratt	2,342
11		18	(a)	Gillingham	L	1-3	Rogers	4,013
12		22	(h)	Newport C	L	1-2	Kirkup	3,970
13		29	(a)	Orient	D	2-2	Neville, Pratt	3,190
14	Nov	2	(h)	Burnley	D	1-1	McEwan (pen)	3,714
15		5	(h)	Port Vale	D	1-1	Francis	3,301
16		12	(a)	Sheffield U	D	2-2	Rogers, Neville	10,334
17		26	(a)	Preston NE	L	1-2	Neville	3,373
18	Dec	3	(h)	Hull C	W	2-1	Atkinson, Pratt	3,099
19		17	(h)	Millwall	W	3-2	Pratt 2, Neville	2,859
20		26	(a)	Plymouth A	D	2-2	Neville, Pratt	10,387
21		27	(h)	Brentford	L	1-2	Pratt	4,252
22		31	(a)	Bournemouth	L	1-3	McEwan	5,133
23	Jan	2	(h)	Oxford U	W	3-1	McEwan, O'Connor, Neville	4,527
24		14	(a)	Walsall	L	1-4	Harrower	5,028
25		21	(h)	Bristol R	L	1-2	Pratt	5,310
26	Feb	3	(h)	Bradford C	L	0-2		3,105
27		11	(a)	Wimbledon	L	1-2	Smith (og)	3,013
28		14	(a)	Burnley	L	0-4		5,951
29		18	(h)	Orient	L	3-4	Pratt 2, McEwan (pen)	2,347
30		25	(a)	Newport C	L	0-1		2,465
31	Mar	3	(h)	Gillingham	D	0-0		2,801
32		5	(a)	Port Vale	D	2-2	Pratt, Neville	4,338
33		10	(h)	Sheffield U	L	1-2	Pratt	3,274
34		17	(a)	Bolton W	L	0-1		5,161
35		23	(h)	Southend U	D	3-3	Pratt 2, Neville	1,782
36		31	(a)	Lincoln C	D	1-1	Neville	1,498
37	Apr	7	(h)	Wigan A	D	1-1	Sims	2,412
38		11	(h)	Scunthorpe U	D	1-1	Francis	2,003
39		14	(a)	Hull C	L	0-1		8,238
40		20	(a)	Brentford	L	0-3		5,620
41		21	(h)	Plymouth A	D	1-1	Pratt	6,870
42		28	(h)	Preston NE	W	2-1	Pratt (pen), Sims	2,005
43	May	1	(a)	Rotherham U	L	0-1		3,636
44		5	(a)	Oxford U	D	1-1	Sims	8,056
45		7	(h)	Bournemouth	L	0-2		2,790
46		12	(a)	Millwall	L	0-3		2,898

FINAL LEAGUE POSITION: 24th in Division Three

Appearances
Sub Appearances
Goals

FA Cup

1	Nov	19	(h)	Maidstone U	D	1-1	
R		23	(a)	Maidstone U	L	1-2	

League Cup

1	Aug	31	(h)	Cardiff C	L	2-3	
	Sep	13	(a)	Cardiff C	L	1-2	

286

Football League appearances and goals grid (players as columns, matches 1–46 as rows).

Bond	Kirkup	Viney	Evans	Harle	McEwan	Neville	Rogers	Kellow	Francis	Ling	Dennis	Lane	Pratt	Howarth	Marker	Auguste	Hicks	Taylor	O'Connor	Musker	Atkinson	Webster	Harrower	McDonough	Sims	Crabtree	#
1	2	3	4	5	6	7	8	9	10	11*	12																1
1		3*	4	5	6	7	8	9	10	11		2	12														2
1	2	3	4	5	6	7	8*	9	10	12	11																3
1	2	3	4	5	6	7		9	10	12	11		8*														4
1		3		5	6	10	8*			11	7		12	2	4	9											5
1		3		8	6	7		9	10	11			12	2	4*	5											6
1		3			6	7	8	9	10	11			12	2	5				4*								7
1	2	3			6	12	8	9	10				4	7	5	11*											8
1	2	3			6	12	8	9	10					7*	5	11											9
1		3			6	12	8		10*				9	2	5	11			4	7							10
1		3			6		8		10				9	2	5	11			4	7							11
1	2	3			6		8		10				9		5	12		11*	4	7							12
1	2	3			6				10				9		5	11			4	7	8						13
1	2	3			6	10	8		12				9*		5	11			4	7							14
1	2	3			6	11	8		10				9*		5	12			4	7							15
1	2	3			6	7	8		10				9		11				4		5						16
1	2	3			6	7	8		10	12					11*				4		9	5					17
1	2	3				7	8		10				9		11*	12			4		6	5					18
1	2	3			6	7	8		10*	12			9		11				4		5						19
1	2	3			6	7	8		10				9			12		11*	4		5						20
1	2	3			6	7	8		10				9						4		11	5					21
1	2	3			6	7	8		10*				9		5				4		11	12					22
1	2	3			6	7	8			11			9						4		5	10					23
1	2				6	7	8			11*			9		12				4	3	5	10					24
1	2				6	7			10*	11			9		12				4	3	5				8		25
1	2	3			6	7				11*			9		12				4		8	5	10				26
1	2	3			6	7				11			9		12				4		8	5*	10				27
1	2	3			6	7			10*	11			9		12				4			5			8		28
1	2	3			6	7				11			9		12				4			5*	10		8		29
1		3				7	8		10	11				2					4		6	5		9			30
1		3				7	8		10	11				2					4		6	5		9			31
1		3				7	8		10				9	2					4		6	5	11*	12			32
1	2	3				7	8		10				9						4		6	5	11				33
1	2	3				7	8		10	12			9						4		6	5	11*				34
1		3				7	8		10				9	2					4		6	5	11				35
1	2	3				7	8		10				9						4		6	5	11*	12			36
1	2	3				7	8		10				9*						4		6	5	11	12			37
1	2	3				7			10										4		6	5	11	9	8		38
1	2	3				7			10						5				4		6		11	9	8		39
1	2	3				7*			10				9						4		6	5	12	11	8		40
	2	3				7*							9			12			4		6	5	10	11	8	1	41
1	2	3				7				11*			9		5	12			4		6		10		8		42
1	2	3				7				11			9		5				4		6		10		8		43
1	2					7				12			9		5				4	3	6	10*	11		8		44
1	2					7				11*			9		5				4	3	6	12	10		8		45
1	2	3				7				12			9		6				4	5*		10	11		8		46
45	36	42	4	6	28	40	25	7	28	23	3	1	30	6	28	7	3	8	38	6	28	26	10	15	12	1	
					3		1						6	1	6	5	3	3					3	1	2		
	1				9	9	5			3			16						1		1			1	3		

1 own-goal

1984-85

Manager: Jim Iley

1	Aug	25	(h)	Northampton T	W	5-0	Brough (og), McDonough, Pratt 2, Sims	3,166
2	Sep	1	(a)	Blackpool	L	0-3		3,663
3		8	(h)	Scunthorpe U	W	2-1	McNichol, Pratt	2,658
4		11	(a)	Wrexham	L	0-2		1,365
5		15	(a)	Aldershot	D	1-1	Pratt	2,372
6		22	(h)	Bury	L	0-2		2,830
7		28	(a)	Southend U	L	0-1		1,952
8	Oct	3	(h)	Mansfield T	D	0-0		2,097
9		13	(h)	Chester C	D	1-1	Viney (pen)	2,347
10		16	(a)	Colchester U	W	4-3	Harrower, Pratt, Sims, Smith	1,846
11		20	(a)	Chesterfield	L	1-5	Pratt	3,457
12		24	(h)	Swindon T	D	1-1	Pratt	2,139
13		27	(h)	Darlington	D	1-1	Neville	2,325
14	Nov	5	(a)	Hartlepool U	D	1-1	Sims	3,657
15		10	(h)	Rochdale	D	1-1	Pratt	2,325
16		24	(a)	Stockport C	L	0-1		1,335
17	Dec	1	(h)	Crewe A	L	0-2		2,413
18		15	(h)	Peterborough U	L	0-1		2,012
19		21	(a)	Tranmere R	L	2-3	Pratt, Morgan	1,115
20		26	(h)	Torquay U	W	4-3	Pratt 3, Smith	3,925
21		29	(h)	Hereford U	D	0-0		3,115
22	Jan	1	(a)	Port Vale	L	1-5	Morgan	3,306
23		5	(a)	Northampton T	L	2-5	McNichol, Morgan	1,475
24		26	(h)	Aldershot	W	3-0	O'Shea, Pratt 2 (1 pen)	2,134
25	Feb	1	(h)	Southend U	W	2-1	Morgan, Pratt	2,337
26		9	(a)	Bury	D	2-2	Morgan, Pratt	2,726
27		13	(h)	Wrexham	W	2-0	Barnard 2	1,885
28		23	(h)	Halifax T	W	1-0	Ling	2,549
29	Mar	2	(a)	Darlington	L	1-2	Todd (og)	2,737
30		5	(a)	Swindon T	L	0-2		2,696
31		9	(h)	Chesterfield	L	0-1		2,401
32		16	(a)	Chester C	W	3-1	Pratt 3	1,400
33		19	(a)	Scunthorpe U	L	1-7	Morgan	1,566
34		23	(h)	Colchester U	L	1-5	Morgan	1,825
35		26	(a)	Halifax T	W	3-2	McNichol, Phillipson-Masters, Watson (og)	1,011
36		30	(h)	Hartlepool U	W	3-2	Ling 2, Morgan	1,578
37	Apr	3	(a)	Mansfield T	D	2-2	Ling 2	1,703
38		6	(a)	Torquay U	D	1-1	O'Shea	3,711
39		8	(h)	Port Vale	W	2-1	McNichol, Morgan	2,427
40		13	(a)	Rochdale	L	0-2		1,181
41		17	(h)	Blackpool	D	1-1	Howarth	1,847
42		20	(h)	Stockport C	L	0-2		1,834
43		27	(a)	Crewe A	D	0-0		1,593
44	May	4	(a)	Peterborough U	D	0-0		1,464
45		6	(a)	Hereford U	W	2-1	Ling, McNichol	2,730
46		11	(h)	Tranmere R	L	0-1		1,859

FINAL LEAGUE POSITION: 18th in Division Four

Appearances
Sub Appearances
Goals

FA Cup

1	Nov	17	(h)	Enfield	D	2-2
R		20	(a)	Enfield	L	0-3

League Cup

1	Aug	29	(h)	Cardiff C	W	1-0
	Sep	4	(a)	Cardiff C	L	0-2

Wood	Rogers	Viney	O'Shea	Marker	McNichol	Neville	McDonough	Sims	Pratt	Ling	Howarth	Kirkup	Harrower	Smith K	Morgan	Smith N	McClure	Davies	Coleman	Burgher	Barnard	King	Phillipson-Masters	Smelt	Clifford	
1	2	3	4	5	6*	7	8	9	10	11	12															1
1	2*	3	4	5	6	7	8	9	10	11		12														2
1		3	4	5	6	7	8	9	10	11		2														3
1	12	3	4	5	6	7	8		10	9	11*	2														4
1	8	3	4	5	6	7			9	10	11*	12	2													5
1	8	3	4	5	6	7			9	10	11*	12	2													6
1	8	3	4	5	6	7			9	10	11*	12	2													7
1	8	3	4	5	6	7			10	11*	9	2	12													8
1	8	3	4	5	6	7		9	10*			2	12	11												9
1		3	4	5	6	11		9*	10	12		2	7	8												10
1		3	4	5	6	7		9	11			2	10	8												11
1	8	3	4*	5	6	7		10	11			2	12	9												12
1	11	3	4	5	6	7		9				12	2*	10	8											13
1		3	4	5	6	7		9	10			12	2	11	8*											14
1		3	4	5	6	7		9	10				2	11	8											15
1		3	4	5	6	7		9	8	10		2	11													16
1		3	4	5	6		8	7		2	11		9	10*	12											17
1		3	4	5	6		10	7	2	12	11	8*	9													18
1		3	4	5	6		10	7	2*	12	8	9			11											19
1		3	4	5	6		10	7		12	8*	9			11	2										20
1		3	4	5	6		10	7		8		9			11	2										21
1		3	4	5	6		10	7	12	8*		9			11	2										22
1		3	4		6		10	7	12	5	8	9			11	2*										23
1		3	4	5	6		10	7		11		9				2	8									24
1		3	4	5	6		10	7		11*	12	9				2	8									25
1		3	4	5	6		10	7		2		9					8*	11								26
1		3	4	5	6		10	7		2	8	9						11								27
1		3	4	5			10	7		2		9					8	11	6							28
1		3	4	5	6*		10	7		2	8	9						11	12							29
1		3	4	5			10	7		2		12	9				8*	11	6							30
1		3	4	5			10	7*			12	9					8	11	2	6						31
1		6	8	5	4		10	7		2		12	9				11*		3							32
1		6	8	5	4		10*	7		2		11	9						3	12						33
		6	8	5	4		10*	7					9				11		3	12	1					34
		3	4	5	6			7		2		10	9				8			11	1					35
		4	5	6				7	12	2		10	9				8*		3	11	1					36
		3	4	5	6			7		2	8	10	9							11	1					37
		3	4	5	6			7		2	8	10	9							11	1					38
		3	4	5	6			7		2	11	10	9					8			1					39
		6	4	5				7	11	2	8	10*	9					12	3		1					40
		3	4	5	6			7	8	2	11		9						10		1					41
		4	8	5	6			7	10	2*	11		9					12	3		1					42
		6	4	5	11			7	10	2	8	9							3		1					43
		6		5	11			7	10	2	8	9*					4		3		1		12			44
		6	4	5	11			7	10	2	8	9							3		1					45
		6	4	5	11			7	10*	2	8	9						12	3		1					46
33	8	45	45	42	16	5	11	33	42	11	35	25	21	27	1		5	6	11	6	15	5	13			
	1								1	8	3	6	4		1		3		1	2		1				
	1	2		5	1	1	3	19	6	1		1	2	9			2		1							

3 own-goals

289

1985-86

Manager: Colin Appleton

					Result		Att
1	Aug	17	(h)	Port Vale	W	1-0 Ling	2,868
2		24	(a)	Aldershot	L	0-4	1,411
3		26	(h)	Northampton T	L	1-2 Kellow	2,392
4	Sep	7	(h)	Southend U	L	0-2	2,213
5		14	(a)	Wrexham	D	1-1 Harrower	2,417
6		18	(h)	Scunthorpe U	W	2-0 Kellow (pen), Harrower	1,723
7		20	(a)	Cambridge U	D	1-1 Gale	1,479
8		28	(h)	Tranmere R	W	1-0 Gale	1,881
9	Oct	1	(a)	Swindon T	L	1-2 Ling	3,118
10		4	(a)	Colchester U	D	1-1 Gale	3,927
11		12	(h)	Orient	D	1-1 Pratt	2,057
12		19	(a)	Mansfield T	L	1-2 Viney	3,289
13		23	(h)	Halifax T	W	1-0 Kellow (pen)	1,719
14		26	(h)	Hartlepool U	L	1-2 Kellow (pen)	1,934
15	Nov	2	(a)	Peterborough U	D	1-1 Kellow (pen)	2,200
16		5	(a)	Rochdale	D	1-1 Harrower	1,243
17		9	(h)	Chester C	L	1-3 Ling	1,888
18		23	(a)	Burnley	L	1-3 Ling	2,874
19		30	(h)	Preston NE	W	3-0 Gale 2, Pratt	1,896
20	Dec	13	(a)	Crewe A	W	1-0 Ling	1,108
21		21	(h)	Aldershot	W	2-0 Crawford, McNichol	1,954
22	Jan	1	(a)	Hereford U	L	1-4 Harrower	3,157
23		11	(h)	Stockport C	W	1-0 Harrower	2,161
24		17	(a)	Port Vale	D	0-0	3,385
25		25	(h)	Wrexham	L	0-1	2,397
26		31	(a)	Southend U	L	0-2	1,653
27	Feb	4	(a)	Halifax T	L	0-1	1,004
28		8	(h)	Mansfield T	L	0-1	1,798
29		21	(h)	Cambridge U	D	0-0	1,369
30		24	(a)	Stockport C	D	1-1 Ward	2,038
31		28	(a)	Tranmere R	W	1-0 McNichol	1,031
32	Mar	4	(h)	Swindon T	L	0-3	2,291
33		8	(h)	Colchester U	D	2-2 Ward, Crawford	1,520
34		15	(a)	Orient	D	2-2 Crawford, Cornwell (og)	2,220
35		19	(h)	Peterborough U	W	1-0 McNichol	1,460
36		22	(a)	Hartlepool U	D	0-0	2,480
37		26	(h)	Torquay U	D	2-2 Ward, Harrower	2,420
38		29	(h)	Hereford U	W	3-2 McNichol, Viney, Kellow (pen)	1,989
39	Apr	1	(a)	Torquay U	W	2-1 Kellow, Ling	2,555
40		4	(h)	Rochdale	W	2-0 Kellow (pen), Jackson	1,713
41		8	(a)	Northampton T	D	2-2 Ling, Friar (og)	2,213
42		12	(a)	Chester C	L	1-2 Kellow	2,899
43		19	(h)	Burnley	L	0-2	2,019
44		22	(a)	Scunthorpe U	L	0-1	1,343
45		26	(a)	Preston NE	D	2-2 Ling, McNichol	3,132
46	May	3	(h)	Crewe A	L	1-2 Jackson	1,777

FINAL LEAGUE POSITION: 21st in Division Four

Appearances
Sub Appearances
Goals

FA Cup

1	Nov	16	(h)	Cardiff C	W	2-1
2	Dec	7	(a)	Bristol C	W	2-1
3	Jan	5	(a)	Everton	L	0-1

League Cup

1	Aug	20	(a)	Plymouth A	L	1-2
	Sep	4	(h)	Plymouth A	W	2-0
2		25	(h)	Aston Villa	L	1-4
	Oct	9	(a)	Aston Villa	L	1-8

290

Football appearances & goals grid (players as columns, match numbers 1–46 as rows; numbers in cells are shirt numbers worn).

No.	Shaw	Kirkup	King	McNichol	McCaffery	Marker	Ling	Kellow	Morgan	Pratt	Crawford	Walsh	Viney	Impey	Kimble A	Kimble G	Williams	Jackson	Harrower	Gale	Gwinnett	Webber	Keough	Ward	Johnson	Massey
1	1	2	3	4	5	6	7	8	9	10	11															
2	1	2	3	4	5	6*	7		9	10	11	12	8													
3	1	2		4	5	6	7	8	9	10	11	3														
4	1	2		4		6	7		9		11	3	5			8	10*	12								
5	1		2	4		6	7		9	12		3	5		10*	8	11									
6	1		2	4		6	7		9			3	5			8	11	10								
7	1		2	4		6	7		9	12		3	5			8	11*	10								
8	1	2		4		6	7		9		11	3	5			8		10								
9			2	4		6	7		9		11	3	5			8		10							1	
10	1	12		4		6	7		9*	10	11	3	5			8	2									
11	1			4	12	6	7				11	3	5			8	2				10	9*				
12	1			4		6	7		9		11	3	5			8	2				10					
13	1			4		6	7		9		11	3	5			8	2				10					
14	1			4		6	7		9		11*	3	5			8	2	12			10					
15	1			4	12	6	7		9		11	3	5			8*	2				10					
16	1			4	2	6	7		9*	12	11	3	5			8					10					
17	1			4	8*	6	7		9	12	11	3	5				2				10					
18	1			4		6	7			12	11	3	5			8	2*				10	9				
19	1			4		6	7	2*		12	11	3	5			8				1	10	9				
20	1			4		6	7		9*	12	11	3	5			8	2				10					
21	1			4		6	7	12	9*		11	3	5			8	2				10					
22	1			4	5	6	7*	12			11	3				8	2				10	9				
23	1			4	5	6	7				11	3				8	2				10	9				
24	1			4		6	7				11	3	5			8	2				10	9				
25	1			4		6	7	12			11*	3	5			8	2				10	9	8			
26	1	11*		4		6	7	12		10		3	5				2				10	9*	8			
27	1	11*		4		6	7			10		3	5				12	2				9	11			
28	1			4		6	7		10*	9		3	5			8	2	12			10					
29	1			4	5	6	7					3				8	2	11			10	9				
30	1			4	5	6	7	12			11	3				8	2				10	9*				
31	1			4	5	6	7				11	3				8	2				10	9				
32	1			4	5	6	7	12			11	3				8*	2				10	9				
33	1			4	5	6	7	12	8*		11	3					2				10	9				
34	1			4	5	6	7	8			11	3					2				10	9				
35	1			4	5	6	7				11	3					2				10	9	8			
36	1			4	5	6	7				11	3					2				10	9	8			
37	1			4	5	6	7				11	3					2				10	9	8*			
38	1			4	5		7				11	3				8	2				10	9				6
39	1			4	5	6	7				11	3				8	2				10	9				
40	1			4	5	6	7				11	3				8	2				10	9				
41	1			4	5	6	7				11	3				8*	12				10	9		2		
42	1			4	5	6	7				11	3				8	12				10	9	8	2*		
43	1	12		4	5	6	7		9		11*	3				8*	2				10					
44	1	10		4	5		7	12	9			3				8*	2						11			6
45	1	9		4	5	6	7	12			11	3				8	2				10*					
46	1	10		4	5		7		9		11	3				8	2									6
Apps	44	8	9	45	31	40	45	24	4	10	33	45	26	1	1	31	36	17	2	1	31	14	5	2		
Sub		2		2				9		8		1						1			1	2	1	1		
Goals		5		8	9		2	3		2			2			2	6	5			3					

2 own-goals

1986-87

Manager: Colin Appleton until December 1986, then Terry Cooper.

1	Aug	23	(h)	Orient	W	1-0	Roberts	2,199
2		29	(a)	Colchester U	D	1-1	Kellow	1,633
3	Sep	6	(h)	Stockport C	W	4-0	Kellow, Priddle, O'Connell 2	1,820
4		13	(a)	Cambridge U	D	2-2	Batty, Roberts	2,791
5		16	(a)	Crewe A	D	2-2	Marker, O'Connell	1,226
6		20	(h)	Cardiff C	D	0-0		3,066
7		27	(a)	Wrexham	D	0-0		2,213
8	Oct	1	(h)	Southend U	D	0-0		2,736
9		4	(a)	Rochdale	D	0-0		1,307
10		11	(h)	Lincoln C	W	2-0	Robson, Roberts	2,499
11		18	(a)	Hereford U	D	1-1	O'Connell	2,461
12		22	(h)	Hartlepool U	W	2-0	O'Connell, Batty	2,660
13		25	(h)	Burnley	W	3-0	O'Connell, Pugh, Robson	3,918
14	Nov	1	(a)	Preston NE	L	1-2	Viney	5,818
15		4	(a)	Halifax T	L	0-2		1,390
16		8	(h)	Peterborough U	D	1-1	Robson	2,701
17		29	(h)	Aldershot	W	4-0	Kellow 2 (1 pen), Roberts 2	2,348
18	Dec	2	(a)	Northampton T	L	0-4		6,639
19		13	(h)	Tranmere R	W	1-0	Roberts	2,084
20		19	(a)	Scunthorpe U	L	1-3	Biggins	1,545
21		26	(h)	Torquay U	D	2-2	Roberts, Kellow	4,327
22		27	(a)	Wolves	D	2-2	Robson, Kellow	4,626
23	Jan	1	(a)	Swansea C	L	0-1		6,057
24		3	(h)	Northampton T	D	1-1	Biggins	4,331
25		17	(h)	Colchester U	W	2-0	Baker (og), Robson	2,553
26		23	(a)	Stockport C	D	0-0		1,975
27		31	(h)	Cambridge U	D	1-1	O'Connell (pen)	2,095
28	Feb	7	(h)	Crewe A	W	1-0	Robson	1,937
29		21	(h)	Wrexham	W	4-2	Kellow 2 (1 pen), Butler, O'Connell	2,267
30		27	(a)	Southend U	L	1-2	Robson	3,156
31	Mar	4	(h)	Preston NE	L	1-2	Kellow (pen)	2,801
32		7	(a)	Burnley	D	0-0		1,787
33		14	(h)	Hereford U	W	1-0	Kellow	2,342
34		18	(a)	Hartlepool U	L	0-1		1,192
35		21	(a)	Lincoln C	D	1-1	Kellow (pen)	1,564
36		28	(h)	Rochdale	D	1-1	Kellow (pen)	1,967
37		31	(a)	Cardiff C	D	0-0		1,825
38	Apr	4	(a)	Peterborough U	D	2-2	Edwards 2	3,523
39		7	(a)	Orient	L	0-2		2,461
40		11	(h)	Halifax T	D	2-2	Edwards 2	1,698
41		18	(h)	Swansea C	D	2-2	Kellow 2	2,330
42		20	(a)	Torquay U	D	1-1	Edwards	2,583
43		25	(h)	Scunthorpe U	D	0-0		1,525
44	May	2	(a)	Aldershot	L	1-2	Watson	2,176
45		4	(h)	Wolves	L	1-3	Kellow (pen)	4,915
46		8	(a)	Tranmere R	L	0-1		6,983

FINAL LEAGUE POSITION: 14th in Division Four

Appearances
Sub Appearances
Goals

FA Cup

1	Nov	15	(h)	Cambridge U	D	1-1
		19	(a)	Cambridge U	L	0-2

League Cup

1	Aug	27	(h)	Newport C	D	0-0
	Sep	2	(a)	Newport C	L	0-1

Gwinnett	Pugh	Viney	Priddle	McCaffery	Watson	Batty	Roberts	Kellow	Keough	Harrower	O'Connell	Shaw	Marker	Gale	Robson	Biggins	Joyce	Taylor	Butler	Williams	Olsson	Massey	Edwards	Jackson	Foley	No.
1	2	3	4	5	6	7	8	9*	10	11	12															1
	2	3	10	5	6	7		12		11	9*	1	4	8												2
	2	3	7	5	6		9	8*	10	11	12	1	4													3
	2	3	7	5	6	11*	9	8	10		12	1	4													4
	2	3	7	5	6			12	10	11	8	1	4	9*												5
	2	3	7	5	6		9	8*	10	11	12	1	4													6
	2	3	7	5	6		9	12	10	11*	8	1	4													7
	2	3	7	5	6	12	9*	11	10		8	1	4													8
	2	3	7	5	6		9*	8	10	11	12	1	4													9
		3	7	5	6	2	9	8*	10		12	1	4		11											10
		3	7	5	6	2	9*	12	10		8	1	4		11											11
		3	7	5	6	2			10		8	1	4		11	9										12
	7	3		5	6	2			10		8	1	4		11	9										13
	7	3		5	6	2			10		8	1	4		11	9										14
	7	3	2*	5	6		8		10	11	12	1	4			9										15
	7	3		5	6	2	12	9*	10		8	1	4		11											16
		3		5	6	2	7	12	10	11	8*	1	4			9										17
		3	5		6	2	9	12	10	7		1	4		11	8*										18
		3	8	5	6	7	9		10	2		1	4		11											19
		3	8	5	6	7	9		10	2		1	4		11											20
	7	3		5	6		9	8	10	2	11	1	4													21
	2	3		5	6		12	10		9*		1	4	8	11			7								22
		3	5	6		12	9		10	2		1	4		8*	11		7								23
		3	5		7*	12	10	2	8	11		1	4		11	9		6								24
		3	5	7*		12	10	2	8	11		1	4		11	9		6								25
		3	d	5	7*		12	10	2	8		1	4		11	9		6								26
	7	3		5		12		10	2	8		1	4		11*	9		6								27
		3	12		5	7*	9	10	2	8		1	4		11			6								28
	7	3			5	6	12	9	10	2		1	4		11				8*							29
		3	5*	6		9	10	12	2	2		1	4		11			7	8							30
		3		5	6		9	10	12	2	11*	1	4					7	8							31
		3			6	9		10	7	2	11	1	4					5	8							32
		3		6*		9	10	11	2	1			4					5			12	8				33
		3	6*		8	9	10	11	2	1			4					5			12	7	4			34
		3		6	8*	9	10	11	2	1	4							5			12	7				35
		3		6	11*	9	10	3	2	1								5			12	7	4	8		36
		3		6*	9		10	11	2	1	4							5			12	7	8			37
		3					11	2	1	4		10						5			12	7	8	6*	9	38
		3					11	2	1	4		10						5		9	7	6	8			39
	5	3			6	11*	9	10	12	2	1	4						7					8			40
	7	3			6		9	10		2	1	4			11			5					8			41
	7	3			6	12			2	1	4			11			5	9*					8	10		42
1	6	3			7	9*		10	2		4			11			5			12			8			43
1	12	3		6				10	2		4			11			5	9*				8	7			44
	7	3			6		9	10	12	2*	1	4		11			5*					8				45
	7	3			6		9	10	2	12	1	4		11		5*						8				46
3	23	45	18	24	29	30	23	22	40	30	34	43	43	2	26	14	1	23	4	3	8	3	11	3	1	
1			1		3	2	11		4	8								7								
1	1	1		1	2	7	15		8		1		7	2			1				5					

1 own-goal

1987-88

Manager: Terry Cooper

1	Aug	15	(h)	Cambridge U	W 3-0	Carter 2, O'Connell	2,650
2		22	(a)	Swansea C	W 2-0	O'Connell, Kellow	5,557
3		29	(h)	Newport C	W 3-0	Batty, Harrower, Cooper	2,628
4		31	(a)	Tranmere R	L 1-2	O'Connell	3,107
5	Sep	5	(h)	Wrexham	D 1-1	Batty	2,719
6		12	(a)	Leyton O	W 3-2	Edwards 2, Kellow	3,613
7		16	(h)	Carlisle U	D 1-1	Williams	3,347
8		19	(h)	Rochdale	D 1-1	Kellow (pen)	2,628
9		25	(a)	Colchester U	W 2-0	Batty, Edwards	1,443
10		30	(a)	Hartlepool U	L 1-3	Edwards	2,973
11	Oct	3	(h)	Torquay U	L 0-1		6,281
12		10	(a)	Scarborough	L 1-3	Phillips	2,472
13		17	(h)	Burnley	L 1-2	Edwards	2,780
14		20	(a)	Bolton W	L 0-1		4,165
15		24	(h)	Crewe A	W 3-1	Massey, Kellow, Batty	2,149
16		31	(a)	Hereford U	D 1-1	O'Connell	2,200
17	Nov	7	(a)	Cardiff C	L 2-3	Rowbotham, Batty	3,474
18		21	(h)	Stockport C	W 2-1	Milton 2	2,217
19	Dec	8	(a)	Darlington	L 1-4	Milton	1,107
20		12	(h)	Scunthorpe U	D 1-1	O'Connell (pen)	1,831
21		18	(a)	Halifax T	L 0-2		1,302
22		26	(h)	Colchester U	L 0-2		2,675
23		28	(a)	Wolves	L 0-3		15,588
24	Jan	1	(a)	Newport C	D 1-1	Olsson	1,691
25		2	(h)	Leyton O	L 2-3	Batty, Edwards	2,568
26		9	(h)	Swansea C	W 3-1	Olsson, O'Connell, Edwards	2,225
27		16	(a)	Rochdale	D 0-0		1,431
28		23	(a)	Carlisle U	D 0-0		1,699
29		30	(h)	Tranmere R	L 0-1		2,261
30	Feb	13	(h)	Wolves	L 2-4	O'Connell 2	3,483
31		19	(a)	Cambridge U	L 1-2	Edwards	1,878
32		27	(a)	Torquay U	D 1-1	Taylor	3,383
33	Mar	2	(h)	Hartlepool U	W 1-0	O'Connell (pen)	1,573
34		5	(a)	Burnley	L 0-3		6,052
35		9	(h)	Peterborough U	L 0-1		1,584
36		12	(h)	Scarborough	W 1-0	Harris	1,738
37		19	(h)	Hereford U	D 2-2	Stevens (og), Hiley	1,628
38		22	(a)	Wrexham	L 0-3		963
39		26	(a)	Crewe A	D 0-0		1,665
40	Apr	2	(h)	Cardiff C	L 0-2		2,649
41		4	(a)	Stockport C	L 1-2	Rowbottam	2,161
42		9	(h)	Bolton W	D 1-1	O'Connell (pen)	1,962
43		23	(a)	Peterborough U	L 1-2	Harrower	2,278
44		30	(h)	Darlington	W 4-1	O'Connell, Edwards 3	1,515
45	May	2	(a)	Scunthorpe U	D 1-1	Edwards	6,736
46		7	(h)	Halifax T	L 1-2	Delve	1,602

FINAL LEAGUE POSITION: 22nd in Division Four

Appearances
Sub Appearances
Goals

FA Cup
1 Nov   14 (a) Leyton O   L 0-2

League Cup
1 Aug   17 (a) Bournemouth   D 1-1
       26 (h) Bournemouth   L 1-3

294

Football appearances/lineup grid (shirt numbers worn per match). Columns are players; rows are matches 1–46.

Shaw	Nisbet	Viney	Marker	Taylor	Carter	Batty	Edwards	O'Connell	Olsson	Harrower	Cooper	Kellow	Massey	Williams	Watson	Philips	Gwinnett	Hiley	Delve	Rowbotham	Collins	Milton	Harris	No.
1	2	3	4	5	6	7	8	9	10*	11	12													1
1	2	3	4		6	7	8	9	10*	11	5	12												2
1	2	3	4		6	7	8	9*	10	11	5	12												3
1	2	3	4		6	7	8	9	10	11	5*	12												4
1	2	3	4		6	7	8	9†	10	11*		12	5	14										5
1	2	3†	4	5	6	7	8	9	10*				14		12	11								6
1	2	3	4	5	6	7	8	9*		11†			14		12		10							7
1	2	3	4	5	6	7	8*	9†					14		12		10	11						8
1	2	3	4		6	7	8		10	11			5				9							9
1	2	3	4	5	6	7	8		10*	11					12		9							10
1	2	3	4	5		7	8		10†	11			14	12		6*	9							11
1	2*	3		5		14	8		12	11	7		4	10	6†		9							12
		3		5	4	7†	8	6*	11	2	10	12	9				1	14						13
		3		5	4	7	8	11	2	9	6		10				1							14
		3		5	4	7	8*	11	2	9	6	12	10				1							15
1		3		5	4	7*	8	9	11	2	12		10		6									16
1		3		5	4	7	8*	9	12	11	2		10		6									17
1		3		5	4		8	9	11	2			6	7	10									18
1		3		5	4	7	8	9†	11	12	2*				6	10	14							19
1		3		5	4	7	9	10	2	8	6								11					20
1		3		5	4	7†	9	10	12	2	8		6*				14	11						21
1		3		5	4	7	9	10	2	8		6					11*		12					22
1		3		5	4	7	9	10	12	2	8	11†	6*				14	11						23
1		3		5	4	7		10	6	2	8	9					11							24
1		3		5	4	7	9	10	6	2	8						11							25
		3		5	4	7	9	10	6	2		12	14		1	8†	11*							26
		3		5	4	7	9*	10	6	2		12			1	8	11							27
		3		5	4	7	9	10	6	2		12			1	8*	11							28
		3*		5	4	7†	9	10	6	2	8	14	12		1		11							29
		3		5	4	7	9	10	6	2		12			1	8*	11							30
		3		5	7	11	9†	10	6	2		4	8*		1	12	14							31
		3		5	7		9	10	2	8	4	6		1	11*	12								32
		3		5	7		9	10	2	8	4	6		1		11								33
		3		5	7		9	10	12	2	8	6*		1		11								34
		3		5	7*		9	10†	6	2	8	4		1	11	12				14				35
		3		5			10		2	8		6	1	7	4	11				9				36
		3		5	12		10	8	2		6	1	7	4*	11					9				37
		3		5	12		14	10	8	2	6*	1	7	4	11					9†				38
		3		5			12	10	8	2	6	4	1	7	11					9*				39
		3		5			12	10	8	2	6	4	1	7	11					9*				40
		3*		5	12		9	10	8	2	6	4	1	7	11									41
		3		5	12		9	10	8	2	6	4	1	7*	11									42
		3		5	4		9†	10	8	2	6	12	1	7*	11				14					43
		3		5	4		9	10	7	2	6	1	12	8*	11									44
		3		5	4	12	9	10	8	2	6	1	7*	11										45
		3		5	4	12	9	10	7	2	6	1	8*	11										46
22	12	46	11	41	37	29	40	39	30	43	30	5	17	4	12	5	24	12	12	20	8	2	5	
		4	3	3		5	3	3	11	6	2	1	1		3	1	3	1					4	
		1	2	6	12	11	2	2	1	4	1	1		1	1	1	2		3	1				

1 own-goal

295

1988-89

Manager: Terry Cooper

1	Aug	27	(h)	Wrexham	L 0-2		2,504
2	Sep	3	(a)	Doncaster R	L 1-2	Neville (pen)	1,525
3		10	(h)	Halifax T	W 4-1	Withey 2, Neville, Rowbotham	1,725
4		17	(a)	Rochdale	L 1-2	Hiley	1,216
5		20	(a)	Darlington	D 2-2	Rowbotham, Langley	1,216
6		24	(h)	Scunthorpe U	D 2-2	Neville, Taylor	1,876
7	Oct	1	(a)	Rotherham U	W 1-0	Johnson (og)	4,075
8		5	(h)	Torquay U	W 3-0	Neville, Batty, Rowbotham	4,243
9		8	(a)	Burnley	L 0-3		7,889
10		15	(h)	Grimsby T	W 2-1	Neville (pen), Taylor	2,232
11		22	(h)	Carlisle U	W 3-0	Rowbotham 2, Langley	2,235
12		25	(a)	Leyton O	L 0-4		3,873
13		29	(h)	Crewe A	L 1-2	Neville (pen)	2,567
14	Nov	4	(a)	Cambridge U	L 0-2		2,063
15		9	(h)	Scarborough	W 1-0	Rowbotham	2,351
16		12	(a)	Lincoln C	L 0-2		3,461
17		26	(a)	Hartlepool U	D 2-2	Rowbotham, Taylor	2,125
18	Dec	3	(h)	Colchester U	W 4-2	Taylor, Neville, Hiley, Rowbotham	2,132
19		17	(a)	Peterborough U	W 1-0	Neville	3,149
20		26	(h)	Hereford U	W 3-1	Taylor, Rowbotham, Cooper	3,229
21		31	(h)	York C	W 2-0	Rowbotham (pen), Neville	3,092
22	Jan	2	(a)	Stockport C	L 0-4		2,936
23		14	(h)	Doncaster R	W 3-0	Rowbotham 2 (1 pen), Neville	2,540
24		21	(a)	Wrexham	L 0-3		2,514
25		28	(h)	Rochdale	W 5-1	Smith 2, Rowbotham, Neville, Tupling	2,428
26	Feb	4	(h)	Darlington	W 2-1	Rowbotham (pen), Neville	2,687
27		11	(a)	Scunthorpe U	L 0-2		4,102
28		18	(h)	Burnley	W 3-0	C.Harris, Benjamin, Neville	3,672
29		25	(a)	Grimsby T	L 1-2	Rowbotham (pen)	4,684
30	Mar	1	(h)	Leyton O	D 1-1	Rowbotham (pen)	2,890
31		4	(a)	Carlisle U	L 0-1		2,601
32		11	(h)	Cambridge U	L 0-3		3,180
33		14	(a)	Crewe A	L 1-2	Hiley	3,156
34		17	(a)	Halifax T	W 3-0	Rowbotham, Taylor, Young	1,473
35		20	(a)	Tranmere R	L 0-2		3,885
36		25	(h)	Stockport C	D 2-2	Rowbotham 2 (1 pen)	3,058
37		27	(a)	Hereford U	L 0-1		2,735
38	Apr	1	(h)	Peterborough U	W 3-1	Banks, Neville, Young	2,522
39		5	(h)	Tranmere R	L 0-1		2,956
40		8	(a)	York C	L 1-3	Hiley	2,052
41		15	(h)	Rotherham U	D 0-0		2,594
42		22	(a)	Torquay U	W 4-0	Young 2, Rowbotham, McDermott	2,939
43		29	(h)	Hartlepool U	W 2-1	Hiley, Benjamin	2,380
44	May	1	(a)	Scarborough	L 1-2	Benjamin	2,513
45		5	(a)	Colchester U	L 0-4		5,256
46		13	(h)	Lincoln C	L 0-1		2,249

FINAL LEAGUE POSITION: 10th in Division Four

Appearances
Sub Appearances
Goals

FA Cup
1	Nov	19	(a)	Bognor R	L 1-2

League Cup
1	Aug	30	(a)	Bristol C	L 0-1
	Sep	7	(h)	Bristol C	L 0-1

Player appearances and goals chart (numbers indicate shirt worn; * and † denote substitutions).

Gwinnett	Banks	Viney	Rogers	Taylor	Cooper	Rowbotham	Hiley	Langley	Neville	Harrower	Harris J	Vinnicombe	Withey	Batty	Dryden	Jones	Harris C	Walter	Roberts	Tupling	Smith	Parker	Benjamin	Heath	McDermott	Young	Miller	No.
1	2*	3	4	5	6	7	8	9	10	11	12																	1
1	2	3	4	5	6	7	8		10	11*	9	12																2
1	2		4	5	6	7	8		10	11				3	9													3
1	2		4	5	6*	7	8	12	10	11				3	9													4
1	2		4	5	6	7	8	12	10	11				3*	9													5
1	2		4	5	6	7	8	12	10	11					9	3*												6
1	2		4	5	6	7	8		10	11					9	3												7
1	2		4	5	6	7	8		10	11					9	3												8
1	2		4	5	6	7	8*		10	11				12	9	3												9
1	2		4	5	6	7	8*	12	10	11					9	3												10
1	2		4	5	6	7	8*	12	10	11					9	3												11
1	2		4	5	6	7		8	10	11				3	9													12
1	2		4	5	6	7	8	3*	10	11			12		9													13
1	2		4	5		7	8	12	10	11				6*	9	3												14
1	2		4	5		7	8	12	10	11				6*	9	3												15
1	2	9*	4	5	6	7	8	10†		11		12	14			3												16
	2		4	5	6	7	8		10	11		12			9	3*		1										17
	2		4	5	6	7	8		10			11			9	3*		1										18
	2		4	5	6	7	8		10			11			9	3		1										19
	2		4	5	6	7	8*		10			11			9			1	2									20
	2		4	5	6	7	14	11†	10*			12			9			1	2	12								21
	2		4	5	6	7	8	11†	10*			12			9			1	2				8					22
	2		4	5	6	7	8		10			11			9		3	1		14								23
	2		4	5	6	7	8	11*	10†			12			9		3	1		14								24
	2		4	5	6	7			10			11*			9		3	1					8	12				25
	2		4	5	6	7			10			11*			9		3	1		14			8†	12				26
	2		4	5	12	7			10*			11			9		3	1		14			8		6†			27
	2		4	5	12	7			10			11*			9		3	1					8		6			28
	2		4	5	12	7			10†			11*			9		3	1	3*	14			8		6			29
	2		4	5	12	7			10			11			9		3	1	3*		12		8		6			30
	2		4	5	10	7						11*			9		3	1					8	12	6			31
	2		4	5		7	11*								9†		3	1		12	14		8		6	10		32
	2		4	5		7	11								9		3	1		12			8		6	10*		33
	2		4	5		7	11								9*		3	1		12			8		6	10		34
			4	5		7	11	9									3	1					8	2	6	10		35
	2		4	5		7	11	9									3	1		12			8		6*	10		36
14			4	5		7	11*	9									3	1		12			8	2†	6	10		37
	2		4	5		7	11	9*	10								3	1					8		6	12		38
	2		4	5		7	11*		10								3	1		12			8		6	9		39
	2		4	5		7	11		10								3*	1		12			8		6	9		40
	2		4	5			11		10							3	7*			12			8		6	9	1	41
	2		4	5		7	11		10							3		1					8		6	9	1	42
	2		4	5		7	11*		10			12			9*		3						8		6		1	43
	2			5		7	11*		10†				4				3		12	1	14		8		6	9		44
14			4	5		7	11		10				2†				3		12	1			8		6*	9		45
	2		4	5		7	11		10				8				3		12	1					6	9*		46
17	43	3	45	46	25	45	36	14	38	18	1	21	5	15	21	5	11	26	3	8	2		20	3	19	13	3	
	2		4			1	7					4	4	2			5			1	13	1		2		1		
1		6	1	20	5	2	14					2	1				1			1	2		3		1	4		

1 own-goal

1989-90

Manager: Terry Cooper

1	Aug	19	(h)	Doncaster R	W 1-0	Neville	3,033
2		26	(a)	Hartlepool U	W 3-0	Dryden, Taylor, Rowbotham	1,726
3	Sep	2	(h)	Carlisle U	D 0-0		3,338
4		9	(a)	Burnley	L 0-1		5,443
5		16	(h)	Cambridge U	W 3-2	Rowbotham 2, Dryden	2,754
6		23	(a)	Scunthorpe U	L 4-5	Neville 2, Vinnicombe, Dryden	2,935
7		27	(h)	Grimsby T	W 2-1	Rowbotham, Taylor	3,702
8		30	(a)	Halifax T	W 2-1	Neville, Dryden	1,720
9	Oct	7	(a)	Peterborough U	L 3-4	Robinson (og), Bailey, Rowbotham	3,831
10		14	(h)	Chesterfield	W 2-1	Rowbotham, Whitehead	3,773
11		17	(a)	Rochdale	L 0-1		1,337
12		21	(h)	Hereford U	W 2-0	McDermott, Dryden	3,269
13		28	(a)	Stockport C	L 1-2	Young	2,767
14	Nov	1	(h)	Colchester U	W 2-1	Neville 2	3,905
15		4	(h)	Lincoln C	W 3-0	McNichol, Rowbotham, Neville	3,674
16		11	(a)	Scarborough	W 2-1	Rowbotham, Batty	2,124
17		25	(h)	Wrexham	D 1-1	Bowbotham	3,522
18	Dec	2	(a)	Maidstone U	L 0-1		1,650
19		16	(h)	Gillingham	W 3-1	Rowbotham 2 (2 pens), Neville	3,818
20		26	(a)	Aldershot	W 1-0	Benjamin	3,101
21		30	(a)	Southend U	W 2-1	Rowbotham 2 (1 pen)	3,761
22	Jan	1	(h)	Torquay U	W 3-0	McNichol, Rowbotham, Whitehead	8,154
23		13	(h)	Hartlepool U	W 3-1	Bennyworth (og), Rowbotham 2	4,959
24		20	(a)	Doncaster R	L 1-2	Neville	3,492
25	Feb	10	(a)	Cambridge U	L 2-3	Whitehead, Rowbotham (pen)	3,508
26		13	(a)	Carlisle U	L 0-1		8,461
27		17	(h)	Maidstone U	W 2-0	Rowbotham, Berry (og)	4,181
28		24	(a)	Wrexham	D 1-1	McNichol	2,128
29	Mar	3	(h)	York C	W 3-1	Neville, Rowbotham 2 (1 pen)	4,632
30		7	(h)	Halifax T	W 2-0	Taylor 2	5,528
31		10	(a)	Grimsby T	L 0-1		6,629
32		17	(h)	Peterborough U	W 2-0	Dryden, Batty (pen)	4,676
33		20	(a)	Chesterfield	L 1-2	Rowe	5,319
34		24	(h)	Rochdale	W 5-0	McNichol 3 (1 pen), Neville 2	4,701
35		28	(h)	Scunthorpe U	W 1-0	Taylor	5,805
36		31	(a)	Hereford U	L 1-2	Dryden	4,243
37	Apr	2	(a)	York C	L 0-3		2,091
38		7	(h)	Stockport C	D 1-1	McNichol (pen)	4,817
39		10	(a)	Colchester U	W 1-0	McNichol	3,369
40		14	(a)	Torquay U	W 2-0	Taylor, McPherson	3,389
41		16	(h)	Aldershot	W 2-0	Neville, Young	6,832
42		21	(a)	Gillingham	D 1-1	Young	3,374
43		25	(h)	Southend U	W 2-1	Neville, McDermott	8,271
44		28	(h)	Scarborough	W 3-2	Kelly 2 (2 pens), Young	6,850
45	May	1	(h)	Burnley	W 2-1	Whitehead, Young	7,544
46		5	(a)	Lincoln C	W 5-1	N.Smith (og), Whitehead, McDermott, Young, Rowe	4,772

FINAL LEAGUE POSITION: 1st in Division Four

Appearances
Sub Appearances
Goals

FA Cup

1	Nov	18	(a)	Dartford	D 1-1	
R		22	(h)	Dartford	W 4-1	
2	Dec	9	(a)	Maidstone U	D 1-1	
R		13	(h)	Maidstone U	W 3-2	
3	Jan	6	(h)	Norwich C	D 1-1	
R		10	(a)	Norwich C	L 0-2	

League Cup

1	Aug	23	(h)	Swansea C	W 3-0	
		29	(a)	Swansea C	D 1-1	
2	Sep	20	(h)	Blackburn R	W 3-0	
	Oct	3	(a)	Blackburn R	L 1-2	
3		25	(h)	Blackpool	W 3-0	
4	Nov	29	(h)	Sunderland	D 2-2	
R	Dec	5	(a)	Sunderland	L 2-5	

Leyland DAF Cup

P1	Jan	15	(h)	Torquay U	W 2-0	
P2		17	(a)	Bristol R	L 0-3	
1		23	(a)	Shrewsbury T	W 1-0	
2	Feb	21	(a)	Maidstone U	L 0-2	

298

	Walter	McNichol	Vinnicombe	Rogers	Taylor	Whitehead	Rowbotham	Bailey	McDermott	Neville	Dryden	Hiley	Young	Benjamin	Rowe	Harrower	Batty	Cooper	Frankland	Coyle	Miller	Elkins	Goddard	Eshelby	Stafford	McPherson	Kelly	Summerfield
1	1	2	3	4	5	6	7	8	9*	10	11†	12	14															
2	1		3	4	5	6*	7	8	9	10	11	2		12														
3	1		3	4*	5	6	7	8	9	10	11	2	12															
4	1		3	4	5	6	7*	8	9	10	11	2	12															
5	1		3	4	5	6	7	8	9		11*	2	10		12													
6	1		3	4	5	6	7	8	9*	10	11	2	12															
7	1		3	4	5	6	7	8	9*	10	11	2	12															
8	1		3	4	5	6	7	8	9	10*	11	2	12															
9	1	4	3		5	6	7	8		10		2	9				11*	12										
10	1	4	3		5	6	7	8	9	10	11	2																
11	1	4	3		5	6	7	8	9*	10	11	2	12															
12	1	4	3		5	6	7*	8	9	10	11	2	12															
13	1	4	3		5	6*	7	8	9	10	11	2	12															
14	1	4	3		5		7	8*	9	10	11	2	12				6											
15	1	4			5		7	8	9	10*	11	2	3	12			6											
16	1	4			5		7	8	9	10	11	2	3*			12	6											
17	1	4			5	6	7	8		10		2				12	9		11	3*								
18	1	4			5	6	7	8		10		2		11		3	9											
19		4			5	6	7	8	9	10		2		3			12	11*			1							
20					5	6	7	8	9	10		2		3					4		1	11						
21		4			5	6	7	8	9	10		2		3							1	11						
22		4			5	6	7*	8	9	10		2		3†				12			1	11	14					
23		4*			5	6	7	8	9	10		2		3				12			1	11						
24		4		12	5	6	7	8	9*	10		2		3							1	11						
25		4			5	6	7*	8	9	10		2		3			12				1				11			
26		4			5	6	7	8	9	10*		2		3			12				1				11			
27		4			5	6*	7	8	9	10		2		3			12		11		1							
28		4			5	6	12	8		10†	11	2			14	3*	9				1			7				
29		4			5	6	7	8	9	10	3	2					11				1							
30		4			5	6	7	8	9	10	3	2					11				1							
31		4			5		7†	8	12	10	3	2			14	6	11*				1					9		
32		4			5		7*	8	9†	10	3	2	12				11		14		1					6		
33		4			5			8		10	3	2	7		9		11				1					6		
34		4			5†			8	7	10*	11	2	9		12						1					3	14	6
35		4			5*	12		8	7	10	11	2	9								1					3		6
36		4			5	9*		8	12	10	11	2			14						1					3	7	6†
37		4			5	6		8	12		11*	2	9		10						1					3	7	
38		4			5	6		8	9	10		2	12								1					3	7	11*
39		4			5	6		8	9	10		2	11								1					3	7	
40		4			5			8	9	10	6	2	11								1					3	7	
41		4			5	12		8	9	10	6	2	11								1					3*	7	
42		4*		12	5	3		8	9		6	2	11		10						1						7	
43				5		3		8	9	10	6	2	11				4				1						7	
44				4	5	3		8	9*	10	6†	2	11		14		12				1						7	
45				4	5	3		8	9	10		2	11			12	6				1						7*	
46				4	5	3		8	9			2	11*		10	12	6				1						7	
	18	33	14	13	45	36	31	46	38	42	30	45	16	10	4	3	15	1	3	1	28	5		1	2	11	11	4
				3		2	1		3			1	12	2	6	4	5	3	1				1				1	
		8	1		6	5	20	1	3	14	7		6	1	2		2									1	2	

4 own-goals

Exeter in the FA Cup

1908-09
1st Qualifying Round
Oct 3 v Weymouth (h) 14-0
Bell 6, McGuigan 4, Copestake 2, Watson, Parnell
Fletcher; Craig, Bulcock, Ambler, Chadwick, Wake,
Parnell, Watson, McGuigan, Bell, Copestake.
Att: 5,000
2nd Qualifying Round
Oct 17 v Longfleet St Mary (a*) 1-1
Copestake
Fletcher; Craig, Bulcock, Ambler, Johnson, Wake,
Parnell, Watson, McGuigan, Bell, Copestake.
Att: 5,000
*Played at Poole
Replay
Oct 21 v Longfleet St Mary (h) 10-1
*Watson 3, McGuigan 2, Bell 2, Copestake, Johnson,
Opp own-goal*
Fletcher; Craig, Bulcock, Ambler, Chadwick, Johnson,
White, Watson, McGuigan, Bell, Copestake.
Att: 1,000
3rd Qualifying Round
Nov 7 v Whiteheads of Weymouth (h) 4-0
Watson 2, Chadwick (pen), McGuigan
Fletcher; Craig, Bulcock, Ambler, Chadwick, Johnson,
White, Watson, McGuigan, Bell, Copestake.
Att: 3,000
4th Qualifying Round
Nov 21 v Kingswood Rovers (a*) 2-0
McGuigan, Watson
Fletcher; Craig, Bulcock, Ambler, Chadwick, Johnson,
White, Watson, McGuigan, Bell, Copestake.
Att: 3,000
*Played at Warmley, Bristol.
5th Qualifying Round
Dec 5 v Barnet Alston (a) 3-0
Bell, Parnell, Chadwick (pen)
Robinson; Craig, Bulcock, Ambler, Chadwick,
Johnson, Parnell, Watson, McGuigan, Bell, Copestake.
Att: 3,000
Round 1
Jan 16 v Wrexham (a) 1-1
Watson
Robinson; Craig, Bulcock, Ambler, Chadwick, Wake,
Parnell, Watson, McGuigan, Bell, Copestake.
Att: 4,000
Replay
Jan 20 v Wrexham (h) 2-1
Chadwick (pen), McGuigan
Robinson; Crelley, Bulcock, Ambler, Chadwick,
Wake, Parnell, Watson, McGuigan, Bell, Copestake.
Att: 5,000
Round 2
Feb 6 v Plymouth Argyle (a) 0-2
Robinson; Craig, Bulcock, Ambler, Chadwick, Wake,
Parnell, Watson, McGuigan, Bell, Copestake.
Att: 20,000

1909-10
4th Qualifying Round
Nov 20 v Nunhead (h) 7-1
Bell 3, Chadwick (pen), Atkinson, Harrison, Watson
Crossthwaite; Crelley, Jones, Atkinson, Chadwick,
Hartley, Green, Watson, Harrison, Bell, Garside.
Att : 3,000

5th Qualifying Round
Dec 4 v Stoke (a) 0-0
Crossthwaite; Crelley, Jones, Atkinson, Chadwick,
Hartley, Green, Watson, Harrison, Bell, Garside.
Att: 7,050

Replay
Dec 8 v Stoke (h*) 1-1
Hartley
R.Sturge; Craig, Jones, Atkinson, Chadwick, Hartley,
Green, Watson, Harrison, Bell, Garside.
Att: 5,500
*Played at County Ground, St Thomas, Exeter.

2nd Replay
Dec 13 v Stoke (n*) 1-2
Watson
Crossthwaite; Crelley, Jones, Atkinson, Chadwick,
Hartley, Green, Watson, Harrison, McGuigan,
Copestake.
Att: 1,500
*Played at Craven Cottage, Fulham.

1910-11
4th Qualifying Round
Nov 19 v Reading (a) 1-1
Garside
W.Whittaker; Evans, Jones, Duffy, Pratt, Prideaux,
Parnell, Watson, Hughes, Bell, Garside.
Att: 4,000

Replay
Nov 23 v Reading (h*) 1-1
Hughes
W.Whittaker; Evans, Jones, Bassett, Pratt, Prideaux,
Parnell, Watson, Hughes, Bell, Garside.
Att: 3,000
*Played at County Ground, Exeter. Match abandoned
ten minutes from time (fog).

Replay
Nov 28 v Reading (h*) 1-0
Bassett
W.Whittaker; Evans, Jones, Bassett, Pratt, Prideaux,
Parnell, Watson, James, Hughes, Garside.
Att: 2,000
*Played at County Ground, Exeter.

5th Qualifying Round
Dec 3 v Nelson (a*) 4-3
Hughes 2, Watson, Jones (pen)
W.Whittaker; Evans, Jones, Bassett, Pratt, Prideaux,
Parnell, Watson, Hughes, James, Garside.
Att: 3,000
*Drawn to be played at Exeter but transferred to
Nelson following the Lancashire club's objection to
the St James' Park pitch.
Round 1
Jan 14 v Burnley (a*) 0-2
W.Whittaker; Evans, Jones, Bassett, Pratt, Prideaux,
E.Whittaker, Watson, Hughes, Bell, Garside.
Att: 16,000
*Tie transferred to Burnley ground for same reason
as Nelson (above).

1911-12
4th Qualifying Round
Nov 18 v Merthyr Town (h) 1-1
Garside
Chapman; Evans, Coates, Rigby, Griffiths, Cornan,
E.Whittaker, Watson, Rutter, Lockett, Garside.
Att: 5,000
Replay
Nov 23 v Merthyr Town (a) 0-0 (after extra-time)
Chapman; Evans, Coates, Bassett, Chadwick,
Prideaux, E.Whittaker, Lockett, Griffiths, Cornan,
Garside.
Att: 3,000
2nd Replay
Nov 27 v Merthyr Town (n*) 0-2
W.Whittaker; Evans, Coates, Bassett, Chadwick,
Prideaux, E.Whittaker, Watson, Griffiths, Lockett,
Parnell.
Att: 700
*Played at Ashton Gate, Bristol City.

1912-13
4th Qualifying Round
Nov 30 v Cardiff City (a) 1-5
Bassett
Pym; Fort, Hurst, Rigby, Pratt, Bassett, Whittaker,
Crompton, Rutter, Lockett, Ives.
Att: 18,000

1913-14
Round 1
Jan 10 v Portsmouth (a) 4-0
Holt 2, Marshall 2
Pym; Fort, Strettle, Rigby, Lagan, Smith, Holt, Lovett,
Whittaker, McCann, Marshall.
Att: 18,379
Round 2
Jan 31 v Aston Villa (h) 1-2
McCann
Pym; Fort, Strettle, Rigby, Lagan, Smith, Holt, Lovett,
Whittaker, McCann, Marshall.
Att: 9,500

1914-15
Round 1
Jan 9 v Aston Villa (a) 0-2
Pym; Marshall, Strettle, Rigby, Lagan, Smith, Holt,
Evans, W.Goodwin, Lovett, Dockray.
Att: 12,000

1919-20
6th Qualifying Round
Dec 20 v Newport County (a) 0-1
Pym; Coleburne, Strettle, Rigby, Popplewell, Mitton,
Oldacre, Makin, Goodwin, Lovett, Dockray.
Att: 10,000

1920-21
Round 1
Jan 8 v Watford (a) 0-3
Pym; Coleburne, Feebury, Rigby, Carrick, Green,
Appleton, Makin, Shields, Vowles, Dockray.
Att: 9,000

1921-22
5th Qualifying Round
Dec 3 v Bristol Rovers (a) 0-0
Watson; Stewart, Pollard, Rigby, Mitton, Graham,
Newman, Crompton, Vowles, Dockray, Congdon.
Att: 20,000
Replay
Dec 7 v Bristol Rovers (h) 0-2
Watson; Stewart, Pollard, Rigby, Mitton, Brown,
Newman, Alf Green, James Green, Crompton,
Congdon.
Att: 5,000

1922-23
4th Qualifying Round
Nov 18 v Bournemouth & Boscombe Athletic (h) 0-0
Flynn; Pollard, Ackroyd, Rigby, Mitton, Crompton,
Matthews, Kirk, Mathieson, Crockford, Shelton.
Att: 4,000
Replay
Nov 22 v Bournemouth & Boscombe Athletic (a) 3-1
Kirk 2, Shelton
Flynn; Pollard, Ackroyd, Rigby, Mitton, Crompton,
Matthews, Kirk, Vowles, Mathieson, Shelton.
Att: 5,000
5th Qualifying Round
Dec 2 v Bath City (h) 1-2
Shelton
Flynn; Pollard, Ackroyd, Rigby, Mitton, Crompton,
Matthews, Kirk, Vowles, Mathieson, Shelton.
Att: 2,000

1923-24
4th Qualifying Round
Nov 17 v Newport County (a) 2-0
Davis 2
Bailey; Coleburne, Charlton, Hunter, McIntosh,
Gilchrist, Matthews, Kirk, Davis, Gallogley, Shelton.
Att: 9,000
5th Qualifying Round
Dec 1 v Bristol Rovers (h) 2-2
Shelton, Matthews
Bailey; Coleburne, Flynn, Hunter, McIntosh, Gilchrist,
Matthews, Kirk, Davis, Gallogley, Shelton.
Att: 9,260
Replay
Dec 5 v Bristol Rovers (a) 1-0
Davis
Bailey; Coleburne, Charlton, Hunter, McIntosh,
Gilchrist, Matthews, Kirk, Davis, Gallogley, Shelton.
Att: 7,000

6th Qualifying Round
Dec 15 v Sittingbourne (a) 2-0
Matthews, Shelton
Bailey; Coleburne, Charlton, Hunter, McIntosh,
Gilchrist, Matthews, Kirk, Davis, Gallogley, Shelton.
Att: 2,000

Round 1
Jan 12 v Grimsby Town (h) 1-0
Davis
Bailey; Coleburne, Charlton, Hunter, Crompton,
Gilchrist, Matthews, Kirk, Davis, Gallogley, Shelton.
Att: 8,250

Round 2
Feb 2 v Watford (h) 0-0
Bailey; Coleburne, Charlton, Hunter, Crompton,
Crawshaw, Lievesley, Kirk, Davis, Gallogley, Shelton.
Att: 11,150

Replay
Feb 6 v Watford (a) 0-1
Bailey; Coleburne, Charlton, Crawshaw, McIntosh,
Gilchrist, Matthews, Gallogley, Davis, Batten, Shelton.
Att: 9,234

1924-25
5th Qualifying Round
Nov 29 v Newport County (h) 1-1
Compton
Bailey; Pollard, Charlton, Coleburne, Pullan, Jones,
Matthews, Kirk, Appleyard, Davis, Compton.
Att: 8,000

Replay
Dec 4 v Newport County (a) 3-3 (after extra-time)
Davis, Kirk, Matthews (pen)
Bailey; Pollard, Charlton, Pullan, Crompton, Jones,
Matthews, Kirk, Davis, Smelt, Compton.
Att: 6,000

2nd Replay
Dec 8 v Newport County (n*) 1-0
Blackmore
Bailey; Pollard, Charlton, Pullan, Crompton, Potter,
Matthews, Blackmore, Davis, Lievesley, Compton.
Att: 5,000
*Played at Ashton Gate, Bristol.

6th Qualifying Round
Dec 13 v Barnet (h) 3-0
Davis, Kirk, Blackmore
Bailey; Pollard, Charlton, Pullan, Crompton, Potter,
Matthews, Kirk, Blackmore, Davis, Compton.
Att: 7,950

Round 1
Jan 10 v Southampton (a) 0-5
Bailey; Pollard, Charlton, Pullan, Crompton, Potter,
Matthews, Kirk, Davis, Lievesley, Compton.
Att: 15,507
Match abandoned after 77 minutes (fog).

Replay
Jan 14 v Southampton (a) 1-3
Kirk
Bailey; Pollard, Charlton, Pullan, Crompton, Potter,
Matthews, Kirk, Davis, Lievesley, Compton.
Att: 12,000

1925-26
Round 1
Nov 28 v Swansea Town (h) 1-3
Compton
Pavey; Pollard, Charlton, Pullan, McDevitt, Potter,
Matthews, Kirk, Blackmore, Myers, Compton.
Att: 10,000
Eleven days before this Cup tie, the Exeter City
grandstand and dressing-rooms were gutted by fire and
burnt to the ground. Players and officials in this match
used tented accommodation.

1926-27
Round 1
Nov 27 v Aberdare Athletic (h) 3-0
Compton 2, Purcell
Bailey; Pollard, Charlton, Pullan, Pool, Potter, Purcell,
McDevitt, Blackmore, Dent, Compton.
Att: 9,000
Round 2
Dec 11 v Northampton Town (h) 1-0
McDevitt
Bailey; Pollard, Charlton, Pullan, Pool, Garratt,
Purcell, McDevitt, Blackmore, Dent, Compton.
Att: 11,314
Round 3
Jan 8 v Accrington Stanley (h) 0-2
Bailey; Pollard, Charlton, Pullan, Pool, Good, Purcell,
McDevitt, Blackmore, Walker, Parkin.
Att: 13,647

1927-28
Round 1
Nov 26 v Aberdare Athletic (h) 9-1
Dent 4, Vaughan 2, Purcell 2, Compton
Holland; Pollard, Charlton, Phoenix, Pool, Gee,
Purcell, McDevitt, Dent, Vaughan, Compton.
Att: 9,378
Round 2
Dec 10 v Ilford (h) 5-3
Dent 2, Purcell 2, McDevitt
Holland; Pollard, Charlton, Phoenix, Pool, Gee,
Purcell, McDevitt, Dent, Vaughan, Compton.
Att: 8,501
Round 3
Jan 14 v Rotherham United (a) 3-3
Vaughan, Mason, Jackson (og)
Holland; Pollard, Miller, Ditchburn, Mason, Gee,
Purcell, McDevitt, Dent, Vaughan, Compton.
Att: 15,500
Replay
Jan 18 v Rotherham United (h) 3-1
Vaughan 2, Purcell
Holland; Pollard, Miller, Ditchburn, Mason, Gee,
Purcell, McDevitt, Dent, Vaughan, Compton.
Att: 11,805
Round 4
Jan 28 v Blackburn Rovers (h) 2-2
Gee (pen), Mason
Holland; Pollard, Miller, Ditchburn, Mason, Gee,
Purcell, McDevitt, Dent, Vaughan, Compton.
Att: 17,330

Replay
Feb 2 v Blackburn Rovers (a) 1-3 (after extra-time)
Compton
Holland; Pollard, Miller, Ditchburn, Mason, Gee, Purcell, McDevitt, Dent, Vaughan, Compton.
Att: 28,348

1928-29
Round 1
Nov 24 v Barking Town (h) 6-0
Purcell, Doncaster, Clarke, Death, Vango (og), Cameron
Holland; Lowton, Miller, Ditchburn, Pool, Clarke, Purcell, McDevitt, Cameron, Doncaster, Death.
Att: 6,000
Round 2
Dec 8 v Torquay United (a) 1-0
Purcell
Holland; Lowton, Miller, Pollard, Pool, Clarke, Purcell, McDevitt, Doncaster, Houghton, Death.
Att: 12,000
Round 3
Jan 12 v Leeds United (h) 2-2
Doncaster, Purcell
Holland; Lowton, Miller, Pollard, Pool, Dennington, Purcell, McDevitt, Doncaster, Houghton, Cameron.
Att: 13,500
Replay
Jan 16 v Leeds United (a) 1-5
Doncaster
Holland; Lowton, Miller, Pollard, Pool, Dennington, Purcell, McDevitt, Doncaster, Houghton, Cameron.
Att: 23,000

1929-30
Round 1
Nov 30 v Walsall (a) 0-1
Alderson; Baugh, Shanks, Clarke, Ditchburn, Dennington, Purcell, Houghton, Guyan, Hemingway, Doncaster.
Att: 7,989

1930-31
Round 1
Nov 29 v Northfleet United (a) 3-0
Maitland og, Houghton, Purcell
Davies; Baugh, Miller, Clarke, Dennington, Barber, Armfield, Purcell, Varco, Houghton, Doncaster.
Att: 5,000
Round 2
Dec 13 v Coventry City (h) 1-1
Varco
Davies; Baugh, Miller, Clarke, Dennington, Barber, Armfield, Purcell, Varco, Houghton, Doncaster.
Att: 9,600
Replay
Dec 18 v Coventry City (a) 2-1
Varco, Doncaster
Davies; Baugh, Miller, Clarke, Dennington, Barber, J.Gumm, Purcell, Varco, Houghton, Doncaster.
Att: 8,690
Round 3
Jan 10 v Derby County (h) 3-2
Varco, Armfield, Houghton
Davies; Baugh, Miller, Clarke, Dennington, Barber, Armfield, Purcell, Varco, Houghton, Doncaster.
Att: 16,500

Round 4
Jan 24 v Bury (a) 2-1
Varco, Houghton
Davies; Baugh, Miller, Clarke, Angus, Barber, Armfield, Purcell, Varco, Houghton, Doncaster.
Att: 15,000
Round 5
Feb 14 v Leeds United (h) 3-1
Armfield 2, Purcell
Davies; Baugh, Miller, Clarke, Angus, Barber, Armfield, Purcell, Varco, Houghton, Doncaster.
Att: 19,130
Round 6
Feb 28 v Sunderland (a) 1-1
Houghton
Davies; Baugh, Miller, Clarke, Angus, Barber, Armfield, Purcell, Varco, Houghton, Doncaster.
Att: 51,642
Replay
Mar 4 v Sunderland (h) 2-4
Varco, Purcell
Davies; Baugh, Miller, Clarke, Angus, Barber, Armfield, Purcell, Varco, Houghton, Doncaster.
Att: 20,984

1931-32
Round 3*
Jan 9 v Grimsby Town (a) 1-4
Woodward
Davies; Gray, Miller, Clarke, Angus, Barber, Armfield, Woodward, Varco, Houghton, Doncaster.
Att: 12,000
*Exeter were given byes in the first two rounds on account of their progress the previous season.

1932-33
Round 1
Nov 26 v Southend United (a) 1-1
Whitlow
Davies; Gray, Miller, Robinson, Childs, Clarke, Scott, Higgins, Whitlow, Houghton, Welsby.
Att: 8,505
Replay
Nov 30 v Southend United (h) 0-1
Davies; Gray, Miller, Robinson, Childs, Clarke, Scott, Higgins, Whitlow, Houghton, Welsby.
Att: 6,500

1933-34
Round 1
Nov 25 v Northampton Town (a) 0-2
Davies; Gray, Hughes, Clarke, Angus, Hardie, J.Gumm, Poulter, Whitlow, Houghton, Hurst.
Att: 8,000

1934-35
Round 1
Nov 24 v Charlton Athletic (a) 2-2
Hurst 2
Chesters; Gray, Miller, Clarke, Webb, Angus, J.Scott, Wrightson, Poulter, T.Scott, Hurst.
Att: 10,000
Replay
Nov 28 v Charlton Athletic (h) 5-2
T.Scott 2, Hurst, Wrightson, J.Scott
Chesters; Gray, Miller, Clarke, Webb, Angus, J.Scott, Wrightson, Poulter, T.Scott, Hurst.
Att: 7,400

303

Round 2
Dec 8 v Yeovil & Petters United (a) 1-4
Angus
Chesters; Gray, Miller, Lewis, Webb, Angus, J.Scott, Wrightson, Poulter, T.Scott, Hurst.
Att: 5,000

1935-36
Round 1
Nov 30 v Gillingham (h) 0-4
Chesters; Gray, Miller, Clarke, Robinson, Angus, J.Scott, Dunn, McCambridge, McLean, Hurst.
Att: 7,500

1936-37
Round 1
Nov 28 v Folkestone (h) 3-0
Keane 2, Williams
Tierney; Stimpson, Boyle, Clarke, Angus, Shadwell, Keane, Johnson, Williams, T.Scott, McGill.
Att: 6,051
Round 2
Dec 12 v Walthamstow Avenue (a) 1-1
Clarke (pen)
Tierney; Stimpson, Boyle, Clarke, Angus, Shadwell, Keane, T.Scott, Williams, Johnson, Urmson.
Att: 11,131
Match abandoned after 65 minutes due to fog, frost and snow.
Replay
Dec 17 v Walthamstow Avenue (a) 3-2
Williams 2, Keane
Tierney; Stimpson, Boyle, Clarke, Angus, Shadwell, Keane, T.Scott, Williams, Johnson, Urmson.
Att: 8,000
Round 3
Jan 16 v Oldham Athletic (h) 3-0
Williams 2, Smith
Chesters; Brown, Stimpson, Clarke, Angus, Young, F.Smith, Bussey, Williams, Pope, Owen.
Att: 12,412
Round 4
Jan 30 v Leicester City (h) 3-1
Williams 2, Bussey
Chesters; Brown, Boyle, Clarke, Angus, Shadwell, F.Smith, Bussey, Williams, Pope, Owen.
Att: 13,731
Round 5
Feb 20 v Preston North End (a) 3-5
Owen 2, F.Smith
Chesters; Brown, Boyle, Clarke, Angus, Shadwell, F.Smith, Bussey, Williams, Pope, Owen.
Att: 28,000

1937-38
Round 1
Nov 27 v Folkestone (h) 1-0
Pope
Church; Brown, Wallace, Shadwell, Bamsey, Angus, Coulston, Bussey, Bowl, Pope, W.Clarke.
Att: 7,281
Round 2
Dec 11 v Hull City (h) 1-2
Liddle
Church; Brown, Wallace, Shadwell, Bamsey, Angus, W.Clarke, Bussey, Bowl, Pope, Liddle.
Att: 10,000

1938-39
Round 1
Nov 26 v Torquay United (a) 1-3
Riley
Church; Brown, B.Clarke, Angus, Fellowes, Walker, Rich, Ebdon, Bowl, Riley, Liddle.
Att: 8,500

1945-46
Round 1 (1st leg)
Nov 17 v Trowbridge Town (a) 3-1
Challis, Walker, Ebdon
Thomson; Murray, Roughton, Jordan, Blood, Lewis, Tickell, Bowden, Walker, Ebdon, Challis.
Att: 4,300
Round 1 (2nd leg)
Nov 24 v Trowbridge Town (h) 7-2
Walker 4, Challis, Tickell, Atack (og)
Thomson; Murray, Roughton, Jordan, Blood, Lewis, Tickell, Walker, Ebdon, Bowden, Challis.
Att: 6,971
Exeter won 10-3 on aggregate.
Round 2 (1st leg)
Dec 8 v Newport County (a) 1-5
Gallagher
Thomson; Murray, Roughton, Gallagher, Blood, Angus, Tickell, Wardle, Ebdon, Walker, Challis.
Att: 4,000
Round 2 (2nd leg)
Dec 15 v Newport County (h) 1-3
Crawshaw
Thomson; Murray, Roughton, Jordan, Blood, Haddock, Challis, Wardle, Crawshaw, Walker, Ebdon.
Att: 7,793
Newport County won 8-2 on aggregate.

1946-47
Round 1
Nov 30 v Bournemouth & Boscombe Athletic (a) 2-4
Regan, Hydes
Singleton; Thompson, Blood, Cutting, Hanford, Walker, Wardle, Hydes, Owen, Wright, Regan.
Att: 16,168

1947-48
Round 1
Nov 29 v Northampton Town (h) 1-1 (after extra-time)
Bartholomew
Singleton; Thompson, Johnstone, Bartholomew, Gibson, Walker, Hutchings, Mackay, Ebdon, Wright, Regan.
Att: 13,143
Replay
Dec 6 v Northampton Town (a) 0-2
Singleton; Thompson, Johnstone, Bartholomew, Gibson, Walker, Hutchings, Dymond, Smart, Wright, Regan.
Att: 9,500

1948-49
Round 1
Dec 4* v Barnet (a) 6-2
Smith 4, Bartholomew, Dymond
Hoyle; Warren, Rowe, Bartholomew, Walker, Evans, Dymond, Smart, Smith, Mackay, Regan.
Att: 5,224
*Original date was 27 November but it was too foggy for play to commence.

304

Round 2
Dec 11 v Hereford United (h) 2-1
Dymond 2
Hoyle; Warren, Rowe, Bartholomew, Walker, Fallon, Dymond, Evans, Smith, Mackay, Regan.
Att: 8,000
Round 3
Jan 8 v Grimsby Town (a) 1-2
Regan
Hoyle; Johnstone, Clark, Bartholomew, Walker, Fallon, Dymond, Smart, Smith, Harrower, Regan.
Att: 18,000

1949-50
Round 1
Nov 26 v Millwall (a) 5-3
Smart 3, Regan, Smith
Hoyle; Johnstone, Rowe, Doyle, Davey, Greenwood, Harrower, Smart, Smith, McClelland, Regan.
Att: 19,487
Round 2
Dec 10 v Chester (h) 2-0
Regan 2 (1 pen)
Hoyle; Johnstone, Rowe, Doyle, Davey, Greenwood, Harrower, Smart, Smith, McClelland, Regan.
Att: 11,025
Round 3
Jan 7 v Nuneaton Borough (h) 3-0
Greenwood, Regan, Fallon
Singleton; Johnstone, Clark, Fallon, Goddard, Powell, Harrower, Smart, Smith, Greenwood, Regan.
Att: 14,365
Round 4
Jan 28 v Liverpool (a) 1-3
Smart
Singleton; Johnstone, Clark, Fallon, Goddard, Davey, Hutchings, Smart, Walker, Greenwood, Regan.
Att: 45,000

1950-51
Round 1
Nov 25 v Glastonbury (a) 2-1
Smith, Mackay
Singleton; Clark, Rowe, Harrower, Doyle, Davey, McClelland, Mackay, Smith, Lynn, Regan.
Att: 4,000
Round 2
Dec 9 v Swindon Town (h) 3-0
Smith, Fallon, Mackay
Singleton; Clark, Rowe, Harrower, Doyle, Davey, McClelland, Fallon, Smith, Mackay, Regan.
Att: 14,764
Round 3
Jan 6 v Grimsby Town (a) 3-3
Mackay 2, McClelland
Singleton; Warren, Clark, Fallon, Doyle, Davey, McClelland, Lynn, Smith, Mackay, Regan.
Att: 13,233
Replay
Jan 10 v Grimsby Town (h) 4-2
McClelland 2, Smith 2
Singleton; Warren, Clark, Harrower, Doyle, Davey, McClelland, Fallon, Smith, Lynn, Regan.
Att: 18,117

Round 4
Jan 27 v Chelsea (h) 1-1
Regan
Singleton; Warren, Clark, Harrower, Goddard, Davey, McClelland, Lynn, Smith, Mackay, Regan.
Att: 20,000
Replay
Jan 31 v Chelsea (a) 0-2
Singleton; Warren, Rowe, Fallon, Goddard, Davey, McClelland, Harrower, Dare, Lynn, Regan.
Att: 40,000

1951-52
Round 1
Nov 24 v King's Lynn (a) 3-1
McClelland 2, Smart
Lear; Warren, Clark, Fallon, Goddard, Davey, McClelland, Smart, Smith, Mackay, Regan.
Att: 12,931
Round 2
Dec 15 v Ipswich Town (a) 0-4
Singleton; Warren, Rowe, Goddard, Doyle, Davey, Digby, Smart, Mitchell, Mackay, McClelland.
Att: 11,819

1952-53
Round 1
Nov 22 v Port Vale (a) 1-2
Murphy
Kelly; Walton, Rowe, Davey, Goddard, Armes, McClelland, Mackay, Dailey, Murphy, Regan.
Att: 14,566

1953-54
Round 1
Nov 21 v Hereford United (h) 1-1
Samuels
Kelly; Storey, Rowe, Booth, Davey, Dodgin, Dailey, Samuels, Donaldson, Mackay, McClelland.
Att: 10,829
Replay
Nov 25 v Hereford United (a) 0-2
Kelly; Storey, Rowe, Booth, Davey, Dodgin, Dailey, Samuels, Donaldson, Mackay, McClelland.
Att: 8,000

1954-55
Round 1
Nov 20 v Millwall (a) 2-3
Murphy, Mackay
Kelly; B.Doyle, Douglass, Setters, Davey, Mitchell, McClelland, Mackay, Ellaway, Murphy, Kaile.
Att: 15,610

1955-56
Round 1
Nov 19 v Coventry City (a) 1-0
Rees
Hunter; Parr, Mitchell, Davey, Harvey, Dunne, Simpson, John, Burke, Murphy, Rees.
Att: 17,919
Round 2
Dec 10 v Hendon (h) 6-2
Rees 2, Iggleden 2, Simpson, Murphy
Hunter; Parr, Mitchell, Davey, Harvey, Dunne, Simpson, John, Iggleden, Murphy, Rees.
Att: 12,044

305

Round 3
Jan 7 v Stoke City (h) 0-0
Hunter; Doyle, Mitchell, Davey, Harvey, Dunne,
Buckle, Burke, Iggleden, Murphy, Rees.
Att: 16,919
Replay
Jan 9 v Stoke City (a) 0-3
Hunter; Doyle, Mitchell, Davey, Harvey, Dunne, John,
Burke, Iggleden, Murphy, Rees.
Att: 14,513

1956-57
Round 1
Nov 17 v Plymouth Argyle (h) 0-2
Hunter; Doyle, Ferrier, John, Harvey, Porteous,
Buckle, Thomas, Mitchell, Currie, Rees.
Att: 13,855

1957-58
Round 1
Nov 16 v Bath City (a) 1-2
Calland
Hunter; John, Mitchell, Butterworth, Harvey,
Waterman, Wilson, Atkinson, Calland, Churms, Dale.
Att: 9,030

1958-59
Round 1
Nov 15 v Brentford (a) 2-3
Calland, Mitchell (pen)
Hunter; Foley, MacDonald, Mitchell, Oliver, John,
Stiffle, Rees, Calland, Nicholls, Dale.
Att: 15,000

1959-60
Round 1
Nov 14 v Barnstaple Town (h) 4-0
Rees 2, Wilkinson, Stiffle
Jones; Foley, MacDonald, Mitchell, Oliver,
Thompson, Stiffle, Rees, Wilkinson, Calland, Dale.
Att: 9,200
Round 2
Dec 5 v Brentford (h) 3-1
Dale, Rees, Stiffle
Jones; Foley, MacDonald, Mitchell, Oliver,
Thompson, Stiffle, Rees, Wilkinson, Micklewright,
Dale.
Att: 13,000
Round 3
Jan 9 v Luton Town (h) 1-2
Daniel (og)
Lobbett; Foley, MacDonald, Mitchell, Oliver,
Thompson, Stiffle, Rees, Wilkinson, Micklewright,
Dale.
Att: 20,000

1960-61
Round 1
Nov 5 v Bournemouth & Boscombe Athletic (h) 1-1
Bond
Lobbett; Whitnall, MacDonald, Harvey, A.Williams,
Thompson, Harrison, Bond, Donaldson, Rees, Dale.
Att: 8,000

Replay
Nov 9 v Bournemouth & Boscombe Athletic (a) 1-3
Bond
Lobbett; Whitnall, MacDonald, Grant, Harvey,
Thompson, Welsh, Bond, Wilkinson, Donaldson,
Dale.
Att: 6,382

1961-62
Round 1
Nov 4 v Dartford (h) 3-3
McMillan 2, Mabey (og)
Jones; Hudson, MacDonald, Hughes, Harvey,
Sullivan, McMillan, Gordon, Carter, Rees, Jenkins.
Att: 6,162
Replay
Nov 8 v Dartford (a) 1-2
Carter
Jones; Hudson, MacDonald, Hughes, Harvey,
Sullivan, McMillan, Rees, Carter, Gordon, Jenkins
Att: 6,777

1962-63
Round 1
Nov 3 v Gravesend & Northfleet (a) 2-3
Carter 2
Tinsley; Smyth, MacDonald, Hughes, Anderson,
Sanders, Welsh, Mitchell, Pierce, Carter, Rees.
Att: 3,552

1963-64
Round 1
Nov 16 v Shrewsbury Town (h) 2-1
Curtis, Anderson
Barnett; Smyth, MacDonald, Mitchell, Harvey,
Anderson, Rees, Northcott, Curtis, Grace, Phoenix.
Att: 8,000
Round 2
Dec 7 v Bristol City (h) 0-2
Barnett; Smyth, MacDonald, Mitchell, Harvey,
Anderson, Rees, Northcott, Curtis, Grace, Phoenix.
Att: 15,000

1964-65
Round 1
Nov 14 v Hayes (h) 1-0
Ley
Barnett; Smyth, MacDonald, Mitchell, Harvey,
Hancock, Welsh, Carter, Curtis, Ley, Rees.
Att: 9,000
Round 2
Dec 5 v Shrewsbury Town (h) 1-2
Mitchell
Shearing; Smyth, MacDonald, Mitchell, Harvey,
Anderson, Welsh, Riding, Curtis, Grace, Ley.
Att: 6,500

1965-66
Round 1
Nov 13 v Bedford Town (h) 1-2
Curtis
Shearing; Smyth, Ley, Mitchell, Harvey, Fulton, Blain,
Banks, McLean, Curtis, Rees.
Att: 6,000

1966-67
Round 1
Nov 26 v Luton Town (h) 1-1
Keeley
Smout; Smyth, Ley, Wilkinson, Harvey, Blain,
Godfrey, Keeley, McLean, Thompson, Buckingham.
Att: 4,744
Replay
Dec 1 v Luton Town (a) 0-2
Smout; Smyth, Ley, Wilkinson, Harford, Thompson,
Godfrey, Keeley, McLean, McNeil, Blain.
Att: 5,000

1967-68
Round 1
Dec 9 v Nuneaton Borough (a) 0-0
Smout; Embury, Smyth, Blain, Newman, Huxford,
Hart, Banks, Curtis, Crawford, Fudge.
Att: 10,750
Replay
Dec 13 v Nuneaton Borough (h) 0-0 (after extra-time)
Smout; Embury, Smyth, Blain, Newman, Huxford,
Hart(Balson), Banks, Curtis, Crawford, Fudge.
Att: 6,909
2nd Replay
Dec 18 v Nuneaton Borough (n*) 1-0
Banks
Smout; Embury, Smyth, Blain, Newman, Huxford,
Fudge, Banks, Curtis, Crawford, Corr.
Att: 5,079
*Played at Ashton Gate, Bristol.
Round 2
Jan 6 v Walsall (h) 1-3
Blain (pen)
Smout; Smyth, Balson, Newman, Harvey, Huxford,
Blain, Banks, Curtis, Crawford, Corr.
Att: 10,133

1968-69
Round 1
Nov 16 v Newport County (h) 0-0
Shearing; Smyth, Blain, Kirkham, Harvey, Newman,
Corr. Banks, Balson, Curtis, Pleat.
Att: 6,045
Replay
Nov 18 v Newport County (a) 3-1
Balson, Williams (og), Wood (og)
Shearing; Smyth, Blain, Kirkham, Harvey, Newman,
Corr, Pinkney, Balson, Curtis, Pleat.
Att: 6,000
Round 2
Dec 7 v Colchester United (a) 1-0
Banks
Shearing; Smyth, Blain, Kirkham, Harvey, Newman,
Corr, Banks, Balson, Mitten, Pleat.
Att: 6,180
Round 3
Jan 4 v Manchester United (h) 1-3
Banks
Shearing; Smyth, Blain, Harvey(Pleat), Sharples,
Newman, Corr, Banks, Pinkney, Mitten, Balson.
Att: 18,500

1969-70
Round 1
Nov 15 v Fulham (h) 2-0
Corr, Banks
Shearing; Crawford, Blain, Morris, Sharples, Balson,
Corr, Banks, Wingate, Pleat(Walker), Mitten.
Att: 9,181
Round 2
Dec 6 v Northampton Town (a) 1-1
Wingate
Shearing; Crawford, Balson, Morris, Sharples, Parker,
Pleat, Banks, Wingate, Gadston, Mitten.
Att: 5,000
Replay
Dec 10 v Northampton Town (h) 0-0 (after extra-time)
Shearing; Crawford, Balson, Morris, Sharples, Parker,
Pleat, Banks, Wingate, Gadston, Mitten.
Att: 8,930
2nd Replay
Dec 15 v Northampton Town (n*) 1-2
Mitten (pen)
Shearing; Crawford, Balson, Morris, Sharples,
Parker(Blain), Corr, Banks, Gadston, Mitten, Walker.
Att: 2,434
*Played at the County Ground, Swindon.

1970-71
Round 1
Nov 21 v Swansea City (a) 1-4
Wingate
Wilson; Crawford, Blain, Sharples, Newman, Wingate,
Rowan, Binney, Gadston, Mitten, Corr.
Att: 7,386

1971-72
Round 1
Nov 20 v Crawley Town (a) 0-0
Wilson; Crawford, Blain, Parker, Jimmy Giles, Balson,
Morrin, Banks, Binney, Wingate, John Giles.
Att: 3,000
Replay
Nov 24 v Crawley Town (h) 2-0
Binney, Rowan
Wilson; Crawford, Blain, Morrin, Jimmy Giles,
Balson, Rowan, Banks, Binney, Wingate, Gadston.
Att: 3,967
Round 2
Dec 11 v Swansea City (a) 0-0
Wilson; Stacey, Blain, Morris, Jimmy Giles, Balson,
Rowan, Banks, Gadston, Wingate, John Giles.
Att: 8,397
Replay
Dec 15 v Swansea City (h) 0-1
Wilson; Stacey, Blain, Morris, Jimmy Giles, Balson,
Rowan, Banks, Gadston, Wingate, John Giles.
Att: 6,858

1972-73
Round 1
Nov 18 v Walton & Hersham (a) 1-2
Stacey
Wilson; Stacey, Parker, Clapham, Giles, Balson,
Wingate, Binney(Banks), Plumb, Morrin, Gibson.
Att: 2,000

1973-74
Round 1
Nov 24 v Alvechurch (h) 0-1
Wilson; Crawford, Blain, Joy, Giles, Clapham, Wallace, Binney, Plumb(Devlin), Neale, Wingate.
Att: 4,698

1974-75
Round 1
Nov 23 v Newport County (h) 1-2
Hodge
Bond; Rutter, Hatch, Morrin, Giles, Clapham (Hooker), Jennings, Templeman, Bowker, Joy, Hodge.
Att: 4,292

1975-76
Round 1
Nov 22 v Cardiff City (a) 2-6
Beer, Bowker
Key; Rutter(Joy), Hooker, Hodge, Saxton, Hatch, Wingate, Bowker, Robertson, Beer, Moxham.
Att: 7,538

1976-77
Round 1
Nov 20 v Southend United (h) 1-1
Hatch
Key; Hore, Hooker, Morrin, Saxton, Hatch, Weeks, Kellow, Robertson, Holman, Jennings.
Att: 4,434
Replay
Nov 22 v Southend United (a) 1-2 (after extra-time)
Kellow
Key; Hore, Hooker, Morrin, Saxton, Hatch, Weeks, Kellow, Robertson, Holman(Hodge), Jennings.
Att: 6,604

1977-78
Round 1
Nov 26 v Newport County (a) 1-1
Bowker
Key; Templeman, Hore, Bowker, Saxton, Hatch, Hodge, Kellow, Randell, Holman, Jennings.
Att: 6,227
Replay
Nov 30 v Newport County (h) 4-2
Roberts, Hatch, Kellow, Templeman
Key; Templeman, Hore, Bowker, Saxton, Hatch, Weeks, Kellow, Randell, Roberts, Jennings.
Att: 5,713
Round 2
Dec 17 v Minehead (a) 3-0
Randell 2, Kellow
Key; Templeman, Hore, Bowker, Saxton, Hatch, Randell, Kellow, Holman, Roberts, Jennings.
Att: 3,200
Round 3
Jan 7 v Wolverhampton Wanderers (h) 2-2
Roberts, Holman
Key; Templeman, Hatch, Bowker, Giles, Saxton, Randell, Kellow, Holman, Roberts, Hore.
Att: 14,377
Replay
Jan 10 v Wolverhampton Wanderers (a) 1-3
Kellow
Key; Templeman, Hatch, Bowker, Giles, Saxton, Randell, Kellow, Holman, Roberts, Hore.
Att: 20,000

1978-79
Round 1
Nov 25 v Brentford (h) 1-0
Forbes
O'Keefe; Templeman, Mitchell, Roberts, Hore, Delve, Forbes, Neville, Ingham, Bowker, Hatch.
Att: 3,782
Round 2
Dec 16 v Maidstone United (a) 0-1
O'Keefe; Hore, Giles, Roberts, Mitchell, Delve, Forbes, Neville, Bowker, Pearson, Hatch.
Att: 3,685

1979-80
Round 1
Nov 24 v Aldershot (a) 1-4
Neville
O'Keefe; Mitchell, Hore, Delve, Giles, Hatch, Forbes, L.Roberts, Bowker, Pearson, Neville.
Att: 5,000

1980-81
Round 1
Nov 22 v Leatherhead (h) 5-0
Kellow 2, Pearson, L.Roberts, Hinshelwood (og)
Bond; M.Rogers, L.Roberts, P.Roberts, Delve, Hatch, Forbes, Pearson, Kellow, P.Rogers, Pullar.
Att: 5,000
Round 2
Dec 13 v Millwall (a) 1-0
P.Rogers
Bond; M.Rogers, L.Roberts, Delve, P.Roberts, Hatch, Forbes, Pearson, Kellow, P.Rogers, Pullar.
Att: 3,426
Round 3
Jan 3 v Maidstone United (a) 4-2
Pullar 2, Kellow, P.Rogers
Bond; M.Rogers, L.Roberts, Delve, P.Roberts, Hatch, Forbes, Pearson, Kellow, P.Rogers, Pullar.
Att: 6,000
Round 4
Jan 24 v Leicester City (a) 1-1
Pullar
Bond; M.Rogers, L.Roberts, P.Roberts, Prince, Hatch, Forbes, Delve, Kellow, P.Rogers, Pullar.
Att: 21,000
Replay
Jan 28 v Leicester City (h) 3-1
Kellow 3 (1 pen)
Main; M.Rogers, L.Roberts, Delve, P.Roberts, Hatch, Forbes, Pearson, Kellow, P.Rogers, Pullar.
Att: 15,268
Round 5
Feb 14 v Newcastle United (a) 1-1
L.Roberts
Bond; M.Rogers, L.Roberts, Delve, P.Roberts, Sparrow, Forbes, Pearson, Kellow, P.Rogers, Hatch.
Att: 37,420
Replay
Feb 18 v Newcastle United (h) 4-0
Hatch, Pearson, P.Roberts, M.Rogers
Bond; M.Rogers, L.Roberts, Delve, P.Roberts, Sparrow, Forbes, P.Rogers, Kellow, Pearson, Hatch.
Att: 17,668

Round 6
Mar 7 v Tottenham Hotspur (a) 0-2
Bond; M.Rogers, L.Roberts, Forbes, P.Roberts,
Sparrow, Pearson, P.Rogers, Kellow, Delve, Hatch.
Att: 41,000

1981-82
Round 1
Nov 21 v Brentford (a) 0-2
Bond; Davey, Shaw, L.Roberts, Cooke, Sparrow,
Lester, Delve, Kellow, P.Rogers, Pullar.
Att: 6,432

1982-83
Nov 20 v Plymouth Argyle (a) 0-2
Bond; M.Rogers, Viney, Harle, Marker, McEwan,
Neville, P.Rogers, Kellow, Delve, Pullar.
Att: 10,202

1983-84
Round 1
Nov 19 v Maidstone United (h) 1-1
O'Connor
Bond; Kirkup, Viney, O'Connor, Atkinson, McEwan,
Neville, Rogers, Auguste, Francis, Taylor.
Att: 3,615
Replay
Nov 23 v Maidstone United (a) 1-2
Neville
Bond; Kirkup, Viney, O'Connor, Atkinson, McEwan,
Neville, Rogers, Howarth, Francis, Taylor.
Att: 4,381

1984-85
Round 1
Nov 17 v Enfield (h) 2-2
Neville, Sims
Wood; Kirkup, Viney, O'Shea, Marker, McNichol,
Neville, Smith, Sims, Pratt, Harrower.
Att: 3,261
Replay
Nov 20 v Enfield (a) 0-3
Wood; Kirkup, Viney, O'Shea, Marker, McNichol,
Neville, Ling, Sims, Pratt, Harrower.
Att: 3,000

1985-86
Round 1
Nov 16 v Cardiff City (h) 2-1
Gale 2
Shaw; Harrower, Viney, McNichol, McCaffery,
Marker, Ling, Jackson, Gale, Keough, Crawford.
Att: 2,772
Round 2
Dec 7 v Bristol City (a) 2-1
Kellow, Crawford
Shaw; Harrower, Viney, McNichol, McCaffery,
Marker, Ling, Jackson, Kellow, Keough, Crawford.
Att: 8,052
Round 3
Jan 5 v Everton (a) 0-1
Shaw; Harrower, Viney, McNichol, Marker,
McCaffery, Ling, Jackson, Gale, Keough, Crawford.
Att: 22,726

1986-87
Round 1
Nov 15 v Cambridge United (h) 1-1
Viney

Shaw; Batty, Viney, Marker, Massey, Watson, Pugh,
O'Connell, Biggins, Keough, Robson.
Att: 3,340
Replay
Nov 19 v Cambridge United (a) 0-2
Shaw; Batty, Viney, Marker, Massey, Watson,
Harrower, O'Connell, Roberts, Priddle, Robson.
Att: 3,618

1987-88
Round 1
Nov 14 v Leyton Orient (a) 0-2
Shaw; Cooper, Viney, Carter, Taylor(Watson),
Massey, Batty, Edwards, O'Connell, Rowbotham
(Olsson), Harrower.
Att: 3,787

1988-89
Round 1
Nov 19 v Bognor Regis (a) 1-2
Rowbotham
Gwinnett; Banks, Viney, Rogers, Taylor, Langley,
Hiley(Withey), Batty, Neville, Harrower, Rowbotham.
Att: 2,000

1989-90
Round 1
Nov 18 v Dartford (a) 1-1
Rowbotham (pen)
Walter; Hiley, Harrower, McNichol, Taylor,
Whitehead, Rowbotham, Bailey, Batty, Neville,
Dryden(Young).
Att: 3,129
Replay
Nov 22 v Dartford (h) 4-1
Bailey, Batty, Harrower, Neville
Walter; Hiley, Harrower(Rowe), McNichol, Taylor,
Whitehead, Rowbotham, Bailey, Batty, Neville
(Benjamin), Frankland.
Att: 4,900
Round 2
Dec 9 v Maidstone United (a) 1-1
Cooper
Miller; Hiley, Benjamin, McNichol, Taylor,
Whitehead, Rowbotham, Bailey, McDermott, Neville
(Batty), Cooper.
Att: 2,385
Replay
Dec 13 v Maidstone United (h) 3-2
Rowbotham 2, McDermott
Miller; Hiley, Benjamin, McNichol, Taylor,
Whitehead, Rowbotham, Bailey, McDermott, Neville,
Cooper(Batty).
Att: 4,125
Round 3
Jan 6 v Norwich City (h) 1-1
Rowbotham
Miller; Hiley, Benjamin, McNichol, Taylor,
Whitehead, Rowbotham, Bailey, McDermott(Batty),
Neville, Frankland.
Att: 9,061
Replay
Jan 10 v Norwich City (a) 0-2
Miller; Hiley, Benjamin, McNichol, Taylor,
Whitehead, Rowbotham, Bailey, McDermott
(Cooper), Neville(Batty), Frankland.
Att: 18,202

Exeter in the League Cup

1960-61
Round 1
Oct 19 v Manchester United (h) 1-1
Rees
Lobbett; Whitnall, MacDonald, Wilson, Harvey, Thompson, Welsh, Gordon, Donaldson, Rees, Harrison.
Att: 16,000
Replay
Oct 26 v Manchester United (a) 1-4
Thompson (pen)
Lobbett; Whitnall, MacDonald, Wilson, Harvey, Thompson, Welsh, Gordon, Donaldson, Rees, Dale.
Att: 15,662

1961-62
Round 1
Sep 11 v Mansfield Town (a) 2-5
Gordon, Blue
Jones; Whitnall, MacDonald, Wilson, Harvey, Sullivan, Rees, Gordon, Blue, Carter, Jenkins.
Att: 5,904

1962-63
Round 1
Sep 5 v Aldershot (a) 0-2
Tinsley; Smyth, Davis, Brown, Anderson, Rutley, Rees, Mitchell, Green, Welsh, McMillan.
Att: 4,000

1963-64
Round 1
Sep 4 v Oxford United (a) 1-0
Cochrane
Barnett; Smyth, MacDonald, Mitchell, Harvey, Anderson, Cochrane, Henderson, Curtis, Grace, Rees.
Att: 5,000
Round 2
Sep 25 v Hull City (a) 0-1
Barnett; Smyth, MacDonald, Mitchell, Harvey, Anderson, Rees, J.Henderson, Redwood, Grace, Ley.
Att: 8,500

1964-65
Round 1
Sep 2 v Gillingham (h) 2-0
Carter, Banks
Barnett; Fulton, MacDonald, Anderson, Harvey, Hancock, Welsh, Banks, Carter, Curtis, Rees.
Att; 7,788
Round 2
Sep 23 v Bradford City (h) 5-3
Curtis 2, Hancock
Shearing; Smyth, Fulton, Rutley, Harvey, Hancock, Rees, Carter, Banks, Curtis, Ley.
Att: 8,000

1965-66
Round 1
Sep 1 v Colchester United (a) 1-2
Curtis
Shearing; Fulton, Peapell, Mitchell, Harvey, Anderson, Welsh, Curtis, McLean, Carter, Ley.
Att: 2,900

1966-67
Round 1
Aug 24 v Torquay United (h) 2-2
McLean, Smyth
Jones; Smyth, Ley, Wilkinson, Harford, Thompson, Godfrey, Keeley, McLean, Kennedy, Blain.
Att: 7,000
Replay
Aug 31 v Torquay United (a) 2-1
McLean, Harford
Jones; Smyth, Ley, Wilkinson, Harford, Thompson, Godfrey, Keeley, McLean, Evans, Blain.
Att: 7,679
Round 2
Sep 14 v Cardiff City (a) 1-0
Harford
Jones; Embury, Smyth, Wilkinson, Harford, Thompson, Godfrey, Keeley, McLean, Evans, Blain.
Att: 5,000
Round 3
Oct 5 v Walsall (h) 1-2
McNeil
Jones; Embury, Ley, Wilkinson, Harford, Thompson, Godfrey, Keeley, Elliott, McNeil, Smith.
Att: 5,487

1967-68
Round 1
Aug 22 v Torquay United (a) 0-0
Smout; Smyth, Blain, Embury, Wilkinson, Crawford, Hart, Stuckey, Balson, Fudge, Whatling.
Att: 6,794
Replay
Aug 28 v Torquay United (h) 0-3
Smout; Smyth, Blain, Balson, Wilkinson, Huxford, Hart, Crawford, Stuckey, Fudge, Whatling.
Att: 5,700

1968-69
Round 1
Aug 14 v Plymouth Argyle (a) 0-0
Shearing; Smyth, Balson, Kirkham, Harvey, Newman, Corr, Banks, Bullock, Mitten, Pleat.
Att: 8,662
Replay
Aug 21 v Plymouth Argyle (h) 0-0 (after extra-time)
Shearing; Smyth, Balson, Kirkham, Harvey, Newman, Blain, Banks, Bullock, Mitten, Pleat.
Att: 13,338

2nd Replay
Aug 26 v Plymouth Argyle (n*) 1-0 (after extra-time)
Kirkham
Shearing; Smyth, Balson, Kirkham, Harvey, Newman,
Blain, Banks, Bullock(Curtis), Mitten, Pleat.
Att: 10,884
*Played at the Plainmoor Ground, Torquay.
Round 2
Sep 4 v Sheffield Wednesday (h) 3-1
Curtis, Corr, Bullock
Shearing; Smyth, Balson, Curtis(Crawford), Harvey,
Newman, Corr, Blain, Bullock, Mitten, Pleat.
Att: 15,962
Round 3
Sep 25 v Tottenham Hotspur (a) 3-6
Banks 2, Mitten
Shearing; Smyth, Blain, Kirkham, Harvey, Newman,
Corr(Curtis), Banks, Bullock, Mitten, Pleat.
Att: 25,796

1969-70
Round 1
Aug 13 v Bristol City (h) 1-1
Banks
Shearing; Crawford, Blain, Balson, Sharples, Newman,
Corr, Giles, Banks, Mitten, Walker.
Att: 8,050
Replay
Aug 19 v Bristol City (a) 2-3
Corr, Parr (og)
Shearing; Crawford, Blain, Giles, Newman, Parker,
Corr, Banks, Wingate, Mitten, Walker.
Att: 10,915

1970-71
Round 1
Aug 18 v Swansea City (h) 0-0
Wilson; Crawford, Blain, Parker, Sharples, Balson,
Corr, Banks, Binney(Wingate), Giles, Mitten.
Att: 4,932
Replay
Aug 25 v Swansea City (a) 2-4 (after extra-time)
Gadston, Mitten
Wilson; Crawford, Blain, Parker, Sharples, Balson,
Rowan, Mitten, Gadston, Wingate, Corr.
Att: 6,739

1971-72
Round 1
Aug 18 v Bristol Rovers (h) 0-3
Wilson; Crawford, Stacey, Parker, Jimmy Giles,
Balson, Morrin, Banks, Gadston, Binney, Wingate.
Att; 6,418

1972-73
Round 1
Aug 16 v Brighton & Hove Albion (a) 1-2
Binney
Wilson; Stacey, Blain, Parker, Giles, Balson, Morrin,
Binney, Plumb, Gibson, Scott.
Att: 10,155

1973-74
Round 1
Aug 28 v Swansea City (a) 1-1
Binney
Wilson; Crawford, Blain, Parker, Giles, Clapham,
Scott, Balson, Binney, Plumb, Wingate.
Att: 8,000

Replay
Sep 5 v Swansea City (h) 2-1 (after extra-time)
Binney 2
Wilson; Crawford, Blain, Joy, Giles, Clapham, Scott,
Binney, Plumb, Balson, Wingate.
Att: 5,023
Round 2
Oct 10 v Rotherham United (a) 4-1
Binney, Parker, Wingate, Joy
Wilson; Crawford, Blain, Parker, Giles, Clapham,
Wingate, Binney, Plumb, Joy, Scott.
Att: 7,000
Round 3
Oct 31 v West Bromwich Albion (a) 3-1
Binney 2, Plumb
Wilson; Crawford, Joy, Morrin, Giles, Clapham,
Wallace, Binney, Plumb, Gibson, Wingate.
Att: 10,783
Round 4
Nov 20 v Wolverhampton Wanderers (a) 1-5
Plumb
Clarke; Crawford, Blain, Joy, Giles, Clapham,
Wallace, Neale, Plumb, Gibson, Wingate.
Att: 7,622

1974-75
Round 1
Aug 21 v Swansea City (h) 3-1
Jennings 3
Wilson; Rutter, Hatch, Morrin, Steele, Clapham(Joy),
Neale, Bowker, Robertson, Templeman, Jennings.
Att: 3,472
Round 2
Sep 11 v Hereford United (h) 0-1
Wilson, Rutter, Hatch, Morrin, Giles, Clapham, Neale,
Bowker, Robertson, Joy, Jennings.
Att: 3,500

1975-76
Round 1
Aug 19 v Newport County (a) 1-1
Bowker
Wilson; Templeman, Hooker, Joy, Wingate, Hatch,
Hodge, Bowker, Robertson, Beer, Jennings.
Att: 2,268
Replay
Aug 26 v Newport County (h) 2-0
Beer, Bowker
Wilson; Templeman, Hooker, Joy, Wingate, Hatch,
Jennings, Bowker, Robertson, Morrin, Beer.
Att: 3,303
Round 2
Sep 10 v Torquay United (a) 1-1
Hatch
Wilson; Templeman, Joy, Morrin, Wingate, Hatch,
Hodge, Bowker, Robertson, Beer, Jennings(Moxham).
Att: 5,186
Replay
Sep 17 v Torquay United (h) 1-2
Beer
Wilson; Templeman, Joy, Morrin, Wingate, Hatch,
Hodge, Bowker, Jordan, Beer, Jennings.
Att: 4,707

1976-77
Round 1 (1st leg)
Aug 14 v Plymouth Argyle (a) 1-0
Kellow
Key; Templeman, Hooker, Hore, Saxton, Hatch,
Hodge, Kellow, Morrin, Beer, Jennings.
Att: 8,500
Round 1 (2nd leg)
Aug 18 v Plymouth Argyle (h) 1-0
Jordan
Key; Templeman, Hooker, Hore, Saxton, Hatch,
Hodge, Kellow, Clapham, Beer, Jordan.
Att: 9,000
Exeter City won 2-0 on aggregate.
Round 2
Aug 31 v Norwich City (h) 1-3
Kellow
Key; Templeman, Hooker, Hore, Saxton(Clapham),
Hatch, Hodge, Kellow, Morrin, Beer, Jordan.
Att: 9,449

1977-78
Round 1 (1st leg)
Aug 13 v Plymouth Argyle (h) 2-2
Robertson 2 (2 pens)
Baugh; Templeman, Hore, Weeks, Saxton, Hatch,
Hodge, Kellow, Robertson, Beer, Jennings.
Att: 6,712
Round 1 (2nd leg)
Aug 16 v Plymouth Argyle (a) 0-0 (after extra-time)
Baugh; Templeman, Hore, Weeks, Saxton, Hatch,
Hodge, Kellow, Bowker, Beer, Jennings.
Att: 7,639
Replay
Aug 23 v Plymouth Argyle (a) 1-0
Beer
Baugh; Templeman, Hore, Weeks, Saxton, Hatch,
Hodge, Kellow, Bowker, Beer, Jennings.
Att: 8,776
Round 2
Aug 31 v Aston Villa (h) 1-3
Robertson
Baugh; Templeman, Hore, Weeks(Robertson), Saxton,
Hatch, Hodge, Kellow, Bowker, Beer, Jennings.
Att: 13,768

Goalkeeper John Baugh, who was ever-present in Exeter's somewhat limited progress in the 1977-8
League Cup.

312

1978-79
Round 1 (1st leg)
Aug 12 v AFC Bournemouth (a) 1-0
Kellow
O'Keefe; Templeman, Hore, Giles, Roberts, Delve, Hodge, Bowker, Randell, Forbes, Kellow.
Att: 5,000
Round 1 (2nd leg)
Aug 15 v AFC Bournemouth (h) 1-1
Delve
O'Keefe; Templeman, Hore, Giles, Roberts, Hatch, Hodge, Bowker, Randell, Delve, Kellow.
Att: 3,500
Exeter City won 2-1 on aggregate.
Round 2
Aug 29 v Blackburn Rovers (h) 2-1
Bowker, Delve
O'Keefe; Templeman, Hore, Giles, Roberts, Hatch, Hodge, Randell, Bowker, Delve, Kellow.
Att: 4,250
Round 3
Oct 4 v Bolton Wanderers (h) 2-1
Delve, Kellow (pen)
O'Keefe; Templeman, Hore, Giles, Roberts, Hatch, Holman, Kellow, Bowker, Delve, Holman.
Att: 9,151
Round 4
Nov 8 v Watford (h) 0-2
O'Keefe; Templeman, Hore, Giles, Roberts, Delve, Neville, Randell, Kellow, Bowker, Hatch.
Att: 14,740
1979-80
Round 1 (1st leg)
Aug 11 v Hereford United (a) 3-1
Bowker 3
O'Keefe; P.Roberts, Hore, Giles, M.Rogers, Delve, Pullar, Pearson, Bowker, Neville, Hatch.
Att: 3,278
Round 1 (2nd leg)
Aug 15 v Hereford United (h) 2-1
Pullar, Pearson
O'Keefe; P.Roberts, Hore, Giles, M.Rogers, Delve, Pullar, Neville, Bowker, Pearson, Hatch.
Att: 4,312
Exeter City won 5-2 on aggregate.
Round 2 (1st leg)
Aug 28 v Doncaster Rovers (a) 1-3
Pullar
O'Keefe; P.Roberts, Hore, Giles, L.Roberts, Delve, Pullar, Neville, Sims, P.Rogers, Hatch.
Att: 4,636
Round 2 (2nd leg)
Sep 5 v Doncaster Rovers (h) 5-1
Bowker 2, Hatch, Neville (pen), Sims
O'Keefe; P.Roberts(Bowker), Hore, Giles, M.Rogers, Delve, Pullar, Neville, Sims, P.Rogers, Hatch.
Att: 3,000
Exeter City won 6-4 on aggregate.
Round 3
Sep 26 v Birmingham City (a) 2-1
Neville 2
O'Keefe; Mitchell, Hore, Giles, Delve, Hatch, Forbes, Pullar, Bowker, Sims, Neville.
Att: 13,669
Round 4
Oct 30 v Liverpool (a) 0-2
O'Keefe; Mitchell, Hore, Giles, Delve, Hatch, Forbes, Pullar, Neville, Bowker, Pearson.
Att: 21,000

1980-81
Round 1 (1st leg)
Aug 9 v Bristol Rovers (h) 1-1
Kellow
Main; Ireland, Prince, Giles, Delve, Hatch, P.Roberts, Pullar, Kellow, P.Rogers, Pearson.
Att: 4,702
Round 1 (2nd leg)
Aug 12 v Bristol Rovers (a) 1-1 (after extra-time)
Kellow
Main; Ireland, Prince, Delve, Giles, Hatch, P.Roberts, Forbes, Neville, Kellow, Pullar.
Att: 4,000
Bristol Rovers won 7-6 on penalties.

1981-82
Round 1 (1st leg)
Sep 2 v Cardiff City (a) 1-2
Cooke
Main; M.Rogers, Hatch, L.Roberts, Cooke, Davey, Lester, Pullar, Pratt, Kellow, P.Rogers.
Att: 3,000
Round 1 (2nd leg)
Sep 16 v Cardiff City (h) 3-1
Fisher, Cooke, Kellow (pen)
Main; Mitchell, L.Roberts, Cooke, P.Roberts, Davey, Lester, Fisher, Kellow, Pratt, Hatch.
Att: 4,500
Exeter City won 4-3 on aggregate.
Round 2 (1st leg)
Oct 7 v Liverpool (a) 0-5
Bond; M.Rogers, Sparrow, Davey, Cooke, Prince, L.Roberts, Delve, P.Rogers, Kellow, Lester.
Att: 11,000
Round 2 (2nd leg)
Oct 28 v Liverpool (h) 0-6
Bond; M.Rogers, Sparrow, Davey, Marker, Pullar, L.Roberts, Delve, Kellow, P.Rogers, Lester.
Att: 11,740
Liverpool won 11-0 on aggregate.

1982-83
Round 1 (1st leg)
Sep 1 v Newport County (h) 1-2
Kellow
Bond; Kirkup, Viney, McEwan, Roberts, Howarth, Harle, P.Rogers, Kellow, Delve, Pullar.
Att: 2,292
Round 1 (2nd leg)
Sep 14 v Newport County (a) 0-6
Bond; Kirkup, Viney, M.Rogers, Roberts, McEwan, Harle, P.Rogers, Kellow, Delve, Pullar.
Att: 2,684
Newport County won 8-1 on aggregate.

1983-84
Round 1 (1st leg)
Aug 31 v Cardiff City (h) 2-3
Kellow, Rogers
Bond; Lane, Viney, Evans, McEwan, Harle, Neville, Rogers, Kellow, Kirkup, Ling.
Att: 4,000
Round 1 (2nd leg)
Sep 13 v Cardiff City (a) 1-2
McEwan
Bond; Howarth, Viney, Harle, Marker, McEwan, Neville, Dennis, Kellow, Francis, Ling.
Att: 3,450
Cardiff City won 5-3 on aggregate.

1984-85
Round 1 (1st leg)
Aug 29 v Cardiff City (h) 1-0
Viney (pen)
Wood; Rogers, Viney, O'Shea, Marker, McNichol, Neville, McDonough, Sims, Pratt, Ling.
Att: 3,469
Round 1 (2nd leg)
Sep 4 v Cardiff City (a) 0-2
Wood; Rogers, Viney, O'Shea, Marker, McNichol, Neville, McDonough, Sims, Pratt, Ling.
Att: 2,000
Cardiff City won 2-1 on aggregate.

1985-86
Round 1 (1st leg)
Aug 20 v Plymouth Argyle (a) 1-2
Pratt (pen)
Shaw; Kirkup, King, McNichol, McCaffery, Marker, Ling, Kellow, Morgan, Pratt, Crawford.
Att: 4,754
Round 1 (2nd leg)
Sep 4 v Plymouth Argyle (h) 2-0
G.Kimble, Marker
Shaw; Kirkup, Viney, McNichol, Impey, Marker, Ling, A.Kimble, Morgan, G.Kimble, Crawford.
Att: 3,362
Exeter City won 3-2 on aggregate.
Round 2 (1st leg)
Sep 25 v Aston Villa (h) 1-4
Kellow
Shaw; Kirkup, Viney, McNichol, Impey, Marker, Ling, Jackson, Kellow, Gale, Crawford.
Att: 5,325
Round 2 (2nd leg)
Oct 9 v Aston Villa (a) 1-8
Crawford
Shaw; Kirkup, Viney, McNichol, Impey, Marker, Ling, Jackson, Kellow, Pratt, Crawford.
Att: 7,678
Aston Villa won 12-2 on aggregate.

1986-87
Round 1 (1st leg)
Aug 27 v Newport County (h) 0-0
Shaw; Pugh, Viney, Marker, McCaffery, Watson, Batty, Gale, O'Connell, Keough, Harrower.
Att: 1,545
Round 1 (2nd leg)
Sep 2 v Newport County (a) 0-1
Shaw; Pugh, Viney, Priddle, McCaffery, Watson, Batty, Gale, Roberts, Keough, Harrower.
Att: 1,600
Newport County won 1-0 on aggregate.

1987-88
Round 1 (1st leg)
Aug 17 v AFC Bournemouth (a) 1-1
O'Connell
Shaw; Nisbet, Viney, Marker, Taylor(Cooper), Carter, Batty, Edwards(Kellow), O'Connell, Olsson, Harrower.
Att: 4,094
Round 1 (2nd leg)
Aug 26 v AFC Bournemouth (h) 1-3 (after extra-time)
O'Connell
Shaw; Nisbet, Viney, Marker, Cooper, Carter, Batty (Williams), Edwards(Kellow), O'Connell, Olsson, Harrower.
Att: 4,000
Bournemouth won 4-2 on aggregate.

1988-89
Round 1 (1st leg)
Aug 30 v Bristol City (a) 0-1
Gwinnett; Banks, Viney, Rogers, Taylor, Cooper, Rowbotham, Hiley, Langley, Neville, Harrower.
Att: 6,005
Round 1 (2nd leg)
Sep 7 v Bristol City (h) 0-1
Gwinnett; Banks, Viney, Rogers, Taylor, Cooper, Rowbotham, Hiley, Batty, Neville, Harrower.
Att: 2,749
Bristol City won 2-0 on aggregate.

1989-90
Round 1 (1st leg)
Aug 23 v Swansea City (h) 3-0
Rowbotham 2, McDermott
Walter; Hiley, Vinnicombe, Rogers, Taylor, Whitehead, Rowbotham, Bailey, McDermott, Neville, Dryden.
Att: 2,777
Round 1 (2nd leg)
Aug 29 v Swansea City (a) 1-1
Rowbotham
Walter; Hiley, Vinnicombe, McNichol, Taylor, Whitehead, Rowbotham, Bailey, McDermott, Neville, Dryden.
Att: 1,987
Exeter City won 4-1 on aggregate
Round 2 (1st leg)
Sep 20 v Blackburn Rovers (h) 3-0
Vinnicombe, Dryden, Young
Walter; Hiley, Vinnicombe, Rogers, Taylor, Whitehead, Rowbotham, Bailey(Young), McDermott, Neville, Dryden.
Att: 4,808
Round 2 (2nd leg)
Oct 3 v Blackburn Rovers (a) 1-2
Rowbotham
Walter; Hiley, Vinnicombe, Rogers, Taylor, Whitehead, Rowbotham, Bailey, Young, Neville, Dryden(Harrower).
Att: 6,608
Exeter City won 4-2 on aggregate
Round 3
Oct 25 v Blackpool (h) 3-0
McNichol, Neville, Rowbotham
Walter; Hiley, Vinnicombe, McNichol, Taylor, Whitehead, Rowbotham, Bailey, McDermott, Neville, Dryden.
Att: 6,508
Round 4
Nov 29 v Sunderland (h) 2-2
Rowbotham, Neville
Walter; Hiley, Harrower, McNichol, Taylor, Whitehead, Rowbotham, Bailey, Batty, Neville, Benjamin.
Att: 8,643
Replay
Dec 5 v Sunderland (a) 2-5
Benjamin, McNichol
Walter; Hiley, Harrower(Cooper), McNichol, Taylor, Whitehead, Rowbotham, Bailey, Batty, Neville, Benjamin(Coyle).
Att: 18,130

City in Other Cup Competitions
Division Three South Cup

1933-34
Round 1
Jan 24 (h) v Crystal Palace 11-6
Whitlow 6 (1 pen), Hurst 2, Wrightson 2, Scott
Davies; Gray, Miller, Clarke, Webb, Hardie, Scott,
Wrightson, Whitlow, Houghton, Hurst.
Att: 2,000
Round 2
Feb 21 v Watford (h) 4-2
Clarke 2, Barnes, Hurst
Chesters; Gray, Miller, Angus, Webb, Hardie, Clarke,
Scott, Hurst, Houghton, Barnes.
Att: 3,000
Round 3
Mar 14 v Coventry City (h) 1-1
Barnes
Davies; Gray, Miller, Clarke, Webb, Angus, Scott,
Wrightson, Whitlow, Barnes, Hurst.
Att: 1,000
Replay
Mar 22 v Coventry City (a) 1-0
Barnes
Davies; Hughes, Miller, Clarke, Webb, Angus, Scott,
Risdon, Hurst, Wrightson, Barnes.
Att: 4,000
Semi-final
Apr 12 v Brighton & Hove Albion (n*) 1-1
Hurst
Chesters; Gray, Miller, Clarke, Webb, Angus, Scott,
Risdon, Hurst, Wrightson, Whitlow.
Att: 3,221
*Played at Craven Cottage, Fulham.
Replay
Apr 23 v Brighton & Hove Albion (h) 1-1 (after extra-time)
Hurst
Chesters; Gray, Miller, Clarke, Webb, Angus, Scott,
Risdon, Hurst, Wrightson, Barnes.
Att: 5,000
2nd Replay
Apr 26 v Brighton & Hove Albion (a) 4-3
Poulter 2, Hurst, Wrightson
Chesters; Gray, Miller, Clarke, Webb, Angus, Scott,
Risdon, Poulter, Wrightson, Hurst.
Att: 7,000
Final
May 2 v Torquay United (n*) 1-0
Hurst
Chesters; Gray, Miller, Clarke, Webb, Angus, Scott,
Poulter, Hurst, Wrightson, Barnes.
Att: 6,000
*Played at Home Park, Plymouth.

1934-35
Round 2
Oct 24 v Aldershot (h) 4-0
T.Scott 2, Dryden 2
Chesters; Angus, Smith, McClure, Webb, Lewis,
J.Scott, T.Scott, Poulter, Dudley, Dryden.
Att: 1,500
Round 3
Feb 20 v Millwall (h) 5-0
Poulter 4, Wrightson
Chesters; Gray, Miller, Risdon, E.Keefe, Angus,
J.Scott, Wrightson, Poulter, Tierney, McArthur.
Att: 2,000
Semi-final
Mar 27 v Bristol Rovers (a) 1-2
Poulter
Chesters; Gray, Miller, Risdon, Webb, Angus, J.Scott,
Wrightson, Poulter, Hurst, Dryden.
Att: 2,000

1935-36
Round 1
Oct 2 v Gillingham (a) 0-0
Chesters; Angus, Miller, Risdon, H.Bamsey, Fantham,
J.Scott, T.Scott, McCambridge, McArthur, McArdle.
Att: 2,000
Replay
Oct 16 v Gillingham (h) 4-2
T.Scott 3, McCambridge
Kirk; Gray, Miller, Clarke, Robinson, Angus, Hurst,
T.Scott, McCambridge, McLean, V.Hoyle.
Att: 2,500
Round 2
Oct 28 v Crystal Palace (a) 2-4
McCambridge, T.Scott
Chesters; Gray, Miller, Clarke, Robinson, Risdon,
Hurst, T.Scott, McCambridge, McLean, V.Hoyle.
Att: 3,500

1936-37
Round 2
Oct 28 v Cardiff City (h) 1-0
Johnson
Tierney; Brown, Boyle, Clarke, Angus, Shadwell,
Keane, Johnson, Williams, McGill, Urmson.
Att: 1,500
Round 3
Nov 11 v Torquay United (a) 1-2
Williams
Tierney; Brown, Boyle, Shadwell, Hobbs, Pollard,
Keane, Johnson, Williams, Young, Urmson.
Att: 1,000

1937-38
Round 1
Sep 22 v Southend United (a) 2-1
Bowl 2
Tierney; Brown, B.Clarke, Kavanagh, Davies, Angus,
Miles, Bussey, Bowl, Ebdon, Liddle.
Att: 3,810
Round 2
Nov 17 v Swindon Town (a) 0-2
Church; Brown, B.Clarke, Shadwell, Bamsey, Farrell,
Coulston, Ebdon, Bowl, Pope, W.Clarke.
Att: 5,000

1938-39
Round 1
Oct 19 v Swindon Town (a) 3-2
Rich 2, Walker
Church; Brown, Little, Shadwell, Fellowes, Walker,
Rich, Ebdon, Clarke, Bowl, Liddle.
Att: 1,000
Round 2
Feb 1 v Bournemouth & Boscombe Athletic (h) 1-2
Riley
Church; Brown, Little, Bussey, Angus, Fellowes,
Turnbull, Riley, Bowl, Ebdon, Liddle.
Att: 1,000

Leyland Daf Cup

(formerly the Football League Trophy, Associate Members' Cup, Freight/Rover Trophy and Sherpa Van Trophy)

1982-3 (Football League Trophy)
Group Match
Aug 14 v Bristol City (h) 2-1
Kellow, Pratt
Bond; Kirkup, Viney, McEwan(Howarth), Roberts,
M.Rogers, Harle, P.Rogers, Kellow, Delve, Pratt.
Att: 1,040.
Group Match
Aug 18 v Newport County (a) 1-5
Howarth
Shepherd(Bond); Howarth, Viney, McEwan, Roberts,
M.Rogers, Pullar, Longden, Pratt, Delve,
Gibson(Walter).
Att: 1,084.
Group Match
Aug 21 v Torquay United (a) 2-3
Pullar, Pratt
Bond; Kirkup, Viney, McEwan, Howarth, M.Rogers,
Harle, P.Rogers, Kellow, Delve, Pullar(Pratt).
Att: 2,384
Exeter City did not qualify for the quarter-final.

1983-4 (Associate Members' Cup)
Southern Section
Round 1
Feb 22 v Bristol City (h) 3-1
Pratt 2, Neville
Bond; Viney, Marker, Webster, Atkinson, O'Connor,
Ling, Pratt, Neville, P.Rogers, McDonough.
Att: 1,754
Round 2
March 14 v Wrexham (a) 0-2
Bond; Harrower(Kirkup), Viney, O'Connor, Webster,
Atkinson, Neville, P.Rogers, Pratt, Francis,
Sims(McDonough).
Att: 834
Exeter City did not qualify for the quarter-final.

1984-5 (Freight/Rover Trophy)
Southern Section
Round 1 (1st leg)
Jan 22 v Newport County (a) 0-3
Wood; Kirkup, Viney, O'Shea, Marker, Coleman,
King, Burgher, Morgan, Pratt, Harrower.
Att: 1,017
Round 1 (2nd leg)
Feb 6 v Newport County (h) 1-1
Marker
Wood; Howarth, Viney, O'Shea, Marker, McNichol,
Ling(Kirkup), Smith(King), Morgan, Burgher,
Harrower.
Att: 1,272
Newport County won 4-1 on aggregate.

1985-6 (Freight/Rover Trophy)
Southern Section
Group Match
Jan 14 v Wolverhampton Wanderers (h) 1-1
McNichol
Shaw; Harrower, Viney, McNichol, McCaffery,
Marker, Ling, Jackson, Gale, Keough, Kellow(Impey).
Att: 1,278
Group Match
Jan 29 v Torquay United (a) 0-1
Shaw; Harrower, Viney, McNichol, Impey, McCaffery,
Ling, Kellow(Pratt), Gale, Keough, Marker.
Att: 1,046
Exeter City did not qualify for the quarter-final.

1986-7 (Freight/Rover Trophy)
Southern Section
Group Match
Nov 26 v Bristol City (h) 1-1
Marker
Shaw; Batty, Viney, Marker, Priddle, Watson,
Harrower, O'Connell, Roberts(Kellow), Keough,
Biggins.
Att: 1,338

Group Match
Jan 7 v Bristol Rovers (a) 1-1
Marker
Shaw; Harrower, Viney, Marker, McCaffery, Taylor, Batty(Massey), Robson, Kellow, Keough, O'Connell.
Att: 1,608
Group Match
Jan 20 v Port Vale (h) 0-1
Shaw; Harrower, Viney, Marker, McCaffery, Taylor, Batty(Kellow), O'Connell, Biggins, Keough, Robson.
Att: 1,635
Exeter City did not qualify for the quarter-final.

1987-8 (Sherpa Van Trophy)
Southern Section
Group Match
Oct 26 v Port Vale (a) 0-2
Shaw; Cooper, Viney, Massey, Taylor, Carter, Batty, Edwards(Williams), Kellow, Delve, Harrower.
Att: 2,176
Group Match
Nov 24 v Newport County (h) 0-1
Shaw; Cooper, Viney, Carter, Massey, Collins, Batty, Edwards(Watson), O'Connell(Hiley), Milton, Harrower.
Att: 1,006
Exeter City did not qualify for the next round.

1988-9 (Sherpa Van Trophy)
Southern Area
Preliminary Round
Dec 6 v Bristol City (a) 0-2
Gwinnett; Banks, Hawkins, Rogers, Taylor, Cooper, Rowbotham, Hiley(Harris), Vinnicombe, Neville, Harrower.
Att: 3,642
Preliminary Round
Dec 14 v Bristol Rovers (h) 1-1
Rowbotham
Walter; Banks, Jones, Rogers, Taylor, Cooper, Rowbotham, Hiley, Vinnicombe, Neville, Harrower(Langley).
Att: 1,609
Exeter City did not qualify for the first round.

1989-90 (Leyland Daf Cup)
Preliminary Round
Jan 15 v Torquay United (h) 2-0
Benjamin, Neville
Miller; Hiley, Benjamin, Rogers, Taylor, Whitehead, Rowbotham, Bailey, McDermott, Neville, Goddard.
Att: 4,737.
Preliminary Round
Jan 17 v Bristol Rovers (a) 0-3
Walter; Hiley, Benjamin, McNichol, Heath, Cooper, Eshelby, Batty, Lock(Bailey), McDermott, Frankland.
Att: 3,136.
Round 1
Jan 23 v Shrewsbury Town (a) 1-0
McDermott
Miller; Hiley, Benjamin, McNichol, Taylor, Whitehead, Rowbotham, Bailey, McDermott, Neville, Goddard.
Att: 1,462.

Round 2
Feb 21 v Maidstone United (a) 0-2
Miller; Batty, Benjamin, McNichol, Taylor, Whitehead, Rowbotham(Rogers), Bailey, McDermott, Neville, Frankland.
Att: 1,685.

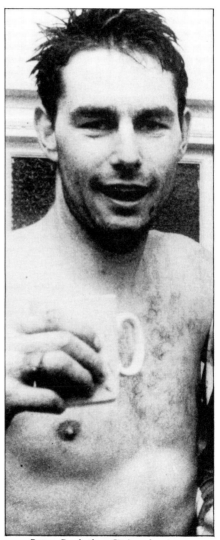

Darren Rowbotham City's goalscoring star.

317

Southern Charity Cup

A competition for professional clubs in the South of England

1909-10
Round 1
Sep 29 v Plymouth Argyle (a) 1-0
Hartley
Crossthwaite; Jones, Crelley, Atkinson, Tierney, Hartley, Copestake, Watson, McGuigan, Bell, Garside.
Att: 3,000
Round 2
Oct 27 v Swindon Town (a) 0-4
Crossthwaite; Craig, Jones, Atkinson, Tierney, Hartley, Copestake, Watson, Harrison, Bell, Garside.
Att: 900

1910-11
Round 1
Sep 7 v Bristol Rovers (a) 0-1
W.Whittaker; Evans, Jones, Bassett, Pratt, Prideaux, Parnell, Watson, James, Bell, Garside.
Att: 1,600

1911-12
Round 1
Sep 20 v Swindon Town (h) 2-0
Watson 2
W.Whittaker; Evans, Coates, Bassett, Pratt, Prideaux, E.Whittaker, Watson, Rutter, Lockett, Garside.
Att: 1,700
Round 2
Oct 18 v Plymouth Argyle (h) 0-0
Chapman; Evans, Coates, Bassett, Prideaux, Griffiths, Parnell, Lockett, Rutter, Cornan, Garside.
4,000
Replay
Dec 13 v Plymouth Argyle (a) 1-2
Watson
Chapman; Evans, Coates, Rigby, Bassett, Prideaux, E.Whittaker, Watson, Griffiths, Bailey, Lockett.

1912-13
Round 1
Nov 13 v Plymouth Argyle (h) 2-0
Cooper 2
Pym; Nevin, Hurst, Rigby, Lagan, Bassett, Whittaker, Cooper, Rutter, Lockett, Ives.
Att: 2,000
Round 2
Feb 12 v Swindon Town (h) 2-0
Crompton, Rutter
Pym; Fort, Hurst, Rigby, Lagan, Lockett, Whittaker, Cooper, Rutter, Crompton, Ives.
Att: 2,500
Semi-final
Apr 3 v Queen's Park Rangers (a) 0-2
Pym; Fort, Hurst, Rigby, Bassett, Lockett, Whittaker, Cooper, Rutter, Crompton, Garside.
Att: 2,500

1913-14
Round 1
Sep 15 v Merthyr Town (a) 1-2
Lovett
Pym; Fort, Strettle, Smith, Lagan, Marshall, Whittaker, Lovett, Brooksbank, Kirby, Orr.
Att: 6,000

1914-15
Round 1
Oct 14 v Merthyr Town (h) 2-1
Green, Lovett
Pym; Marshall, Strettle, Rigby, Smith, Evans, Holt, Green, W.Goodwin, Lovett, F.Goodwin.
Att: 1,000
Round 2
Feb 10 v Plymouth Argyle (a) 0-1
Pym; Marshall, Strettle, Rigby, Lagan, Smith, Holt, Evans, W.Goodwin, Lovett, Dockray.
Att: 1,000

Plymouth Argyle reached the final, as did Luton Town, and the match resulted in a 0-0 draw. As far as is known, there was no replay and no further matches were played after World War One.

List of winners:-
1902 Tottenham Hotspur
1903 Portsmouth
1904 Millwall
1905 Reading and Tottenham Hotspur joint holders
1906 Woolwich Arsenal
1907 Tottenham Hotspur
1908 Southampton
1909 Brentford
1910 Brighton & Hove Albion
1911 Swindon Town
1912 Southend United
1913 Queen's Park Rangers
1914 Coventry City
1915 see above.

City Internationals

ALTHOUGH the selectors do not come to places like Exeter when looking for prospective international stars, 46 players and managers of the City club have, at different times in their careers, been chosen to take part in international and other representative matches.

Apart from these men, mention should also be made of Evelyn Henry Lintott, of Godalming, who played a couple of matches for Exeter City Reserves whilst a student at St Luke's Training College, Exeter, in 1905. He afterwards played for Woking, Plymouth Argyle, Queen's Park Rangers and, turning professional in May 1908, Bradford City and Leeds City. He made seven appearances for England in full internationals, besides winning several Amateur caps, and also played for Surrey County. He became a schoolmaster and was also secretary of the Players' Union (now the Professional Footballers' Association). Lintott was killed in action on the Somme on 1 July 1916, whilst serving as an officer with the 1st Yorkshire Regiment. Another even more famous footballing personality who had connections with Exeter City was Stanley Rous, later Sir Stanley, secretary of the FA and president of FIFA, who turned out as goalkeeper several times for Exeter City Reserves whilst at St Luke's in 1919. Here is the full list.

JOHN ALDERSON Goalkeeper. With Crystal Palace, England v France 1923, Southern League v Brentford (League Champions) 1919, v Corinthians 1919; with Pontypridd, Welsh League v League of Ireland 1925.

COLIN APPLETON Left-half. With Leicester City, Football League v Irish League 1962.

CLIFF BASTIN Inside-left and outside-left. With Arsenal, 21 English international caps 1932 to 1938, Football League v Scottish League 1931, 1934, 1936, v Irish League 1933, also English international trial matches.

FRANK BROOME Inside or wing-forward. With Aston Villa, 7 English international caps 1938 and 1939, England v Scotland 1940; with Notts County, England v Australia (2 matches) 1951.

JACK BULCOCK Full-back. With Crystal Palace, England v South Africa 1910, Southern League v Football League 1910.

ARTHUR CHADWICK Centre-half. With Southampton, England v Scotland and Wales 1900.

STAN CHARLTON Left-back. With Exeter City, English FA XI v Australia (5 matches) 1925, Professionals v Amateurs for the FA Charity Shield, the match also serving as an English international trial 1926.

TERRY COOPER Left-back. With Leeds United, 17 English international caps 1969 to 1972.

WYNNE CROMPTON Left-back. With Wrexham, Wales v England, Scotland and Northern Ireland 1931.

DERMOT CURTIS Centre-forward. With Shelbourne, Republic of Ireland v Denmark and Germany 1957, League of Ireland v Football League 1956; with Bristol City, Republic of Ireland v England (2 matches), Poland, Denmark and Austria 1958; with Ipswich Town, 9 caps for Republic of Ireland; with Exeter City, Republic of Ireland v Austria 1964.

ARTHUR DAVIES Goalkeeper. With Everton, Football League v Irish League 1929.

FRED DENT Centre-forward. With Mid-Rhondda, Welsh League v League of Ireland 1925.

JOHN DOCKRAY Outside-left. With Exeter City, Southern League v Welsh League 1921, 1922.

JIMMY DUNN Inside-right. With Hibernian, Scotland v Wales and Northern Ireland 1925, v Northern Ireland 1927, v England and Northern Ireland 1928; with Everton, v Wales 1929.

TOMMY DUNNE Right-half. With St Patrick's Athletic, League of Ireland v Football League 1956, 1957, 1959, v Irish League (2 matches) 1957 and (2 matches) 1958, v Scottish League 1957.

TOM EDGE Outside-right. With Exeter City, Southern League v Central League 1922.

JAMES EDMONDSON Centre-forward. With Swansea Town, Welsh League v Irish League 1923.

P.CHAD EVANS Inside-forward. With Exeter City, Wales v England (amateur) 1910.

WILLIE FALLON Outside-left. With Shelbourne, League of Ireland v Irish League 1941, 1944; With Dundalk, v Irish League 1945 (2 matches).

THEO FOLEY Right-back. With Northampton Town, 9 international caps for the Republic of Ireland 1964 to 1967.

JACK FORT Right-back. With Exeter City, Southern League v Football League 1914; with Millwall, England v Belgium 1921, English international trial 1921, Football League v the Army 1921.

GERRY FRANCIS Inside-forward or midfield. With Queen's Park Rangers, 12 English international caps 1975 and 1976, sometimes as captain.

JIM GARSIDE Outside-left. With Exeter City, Southern League v Irish League 1911.

DAVID GIBSON Inside-left. With Leicester City, 7 Scottish international caps 1963 to 1965.

BRIAN GODFREY Inside-right. With Preston North End, Wales v Northern Ireland 1964, v Denmark and Italy 1965.

HARRY HADDOCK Left-back. With Clyde, 6 Scottish international caps 1955 to 1958.

HARRY HANFORD Centre-half. With Swansea Town, Wales v Northern Ireland 1934, v Scotland 1935, v England 1936; with Sheffield Wednesday, v Northern Ireland 1936, v England and Scotland 1938, v France 1939.

CARL HARRIS Outside-left. With Leeds United, 24 Welsh international caps 1976 to 1982.

HAROLD HOUGHTON Inside-left. With Exeter City, FA XI v Canada 1931.

JIM ILEY Left-half. With Sheffield United, Football League v League of Ireland 1956; with Tottenham Hotspur, v Scottish League 1958.

HUGH KELLY Goalkeeper. With Belfast Celtic, Irish League v League of Ireland 1944, 1945, 1947, 1948, Irish League v Football League 1947; with Fulham, Northern Ireland v England and Wales 1950; with Southampton, Northern Ireland v England and Scotland 1951.

JIM McCAMBRIDGE Centre-forward. With Ballymena, Northern Ireland v Scotland and Wales 1930; with Cardiff City, Northern Ireland v Wales 1931, v England 1932.

JOE McCLURE Right-half. With Everton, FA XI v Canada 1931.

DAVID McMULLAN Outside-left and left-half. With Belfast Distillery, Irish League v Scottish League 1919, 1924, v Football League 1924, 1925; with Liverpool, Northern Ireland v England and Wales 1926, v Scotland 1927.

ALAN MATHIESON Inside-left. With Luton Town, Ireland v Wales 1921, v England 1922.

JIMMY NICHOLLS Inside-left. With West Bromwich Albion, England v Scotland and Yugoslavia 1954.

LEIGHTON PHILLIPS Forward. With Cardiff City, Aston Villa, Swansea City, Charlton Athletic, 58 Welsh international caps 1971 to 1982.

DICK PYM Goalkeeper. With Exeter City, English Clubs v Welsh Clubs 1920; with Bolton Wanderers, Football League v Irish League 1923, v Scottish League 1925, England v Wales and Scotland 1925, v Scotland 1926, also 3 appearances in English international trial matches 1925 and 1926.

PHIL ROBERTS Defender. With Portsmouth, Wales v England 1974, v Austria, Hungary and Luxembourg 1975.

JACK ROBINSON Goalkeeper. With Derby County, England v Scotland and Ireland 1897; with New Brighton Tower, v Scotland, Wales and Ireland 1898; with Southampton, v Wales and Scotland 1899, v Scotland, Wales and Ireland 1900, v Ireland 1901, also English international trial matches.

GEORGE ROUGHTON Left-back. With Huddersfield Town, FA XI v Canada 1931.

PETER TAYLOR Outside-left. With Crystal Palace, England v Wales, Northern Ireland and Scotland 1976.

GEORGE THOMPSON Right-back. With Sligo Rovers, League of Ireland v Irish League 1940; with St James' Gate, v Irish League 1942.

LANCE TIERNEY Goalkeeper. With Belfast Distillery, Northern Ireland v League of Ireland 1941.

BILL WAKE Left-half. With Queen's Park Rangers, Southern League v Scottish League 1912.

TIM WARD Right-half. With Derby County, England v Belgium 1948, v Wales 1949.

DAVID WILSON Left-half. With Oldham Athletic, Scotland v England 1913.

ERIC WELSH Outside-right. With Carlisle United, Northern Ireland v Wales, West Germany, Mexico 1966, v Wales 1967.

Dermot Curtis playing for the Republic of Ireland against England in 1958. The England player is skipper Billy Wright.

Exeter City Abroad

IN the summer of 1914, Exeter City became the first English football club to undertake a tour of South America. The Exeter party consisted of directors McGahey, Parkhouse and Middleweek, and players J.Fort, F.Goodwin, A.Harding, H.Holt, W.Hunter, J.Lagan, R.Loram, W.Lovett, F.Marshall, C.Pratt, R.Pym, J.Rigby, W.Smith, S.Strettle and F.Whittaker.

City embarked from Southampton on 22 May and played five matches in the Argentine and three in Brazil. Their only defeat came 12 hours after disembarking from a three-week sea voyage and the only other team to avoid defeat by Exeter was the full Brazilian national side.

The trip was certainly full of incident. When City scored against Racing Club, the Argentinian League champions, the Racing secretary drew a revolver and threatened to shoot the referee. The official quickly stopped the game and brought the players off the field, allowing the match to continue only after a great deal of persuasion.

Against the Rosarian League, City were leading 3-0 with about ten minutes remaining. At that point the Argentinians were awarded a penalty, from which they scored. The crowd went absolutely wild, letting off fireworks, screaming and shouting, and the band marched on to the pitch to play the Argentine national anthem half a dozen times.

The Exeter party were given many gifts whilst they were on tour. One of these was a beautiful parrot of bright and colourful hue. Unfortunately, the poor bird, unable to withstand the rigours of the English climate, died shortly after the start of the new football season and was buried by the players, with suitable ceremony, behind the goal at the St James' Road end of the ground.

Weeks later, legend has it, the players realized that no goals were being scored by them at that end of St James' Park and the dead parrot was blamed. Consequently, the body of the innocent bird was dug up again and reburied, this time underneath the centre spot, this being considered less likely to have any effect on the goalscoring. This may be a tall story, but it is true to say that, from then onwards, the goal at the St James' Road end became equally productive for Exeter.

The sick parrot notwithstanding, City considered the tour most beneficial. It not only enabled the directors to retain the services of nearly the whole of the 1913-14 side, but also served to blood Clapton Orient's Hunter, the best of the new players engaged for 1914-15.

Results

v Argentine North	L 0-1
v Argentine South	W 3-0
v Racing Club of Buenos Aires	W 2-0
v Rosarian League XI	W 3-1
v Combinadoes	W 5-0
v Rio de Janeiro	W 3-0
v Fluminense	W 5-3
v Brazil	D 3-3

The City party returned home on Sunday, 9 August, docking at Liverpool and having survived three separate incidents when shots were put across the bows of their ship, for whilst they had been away, war had been declared between Britain and Germany.

Exeter City's next experience of foreign football materialized about ten years later. On 14 March 1925, they travelled to Norwich for a Third Division South game. On the following day, the team made the short journey to the docks at Harwich, from where they were ferried across the North Sea by steamer to the Hook of Holland. In the afternoon they made the next step of their journey, this time to Amsterdam, where they opposed Ajax, in a friendly match.

Ajax were not quite at full strength, owing to some members of the team being engaged in an international against Belgium. City, who substituted Blackmore for Davis at centre-forward, won 5-1 before a crowd of 15,000. Exeter's scorers were Kirk (3), Charlton (penalty) and Lievesley. The team was: Bailey; Pollard, Charlton, Pullan, Potter, Shelton, Matthews, Kirk, Blackmore, Lievesley and Compton.

City's next trip to the Netherlands was not until 1951 when they won their opening match, 3-0 against DOS at Utrecht on 20 May. Mackay scored twice and McClelland once, all the goals coming in the second half. The game, played in heatwave conditions, was thoroughly enjoyed by a large crowd.

The second match, 23 May, was against Haarlem Eftal. In beating them 5-3, Exeter overcame a strong team which included no fewer than seven full internationals and a Youth international outside-right. The match was watched by 15,500 people and fast, open football was the rule on both sides.

In a sensational start, a long ball was sent down the middle, McClelland chased it, outpaced the Dutch centre-half, drew the goalkeeper and shot low into an empty net.

Showing more determination than their hosts, Exeter continued to prove dangerous, but Haarlem played the cleverer football and on one occasion their centre-forward shot wide of an open goal. Against this, however, must be balanced two escapes which Haarlem enjoyed when they kicked the ball off their line with the goalkeeper beaten.

City's crisp first-time methods brought another goal in the 35th minute, from McClelland, and straight from the kick-off Smart made it 3-0. Haarlem reduced the margin just before half-time and this inspired the Dutch to greater efforts.

Against a reshuffled team, from which Fred Davey, suffering from a wrenched ankle, was missing in the second half, Haarlem piled on the pressure. Harrower dropped back from outside-right to occupy Davey's place and Digby came in on the right wing.

Haarlem scored their second goal within two minutes of the restart and it now looked anybody's game until Digby gave Smart a through pass from which the City inside-right increased his side's lead.

McClelland, who had a useful match at centre-forward, scored Exeter's fifth, following a scramble in the goalmouth, and the Dutch netted for their third goal five minutes from the end. Goddard was outstanding in Exeter's defence, whilst McClelland and Digby took the honours in the forward line.

After dominating the play before the interval and establishing a two-goal lead in the first 30 minutes, Exeter lost the third match of the tour, 4-2 against Hertogenbosch in front of a 12,000 crowd.

Disappointed, the City players went into serious training for the last match of their tour, against the Combined Hague XI on Wednesday, 30 May.

Facing the strong sun in the first half, City used the long ball, and it was during one of several fast, open movements that McClelland was fouled just outside the penalty area in the 15th minute.

Taking the free-kick himself, he scored with a rocket-like shot which zoomed into the net via the underside of the crossbar. End-to-end exchanges were now the order and neither side gave an inch.

After the interval, however, it became obvious that the City's greater stamina would tell. The standard of refereeing was not as good as in the earlier games, and the official was guilty of several very strange decisions, notably 15 minutes from the end when Smart, taking over a pass from Fallon, went through on his own and netted.

To everyone's amazement the 'goal' was disallowed for offside, but City did not lose heart and Regan scored for them with three minutes left.

Exeter City chairman Ivor Doble with newly-appointed manager Terry Cooper in May 1988.

No Mean Rivals, City v Argyle

Devonshire's first professional football club was Plymouth Argyle in 1903. Exeter City followed five years later. From then onwards, the keenest of rivalry has existed between the two clubs, and here is a list which shows the outcome of these 'Devon Derbies'.

1908

Nov 11	City 2	Argyle 1	(h)	Southern League
Dec 26	City 1	Argyle 0	(a)	Friendly

1909

Feb 6	Argyle 2	City 0	(a)	FA Cup 2nd round
Mar 10	Argyle 4	City 0	(a)	Southern League
Apr 12	Argyle 1	City 0	(h)	Friendly
Sep 29	City 1	Argyle 0	(a)	Southern Charity Cup 1st round
Nov 24	City 2	Argyle 1	(h)	Friendly
Dec 25	Argyle 1	City 0	(a)	Southern League
Dec 26	Argyle 4	City 2	(h)	Southern League

1910

Mar 9	Argyle 3	City 1	(a)	Benefit match for J.Sutcliffe
Apr 13	Argyle 4	City 0	(a)	Friendly
Sep 24	Argyle 0	City 0	(a)	Southern League
Oct 26	City 3	Argyle 1	(h)	Benefit match, Exeter shopping week

1911

Jan 28	Argyle 3	City 1	(h)	Southern League
Mar 15	Argyle 8	City 3	(a)	Friendly
Sep 27	Argyle 1	City 1	(a)	Friendly
Oct 18	City 0	Argyle 0	(h)	Southern Charity Cup 2nd round
Dec 13	Argyle 2	City 1	(a)	Southern Charity Cup replay
Dec 25	Argyle 3	City 1	(a)	Southern League
Dec 26	Argyle 1	City 0	(h)	Southern League

1912

Mar 20	City 1	Argyle 0	(h)	Friendly
Sep 28	Argyle 3	City 0	(a)	Southern League
Nov 12	City 2	Argyle 0	(h)	Southern Charity Cup 1st round

1913

Jan 25	City 1	Argyle 0	(h)	Southern League

1914

Apr 10	Argyle 0	City 0	(a)	Southern League
Apr 13	City 0	Argyle 0	(h)	Southern League
Apr 29	City 1	Argyle 0	(a)	Spooner Cup Final

1915

Feb 10	Argyle 1	City 0	(a)	Southern Charity Cup 2nd round
Apr 2	City 3	Argyle 1	(a)	Southern League
Apr 5	City 1	Argyle 1	(h)	Southern League

1919

Apr 18	City 2	Argyle 1	(a)	Friendly
Apr 21	City 2	Argyle 1	(h)	Friendly
Jul 26	Argyle 1	City 1	(a)	Peace match
Dec 25	Argyle 3	City 1	(a)	Southern League
Dec 26	Argyle 1	City 0	(h)	Southern League

1920

Dec 25	Argyle 0	City 0	(a)	League Division Three
Dec 27	City 1	Argyle 1	(h)	League Division Three

1921

Dec 26	Argyle 2	City 0	(h)	League Division Three South
Dec 27	Argyle 0	City 0	(a)	League Division Three South

1922

Mar 15	Argyle 2	City 0	(h)	Spooner Cup Final

1923

Mar 30	Argyle 5	City 1	(a)	League Division Three South
Apr 2	City 0	Argyle 0	(h)	League Division Three South
Apr 25	Argyle 3	City 0	(a)	Spooner Cup Final
Oct 10	Argyle 2	City 0	(a)	Devon Professional Champ'ship
Dec 25	Argyle 4	City 0	(a)	League Division Three South
Dec 26	Argyle 4	City 0	(h)	League Division Three South

1924

Dec 25	Argyle 1	City 1	(a)	League Division Three South
Dec 26	City 3	Argyle 0	(h)	League Division Three South

1925

Apr 1	Argyle 3	City 2	(h)	Devon Professional Champ'ship
Dec 25	City 4	Argyle 0	(h)	League Division Three South
Dec 26	Argyle 2	City 1	(a)	League Division Three South

1926

Mar 10	City 2	Argyle 1	(a)	Devon Professional Champ'ship
Dec 25	Argyle 2	City 0	(a)	League Division Three South
Dec 27	Argyle 2	City 0	(h)	League Division Three South

1927

Mar 9	City 3	Argyle 1	(h)	Devon Professional Champ'ship
Dec 26	City 2	Argyle 0	(h)	League Division Three South
Dec 27	City 2	Argyle 1	(a)	League Division Three South

1928

Apr 30	City 4	Argyle 2	(h)	Devon Professional Champ'ship
Oct 27	Argyle 2	City 1	(h)	League Division Three South

1929
Mar 9	Argyle 0	City 0	(a)	League Division Three South
Apr 24	Argyle 3	City 2	(h)	Devon Professional Champ'ship
Oct 26	Argyle 4	City 1	(a)	League Division Three South

1930
Mar 1	City 1	Argyle 1	(h)	League Division Three South
Apr 30	Argyle 2	City 1	(a)	Devon Professional Champ'ship
May 2	Argyle 4	City 2	(h)	Benefit match for George Purcell

1932
Apr 20	Argyle 2	City 0	(a)	Devon Professional Champ'ship

1933
May 1	City 3	Argyle 2	(h)	Benefit match for Charlie Miller
May 3	Argyle 5	City 0	(a)	Benefit match for Alf Matthews
Sep 27	Argyle 3	City 2	(h)	Devon Professional Champ'ship

1935
Apr 29	Argyle 1	City 0	(a)	Benefit match for Plymouth Albion RFC
Oct 9	Argyle 5	City 0	(a)	Devon Professional Champ'ship

1936
Apr 29	Argyle 4	City 2	(n)	Exhibition match

(Played at Barnstaple)

1937
Apr 21	City 2	Argyle 1	(a)	Devon Professional Champ'ship
Dec 1	Argyle 5	City 2	(a)	Devon Professional Champ'ship

1938
Aug 20	Argyle 5	City 3	(a)	Football League Jubilee Fund
Sep 28	Argyle 6	City 4	(a)	Devon Professional Champ'ship

1939
Aug 19	Argyle 2	City 1	(h)	Football League Jubilee Fund
Aug 30	City Past 7	Argyle Past 1	(h)	Friendly

1945
Jan 20	City 2	Argyle 2	(h)	Friendly
Mar 10	Argyle 5	City 1	(a)	Friendly
Apr 1	City 5	Argyle 1	(h)	Friendly

1946
Apr 10	City 2	Argyle 1	(h)	Devon Professional Champ'ship

1948
Mar 15	City 1	Argyle 1	(h)	Benefit for Jack Angus and Dick Ebdon
Apr 5	Argyle 2	City 1	(a)	Devon Professional Champ'ship

1950
May 3	Argyle 2	City 1	(h)	Devon Professional Champ'ship
Sep 23	City 1	Argyle 0	(a)	League Division Three South

1951

Feb 3	City 3	Argyle 2	(h)	League Division Three South
Apr 11	Argyle 2	City 0	(h)	Devon Professional Champ'ship

1952

Jan 12	City 1	Argyle 0	(h)	League Division Three South
Apr 14	City 1	Argyle 0	(h)	League Division Three South
May 2	Argyle 1	City 0	(a)	Devon Professional Champ'ship

1953

Mar 9	Argyle 3	City 0	(h)	Inauguration of St James' Park floodlights
Apr 29	Argyle 4	City 1	(a)	Devon Professional Champ'ship
Oct 26	Argyle 3	City 1	(a)	Friendly (floodlit)

1956

Apr 18	Argyle 3	City 0	(a)	Devon Professional Champ'ship
May 1	City 2	Argyle 2	(h)	Friendly
Nov 17	Argyle 2	City 0	(h)	FA Cup 1st round
Dec 26	City 2	Argyle 1	(h)	League Division Three South

1957

Jan 5	Argyle 5	City 0	(a)	League Division Three South
May 2	Argyle 4	City 2	(a)	Devon Championship Bowl
Sep 28	Argyle 1	City 0	(a)	League Division Three South

1958

Feb 8	City 4	Argyle 2	(h)	League Division Three South

1959

Apr 4	City 6	Argyle 0	(h)	Devon Professional Champ'ship (Reserves)
May 6	City 6	Argyle 3	(n)	Benefit match for Rotary Club funds

(Played at Falmouth)

1961

Apr 19	Combined City & Torquay U 2 Argyle 1	(n)	Devon Professional Bowl

(Played at Torquay)

1962

Mar 20	City 3	Argyle 1	(h)	Devon Championship Bowl

1963

May 6	City 1	Argyle 0	(h)	Devon Championship Bowl

1964

Apr 28	City 4	Argyle 0	(h)	Devon Championship Bowl

1965

Apr 29	City 1	Argyle 0	(a)	Devon Championship Bowl

1966

May 4	Argyle 3	City 2	(a)	Devon Championship Bowl

1967

Mar 15	Argyle 1	City 0	(h)	Devon Championship Bowl

1968

May 13	City 2	Argyle 0	(h)	Devon Championship Bowl
Aug 14	Argyle 0	City 0	(a)	Football League Cup 1st round
Aug 21	City 0	Argyle 0	(h)	Football League Cup replay
Aug 26	City 1	Argyle 0	(n)	Football League Cup replay

(Played at Torquay)

1969

Feb 17	Argyle 1	City 0	(a)	Devon Championship Bowl

1971

Mar 9	Argyle 2	City 1	(a)	Devon Championship Bowl
Jul 31	Argyle 2	City 1	(h)	Friendly

1972

May 4	City 2	Argyle 1	(h)	Devon Championship Bowl

1973

May 4	Argyle 2	City 1	(a)	Devon Championship Bowl

1976

Aug 14	City 1	Argyle 0	(a)	League Cup 1st round 1st leg
Aug 18	City 1	Argyle 0	(h)	League Cup 1st round 2nd leg

1977

Aug 13	City 2	Argyle 2	(h)	League Cup 1st round 1st leg
Aug 16	Argyle 0	City 0	(a)	League Cup 1st round 2nd leg
Aug 20	City 1	Argyle 0	(a)	League Cup 1st round replay
Dec 26	Argyle 2	City 2	(a)	League Division Three

1978

Mar 28	City 0	Argyle 0	(h)	League Division Three

1979

Feb 27	Argyle 4	City 2	(a)	League Division Three
Apr 17	City 1	Argyle 0	(h)	League Division Three

1980

Jan 1	City 2	Argyle 2	(h)	League Division Three
Apr 7	Argyle 2	City 0	(a)	League Division Three
Dec 26	City 2	Argyle 0	(a)	League Division Three

1981

Apr 21	City 1	Argyle 1	(h)	League Division Three
Dec 28	City 1	Argyle 1	(h)	League Division Three

1982

Apr 9	Argyle 2	City 1	(a)	League Division Three
Nov 20	Argyle 2	City 0	(a)	FA Cup 1st round
Dec 27	City 1	Argyle 0	(h)	League Division Three

1983
| Apr 1 | Argyle 1 | City 0 | (a) League Division Three |
| Dec 26 | Argyle 2 | City 2 | (a) League Division Three |

1984
| Apr 21 | City 1 | Argyle 1 | (h) League Division Three |
| Apr 24 | Argyle 2 | City 1 | (a) Associate Members' Cup |

1985
May 13	City 1	Argyle 1	(h) Devon Professional Bowl*
Aug 20	Argyle 2	City 1	(a) League Cup 1st round 1st leg
Sep 4	City 2	Argyle 0	(h) League Cup 1st round 2nd leg

City won 6-5 on penalties

1986
| May 7 | Argyle 2 | City 4 | (a) Devon Professional Bowl |

1987
| Aug 3 | City 1 | Argyle 0 | (h) Devon Professional Bowl |

Cliff Bastin (right) shows some of his collection of football medals to Maurice Golesworthy over the bar of Bastin's public house in Exeter. The picture was taken about 1956.

This photograph appeared in a local newspaper in the early 1930s and was described as 'the first Exeter City team of 1893-4'. In fact it is Exeter United. The personnel are: Back row (left to right): A.E.Denning (honorary secretary), Littlehales, Bayles, Carey. Middle row: Garland, Byrne, Addis. Front row: Davey, Nelson, McDermott, Fletcher, Smith. Outside-right R.G.Davey was still alive when the photograph was published and was the postmaster in Queen Street, Exeter.

EXETER CITY CAREER RECORDS

Southern League (1908-09 to 1919-20)

Below are the career records for all Exeter City players who played in the Southern League and FA Cup. The 'Played' section signifies the first year played to the last. Where a (P-m) appears after a club name the player became the player-manager. An asterisk (*) indicates they subsequently played for Exeter City in the Football League.

Player	Birthplace	From	To	Played	League App	League Gls	FA Cup App	FA Cup Gls
AMBLER, Albert	Manchester	Stockport C	Colne	1908-10	56	9	9	0
ATKINSON, James	Manchester	Brighton & HA	Barrow	1909-10	40	0	4	1
BANKS, John	West Bromwich	Plymouth A	Retired	1908-09	2	0	0	0
BASSETT, Spencer	Blackheath	W Arsenal	Swansea T	1910-13	81	3	6	2
BELL, James	Eston	Barrow	Portsmouth	1908-11	105	51	14	12
BROOKSBANK, Clifford	Halifax	Blackburn R	Bristol C	1912-14	35	5	0	0
BULCOCK, Joseph	Burnley	Macclesfield T	Crystal P	1908-09	23	0	9	0
CADDY, William	Plymouth	Woodland Villa	Royal Navy	1911-12	2	0	0	0
CHADWICK, Arthur	Church, Lancs	Northampton T	Manager	1908-12	41	6	14	4
CHAPMAN, John	Bolton	Bolton W	Army	1911-13	6	0	2	0
CHENNEOUR, Fred	Exeter	Local	Retired	1910-12	2	0	0	0
COATES, Arthur	Wensleydale	Heywood U	Southampton	1910-12	41	0	3	0
COLEBURNE, Joseph*	Tyldesley	Atherton	Third Division	1919-20	42	0	1	0
CONNOR, Edwin	Sheffield	Fulham	Rochdale	1919-20	14	1	0	0
COOKE, Arthur	Australia	Sheffield W	Retired	1910-11	4	0	0	0
COOPER, Thomas	Birkenhead	South Liverpool	South Liverpool	1912-13	28	9	0	0
COPESTAKE, Levi	Sheffield	Bristol C	Retired	1908-10	62	10	10	4
CORNAN, Frank	Sunderland	Nelson		1911-12	28	6	2	0
COWIE, Stanley	Accrington	Blackpool	Barry	1914-20	1	0	0	0

Player	Birthplace	From	To	Played	League App	League Gls	FA Cup App	FA Cup Gls
COX, Samuel	Plymouth	Army	Caerphilly	1914-19	2	0	0	0
CRAIG, Thomas	Manchester	Stockport C		1908-10	51	0	9	0
CRAWSHAW, William*	Darwen	Amateur	Accrington S	1919-20	15	0	0	0
CRELLEY, John	Liverpool	Everton	St Helens Rec	1908-10	48	0	4	0
CROMPTON, Ellis*	Ramsbottom	Tottenham H	Bristol R	1912-13	31	10	1	0
CROSSTHWAITE, Herbert	Preston	Fulham	Birmingham	1909-10	41	0	3	0
CRUTE, William	Paignton	Babbacombe	Retired	1911-12	3	0	0	0
DOCKRAY, John*	Carlisle	Bury	Third Division	1914-20	64	5	2	0
DRAIN, Thomas	Pollokshaw	Kilmarnock	W Arsenal	1908-09	14	1	0	0
DUFFY, John	Cleator Moor	Bradford C		1910-11	7	0	1	0
EVANS, Arthur	Bolton	Manchester C	Killed in war	1913-15	26	1	1	0
EVANS, Nolan	Wigan	St Helen's Rec	Clapton O	1910-12	63	2	7	0
EVANS, PC 'Crad'	Torquay	Plymouth A	Plymouth A	1909-10	3	2	0	0
FLETCHER, James	Bury	Carlisle U		1908-09	11	0	5	0
FORT, John	Leigh	Atherton	Millwall	1911-14	85	0	3	0
GARSIDE, James	Manchester	Accrington S		1909-13	101	20	9	2
GILL, W	Bury	Bury	Wolves	1919-20	3	0	0	0
GOLIGHTLY, Martin	Gateshead	Gateshead	Bideford (P-m)	1912-13	7	0	0	0
GOODWIN, Frederick	Macclesfield	West Ham U	Retired	1913-15	40	5	0	0
GOODWIN, William	Staveley	Blackburn R	Manchester U	1914-20	73	40	2	0
GREEN, Alfred*	Rotherham	Rotherham T	Third Division	1914-20	17	8	0	0
GREEN, Thomas	Rockferry	Stockport C		1909-10	31	8	4	0
GRIFFITHS, Thomas	Manchester	Blackburn R	Clapton O	1910-12	22	2	3	0
HARDING, Augustus	Chesham	Chelsea	Killed in war	1913-15	7	0	0	0
HARRISON, Richard	Manchester	Manchester C		1909-10	8	5	4	1
HARTLEY, Percival	Bolton	Chorley	Rochdale	1909-10	34	4	4	1
HENDERSON, James	South Shields	South Shields	Caerphilly	1919-20	6	3	0	0
HETHERINGTON, Sydney*	Monkswearmouth	Army	Third Division	1919-20	1	0	0	0

Player	Birthplace	From	To	Played	League App	League Gls	FA Cup App	FA Cup Gls
HOLT, Harold	Bolton	Bolton W	Plymouth A	1913-15	68	7	3	2
HUGHES, Archibald	Barrhead	Manchester C	Bristol R	1910-11	18	7	4	2
HUNTER, William	Sunderland	Clapton O		1914-19	5	1	0	0
HURST, George	Radcliffe, Lancs	Walkden Central	Retired	1912-13	35	0	1	0
IVES, Benjamin	Hackney	Barrow	Queen's Park R	1912-13	29	8	1	0
JAMES, Francis	Brownhills	Manchester C		1910-11	24	6	2	0
JOHNSON, Samuel	Manchester	Blackpool	Coventry C	1908-09	23	0	5	1
JONES, Edwin	Tydesley	Chorley	Bristol C	1909-11	63	2	8	1
KENT, TR	Exeter	St Luke's College	Retired	1910-12	13	2	0	0
KIRBY, William	Preston	Preston NE	Merthyr T	1913-14	5	0	0	0
LAGAN, James	Felling-on-Tyne	West Stanley	Retired	1912-15	63	0	3	0
LEE, John	Morpeth	Clapton O		1913-14	6	1	0	0
LEWIS, Ernest	Exeter	Local		1912-15	3	0	0	0
LINCOLN, Charles	Exeter	Local	Torquay T	1919-20	2	0	0	0
LOCKETT, Henry	Market Drayton	Nottingham F	Chesterfield	1911-13	70	6	4	0
LOVETT, William	Bolton	Rochdale	Blackpool	1913-20	87	15	4	0
McCANN, Henry	Scotland	Barnsley	Bristol R	1913-14	35	11	2	1
McGUIGAN, Andrew	Newton Stuart	Barrow	Retired	1908-10	44	20	10	9
MAKIN, James*	Bury	Army	Third Division	1919-20	31	14	1	0
MARSHALL, Frederick	Newmills	Hyde U	Retired (war wounds)	1913-15	55	4	3	2
MAXSTED, James	Scotland	Royal Artillery	Royal Artillery	1910-11	1	0	0	0
MEDCALF, Henry	Westward Ho!	South Molton	Swindon T	1919-20	5	0	0	0
MITTON, John*	Ramsbottom	Burnley	Third Division	1919-20	42	0	1	0
NEVIN, Ralph	Lintz Colliery	Gateshead		1912-13	7	0	0	0
NUTLAND, Percival	Yeovil	Yeovil T	Yeovil T	1919-20	1	0	0	0
OLDACRE, Percival	Stoke	Stoke	Castleford T	1919-20	33	8	1	0
ORR, Henry	Little Lever	Barnsley	Barry	1913-14	2	0	0	0
PARNELL, Frederick	Sutton-in-Ashfield	Leeds C	Preston NE	1908-09	29	3	6	2

Player	Birthplace	From	To	Played	League App	League Gls	FA Cup App	FA Cup Gls
Parnell, Frederick cont......	....	Preston NE	Rochdale T	1910-12	50	5	4	0
PLANT, W	(Unknown)	St Luke's College	Retired	1908-09	1	0	0	0
POPPLEWELL, Stanley	Bolton	Blackpool	Blackpool	1919-20	41	4	1	0
POTTER, Benjamin	Manchester	Barrow	Yeovil	1919-20	2	0	0	0
PRATT, Charles	Birmingham	Everton	Trainer	1910-20	99	1	5	0
PRIDEAUX, Frederick	Torpoint	Torpoint	Swansea T	1910-12	47	0	6	0
PRIDHAM, WA	Torquay	Torquay T	Torquay T	1913-15	2	0	0	0
PYM, Richard*	Topsham	Topsham	Third Division	1911-20	164	0	5	0
READER, George	Birmingham	St Luke's College	Southampton	1919-20	1	1	0	0
RIGBY, James*	Bolton	Accrington S	Third Division	1911-20	157	2	6	0
ROBINSON, John	Derby	Green Waves (Plymouth)	Stoke	1908-09	29	0	4	0
RUTTER, Arthur	South Shields	Barnsley	Plymouth A	1911-13	64	19	2	0
SHREEVE, Charles	South Shields	Army		1919-20	2	0	0	0
SMITH, William	Newcastle	S Shields Adelaide	Burnley	1910-11	12	4	0	0
SMITH, William	Hyde, Cheshire	Hyde U	Leg amputated 1919	1913-15	66	3	0	0
SOUTHCOMBE, Christopher	Ilfracombe	South Molton	South Molton	1919-20	1	0	0	0
STRETTLE, Samuel	Warrington	Chesterfield	Northwich V	1913-20	110	0	4	0
STURGE, Harold	Exmouth	Exmouth U	Exmouth U	1908-10	1	0	1	0
TIERNEY, Herbert	Bury	Bolton W	Retired (war wounds)	1908-10	32	2	0	1
TOMPKINSON, A	Burslem	Glossop		1911-12	1	0	1	1
WAKE, William	Banbury Castle	Plymouth A	Queen's Park R	1908-09	30	0	5	0
WATSON, Robert	Middlesbrough	W Arsenal	Stalybridge C	1908-12	137	25	19	11
WHITE, Thomas	Tring	Carlisle U	Watford	1908-09	19	0	3	0
WHITTAKER, Enos	Nelson	Haslingden	Stoke C	1910-12	33	3	4	0
WHITTAKER, Frederick	Burnley	Northampton T	Millwall	1912-14	68	17	3	0
WHITTAKER, Walter	Manchester	Clapton O	Swansea T (P-m)	1910-12	59	0	5	0

EXETER CITY CAREER RECORDS

Football League (1920-21 to 1989-90)

Below are the career records for all Exeter City players who played in the Football League, FA Cup and Football League Cup. The 'Played' section signifies the first year played to the last and where only one year is listed the player appeared in only that year. A hyphen following a single year thus, 1989-, means the player is still with the club. Where an (L) appears after a club name the player was on loan and likewise (Am) = amateur, (P-m) = player-manager, (M) = manager, (P-c) = player-coach, (app) = apprentice, YTS = Youth Training Scheme. A dagger (†) indicates they also played for Exeter City in the Southern League prior to 1920.

Player	Birthplace	From	To	Played	League		FA Cup		FL Cup	
					App	Gls	App	Gls	App	Gls
ACKROYD, John	Rotherham	Scunthorpe U	Grimsby T	1922-23	30	0	3	0	0	0
ALDERSON, John	Crook	Sheffield U	Retired	1929-30	36	0	1	0	0	0
ANDERSON, Alexander	Monifieth	Southampton	Retired	1952-53	6	0	0	0	0	0
ANDERSON, Desmond	Templepatrick	Glenavon	Chesterfield	1962-66	142/2	1	4	1	5	0
ANDERSON, John	South Molton	South Molton	South Molton	1925-26	1	0	0	0	0	0
ANDERSON, John	Glasgow	Northampton T	Dundee	1954-55	7	0	0	0	0	0
ANDERSON, John	Earby	Torquay U	Merthyr T	1927-28	2	0	0	0	0	0
ANDREWS, Harold	Amble	Scunthorpe U	Sidmouth	1930-49	246	1	19	1	0	0
ANGUS, John	Bamfurlong	Blackpool	Southport	1920-21	37	2	1	0	0	0
APPLETON, Leonard	Rawmarsh	Barnsley	Torquay U	1924-25	8	1	1	0	0	0
APPLEYARD, George	Lowestoft	Norwich C	Lowestoft	1951-53	14	2	1	0	0	0
ARMES, Ivan	Handsworth	Aston Villa	Gillingham	1929-32	72	14	8	3	0	0
ARMFIELD, William	Exeter	Local	Peterborough U	1957-60	3	3	0	0	0	0
ATKINS, Trevor	Dublin	Wolves	York C	1983-84	28	1	2	0	0	0
ATKINSON, Hugh	Carlisle	Carlisle U		1957-58	8	2	1	0	0	0
AUGUSTE, Joseph	Trinidad	Hounslow		1983-84	7/3	0	1	0	0	0

337

Alan Banks (under the banner) at Exeter railway station where supporters greeted the team after their goalless draw at Workington in April 1964 which assured the Grecians of promotion to Division Three. Club chairman Reg Rose is the man on the extreme left in the foreground.

Player	Birthplace	From	To	Played	League App	League Gls	FA Cup App	FA Cup Gls	FL Cup App	FL Cup Gls
BAILEY, Danny	Leyton	Wealdstone	Brentford	1989-	46	1	6	1	7	0
BAILEY, Harry	Macclesfield	Luton T	Retired	1923-27	143	0	15	0	0	0
BALSON, Michael	Bridport	Local	Retired	1965-74	273/3	9	14/1	1	13	0
BAMSEY, Hiley	Woodbury	Woodbury	Barrow	1934-39	42	0	2	0	0	0
BANKS, Alan	Liverpool	Cambridge C	Plymouth A	1963-66	85	43	1	0	2	1
		Plymouth A	Retired	1967-73	160/13	58	16/1	4	8	3
BANKS, Christopher	Stoke	Port Vale	Bath C	1988-89	43/2	1	1	0	2	0
BARBER, Stanley	Wallsend-on-Tyne	Bristol C	Brighton & HA	1930-34	118	10	9	0	0	0
BARNARD, Leigh	Worsley	Swindon T (L)	Swindon T	1985	6	2	0	0	0	0
BARNES, John	Atherstone	Watford	York C	1933-34	18	1	0	0	0	0
BARNETT, Alan	Croydon	Grimsby T	Torquay U	1963-66	57	0	3	0	3	0
BARTHOLOMEW, Henry	Motherwell	Motherwell	Bournemouth & BA	1947-49	66	6	5	2	0	0
BASTIN, Clifford	Exeter	Local	Arsenal	1927-29	17	6	0	0	0	0
BATTEN, John	Galston	Bradford	Kidderminster H	1923-24	9	1	1	0	0	0
BATTY, Paul	East Dington	Chesterfield	Kidderminster H	1986-	89/11	11	6/4	1	7	0
BAUGH, John	Uganda	St Luke's College	Retired	1976-78	20	0	0	0	4	0
BAUGH, Richard	Wolverhampton	West Bromwich A	Kidderminster H	1929-32	53	5	9	0	0	0
BEBY, John	Gillingham	Darlington		1936	10	0	0	0	0	0
BEER, Alan	Swansea	Weymouth	Assistant manager	1974-77	114	52	1	1	11	3
BEER, Colin	Exeter	Exbourne	Bideford	1956-58	5	2	0	0	0	0
BELL, Alec	Ayr	Partick T	Grimsby T	1954-58	40	0	0	0	0	0
BELL, Andrew	Taunton	Taunton T		1979-80	2/1	0	0	0	0	0
BELL, Edwin	Bristol	Welton R	Bath C	1922-23	1	0	0	0	0	0
BENJAMIN, Ian	Nottingham	Chester C	Southend U	1989-90	30/2	4	4/1	1	2	1
BENNETT, Peter	Plymstock	Plymstock	Falmouth	1959-61	6	5	0	0	0	0
BENSON, John	Arbroath	AFC Bournemouth	AFC Bournemouth	1973	4	0	0	0	0	0
BETTERIDGE, W	Boscombe	Boscombe A	Maidstone U	1920-21	2	0	0	0	0	0
BIGGINS, Stephen	Walsall	Telleborg FF	Telford	1986-87	14	2	1	0	0	0

Player	Birthplace	From	To	Played	League App	League Gls	FA Cup App	FA Cup Gls	FL Cup App	FL Cup Gls
BINNEY, Frederick	Plymouth	Torquay U	Brighton & HA	1969-74	177	90	5	1	7	7
BIRCH, Brian	Salford	Barrow	Oldham A	1958-60	19	1	0	0	0	0
BLACK, Neville	Ashington	Newcastle U	Rochdale	1953-53	4	0	0	0	0	0
BLACKMORE, Harold	Silverton	Local	Bolton W	1924-27	71	45	6	2	0	0
BLAIN, James	Liverpool	Carlisle U	Retired	1965-74	310/10	14	18/1	1	18	0
BLOOD, John	Nottingham	Notts C	Peterboro' U (P-m)	1939-48	39	1	5	0	0	0
BLORE, Vincent	Uttoxeter	Crystal P	Retired	1938-45	4	0	0	0	0	0
BLUE, Archibald	Glasgow	Hearts	Carlisle U	1961-62	34	6	0	0	1	1
BOAG, James	Blairhall	Bath C	Bath C	1962-63	2	0	0	0	0	0
BOLAM, David	Newcastle	Lincoln C		1925-26	1	0	0	0	0	0
BOND, Graham	Torquay	Torquay U	Weymouth T	1960-61	10	4	2	2	0	0
BOND, Leonard	Ilminster	Bristol C	Bristol C	1974-75	30	0	1	0	0	0
		Brentford	Weymouth T	1980-84	138	0	11	0	6	0
BOOTH, Samuel	Shotts	Derry C	Bradford C	1951-54	62	0	2	0	0	0
BOUNDY, Ronald	Wallasey	Wallasey	Southport	1933-34	2	0	0	0	0	0
BOWDEN, Albert	Exeter	Local	Retired	1945-47	0	0	2	0	0	0
BOWKER, Keith	West Bromwich	Birmingham C	Cambridge U	1973-76	110	38	8	1	6	2
		Northampton T	Torquay U	1977-80	93/9	28	3	1	12/1	6
BOWL, Henry	Clanfield	Blackpool	Lancaster T	1937-45	76	42	4	0	0	0
BOYLE, Michael	Bearpark	Reading	Darlington	1936-37	23	0	4	0	0	0
BRAYSHAW, Walter	Mexborough	Sheffield U	Blackburn R	1920-21	5	0	0	0	0	0
BRIGHT, Stanley	Hemyock	Cullompton	Bournemouth & BA	1929-34	1	0	0	0	0	0
BROWN, Alan	Lewes	Brighton & HA	Hastings U	1961-62	11	3	1	0	1	0
BROWN, Frank	Rotherham	Blackpool	Pontypridd	1921-22	6	0	0	0	0	0
BROWN, William	Bishop Auckland	Watford	Darlington	1936-39	86	6	6	0	0	0
BROWN, William	Kilsyth	Reading	Yeovil T	1951-52	7	0	1	0	0	0
BUCKINGHAM, Colin	Plymouth	Plymouth A	Falmouth	1965-67	29	0	1	0	0	0
BUCKLE, Edward	Southwark	Everton	Wigan A	1955-57	65	12	2	0	0	0

Player	Birthplace	From	To	Played	League App	League Gls	FA Cup App	FA Cup Gls	FL Cup App	FL Cup Gls
BULLOCK, Eli	Stoke	Macclesfield T		1921-22	27	4	0	0	0	0
BULLOCK, Peter	Stoke	Colchester U	Walsall	1968	14	2	0	0	0	0
BURGHER, Symon	Birmingham	Schoolboy		1984-85	11/3	0	0	0	0	0
BURKE, John	Motherwell	Sheffield U	Chester	1983	3	0	0	0	0	0
BURKE, Ronald	Marske	Rotherham U	Biggleswade T	1955-57	42	14	3	1	0	0
BUSSEY, Walter	Eckington	Swansea T	Retired	1936-39	75	16	5	0	0	0
BUTLER, Martin	Hull	York C (L)	York C	1987	4	1	0	0	0	0
BUTTERWORTH, David	Bristol	Guildford C	Hyde U	1957-60	26	0	1	0	0	0
CALLAN, Dennis	Merthyr Tydfil	Cardiff C	Cardiff C	1954	10	1	0	0	0	0
CALLAND, Edward	Durham	Torquay U	Port Vale	1957-60	105	49	3	2	0	0
CAMERON, Edward	Glasgow	Stafford R		1928-29	24	9	3	1	0	0
CAMPBELL, James	Dalry	Partick T		1928-29	17	0	0	0	0	0
CARRICK, James	Boothstown	Plank Lane	Oldham A	1920-21	41	3	1	3	0	0
CARTER, Raymond	West Heathley	Torquay U	Crawley	1960-63	105	50	3	3	1	0
CARTER, Roy	Torpoint	Newport C		1987-88	37/4	2	1	0	2	0
CARTER, Stanley	Exeter	Heavitree U	Barnstaple T	1949-52	2	0	0	0	0	0
CARTER, Wilfred	Wednesbury	Plymouth A	Bath C	1964-66	48	6	1	0	3	1
CASSON, Walter	Blyth	Pontypridd	South Shields	1925-26	8	3	0	0	0	0
CHALLIS, Stanley	Lympstone	Lympstone	Lympstone	1945-47	4	1	4	2	0	0
CHAMBERS, Robert	Newcastle	Carlisle U	New Brighton	1927-29	1	0	0	0	0	0
CHARLTON, Stanley	Little Hulton	Rochdale	Crystal P	1923-28	163	10	17	0	0	0
CHESTERS, Arthur	Pendleton	Manchester U	Crystal P	1933-37	95	0	7	0	0	0
CHILDS, Arthur	Acomb	Hull C	Darlington	1931-34	62	4	2	0	0	0
CHRISTIE, Alexander	Paisley	Rochdale		1928-29	4	0	0	0	0	0
CHURCH, Henry	Castleford	Oldham A	Retired	1937-39	66	0	3	0	0	0
CHURMS, Dennis	Rotherham	Coventry C	Folkestone T	1957-58	44	8	1	0	0	0
CLAPHAM, Keith	Fareham	Bournemouth & BA	Australia	1972-77	79/21	0	3	0	8/1	0
CLARK, James	Dornoch	Aberdeen	Bradford C	1948-53	92	5	9	0	0	0

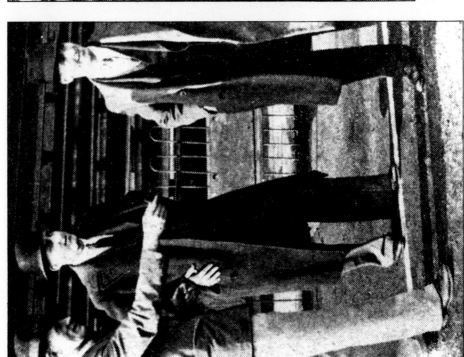

Left: Charlie Miller, the Exeter City captain, introduces Fred Wrightson (centre) and Harold Webb to St James' Park after their move from Fulham in March 1933. Above: Nobby Clarke leads out the Exeter team for his benefit match against Leicester City in September 1933. Behind him are Harold Webb and a young Jack Angus.

Player	Birthplace	From	To	Played	League App	League Gls	FA Cup App	FA Cup Gls	FL Cup App	FL Cup Gls
CLARKE, Allan	Crayford	Charlton A		1972-74	16	0	0	0	1	0
CLARKE, Benjamin	Dungannon	Sheffield U	Retired	1937-39	40	1	1	0	0	0
CLARKE, Horace	Pleasley	Chesterfield		1922-23	16	0	0	0	0	0
CLARKE, Reginald	Seaton	Friernhay	Aldershot	1926-37	315	18	23	1	0	0
CLARKE, William	Leicester	Leicester C	Southampton	1937-38	12	1	2	0	0	0
CLIFFORD, Darren	Bristol	Apprentice		1984-85	0/1	0	0	0	0	0
COCHRANE, John	Belfast	Brighton & HA	Ards	1963-64	2	0	1	0	0	0
COLEBURNE, Joseph	Tyldesley	Atherton	Swindon T	1920-21	30	0	1	0	0	0
		Swindon T	Taunton T	1923-24	45	3	8	3	0	0
COLEMAN, Philip	Woolwich	Colchester U	Aldershot	1984	6	0	0	0	0	0
COLES, Arthur	Crediton	Copplestone	Coleraine	1936-38	2	0	0	0	0	0
		RAF	Barnstaple T	1939-49	14	0	0	0	0	0
COLEY, William	Wolverhampton	Northampton T	St Austell	1951-52	8	0	0	0	0	0
COLLINS, Eamon	Dublin	Portsmouth (L)	Portsmouth	1987-88	8/1	0	0	0	0	0
COMPTON, William	Bedminster	Bristol C	Bristol R	1924-28	151	39	14	6	0	0
CONGDON, James	Plymouth	Millbrook	Accrington S	1921-22	6	1	2	0	0	0
CONNABOY, Michael	Edinburgh	Wolves	Darlington	1932-33	4	0	0	0	0	0
COOKE, Joseph	Dominica	Oxford U	Bradford C	1981-82	17	3	1	1	3/1	0
COOPER, Mark	Wakefield	Bristol C		1989-	1/3	0	2/1	1	0/1	0
COOPER, Richard	London	Lincoln C		1987-89	55/7	2	1	0	3/1	0
COOPLAND, Ernest	Sheffield	Arsenal	Aberdare	1923	9	0	0	0	0	0
CORR, John	Glasgow	Arsenal	Cheltenham T	1967-71	73/6	19	9	1	7	2
COUGHLIN, Dennis	Houghton-le-Spring	Swansea (L)	Swansea T	1968	13	2	1	0	0	0
COULSTON, Walter	Warwell Sampford	Crystal P	Barnsley	1937-38	32	2	1	0	0	0
COURTNEY, Frederick	Peverell	South Molton	South Molton	1930-33	3	0	0	0	0	0
COYLE, Anthony	Glasgow	Northwich V (L)	Northwich V	1989-90	1	0	0	0	0/1	0
CRABTREE, Richard	Exeter	Torquay U	Dawlish T	1983-84	1	0	0	0	0	0
CRAWFORD, Alan	Rotherham	Bristol C	Weston-super-Mare	1985-86	33	3	3	1	4	1

Player	Birthplace	From	To	Played	League App	League Gls	FA Cup App	FA Cup Gls	FL Cup App	FL Cup Gls
CRAWFORD, Campbell	Alexandria	West Bromwich A	Kidderminster H	1967-74	224/10	3	12	0	12/1	0
CRAWSHAW, Cyril	Barton on Irwell	Queen of South	Hull C	1939-46	0	0	1	1	0	0
CRAWSHAW, William	Darwen	Southern League	Accrington S	1920-21	28	0	1	0	0	0
		Accrington S	Taunton	1923-25	11	0	2	0	0	0
CROCKFORD, Harold	Derby	Fulham	Port Vale	1922-23	30	17	1	0	0	0
CROMPTON, Ellis	Ramsbottom	Bristol R	Barnstaple T	1921-26	145	6	11	0	0	0
CROMPTON, Wynne	Cefnyhedd	Crystal P		1935-36	7	0	0	0	0	0
CROWN, David	Enfield	Portsmouth (L)	Portsmouth	1983	6/1	3	0	0	0	0
CURRIE, James	Glasgow	Falkirk	Workington	1956-57	54	19	1	0	0	0
CURTIS, Dermot	Dublin	Ipswich T	Torquay U	1963-66	91	23	5	2	4	3
		Torquay U	Bideford	1967-69	64/2	10	6	0	1/2	1
CUTTING, Stanley	Saint Frith's	Southampton	Assistant trainer	1939-50	38	2	1	0	0	0
DAILEY, James	Glenboig	Birmingham C	Workington	1952-53	45	13	3	0	0	0
DALE, Gordon	Manton	Portsmouth	Chelmsford C	1957-61	124	8	7	1	1	0
DARE, Reginald	Blandford	Southampton		1950-51	6	0	1	0	0	0
DARKE, Peter	Exeter	Plymouth A	Torquay U	1976-77	5	0	0	0	0	0
DAVEY, Frederick	Crediton	Crediton	Bridgwater	1947-56	276	3	19	0	0	0
DAVEY, Stephen	Plymouth	Portsmouth	Bideford	1981-82	15	0	1	0	4	0
DAVIES, Arthur	Wallasey	Everton	Plymouth A	1930-35	165	0	12	0	0	0
DAVIES, Grant	Barrow	Newport C	Newport C	1983	7	0	0	0	0	0
DAVIES, Ian	Bristol	Carlisle U	Bristol R	1984-85	5	0	0	0	0	0
DAVIES, Thomas	Troedyrhiw	Watford	Walsall	1937-38	14	0	0	0	0	0
DAVIS, Robert	London	Queen's Park R	Yeovil T	1962-63	0	0	0	0	1	0
DAVIS, John	Plymouth	Torquay U	Newport C	1922-25	68	18	12	6	0	0
DEATH, William	Rotherham	Sunderland	Gillingham	1928-30	25	6	2	1	0	0
DELVE, John	Iselworth	Plymouth A	Hereford U	1978-83	215	20	13	0	17	3
		Hereford U	Taunton T	1987-88	12/1	1	0	0	0	0
DENNINGTON, Leslie	West Bromwich	Reading	Retired	1928-31	65	0	7	0	0	0

Exeter City, 1949–50. Back row (left to right, players only): Cyril Johnstone, Fred Davey, Ray Goddard, Ken Powell, Bernard Singleton, Bill Harrower, Jim Clark, Steve Walker. Front row: Peter Fallon, Dick Smart, Archie Smith, John Greenwood, Doug Regan.

345

Player	Birthplace	From	To	Played	League App	League Gls	FA Cup App	FA Cup Gls	FL Cup App	FL Cup Gls
DENNIS, Anthony	Taplow	Plymouth A	Bideford	1983	3/1	0	0	0	1	0
DENT, Frederick	Sheffield	Bristol C	Merthyr T	1926-28	48	29	8	6	0	0
DEVLIN, Alan	Edinburgh	Dundee U		1973-74	1	0	0/1	0	0	0
DEVLIN, William	Newcastle	Newport C		1922-23	12	5	0	0	0	0
DIGBY, Derek	Teignmouth	Dawlish T	Southampton	1949-53	31	2	1	0	0	0
DITCHBURN John 'Jock'	Leeds	Sunderland	Sthn Railway	1926-28	50	4	0	0	0	0
		Sthn Railway	Retired	1929-34	35	2	0	0	0	0
DIVERS, John	Glasgow	Clyde	E Stirling	1956-57	12	1	0	0	0	0
DOCKRAY, John	Carlisle	Bury	Bideford	1920-24	141	12	2	2	0	0
DODGIN, Norman	Gateshead	North'ton T (P-m)	Manager	1953-57	33	1	2	0	0	0
DONALDSON, Andrew	Newcastle	Peterborough U	Peterborough U	1953-55	39	16	2	0	0	0
DONALDSON, Frederick	Stoke	Port Vale	Chester	1960-61	36	6	2	2	0	0
DONCASTER, Arthur	Barry Dock	Bolton W	Crystal P	1928-32	126	31	14	4	0	0
DOUGLASS, Norman	Durham	Chelsea	Peterborough U	1953-56	63	0	1	0	0	0
DOYLE, Brian	Salford	Stoke C	Bristol R	1954-57	100	0	4	0	0	0
DOYLE, Leslie	Liverpool	Everton	Bideford	1949-55	82	0	7	0	0	0
DRYDEN, John	Broomhill	Newcastle U	Sheffield U	1934-35	20	5	0	0	0	0
DRYDEN, Richard	Stroud	Bristol R		1988-	51	7	1	0	5	1
DUDLEY, Samuel	Dudley	Chelsea		1934-35	8	1	0	0	0	0
DUKE, John	Mauchline	Scunthorpe U	Bristol C	1922-23	1	0	0	0	0	0
DUNLOP, William	Airdrie	Dunfermline	Northwich V	1950-52	4	0	0	0	0	0
DUNN, James	Glasgow	Everton	Runcorn	1935-36	22	4	1	0	0	0
DUNNE, Thomas	Dublin	Leicester C	Shrewsbury T	1954-56	37	1	4	0	0	0
DURRANT, Frederick	Dover	Queen's Park R	Dover	1949-50	17	5	0	0	0	0
DYMOND, William	Kenton	Bristol C	Hereford U	1947-49	41	7	4	3	0	0
EBDON, Richard	Ottery St Mary	Ottery St Mary	Torquay U	1935-48	138	50	6	1	0	0
EDGAR, John	Barnsley	Hartlepools U	Matlock	1963-64	6	0	0	0	0	0
EDGE, Thomas	Leigh	Oldham A	Blackpool	1921-22	3	0	0	0	0	0

Player	Birthplace	From	To	Played	League App	League Gls	FA Cup App	FA Cup Gls	FL Cup App	FL Cup Gls
EDMONDSON, James	Carleton	Swansea T	Retired	1923-24	6	1	0	0	0	0
EDWARDS, Dean	Wolverhampton	Wolves	Torquay U	1986-88	51/3	17	1	0	2	0
EDWARDS, Thomas	Aberdare	Aberdare A		1927-28	3	0	0	0	0	0
ELKINS, Gary	Wallingford	Fulham (L)	Fulham	1989	5	0	0	0	0	0
ELLAWAY, William	Crediton	Barnstaple T	Bournemouth & BA	1954-56	31	9	1	0	0	0
ELLIOTT, Raymond	Southampton	Charlton A	Poole T	1965-67	28	3	0	0	1	0
EMBURY, Benjamin	Barking	Tottenham H	Barnet	1966-68	36/3	0	3	0	3	0
ESHELBY, Paul	Sheffield	Sheffield Bankers		1989-	1	0	0	0	0	0
EVANS, Henry	Lambeth	Southampton	Aldershot	1947-49	41	6	2	0	0	0
EVANS, Ian	Egham	Barnsley (L)	Barnsley	1983-84	4	0	0	0	1	0
EVANS, John	Liverpool	Carlisle U	Barnsley	1966-67	11/1	2	0	0	2	0
FALLON, Peter	Dublin	RAF	Queen's Park R	1947-53	110	8	9	2	0	0
FALLON, William	Dublin	Notts C	Peterborough U	1947-48	8	2	0	0	0	0
FANTHAM, John	Wolverhampton	Chester	Rhyl	1935-36	6	1	0	0	0	0
FARRELL, Vincent	Preston	Clapton O	Clapton O	1937-38	6	4	0	0	0	0
FEEBURY, John	Nottingham	Bolton W	Brighton & HA	1920-21	42	2	1	0	0	0
FELLOWES, William	Bradford	Luton T	Tavistock T	1938-47	56	1	1	0	0	0
FERRIER, John	Edinburgh	Clyde	Yeovil T	1956-57	31	0	1	0	0	0
FISHER, Philip	Carmarthen	Bridgend	Swansea	1981-82	9/2	1	0	0	0	1
FLYNN, Andrew	Sheffield	Mexborough	York C	1922-26	34	1	4	0	0	0
FOLEY, Peter	Bicester	Oxford U		1987	1	0	0	0	0	0
FOLEY, Theophilus	Dublin	Home Farm (Dubl)	Northampton T	1955-61	155	1	4	0	1	0
FORBES, Richard	Ashford	Woking	Plymouth A	1977-82	55/4	5	11	1	4	0
FOSTER, George	Plymouth	Plymouth (L)	Plymouth A	1981-82	28	0	0	0	0	0
FRANCIS, Gerald	Chiswick	Coventry C	Cardiff C	1983-84	28	3	2	0	1	0
FRANKLAND, Tony	Basingstoke	Schoolboy		1989-	3/1	0	0	0	0	0
FRYER, Henry	Luton	Luton Clarence	Torquay U	1921-23	58	0	3	0	0	0
FUDGE, Michael	Bristol	West Bromwich A	Wellington T	1967-68	32/2	6	3	0	2	0

Exeter City, 1946-7, the first post-war Football League season. Back row (left to right): R.Ebdon, J.Long, A.Hydes, R.Wright, S.Walker, H.Hanford. Middle: N.Foot (secretary), G.Thompson, S.Challis, W.Fellows, A.Coles, H.Hoyle, A.Hammond, J.Murray, G.Vaughan, J.Gallagher (trainer). Front: G.Wardle, W.Mustard, S.Cutting, G.Roughton (manager), R.Smart, A.Bowden, D.Regan.

348

Player	Birthplace	From	To	Played	League App	League Gls	FA Cup App	FA Cup Gls	FL Cup App	FL Cup Gls
FULTON, Bryce	Prestwick	Plymouth A	Stockport C	1964-67	37	0	1	0	3	0
GADSTON, Joseph	Hanwell	Bristol R	Aldershot	1969-72	85	31	7	0	2	1
GALE, Darren	Port Talbot	Swansea C	Retired	1985-87	19/1	5	2	2	3	0
GALLAGHER, James	Bury	Notts C	Trainer	1939-49	1	0	1	1	0	0
GALLOGLEY, Thomas	Larkhall	Plymouth A	Retired	1923-24	21	1	7	0	0	0
GARRATT, John	Halesowen	Torquay U		1926-27	10	0	1	0	0	0
GASKELL, Richard	Ashton-under-Lyne	Ashton National	Torquay U	1921-22	14	0	0	0	0	0
GAY, Geoffrey	Romford	Bolton W	Southport	1976-77	5/1	0	0	0	0	0
GEE, Harold	Haydock	New Brighton	Retired	1927-28	29	2	6	1	0	0
GIBSON, Aidan	Clayton	Derby C	Stourbridge	1982-83	17/1	1	0	0	0	0
GIBSON, David	Winchburgh	Aston Villa	Retired	1972-74	69/2	3	1	0	3	0
GIBSON, Reginald	Tideswell	Plymouth A	Retired	1947-50	40	0	2	0	0	0
GILCHRIST, Donald	Campbeltown	Portsmouth	Workington	1923-24	29	1	6	0	0	0
GILES, James	Kidlington	Aldershot	Charlton A	1971-75	183	8	7	0	8	0
		Charlton A	Retired	1977-82	130	5	4	0	13	0
GILES, John	Bristol	Bradford	Bath C	1969-72	55/5	2	3	0	3	0
GILES, Paul	Cardiff	Cardiff C	Excelsior (Holl)	1981-83	9	1	0	0	0	0
GODDARD, Karl	Leeds	Bradford C	Bradford C	1990	0/1	0	0	0	0	0
GODDARD, Raymond	Birmingham	Plymouth A	Bideford (P-m)	1949-54	130	2	7	0	0	0
GODFREY, Peter	Woolwich	Chesterfield		1966-67	42	4	2	0	4	0
GOOD, Hugh	Motherwell	Middlesbrough	Bristol C	1926-27	4	0	1	0	0	0
GORDON, Peter	Northampton	Watford	Newport C	1960-62	67	11	2	0	3	1
GRACE, Derek	Chiswick	Queen's Park R	Gillingham	1962-65	40	4	3	0	2	0
GRAHAM, Joseph	Hebburn-on-Tyne	Stockport C	New Brighton	1921-22	12	0	1	0	0	0
GRANT, Alan	Havant	Brighton & HA		1960-61	4	0	1	0	0	0
GRANT, Bernard	Airdrie	Third Lanark		1947-49	2	0	0	0	0	0
GRANVILLE, Trevor	Newport	Newport C	Gillingham	1946-48	20	1	0	0	0	0
GRAY, James	Glasgow	Liverpool	Retired	1930-36	213	0	8	0	0	0

Player	Birthplace	From	To	Played	League App	League Gls	FA Cup App	FA Cup Gls	FL Cup App	FL Cup Gls
GREEN, Alfred	Rotherham	Pre-war	Retired	1920-22	43	0	2	0	0	0
GREEN, Brian	Heywood	Barrow	Chesterfield	1962-63	9	1	0	1	0	0
GREEN, Jasper	Preston	Preston NE	Bideford	1921-22	6	0	1	0	0	0
GREEN, Mike J	Southend	Apprentice		1975-76	0/1	0	0	0	0	0
GREENAWAY, Arthur	Swindon	Plymouth A	Swansea T	1950-51	1	0	0	0	0	0
GREENWOOD, John	Manchester	Manchester U	Aldershot	1949-51	31	2	4	1	0	0
GRINNEY, Ian	Crediton	Crediton	Crediton	1954-59	2	0	0	0	0	0
GUMM, James	Exeter	Local amateur	Retired	1928-34	5	0	2	0	0	0
GURKIN, John	Murton	Stalybridge C	Retired	1929-30	2	0	0	0	0	0
GUYAN, George	Aberdeen	Connah's Quay	Swindon T	1929-30	28	14	1	1	0	0
GWINNETT, Melvyn	Worcester	Bradford C	Weymouth T	1985-89	46	0	1	0	2	0
HADDOCK, Henry	Glasgow	Renfrew Jnrs	Clyde	1945-47	1	0	1	0	0	0
HALLIDAY, Thomas	Browney Colliery	Norwich C	Retired	1939-45	14	0	0	0	0	0
HALLIDAY, William	Dumfries	Connah's Quay		1930-32	11	4	0	0	0	0
HAMILTON, Ian	Bristol	Bristol R (L)	Bristol R	1967-68	4	1	0	0	0	0
HAMMOND, Albert	Hanwell	Brentford	Hastings U	1946-47	2	0	0	0	0	0
HANCOCK, David	Exeter	Torquay U	Retired	1964-65	40	3	1	0	2	0
HANFORD, Henry	Blaingwyfi	Sheffield W	Haverfordwest	1946-47	36	0	1	0	0	0
HARDIE, Alexander	Kilsyth	Plymouth A	Truro C	1933-34	18	1	1	0	0	0
HARFORD, Raymond	Halifax	Charlton A	Lincoln C	1965-67	55	1	1	0	4	2
HARLE, David	Denaby	Doncaster R	Doncaster T	1982-83	42/1	6	1	0	4	2
HARRIS, Carl	Neath	YTS		1988-89	11/5	2	0	0	0	0
HARRIS, James	Exeter	YTS	Exmouth T	1987-89	5/4	0	0	0	0	0
HARRISON, Bernard	Worcester	Southampton	Poole T	1960-61	18	4	1	1	1	0
HARROWER, Stephen	Exeter	Dawlish T		1983-	165/22	10	10	1	8/1	1
HARROWER, William	Dunfermline	Torquay U	Bideford	1948-52	85	11	9	0	0	0
HART, Stuart	Derby	Long Eaton U	Ilkeston T	1967-68	20/2	1	2	0	2	0
HARVEY, Keith	Crediton	Crediton	Retired	1952-69	483	28	21	0	13	0

Exeter City skipper Keith Harvey (right) and Czechoslovakian World Cup star Jan Popluhár, pictured before the start of a friendly game between the Grecians and Slovan Bratislava in the 1965-6 season. The referee is Ernie Edworthy of Exeter.

Player	Birthplace	From	To	Played	League App	League Gls	FA Cup App	FA Cup Gls	FL Cup App	FL Cup Gls
HATCH, Peter	Wargrave	Oxford U	Bideford	1973-82	343/3	18	20	3	27	2
HATTER, Stephen	London	Fulham	Wimbledon	1982	11	1	0	0	0	0
HAWKINS, Horace	Mexborough	Denaby U		1925-26	4	0	0	0	0	0
HEALE, Garry	Canvey Island	Luton T	Reading	1977-79	3/1	0	0	0	0	0
HEATH, Herbert	Wolverhampton	Darlaston		1989-	3/2	0	0	0	0	0
HEMINGWAY, Cryil	Rotherham	Torquay U	Wolves	1929-30	39	19	1	0	0	0
HENDERSON, John	Johnshaven	Charlton A	Doncaster R	1962-64	46	14	0	0	2	0
HENDERSON, William	Edinburgh	Torquay U	Retired	1929-30	5	0	0	0	0	0
HESMONDHALGH, Thomas	Bolton	Rochdale		1920-21	1	0	0	0	0	0
HETHERINGTON, Sydney	Monkswearmouth	Southern League	Southwick	1920-21	8	1	0	0	0	0
HICK, William	West Pelton	Bristol C	Grays A	1929	16	8	0	0	0	0
HICKS, James	Ipswich	Exeter University		1983	3	0	0	0	0	0
HIGGINS, Andrew	Gartsherrie	Millwall	Newport C	1932-33	22	9	2	0	0	0
HILEY, Scott	Plymouth	YTS		1987-	93/5	6	7	0	9	0
HILL, Dilwyn	Porth	Pontypridd	Salisbury C	1955-60	14	3	0	0	0	0
HILL, Percival	Luton	Luton T	Torquay U	1921-22	14	2	0	0	0	0
HILTON, Percival	Eagley	Everton	Torquay U	1920-21	1	0	0	0	0	0
HINTON, John	Barnstaple	Thorneycrofts		1921	4	1	0	0	0	0
HOBBS, Ernest	Wellingborough	Northampton T	Tunbridge Wells	1936-37	11	0	0	0	0	0
HODGE, Robert	Exeter	Local	Colchester U	1974-78	120/8	18	3/1	1	13	0
HOLLAND, Thomas	Sheffield	Weymouth	Watford	1927-30	59	0	10	0	0	0
HOLMAN, Henry	Exeter	Local	Southampton	1946-47	4	2	0	0	0	0
HOLMAN, Henry	Exeter	Chelsea (app)	Peterborough U	1976-78	47/5	9	6	1	1	1
HOOKER, Alan	Exmouth	Local	Dorchester T	1974-77	46/4	0	3/1	0	5	0
HORE, John	St Austell	Plymouth A	Plymouth A (M)	1976-81	193	0	10	0	18	0
HOUGHTON, Frank	Preston	Newcastle U	Asst trainer	1954-57	28	10	0	0	0	0
HOUGHTON, Harold	Liverpool	Everton	Norwich C	1928-34	207	79	16	4	0	0
HOWARTH, Frank	Budleigh Salterton	Apprentice		1981-85	21/16	1	1	1	2	0

Exeter City, 1934-5. Back row (left to right): J.Scott, J.McClure, M.Lock, D.Lewis, F.P.Nichols (director), A.Chesters, W.McDevitt (manager), C.Miller, S.H.Thomas (secretary), E.Keefe, R.Clarke. Middle row: J.Lake (director), E.Edwards (trainer), F.Wrightson, H.Poulter, J.Angus, H.Webb, A.Davies, W.Smith, J.Dryden, F.Jasper, E.Head (director), R.Loram (assistant trainer), Captain Hunter (director). Front row: H.Greenaway (groundsman), S.Risdon, J.Gray, S.Hurst, M.J.McGahey (chairman), E.McArthur, C.Tierney, S.Dudley, 'Jazzo' (club mascot).

Player	Birthplace	From	To	Played	League App	League Gls	FA Cup App	FA Cup Gls	FL Cup App	FL Cup Gls
HOWELLS, Raymond	Rhondda	Crystal P	Barnstaple T	1951-53	15	3	0	0	0	0
HOWSON, George	Bristol	Bath C	Bath C	1929-30	13	0	0	0	0	0
HOYLE, Herbert	Basildon	Wolves	Bristol R	1946-50	82	0	5	0	0	0
HOYLE, Victor	Exeter	Local	Torquay U	1935-36	6	1	0	0	0	0
HUDSON, Geoffrey	Leeds	Halifax T	Crewe A	1961-62	41	0	2	0	0	0
HUGHES, Michael	Llandiloes	Cardiff C	Chesterfield	1961-63	36	0	3	0	0	0
HUGHES, Richard	Sunderland	Bristol C	Retired	1932-34	26	0	1	0	0	0
HUNTER, George	South Shields	Sunderland	Workington	1923-24	18	0	6	0	0	0
HUNTER, George	Troon	Derby C	Yiewsley	1955-60	147	0	7	0	0	0
HURST, Stanley	Crediton	Tipton St John	Watford	1931-36	107	25	5	3	0	0
HUTCHINGS, Dennis	Axminster	Axminster	Barnstaple T	1947-52	82	13	3	0	0	0
HUXFORD, Clifford	Stroud	Southampton	Aldershot	1967-68	40/1	1	4	0	1	0
HYDES, Arthur	Barnsley	Newport C	Scunthorpe U	1946-47	4	0	1	0	0	0
IGGLEDEN, Horatio	Hull	Leeds U	Goole T	1955-56	27	8	3	2	0	0
IMPEY, John	Minehead	Torquay U	Torquay U	1985-86	26	0	0	0	3	0
INGHAM, Frederick	Manchester	Falmouth T	Retired	1977-79	4/4	1	1	0	0	0
INGLIS, William	Hebbern-on-Tyne	Reading	Stockport C	1930-31	15	0	0	0	0	0
IRELAND, Roy	Exeter	Apprentice	Yeovil T	1979-82	17/4	0	0	0	2	0
JACKSON, Garry	Swinton	Manchester C		1985-87	34/1	2	3	0	2	0
JASPER, Frederick	Budleigh Salterton	Budleigh Salterton	Budleigh Salterton	1933-35	1	0	0	0	0	0
JEFFREY, Robert	Aberdeen	Aberdeen	Weymouth	1947-49	7	0	2	0	0	0
JENKINS, Brian	Treherbert	Cardiff C	Bristol R	1961-63	73	11	2	0	1	0
JENKINS, Reginald	Millbrook	Plymouth A	Torquay U	1960-61	20	6	0	0	0	0
JENKINS, Thomas	Merthyr Tydfil	Merthyr T	Southend U	1927-28	4	0	0	0	0	0
JENNINGS, Nicholas	Wellington	Aldershot (L)	Retired	1974-78	119/5	15	6	0	11	3
JOHN, Raymond	Swansea	Barnsley	Oldham A	1954-58	144	18	6	0	0	0
JOHNSON, Henry	Radcliffe	Southend U	Scunthorpe U	1936-37	11	1	2	0	0	0
JOHNSON, Peter	Harrogate	Crewe A	Southend U	1985-86	5	0	0	0	0	0

Player	Birthplace	From	To	Played	League App	League Gls	FA Cup App	FA Cup Gls	FL Cup App	FL Cup Gls
JOHNSTON, David	Bishop Auckland	Leicester C	Stockport S	1962-63	10	0	0	0	0	0
JOHNSTON, Ronald	Glasgow	Rochdale	Weymouth T	1948-49	10	2	0	0	0	0
JOHNSTONE, Cyril	Hamilton	Hamilton A	Retired	1947-52	134	0	7	0	0	0
JONES, Alan	Wrexham	Cardiff C	Norwich C	1959-62	90	0	4	0	1	0
JONES, Frederick	Disley	Manchester C	Yeovil T	1930-32	5	0	0	0	0	0
JONES, Kenneth	Aberdare	Charlton A	Yeovil T	1966-67	17	0	0	0	0	0
JONES, Mark	Brownhills	Walsall (L)	Walsall	1988	5	0	0	0	0	0
JONES, Richard	Ashton-in-Makerf'd	Stockport C	Bristol R	1924-25	10	0	2	0	0	0
JORDAN, Michael	Exeter	Local	Bideford	1975-78	15/3	3	0	0	3	1
JORDAN, William	Southport	Southport	Prescot Cables	1945-46	0	0	3	0	0	0
JOY, Brian	Manchester	Doncaster R	York C	1973-76	89/1	2	2/1	0	9/1	1
JOYCE, Sean	Doncaster	Doncaster R (L)	Doncaster R	1986-87	1	0	0	0	0	0
KAILE, Gordon	Pimperne	Preston NE	St Luke's College	1954-55	6	1	1	0	0	0
KAVANAGH, Terrance	Dublin	Notts C		1937-38	6	0	0	0	0	0
KEANE, John	Newcastle	Falkirk (trial)	Gateshead	1936-37	13	1	2	3	0	0
KEEFE, Edward	Exeter	Exminster	Retired	1931-35	2	0	0	0	0	0
KEELEY, Raymond	Wandsworth	Charlton A	Mansfield T	1966-67	45/1	10	2	1	4	0
KELLOW, Anthony	Budock Water	Falmouth T	Blackpool	1976-78	107	40	7	4	12	4
		Blackpool	Plymouth A	1980-83	140/3	61	10	6	10	5
KELLY, Hugh	Lurgan	Newport C	Comm manager	1985-88	51/31	28	1	1	3/2	1
KELLY, Tom	Bellshill	Southampton	Weymouth T	1952-56	99	0	4	0	0	0
KENNEDY, John	Blyth	York C		1990-	11/1	2	0	0	0	0
KENNEDY, John	Kilwinning	Tranmere R	Torquay U	1932-33	16	3	0	0	1	0
KEOUGH, Daniel	Rawtenstall	Charlton A	Arcadia U (SA)	1965-67	40/1	6	0	0	1	0
KEY, Richard	Coventry	Bury	West Germany	1985-87	71/1	0	4	0	2	0
KIMBLE, Alan	Poole	Coventry C (Am)	Cambridge U	1975-78	109	0	8	0	3	0
KIMBLE, Garry	Poole	Charlton A (L)	Charlton A	1985	1	0	0	0	1	0
	Poole	Charlton A (L)	Charlton A	1985	1	0	0	0	1	1

Exeter City at the start of 1984-5. Back row (left to right): Martin Rogers, Graeme Kirkup, Jim McNichol, Roy McDonough, John Sims, Jim Iley (manager), Nick Marker, Ray Pratt, Danny O'Shea, Symon Burgher, Phil King. Middle row: Malcolm Musgrove (chief coach), Steve Neville, Martin King, Keith Viney, Steve Harrower, Frank Howarth, Mike Radford (youth development officer). Front row: Neville Crocker, Michael Lane, Andy Phillips, Darren Clifford.

356

Player	Birthplace	From	To	Played	League App	League Gls	FA Cup App	FA Cup Gls	FL Cup App	FL Cup Gls
KING, Philip	Bristol	Apprentice	Torquay U	1984-86	24/3	0	0	0	1	0
KIRK, Clifford	Cardiff	Liverpool	Barnsley	1935-36	3	0	0	0	0	0
KIRK, Harold	Sheffield	Bristol C	Plymouth A	1921-22	14	9	0	0	0	0
KIRK, Robert	Clydebank	Plymouth A	Charlton A	1922-26	126	36	14	5	0	0
KIRKHAM, John	Wednesbury	Bristol C	Blackpool	1927-28	10	0	0	0	0	0
KIRKMAN, Norman	Bolton	Peterborough U	Horwich RMI	1968-69	31/1	6	3	0	4	1
KIRKUP, Graham	Newcastle	Southampton(P-m)	Bradford (M)	1952-53	11	1	0	0	0	0
KNIGHT, John	Bolton	Apprentice	Torrington	1981-86	102/5	1	4	0	7	0
LACKENBY, George	Newcastle	Chesterfield	Bath C	1953-54	56	6	0	0	0	0
LAKIN, William	Sheffield	Newcastle U	Carlisle U	1956-57	24	4	0	0	0	0
LANE, Michael	Wellington	Barnsley	Retired	1920-21	6	0	0	0	0	0
LANGLEY, Thomas	Lambeth	Apprentice	Minehead	1983-84	1	0	0	1	0	0
LEAR, Graham	Exmouth	Aldershot	Slough T	1988-89	14/7	2	1	1	1	0
LESTER, Michael	Manchester	Local amateur	Leytonstone	1950-52	20	0	1	0	0	0
LEWIS, Dudley	London	Barnsley	Bradford C	1981-82	18/1	6	1	0	4	0
LEWIS, Geoffrey	Abertillery	Bristol R	Newport C	1934-35	16	2	1	0	0	0
LEY, George	Exminster	Royal Marines(Am)		1945-46	0	0	2	0	0	0
LIDDLE, James	Newcastle	Local amateur	Portsmouth	1963-67	93	7	5	1	6	0
LIEVESLEY, Wilfred	Staveley	Coventry C	Retired	1937-39	43	9	2	1	0	0
LIGHTLY, Brian	Portsmouth	Manchester U	Wigan B	1923-28	97	38	3	0	0	0
LING, Martin	West Ham	Portsmouth (Am)		1957-59	4	0	0	0	0	0
LISTER, Robert	Fife	Apprentice	Swindon T	1983-86	110/8	14	4	0	8	0
LITTLE, John	Dunston-on-Tyne	West Ham U	Rhyl Athletic	1930-31	8	1	0	0	0	0
LOBBETT, John	Exeter	Northampton T	Southport	1938-39	25	0	0	0	0	0
LONG, John	Lancashire	Local amateur	Barnstaple T	1957-61	44	0	3	0	2	0
LOWSON, Frank	Forfar	Chester (Am)	Boston U	1945-47	1	0	0	0	0	0
LOWTON, Frank	Exeter	Bradford	Barrow	1923-24	4	0	0	0	0	0
LOWTON, Wilfred	Exeter	Heavitree U (Am)	Wolves	1924-29	75	9	4	0	0	0

An expert tactician, Norman Dodgin is seen here imparting some of his knowledge before Exeter met Plymouth Argyle in the FA Cup in 1956-7. Pictured are: Back (left to right): John Porteous, George Hunter, Ray John, Keith Thomas, Harry Hanford (trainer). Front row: John Ferrier, Ted Buckle, Arnold Mitchell, Brian Doyle, Keith Harvey and Jim Currie.

Player	Birthplace	From	To	Played	League App	League Gls	FA Cup App	FA Cup Gls	FL Cup App	FL Cup Gls
Lowton, Wilfred cont........		Wolves	Asst trainer	1935-36	18	0	0	0	0	0
LYNN, Joseph	Cramlington	Huddersfield T	Rochdale	1950-51	29	2	5	0	0	0
McARDLE, Peter	Durham	Stoke C	Barnsley	1935-36	9	1	0	0	0	0
McARTHUR, Edward	Cowdenbeath	Middlesbrough	Torquay U	1934-36	23	7	0	0	0	0
McCAFFERY, Aidan	Newcastle	Bristol R	Whitley Bay	1985-87	55/3	0	3	0	3	0
McCAMBRIDGE, James	Larne	Bristol R	Sheffield W	1935-36	23	14	1	0	0	0
McCLELLAND, Charles	Manchester	Blackburn R	Portland U	1949-55	183	60	14	5	0	0
McCLURE, Doug	Islington	Queen's Park R	Torquay U	1984	0/1	0	0	0	0	0
McCLURE, Joseph	Workington	Brentford	Nuneaton T (P-m)	1934-36	5	0	0	0	0	0
McCOSH, John	Colyton (Ayr)	Queen of South	New Brighton	1930-31	1	0	0	0	0	0
McCULLOCH, John	Scotland	Dykeshead		1921	1	0	0	0	0	1
McDADE, Patrick	Clydebank	Liverpool	Morton	1927-28	2	0	0	0	0	0
McDERMOTT, Brian	Slough	Cardiff C		1989-	57/3	4	4	1	4	0
McDEVITT, William	Belfast	Liverpool	Manager	1925-30	125	9	14	2	0	0
MacDONALD, Leslie	Newcastle	Portsmouth	Weymouth T	1957-66	294	0	13	0	6	0
McDONOUGH, Roy	Solihull	Southend U	Cambridge U	1983-84	20/1	1	0	0	2	1
McEWAN, Stanley	Cambuskenneth	Blackpool	Hull C	1982-84	65	15	3	0	4	0
McGILL, Patrick	Glasgow	Hearts	Distillery (Belfast)	1936-38	34	1	1	0	0	0
McINTOSH, George	Govan	Workington	Accrington S	1923-24	16	0	5	0	0	0
MacINTYRE, Thomas	Dumfries	Services	Crewe A	1920-21	5	0	0	0	0	0
MACKAY, Angus	Glasgow	Ipswich T	Millwall	1947-55	257	78	13	5	0	0
MacKECHNIE, John	Inverness	Northampton T	Stockport C	1921-22	18	0	0	0	0	0
McLEAN, George	Paisley	Grimsby T	Workington	1965-67	47	12	3	0	4	2
McLEAN, Peter	East Fife	Reading	Bath C	1953-54	15	0	0	0	0	0
McLEAN, Thomas	Lochgelly	Blackburn R	Barrow	1935-37	21	1	1	0	0	0
McMILLAN, John	Dumbarton	Cardiff C	Margate	1961-63	20	1	2	0	1	0
McMULLAN, David	Belfast	Distillery (Belfast)		1929-30	19	0	0	0	0	0
McNEIL, Richard	Melton Mowbray	Leicester C	Northampton T	1966-67	32	11	1	0	1	1

Player	Birthplace	From	To	Played	League App	League Gls	FA Cup App	FA Cup Gls	FL Cup App	FL Cup Gls
McNICHOL, James	Glasgow	Brentford	Torquay U	1984-86	87	10	5	0	6	0
McPHERSON, Angus	Glasgow	Torquay U	Glasgow Rangers	1989-	33	8	6	0	4	2
MAIN, Ian	Swindon	Glasgow Rangers (L)		1990	11	1	0	0	0	0
MAKIN, James†	Bury	Gloucester C	Accrington S	1978-82	78	0	1	0	4	0
MARKER, Nicholas	Budleigh Salterton	Apprentice	Plymouth A	1981-87	196/6	3	8	0	11	1
MASON, Samuel	Feldhouse	Gillingham	Retired	1927-30	53	2	4	2	0	0
MASSEY, Richard	Selsdon	YTS	Kettering T	1985-88	22/6	1	3	0	0	0
MATHIESON, Allan	Belfast	Luton T	New Brighton	1922-23	26	4	3	0	0	0
MATTHEWS, Alfred	Bristol	Bristol C	Plymouth A	1922-26	138	13	15	4	0	0
MERRIE, Alexander	Saltcoats	Aldershot	Workington	1936	4	2	0	0	0	0
MICKLEWRIGHT, Andrew	Birmingham	Swindon T	Nuneaton B	1959-60	38	11	2	0	0	0
MILES, Idris	Cardiff	Clapton O	Worcester C	1937-38	10	0	0	0	0	0
MILLAR, James	Coatbridge	Benburb	Retired	1938-39	9	3	0	0	0	0
MILLER, Charles	Bellshill	Plymouth A	Retired	1926-36	274	0	23	0	0	0
MILLER, James	Scotland	Kilmarnock	Galston	1937	1	0	0	0	0	0
MILLER, Kevin	Falmouth	Newquay		1989-	31	0	4	0	0	0
MILTON, Simon	London	Ipswich T (L)	Ipswich T	1987	2	3	0	0	0	0
MITCHELL, Anthony	London	Leatherhead	Sutton U	1978-82	60	0	3	0	3	0
MITCHELL, Arnold	Rawmarsh	Notts C	Taunton T	1952-66	495	44	18	2	4	0
MITCHELL, Robert	Campbel Town	Third Lanark		1951-52	3	0	0	0	0	0
MITCHELL, Ronald	Barrhead	Glasgow Celtic	Third Lanark	1949-50	2	0	0	0	0	0
MITTEN, John	Manchester	Plymouth A	Retired	1968-71	96/4	17	7	1	9	1
MITTON, James	Brierfield	Stockport C	Nelson	1921-23	72	2	5	0	0	0
MITTON, John†	Ramsbottom	Southern League	Sunderland	1920-21	11	0	0	0	0	0
MOLYNEUX, Frederick	Wallasey	Plymouth A	Tranmere R	1970-71	2	0	0	0	0	0
MORGAN, Trevor	Forest Gate	Bristol C	Bristol R	1984-85	31	9	0	0	2	0
MORRIN, Anthony	Manchester	Barrow	Stockport C	1971-77	180/2	15	4	0	10	0

Exeter City, 1933-4. Back row (left to right): Reg Clarke, Dick Hughes, Arthur Davies, Reg Loram (trainer), Charlie Miller, Jack Angus. Front row: Jack Scott, Stan Risdon, Stan Hurst, Frank Wrightson, Jack Barnes, Harry Webb.

361

Player	Birthplace	From	To	Played	League App	League Gls	FA Cup App	FA Cup Gls	FL Cup App	FL Cup Gls
MORRIS, Stephen	Bristol	Bristol C	Bideford	1969-72	61/11	2	6	0	0	0
MORTON, Geoffrey	Aston	Fulham		1954-55	6	0	0	0	0	0
MOXHAM, Graham	Exeter	Bideford	Bideford	1975-76	4/2	0	1	0	0/1	0
MUNKS, David	Sheffield	Swindon T		1975-76	20	0	0	0	0	0
MURPHY, Edward	Hamilton	Barnsley	Bridgwater T	1952-56	94	13	6	3	0	0
MURPHY, James	Barrhead	Stirling A	Retired	1949-50	2	0	0	0	0	0
MURRAY, James	Denny	Reading	Retired	1923-25	20	1	0	0	0	0
MURRAY, James	Glasgow	Shawfield Jnrs	Retired	1945-47	1	0	4	0	0	0
MUSKER, Russell	Liverpool	Bristol C (L)	Bristol C	1983	6	0	0	0	0	0
MUSTARD, William	South Shields	Bath C	Bideford	1946-47	14	0	0	0	0	0
MYERS, Colin	Ecclesfield	Queen's Park R	Hartlepools U	1925-26	19	3	1	0	0	0
NASH, Robert	London	Queen's Park R	Retired	1966-67	1	0	0	0	0	0
NEALE, John	Barnstaple	Barnstaple T	Torquay U	1972-75	51/14	5	1	0	3	0
NEVILLE, Stephen	Walthamstow	Southampton	Sheffield U	1978-80	90/3	22	3	1	8	3
		Sheffield U	Bristol C	1982-84	89/3	27	5	2	4	0
		Bristol C		1988-	80	28	7	1	9	2
NEWMAN, Frank	Nuneaton	Port Vale	Halifax T	1921-23	42	1	2	0	0	0
		Halifax T	Yeovil T	1924-27	16	1	2	0	0	0
NEWMAN, John	Hereford	Plymouth A	Manager	1967-71	91/1	1	9	0	7	0
NICHOLLS, John	Wolverhampton	Cardiff C	Worcester C	1957-59	56	23	1	0	0	0
NISBET, Gordon	Wallsend-on-Tyne	Plymouth A	Retired	1987-88	12	0	0	0	2	0
NORTHCOTT, George	Torquay	Torquay U	Cheltenham T	1963-64	1	0	0	0	0	0
NUTE, Stephen	Saltash	Apprentice	Bideford	1978-81	5	0	2	0	0	0
O'CONNELL, Brendon	London	Portsmouth	Burnley	1986-88	73/8	19	3	0	3	2
O'CONNOR, Mark	Rochdale	Queen's Park R (L)	Queen's Park R	1983-84	38	1	2	0	1	0
O'KEEFE, Vincent	Birmingham	AP Leamington	Torquay U	1978-80	53	0	3	0	11	0
OLIVER, Kenneth	Loughborough	Derby C	Retired	1958-60	92	0	4	0	0	0
OLSSON, Paul	Hull	Hull C	Scarborough	1986-88	38/5	2	0/1	0	2	0

Player	Birthplace	From	To	Played	League App	League Gls	FA Cup App	FA Cup Gls	FL Cup App	FL Cup Gls
O'SHEA, Daniel	Kennington	Arsenal	Southend U	1984-85	45	2	2	0	2	0
OWEN, Willian	Liverpool	Newport C	Barry T	1946-47	20	9	1	0	0	0
OWEN, William	Manchester	Reading	Newport C	1936-37	24	6	3	2	0	0
OWENS, John	Llanwonet	Pontypridd	Bournemouth & BA	1953-55	14	0	0	0	0	0
PACKER, Norman	Ynysybul	Pontypridd	Bridgwater T	1955-61	18	0	0	0	0	0
PARKER, Graham	Coventry	Lincoln C	Torquay U	1969-74	180/1	12	5	0	7	1
PARKER, Martin	Exeter	Local amateur		1988-	0/1	0	0	0	0	0
PARKER, William	Liverpool	Swindon T	Retired	1953-54	18	2	0	0	0	0
PARKHILL, James	Belfast	Cliftonville	Taunton T	1963-64	1	0	0	0	0	0
PARKIN, Thomas	Newcastle	Durham C	Merthyr T	1926-28	8	1	1	0	0	0
PARR, Stephen	Preston	Liverpool	Rochdale	1955-56	8	0	2	0	0	0
PARSONS, Jacob	Whitehaven	Accrington S	Thames	1930-31	3	0	0	0	0	0
PATRICK, Roy	Overseal	Southampton	Burton A	1963-65	50	0	1	0	0	0
PAVEY, Sydney	Taunton	Taunton T		1922-26	27	0	1	0	0	0
PEAPELL, Dennis	Swindon	Swindon T	Bideford	1965-66	23/1	1	0	0	1	0
PEARSON, IAN	Leeds	Millwall	Bideford	1978-81	67/2	10	9	2	4	1
PHILLIPS, Leighton	Briton Ferry	Swansea C	Retired	1983	10	0	0	0	0	0
PHILLIPS, Stephen	Edmonton	Peterborough U (L)	Peterborough U	1987-88	5/1	1	0	0	0	0
PHILLIPSON-MASTERS, Forbes	Boscombe	Southampton (L)	Southampton	1976-77	6	0	0	0	0	0
		Bristol C (L)	Bristol C	1985	5/2	1	0	0	0	0
PHOENIX, Arthur	Patricroft	Barnsley	Wigan B	1926-29	52	9	2	0	0	0
PHOENIX, Eric	Manchester	Gillingham	Dover T	1956-57	5	0	0	0	0	0
PHOENIX, Peter	Manchester	Rochdale	Southport	1963-64	15	1	2	0	0	0
PIERCE, Barry	Liverpool	York C	Salisbury C	1962-63	28	3	1	0	0	0
PINKNEY, Alan	Battersea	St Luke's College	Crystal P	1967-69	7	1	2	0	0	0
PLEAT, David	Nottingham	Shrewsbury T	Peterborough T	1968-70	66/2	13	6/1	0	5	0
PLUMB, Richard	Swindon	Charlton A	Retired	1972-73	59	17	2	0	6	2
POLLARD, Henry	Liverpool	Sheffield W	Rochdale	1936-39	4	0	0	0	0	0

Exeter City, 1968-9. Back row (left to right): F.Broome (manager), J.Blain, P.Bullock, K.Harvey, P.Shearing, M.Balson, J.Kirkham, D.Pleat, B.Edwards (trainer). Front: J.Corr, A.Banks, J.Mitten, J.Newman, C.Smyth, C.Crawford, K.Whatling.

Player	Birthplace	From	To	Played	League App	League Gls	FA Cup App	FA Cup Gls	FL Cup App	FL Cup Gls
POLLARD, Robert	Plattbridge	Plank Lane	Queen's Park R	1920-29	246	0	23	0	0	0
POOL, Alexander	Annan	Bristol C	Stalybridge C	1926-29	74	3	9	0	0	0
POPE, Stanley	Tiverton	Tiverton (Am)	Torquay U	1936-38	26	10	5	1	0	0
PORTEOUS, John	Motherwell	Plymouth A	Truro C	1956-57	40	0	1	0	0	0
POTTER, Albert	Exeter	Pinhoe (Am)	Wigan B	1922-27	89	3	5	0	0	0
POULTER, Henry	Sunderland	Sunderland (Am)	Retired	1932-36	50	33	4	3	0	0
POWELL, Kenneth	Chester	Cardiff C	Bristol R	1948-51	22	1	1	0	0	0
PRATT, Raymond	Barry Port	Merthyr T	Chard T	1979-86	126/46	61	2	3	6	1
PRIDDLE, Sean	Hammersmith	Crewe A	Brentford	1986-87	18	1	1	0	1	0
PRIESTLEY, Gerald	Halifax	Nottingham F	Grimsby T	1953-55	42	6	1	0	0	0
PRINCE, Francis	Penarth	Bristol R	Retired	1980-82	27/4	2	1	0	3	0
PUGH, Stephen	Wolverhampton	Torquay U	Weymouth	1986-87	23/1	1	1	0	2	0
PULLAR, Robert	Darlington	Bristol C	Yeovil T	1924-27	103	2	9	0	0	0
PULLAR, David	London	Portsmouth	Crewe A	1979-83	124/6	22	7	3	12	2
PURCELL, George	Sheffield	Swindon T	Gillingham	1926-32	227	51	22	12	0	0
PYM, Richard	Topsham	Pre-war	Bolton W	1920-21	39	0	1	0	0	0
RANDALL, Oswald	Thatcham	Swindon T		1926-27	14	0	0	0	0	0
RANDELL, Colin	Skewen	Plymouth A	Plymouth A	1977-79	78	4	5	2	5	0
RAPLEY, Peter	Portsmouth	Portsmouth (Am)	Cambridge U	1957-60	10	4	0	0	0	0
REDWOOD, Barry	Torquay	Apprentice	Retired	1964	1	0	0	0	1	0
REES, Graham	Pontypridd	Pontypridd YC(Am)	Yeovil T	1954-66	345	85	17	6	8	1
REGAN, Douglas	Yeovil	Royal Navy (Am)	Bristol C	1946-52	206	63	18	7	0	0
REW, Roy	Belfast	Seamills (Am)	Glastonbury	1948-50	4	1	0	0	0	0
RICH, Leonard	Camelford	Luton T	Stockport C	1938-39	32	4	1	0	0	0
RIDING, Alan	Tynemouth	Local amateur	Yeovil T	1964-66	1	0	1	0	0	0
RIGBY, James	Bolton	Pre-war	Retired	1920-23	60	0	6	0	0	0
RILEY, Harold	Oldham	Northampton T	Retired	1938-45	26	9	1	1	0	0
RISDON, Stanley	Exeter	Local amateur	Brighton & HA	1932-36	35	1	0	0	0	0

Dick Walton

Ray Iggleden

Charlie Vowles

Dick Gaskell

Eli Bullock

J.Coleburne

Horace Clarke

Tommy Edge

Alex Christie

Bob Pullan

A.V. Green

Edwin Bell

Jasper Green

Jimmy Mitton

366

Player	Birthplace	From	To	Played	League App	League Gls	FA Cup App	FA Cup Gls	FL Cup App	FL Cup Gls
ROBERTS, Dean	Mexborough	Bolton W	Heavitree U	1986-87	23/2	7	1	0	1	0
ROBERTS, Lee	Market Drayton	Shrewsbury T		1977-83	131/11	12	12	2	10	0
ROBERTS, C Leslie	Halesowen	Manchester C	Crystal P	1932-32	11	4	0	0	0	0
ROBERTS, Paul	London	Aldershot	Southend U	1988-89	3	0	0	0	0	0
ROBERTS, Philip	Cardiff	Hereford U	Chard T	1979-82	112/2	0	12	3	9	0
ROBERTSON, Lammie	Paisley	Brighton & HA	Leicester C	1974-77	132/1	25	3	0	6/1	3
ROBERTSON, Stuart	Glasgow	West Bromwich A	Cardiff C	1982	5/1	0	0	0	0	0
ROBINSON, Charles	Pegswood	Blackpool	Gillingham	1931-33	8	0	2	0	0	0
ROBINSON, David	Exeter	Whipton (Am)	Oldham A	1954-59	16	4	0	0	0	0
ROBINSON, Reginald	Scunthorpe	Huddersfield T	Watford	1935-36	30	1	1	0	0	0
ROBSON, Mark	Newham	YTS	Tottenham H	1986-87	26	7	2	0	0	0
ROGERS, Lee	Doncaster	Bristol C		1988-	58/3	0	1	0	5	0
ROGERS, Martyn	Bristol	Bath C	Tiverton T	1979-84	128/3	5	9	1	7	0
ROGERS, Peter	Bristol	Bath C	Weymouth	1979-84	194/11	39	12	2	9	1
ROSE, Kenneth	Eckington	Chesterfield	Rochdale	1952-53	11	3	0	0	0	0
ROUGHTON, George	Manchester	Manchester U	Manager	1945-46	0	0	4	0	0	0
ROWAN, Barry	Willesden	Plymouth A	Retired	1970-73	76/5	14	4	1	1	0
ROWBOTHAM, Darren	Cardiff	Plymouth A		1987-	96/4	42	8	5	9	6
ROWE, Ben	Hull	Bristol C (Am)		1989-	4/6	2	0/1	0	0	0
ROWE, Stanley	Exeter	Local amateur	Bridgwater T	1947-55	142	0	11	0	0	0
ROWLANDS, John	Liverpool	Torquay U	Stockport C	1969	1	0	0	0	0	0
ROY, Andrew	Tillicoultry	Dunfermline A	Alloa A	1949	2	0	0	0	0	0
RUTLEY, Peter	Exeter	Apprentice	Leicester C	1962-65	16	0	0	0	2	0
RUTTER, John	Warrington	Bournemouth & BA	Stockport C	1974-76	31/1	1	2	0	2	0
RYAN, James P	Rhyl	Hastings U	Dover	1966-67	20	5	0	0	0	0
SALTER, Kenneth	Cullompton	Cullompton (Am)	Bideford	1949-52	1	0	0	0	0	0
SAMUELS, Leslie	Oldham	Burnley	Wrexham	1953-54	12	1	2	1	0	0
SANDERS, James	Marlborough	Rochdale	Retired	1962-64	20	1	1	0	0	0

Player	Birthplace	From	To	Played	League App	League Gls	FA Cup App	FA Cup Gls	FL Cup App	FL Cup Gls
SAXTON, Robert	Bagby	Plymouth A	Manager	1975-79	92	3	8	0	7	0
SCOTT, Anthony	Huntingdon	Bournemouth & BA	Retired	1972-74	51	2	0	0	4	0
SCOTT, John	Sunderland	Northampton T	Hartlepools U	1932-36	133	20	6	1	0	0
SCOTT, Thomas	Newcastle	Norwich C	Hartlepools U	1934-37	56	16	5	2	0	0
SELLS, Charles	Paddington	Wealdstone	Guildford	1962-63	14	3	0	0	0	0
SETTERS, Maurice	Honiton	Local amateur	West Bromwich A	1952-55	10	0	1	0	0	0
SHADWELL, John	Bury	Manchester C	Retired	1936-46	85	2	6	0	0	0
SHANKS, Robert	Cowpen Bewley	Huddersfield T	Stockport C	1929-31	41	1	1	0	0	0
SHARPLES, Brian	Bradford	Birmingham C	Retired	1968-71	68	4	6	0	3	0
SHAW, John	Stirling	Bristol C	Gloucester C	1985-88	109	0	6	0	8	0
SHAW, Peter	Northolt	Charlton A	Gillingham	1981-82	3	0	1	0	0	0
SHEARING, Peter	Uxbridge	Portsmouth	Plymouth A	1964-66	80	0	2	0	2	0
		Plymouth A	Bristol R	1968-71	79	0	8	0	7	0
SHEFFIELD, Alexander	Nottingham	Mansfield T	Bristol C	1928-30	24	0	0	0	0	0
SHELTON, George	Sheffield	Sheffield W	New Brighton	1922-26	75	8	10	4	0	0
SHEPHERD, Peter	Edrington	Local amateur	Ottery St Mary	1982-83	1	0	0	0	0	0
SHIELDS, Robert	Newbiggin	Huddersfield T	Brentford	1920-21	19	4	1	0	0	0
SHORT, Alan	Tamerton Foliot	Tamerton (Am)	Yeovil T	1950-51	5	1	0	0	0	0
SIMPSON, Dennis	Coventry	Reading	Exmouth T	1955-57	30	4	0	0	0	0
SIMPSON, Noël	Mansfield	Coventry C	Retired	1957-58	33	0	0	0	0	0
SIMS, John	Belper	Notts C	Plymouth A	1978-79	33/1	11	0	0	3	0
		Torquay U	Torquay U (P-m)	1984-85	23/2	6	2	1	2	0
SINGLETON, Bernard	Conisbrough	Wolves	Yeovil T	1946-54	177	1	12	1	0	0
SMART, Richard	Bishop Auckland	Stanley U	Bideford	1946-52	103	33	9	5	0	0
SMELT, Lee	Edmonton	Cardiff C (L)	Cardiff C	1985	13	0	0	0	0	0
SMELT, Tom	Rotherham	Accrington S	Chesterfield	1924-25	5	1	1	1	0	0
SMITH, Archibald	Larkhall	Hamilton A	Barnstaple T	1948-52	113	43	12	9	0	0
SMITH, Charles	Aberdeen	Local amateur	Yeovil T	1936-37	5	0	0	0	0	0

Exeter City at the start of 1977-8, when the Grecians were newly-promoted to the Third Division. Back row (left to right): Keith Ford, Keith Bowker, Harry Holman, Bobby Saxton (manager). Middle row: Lammie Robertson, John Templeman, John Baugh, Richard Key, Phil Howe, Bobby Hodge, Peter Hatch. Seated: Jack Edwards (coach), Nicky Jennings, Graham Weeks, John Hore, Tony Kellow, Alan Beer, Tommy Long (trainer). On ground: Paul Smythe, Roy Ireland.

369

Player	Birthplace	From	To	Played	League App	League Gls	FA Cup App	FA Cup Gls	FL Cup App	FL Cup Gls
SMITH, Frederick	Darlington	Darlington	Gillingham	1936-37	24	4	3	2	0	0
SMITH, Keith	Sheffield	Cambridge U	Alfreton T	1988-89	2/13	2	0	0	0	0
SMITH, Kevin	St Paul's Cray		Torquay U	1984-85	22/4	2	1	0	0	0
SMITH, Nigel	Bath	Bristol C (L)	Bristol C	1984-85	1	0	0	0	0	0
SMITH, Roger	Welwyn G'den City	Tottenham H	Ashford T	1966-67	6	3	0	1	0	0
SMITH, William	Glasgow	Norwich C	Stenhousemuir	1934-35	13	0	0	0	0	0
SMOUT, John	Newtown	Crystal P	Retired	1966-68	75	0	6	0	2	0
SMYTH, Cecil	Belfast	Distillery	Torquay U	1962-69	270/3	1	16	0	14	1
SMYTH, Peter	Derry	Albion R	Southport	1950-51	5	1	0	0	0	0
SOUTHCOMBE, Roy	South Molton	Bideford (Am)	Retired	1938-39	2	0	0	0	0	0
SOUTHWAY, Leonard	Bristol	Bristol C	Aberdare	1922-23	15	0	0	2	0	0
SPARROW, John	Bethnal Green	Chelsea	Retired	1980-83	62/1	3	4	0	2	0
SPIERS, George	Belfast	Crusaders (Belfast)	Retired	1963-64	5	0	0	0	0	0
SQUIRES, Charles	Mardy	Mardy	Torquay U	1922	2	0	0	0	0	0
SQUIRES, Robert	Selby	Doncaster R	Weymouth	1949-50	1	0	0	0	0	0
STACEY, Stephen	Bristol	Bristol C	Retired	1971-73	57/2	0	3	1	2	0
STEELE, Hedley	Barnsley	Local amateur	Dorchester T	1974-76	6/1	1	0	0	1	0
STAFFORD, Clive	Ipswich	Colchester U (L)	Colchester U	1990	2	0	2	0	0	0
STEWART, Robert	Loanhead	Oldham A	Wigan B	1921-22	25	0	4	2	0	0
STIFFLE, Nelson	India	Bournemouth & BA	Coventry C	1958-60	94	17	0	0	0	0
STIMPSON, George	Gillbrook	Rhyl	Mansfield T	1936-37	29	0	3	0	0	0
STOREY, James	Rowlands Green	Newcastle U	Bournemouth & BA	1953-54	9	0	2	0	0	0
STOREY, William	Jarrow	Swindon T	Gateshead	1937-38	5	2	0	0	0	0
STREETS, Stanley	Newark	Clapton O	Retired	1928-29	9	2	0	0	0	0
STUCKEY, Bruce	Torquay	Apprentice	Sunderland	1965-67	37/2	6	0	2	2	0
SULLIVAN, Derek	Newport	Cardiff C	Newport C	1961-62	44	0	2	0	1	0
SUMMERFIELD, Kevin	Walsall	Plymouth A (L)	Plymouth A	1990-	4	0	0	0	0	0
SUTHERLAND, Henry	Salford	Leeds U	Bournemouth & BA	1947-48	14	3	0	0	0	0

Exeter City, 1964-5. Back row (left to right): K.Harvey, B.Stuckey, D.Grace, L.MacDonald, R.Patrick, P.Davis, A.Barnett, P.Shearing, W.Carter, B.Fulton, D.Anderson. Middle: S.Clark (groundsman), A.Mitchell, A.Banks, B.Redwood, P.Rutley, E.Welsh, C.Smyth, D.Curtis, A.Thorne, D.Hancock, A.Riding, G.Rees, G.Ley. Front: Jack Edwards (manager), L.Kerslake (director), F.Dart (director), R.Rose (chairman), G.Gillin (director), K.Honey (secretary), F.Elston (commercial manager).

Player	Birthplace	From	To	Played	League App	League Gls	FA Cup App	FA Cup Gls	FL Cup App	FL Cup Gls
SUTHERLEY, Charles	Chudleigh	Chudleigh (Am)	Penzance	1934-46	9	1	0	0	0	0
SWORD, Alan	Michley	Newcastle U	Bridgwater T	1953-57	9	4	0	0	0	0
TAYLOR, George	Burtonwood	Skelmersdale U	Skelmersdale U	1920-21	6	0	0	0	0	0
TAYLOR, James	Ashton-under-Lyne	Droylesden	Southport	1928-28	2	0	0	0	0	0
TAYLOR, Peter	Southend	Maidstone U	Maidstone U	1983	8	0	2	0	0	0
TAYLOR, Shaun	Plymouth	Bideford		1986-	155	13	8	0	10	0
TEMPLEMAN, John	Yapton	Brighton & HA	Swindon T	1974-79	205/1	7	7	1	17	0
THOMAS, Alwyn	Tonypandy	Torquay U		1929-30	1	0	0	0	0	0
THOMAS, W Keith	Oswestry	Plymouth A	Hereford U	1956-57	43	6	1	0	0	0
THOMAS, Patrick	Sidmouth	Sidmouth T (Am)	Sidmouth T	1982-83	0/1	0	0	0	0	0
THOMAS, Peter	Cardiff	Cardiff C	Newport C	1954-56	30	4	0	0	0	0
THOMPSON, Aldred	Durham	Hartlepools	Hartlepools U	1936-37	3	0	0	0	0	0
THOMPSON, George	Maltby	Huddersfield T	Rochdale	1946-48	63	4	4	0	0	0
THOMPSON, James	Chadderton	Oldham A	Rochdale	1958-61	105	10	5	0	2	1
THOMPSON, Kenneth	Ipswich	Ipswich T	Yeovil T	1966-67	38/1	1	2	0	4	0
THOMSON, Charles	Perth	Brighton & HA	Retired	1939-46	0	0	4	0	0	0
THORNE, Adrian	Brighton	Plymouth A	Leyton O	1963-65	41	8	0	0	0	0
TICKELL, Roy	Bootle	Tranmere R	Southport	1945-47	0	0	3	1	0	0
TIERNEY, Cornelius	Kilbirnie	Guildford C		1934-35	18	1	0	0	0	0
TIERNEY, Patrick	Renfrew	Vale of Clyde	Crystal P	1936-38	29	0	2	0	0	0
TINSLEY, Colin	Redcar	Darlington	Luton T	1961-63	56	1	1	0	1	0
TOLCHARD, Jeffrey	Torquay	Torquay U	Loughborough U	1965-66	1	0	0	0	0	0
TOPPING, Henry	Kearsley	Manchester C	New Brighton	1937-38	1	0	0	0	0	0
TOWNSEND, Thomas	Babbacombe	Torquay U	Torquay U	1922	7	0	0	0	0	0
TUPLING, Stephen	Wensleydale	Cardiff C (L)	Cardiff C	1989	8/1	1	0	0	0	0
TURNBULL, Alexander	Droylsden	Droylesden	Retired	1938-39	13	1	0	0	0	0
URMSON, Fred	Little Hulton	Tranmere R	Stalybridge C	1936-37	10	1	0	0	0	0
VARCO, Percival	Fowey	Norwich C	Brighton & HA	1930-32	81	41	9	5	0	0

Members of the City Supporters' Club and Grecians Association, pictured in 1966 working on levelling the site of their new offices at St James' Park.

Player	Birthplace	From	To	Played	League App	League Gls	FA Cup App	FA Cup Gls	FL Cup App	FL Cup Gls
VAUGHAN, Glyn	Oldham	Oldham A	Peterborough U	1946-48	6	6	0	0	0	0
VAUGHAN, William	Willenhall	Burton T	Merthyr T	1927-28	33	9	6	5	0	0
VINEY, Keith	Portsmouth	Portsmouth	Torrington	1982-89	270	8	12	1	15	1
VINNICOMBE, Chris	Exeter	Trainee	Glasgow Rangers	1988-89	35/4	1	0	0	5	1
VOWLES, Charles	Bristol	Army amateur	Barrow	1920-23	64	20	4	0	0	0
WADE, Edward	Blackpool	New Brighton	Retired	1928-29	9	5	0	0	0	0
WAINWRIGHT, Thomas	Sheffield	Cardiff C	Tunbridge Wells	1927-28	13	0	0	0	0	0
WALKER, Bruce	West Woodhay	Bradford C	Hereford U	1969-70	21/2	2	1/1	0	2	0
WALKER, James	Rutherglen	Plymouth A	Wigan B	1926-27	12	2	1	0	2	0
WALKER, Stephen	Sheffield	Sheffield U	Minehead (P-c)	1938-50	141	3	12	5	0	0
WALLACE, Kenneth	Islington	Hereford U		1973-74	8/2	1	1	0	2	2
WALLACE, Robert	Newcastle	Plymouth A	Died 14 Sept 1938	1937-38	38	0	2	0	0	0
WALLER, Charles	Plymouth	Army amateur	Army amateur	1920-21	3	0	0	0	0	0
WALSH, Mark	Preston	New Zealand	Retired	1985-86	0/1	0	0	0	0	0
WALTER, David	Barnstaple	Bideford	Plymouth A	1988-90	44	0	2	0	7	0
WALTERS, Thomas	Merthyr Tydfil	Crystal P	Torquay U	1933	6	4	0	0	0	0
WALTON, Richard	Hull	Leyton O	Tonbridge	1951-56	135	6	1	0	0	0
WARD, Warren	Plymstock	Lincoln C (L)	Lincoln C	1986	14	3	0	0	0	0
WARDLE, George	Kimblesworth	Middlesbrough	Cardiff C	1939-47	38	6	3	0	0	0
WARREN, Derek	Colyton Raleigh	Local amateur	Retired	1948-52	55	0	8	0	0	0
WARREN, Henry	Newhall	Blackpool	Merthyr T	1927-28	1	0	0	0	0	0
WATERMAN, Derek	Guildford	Guildford C	Worcester C	1957-58	4	0	1	0	0	0
WATSON, Andrew	Huddersfield	Huddersfield T	Mossley	1986-88	41/1	1	2/1	0	2	0
WATSON, James	Motherwell	Luton T		1921-22	10	0	2	0	0	0
WEBB, Harold	London	Fulham	Coventry C	1933-35	69	5	3	0	0	0
WEBBER, Andrew	Port Talbot	Swansea C		1985-86	1	0	0	0	0	0
WEBSTER, Simon	Earl Shilton	Tottenham H (L)	Tottenham H	1983-84	26	1	3	0	0	0
WEEKS, Graham	Exeter	Apprentice	Bournemouth & BA	1976-78	49/4	1	3	0	4	0

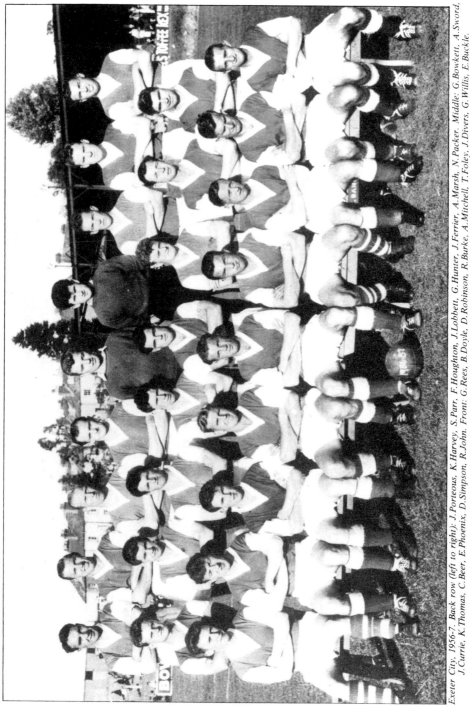

Exeter City, 1956-7. Back row (left to right): J.Porteous, K.Harvey, S.Parr, F.Houghton, J.Lobbett, G.Hunter, J.Ferrier, A.Marsh, N.Packer. Middle: G.Bowkett, A.Sword, J.Currie, K.Thomas, C.Beer, E.Phoenix, D.Simpson, R.John. Front: G.Rees, B.Doyle, D.Robinson, R.Burke, A.Mitchell, T.Foley, J.Divers, G.Willis, E.Buckle.

Player	Birthplace	From	To	Played	League App	League Gls	FA Cup App	FA Cup Gls	FL Cup App	FL Cup Gls
WELSBY, Arthur	North Ashton	Sunderland	Stockport C	1932-34	39	8	2	0	0	0
WELSH, Eric	Belfast	Distillery	Carlisle U	1959-65	105	19	4	0	5	0
WHATLING, Keith	Worlingworth	Ipswich T	Retired	1967-69	19/3	3	0	0	2	0
WHELAN, Hugh	Airdrie	Bradford C		1923-24	2	0	0	0	0	0
WHITEHEAD, Clive	Birmingham	Portsmouth		1989-	36/2	5	6	0	7	0
WHITESIDE, Roy	Belfast	Portadown	Scunthorpe U	1955-56	3	1	0	0	0	0
WHITLOW, Frederick	Bristol	Charlton A	Cardiff C	1931-34	83	61	3	1	0	0
WHITNALL, Brian	Doncaster	Scunthorpe U	Bath C	1958-62	36	0	2	0	3	0
WILKINS, Kenneth	Salford	Southampton	Southampton	1951-52	3	0	0	0	0	0
WILKINSON, Ernest	Chesterfield	Arsenal	Rochdale	1966-68	59/1	0	2	0	6	0
WILKINSON, Harold	Sunderland	Chelsea	Colchester U	1950-51	1	0	0	0	0	0
WILKINSON, John	Middlewich	Poole T	Wellington T	1959-61	48	26	4	1	0	0
WILLIAMS, Alvan	Penmon	Bradford	Retired	1960-61	19	1	1	0	0	0
WILLIAMS, Evan	Swansea	Cardiff C	Aldershot	1954-55	1	0	0	0	0	0
WILLIAMS, George	Netley	Southampton	Retired	1921-22	11	1	0	0	0	0
WILLIAMS, Osher	Stockton	Southampton	Stockport C	1978-79	2/1	0	0	0	0/1	0
WILLIAMS, Paul	Newton Abbot	Bury	Bath C	1985-88	8/10	1	0	0	0	0
WILLIAMS, Peter	Plymouth	Plymouth (Am)	Retired	1960-61	1	0	0	0	0	0
WILLIAMS, Roderick	Newport	Norwich C	Reading	1936-37	41	29	5	7	0	0
WILLIS, George	Newcastle	Plymouth A	Taunton T	1956-58	26	3	0	0	0	0
WILSON, Glen	Newcastle	Brighton & HA(P-m)	Retired	1960-62	36	2	0	0	3	0
WILSON, Henry	Exeter	Local amateur	Retired	1920-23	4	0	0	0	0	0
WILSON, Robert	Birmingham	Cardiff C	Retired	1970-76	205	0	7	0	14	0
WILSON, Thomas	Ayr	Reading	Bridgwater	1957-58	22	2	1	0	0	0
WINGATE, John	Budleigh Salterton	Dawlish T (Am)	Bournemouth & BA	1966-74	187/16	32	10	2	8/1	1
		Bournemouth & BA	Retired	1975-76	44/1	2	1	2	4	0
WITHEY, Graham	Bristol	Cheltenham T		1988-89	5/2	2	0	0	0	0
WOOD, Francis	Manchester	Shrewsbury T	Rochdale	1953	8	0	0/1	0	0	0

Nobby Clarke

Arthur Phoenix

Frank Wrightson

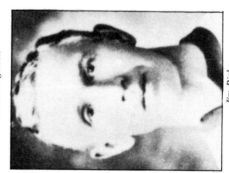

Jim Rigby

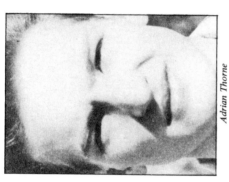

Adrian Thorne

Stan McEwan

Jack Barnes

Dick Baugh

Player	Birthplace	From	To	Played	League App	League Gls	FA Cup App	FA Cup Gls	FL Cup App	FL Cup Gls
WOOD, Jeffrey	Harlow	Colchester U	Finland	1984-85	33	0	2	0	2	0
WOODWARD, William	West Auckland	Spennymoor U	Bath C	1931-32	7	2	1	1	0	0
WORTHINGTON, Fred	Manchester	Leicester C	Oldham A	1955-56	16	1	0	0	0	0
WRIGHT, Raymond	Pontefract	Wolves	Yeovil T	1946-48	56	11	3	0	0	0
WRIGHT, William	Seaforth	Tranmere R	Huddersfield T	1920	17	9	0	0	0	0
WRIGHTSON, Frank	Shildon	Fulham	Chester	1933-35	71	25	3	1	0	0
YOUNG, Archibald	Twechar	Bristol R	Gillingham	1936-37	19	0	1	0	0	0
YOUNG, Richard	Nottingham	Southend U		1989-	29/13	10	0/1	0	1/1	1

Exeter City, 1957-8. Back row (left to right): D.Buterworth, not known, E.Calland, P.Rapley, D.Churns, N.Packer, A.Bell, G.Hunter, D.Hill, T.Wilson, K.Harvey, J.Currie, A.Mitchell. Middle: H.Hanford (trainer), S.Clarke (groundsman), D.Waterman, T.Atkins, not known, G.Rees, D.Robinson, L.MacDonald, N.Simpson, M.Cleverley, T.Skuse, R.John, T.Foley, F.Houghton (assistant trainer-coach). Front: J.Rigby (director), A.W.Crawshaw (director), A.S.Line (chairman), S.H.Thomas (president), A.Ford (director), J.Watts (director), G.Gilbert (secretary).

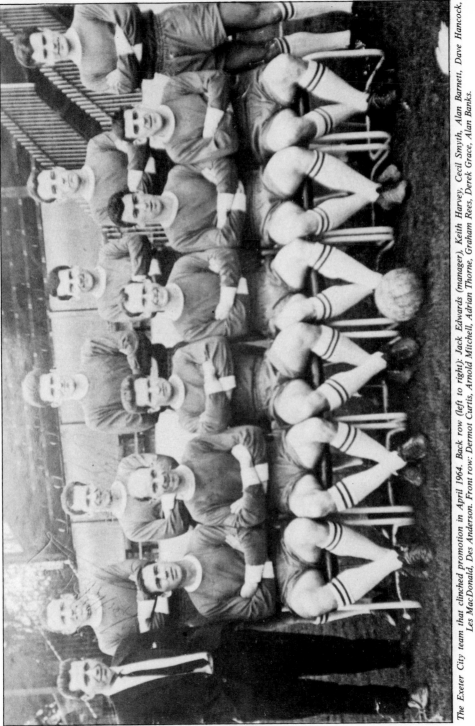

The Exeter City team that clinched promotion in April 1964. Back row (left to right): Jack Edwards (manager), Keith Harvey, Cecil Smyth, Alan Barnett, Dave Hancock, Les MacDonald, Des Anderson. Front row: Dermot Curtis, Arnold Mitchell, Adrian Thorne, Graham Rees, Derek Grace, Alan Banks.

SUBSCRIBERS

4 Alex Wilson
(In Memoriam)
5 Mrs G Wilson
6 Mr & Mrs Alex Wilson
7 Garth Dykes
8 Maurice Golesworthy
9 J A Harris
10 Raymond Shaw
11 A N Other
12 K P Wood
13 John Lathan
14 Derek Hyde
15 Harry Kay
16 William James Grier
17 Dave Parine
18 Roberto J Gamble
19 David Earnshaw
20 Errick Peterson
21 Peter Lunn
22 R K Shoesmith
23 Douglas Lamming
24 Harald Löhr
25 B H Standish
26 Moira & Frederick
Furness
27 John Motson
28 Duncan Watt
29 Denzil Lush
30 P H Whitehead
31 D T Bryant
32 Sports Marketing
(Australia)
33 Brian H Hobbs
34 Ian Willott
35 Chris Minchin
36 Gordon Small
37 David Downs
38 Angus W Rodger
39 Colin Cameron
40 Andrew Till
41 Paul H Bannister
42 Richard Shore
43 Giles Ashman
44 J Ringrose

45 Douglas Bidgood
46 David J Godfrey
47 Lars-Olof Wendler
48 Gilbert Monnereau
49 John Treleven
50 J Mulrennan
51 P Marks
52 Myles W Sutherland
53 David Keats
54 Gareth M Davies
55 J D M Whitaker
56 Nick House
57 Andrew & Janet
Waterman
58 Kevin C Wyatt
59 Paul Snape
60 Paul Vibert
61 Christer Svensson
62 D F Sercombe
63 Richard D N Wells
64 Gary Wynne
65 R Gray
66 Colin Beer
67 Mrs J Courtney
68 Martin Weiler
69 Paul Sanders
70 Timothy Adkin
71 Steve Somers
72 James Green
73 P J Reynolds
74 Kevin Newcombe
75 William Cox
76 E G Sansom
77 Simon Priest
78 B J Brooks
79 Martin Woodgates
80 Darren Beggs
81 Keith Coburn
82 Roger Hudson
83 W D Phillips
84 Alex Young
85 Richard 'Saxon' Kitson
86 Steven Darke
87 Paul M Fernbank

88 Wally Phillips
89 Dr Patrick Woodland
90 Alan Woodland
91 Chris Randall
92 Tony Ellis (Football
League Referees Assessor)
93 John Hurrell
94 R G Baker
95 Peter Heard
96 Mark Worwood
97 William H Lewis
98 Barry Durnford
99 David Edmonds
100 Geoffrey R Pejberthy
101 Mike Atkins
102 Clock Tower Guest
House
103 Morris Elliott
104 Paul Elliott
105 G L L Edmunds
106 Ian Aplin
107 Trefor Thynne
108 Dennis Michael Berry
109 Carl Newman
110 James Coombes
111 R G Harris
112 Paul Sleeman
113 M J Mears
114 P H Fenn
115 D M Kirby
116 Paul Knowles
117 Richard Leslie Scant
118 Mark Richard Griffin
119 John Waddington
120 Andrew McLarin
121 L H Woodgates
122 Andrew N George
123 Roger Wash
124 Diamant Yosef
125 Alan Gerald Woods
126 Mike Butler
127 Brian H Horne
128 John Snook
129 Marian Stanford

130 J H Wilson	180 Richard Slack	230 J Burrows
131 Stephen Davies	181 D Leaman	231 I K Jordan
132 Martyn Hodge	182 L William Short	232 A Dockray
133 Nicholas John Ware	183 Clive Taylor	233 J S Pyke
134 Geir Juva	184 Robert Taylor	234 C J Morton
135 Michael John Salter	185 N S Barnes	235 Terry Frost
136 R Sullivan	186 Paul Barnard	236 G Chudley
137 G B Dyer	187 Stephen Ellis	237 David Lashbrook
138 S G Dyer	188 David Morgan	238 G Potbury
139 Paul Simmonds	189 Matthew David Roach	239 John Clarke
140 I W Jubb	190 Dave Slocombe	240 David Goad
141 S J Davey	191 R Bickel	241 Gary James — 'The Blue'
142 W Davey	192 Andrew Paul Marchant	242 David Gregg
143 Dennis Goss	193 Peter Greenslade	243 Peter Baxter
144 Allan Philip Woodland	194 A T Gumbrill	244 Dave Harrison
145 Gerald Shepherd	195 A C J Pullen	245 Anthony Taylor
146 Robert Doidge	196 Stephen R Weston	246 Simon Taylor
147 Richard Davey	197 Roger Wellman	247 P Bowditch
148 Martyn Ashmead	198 Adrian Paul Autton	248 John Spencer Stoodley
149 David Fisher	199 A Sarsfield	249 L A Zammit
150 Harry Thompson	200 Trond Isaksen	250 J Caddy
151 Fred Lee	201 Mrs M I Mountain	251 W G Porter
152 Mark Bendell	202 Mrs M I Mountain	252 W T Porter
153 Chris Binstead	203 David Hutchings	253 Mike Blackstone
154 Peter Robinson	204 Neil Williams	254 M J Price
155 A J Farley	205 Ricky Montgomery	255 Brian Tabner
156 Lewis Jones	206 Brian J Peeke	256 Cyril Saunders
157 Francis P J Sealey	207 Larry Overend	257 Martyn Robb
158 Roger Carpanini	208 R Banham	258 John Willett
159 K S V Chambers	209 Leslie Hewitt	259 Jim Field
160 Keith B Ducker	210 D Yeo	260 J Tayler
161 Julie A Dunlop	211 Raymond A Kelly	261 Gary Curl
162 Simon Daddow	212 Ian Watts	262 T Anderson
163 David Knowles	213 C Bastyan	263 Ian Townsend
164 Steve Stentiford	214 Jason Warren	264 Michael Briggs
165 Norman Shiel	215 Michael J Endacott	265 Mrs A Smyth
166 Graham Clatworthy	216 Paul Stephen Morrish	266 Mrs V Thomas
167 E Heseltine	217 T D Culshaw	267 Mrs V Thomas
168 Nigel Skinner	218 Alan Davies	268 Chris Stone
169 Nicholas Drew	219 T T Lipscombe	269 David Coulson
170 M A Welch	220 Gary Salter	270 D Baker
171 G C Welch	221 A Williams	271 Nigel Beer
172 John Fox	222 A Williams	272 Gareth George
173 N R J Down	223 Nigel Tamlin	273 Ann Anderson
174 James Channon	224 Alan Brend	274 John Parr
175 Heidi Viles	225 Graham Brend	275 Jenny Croucher
176 A & J Goodrich	226 C J Radway	276 Michael Smerdon
177 Mrs Doreen Polter	227 Roy Willis	277 F Beale
178 Philip Scoble	228 Stewart Fell	278 Trevor Lobb
179 J Gardiner	229 John van den Elsen	279 Michael John Wilde

280 P R J Taylor
281 Paul Jerome
282 Dave Hillam
283 Hugh C Betteridge
284 Stephen D Larne
285 Gordon F Edwards
286 Peter R Edwards
287 John P Edwards
288 Nigel D Edwards
289 Alan Wheatley
290 B R Butler
291 Eric Heesom
292 Michael Joyce
293 Jon Robinson
294 Mike Purkiss
295 K M Brimacombe
296 Paul Greenaway
297 David J Gumm
298 Andrew Anderson
299 Stanley A Robinson
300 Alan Hindley
301 Keith Perryman
302 Tim Long
303 Julie Jeary
304 Jim Walker
305 M R Pearce
306 David Dickens
307 Geoffrey Wright
308 Tony Bluff
309 Riccardo Rossi
310 Dave Green
311 Mervyn Powell
312 Aidan Oliver Baker
313 Jeffery J Tolman
314 Richard Stocken
315 Norman Green
316 A N Davis
317 David Pease
318 Peter Pickup
319 A F Webber
320 Paul Farley
321 Frances Farley
322 Arthur Frank Pearson
    Junior
323 J Buitenga
324 D Samuels
325 Kevin Blaker
326 Mrs L Wonnacott
327 Kevin Stone
328 Trevor Manley

329 Philip Manley
330 Oswald Manley
331 Alan Couch
332 Nicholas C King
333 Gerald Hill
334 James H W Davey
335 Tasos Botsis
336 Kostas Fotopoulos
337 Ian Griffiths
338 Barrie Burnett
339 Sylvia Elcoate
340 William Clarke
341 Andrew Gillard
342 Ian Huxham
343 Surapot Saengchote
344 Edward Lavis
345 R H Main
346 G R Guppy
347 Philip Aggett
348 John Farrant
349 Edward Liddell
350 A D Mack
351 Richard Eric George
    Newton
352 Anthony May
353 H W J Parker
354 A V Phillips
355 I J Totterdell
356 Paul Phillips
357 Robert J Hammett
358 Daniel J Hammett
359 Robert Knapman
360 W V C Glasspoole
361 Francis Welland
362 R Bolt
363 Peter Overton
364 L J Haydon
365 Rick Norman
366 Martin Brittain
367 C J Maeer
368 A T Bolt
369 Mike Vosper
370 P & K Bastyan
371 Gary Norman
372 John Hobbs
373 Norman George Seward
374 L F Linscott
375 Russell Smith
376 J W Reynolds
377 Philip A Uzzell

378 Gerald S Uzzell
379 F J Stiles
380 E J Holman
381 Raymond M F Gale
382 David Pearse
383 Ronald White
384 Victor J King
385 Geoff Allman
386 S J Gillam
387 Francis Leslie Bevan
388 Steve Upton
389 Ted Drawer
390 Pauline Howe
391 Donald Brealy
392 Paul Auchterlonie
393 Mark Jenkins
394 Richard Green
395 Jamie R Short
396 David R Robbins
397 John Palmer
398 D Palmer
399 D J Hooper
400 G M Langworthy
401 F A Peters
402 Richard Somerwill
403 Stephen Parsons
404 Frank Grande
405 S P Tomlin
406 A H Atkins
407 A Young
408 M Swart
409 P W Stevenson
410 Anders Johansson
411 Q C M Olsthoorn
412 G D Painter
413 Tonny Otten
414 Patricia Arthur
415 R G Woolman
416 R W Lane
417 Simons Martin
418 David Lumb
419 David Helliwell
420 S J Rendell
421 G J Needs
422 Ian Andrews
423 Roger Cook
424 Paul Mason
425 Geoff Walpole
426 Michael Flack
427 Stephen Clark

428 J J McCormack	476 Dave Richards	526 Garry Alexander
429 Lawrence I M Bovey	477 A J Cole	527 James Nash
430 Richard L Bovey	478 Adrian Tripp	528 Nicholas Short
431 Martin J Bovey	479 Reverend Peter Pengelley	529 M F Abnett
432 A S Hockin	480 Polly Extence	530 Martin Sprague
433 B Downton	481 H J Ware	531 P A Cotton
434 S Downton	482 J R Summers	532 John Adcock
435 A J Kavanagh	483 Charles E Sutherley	533 P R Satterly
436 W A Phillips	484 Hugh Elwood	534 Mark Curl
437 H J A Preston	485 John Gillard	535 I Doble
438 W J Green	486 Steve Swan	536 P Carter
439 Robin Bostock-Smith	487 David Mitchell	537 Michael Holladay
440 Jim Tucker	488 Christopher Roy Ware	538 Graham Sparks
441 Dean Reed	489 Andrew Burvill	539 Colin Wheatcroft
442 Colin James Hall	490 K J Dymond	540 Richard Chewter
443 David Phillips	491 A Lyne	541 Stuart Brailey
444 Nigel Phillips	492 G Nelson	542 Robin Middleton
445 Alan R Baker	493 Kevin Bamsey	543 John Bond
446 Simon Lobb	494 Jonathan Hall	544 Michael Jordan
447 Jack Guy	495 Nicholas Tucker	545 Anna Laskey
448 W King	496 Malcolm Dommett	546 K G Baker
449 Leslie Roy Skinner	497 R M Peard	547 C P Baker
450 Brian Robert Fear	498 P Porter	548 Mrs M Saunders
451 Peter John William Chambers	499 Graham P Oglesby	549 John Goodridge
	500 H J Webber	550 F J Vosper
452 Rex Tapp	501 M F Bray	551 E J Wilde
453 Peter Parkhouse	502 M F Bray	552 Ryan Lock
454 Malcolm MacDonald	503 Bill Gubb	553 Allen Trump
455 Darryl Thomas	504 Malcolm Flack	554 Tony Selley
456 Graham John Parish	505 R Buckman	555 Mark Selley
457 Mrs L M Bowers	506 William Flack	556 Mark Abbott
458 Vince Davies	507 Stephen Powell	557 Trevor Hibberd
459 Tony Davies	508 Reese Phare	558 David Crawford
460 Kevin Redwood	509 Stephen Ankers	559 B H Kelland
461 M H F Morgan	510 Lesley Phare	560 Trevor John Marks
462 Chris & Grant	511 Stafford Spurway	561 R V Calmels
463 R L D Bradford	512 Nicholas Sparey	562 Esa Kautonen
464 Miss Lesley K Matthews	513 John Mills	563 Peter Yates
465 N W Lawrence	514 John Bowles	564 Samuel Jeremy Richard Mather
466 Ian Lewis	515 Christopher Richards	
467 Jim Clark (Exeter City FC 1948-1953)	516 D G French	565 J T Moore
	517 Paul Hunkin	566 H C Saunders
468 Gary Dart	518 F A Davey	567 John A Pitts
469 Michael John Moore	519 Samuel Gregory Weekes	568 Ann Whitchelo
470 W C Cockings	520 Miss S J Bowen	569 Marjorie Litt
471 Philip Harris	521 John Sanders	570 P Roberts
472 R S F James	522 K J Staddon	571 Frank & Elsa Broome
473 Simon Miller	523 Phil Hollow	
474 Maurice Crockford	524 P G Cruwys	
475 Keith Urro	525 Rodney Fry	